C000229462

ROAD ATLAS

COMPACT BRITAIN

CONTENTS

www.philips-maps.co.uk

First published in 2006 by Philip's
a division of Octopus Publishing Group Ltd
Carmelite House, 50 Victoria Embankment
London EC4Y 0DZ
An Hachette UK Company
www.hachette.co.uk

Eighth edition 2019
First impression 2019

ISBN 978-1-84907-506-0

Cartography by Philip's

Information for National Parks, Areas of Outstanding Natural Beauty, National Trails and Country Parks in Wales supplied by the Countryside Council for Wales.

Information for National Parks, Areas of Outstanding Natural Beauty, National Trails and Country Parks in England supplied by Natural England.

Data for Regional Parks, Long Distance Footpaths and Country Parks in Scotland provided by Scottish Natural Heritage.

Gaelic name forms used in the Western Isles provided by Comhairle nan Eilean.

Data for the National Nature Reserves in England provided by Natural England.

Data for the National Nature Reserves in Wales provided by Countryside Council for Wales. Darparwyd data'n ymwneud â Gwarchodfeydd Natur Cenedlaethol Cymru gan Gyngor Cefn Gwlad Cymru.

Information on the location of National Nature Reserves in Scotland was provided by Scottish Natural Heritage.

Data for National Scenic Areas in Scotland provided by the Scottish Executive Office. Crown copyright material is reproduced with the permission of the Controller of HMSO and the Queen's Printer for Scotland. Licence number C02W0003960.

Printed in Malaysia

Key to Map Pages

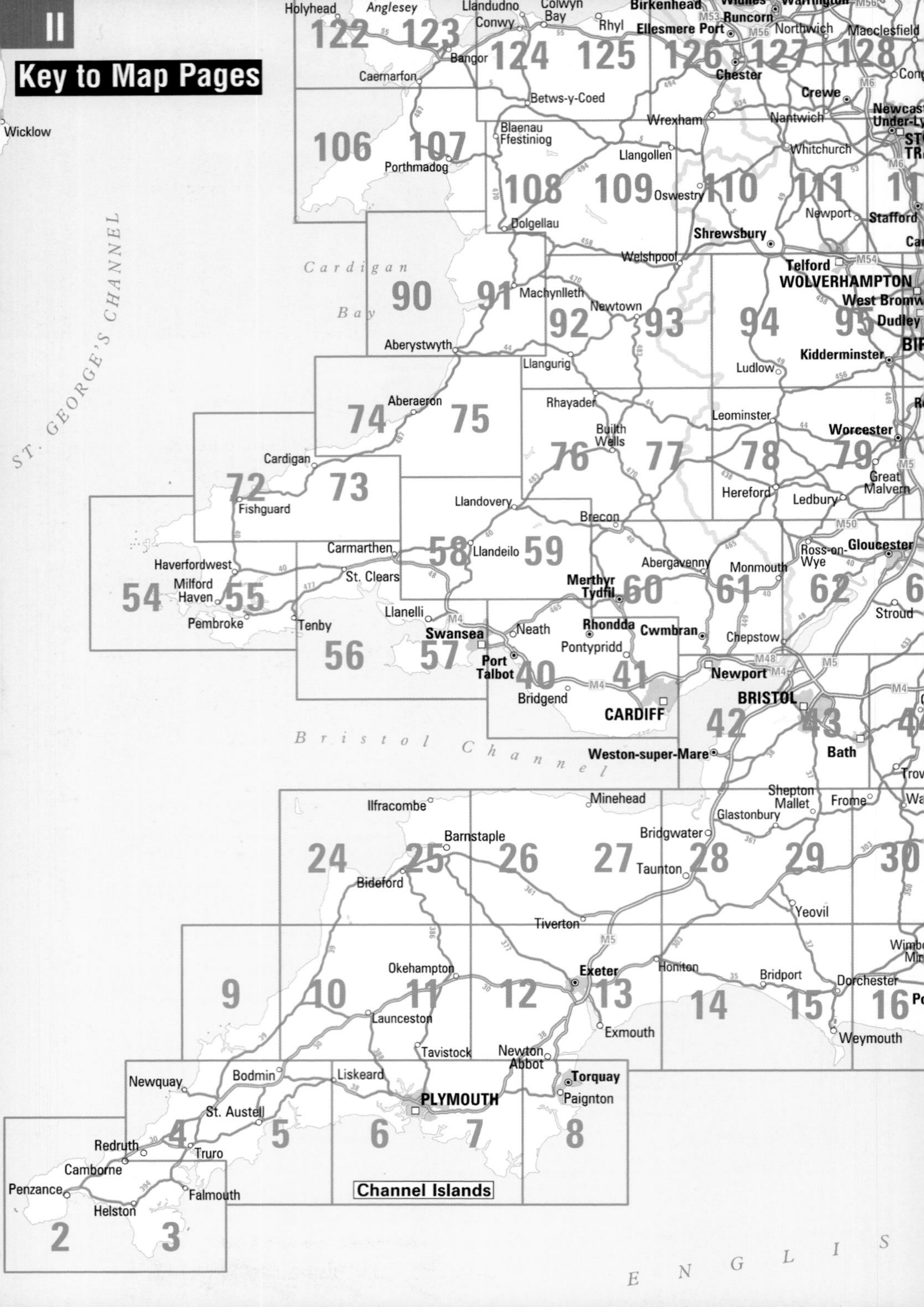

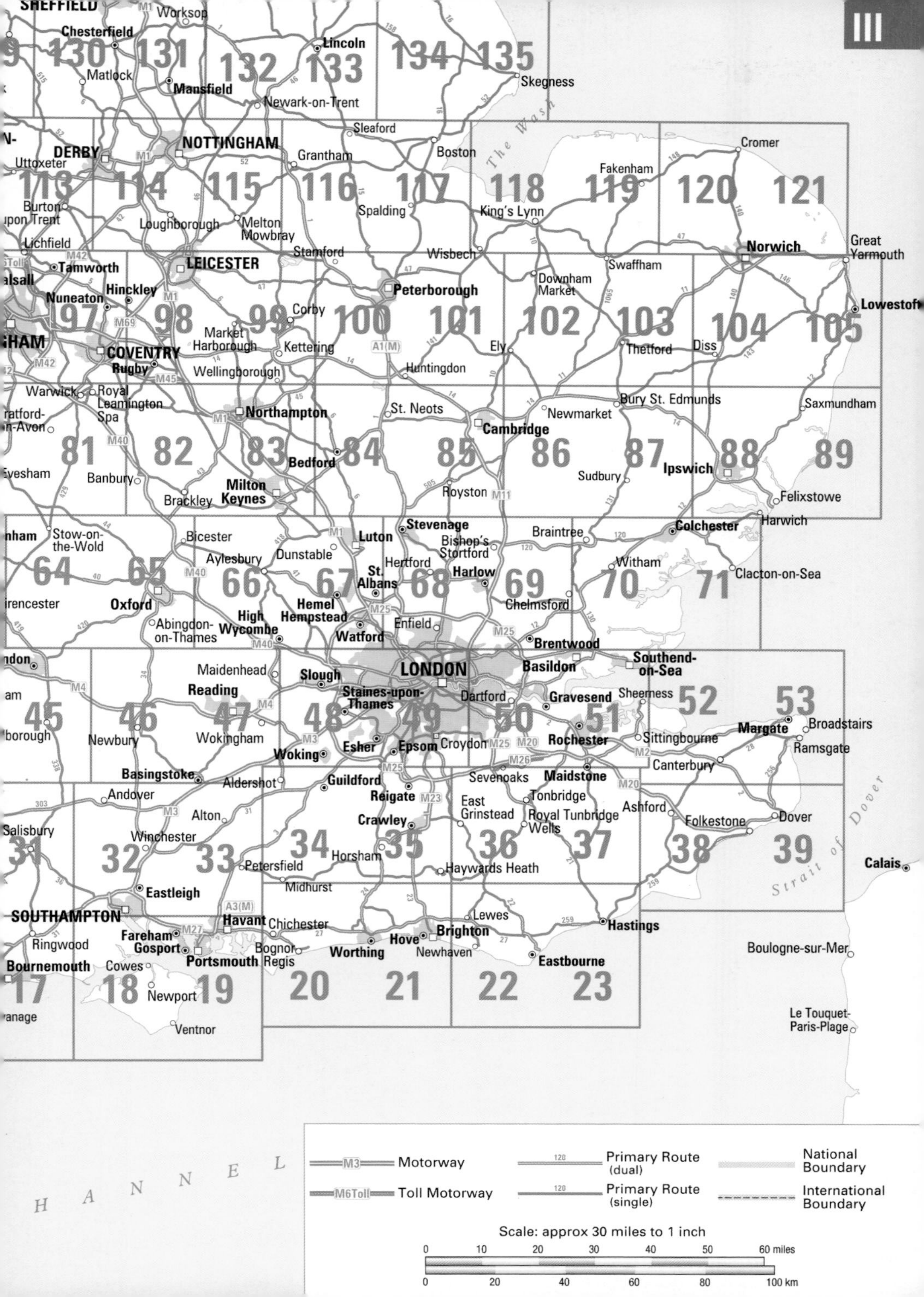
SHEFFIELD
Worksop
Chesterfield
Lincoln
130
131
132
133
134
135
Matlock
Mansfield
Skegness
Newark-on-Trent
The Wash
Sleaford
NOTTINGHAM
DERBY
Boston
Cromer
Uttoxeter
Grantham
Fakenham
113
114
115
116
117
118
119
120
121
Burton upon Trent
Spalding
King's Lynn
Loughborough
Melton Mowbray
Lichfield
Stamford
Wisbech
Norwich
Great Yarmouth
Tamworth
LEICESTER
Swaffham
Downham Market
Hinckley
Peterborough
Nuneaton
Corby
Lowestoft
97
98
99
100
101
102
103
104
105
Market Harborough
Kettering
Ely
Thetford
Diss
COVENTRY
Rugby
Huntingdon
Wellingborough
Warwick
Royal Leamington Spa
Bury St. Edmunds
Saxmundham
Northampton
St. Neots
Newmarket
Cambridge
81
82
83
84
85
86
87
88
89
Bedford
Evesham
Banbury
Milton Keynes
Sudbury
Ipswich
Royston
Felixstowe
Brackley
Harwich
Stow-on-the-Wold
Bicester
Stevenage
Luton
Braintree
Colchester
Bishop's Stortford
Aylesbury
Dunstable
Hertford
Witham
64
65
66
67
68
69
70
71
St. Albans
Harlow
Clacton-on-Sea
Oxford
Hemel Hempstead
Chelmsford
High Wycombe
Abingdon-on-Thames
Enfield
Watford
Brentwood
Maidenhead
LONDON
Basildon
Southend-on-Sea
Slough
Reading
Staines-upon-Thames
Dartford
Gravesend
Sheerness
45
46
47
48
49
50
51
52
53
Newbury
Wokingham
Rochester
Sittingbourne
Margate
Broadstairs
Ramsgate
Woking
Esher
Epsom
Croydon
Basingstoke
Canterbury
Sevenoaks
Maidstone
Aldershot
Guildford
Andover
Reigate
Tonbridge
East Grinstead
Royal Tunbridge Wells
Ashford
Alton
Crawley
Salisbury
Winchester
Folkestone
Dover
Strait of Dover
31
32
33
34
35
36
37
38
39
Horsham
Petersfield
Haywards Heath
Calais
Eastleigh
Midhurst
SOUTHAMPTON
Havant
Chichester
Lewes
Hastings
Fareham
Gosport
Brighton
Hove
Worthing
Newhaven
Ringwood
Bognor Regis
Eastbourne
Boulogne-sur-Mer
Bournemouth
Cowes
Portsmouth
17
18
19
20
21
22
23
Newport
Ventnor
Le Touquet-Paris-Plage
CHANNEL
M3 Motorway
M6Toll Toll Motorway
120 Primary Route (dual)
120 Primary Route (single)
National Boundary
International Boundary
Scale: approx 30 miles to 1 inch
0 10 20 30 40 50 60 miles
0 20 40 60 80 100 km

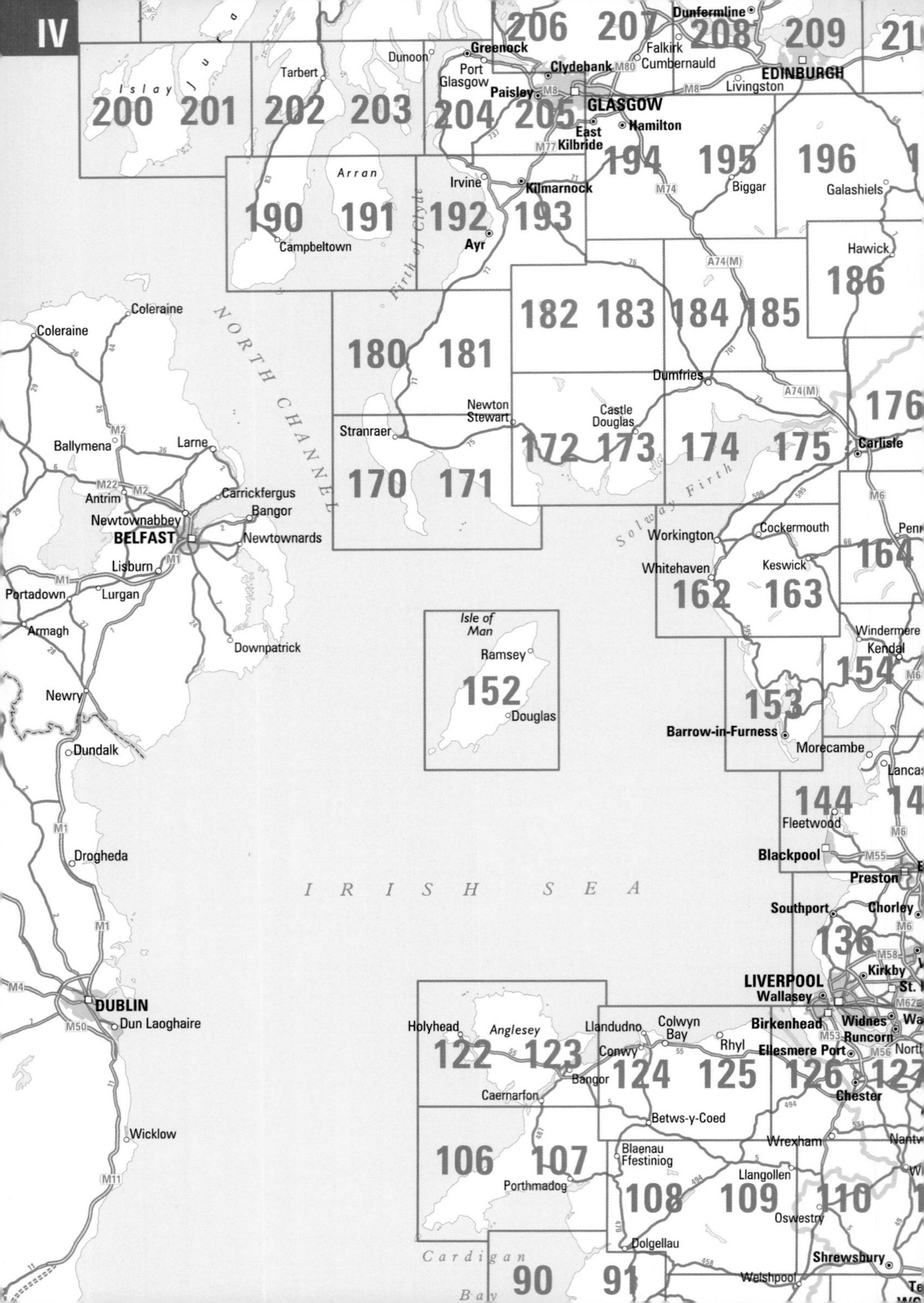

Islay
Jura
200
201
Tarbert
202
203
Dunoon
Greenock
Port Glasgow
204
Paisley
205
Clydebank
GLASGOW
East Kilbride
Hamilton
206
207
Dunfermline
Falkirk
208
Cumbernauld
209
EDINBURGH
Livingston
Arran
190
191
Campbeltown
Firth of Clyde
Irvine
Kilmarnock
192
193
Ayr
194
195
Biggar
196
Galashiels
Hawick
186
182
183
184
185
180
181
NORTH CHANNEL
Coleraine
Coleraine
Ballymena
Larne
Antrim
Carrickfergus
Newtownabbey
Bangor
BELFAST
Newtownards
Lisburn
Portadown
Lurgan
Armagh
Downpatrick
Newry
Dundalk
Drogheda
Newton Stewart
Stranraer
170
171
Dumfries
Castle Douglas
172
173
174
175
Carlisle
176
Solway Firth
Workington
Cockermouth
Whitehaven
Keswick
162
163
164
Penr
Isle of Man
Ramsey
152
Douglas
Windermere
Kendal
154
153
Barrow-in-Furness
Morecambe
Lancas
144
Fleetwood
Blackpool
Preston
IRISH SEA
Southport
Chorley
136
Kirkby
LIVERPOOL
Wallasey
St.
Birkenhead
Widnes
Runcorn
Ellesmere Port
North
126
Chester
DUBLIN
Dun Laoghaire
Wicklow
Holyhead
Anglesey
122
123
Llandudno
Colwyn Bay
Conwy
Rhyl
124
125
Bangor
Caernarfon
Betws-y-Coed
Wrexham
Nantw
106
107
Porthmadog
Blaenau Ffestiniog
Llangollen
108
109
110
Oswestry
Dolgellau
Shrewsbury
Cardigan Bay
90
91
Welshpool

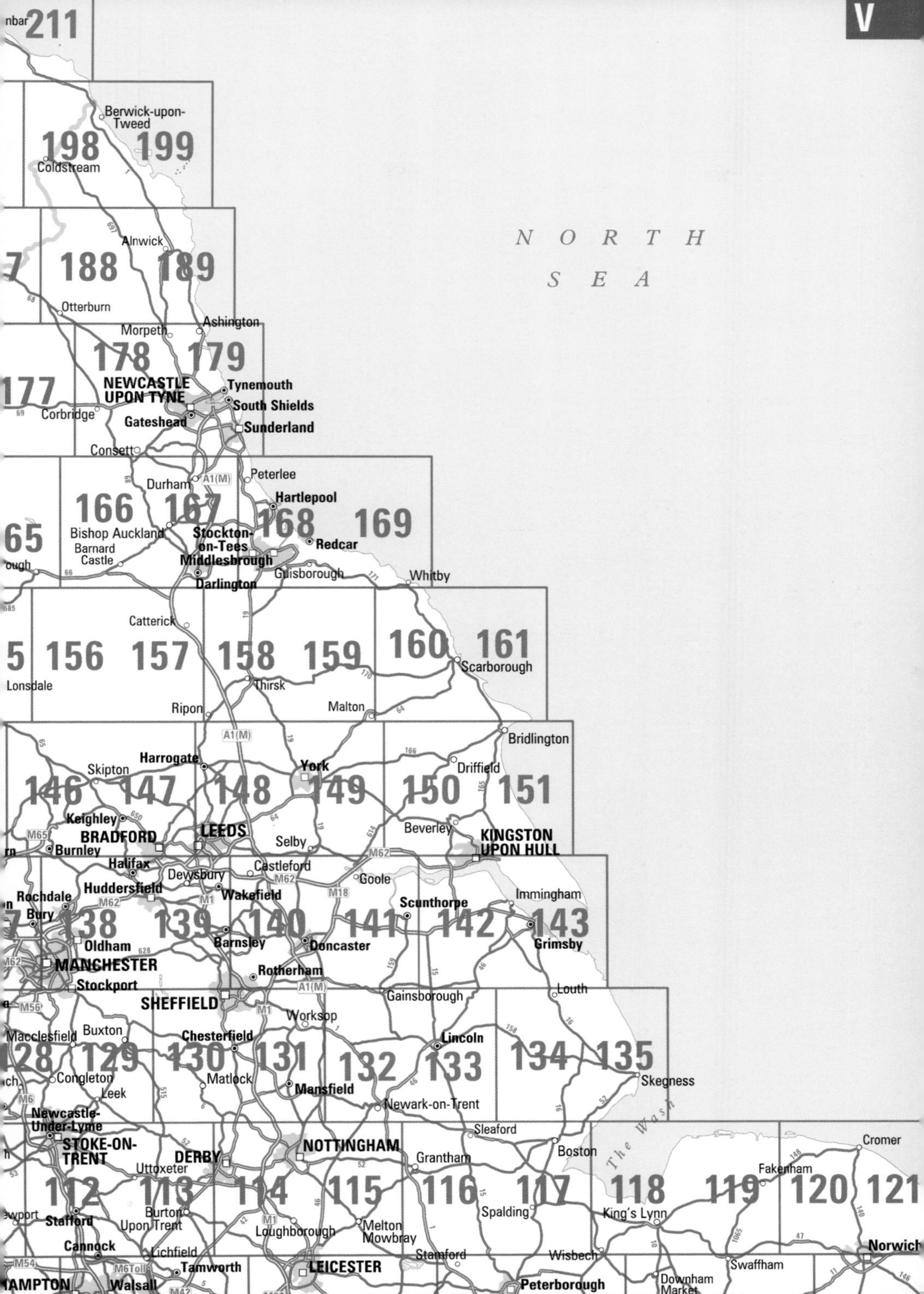
V
NORTH SEA
211
198
199
Berwick-upon-Tweed
Coldstream
188
189
Alnwick
Otterburn
Morpeth
Ashington
178
179
177
NEWCASTLE UPON TYNE
Tynemouth
South Shields
Corbridge
Gateshead
Sunderland
Consett
Durham
Peterlee
Hartlepool
166
167
168
169
165
Bishop Auckland
Stockton-on-Tees
Redcar
Barnard Castle
Middlesbrough
Guisborough
Whitby
Darlington
Catterick
156
157
158
159
160
161
Scarborough
Lonsdale
Thirsk
Ripon
Malton
Bridlington
Skipton
Harrogate
York
Driffield
146
147
148
149
150
151
Keighley
BRADFORD
LEEDS
Beverley
KINGSTON UPON HULL
Burnley
Selby
Halifax
Castleford
Dewsbury
Goole
Huddersfield
Wakefield
Rochdale
Scunthorpe
Immingham
Bury
138
139
140
141
142
143
Oldham
Barnsley
Doncaster
Grimsby
MANCHESTER
Rotherham
Stockport
SHEFFIELD
Gainsborough
Louth
Worksop
Macclesfield
Buxton
Chesterfield
Lincoln
128
129
130
131
132
133
134
135
Congleton
Matlock
Skegness
Leek
Mansfield
Newark-on-Trent
The Wash
Newcastle-Under-Lyme
STOKE-ON-TRENT
Sleaford
Cromer
NOTTINGHAM
DERBY
Boston
Grantham
Fakenham
Uttoxeter
112
113
114
115
116
117
118
119
120
121
Stafford
Burton Upon Trent
Spalding
King's Lynn
Loughborough
Melton Mowbray
Cannock
Lichfield
Stamford
Wisbech
Swaffham
Norwich
Tamworth
LEICESTER
Walsall
Peterborough
Downham Market
A1(M)
M1
M6
M18
M56
M62
M65
M42
M54
M6Toll

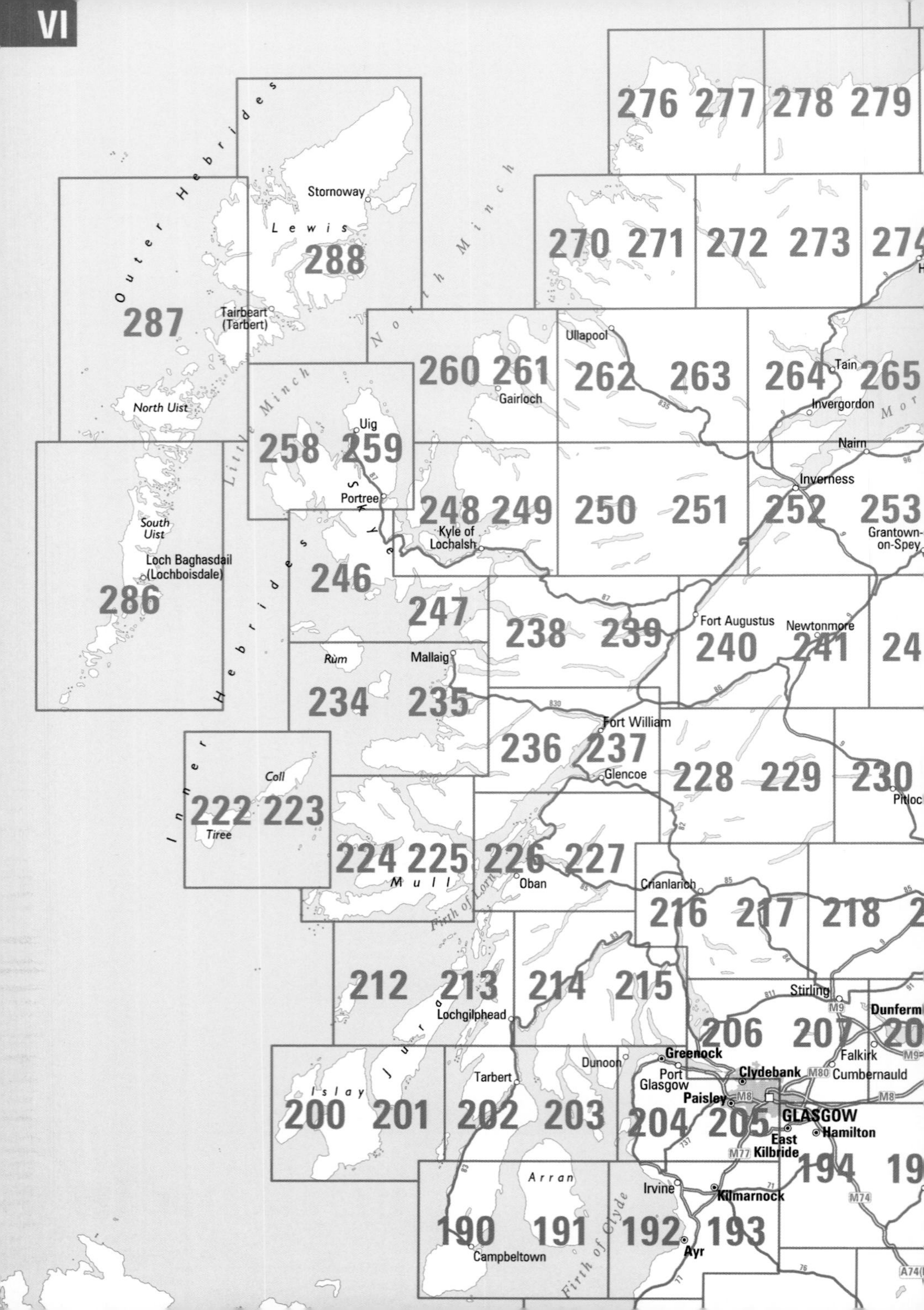
Outer Hebrides
Stornoway
Lewis
288
287
Tairbeart (Tarbert)
North Minch
North Uist
Little Minch
258
259
Uig
Portree
South Uist
Loch Baghasdail (Lochboisdale)
286
Skye
Inner Hebrides
276
277
278
279
270
271
272
273
Ullapool
260
261
262
263
264
Tain
265
Gairloch
Invergordon
Nairn
Inverness
248
249
250
251
252
253
Kyle of Lochalsh
Grantown-on-Spey
246
247
238
239
Fort Augustus
240
Newtonmore
241
Rùm
Mallaig
234
235
Fort William
236
237
Glencoe
228
229
230
Coll
222
223
Tiree
224
225
226
227
Mull
Oban
Firth of Lorn
Crianlarich
216
217
218
212
213
214
215
Lochgilphead
Jura
Stirling
206
207
Dunferm
Falkirk
Cumbernauld
Dunoon
Greenock
Port Glasgow
Clydebank
Paisley
GLASGOW
Hamilton
East Kilbride
Islay
200
201
Tarbert
202
203
204
205
194
Arran
Irvine
Kilmarnock
190
191
192
193
Firth of Clyde
Ayr
Campbeltown
M8
M9
M77
M80
M74
A74

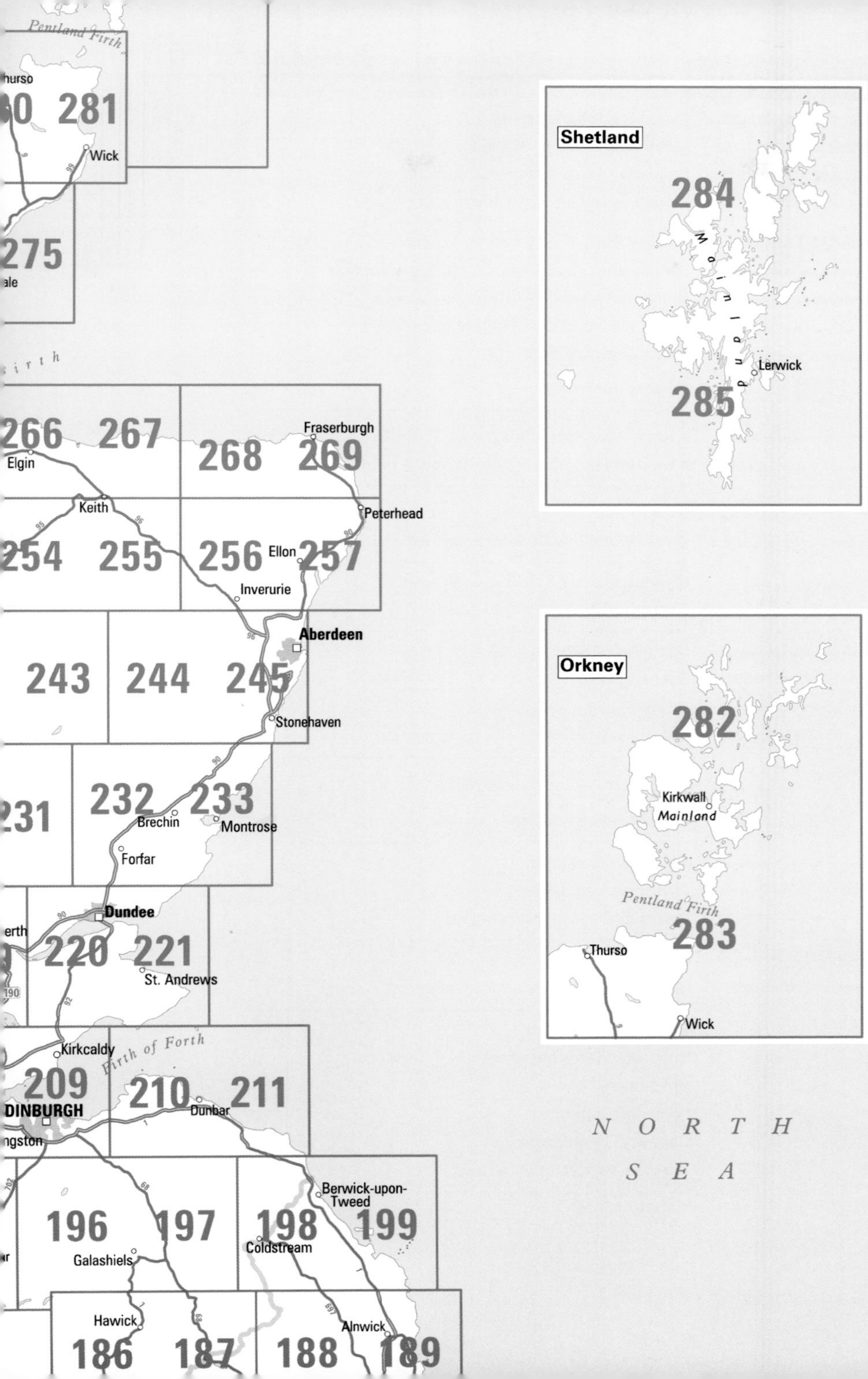

Pentland Firth
Thurso
281
Wick
275
Firth
266 267
Elgin
268 269
Fraserburgh
Keith
Peterhead
254 255
256 257
Ellon
Inverurie
Aberdeen
243 244 245
Stonehaven
231
232 233
Brechin
Montrose
Forfar
Dundee
Perth
220 221
St. Andrews
Kirkcaldy
Firth of Forth
209
210 211
Dunbar
EDINBURGH
196 197 198 199
Berwick-upon-Tweed
Coldstream
Galashiels
Hawick
Alnwick
186 187 188 189

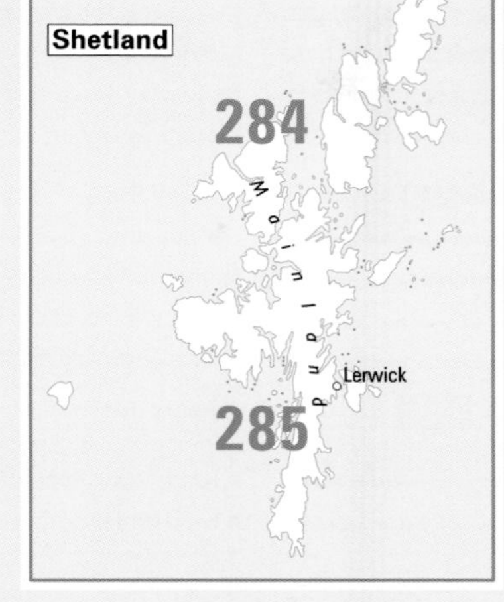

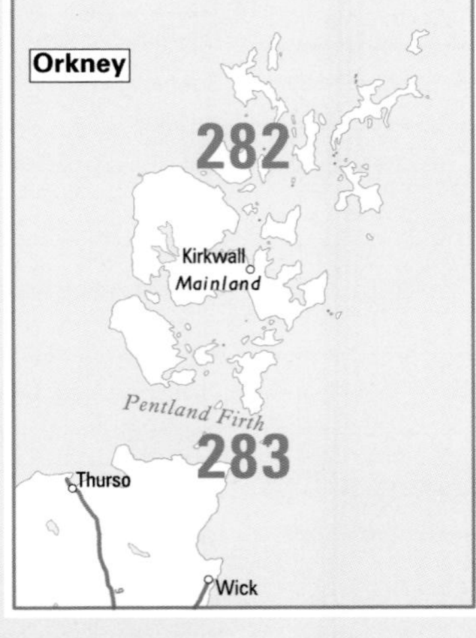

N O R T H
S E A

Road map symbols

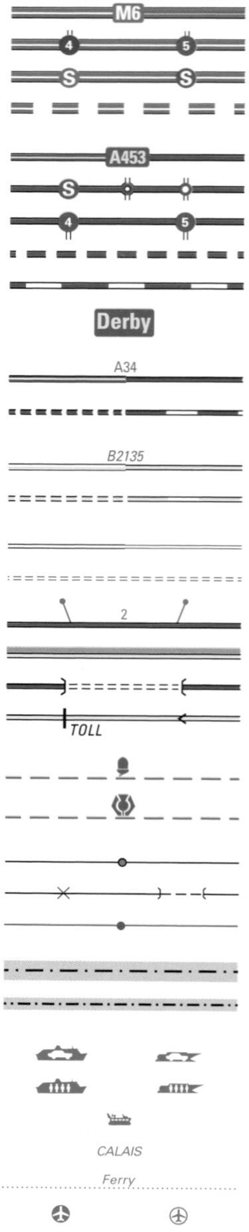

Motorway, toll motorway

Motorway junction – full, restricted access

Motorway service area – full, restricted access
Motorway under construction

Primary route – dual, single carriageway

Service area, roundabout, multi-level junction

Numbered junction – full, restricted access
Primary route under construction
Narrow primary route

Primary destination

A road – dual, single carriageway
A road under construction, narrow A road

B road – dual, single carriageway
B road under construction, narrow B road

Minor road – over 4 metres, under 4 metres wide
Minor road with restricted access

Distance in miles
Scenic route
Tunnel

Toll, steep gradient – arrow points downhill

National trail – England and Wales
Long distance footpath – Scotland

Railway with station
Level crossing, tunnel
Preserved railway with station

National boundary
County / unitary authority boundary

Car ferry, catamaran
Passenger ferry, catamaran
Hovercraft

Ferry destination

Car ferry – river crossing
Principal airport, other airport

Road map symbols

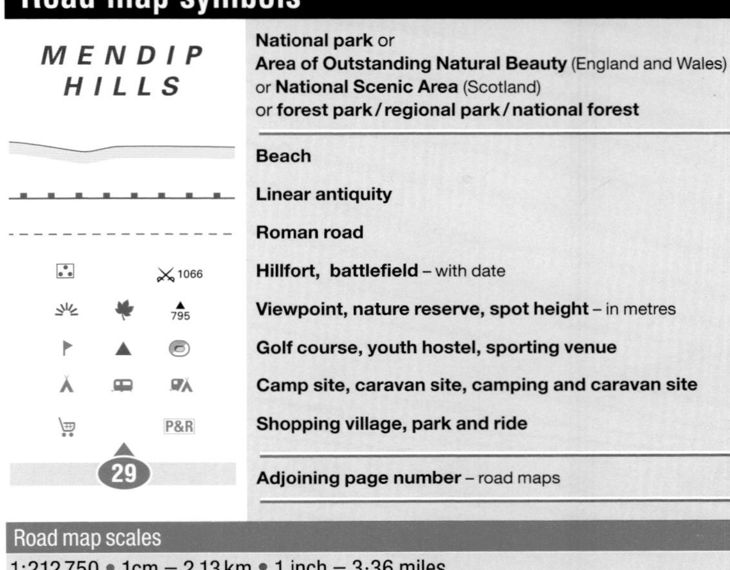

National park or
Area of Outstanding Natural Beauty (England and Wales)
or **National Scenic Area** (Scotland)
or **forest park / regional park / national forest**

Beach

Linear antiquity

Roman road

Hillfort, battlefield – with date

Viewpoint, nature reserve, spot height – in metres

Golf course, youth hostel, sporting venue

Camp site, caravan site, camping and caravan site

Shopping village, park and ride

Adjoining page number – road maps

Road map scales

1:212 750 • 1cm = 2.13 km • 1 inch = 3·36 miles

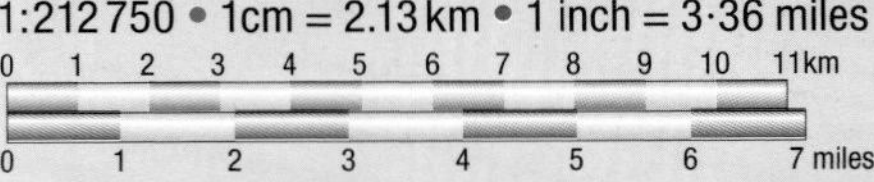

Outer Hebrides, Orkney and Shetland

1:425 700 • 1 cm = 4.25 km • 1 inch = 6.72 miles

Tourist information

- **Abbey, cathedral or priory**
- **Ancient monument**
- **Aquarium**
- **Art gallery**
- **Bird collection or aviary**
- **Castle**
- **Church**
- **Country park**
  England and Wales
  Scotland
- **Farm park**
- **Garden**
- **Historic ship**
- **House**
- **House and garden**
- **Motor racing circuit**
- **Museum**
- **Picnic area**
- **Preserved railway**
- **Race course**
- **Roman antiquity**
- **Safari park**
- **Theme park**
- **Tourist information centre** open all year
  open seasonally
- **Zoo**
- **Other place of interest**

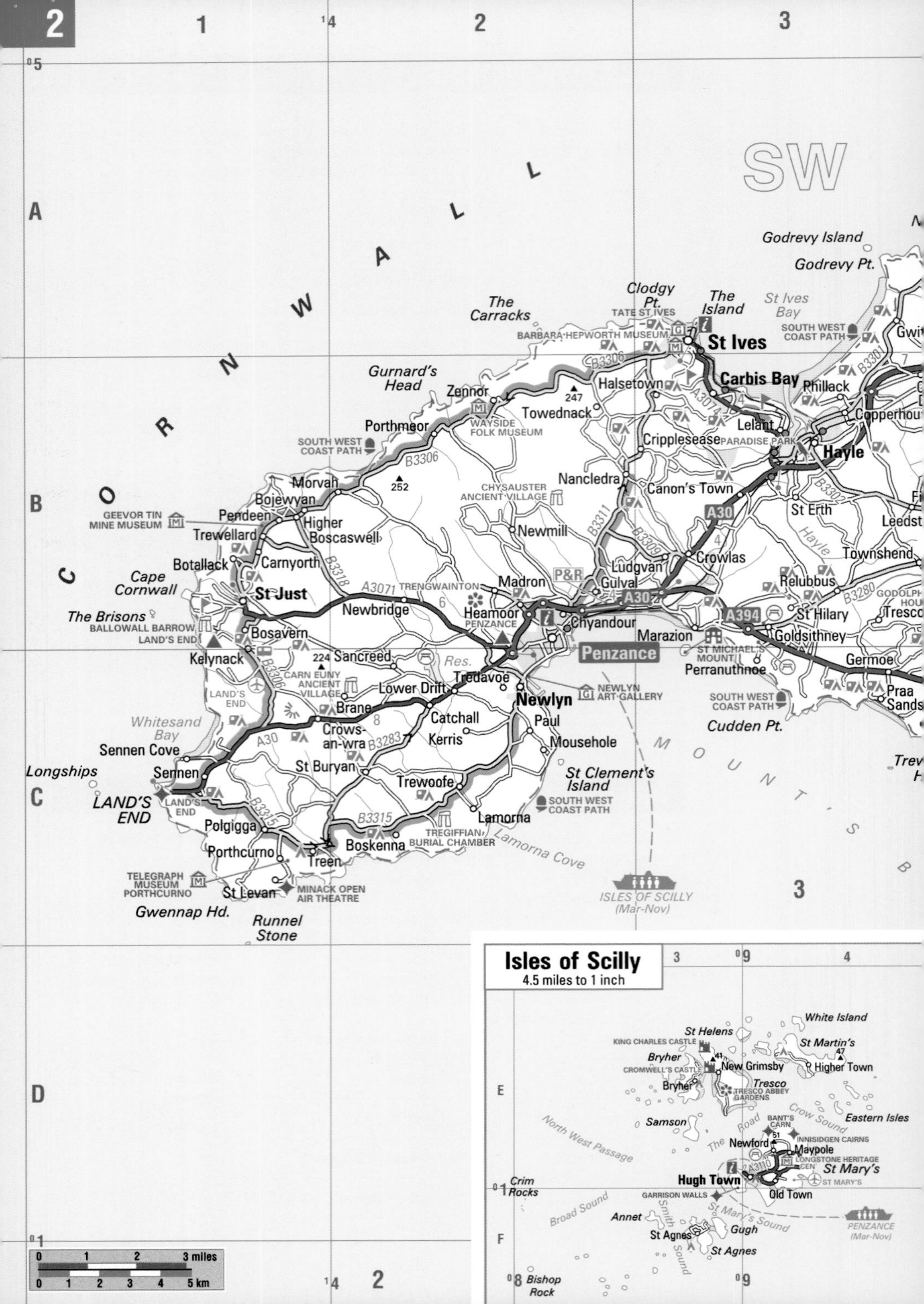
1
2
3
A
B
C
D
E
F
SW
C O R N W A L L
Godrevy Island
Godrevy Pt.
Clodgy Pt.
The Island
St Ives Bay
The Carracks
TATE ST IVES
BARBARA HEPWORTH MUSEUM
St Ives
SOUTH WEST COAST PATH
Carbis Bay
Phillack
Gurnard's Head
Zennor
247
Halsetown
Towednack
Lelant
Copperhouse
WAYSIDE FOLK MUSEUM
Porthmeor
Cripplesease
PARADISE PARK
Hayle
B3306
A3074
B3301
B3302
252
Morvah
Nancledra
Canon's Town
CHYSAUSTER ANCIENT VILLAGE
Bojewyan
GEEVOR TIN MINE MUSEUM
Pendeen
Higher Boscaswell
St Erth
Leedstown
A30
Trewellard
Newmill
B3311
B3309
Crowlas
Townshend
Botallack
Carnyorth
B3318
Ludgvan
P&R
Cape Cornwall
St Just
A3071
TRENGWAINTON
Madron
Gulval
Relubbus
B3280
GODOLPHIN HOUSE
The Brisons
Newbridge
Heamoor
PENZANCE
Chyandour
A394
St Hilary
Tresco
BALLOWALL BARROW
Marazion
Goldsithney
LAND'S END
Bosavern
Kelynack
224
Sancreed
Res.
Penzance
ST MICHAEL'S MOUNT
Germoe
Perranuthnoe
CARN EUNY ANCIENT VILLAGE
Tredavoe
LAND'S END
Lower Drift
NEWLYN ART GALLERY
Praa Sands
Newlyn
SOUTH WEST COAST PATH
Brane
Catchall
Paul
Whitesand Bay
Cudden Pt.
Crows-an-wra
B3283
Kerris
Mousehole
Sennen Cove
M O U N T ' S B
Longships
Sennen
St Buryan
St Clement's Island
LAND'S END
Trewoofe
LAND'S END
SOUTH WEST COAST PATH
Lamorna
Polgigga
B3315
TREGIFFIAN BURIAL CHAMBER
Porthcurno
Boskenna
Lamorna Cove
Treen
TELEGRAPH MUSEUM PORTHCURNO
St Levan
MINACK OPEN AIR THEATRE
ISLES OF SCILLY (Mar-Nov)
Gwennap Hd.
Runnel Stone
Isles of Scilly
4.5 miles to 1 inch
White Island
St Helens
KING CHARLES CASTLE
St Martin's
Bryher
New Grimsby
Higher Town
CROMWELL'S CASTLE
Bryher
Tresco
TRESCO ABBEY GARDENS
Samson
BANT'S CARN
Crow Sound
Eastern Isles
North West Passage
The Road
Newford
INNISIDGEN CAIRNS
Maypole
LONGSTONE HERITAGE CEN
A3110
St Mary's
Hugh Town
ST MARY'S
Crim Rocks
GARRISON WALLS
Old Town
Broad Sound
Annet
Smith Sound
St Mary's Sound
PENZANCE (Mar-Nov)
St Agnes
Gugh
St Agnes
Bishop Rock
0 1 2 3 miles
0 1 2 3 4 5 km

3
St Agnes
Mithian
Trevellas
Callestick
St Allen
Trispen
St Erme
Ladock
Goonbell
Marazanvose
Allet
Porthtowan
Mount Hawke
Shortlanesend
Three Burrows
Blackwater
Tresillian
Portreath
Mawla
Truro
Kenwyn
Tresawle
Scorrier
Chacewater
Threemilestone
Merther
Illogan
Baldhu
Kea
St Clement
Roscroggan
St Day
Twelve Heads
Malpas
Ruan Lanihorne
Redruth
Bissoe
Playing Place
Old Kea
St Michael Penkevil
Lamorran
Pool
Tuckingmill
Cambrea
Carharrack
Carnon Downs
Carnkie
Gwennap
Treworga
CAMBORNE
Lanner
Penpol
Trelissick
Philleigh
Roseworthy
Four Lanes
Perranarworthal
Devoran
Feock
Barripper
Troon
Ponsanooth
Treworlas
Carnhell Green
Penhalvaen
Stithians
Burnthouse
Mylor Bridge
Trewithian
Praze-an-Beeble
Penmarth
St Just in Roseland
Crowan
Burras
Penryn
Gerrans
Portscatho
Carnkie
Flushing
Drym
Releath
Rame
Longdowns
Mabe Burnthouse
Falmouth
St Mawes
Greeb Pt.
Porkellis
Nancegollan
Bohortha
Budock Water
Godolphin Cross
Wendron
Seworgan
Treverva
Pendennis Pt.
Zone Pt.
Crowntown
Penjerrick
Constantine
Sithney
Breage
Mawnan Smith
Trewennack
Porth Navas
Rosemullion Hd.
Helston
Helford Passage
Mawnan
Porthleven
Gweek
Helford
St Anthony-in-Meneage
Mawgan
Manaccan
Nare Pt.
Porthleven Sands
Garras
St Martin
Berepper
Newtown
Tregidden
Porthallow
Gunwalloe
Porthoustock
Cury
Cross Lanes
St Keverne
Manacle Pt.
Traboe
The Manacles
Lowland Pt.
Mullion
Goonhilly Downs
Penhale
Trelan
Coverack
Mullion Cove
Mullion Island
Gwenter
Chynhalls Pt.
Kuggar
Black Hd.
Predannack Wollas
Vellan Hd.
St Ruan
Ruan Minor
Grade
Cadgwith
Lizard
Kynance Cove
Hot Pt.
LIZARD POINT
CORNWALL

4
1
2
3
4
A
B
C
D
SW
Porthcothan
Park Hd.
Penrose
St Ervan
Rumford
St Issey
Tredinnick
St Jidgey
CREALY GREAT ADVENTURE PARK
St Eval
Trenance
Berryl's Pt.
Trevarrian
St Mawgan
CORNISH BIRDS OF PREY CENTRE
Talskiddy
WATERGATE BAY
Tregurrian
NEWQUAY CORNWALL
St Columb Major
Towan Hd.
Newquay Bay
Porth
St Columb Minor
CASTLE AN DINAS
Fistral Bay
Pentire
Trebudannon
Colan
SPRINGFIELDS FUN & PONY CENTRE
NEWQUAY ZOO
Kelsey Hd.
BLUE REEF AQUARIUM
Newquay
Quintrell Downs
Mountjoy
Ruthvoes
West Pentire
Crantock
Lane
Trevarren
Indian Queens
Penhale Pt.
HOLYWELL BAY FUN PARK
Kestle Mill
St Columb Road
Holywell
Carines
DAIRY LAND FARM WORLD
Fraddon
Penhale
St Dennis
Cubert
TRERICE
St Enoder
Ligger or Perran Bay
Penhale Sands
St Newlyn East
Gummow's Shop
Retew
Mount
Rejerrah
LAPPA VALLEY STEAM RAILWAY
Summercourt
Treviscoe
SOUTH WEST COAST PATH
Rose
PERRAN ROUND
Brighton
Trethosa
Perranporth
PERRANPORTH
Newlyn Downs
Mitchell
Goonhavern
Carland Cross
Bolingey
Trelassick
St Stephen
Perranzabuloe
Zelah
St Agnes Hd.
Trevellas
New Mills
Coombe
St Agnes
Mithian
St Allen
St Erme
Ladock
Grampound Road
192
Callestick
Trispen
HEALEYS CYDER FARM
Marazanvose
Goonbell
Allet
Probus
Grampound
TREWITHEN
Porthtowan
Mount Hawke
Shortlanesend
Three Burrows
P&R
Tresillian
Creed
Blackwater
Kenwyn
Truro
Tresawle
Portreath
Mawla
CATHEDRAL
Merther
Tregony
PORTREATH
CORNISH GOLD TOLGUS MILL
Scorrier
Threemilestone
Illogan
Chacewater
ROYAL CORNWALL MUS
St Clement
CORNISH MINES & ENGINES
St Day
Baldhu
Kea
Ruan Lanihorne
Twelve Heads
Malpas
Redruth
Bissoe
Playing Place
Old Kea
St Michael Penkevil
Lamorran
Pool
225
Carnbrea
Carharrack
Tuckingmill
Carnon Downs
Treworga
Carnkie
GWENNAP PIT
Gwennap
Trelissick
Philleigh
CAMBORNE
Lanner
Perranarworthal
Penpol
SHIRE HORSE FARM
Four Lanes
Devoran
Feock
TRELISSICK
Veryan
Troon
Ponsanooth
Treworlas
Carne
Penhalvaen
Gerrans Bay
252
Stithians
Burnthouse
Trewithian
Nare Hd.
Stithians Res.
Mylor Bridge
St Just in Roseland
Penmarth
Carrick Roads
Gerrans
Portscatho
Burras
Carnkie
Penryn
Flushing
Rame
Longdowns
Mabe Burnthouse
Falmouth
St Mawes
Greeb Pt.
Releath
Porkellis
ART GALLERY
NATIONAL MARITIME
Bohortha
Nancegollan
POLDARK MINE
181
Budock Water
PENDENNIS CASTLE
Wendron
Seworgan
Treverva
Pendennis Pt.
Zone Pt.
Penjerrick
Falmouth Bay
Constantine
Mawnan Smith
SOUTH WEST COAST PATH
Porth Navas
GLENDURGAN
Rosemullion Hd.
A30
A39
A390
A392
A394
A3075
A3076
A3058
A3059
A3078
A393
A3047
B3276
B3274
B3275
B3279
B3284
B3285
B3277
B3298
B3301
B3289
B3292
B3280
B3297
0 1 2 3 miles
0 1 2 3 4 5 km

St Breock
Egloshayle
PENCARROW HOUSE
Helland
268
Maidenwell
Lake
Siblyback Lake
A389
9
Burlawn
Millpool
10
BODMIN
Washaway
Bodmin Forest
Commonmoor
Warleggan
GOLITHA FALLS
T.BREOCK DOWNS MONOLITH
A30
Cardinham
KING DONIERT'S STONE
St Neot
St Cleer
Bodmin
Mount
Nanstallon
Ruthernbridge
BODMIN TOWN MUSEUM
CARNGLAZE SLATE CAVERNS
Ley
Rosenannon
St Lawrence
Withiel
BODMIN AND WENFORD RAILWAY
Fowey
Wenn
Dobwalls
A38
Tregonetha
B3268
LANHYDROCK HOUSE
East Taphouse
A390
Doublebois
West Taphouse
Lanivet
St Pinnock
Trebyan
227
Belowda
Victoria
A30
RESTORMEL CASTLE
Sweethouse
Braddock
Lockengate
Redmoor
B3269
Herodsfoot
St Keyne
Tregoss
Bilberry
Lostwithiel
6
Trewidland
GOSS MOOR
Roche
Trezaise
Lanlivery
208
Bugle
Couch's Mill
Duloe
B3274
B3254
Hensbarrow
Downs
312
A391
Milltown
Luxulyan
Bocaddon
FOLK & FARM MUSEUM
Lerryn
Stenalees
B3374
B3359
Sandplace
itemoor
A390
Penpillick
Lanreath
Nanpean
Penwithick
Muchlarnick
Carthew
GOLANT
Golant
Pelynt
Trethurgy
St Veep
Foxhole
WHEAL MARTYN CHINA CLAY CTRY PARK & MUS
EDEN PROJECT
St Blazey
B
Penpoll
Tywardreath
Looe
Carclaze
High Street
Boscoppa
Lanteglos Highway
Trenewan
St Austell
Par
West Looe
Trewoon
Holmbush
A3082
Bodinnick
Porthallow
St Mewan
SHIPWRECK & HERITAGE CENTRE
Polkerris
Fowey
Ferry
Charlestown
Menabilly
Lansallos
Talland Bay
Sticker
ST AUSTELL BREWERY
ST CATHERINE'S CASTLE
Polruan
Polperro
HERITAGE MUSEUM
Polgooth
Porthpean
ST. AUSTELL BAY
SOUTH WEST COAST PATH
Pencarrow Hd.
Hewas Water
Gribbin Hd.
Trenarren
B3273
Black Hd.
SX
THE LOST GARDENS OF HELIGAN
Pentewan
St Ewe
Mevagissey Bay
Kestle
C
lmassick
WORLD OF MODEL RAILWAYS
Mevagissey
Portmellon
Chapel Pt.
Trevarrick
Gorran Churchtown
St Michael Caerhays
Gorran Haven
Boswinger
BOSWINGER
Penare
114
Veryan Bay
Dodman Pt.
D
4
20
5
6
22
7
03

Liskeard
Saltash
Looe
Torpoint
Devonport
Callington
Tamar Valley
Whitsand Bay
Rame Hd.
Looe Bay
St George's or Looe I.
Talland Bay
Polperro
Dobwalls
St Cleer
St Ive
St Mellion
Menheniot
Tideford
Trerulefoot
Hessenford
St Germans
Sheviock
Crafthole
Antony
Millbrook
Kingsand
Cawsand
Rame
Freathy
Portwrinkle
Downderry
Seaton
Polbathic
Widegates
Morval
Sandplace
Duloe
Trewidland
St Keyne
Pelynt
Gunnislake
Calstock
Bere Alston
Bere Ferrers
Landulph
Cremyll
St Budeaux
Drake's I.
The Sound
ROSCOFF SANTANDER (Mar-Nov) ST MALO (Nov-Mar)
0 1 2 3 miles
0 1 2 3 4 5 km
Guernsey
5 miles to 1 inch
St Peter Port
Herm
Jethou
Sark
Jersey
5 miles to 1 inch
St Helier
St Aubin
Gorey
St Clements
Grouville
St Martin's
Trinity
St John's
St Mary's
St Ouens
St Brelade
La Rocque Pt.
Corbière Pt.
Grosnez Pt.

DARTMOOR NATIONAL PARK
Ashburton
Buckfastleigh
Buckfast
Yelverton
Walkhampton
Dousland
Sheepstor
Meavy
Burrator Res.
Whiteworks
Poundsgate
Holne
RYDER'S HILL
UPPER PLYM VALLEY
Clearbrook
Shaugh Prior
Bickleigh
Roborough
Wotter
Lee Moor
SHELL TOP
DENDLES WOOD
Ugborough Moor
Didworthy
South Brent
Dean
Dean Prior
PENNYWELL FARM & WILDLIFE CENTRE
DARTINGTON CIDER PRESS CENTRE
BUCKFAST BUTTERFLIES & DARTMOOR OTTER SANCTUARY
BUCKFAST ABBEY
RIVER ART ADVENTURES
Woodland
Forder Grn.
Landscove
Rattery
Tigley
Cott
Belsford
Harberton
Harbertonford
Lincombe
Avonwick
Diptford
Plym Forest
Drakeland Corner
Lutton
Cornwood
Harford
UGBOROUGH BEACON
Cheston
Bittaford
DARTMOOR ZOOLOGICAL PARK
Sparkwell
Eggbuckland
PLYM VALLEY RAILWAY
Plympton
Lee Mill
Ivybridge
Ugborough
North Huish
Crabadon
Curtisknowle
SALTRAM
Elburton
Brixton
Yealmpton
Westlake
Ermington
Modbury
Brownston
Moreleigh
Halwell
Woodford
Millcombe
Staddiscombe
Down Thomas
Knighton
Wembury
Wembury Bay
Holbeton
Luson
Newton Ferrers
Battisborough Cross
Noss Mayo
Mothecombe
Worswell
Stoke Pt.
SOUTH WEST COAST PATH
Kingston
Ringmore
St Ann's Chapel
Bigbury
Loddiswell
Woodleigh
Aveton Gifford
East Allington
Goveton
Churchstow
West Alvington
Kingsbridge
Sherford
Bigbury on Sea
Burgh I.
BIGBURY BAY
Bantham
Buckland
South Milton
Thurlestone
Frogmore
Chillington
Charleton
Woolston
Kernborough
South Pool
Galmpton
Hope
Malborough
Bolt Tail
Bolberry
Salcombe
East Portlemouth
Kellaton
South Allington
Soar
SALCOMBE
OVERBECKS MUSEUM AND GARDEN
Bolt Hd.
East Prawle
Prawle Pt.
SOUTH DEVON
SX
Alderney
5 miles to 1 inch
DIELETTE
ST. PETER PORT
(Apr-Sept)
Quesnard Pt.
Brehou
Braye
Longis Bay
Clonque Bay
St Anne
ALDERNEY
Telegraph Bay

NEWTON ABBOT
A38
A383
12
West Ogwell
East Ogwell
BRADLEY
Wolborough
Combeinteignhead
Netherton
PLANT WORLD
Stokeinteignhead
SHALDON WILDLIFE TRUST
SOUTH WEST COAST PATH
13
BABBACOMBE BAY
PRICKLY BALL FARM
DECOY
Woodland
Denbury
Abbotskerswell
Coffinswell
Kingskerswell
Maidencombe
Forder Grn.
Torbryan
Ipplepen
North Whilborough
Barton
A3022
Watcombe
Landscove
BUCKFAST BUTTERFLIES & DARTMOOR OTTER SANCTUARY
Broadhempston
Shiphay
MODEL VILLAGE
Babbacombe
A
Compton
COMPTON CASTLE
A380
Torquay
A384
A381
Staverton
Cockington
Torre
TORRE ABBEY
KENT'S CAVERN PREHISTORIC CAVES
Wellswood
Hope's Nose
Dartington
DARTINGTON HALL
Littlehempston
Marldon
LIVING COASTS
DARTINGTON CIDER PRESS CENTRE
Shinner's Bridge
BERRY POMEROY CASTLE
Hollicombe
SOUTH DEVON RAILWAY
Blagdon
A385
Cott
Totnes
Berry Pomeroy
KIRKHAM
Paignton
CASTLE
Tigley
Collaton St Mary
DARTMOUTH STEAM RAILWAY
TORBAY
ZOO
TOR BAY
Belsford
7
Harberton
Dart
Goodrington
GOLDEN HIND
Brixham
BERRY HEAD
Berry Head
Ashprington
Stoke Gabriel
Harbertonford
Galmpton
Churston Ferrers
GREENWAY
BERRY HEAD
St Mary's Bay
Tuckenhay
Cornworthy
B
Crabadon
Washbourne
Dittisham
RIVER DART
P&R
Sharkham Pt.
A379
Hillhead
SX SY
Halwell
Allaleigh
Capton
B3205
Moreleigh
A3122
WOODLANDS LEISURE PARK
Dartmouth
Ferry
NEWCOMEN ENGINE HOUSE
Woodford
Blackawton
Kingswear
Scabbacombe Hd.
Ferry
Millcombe
BAYARDS COVE FORT
Warfleet
COLETON FISHACRE
Bowden
DARTMOUTH CASTLE
Mew Stone
East Allington
Stoke Fleming
Blackpool
Strete
Goveton
SOUTH WEST COAST PATH
Harleston
Slapton
C
Sherford
Slapton Sands
Frittiscombe
SLAPTON LEY
Kingsbridge
Stokenham
Frogmore
Chillington
START BAY
Torcross
Kernborough
Beeson
South Pool
Beesands
Kellaton
East Portlemouth
Hallsands
South Allington
START POINT
East Prawle
Lannacombe Bay
D
Prawle Pt.
SOUTH DEVON
0 1 2 3 miles
0 1 2 3 4 5 km
2
29
3
30
4

4
5
6
SR
SS
SW
SX
10
A
B
C
D
CORNWALL
Fire Beacon Pt.
BOSCASTLE
Trevalga
CASTLE
Tintagel Hd.
OLD POST OFFICE
TINTAGEL
Bossiney
Tintagel
308
Treknow
Trewarmett
B3263
Start Pt.
Trebarwith
Treligga
SOUTH WEST COAST PATH
Delabole
Valley Truckle
Port Isaac Bay
B3314
B3267
Helstone
Port Isaac
Port Quin
Port Gaverne
St Teath
Pentire Pt.
Port Quin Bay
New Polzeath
LONG CROSS
Trelights
Pendoggett
Treveighan
Gulland Rock
Padstow Bay
Polzeath
St Endellion
Trelill
A39
Michaelstow
Trebetherick
Gunver Hd.
St Minver
TREVOSE HEAD
Crugmeer
Pityme
Trewethern
St Kew
St Tudy
PRIDEAUX PLACE
Trevone
Chapel Amble
B3314
Rock
St Kew Highway
Constantine Bay
Constantine Bay
St Merryn
NATIONAL LOBSTER HATCHERY
Padstow
TREYARNON
Treyarnon
Camel
Bodieve
B3266
SOUTH WEST COAST PATH
Shop
Trevanson
St Mabyn
Little Petherick
Wadebridge
Porthcothan
B3276
Whitecross
St Breock
Egloshayle
A389
PENCARROW HOUSE
Camel
Helland
Park Hd.
Penrose
St Ervan
St Issey
A389
Rumford
Tredinnick
A39
Burlawn
St Jidgey
Washaway
Bodmin Forest
CREALY GREAT ADVENTURE PARK
ST BREOCK DOWNS MONOLITH
St Eval
A30

1
2
3
4
A
B
C
D
24
9
5
6
Coombe
Kilkhampton
Alfardisworthy
Stibb
Soldon Cross
A39
Poughill
Hersham
Grimscott
DUNSDON
Flexbury
Stratton
Bude Haven
1643
BUDE
BAY
Bude
Launcells
A3072
Pancrasweek
Upton
Marhamchurch
B3254
Tamar
Derril
Bridgerule
Derriton
Pyworthy
162
Widemouth Bay
Widemouth Sand
Budd's Titson
Leworthy
Coppathorne
Millook
Dizzard Pt.
Poundstock
SOUTH WEST COAST PATH
Tregole
Treskinnick Cross
Whitstone
North Tamerton
St Gennys
Trewint
Week St Mary
PENHALLAM
Cambeak
Crackington Haven
Rosecare
Jacobstow
Tetcott
Lana
Wainhouse Corner
Luffincott
Tresparrett Posts
B3263
West Curry
South Wheatley
Fire Beacon Pt.
260
Beeny
Maxworthy
Marshgate
Bennacott
Boyton
BOSCASTLE
Tresparrett
Canworthy Water
Brazacott
Boscastle
Lesnewth
Otterham
256
Warbstow
TAMAR OTTER & WILDLIFE CENTRE
Trevalga
Trelash
Langdon
Tremaine
Ottery
Bridgetown
Bossiney
B3266
B3262
North Petherwin
Tintagel
Hallworthy
Treneglos
308
Davidstow
Yeolmbridge
Trewarmett
Tremail
13
Tresmeer
Egloskerry
Langore
Trewassa
THE ARTHURIAN CENTRE
Tregeare
CORNWALL AT WAR
Davidstow Moor
St Stephen's
Trebarwith
Cold Northcott
HIDDEN VALLEY DISCOVERY PARK
B3314
A395
Piper's Pool
Launceston
Delabole
TRETHORNE LEISURE FARM
Tregadillett
CASTLE
Camelford
St Clether
Laneast
A30
Valley Truckle
Crowdy Res.
Trewen
Daw's House
Polyphant
Helstone
B3267
South Petherwin
Inny
High Moor
Altarnun
Lewannick
St Teath
400 ROUGH TOR
Treveighan
420 BROWN WILLY
Trewint
B3257
Lezant
369
Michaelstow
Codda
Congdon's Shop
331 GARROW TOR
Trebullett
St Breward
MUSEUM OF SMUGGLING
Trebartha
Row
Coad's Green
St Tudy
Bolventor
North Hill
Bray Shop
Bradford
BODMIN
Wenfordbridge
396 KILMAR TOR
Bathpool
Dozmary Pool
Henwood
Linkinhorne
Blisland
St Mabyn
MOOR
Rilla Mill
South Hill
Temple
342
Upton Cross
Camel
Colliford Lake
THE HURLERS STONE CIRCLES
Helland
268
Minions
369
Maidenwell
CARADON HILL
Millpool
Siblyback Lake
Pensilva
Trevigro
Commonmoor
Darite
Warleggan
GOLITHA FALLS
TRETHEVY QUOIT
KING DONIERT'S STONE
St Neot
Tremar
Gang
A390
0 1 2 3 miles
0 1 2 3 4 5 km

11
Milton Damerel
Torridge
Buckland Filleigh
25
Merton
Huish
Dolton
Hollocombe
Dowland
Shebbear
Thornbury
Petrockstow
Meeth
Iddesleigh
138
Winkleigh
Woodacott
Bradford
A386
Sheepwash
Broadwood Kelly
Black Torrington
SS
Monkokehampton
A3124
Cookbury
Holemoor
Bondleigh
Highampton
Hatherleigh
A3072
Holsworthy
Brandis Corner
Whimble
Hollacombe
Graddon Moor
WINSFORD WALLED GARDEN
B3216
Honeychurch
Chilla
193
150
Exbourne
A3079
Lew
Jacobstowe
Halwill Junction
Sampford Courtenay
Halwill
Beaworthy
Northlew
Inwardleigh
12
Clawton
Oak Cross
A388
Patchacott
Ashbury
DARTMOOR RAILWAY
Quoditch
Folly Gate
Taw Green
B3215
BROADBURY
Okehampton
WHITEHOUSE SERVICES
Ashwater
Eworthy
A30
Sticklepath
Henford
FINCH FOUNDRY
Carey
Germansweek
Boasley Cross
Thorndon Cross
Belstone
Virginstow
OKEHAMPTON (Dartmoor)
CASTLE
Okehampton Camp
Roadford Res.
SOURTON CROSS SERVICES
East Panson
Grinacombe Moor
Meldon
BRACKEN TOR
Bratton Clovelly
Okehampton Common
550
COSDON HILL
Gridley Corner
Sourton
619
YES TOR
Taw
Broadwoodwidger
Bridestowe
BLACK-A-TOR COPSE
621
HIGH WILLHAYS
Thrushel
Bridestowe and Sourton Common
Cross Green
Thrushelton
585
566
OKEMENT HILL
DINGLE'S FAIRGROUND HERITAGE CENTRE
Stowford
Lewdown
262
Shortacombe
Liftondown
Portgate
Lewtrenchard
604
HANGINGSTONE HILL
Lifton
Tinhay
Lydford
LYDFORD
DARTMOOR
Coryton
LYDFORD GORGE
SX
604
CUT HILL
537
SITTAFORD TOR
Lawhitton
Tamar
North Brentor
Black Down
Willsworthy
Kelly
Chillaton
DARTMOOR
Bradstone
Horndon
Milton Abbot
Mary Tavy
546
ROUGH TOR
Dunterton
B3362
Cudliptown
Rezare
NATIONAL
A386
Peter Tavy
FOREST
Sydenham Damerel
Lamerton
539
GT. MIS TOR
WISTMAN'S WOOD
Wilminstone
Tavy
Merrivale
PREHISTORIC SETTLEMENT
Two Bridges
Stoke Climsland
Horsebridge
B3357
Rundlestone
Tavistock
HIGH MOORLAND VISITOR CENTRE
Luckett
Latchley
A390
W. Dart
Princetown
Downgate
Whitchurch
Chilsworthy
Gulworthy
Sampford Spiney
Hexworthy
B3257
TOLL
Gunnislake
Grenofen
Kelly Bray
333
KIT HILL
St Ann's Chapel
PARK
B3212
Drakewalls
Higher Walreddon
Whiteworks
Albaston
Callington
Harrowbarrow
6
Horrabridge
Walkhampton
7
DUPATH WELL HOUSE
COTEHELE
Calstock
Buckland Monachorum
THE GARDEN HOUSE
Dousland
Burrator Res.

Hollocombe
Ashley
Wembworthy
Eastington
Black Dog
Puddington
Pennymoor
Morchard
Winkleigh
Brushford
Coldridge
Nymet Rowland
Lapford
Morchard Bishop
Woolfardisworthy
Poughill
Upham
Kennerleigh
Stockleigh English
Broadwood Kelly
Oldborough
Cheriton Fitzpaine
West Leigh
Ash Bullayne
East Village
Bondleigh
East Leigh
Zeal Monachorum
Down St Mary
Newbuildings
Honeychurch
Copplestone
Sandford
Upton Hellions
Exbourne
Knowle
THE COLLEGIATE CHURCH OF THE HOLY CROSS
Shobrooke
North Tawton
Bow
Sampford Courtenay
Nymet Tracey
Coleford
Crediton
Colebrooke
Itton
Sweetham
Hillerton
Yeoford
Uton
Hookway
DARTMOOR RAILWAY
Venny Tedburn
Newton St Cyres
Taw Green
Spreyton
WHITEHOUSE SERVICES
Hittisleigh
Sticklepath
South Tawton
Tedburn St Mary
FINCH FOUNDRY
South Zeal
Whitestone
Belstone
Whiddon Down
Cheriton Bishop
OKEHAMPTON (Dartmoor)
Crockernwell
Drewsteignton
Longdown
550 COSDON HILL
Throwleigh
CASTLE DROGO
Wonson
Sandypark
Teign
Easton
Dunsford
Gidleigh
Murchington
Chagford
Teigncombe
Doccombe
Bridfordmills
566
604 HANGINGSTONE HILL
Moretonhampstead
Bridford
Doddiscombsleigh
Frenchbeer
Christow
Higher Ashton
DARTMOOR
Lettaford
THE MINIATURE PONY CENTRE
North Bovey
Lower Ashton
537 SITTAFORD TOR
CANONTEIGN FALLS
Trusham
DARTMOOR
GRIMSPOUND
Manaton
Lustleigh
529 HAMELDOWN TOR
Water
Bovey
Hennock
Chudleigh
POSTBRIDGE INFORMATION CENTRE
546 ROUGH TOR
Postbridge
EAST DARTMOOR WOODS & HEATHS
Bovey Tracey
HOUND TOR
Chudleigh Knighton
NATIONAL
UGBROOKE HOUSE
FOREST
Bellever
Bonehill
Haytor Vale
Brimley
CRAFT CENTRE
Ideford
WISTMAN'S WOOD
BELLEVER (Dartmoor)
Widecombe in the Moor
HAYTOR INFORMATION CENTRE
Ilsington
Heathfield
473 RIPPON TOR
Liverton
STOVER
Preston
Coldeast
TRAGO MILLS
431
Ponsworthy
Teigngrace
Sigford
Princetown
W. Dart
Dartmeet
Kingsteignton
Hexworthy
Buckland in the Moor
Bickington
Highweek
NEWTON ABBOT
Poundsgate
PARK
Dart
RIVER DART ADVENTURES
NEWTON ABBOT
Whiteworks
West Ogwell
BRADLEY
Ashburton
East Ogwell
Wolborough
PRICKLY BALL FARM
DECOY
Holne
Woodland
Denbury
Abbotskerswell
BUCKFAST
0 1 2 3 miles
0 1 2 3 4 5 km
A3124
A377
A3072
A30
A382
A38
A383
B3220
B3042
B3215
B3212
B3206
B3193
B3357
B3387
B3344
26
11
7
8
SS
SX
EX

Cotteylands
Tiverton
237
Ash Thomas
Craddock
Smithincott
Ashill
27
Willand
DIGGERLAND
Abbey
Smeatharpe
Well Town
Cadeleigh
Butterleigh
BICKLEIGH MILL
DEVON RAILWAY CENTRE
Bickleigh
CULLOMPTON SERVICES
Cullompton
28
A373
Blackborough
BLACKDOWN HILLS
Sheldon
Dunkeswell
Kentisbeare
Upottery
283
BLACK DOWN
Luppitt
Rawridge
Cadbury
261
Colebrook
Dulford
Kerswell
Beacon
FURSDON HOUSE
Mutterton
Bradninch
Westcott
Norman's Green
Broadhembury
Wick
261
A30
Silverton
Culm
Exe
Tale
Monkton
Thorverton
Up Exe
Hele
Langford
Clyst Hydon
Plymtree
Payhembury
A373
Combe Raleigh
Ellerhayes
B3181
164
Tale
Awliscombe
Nether Exe
KILLERTON HOUSE
Clyst St Lawrence
Colestocks
Buckerell
14
Brampford Speke
Rewe
Budlake
Westwood
Talaton
Feniton
A30
Honiton
Offwell
A396
Clyst
Fenny Bridges
254
Stoke Canon
M5
ESCOT PARK
Gittisham
Upton Pyne
Broadclyst
Whimple
B3177
Alfington
A375
Poltimore
Dog Village
Jack in the Green
Fairmile
Ottery St Mary
Church Green
Cranbrook
Rockbeare
B3174
Farway
Pinhoe
Clyst Honiton
EAST DEVON
B3212
Whipton
EXETER INTERNATIONAL
West Hill
Otter
Broad Down
CATHEDRAL
P&R
29
A30
Marsh Green
Wiggaton
Heavitree
Sowton
EXETER SERVICES
Tipton St John
Sidbury
BLACKBURY CAMP
St Thomas
A3015
P&R
30
Clyst St Mary
Aylesbeare
B3180
Venn Ottery
Farringdon
224
Harcombe
Countess Wear
A3052
CREALY GREAT ADVENTURE PARK
Harpford
Bowd
Sidford
A3052
BEER QUARRY CAVES
Alphington
EXETER
P&R
Clyst St George
Woodbury Salterton
A3052
Newton Poppleford
Weston
Vicarage
B3179
Hawkerland
B3176
A375
Sid
Salcombe Regis
Branscombe
31
Topsham
MUS.
Ebford
A376
Woodbury
Colaton Raleigh
B3178
Cotmaton
A379
Exminster
Exton
BICTON PARK
Sidmouth
DORSET & EAST DEVON COAST WORLD HERITAGE SITE
Kennford
River Exe
BLACK HILL
167
Yettington
Otterton
Kenn
Ladram Bay
C
Powderham
Lympstone
A LA RONDE
B3179
East Budleigh
OTTERTON MILL
POWDERHAM CASTLE
SOUTH WEST COAST PATH
Kenton
Withycombe Raleigh
B3178
Knowle
B3178
Starcross
Budleigh Salterton
Danger Pt.
Littleham
FAIRLYNCH ARTS CENTRE AND MUSEUM
Cockwood
Exmouth
WORLD OF COUNTRY LIFE
Ashcombe
DAWLISH WARREN
EXMOUTH MODEL RAILWAY
Straight Pt.
DAWLISH
B3192
A379
SX
Dawlish Warren
Dawlish
Little Haldon
SY
D
247
Holcombe
Bishopsteignton
A381
Teignmouth
Teign
Shaldon
SHALDON WILDLIFE TRUST
Combeinteignhead
SOUTH WEST COAST PATH
Stokeinteignhead
8
BABBACOMBE BAY
A379
Maidencombe
4
5
6

Whitestaunton
St Nicholas
Cricket Malherbie
Chillington
Abbey
Smeatharpe
Marsh
A303
28
Wadeford
Cudworth
Chaffcombe
Crewkerne
BLACKDOWN
Newcott
Howley
A30
Cricket St Thomas
Hewish
Dunkeswell
Yarcombe
Wambrook
Chard
B3165
Upottery
261
B3162
Whatley
Wayford
Forton
Winsham
Clapton
Luppitt
Rawridge
A30
Tatworth
HILLS
Beacon
South Chard
Drimpton
A
Stockland
Furley
FORDE ABBEY AND GARDENS
Wick
261
Millhayes
Chardstock
B3167
Monkton
Membury
Tytherleigh
Thorncombe
Burstock
B3162
Combe Raleigh
Heathstock
Alston
Holditch
Cotleigh
218
Yarty
Churchill
A358
B3165
THE CRAFT AND DESIGN CENTRE
Ham
277
Birdsmoorgate
B3164
Dalwood
Smallridge
Axe
Hawkchurch
Wilmington
Marshalsea
Bettiscombe
Honiton
BURROW FARM
Weycroft
Marshwood
Offwell
13
AXE VALLEY WILDLIFE PARK
Axminster
Pilsdon
254
223
A35
256
A375
Shute
Kilmington
B3261
SHUTE BARTON
Church Green
A358
Wootton Fitzpaine
Northleigh
Whitchurch Canonicorum
Farway
Whitford
Ryall
EAST DEVON
B3165
Musbury
Char
Colyton
Morcombelake
Southleigh
Symondsbury
Broad Down
Charmouth
Uplyme
Combpyne
CHARMOUTH HERITAGE COAST CENTRE
Lyme Regis
Chideock
BLACKBURY CAMP
Colyford
A35
A3052
Rousdon
AQUARIUM
Seatown
Harcombe
B3172
DINOSAURLAND
155
Axmouth
A3052
SEATON TRAMWAY
SOUTH WEST COAST PATH
B3174
AXMOUTH TO LYME REGIS UNDERCLIFFS
Sidford
BEER QUARRY CAVES
BEER
Weston
Vicarage
Seaton
Charlton Bay
Beer
MARINE HOUSE
SOUTH WEST COAST PATH
Seaton Bay
LYME BAY
Salcombe Regis
Branscombe
DORSET & EAST DEVON COAST WORLD HERITAGE SITE
Beer Hd.
C
13
D
0 1 2 3 miles
0 1 2 3 4 5 km
2
3
4

15
Hardington Mandeville
Haselbury Plucknett
North Perrott
Hardington Marsh
182
Pendomer
Closworth
Ryme Intrinseca
Beer Hackett
29
Holwell
Crouch Hill
Holnest
Leigh
Chetnole
Glanvilles Wootton
Pulham
Halstock
South Perrott
Melbury Osmond
Melbury Sampford
Melbury Bubb
Hermitage
Middlemarsh
Westfields
Mosterton
Chedington
Corscombe
West Chelborough
Evershot
Hilfield
Lyon's Gate
Dunttish
Mappowder
238
Holywell
Batcombe
Minterne Magna
265
MINTERNE HOUSE & GARDENS
Buckland Newton
Alton Pancras
Higher A
Melcon
261
Bingh
Rampisham
Frome St Quintin
Up Cerne
Plush
Beaminster
CERNE ABBAS GIANT
Up Sydling
Cerne Abbas
16
Stoke Abbott
Wraxall
Cattistock
Sydling St Nicholas
Piddletrenthide
Mapperton
MAPPERTON
Hooke
Toller Porcorum
Chilfrome
Maiden Newton
Nether Cerne
White Lackington
Melplash
North Poorton
Toller Fratrum
HOG CLIFF
Godmanstone
Piddlehinton
Salwayash
West Milton
Powerstock
Nettlecombe
Wynford Eagle
Forston
Dottery
D O R S E T
135
Charlton Down
Bradpole
Eggardon Down
252
Frampton
Puddletown
Loders
Uploders
West Compton
Grimstone
Muckleford
Stratton
Charminster
HARDY'S COTTAGE GARDEN
Bridport
Askerswell
Compton Valence
Bradford Peverell
Dorchester
Walditch
170
Kingston Russell
Bothenhampton
Winterbourne Abbas
Stinsford
Kingston Maurward
Shipton Gorge
Chilcombe
THE TUTANKHAMUN EXHIBITION
Poundbury
Long Bredy
Litton Cheney
NINE STONES
MILITARY MUSEUM
THE DINOSAUR MUSEUM
West Stafford
West Bay
POOR LOT BARROWS
LITTON CHENEY
Winterbourne Steepleton
Martinstown
Burton Bradstock
132
Littlebredy
MAIDEN CASTLE
Whitcombe
Punckowle
Black Down
Winterborne Monkton
Winterborne Herringston
Swyre
VALLEY OF STONES
HARDY MONUMENT
West Knighton
KINGSTON RUSSELL STONE CIRCLE
West Bexington
SOUTH WEST COAST PATH
Broadmayne
Portesham
DORSET & EAST DEVON COAST WORLD HERITAGE SITE
Abbotsbury
SUB TROPICAL GARDENS
ABBOTSBURY CHILDREN'S FARM
ST CATHERINES CHAPEL
96
Rodden
Upwey
WHITE HORSE
Bincombe
Poxwell
Broadwey
Littlemoor
Preston
SWANNERY
SOUTH WEST COAST PATH
Nottington
Overcombe
Osmington
Langton Herring
JORDAN HILL ROMAN TEMPLE
Radipole
Osmington Mills
CHESIL BEACH
BENNETTS WATER GARDENS
SEA LIFE
Chickerell
Melcombe Regis
Ringstead Bay
Westham
Weymouth
Charlestown
NOTHE FORT
BREWER'S QUAY AND TIMEWALK
WEYMOUTH BAY
Rodwell
Wyke Regis
Portland Harbour
SY
WEYMOUTH & PORTLAND NATIONAL SAILING ACADEMY
PORTLAND
PORTLAND CASTLE
Fortuneswell
West Bay
130
Grove
Easton
Weston
PORTLAND
MUSEUM
Southwell
Bill of Portland
A37
A30
A3066
A356
A352
A35
A354
A353
B3163
B3146
B3143
B3142
B3159
B3157
B3156
4
5
6
7
A
B
C
D

Woodbridge
King's Stag
Fifehead Neville
Okeford Fitzpaine
Shillingstone
A350
30
Tarrant Hinton
St Michael
Long Crichel
Kingston
Stourpaine
Pimperne
Tarrant Launceston
Hazelbury Bryan
Ibberton
Durweston
Turnworth
Tarrant Monkton
ROYAL SIGNALS MUSEUM
Manswood
Pulham
Woolland
Blandford Forum
Bryanston
Tarrant Rawston
Witchampton
Westfields
Duntish
Mappowder
Stoke Wake
274
Blandford St Mary
Tarrant Rushton
ST
Winterborne Houghton
Winterborne Stickland
Tarrant Keyneston
Higher Ansty
Charlton Marshall
Tarrant Crawford
B3082
Melcombe Bingham
261
Hilton
Winterborne Clenston
Thorncombe
MILTON ABBEY
A354
Whatcombe
Spetisbury
Plush
Milton Abbas
B3143
127
Charlton Down
A350
Shapwick
KINGSTON LACY
15
Winterborne Whitechurch
Sturminster Marshall
Pamphill
Piddletrenthide
Cheselbourne
Almer
White Lackington
Dewlish
13
Winterborne Kingston
Winterborne Zelston
A31
Piddlehinton
Milborne St Andrew
Anderson
Corfe Mullen
A31
A354
Morden
A350
Hill View
B3142
MARTYRS MUSEUM
6
A35
109
East Morden
Lytchett Matravers
92
Puddletown
Bloxworth
Tolpuddle
Bere Regis
B3075
Athelhampton
Burleston
Slepe
Lytchett Minster
Turners Puddle
A35
Upton
Affpuddle
Briants Puddle
ATHELHAMPTON
FARMER PALMER'S FARM PARK
HARDY'S COTTAGE GARDEN
Tincleton
Lane End
Wareham Forest
A35
MORDEN BOG
Holton Heath
B3390
Hamworthy
Stinsford
88
Kingston Maurward
Woodsford
CLOUD'S HILL
A351
THE DINOSAUR MUSEUM
West Stafford
Piddle or Trent
Trigon Hill
Moreton
Bovington Camp
Sandford
P&R
Whitcombe
MORETON
Frome
MONKEY WORLD
Northport
Arne
TANK MUSEUM
Crossways
Winterborne Herringston
Wareham
Stokeford
West Knighton
A352
MILL HOUSE CIDER MUSEUM
East Burton
Stoborough
Ridge
Broadmayne
Wool
East Stoke
A352
Warmwell
West Holme
Stoborough Green
STOBOROUGH HEATH
HARTLAND MOOR
12
Owermoigne
East Knighton
WHITE HORSE
Poxwell
Winfrith Newburgh
Coombe Keynes
Middlebere Heath
Wytch Heath
13
B3071
B3070
Grange Heath
THE BLUE POOL
P&R
A353
Preston
Upton
Holworth
Chaldon Herring or East Chaldon
Norden Heath
LULWORTH CASTLE
Osmington
TOLL
East Creech
199
ISLE OF
Corfe Castle
B3351
D O R S E T
CASTLE
Chaldon Down
Church Knowle
MODEL VILLAGE & GARDENS
Osmington Mills
SOUTH WEST COAST PATH
West Lulworth
East Lulworth
PURBECK HILLS
SEA LIFE
Ringstead Bay
B3071
LULWORTH COVE
Steeple
PURBECK
168
Weymouth
15
Durdle Door
HERITAGE CENTRE
Tyneham
Kingston
B3069
Lulworth Cove
Worbarrow Bay
ETCHES COLLECTION MUSEUM
Kimmeridge
WEYMOUTH BAY
203
Kimmeridge Bay
LANGTON MATRAVERS
Acton
Worth Matravers
SY
St Alban's Head
WEYMOUTH & PORTLAND NATIONAL SAILING ACADEMY
PORTLAND
130
Grove
Easton
PORTLAND
MUSEUM
0 1 2 3 miles
0 1 2 3 4 5 km
A
B
C
D
1
2
3

Verwood
Ringwood Forest
Ringwood
Wimborne Minster
Ferndown
West Moors
St Leonards
Poole
Bournemouth
Boscombe
CHRISTCHURCH
Highcliffe
New Milton
Barton on Sea
Milford on Sea
LYMINGTON
Brockenhurst
Burley
NEW FOREST NATIONAL PARK
Christchurch Bay
Hengistbury Head
POOLE BAY
SZ
Sandbanks
Studland
The Foreland
Swanage
Peveril Pt.
Durlston Head
Tilly Whim Caves
CHERBOURG
GUERNSEY
JERSEY (April-Oct)
ST. MALO (May-Sept)
The Needles
Alum Bay
Totland Bay

SOUTHAMPTON
NEW FOREST NATIONAL PARK
Lyndhurst
Emery Down
Newtown
Woodlands
Ashurst
Pooksgreen
NEW FOREST WILDLIFE PARK
LONGDOWN ACTIVITY FARM
SEA CITY MUS
Marchwood
Itchen
Sholing
Woolston
Old Netley
Netley
NETLEY ABBEY
Bursledon
Hound
Lowford
Burridge
Swanwick
Lower Swanwick
Park Gate
HOLLY HILL WOODLAND PARK
Locks Heath
Warsash
Titchfield
Newtown
TITCHFIELD HAVEN
Hamble-le-Rice
ST ANDREWS
ROYAL VICTORIA
SOUTHAMPTON WATER
Hythe
Dibden
Dibden Purlieu
Buttsash
Hardley
Holbury
Fawley
Ashlett
Blackfield
Langley
Calshot
CALSHOT CASTLE
CALSHOT ACTIVITIES CENTRE
Hill Head
Lee-on-the
Stubbington
NEW FOREST CENTRE
REPTILIARY
Clayhill
Bank
Denny Lodge
New Park
Balmerlawn
Brockenhurst
Beaulieu Heath
Hill Top
PALACE HO
NATIONAL MOTOR MUS
ABBEY
Beaulieu
Hatchet Gate
East Boldre
Beaulieu Heath
Setley
Battramsley
Bull Hill
Bucklers Hard
MARITIME MUSEUM
EXBURY
Exbury
LEPE
Lepe
Stone Pt.
Needs Ore Pt.
Wootton
Sway
Boldre
Pilley
SPINNERS
Norleywood
East End
Portmore
Mount Pleasant
Golden Hill
Hordle
Buckland
Walhampton
LYMINGTON
Pennington
Waterford
Woodside
Ashley
Everton
Milton
BRAXTON
Downton
Lymore
Lower Pennington
KEYHAVEN & PENNINGTON MARSHES
Milford on Sea
Keyhaven
HURST CASTLE
Sconce Pt.
FORT VICTORIA
ISLAND PLANETARIUM
Norton
Yarmouth
Colwell Bay
Totland
Totland Bay
TOTLAND BAY
Pound Green
Freshwater
Norton Green
Freshwater Bay
Alum Bay
The Needles
THE NEEDLES PARK
THE NEEDLES OLD BATTERY
Freshwater Bay
Afton
Cowes
MARITIME MUSEUM
East Cowes
OSBORNE HOUSE
Gurnard Bay
Gurnard
Rew Street
Northwood
Thorness Bay
Whippingham
Medina
Newtown Bay
NEWTOWN HARBOUR
Porchfield
Parkhurst
Parkhurst Forest
Hamstead
OLD TOWN HALL
Newtown
Cranmore
Thorley Street
Shalfleet
Ningwood
Gunville
Carisbrooke
Hunny Hill
NEWPORT
ROMAN VILLA
Shide
BUTTERFLY WORLD
Staplers
Wellow
Newbridge
CALBOURNE WATER MILL
Calbourne
CHESSELL POTTERY BARNS
Clatterford
CARISBROOKE CASTLE
Bowcombe
Blackwater
ARRETON MANOR
Merstone
Rookley
ISLE OF WIGHT
Shalcombe
Brighstone Forest
Gatcombe
Chillerton
Hulverstone
Brook
Mottistone
Moortown
Shorwell
Limerstone
Brighstone
BRIGHSTONE
Kingston
Yafford
Thorncross
Godshill
The Undercliff
Brighstone Bay
Little Atherfield
Roud
Chale Green
Pyle
Atherfield Pt.
Chale
Chale Bay
Blackgang
Blackgang Chine
BLACKGANG CHINE
ST CATHERINE'S ORATORY
Niton
Whitwell
St Catherine's Point
THE SOLENT
A35
A337
A326
B3056
B3055
B3054
B3053
A3054
A3020
A3021
A3055
B3401
B3399
B3323
A3056
B3058
B3397
A3025
A27
17
32
164
167
83
236
C
D
2
3
4
0 1 2 3 miles
0 1 2 3 4 5 km

PORTSMOUTH
GOSPORT
HAVANT
RYDE
Waterlooville
Purbrook
Portchester
Southsea
Emsworth
Southbourne
Bosham
South Hayling
HAYLING ISLAND
East Wittering
Selsey
Bembridge
Sandown
Shanklin
Ventnor
SPITHEAD
CHICHESTER HARBOUR
Portsmouth Harbour
Langstone Harbour
Chichester Harbour
Stokes Bay
Sandown Bay
Whitecliff Bay
Culver Cliff
Luccombe Chine
Dunnose
Nettlestone Pt.
Gilkicker Pt.
FOREST OF BERE
Ports Down
CAEN
LE HAVRE
ST. MALO
BILBAO
SANTANDER
GUERNSEY
JERSEY
CHERBOURG (April-Sept)
SZ
20

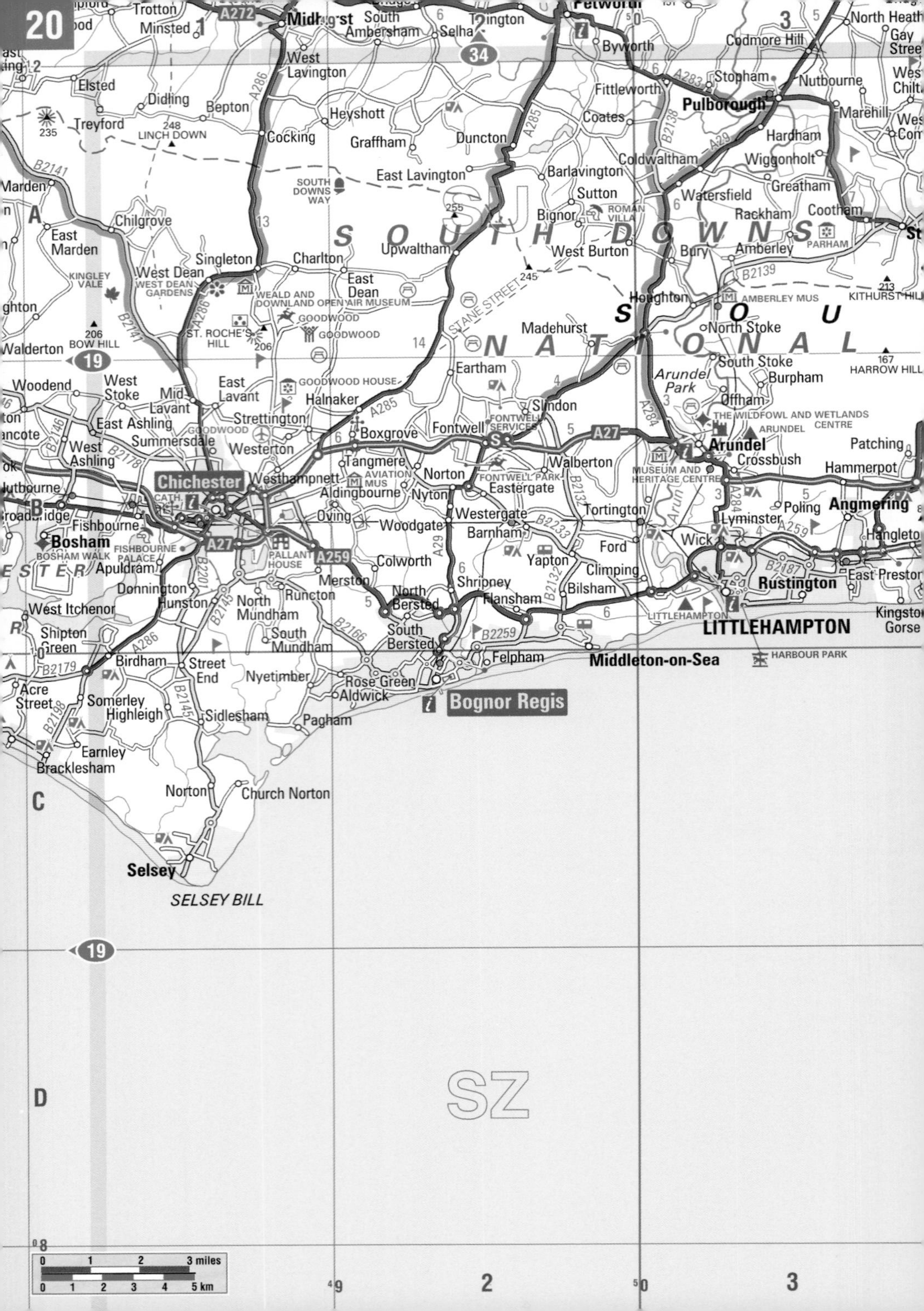
Trotton
Minsted
A272
Midhurst
South
Ambersham
Selham
Tillington
34
Petworth
Byworth
North Heath
Codmore Hill
Gay Street
Stopham
Nutbourne
West Chiltington
Pulborough
Marehill
West Lavington
Elsted
Didling
Bepton
A286
Fittleworth
Coates
Heyshott
Treyford
248
LINCH DOWN
235
Cocking
Graffham
Duncton
A285
B2138
Hardham
A29
Coldwaltham
Wiggonholt
East Lavington
Barlavington
B2141
Marden
SOUTH DOWNS WAY
Sutton
Watersfield
Greatham
255
ROMAN VILLA
Bignor
Rackham
Cootham
Chilgrove
East Marden
SOUTH DOWNS
Upwaltham
West Burton
Bury
Amberley
PARHAM
Singleton
Charlton
KINGLEY VALE
West Dean
WEST DEAN GARDENS
East Dean
WEALD AND DOWNLAND OPEN AIR MUSEUM
STANE STREET
245
B2139
Houghton
AMBERLEY MUS
KITHURST HILL
213
GOODWOOD
ST. ROCHE'S HILL
206
Madehurst
North Stoke
SOUTH DOWNS NATIONAL
206
BOW HILL
Walderton
19
South Stoke
167
HARROW HILL
Eartham
Arundel Park
Burpham
Woodend
West Stoke
Mid Lavant
East Lavant
GOODWOOD HOUSE
Halnaker
A285
Slindon
Offham
THE WILDFOWL AND WETLANDS CENTRE
ARUNDEL
East Ashling
Strettington
GOODWOOD
Boxgrove
Fontwell
FONTWELL SERVICES
A27
A284
Arundel
Patching
West Ashling
Summersdale
Westerton
Tangmere
AVIATION MUS
Walberton
MUSEUM AND HERITAGE CENTRE
Crossbush
Hammerpot
B2178
B2146
Chichester
CATH.
Westhampnett
Aldingbourne
Norton
FONTWELL PARK
Eastergate
B2132
Nyton
Westergate
Tortington
Poling
Angmering
Broadbridge
Fishbourne
Oving
Woodgate
Barnham
B2233
Arun
Lyminster
A259
Bosham
BOSHAM WALK
FISHBOURNE PALACE
A27
PALLANT HOUSE
A259
Colworth
A29
Ford
Wick
Hangleton
Apuldram
B2201
Yapton
Climping
B2187
East Preston
Donnington
Merston
Runcton
Shripney
Rustington
West Itchenor
Hunston
B2145
North Mundham
North Bersted
Flansham
Bilsham
Kingston Gorse
LITTLEHAMPTON
Shipton Green
South Mundham
B2166
South Bersted
B2259
LITTLEHAMPTON
Felpham
Middleton-on-Sea
HARBOUR PARK
B2179
Birdham
A286
Street End
Nyetimber
Rose Green
Aldwick
Acre Street
Somerley
Highleigh
B2145
Sidlesham
Bognor Regis
Pagham
B2198
Earnley
Bracklesham
Norton
Church Norton
Selsey
SELSEY BILL
19
SU
SZ
0
1
2
3 miles
0
1
2
3
4
5 km

West Grinstead
Cowfold
Kent Street
Wineham
Twineham
Sayers Common
ALL ENGLAND JUMPING COURSE
BURGESS HILL
Wivelsfield
Wivelsfield Green
Chailey
South Street
DITCHLING COMMON
Broomer's Corner
Goose Green
Dial Post
Partridge Green
Spear Hill
Thakeham
Ashington
Ashurst
West End
Blackstone
Albourne
WASHBROOKS FARM CENTRE
Hurstpierpoint
Hurst Wickham
Plumpton Green
Henfield
Woodmancote
Hassocks
Keymer
Ditchling
MUS OF ART & CRAFT
Streat
Chiltington
East Chiltington
Rock
Wiston
Clayton
Westmeston
Cooksbridge
Washington
Small Dole
Poynings
Pyecombe
Plumpton
DITCHLING BEACON
Offham
MT. HARRY
Fulking
Steyning
Bramber
Edburton
Saddlescombe
STANMER PARK
Upper Beeding
TRULEIGH HILL
DEVIL'S DYKE
Wellands Park
ST MARY'S HOUSE
Botolphs
Findon
Stanmer
Patcham
Coldean
Falmer
Coombes
Mile Oak
Westdene
Withdean
Kingston near Lewes
High Salvington
North Lancing
Portslade
West Blatchington
PRESTON MANOR
Moulsecoomb
Bevendean
CASTLE HILL
Preston
BRIGHTON
Kingston by Sea
Southwick
SHOREHAM
Woodingdean
Sompting
Lancing
MUS & ART GAL
ROYAL PAVILION
Broadwater
SHOREHAM-BY-SEA
Portslade-by-Sea
HOVE
Kemp Town
Ovingdean
South Lancing
BRITISH AIRWAYS i360 TOWER
Telscombe
East Worthing
MARLIPINS MUSEUM
BRIGHTON
BRIGHTON SEA LIFE
Saltdean
Rottingdean
Worthing
Goring-by-Sea
West Worthing
VOLK'S ELECTRIC RAILWAY
BRIGHTON MARINA
Telscombe Cliffs
Peacehaven
SOUTH DOWNS
TQ
TV
22

Uckfield
Newick
North Chailey
Chailey
South Street
Spithurst
Isfield
Ridgewood
Little Horsted
Halland
East Hoathly
Framfield
Blackboys
Heathfield
Cade Street
Old Heathfield
Waldron
Little London
Foxhunt Green
Maynard's Green
Vine's Cross
Warbleton
Rushlake Green
Horam
Burlow
Foul Mile
Cowbeech
Chiddingly
Gun Hill
Herstmonceux
Hellingly
Lower Horsebridge
Upper Horsebridge
Magham Down
Hailsham
Golden Cross
Lower Dicker
Upper Dicker
Whitesmith
Laughton
Shortgate
Rose Hill
Barcombe Cross
Barcombe
Chiltington
East Chiltington
Plumpton Green
Plumpton
Cooksbridge
Hamsey
Offham
Broyle Side
Ringmer
Lewes
South Malling
Glyndebourne
Mark Cross
Ripe
Chalvington
Wallands Park
Glynde
Falmer
Kingston near Lewes
Beddingham
Iford
Rodmell
Southease
Woodingdean
Ovingdean
Telscombe
Piddinghoe
Saltdean
Rottingdean
Telscombe Cliffs
Peacehaven
Newhaven
Tarring Neville
South Heighton
Denton
Norton
Bishopstone
West Firle
Alciston
Selmeston
Arlington
Berwick
Wilmington
Folkington
Alfriston
Litlington
Willingdon
Jevington
Polegate
Stone Cross
Westham
Pevensey
Hankham
Friday Street
Hampden Park
Roselands
Eastbourne
Seaford
East Blatchington
Westdean
Friston
East Dean
Holywell
Birling Gap
BEACHY HEAD
DIEPPE
SOUTH DOWNS WAY
SEVEN SISTERS
WILLINGDON HILL
FIRLE BEACON
CHARLESTON FARMHOUSE
GLYNDE PLACE
LEWES DOWNS (MOUNT CABURN)
CLIFFE HILL
ANNE OF CLEVES HO
MONKS HO
CASTLE HILL
MT. HARRY
STANMER PARK
LAVENDER LINE STEAM RAILWAY
E.SUSSEX NATIONAL
CHIDDINGLY PARISH CHURCH
MICHELHAM PRIORY
DRUSILLAS PARK
CLERGY HOUSE
THE LONG MAN OF WILMINGTON
LULLINGTON HEATH
NEWHAVEN FORT
PARADISE PARK
TOWNER GALLERY
A22
A26
A27
A259
A275
A272
A267
A295
A271
A2270
B2192
B2124
B2116
B2102
B2123
B2104
B2191
B2203
1 2 3 4
A B C D
0 1 2 3 miles
0 1 2 3 4 5 km

Brightling
Darwell Hole
Dallington
Netherfield
Mountfield
Penhurst
Whatlington
Canadia
Battle
John's Cross
Vinehall Street
Cripp's Corner
Sedlescombe
Sedlescombe Street
BREDE STEAM GIANTS
Broad Oak
Broadland Row
Udimore
Brede
Rye
Foreign
Playden
RYE HERITAGE CENTRE
Rye Harbour
CAMBER CASTLE
Winchelsea
WINCHELSEA COURT HALL MUS
Winchelsea Beach
Rye Bay
Guestling Thorn
Icklesham
Three Oaks
Westfield
Pett
Guestling Green
Cliff End
Fairlight
Fairlight Cove
HASTINGS
Ore
St Helen's
ST CLEMENT'S CAVES
UNDERWATER WORLD
Hastings
Baldslow
Kent Street
Telham
1066 ABBEY
Catsfield
Henley's Down
Crowhurst
Hollington
Ninfield
Boreham Street
Lunsford's Cross
Hooe Common
Hooe
Little Common
Sidley
COMBE VALLEY
Silverhill
St Leonards
Bulverhythe
West Marina
Cooden
BEXHILL
DE LA WARR PAVILION
PEVENSEY SERVICES
Norman's Bay
Pevensey Bay
TQ
TV
A21
A259
A2100
A271
A269
A2691
A2690
A2036
B2089
B2244
B2096
B2204
B2095
B2092
B2182
37
38
A
B
C
D
4
5
6
7

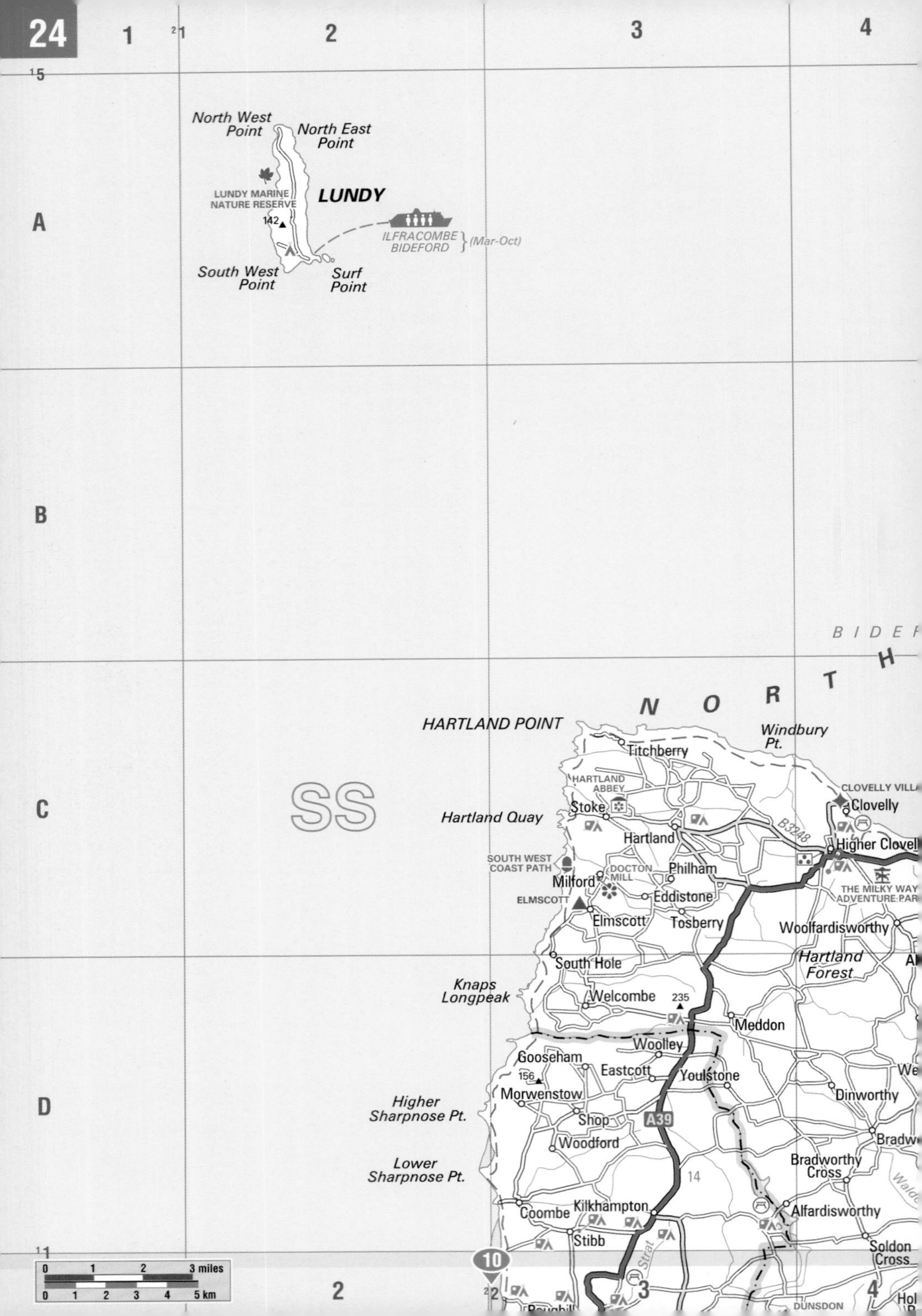
1
2
3
4
A
B
C
D
North West Point
North East Point
LUNDY
LUNDY MARINE NATURE RESERVE
142
ILFRACOMBE
BIDEFORD
(Mar-Oct)
South West Point
Surf Point
BIDEF
NORTH
HARTLAND POINT
Titchberry
Windbury Pt.
HARTLAND ABBEY
Stoke
Hartland Quay
Hartland
CLOVELLY VILL
Clovelly
B3248
Higher Clovell
SOUTH WEST COAST PATH
DOCTON MILL
Milford
Philham
THE MILKY WAY ADVENTURE PAR
ELMSCOTT
Eddistone
Elmscott
Tosberry
Woolfardisworthy
SS
South Hole
Hartland Forest
Knaps Longpeak
Welcombe
235
Meddon
Woolley
Gooseham
156
Eastcott
Youlstone
Morwenstow
Dinworthy
Higher Sharpnose Pt.
Shop
A39
Woodford
Bradworthy Cross
Lower Sharpnose Pt.
14
Alfardisworthy
Coombe
Kilkhampton
Stibb
Soldon Cross
Strat
10
3
DUNSDON
0 1 2 3 miles
0 1 2 3 4 5 km

25
4
5
6
7
LUNDY (Mar-Oct)
HELE CORN MILL
Rillage Pt.
Combe Martin Bay
Ilfracombe
ILFRACOMBE MUSEUM
Hele
WATERMOUTH CASTLE
Girt Down
Trentishoe
Heale
Bull Pt.
Rockham Bay
Lee
Whitestone
Slade
Berrynarbor
Combe Martin
Sterridge
WILDLIFE & DINOSAUR PARK
Morte Point
Mortehoe
A361
B3230
A399
A3123
Woolacombe
MORTE BAY
Trimstone
Berry Down Cross
Kentisbury
Cheglinch
Berry Down
B3229
Patchole
Kentisbury Ford
B3343
Woolacombe Sand
Dean
SOUTH WEST COAST PATH
Bittadon
West Down
East Down
Pickwell
North Buckland
EXMOOR ZOO
Baggy Pt.
Putsborough
Churchill
Arlington
Georgeham
ARLINGTON COURT
26
Croyde Bay
Nethercott
Halsinger
Milltown
Loxhore
Knightacott
Croyde
Darracott
Muddiford
B3231
Lobb
Knowle
Marwood
Guineaford
Shirwell
Bratton Fleming
Saunton
Pippacott
Kingsheanton
Shirwell Cross
Braunton
Yeo
Stoke Rivers
ELLIOT GALLERY
Heanton
MARWOOD HILL GARDENS
Prixford
BROOMHILL
Saunton Sands
Punchardon
Wrafton
Ashford
Burridge
TOLL
Braunton Burrows
Chivenor
Barnstaple
Goodleigh
Gunn
LUNDY (Mar-Oct)
Taw
Pilton
MUSEUM OF BARNSTAPLE & NORTH DEVON
DEVON
Fremington
Westacott
Yelland
Bickington
P&R
Newport
West Buckland
B3233
Bickleton
A39
Landkey
D BAY
NORTH DEVON MARITIME MUSEUM
Bishops Tawton
NORTHAM BURROWS
Instow
Swimbridge Newland
Appledore
A361
Torridge
TAPELEY PARK GDNS
Tawstock
Swimbridge
Westward Ho!
Westleigh
Northam
A386
Orchard Hill
Horwood
Newton Tracey
Eastleigh
Herner
Cobbaton
THE BIG SHEEP
Bideford
Ensis
East Stowford
Abbotsham
BURTON ART GALL & MUS
Hiscott
Chapelton
COBBATON COMBAT COLLECTION
East-the-Water
Woodtown
Chittlehampton
Handy Cross
Alverdiscott
Fishleigh Barton
A39
ATLANTIC VILLAGE
Fairy Cross
Ford
Landcross
A377
Horns Cross
Woodtown
B3232
Umberleigh
Yarnscombe
Atherington
Littleham
Goldworthy
Warkleigh
A386
Langridge Ford
Weare Giffard
B3217
Parkham
Buckland Brewer
Sherwood Green
Chittlehamholt
Monkleigh
High Bullen
B3227
High Bickington
Parkham Ash
216
DARTINGTON CRYSTAL
St Giles in the Wood
Frithelstock
Frithelstock Stone
Great Torrington
Taddiport
Tythecott
Kingscott
Roborough
A388
B3227
R.H.S. GARDEN ROSEMOOR
205
Burrington
East Putford
Little Torrington
GNOME RESERVE & GARDEN
Langtree
Beaford
D
Bulkworthy
Stibb Cross
A3124
Riddlecombe
Peters Marland
B3217
Ashreigney
Abbots Bickington
Newton St Petrock
Woollaton
Winswell
Merton
Dolton
Huish
Milton Damerel
Hollocombe
170
Torridge
Buckland Filleigh
Dowland
11
Petrockstow
Shebbear
Thornbury
Meeth
Iddesleigh
Winkleigh

1
2
3
Highveer Pt.
Foreland Pt.
Lynmouth Bay
Woody Bay
CLIFF RAILWAY
Lynmouth
Countisbury
Lynton
Trentishoe
Martinhoe
WATERSMEET HOUSE
Brendon
Malmsmead
CULBONE HILL
413
TOLL
Porlock Bay
Porlock Weir
Bossingt
Oare
B3225
Barbrook
East Ilkerton
Cheriton
Heale
349
LYNTON AND BARNSTAPLE RLY
A39
Martinhoe Cross
WILDLIFE & DINOSAUR PARK
A399
Parracombe
West Lyn
Furzehill
Shallowford
B3223
E X M O O R
Brendon Common
HAWKCOMBE WOODS
Holnicote Estate
Kentisbury
B3229
Blackmoor Gate
EXMOOR FOREST
465
Patchole
Kentisbury Ford
Challacombe Common
Pinkworthy Pond
487
THE DUNKERY & HORNER WOOD
25
EXMOOR ZOO
B3358
PINKERY
Exe Plain
Challacombe
Arlington
ARLINGTON COURT
Exe
N A T I O N A
329
Shoulsbarrow Common
Simonsbath
B3223
Edgcott
Loxhore
Knightacott
Leworthy
Exford
EXFORD
Shirwell
Yeo
Bratton Fleming
Bray
Barle
Shirwell Cross
Stoke Rivers
Benton
A399
Lydcott
493
443
HORSEN HILL
Withypool
Withypool Common
WINSFORD HILL
B
Goodleigh
13
Brayford
North Radworthy
Gunn
265
High Bray
North Heasley
P A R K
426
Liscombe
Charles
Heasley Mill
South Radworthy
TARR STEPS
West Buckland
East Buckland
377
Molland Common
Dane's Brook
Hawkridge
224
Swimbridge
10
A361
Twitchen
North Molton
Anstey Common
Filleigh
Mole
West Anstey
Molland
Cobbaton
QUINCE HONEY FARM
SS
East Anstey
East Stowford
Yeo
Yeo Mill
COBBATON COMBAT COLLECTION
B3227
Chittlehampton
B3226
South Molton
Bish Mill
Newtown
B3227
Oldways End
C
Umberleigh
Clapworthy
173
Bishops Nympton
Ash Mill
Knowstone
Roachill
Warkleigh
Satterleigh
George Nympton
Alswear
Mariansleigh
B3217
High Bickington
Chittlehamholt
Rose Ash
17
Taw
25
Romansleigh
Meshaw
A361
King's Nympton
238
Creacombe
STOODLEIGH BEACON
A377
Rackenford
301
B3137
Cadbury Barton
205
Burrington
26
Week
Elstone
Dart
Queen Dart
Lutworthy
Little
D
B3096
Templeton Bridge
Chulmleigh
West Worlington
East Worlington
Witheridge
Ashreigney
Cheldon
Drayford
Templeton
Nomansland
B3042
Thelbridge Barton
Washford Pyne
B3137
Chawleigh
Cruwys Morchard
Ashley
Hollocombe
B3042
Pennymoor
Dalch
Filleigh
Black Dog
Puddington
Wembworthy
12
Eastington
0 1 2 3 miles
0 1 2 3 4 5 km
Winkleigh
Coldridge
Lapford
Morchard
Woolfardisworthy
Poughill

4
30
5
31
6
BRIDGWATER
BAY
ST
SOUTH WEST COAST PATH
SELWORTHY BEACON
308
Selworthy
Woodcombe
Minehead
WEST SOMERSET RAILWAY
BUTLINS
Alcombe
A39
Periton
Luccombe
Marsh Street
MINEHEAD
DOLL MUS
Blue Anchor Bay
ENGLAND COAST PATH
Wootton Courtenay
DUNKERY VINEYARD
Dunster
MILL & YARN MARKET
DUNSTER CASTLE
Cowbridge
Timberscombe
Carhampton
Blue Anchor
Old Cleeve
B3191
Watchet
MARKET HOUSE MUS
West Quantoxhead
East Quantoxhead
Kilton
Burton
Lilstock
Stringston
Kilve
A39
TROPIQUARIA
A396
BRENDON
Withycombe
Bilbrook
Washford
Williton
Staple
QUANTOCK
Holford
28
Nether Stowey
CLEEVE ABBEY
Sampford Brett
CROYDON HILL
FOREST
365
Rodhuish
Bicknoller
COLERIDGE COTTAGE
Cutcombe
Wheddon Cross
Yard
B3188
Vellow
Roadwater
Luxborough
Over Stowey
358
423
LYPE HILL
Kingsbridge
290
Monksilver
Stogumber
WEST SOMERSET RAILWAY
A358
QUANTOCK FOREST
B3224
BRENDON HILLS
Treborough
B3190
Crowcombe
412
Elworthy
Flaxpool
Lower Vexford
384
HILLS
Exton
B3224
West Bagborough
Willett
Withiel Florey
Clatworthy Res.
Lydeard St Lawrence
16
Brompton Regis
Tolland
B3224
Brompton Ralph
East Combe
Combe Florey
Cothelstone
27
Clatworthy
Tarr
Cushuish
A396
Wimbleball Lake
Langley Marsh
Ash Priors
Huish Champflower
Bishops Lydeard
Upton
355
HADDON HILL
Maundown
B3188
Fitzhead
A358
B3222
HEYDON HILL
338
Wiveliscombe
Halse
Skilgate
Chipstable
VALE OF TAUNTON DEANE
Bury
B3190
Preston Bowyer
B3227
Heathfield
Barle
Milverton
Hillcommon
Norton Fitzwarren
Waterrow
Morebath
Oake
Petton
B3227
Hillfarance
Exebridge
Bathealton
B3187
267
Shillingford
East Nynehead
Bradford-on-Tone
239
Bampton
Langford Budville
Nynehead
Clayhanger
A38
Kittisford
SHEPPY'S CIDER
Runnington
Oakford
Appley
COTHAY
Wellington
Thorne St Margaret
Ashbrittle
Rockwell Green
West Buckland
Huntsham
Holywell Lake
26
28
Hockworthy
Cove
9
286
Stoodleigh
Holcombe Rogus
Sampford Arundel
Angersleigh
8
Wrangway
Ford Street
A396
Westleigh
EXE VALLEY
M5
East Mere
BLACKDOWN HILLS
Washfield
Chevithorne
Nicholashayne
Burlescombe
Whitnage
Clayhidon
Uplowman
KNIGHTSHAYES COURT
7
Bolham
Rosemary Lane
A38
Appledore
Chettiscombe
Calverleigh
A361
27
Culm Valley
Culmstock
BLACKDOWN
TIVERTON CASTLE
Sampford Peverell
Halberton
Uffculme
Stapley
Cowleymoor
B3391
Hemyock
TIVERTON SERVICES
COLDHARBOUR MILL
258
HACKPEN HILL
GRAND WESTERN CANAL
Craddock
Bolham Water
Cotteylands
Tiverton
B3440
237
Smithincott
Ash Thomas
Ashill
HILLS
4
Abbey
Smeatharpe
Willand
DIGGERLAND
13
Well Town
A396
Blackborough
4
5
CULLOMPTON SERVICES
6
Cadeleigh
Butterleigh
Sheldon
Dunkeswell
Cullompton
Kentisbeare
A
B
C
D

Burnham-on-Sea
Berrow
Brent Knoll
East Brent
Edithmead
Stone Allerton
Chapel Allerton
Cocklake
West Stoughton
Mark Causeway
Mark
Blackford
STERT FLATS
BRIDGWATER BAY
Highbridge
Watchfield
Westham
Heath House
Stolford
Steart
Huntspill
Bason Bridge
SECRET WORLD
East Huntspill
WWT STEART MARSHES NAT RESERVE
Lilstock
Kilton
Burton
Shurton
Stockland Bristol
Stretcholt
HUNTSPILL RIVER
Burtle
Brue
Kilve
Stringston
Stogursey
Otterhampton
Combwich
Pawlett
Puriton
Woolavington
Westhay
Holford
Nether Stowey
Fiddington
Parrett
Dunball
Cossington
Chilton Polden
Edington
THE PEAT MOOR VISITOR CENTRE
COLERIDGE COTTAGE
CANNINGTON COLLEGE
Rodway
Cannington
Bawdrip
POLDEN HILLS
Catcott
Over Stowey
Chilton Trinity
Stawell
Shapwick
QUANTOCK FOREST
Charlynch
BLAKE MUS
Wembdon
BRIDGWATER AND TAUNTON CANAL AND DOCKS
Chedzoy
Moorlinch
Greinton
Crowcombe
Spaxton
Four Forks
Durleigh
Bridgwater
Sutton Mallet
Pedwell
Flaxpool
Lower Aisholt
Enmore
BRIDGWATER SERVICES
Westonzoyland
West Bagborough
Courtway
Goathurst
North Petherton
Huntworth
King's Sedge Moor
TEMPLE OF HARMONY
WESTONZOYLAND PUMPING STATION
SOMERSET LEVELS
QUANTOCK HILLS
FYNE COURT
Middlezoy
East Combe
Cothelstone
Broomfield
Northmoor Green or Moorland
Othery
Pathe
High Ham
Cushuish
North Newton
Thurloxton
BRIDGWATER & TAUNTON CANAL MAUNSEL LOCKS
Burrow-bridge
Lyng
Aller
Bishops Lydeard
Fulford
Pickney
Kingston St Mary
HESTERCOMBE GARDENS
Hedging
Stathe
Athelney
Nailsbourne
West Monkton
A361
Durston
West Lyng
Halse
DEANE
Heathfield
Cheddon Fitzpaine
Monkton Heathfield
Creech Heathfield
Tone
Stoke St Gregory
Langport
Staplegrove
Bathpool
North End
Meare Green
WILLOWS & WETLANDS VISITOR CENTRE
West Sedge Moor
Huish Episcopi
Norton Fitzwarren
P&R
Creech St Michael
Knapp
Curry Rivel
Bishop's Hull
Hillfarance
SOMERSET CRICKET MUS
Ruishton
North Curry
Drayton
ABBEY
East Nynehead
Bradford-on-Tone
Taunton
Thornfalcon
A378
Henlade
Fivehead
SHEPPY'S CIDER
Trull
Stoke St Mary
Isle
Staplehay
TAUNTON
Wrantage
Curry Mallet
Isle Brewers
TAUNTON DEANE SERVICES
Orchard Portman
Thurlbear
West Hatch
Hatch Beauchamp
Isle Abbotts
Hambridge
West Buckland
M5
Beercrocombe
Pitminster
Corfe
Hatch Green
Westport
East Lambrook
West Lambrook
Staple Fitzpaine
A358
E. LAMBROOK MANOR
Angersleigh
Blagdon Hill
Puckington
BARRINGTON COURT
Ford Street
Bickenhall
Ilton
Barrington
South Petherton
BLACKDOWN HILLS
BARRINGTON HILL
Ashill
Stocklinch
ILMINSTER SERVICES
Shepton Beauchamp
STAPLE HILL
Curland
Windmill Hill
Broadway
Ashwell
Seavington St Michael
Clayhidon
Churchstanton
Horton
Ilminster
Fyfett
Donyatt
Seavington St Mary
Lopen
BLACKDOWN
Buckland St Mary
Crock Street
PERRYS CIDER
Kingstone
Dinnington
Stapley
Churchinford
Hemyock
Bishopswood
Dowlish Wake
Hinton St George
Bolham Water
Combe St Nicholas
Cricket Malherbie
HILLS
Marsh
Whitestaunton
Chillington
Smeatharpe
HORNSBURY MILL
Wadeford
Cudworth
A303
Chaffcombe
Crewkerne
Newcott
Howley
Cricket St Thomas
Yarcombe
Wambrook
Chard
Hewish
Dunkeswell
0 1 2 3 miles
0 1 2 3 4 5 km

Draycott
Rodney Stoke
RODNEY STOKE
Priddy
Green Ore
Emborough
Chilcompton
Charlton
Stratton on the Fosse
Buckland
43
Binegar
Gurney Slade
Ashwick
Holcombe
Highbury
Mells
Great Elm
Westbury-sub-Mendip
305
WOOKEY HOLE CAVES & PAPERMILL
West Horrington
Nettlebridge
Coleford
Vobster
Little Green
EBBOR GORGE
Easton
Wookey Hole
Oakhill
Stoke St Michael
Leigh upon Mendip
Whatley
Theale
East Horrington
Chantry
NUNNEY CASTLE
Nunney
Wookey
Wells
CATH
Downside
Downhead
Henton
THE BISHOP'S PALACE
BURCOTT MILL
99
Dinder
Croscombe
Heale
WESTHAY MOOR
Dulcote
Dean
Coxley
Shepton Mallet
East Cranmore
Leighton
Trudoxhill
Polsham
Worminster
WOOTTON VINEYARD
West Compton
Doulting
West Cranmore
EAST SOMERSET RAILWAY
Godney
Southway
North Wootton
East Compton
Cannard's Grave
Chesterblade
Wanstrow
Whitelake
Pilton
Prestleigh
30
Witham
HAM WALL
PILTON MANOR VINEYARD
Stoney Stratton
Westcombe
Upton Noble
Glastonbury
GLASTONBURY TOR
Batcombe
Northover
West Pennard
Pylle
Evercreech
CLARKS VILLAGE
ABBEY
Edgarley
East Pennard
Milton Clevedon
West Bradley
Ditcheat
North Brewham
Street
Walton
SHOE MUS
Parbrook
Wraxall
Lamyatt
South Brewham
Overleigh
Butleigh Wootton
Ham Street
Alhampton
Bruton
STREET
Baltonsborough
Hardway
ALFRED'S TOWER
Hornblotton Green
Sutton
Ansford
Cole
161
Redlynch
Stoney Stoke
Butleigh
Southwood
Pitcombe
Compton Dundon
Brue
Castle Cary
Penselwood
Dundon
Barton St David
West Lydford
East Lydford
Alford
Shepton Montague
Kingweston
Lovington
TOWER MILL
Littleton
Keinton Mandeville
Lydford-on-Fosse
HADSPEN GARDEN
Charlton Musgrove
Leigh Common
Galhampton
WINCANTON
Bratton Seymour
Charlton Adam
Somerton
Babcary
North Barrow
Bayford
Yarlington
Wincanton
Stoke
HAYNES INTERNATIONAL MOTOR MUS
Charlton Mackerell
South Barrow
North Cadbury
Cucklington
LYTES CARY MANOR
Cary Fitzpaine
Holton
Sparkford
Maperton
Cale
Kingsdon
PODIMORE SERVICES
Lattiford
Long Sutton
South Cadbury
Compton Pauncefoot
Blackford
North Cheriton
South Cheriton
Podimore
West Camel
Queen Camel
Northover
Bridgehampton
Sutton Montis
196
185
Horsington
Yeo
FLEET AIR ARM MUS
Marston Magna
Charlton Horethorne
Abbas Combe
Long Load
Ilchester
Yeovilton
Chilton Cantelo
Corton Denham
Limington
SANDFORD ORCAS MANOR HOUSE
Stowell
Templecombe
Stapleton
Rimpton
Ashington
Yenston
Ash
Adber
Sandford Orcas
Milborne Wick
Henstridge Ash
Coat
Tintinhull
TINTINHULL GARDEN
TREASURER'S HO
Poyntington
Henstridge
Yeovil Marsh
Mudford
Chilthorne Domer
Milborne Port
Hurst
Trent
Oborne
MONTACUTE HOUSE
Nether Compton
SHERBORNE OLD CASTLE
Stoke sub Hamdon
Goathill
Purse Caundle
Stalbridge
STOKE-SUB-HAMDON PRIORY
Preston Plucknett
Yeovil
Montacute
Over Compton
Sherborne
Stalbridge Weston
SHERBORNE CASTLE
Odcombe
Brympton
HAM HILL
YEOVIL
North Wootton
Haydon
Stourton Caundle
Chiselborough
West Coker
Alweston
Bishop's Caundle
West Chinnock
Barwick
Bradford Abbas
158
Lydlinch
North Coker
Folke
Stoford
Thornford
East Coker
East Chinnock
HARDINGTON MOOR
Lillington
Longburton
Woodbridge
Hardington Mandeville
Ryme Intrinseca
Beer Hackett
Holwell
King's Stag
Haselbury Plucknett
Res.
Closworth
Yetminster
Crouch Hill
Pendomer
North Perrott
Hardington Marsh
15
Holnest
182
Leigh
Glanvilles Wootton
Lydden
Hazelbury
BLACKMOOR VALE
A37
A39
A361
A371
A359
A303
A3088
A30
A372
A352
A357
A3030
B3139
B3135
B3114
B3151
B3153
B3165
B3081
B3152
B3145
B3148
B3146
B3143
B3356
FOSSE WAY
4
5
6
7
A
B
C
D

Hardington
Lullington
Beckington
Rudge
BRATTON CAMP & WHITE HORSE
230
Littleton Down
Buckland Dinham
Oldford
A36
44
Westbury
Mells
Great Elm
Clink
Berkley
Dilton Marsh
Summer Down
West Lavington Down
Vobster
Little Green
A3098
Upton Scudamore
A350
Whatley
Frome
Chapmanslade
Leigh upon Mendip
Chantry
The Butts
Corsley
A362
NUNNEY CASTLE
WARMINSTER SERVICES
Warminster
S A L
Downhead
Nunney
Corsley Heath
245
A36
A
A361
Tytherington
WARMINSTER DEWEY MUSEUM
Bugley
Boreham
West Woodlands
LONGLEAT
Chitterne
Leighton
Trudoxhill
Bishopstrow
B3414
Norton Bavant
Heytesbury
B390
Frome
Crockerton
LONGLEAT FOREST VILLAGE
Shear Cross
Horningsham
Sutton Veny
Knook
P
Wanstrow
Upton Lovell
29
Witham Friary
Tytherington
Corton
188
A36
Codford St Peter
Codford St Mary
Upton Noble
Gare Hill
Longbridge Deverill
Bruton Forest
284
Boyton
Batcombe
Maiden Bradley
Sherrington
Monkton Deverill
Brixton Deverill
Wylye
A350
Stockton
257
B3092
Kilmington
C R A N B O R N E
North Brewham
Kingston Deverill
Great Ridge
Norton Ferris
Pertwood
South Brewham
B3095
Keysley Down
Chicklade
B
Hardway
ALFRED'S TOWER
STOURHEAD
246
WHITE SHEET HILL
A303
Stourton
STOURTON HOUSE
13
Berwick St Leonard
Fonthill Bishop
B3089
Stoney Stoke
WEST KNOYLE
West Knoyle
Hindon
Chilmark
B3081
Penselwood
Zeals
Mere
The Green
Ridge
Queen Oak
Fonthill Gifford
C H A S E
Teffont Evias
Charlton Musgrove
Leigh Common
Bourton
Barrow Street
East Knoyle
237
Chicksgrove
WINCANTON
Huntingford
Tisbury
Bayford
A350
Wincanton
A303
Stoke Trister
Milton on Stour
Sedgehill
Newtown
Hatch
193
Sutton Mandeville
Cucklington
Swallowcliffe
Gillingham
Elm Hill
Semley
OLD WARDOUR CASTLE
Ansty
Lattiford
Wyke
Ham Common
AND WEST
PRESCOMBE DOWN
North Cheriton
Buckhorn Weston
Donhead St Andrew
242
West End
South Cheriton
Motcombe
WHITE SHEET HILL
Horsington
Knap Corner
244
Donhead St Mary
B3081
Milkwell
Abbas Combe
Kington Magna
West Stour
Ivy Cross
GOLD HILL MUS
A30
Berwick St John
Alvediston
East Stour
210
Shaftesbury
Ludwell
Templecombe
A30
Charlton
Wood
Fifehead Magdalen
Yenston
Stour Provost
Cann
Cann Common
277
Stour Row
Henstridge Ash
Guy's Marsh
W I L T S H I R E
Henstridge Marsh
Win Green
Todber
Melbury Abbas
Melbury Down
Henstridge
Pillwell
Milborne Port
29
Marnhull
Tollard Royal
Margaret Marsh
Stalbridge
Bedchester
Compton Abbas
Ashmore
Woodcutts
Purse Caundle
East Orchard
LARMER TREE GARDENS
Sixpenny Handley
B3081
Stalbridge Weston
Hinton St Mary
West Orchard
Fontmell Magna
B3092
Manston
Dean
B3091
Sutton Waldron
Stourton Caundle
Sturminster Newton
Farnham
Iwerne Courtney or Shroton
Iwerne Minster
FIDDLEFORD MANOR
Hammoon
Stubhampton
Bishop's Caundle
Lydlinch
MILL
Fiddleford
C R A N B O R N E
Chettle
Cashmoor
A357
Newton
Child Okeford
Broad Oak
Tarrant Gunville
Holwell
Woodbridge
HAMBLEDON HILL
Gussage St Michael
Fifehead Neville
A357
King's Stag
Shillingstone
Tarrant Hinton
A354
Okeford Fitzpaine
A350
D O W N S
Long Crichel
B3143
16
Stourpaine
Tarrant Launceston
Moor Crichel
Pimperne
Durweston
Tarrant
0 1 2 3 miles
0 1 2 3 4 5 km

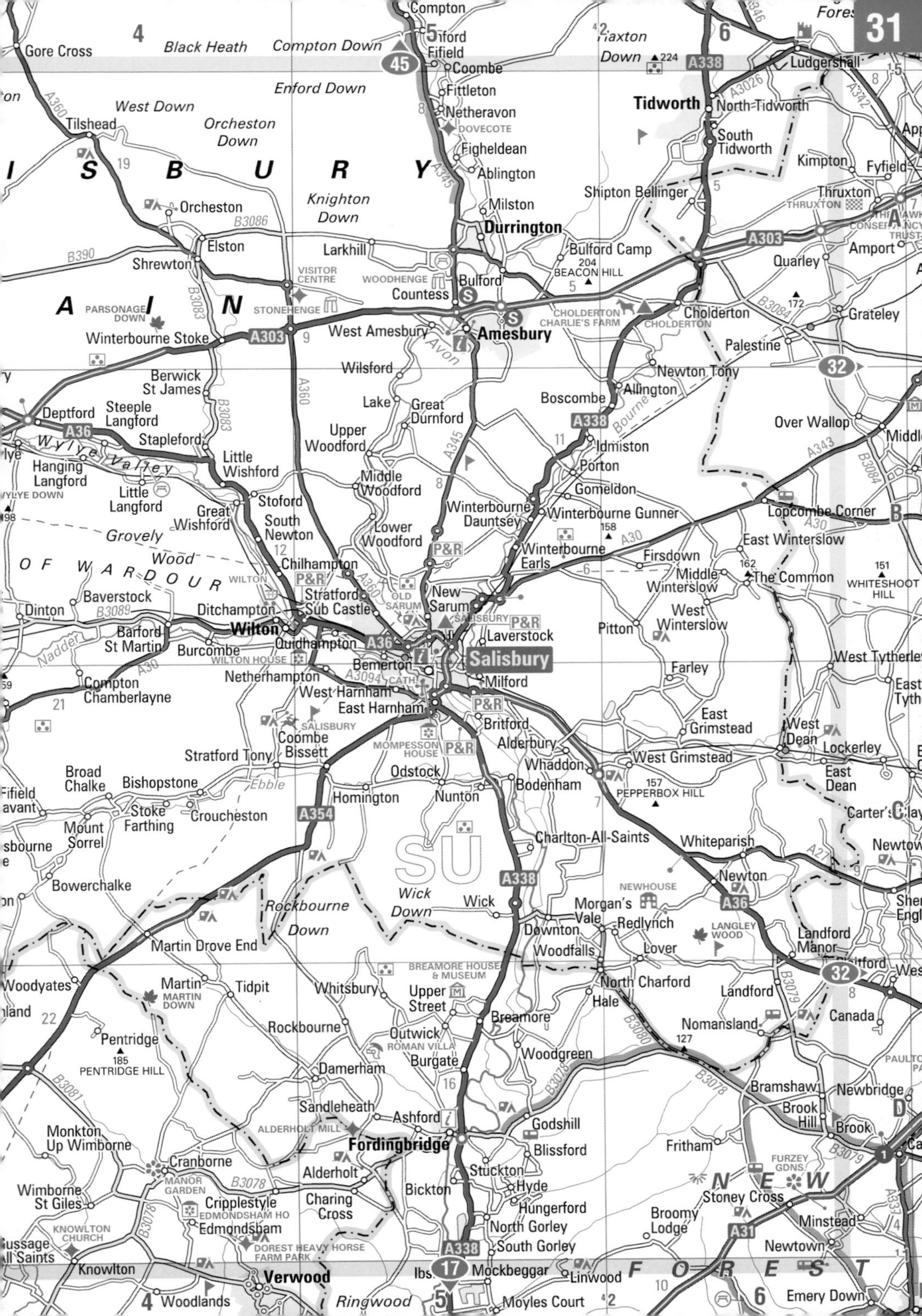
Gore Cross
Black Heath
Compton Down
Compton
Enford Down
West Down
Orcheston Down
Tilshead
Fittleton
Netheravon
Figheldean
Ablington
Milston
Durrington
Knighton Down
Orcheston
Elston
Shrewton
Larkhill
Stonehenge
Woodhenge
Bulford
Countess
Amesbury
West Amesbury
Winterbourne Stoke
Parsonage Down
Berwick St James
Wilsford
Lake
Great Durnford
Upper Woodford
Middle Woodford
Lower Woodford
Deptford
Steeple Langford
Stapleford
Hanging Langford
Little Langford
Little Wishford
Great Wishford
Stoford
South Newton
Grovely Wood
Wylye Valley
Chilhampton
Stratford Sub Castle
Old Sarum
New Sarum
Wilton
Ditchampton
Baverstock
Dinton
Barford St Martin
Burcombe
Quidhampton
Netherhampton
Bemerton
Salisbury
Milford
Laverstock
West Harnham
East Harnham
Compton Chamberlayne
Coombe Bissett
Britford
Alderbury
Stratford Tony
Broad Chalke
Bishopstone
Stoke Farthing
Croucheston
Mount Sorrel
Bowerchalke
Homington
Odstock
Nunton
Bodenham
Whaddon
Charlton-All-Saints
Rockbourne Down
Wick Down
Wick
Downton
Martin Drove End
Martin
Martin Down
Tidpit
Whitsbury
Upper Street
Breamore
Breamore House & Museum
Rockbourne
Outwick
Roman Villa
Burgate
Woodgreen
Damerham
Pentridge
Pentridge Hill
Woodyates
Sandleheath
Ashford
Alderholt Mill
Fordingbridge
Alderholt
Godshill
Blissford
Stuckton
Hyde
Hungerford
North Gorley
South Gorley
Bickton
Charing Cross
Cranborne
Manor Garden
Cripplestyle
Edmondsham
Edmondsham Ho
Monkton Up Wimborne
Wimborne St Giles
Knowlton Church
Knowlton
Verwood
Dorest Heavy Horse Farm Park
Woodlands
Ringwood
Mockbeggar
Moyles Court
Linwood
Tidworth
North Tidworth
South Tidworth
Ludgershall
Kimpton
Fyfield
Thruxton
Shipton Bellinger
Bulford Camp
Beacon Hill
Amport
Quarley
Cholderton
Cholderton Charlie's Farm
Grateley
Palestine
Newton Tony
Allington
Boscombe
Idmiston
Porton
Gomeldon
Over Wallop
Lopcombe Corner
Winterbourne Dauntsey
Winterbourne Gunner
Winterbourne Earls
Firsdown
East Winterslow
Middle Winterslow
The Common
Whiteshoot Hill
West Winterslow
Pitton
Farley
West Tytherley
East Grimstead
West Grimstead
West Dean
Lockerley
East Dean
Pepperbox Hill
Whiteparish
Newton
Newhouse
Morgan's Vale
Redlynch
Langley Wood
Lover
Woodfalls
North Charford
Hale
Landford Manor
Landford
Nomansland
Canada
Bramshaw
Newbridge
Brook Hill
Brook
Fritham
Furzey Gdns.
Stoney Cross
Minstead
Broomy Lodge
Newtown
Emery Down
New Forest
Salisbury Plain
Forest of Wardour
A303
A338
A36
A354
A30
A360
A345
A343
A31
A3026
B3086
B390
B3083
B3089
B3094
B3081
B3078
B3080
B3079
B3084
Avon
Bourne
Nadder
Ebble
Wylye
SU

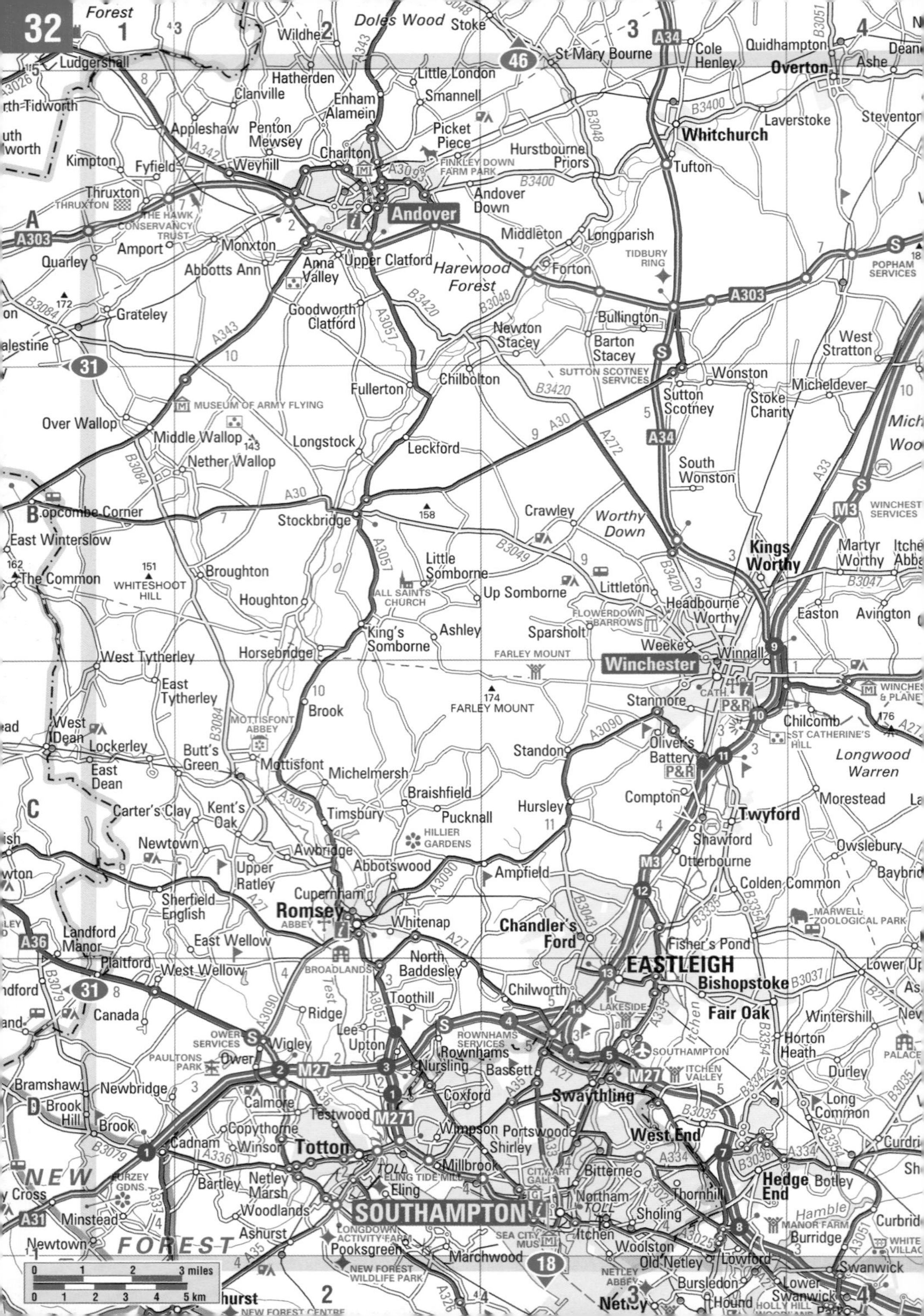

Forest
Wildhern
Doles Wood
Stoke
St Mary Bourne
46
Cole Henley
Quidhampton
Overton
Ashe
Ludgershall
Hatherden
Little London
Clanville
Enham Alamein
Smannell
Whitchurch
Laverstoke
Steventon
Appleshaw
Penton Mewsey
Picket Piece
Hurstbourne Priors
Tufton
Kimpton
Fyfield
Weyhill
Charlton
FINKLEY DOWN FARM PARK
Thruxton
THRUXTON
THE HAWK CONSERVANCY TRUST
Andover
Andover Down
A303
Amport
Monxton
Middleton
Longparish
Quarley
Abbotts Ann
Anna Valley
Upper Clatford
Harewood Forest
Forton
TIDBURY RING
POPHAM SERVICES
Grateley
Goodworth Clatford
Bullington
Newton Stacey
Barton Stacey
West Stratton
31
SUTTON SCOTNEY SERVICES
Wonston
Chilbolton
Fullerton
Sutton Scotney
Stoke Charity
Micheldever
MUSEUM OF ARMY FLYING
Over Wallop
Middle Wallop
Longstock
Leckford
Nether Wallop
South Wonston
Stockbridge
Crawley
Worthy Down
East Winterslow
WINCHESTER SERVICES
Little Somborne
Kings Worthy
Martyr Worthy
The Common
WHITESHOOT HILL
Broughton
Up Somborne
Littleton
Houghton
ALL SAINTS CHURCH
Headbourne Worthy
Easton
Avington
FLOWERDOWN BARROWS
King's Somborne
Ashley
Sparsholt
West Tytherley
Horsebridge
FARLEY MOUNT
Weeke
Winnall
Winchester
East Tytherley
FARLEY MOUNT
Brook
Stanmore
Chilcomb
ST CATHERINE'S HILL
West Dean
MOTTISFONT ABBEY
Lockerley
Standon
Oliver's Battery
Longwood Warren
East Dean
Butt's Green
Mottisfont
Michelmersh
Braishfield
Compton
Morestead
Carter's Clay
Kent's Oak
Timsbury
Pucknall
Hursley
Twyford
HILLIER GARDENS
Shawford
Newtown
Awbridge
Owslebury
Upper Ratley
Abbotswood
Ampfield
Otterbourne
Colden Common
Cupernham
Sherfield English
Romsey
ABBEY
Whitenap
Chandler's Ford
MARWELL ZOOLOGICAL PARK
Landford Manor
East Wellow
Fisher's Pond
North Baddesley
EASTLEIGH
Plaitford
West Wellow
BROADLANDS
Bishopstoke
Chilworth
Toothill
Fair Oak
Canada
Ridge
LAKESIDE
Wintershill
Lee
ROWNHAMS SERVICES
Upton
Horton Heath
Wigley
Rownhams
SOUTHAMPTON
PAULTONS PARK
Ower
Nursling
Bassett
ITCHEN VALLEY
Durley
Bramshaw
Newbridge
M27
Calmore
Coxford
Swaythling
Long Common
Brook Hill
Brook
Testwood
M271
Wimpson
Portswood
West End
Copythorne
Cadnam
Winsor
Totton
Shirley
Millbrook
Bitterne
Hedge End
Botley
NEW
FURZEY GDNS.
Bartley
Netley Marsh
ELING TIDE MILL
Eling
CITY ART GALL
Northam
Thornhill
Minstead
Woodlands
SOUTHAMPTON
Sholing
Hamble
MANOR FARM
Burridge
Curbridge
Ashurst
LONGDOWN ACTIVITY FARM
SEA CITY MUS
Itchen
Newtown
FOREST
Pooksgreen
Woolston
Marchwood
18
Old Netley
Lowford
Swanwick
NEW FOREST WILDLIFE PARK
NETLEY ABBEY
Bursledon
Lower Swanwick
Netley
Hound
HOLLY HILL
NEW FOREST CENTRE
0 1 2 3 miles
0 1 2 3 4 5 km

NORTH DOWNS
SOUTH DOWNS NATIONAL PARK
FOREST OF BERE
Basingstoke
Odiham
Alton
Farnham
Bordon
Liphook
Petersfield
New Alresford
Horndean
Waterlooville
Church Crookham
Shirrell Heath
Micheldever Forest
Wey
Rother
Meon Valley
Mid-Hants Railway
Jane Austen's Ho
Curtis Museum
Gilbert White's House & the Oates Museum
Birdworld
Butser Hill
Queen Elizabeth
Uppark
Stansted Park
Kingley Vale
West Dean Gardens
Hinton Ampner
Ashford Hangers
St Peter's Church
Old Winchester Hill
Beacon Hill
South Downs Way
Southwick Brewhouse
Northington Grange
Staunton

Cobham
Oxshott
EPSOM
Belmont
Purley
Sanderstead
Farleigh
Woodmansterne
Stoke D'Abernon
Wood Field
BANSTEAD
Kenley
Hamsey Green
Coulsdon
Warlingham
Downside
Great Burgh
Whyteleafe
Leatherhead Common
Ashtead
Burgh Heath
Chipstead
Old Coulsdon
Cobham Services
Epsom Downs
Tatsfield
Fetcham
Leatherhead
Tadworth
Kingswood
Hooley
Woldingham
Little Bookham
Walton on the Hill
Chaldon
CATERHAM
Lower Kingswood
Headley
Titsey
Great Bookham
Bocketts Farm Park
Walton Heath
Limpsfield
Mickleham
Polesden Lacey
Merstham
Brewer Street
Godstone
Oxted
Westhumble
Box Hill
Tanners Hatch
Church Town
Buckland
Redhill
Nutfield
Ranmore Common
Dorking
Pixham
Bletchingley
Godstone Farm
Tandridge
Betchworth
Earlswood
Brockham
Reigate
South Nutfield
North Downs Way
Crowhurst Lane End
Westcott
Strood Green
Doversgreen
Ridge Green
South Godstone
Redhill
Wotton
North Holmwood
Leigh
Sidlow
Salfords
Crowhurst
Abinger Common
Mole
Blindley Heath
Haxted Watermill
Nalderswood
Outwood
South Holmwood
Meath Green
Horne
Lingfield
Holmbury St Mary
Coldharbour
Parkgate
Norwood Hill
Weatherhill
Leith Hill
Beare Green
Hookwood
Horley
Smallfield
Lingfield Park
Newdigate
Newchapel
Gatwick Airport
London Gatwick
Charlwood
Burstow
Felcourt
Forest Green
Capel
Ockley
Clark's Green
Copthorne
Felbridge
Walliswood
County Oak
Ifield
Three Bridges
East Grinstead
Oakwoodhill
Rusper
Kingsfold
Lambs Green
Crawley Down
Sunnyside
Ifield Watermill
Pound Hill
Worth
Crawley
Turners Hill
Saint Hill
Stane Street
Holmbush Farm
Broadfield
Faygate
Tilgate
Selsfield Common
Warnham
Buchan
Pease Pottage
Pease Pottage Services
Tilgate
West Hoathly
Balcombe Lane
Sharpthorne
Strood Green
Broadbridge Heath
Roffey
Colgate
Tilgate Forest Row
Priest House
Wakehurst Place
St Leonard's Forest
The High Beeches
Slinfold
Horsham
Balcombe
Wings Mus
Highbrook
Handcross
Nymans Garden
Ashfold Crossways
Ardingly
Horsted Keynes
Itchingfield
Mannings Heath
Staplefield
Southwater Street
Monk's Gate
Slaugham
Brook Street
Borde Hill Garden
The Bluebell Railway
Lower Beeding
Nuthurst
Slough Green
Southwater
Warninglid
Whitemans Green
Heaven Farm
Ouse
Brooks Green
Copsale
Crabtree
Leonardslee Lakes & Gdns
Cuckfield
Lindfield
HAYWARDS HEATH
Maplehurst
Coneyhurst
Bolney
Ansty
Scayne's Hill
Coolham
Coolham Airfield D-Day Memorial
Shipley
Cowfold
West Grinstead
Whitehall
Kent Street
Broomer's Corner
Hickstead
Wivelsfield
Wivelsfield Green
North Chailey
Wineham
Adur
Goose Green
Dial Post
Partridge Green
BURGESS HILL
Chailey
Sayers
Ditchling Common
South Street
A3
A243
A24
A240
A217
A23
M25
A22
A25
A2003
M23
A264
A272
A29
A281
A273
B2028
B2036
B2110
B2115
B2116
B2135
B2139
P&R
49
36
21

Leaves Green
Downe
Pratt's Bottom
Badger's Mount
M25
Shoreham
Fairseat
Hamsey Green
Farleigh
DARWIN MUSEUM
Halstead
M20
BIGGIN HILL
50
Biggin Hill
Cudham
Knockholt Pound
Otford
Wrotham
Warlingham
Knockholt
Kemsing
Heaverham
South Street
Chevening
M26
Borough Green
Tatsfield
NORTH DOWNS WAY
Dunton Green
Seal
Platt
Chipstead
Ightham
Woldingham
B2024
Riverhead
GREAT COMP
CLACKET LANE SERVICES
KENT
Stone Street
Crouch
A
Titsey
Sundridge
Sevenoaks
Claygate Cross
A22
M25
Westerham
Brasted
QUEBEC HO
Brasted Chart
3 KNOLE
Ivy Hatch
Plaxtol
Limpsfield
The Chart
Cross Keys
IGHTHAM MOTE
OLD SOAR MANOR
Limpsfield Chart
EMMETTS
Whitley Row
A21
Dunk's Green
Oxted
CHARTWELL
Ide Hill
Underriver
West Peckham
Church Town
Tandridge
Crockham Hill
Toy's Hill
Sevenoaks Weald
Oakhurst
Shipbourne
GODSTONE FARM
35
Coldharbour
BROADVIEW GARDEN
Pittswood
Pootings
A26
Crowhurst Lane End
Marlpit Hill
Four Elms
Hildenborough
Higham Wood
Hilden Park
Golden Green
South Godstone
Crowhurst
Crouch House Green
B2027
Chiddingstone Causeway
Medway
TONBRIDGE CASTLE
Blindley Heath
HAXTED WATERMILL
Edenbridge
How Green
Bough Beech
Leigh
Brook Street
TONBRIDGE
Five Oak Green
CHIDDINGSTONE CASTLE
B
Hever
Chiddingstone
Tudeley
B2029
Eden
Marsh Green
HEVER CASTLE AND GARDENS
PENSHURST PLACE
HAYSDEN
ALL SAINTS CHURCH
Lingfield
Bidborough
A21
A22
B2028
Penshurst
B2176
LINGFIELD PARK
Markbeech
Southborough
High Brooms
Newchapel
Dormansland
Chiddingstone Hoath
Speldhurst
Felcourt
B2188
Pembury
Cowden
MUS & ART GALL
A26
Lullenden
Fordcombe
Rusthall
A264
Hammerwood
Blackham
Felbridge
ROYAL TUNBRIDGE WELLS
Blackwell
Ashurst
Langton Green
East Grinstead
HAMMERWOOD PARK
Hawkenbury
Crawley Down
SPA VALLEY RAILWAY
Sunnyside
Ashurstwood
B2110
Groombridge
Bells Yew Green
B2110
B2169
Saint Hill
STANDEN
Hartfield
FOREST WAY
Forest Row
Withyham
Eridge Green
Frant
C
Res.
HIGH WEALD
B2110
B2099
West Hoathly
Upper Hartfield
Lye Green
Wood's Green
Coleman's Hatch
Friar's Gate
Boarshead
Sharpthorne
A22
A267
PRIEST HOUSE
Wych Cross
Mark Cross
Durgates
B2188
Bestbeech
35
THE LLAMA PARK
Crowborough
B2100
Riseden
Chelwood Gate
Highbrook
Poundfield
Town Row
ASHDOWN FOREST
Tidebrook
B2100
Rotherfield
Horsted Keynes
Chelwood Common
A26
Jarvis Brook
B2028
Nutley
Duddleswell
Danehill
Coggins Mill
Ouse
HEAVEN FARM
Cackle Street
Fairwarp
High Hurstwood
Mayfield
Butcher's Cross
Lindfield
Sheffield Green
Splayne's Green
HAYWARDS HEATH
D
Hadlow Down
Rother
SHEFFIELD PARK
Maresfield
Pound Green
Five Ashes
Fletching
A272
BLUEBELL RAILWAY
Scayne's Hill
Buxted
A22
Ringles Cross
Cross in Hand
Broad Oak
A265
BLACKBOYS
Grisling Common
A272
Uckfield
Cade Street
Wivelsfield Green
North Chailey
Newick
Framfield
Heathfield
Punnett's Town
B2102
Blackboys
Old Heathfield
22
Ridgewood
Little London
B2192
Waldron
Maynard's Green
E. SUSSEX NATIONAL
Foxhunt
DITCHLING COMMON
Rushlake Green
0 1 2 3 miles
0 1 2 3 4 5 km

Snodland
Birling
Kit's Coty House
Leybourne Lake
Eccles
Bredhurst
M2
Stockbury
Tyland Barn
Wood
51
South Green
Bredgar
Bredgar & Wormshill Lt Rly
Swanton Street
Milstead
Doddington Place
Doddington
Ryarsh
New Hythe
The Friars
Aylesford
Boxley
M20
Addington
Leybourne
West Malling
Ditton
British Legion Village
Sandling
Mus of Kent Life
Detling
Thurnham
Hucking
Bicknor
Frinsted
Wormshill
Wichling
East Malling
Manor Park
Maidstone
Newnham Court
Broad Street
Bearsted Maidstone Services
Hollingbourne
Roseacre
East Barming
Tovil
Bearsted
Eyhorne Street
West Street
King's Hill
A228
Teston
Wateringbury
East Farleigh
West Farleigh
Shepway
Otham
Stoneacre
Leeds
Leeds Castle
Harrietsham
North Downs Way
Warren Street
A229
A274
A249
A20
A26
A21
B2010
B2163
Nettlestead
Nettlestead Green
Loose
Boughton Monchelsea
Langley
Langley Heath
Broomfield
Lenham
Sandway
Kingswood
Coxheath
Warmlake
Lenham Heath
38
Yalding
Hunton
Linton
Chart Corner
Chart Sutton
Sutton Valence
Grafty Green
Boughton Malherbe
Charing Heath
Hale Street
Benover
Laddingford
Beltring
The Hop Farm
Chainhurst
Rabbit's Cross
Ulcombe
Egerton
Little Chart
Queen Street
Collier Street
Milebush
Cross-at-Hand
Beult
Southernden
Egerton Forstal
Pluckley
Pluckley Thorne
Paddock Wood
Claygate
Marden
Hawkenbury
Headcorn
Staplehurst
Headcorn
Smarden Bell
Maltman's Hill
Castle Hill
Marden Beech
Marden Thorn
Farm Mus
Iden Croft Herbs
Sinkhurst Green
Smarden
Brenchley
Knox Bridge
Frittenden
Haffenden Quarter
Wissenden
Petteridge
Horsmonden
Winchet Hill
Curtisden Green
Lashenden
Bethersden
Hazel Street
Collier's Green
Cranbrook Common
Sissinghurst Castle
Three Chimneys
Standen
Biddenden
Tanden
Shadoxhurst
Goudhurst
A262
Iden Green
Wilsley Pound
Sissinghurst
High Halden
A28
Cranbrook Museum
Union Mill
Biddenden Vineyard
Scotney Castle
Kilndown
Cranbrook
East End
St Michael's
Shirkoak
Hartley
Kent & East Sussex Railway
Parkgate
Woodchurch
Bedgebury Pinetum
Bedgebury Forest
Tenterden
Brook Street
Bewl Water
B2086
Benenden
CM Booth Collection
Leigh Green
Kenardington
Three Leg Cross
Gill's Green
Colonel Stephens Railway Museum
Iden Green
Flimwell
High Street
Hawkhurst
Dingleden
Rolvenden
Small Hythe
Reading Street
Appledore Heath
B2099
Union Street
A268
Four Throws
Rolvenden Layne
Smallhythe Place
Isle of Oxney
Appledore
Wallcrouch
Ticehurst
Horns Corner
The Moor
Pashley Manor Gardens
Swiftsden
Sandhurst
Linkhill
Peening Quarter
Stone
Stonegate
Hurst Green
Sandhurst Cross
Newenden
Wittersham
The Stocks
Rother
Ham Green
Etchingham
A265
B2244
Bodiam
Great Dixter
Rother Levels
Farm World
Northbridge Street
Northiam
Burwash
Bateman's
Salehurst
Ewhurst Green
Beckley
Four Oaks
Rother Valley Rly
Robertsbridge
Millcorner
Clayhill
Iden
Houghton Green
A259
Peasmarsh
Oxley's Green
Staple Cross
B2165
Horns Cross
Rye Foreign
Playden
East Guldeford
John's Cross
B2089
Cripp's Corner
Brightling
Vinehall Street
Tillingham
Rye
Res.
Mountfield
23
Broad Oak
Broadland Row
Rye Heritage Centre
Darwell Hole
B2096
Udimore
Rye Harbour
Dallington
Netherfield
Whatlington
Sedlescombe
Brede

Molash
Challock
NORTH DOWNS WAY
52
Godmersham
KENT DOWNS
Petham
Bishopsbourne
Kingston
Upper Hardres Court
Lenham Heath
Charing
Charing Heath
M20
A20
A252
A251
A28
Bilting
Boughton Aluph
Westwell Leacon
Westwell
Boughton Lees
Sole Street
Crundale
Waltham
Bossingham
Derrings
ELHAM VALLEY VINEYARD
Stelling Minnis
Hassell Street
WYE CROWN
Wye
Bodsham
Elmsted
Lyminge Forest
Egerton
Egerton Forstal
Little Chart
Ram Lane
Goat Lees
Pluckley
Pluckley Thorne
Hothfield
GODINTON HOUSE
Kennington
Brook
Hastingleigh
WYE
CONNINGBROOK LAKES
Elham
Maltman's Hill
Great Chart
Ashford
ASHFORD
Willesborough
Hinxhill
Willesborough Lees
Brabourne
Lymbridge Green
B2068
Rhodes Minnis
Ottinge
KENT BATTLE OF BRITAIN MUSEUM
Wissenden
Sevington
Stowting
Brabourne Lees
Lyminge
Paddlesworth
Bethersden
37
Stubbs Cross
Kingsnorth
Mersham
Smeeth
STOP 24 SERVICES
Postling
Etchinghill
CHANNEL TUNNEL
Tanden
Shadoxhurst
Cheeseman's Green
Sellindge
Sellindge Lees
Beachborough
Stanford
Newington
High Halden
Bromley Green
Aldington Frith
Clap Hill
E. Stour
Aldington
Henghurst
Bonnington
Newingreen
Pedlinge
ELHAM VALLEY RLY MUS
Cheriton
Shirkoak
Court-at-Street
Lympne
A261
Saltwood
Woodchurch
Orlestone
SOUTH OF ENGLAND RARE BREEDS CEN
HAM STREET WOODS
B2067
Bilsington
PORT LYMPNE WILD ANIMAL PARK AND GARDENS
BROCKHILL
Hythe
Brook Street
Ruckinge
Military
Canal
West Hythe
Palmarsh
Kenardington
Hamstreet
Royal
Warehorne
Burmarsh
Newchurch
A259
B2080
Reading Street
Appledore Heath
A2070
ROMNEY, HYTHE AND DYMCHURCH RAILWAY
SMALLHYTHE PLACE
HORNE'S PLACE CHAPEL
Snave
ISLE OF OXNEY
Appledore
ROMNEY MARSH
Dymchurch
MARTELLO TOWER
St Mary in the Marsh
Snargate
Stone
Ivychurch
Brenzett
AERONAUTICAL MUSEUM
ROMNEY WARREN
St Mary's Bay
The Stocks
Ham Green
B2082
Brookland
Old Romney
New Romney
Littlestone on Sea
Romney Sands
Iden
Houghton Green
Walland Marsh
Greatstone on Sea
B2075
Playden
East Guldeford
Lydd
LYDD (LONDON ASHFORD)
Lydd on Sea
Rye
B2089
RYE HERITAGE CENTRE
Denge Marsh
Camber
LYDD INTERNATIONAL RACEWAY
Rye Harbour
DUNGENESS
Denge Beach
CAMBER CASTLE
Rye Bay
DUNGENESS POWER STATION & INFORMATION CENTRE
DUNGENESS
THE OLD LIGHTHOUSE
Winchelsea Beach
WINCHELSEA COURT HALL MUSEUM
End
Cove
0 1 2 3 miles
0 1 2 3 4 5 km

DEAL CASTLE
THE DOWNS
Northbourne
Tilmanstone
Elvington
Womenswold
Barfrestone
EAST KENT RLY
Woolage Green
Eythorne
Shepherdswell
Coxhill
Coldred
LYDDEN
Wootton
Selsted
Lydden
ST JOHN'S COMMANDERY
LYDDEN TEMPLE EWELL
Ewell Minnis
Swingfield Street
Swingfield Minnis
Densole
Drellingore
Alkham
Hawkinge
West Hougham
Farthingloe
Maxton
Capel le Ferne
EAST CLIFF & WARREN
East Wear Bay
Folkestone
ROTUNDA
CLIFF LIFT
Great Mongeham
Walmer
WALMER CASTLE AND GARDENS
Ripple
East Studdal
Sutton
Ringwould
Kingsdown
West Langdon
East Langdon
Martin
Martin Mill
Whitfield
Guston
St Margaret's at Cliffe
THE BAY MUSEUM
St Margaret's Bay
West Cliffe
THE PINES GARDEN
SOUTH FORELAND
Temple Ewell
CRABBLE CORN MILL
Buckland
ROMAN PAINTED HOUSE
WHITE CLIFFS
CASTLE & HELLFIRE CORNER
DOVER
CALAIS DUNKERQUE
Aycliff
DE BRADELEI WHARF
SAMPHIRE HOE
A2
A20
A256
A258
A260
B2011
53
CHANNEL TUNNEL
TR
ENGLISH CHANNEL
A
B
C
D
4
5
6

Climaen gwyn
Ynys-meudwy
Rhyd-y-fro
Morfa Glas
Rhigos
Cwm-hwnt
Crynant
Mynydd March-Hywel
Rheola Forest
VALE OF NEATH
CWM NEDD
Blaengwrach
Cwmgwrach
Pontardawe
GLANTAWE RIVERSIDE PARK
Cilybebyll
Gellinudd
Rhôs
Alltwen
Trebanos
Craig-cefn-parc
Rhyd-y-gwin
Rhyd-y-pandy
Faerdre
Clydach
Ynystawe
Pant-lasau
Glais
CEFN COED COLLIERY MUS
Resolven
RESOLVEN MTN.
Melincourt
Cilfrew
FALLS
Aberdulais
Clyne
Blaenrhondda
Tynewydd
Treherbert
Bryn-coch
Heol-las
Birchgrove
Rhydding
Neath Abbey
Tonna
Cadoxton-Juxta-Neath
NEATH MUSEUM
Neath
(Castell-Nedd)
Glyncorrwg
Morriston
Skewen
Llansamlet
Pentre-dwr
Cimla
Cwm
Bon-y-maen
Llandarcy
Swansea
(Abertawe)
Foxhole
PLANTASIA
Port Tennant
CRYMLYN BOG AND PANT-Y-SAIS
SWANSEA MUSEUM
NATIONAL WATERFRONT MUSEUM
Briton Ferry
GNOLL
Pontrhydyfen
VISITOR CENTRE
Duffryn
Cymer
Croeserw
Blaen-gwynfi
Aber-gwynfi
Cwm-parc
SOUTH WALES MINERS MUSEUM
Caerau
Spelter
FOEL Y DYFFRYN
Dyffryn
AFAN FOREST PARK
WERFA
Nant-y-moel
Blaengarw
Baglan
Pwll-y-glaw
Brynbryddan
MYNYDD DINAS
Bryn
Nantyffyllon
Wyndham
Cwmafan
Pontycymer
MAESTEG
Garth
Cwmfelin
Aberavon
SWANSEA BAY
BAE ABERTAWE
Port Talbot
Goytre
Llangynwyd
Pont Rhyd-y-cyff
Ogmore Vale
Taibach
MYNYDD MARGAM
Margam
Groes
MOEL TON-MAWR
Bettws
Llangeinor
MARGAM
MARGAM ABBEY AND STONES MUSEUM
BRYNGARW
Brynmenyn
Coytrahen
Tondu
Bryncethin
Aberkenfig
BEDFORD
Kenfig Hill
Cefn Cross
SARN PARK SERVICES
Sarn
BRIDGEND
Kenfig
Mawdlam
KENFIG POOL AND DUNES
Kenfig Burrows
North Cornelly
Pyle
(Y Pîl)
Cefn Cribbwr
Pen-y-fai
Pendre
Coity
COITY CASTLE
Bridgend
(Pen-y-bont ar Ogwr)
NEWCASTLE
South Cornelly
Laleston
Coychurch
ROYAL PORTHCAWL
Tythegston
Nottage
Newton
Treoes
Corntown
Hutchwns
Clevis
Merthyr Mawr
OGMORE CASTLE
Ogmore
Ewenny
Porthcawl
MERTHYR MAWR WARREN
CONEY BEACH
SS
Ogmore-by-Sea
St Brides Major
Colwinston
Tusker Rock
Penuchadre
Southerndown
GLENMORGAN HERITAGE COAST CENTRE
WALES COAST PATH
Wick
Broughton
Monknash
Marcross
Nash Pt.
Trwyn yr As
St Donat's
0 1 2 3 miles
0 1 2 3 4 5 km

41
Hirwaun
Gellideg
Pen-yr-Heolgerrig
Merthyr Tydfil
(Merthyr Tudful)
Tre-Gibbon
Trecynon
Llwydcoed
Cwmdare
ABERDARE
(ABERDÂR)
Aber-nant
Cwmbâch
Aberaman
Pentrebach
Abercanaid
Troedyrhiw
YNYSFACH ENGINE HOUSE HERITAGE CENTRE
Pontlottyn
Abertysswg
New Tredegar
(Tredegar Newydd)
Tirphil
PARC CWM DARREN
Deri
Bedlinog
Cwmfelin
Aberfan
Merthyr Vale
Cwmaman
MOUNTAIN ASH
(ABERPENNAR)
Penrhiwceiber
Treharris
Trelewis
Bargoed
(Bargod)
TAF BARGOED
ABERBARGOED GRASSLANDS
Gilfach
Gelligaer
LLANCAIACH FAWR MANOR
Nelson
Hengoed
Ystrad-mynach
Rhymney Valley
Waunlwyd
FESTIVAL PARK
Cwm
Man-moel
Hollybush
Markham
PEN-Y-FAN POND
Argoed
Trinant
Abertillery
(Abertyleri)
Aberbeeg
St Illtyd
Brynithel
Llanhilleth
(Llanhiledd)
Crumlin
(Crymlyn)
Newbridge
Oakdale
Pengam
Blackwood
(Coed Duon)
Pontllanfraith
Maesycwmmer
Wyllie
Ynysddu
Cwmfelinfach
Sirhowy Valley
SIRHOWY VALLEY
Ebbw Vale
Lanfach
Abercarn
Cwmcarn
Pontywaun
Crosskeys
Risca
(Rhisga)
Maerdy
Treorchy
(Treorci)
Pentre
Ferndale
St Gwynno Forest
RHONDDA
Ystrad
Ton-Pentre
Gelli
Tylorstown
Pont-y-gwaith
Wattstown
Ynysboeth
Abercynon
Ynysybwl
Llwynypia
Clydach Vale
CLYDACH VALE
Trealaw
Ynyshir
Tonypandy
Penygraig
Porth
RHONDDA HERITAGE PARK
Trehafod
Glyncoch
Cilfynydd
Trebanog
PONTYPRIDD
Senghenydd
Abertridwr
Llanbradach
Bedwas
Machen
Lower Machen
Glyntaff
Treforest
Pen-y-coedcae
Rhydyfelin
Bryn Golau
Tonyrefail
Hendreforgan
Penyrheol
Trecenydd
CAERPHILLY
(CAERFFILI)
Rudry
Rhiwderin
Hawthorn
Castellau
Upper Church Village
Llantwit Fardre
Church Village
Coedely
Nantgarw
MYNYDD MAENDY
Beddau
Thornhill
Efail Isaf
MODEL HOUSE CENTRE
PARC CEFN ONN
CARDIFF GATE SERVICES
Brynna
Llanharan
Talbot Green
Llantrisant
Taff's Well
CASTELL COCH
Tongwynlais
Lisvane
Llanedeyrn
Bryncae
Dolau
Cross Inn
Pontyclun
Creigiau
Pentyrch
Llanishen
Rhiwbina
Cyncoed
Llanilid
FOREST FARM
Whitchurch
St Mellons
Llanrumney
Llanharry
Brynsadler
Miskin
Groes-faen
Capel Llanilltern
Radyr
Rumney
Talygarn
LLANERCH VINEYARD
CARDIFF WEST SERVICES
Birchgrove
Heath
Craig Penllyn
St Brides super Ely
NATIONAL HISTORY MUSEUM
Llandaff
Cathays
Roath
Newton
Llansannor
Ystradowen
Peterston super-Ely
St George's
St Fagans
Canton
Ely
PRINCIPALITY STADIUM
NAT MUS OF WALES
CARDIFF
Maendy
Penllyn
Aberthin
Welsh St Donats
Pendoylan
Michaelston-super-Ely
Caerau
Butetown
Grangetown
(CAERDYDD)
MILLENNIUM CENTRE
Cowbridge
(Y Bont-Faen)
Llanblethian
St Nicholas
Leckwith
Michaelston-le-Pit
Bonvilston
Llandough
St Hilary
Llantrithyd
Wallston
St Lythans
Wenvoe
TECHNIQUEST
Llandough
Cogan
CARDIFF BAY BARRAGE
DYFFRYN GARDENS
St Mary Church
OLD BEAUPRE CASTLE
St Andrews Major
TURNER HOUSE GALLERY
Sigingstone
Walterston
Dinas Powys
PENARTH
Flemingston
Moulton
Cadoxton
Llanmaes
Eglwys-Brewis
Llanbethery
Llancarfan
Colcot
COSMESTON LAKES
Lower Penarth
WELSH HAWKING CENTRE
Merthyr-Dyfan
Penmark
Sully
MEDIEVAL VILLAGE
Lavernock Pt.
Trwyn Larnog
Boverton
St Athan
CARDIFF (MAES AWYR CAERDYDD-CYMRU)
PORTHKERRY
BARRY
(Y BARRI)
Barry Island
BARRY ISLAND PLEASURE PARK
Sully Island
Ynys Sili
Gileston
East Aberthaw
Rhoose
(Y Rhws)
Porthkerry
Breaksea Pt.
Trwyn Breaksea
Flat Holm
A465
A470
A4059
A4054
A469
A4046
A467
A4048
A4049
A4254
A472
A4233
B4275
B4273
A4058
B4278
A4119
A468
B4263
B4600
A4055
B4595
A473
A48(M)
B4562
A4232
A4222
M4
A4119
B4487
A48
A4160
B4270
B4268
A4226
A4050
A4231
B4265
B4267
B4266
B4251
B4255
B5464
A4093
4
5
6
7
A
B
C
D
E

Crosskeys
Risca
(Rhisga)
SIRHOWY VALLEY
Machen
Lower Machen
Rogerstone
FOURTEEN LOCKS
Bettws
Malpas
LEGIONARY MUS.
Caerleon
(Caerllion)
61
Christchurch
Maindee
Newport
(Casnewydd)
CATH.
MUS.& GALLERY
Liswerry
GERAINT THOMAS NAT. VELODROME OF WALES
Cat's Ash
Seymour
Llanvaches
Llanbeder
Penhow
PENHOW WOODLANDS
Langstone
Llanmartin
M4
Llanwern
Wilcrick
Bishton
Llandevenny
Magor
MAGOR SERVICES
St Bride's Netherwent
Caerwent
Highmoor Hill
Crick
RUNSTON CHAPEL
M48
Rogiet
Llanfihangel Rogiet
Caldicot
Undy
A4810
Caldicot Level
Summerleaze
Redwick
WALES COAST PATH
Whitson
Goldcliff
NEWPORT WETLANDS
Nash
Pye Corner
Usk (Wysg)
Rhiwderin
Rudry
Pentre-poeth
Bassaleg
Duffryn
TREDEGAR HOUSE
(Rhymni)
Rhymney
Michaelston-y-Fedw
CARDIFF GATE SERVICES
A48
Castleton
Coedkernew
Lisvane
Llanedeyrn
A48(M)
Marshfield
St Brides Wentlooge
B4239
Blacktown
Cyncoed
P&R
St Mellons
Llanrumney
Peterstone Wentlooge
Rumney
Newton
Roath
41
NAT. MUS. OF WALES
CARDIFF
(CAERDYDD)
MILLENNIUM CENTRE
CARDIFF BAY BARRAGE
TURNER HOUSE GALLERY
PENARTH
Lavernock Pt.
Flat Holm
ABER HAFREN
MOUTH OF THE SEVERN
ST
Battery Pt.
Portishead
West Hill
Redcliff Bay
Sheepway
A369
Weston-in-Gordano
Clapton-in-Gordano
B3124
Walton-in-Gordano
GORDANO VALLEY
CLEVEDON COURT
Clevedon
Stone-edge Batch
B3130
Tickenham
Nailsea
West End
Kenn
East End
Farleigh
M5
Chelvey
Brockley
West Town
Kingston Seymour
North End
Claverham
Yatton
Cleeve
Sand Pt.
Wick St Lawrence
Bourton
Hewish
Yeo
B3133
A370
Congresbury
Wrington
Sand Bay
Kewstoke
TOLL
Worle
Milton
Puxton
PUXTON PARK
Brinsea
NORTH SOMERSET
Weston-super-Mare
B3440
West Wick
21
Lower Langford
Steep Holm
Weston Bay
SEAQUARIUM
HELICOPTER MUS.
Locking
COURT FARM
Banwell
Churchill
Sandford
A368
Burrington
A371
Brean Down
Hutton
Uphill
BLEADON HILL
134
Christon
175
Star
Shipham
325
Winscombe
Sidcot
Bleadon
Brean
Loxton
Compton Bishop
233
KING JOHN'S HUNTING LODGE
Charterhouse
BERROW
BREAN LEISURE PARK
FLATS
Eastertown
Cross
Lower Weare
A38
Axbridge
Cheddar Res.
CHEDDAR
Cheddar
CHEDDAR CAVES & GORGE
B3135
Lympsham
Biddisham
Weare
SEDGEMOOR SERVICES
Gore Sands
B3140
East Brent
Rooks Bridge
Badgworth
Clewer
B3151
Axe
Draycott
Brent Knoll
137
Stone Allerton
ASHTON WINDMILL
Berrow
Chapel Allerton
Rodney Stoke
Burnham -on-Sea
Edithmead
28
Cocklake
West Stoughton
22
Mark
Mark Causeway
Blackford
Wedmore
0 1 2 3 miles
0 1 2 3 4 5 km

(Cas-gwent)
Beachley
SEVERN ROAD BRIDGE
PONT HAFREN
SEVERN VIEW SERVICES
Mathern
Littleton-on-Severn
Thornbury
Whitfield
Morton
Kingswood
ABBEY GATEHOUSE
Cromhall
Churchend
Alderley
Cromhall Common
Hillesley
Aust
Portskewett
Sudbrook
Ingst
Elberton
Alveston
OLDOWN
Tytherington
Wickwar
Hawkesbury Upton
Hawkesbury
Northwick
Olveston
Rudgeway
Itchington
Redwick
Tockington
Rangeworthy
HORTON COURT
Pilning
Awkley
Severn Beach
Almondsbury
Latteridge
Engine Common
Horton
Iron Acton
Little Sodbury
THE WAVE
Over
Frampton Cotterell
Nibley
Yate
Old Sodbury
Badminton
Easter Compton
Bradley Stoke
Chipping Sodbury
Patchway
Hallen
Catbrain
AEROSPACE BRISTOL
Stoke Gifford
Winterbourne
Coalpit Heath
Winterbourne Down
Wapley
Dodington
Acton Turvil
Tormarton
Westerleigh
FILTON
Henbury
Horfield
Hambrook
Codrington
Frenchay
Blackhorse
Emersons Green
Downend
West King
Shirehampton
Westbury on Trym
Hinton
MANGOTSFIELD
Pucklechurch
DYRHAM PARK
West Littleton
Pill
Ham Green
Stapleton
Fishponds
Siston
BRISTOL ZOO
Easton-in-Gordano
Abbots Leigh
Redland
Eastville
Soundwell
Abson
Dyrham
Kingswood
Clifton
Warmley
Bridge Yate
Doynton
Marshfield
LEIGH WOODS
Leigh Woods
CLIFTON SUSPENSION BRIDGE
BRISTOL
Hanham
Wick
Cold Ashton
Warmley Tower
TYNTESFIELD HOUSE
SS GREAT BRITAIN
AVON VALLEY RAILWAY
Failand
Long Ashton
Bedminster
Knowle
Brislington
Oldland
Upton Cheyney
GRENVILLE'S MON
St Catherine
ARNOLFINI GALLERY
Willsbridge
Bitton
North Stoke
Langridge
Flax Bourton
Woolley
Northend
Bishopsworth
KEYNSHAM
Whitchurch
Swainswick
Batheaston
Barrow Gurney
DUNDRY HILL
Dundry
Kelston
Charlcombe
Saltford
Weston
Bath
Bathford
Upper Town
North Wick
Norton Malreward
Queen Charlton
Chewton Keynsham
Corston
ROYAL CRESCENT
Bathampton
Felton
Winford
Norton Hawkfield
Burnett
Newton St Loe
Twerton
ABBEY
AMERICAN
STONE CIRCLES
Chew Magna
Pensford
Compton Dando
The Oval
ROMAN BATHS
Claverton
Stanton Drew
Stanton Prior
Englishcombe
Odd Down
PRIOR PARK
Combe Down
Ridgehill
Chew Stoke
Chelwood
Hunstrete
Marksbury
Inglesbatch
Monkton Combe
Butcombe
Stanton Wick
PRISTON MILL
Priston
Southstoke
Nempnett Thrubwell
Limpley Stoke
Winsley
Chew Valley Lake
Blagdon Lake
Farmborough
Combe Hay
Bishop Sutton
Clutton
Dunkerton
Twinhoe
Timsbury
Carlingcott
Ubley
Sutton Wick
Temple Cloud
High Littleton
Wellow
Hinton Charterhouse
Farleigh Hungerford
Camerton
Peasedown St John
Compton Martin
South Widcombe
Hinton Blewett
Hallatrow
Paulton
LONG BARROW
West Harptree
Norton St Philip
Clandown
Shoscombe
East Harptree
Farrington Gurney
RADSTOCK MUSEUM
Radstock
Tellis
Midsomer Norton
Litton
Ston Easton
Writhlington
Faulkland
Woolverton
Chewton Mendip
SOMERSET & DORSET RAILWAY HER TRUST
Hemington
Kilmersdon
Chilcompton
Laverton
Charlton
Hardington
Lullington
Emborough
Buckland Dinham
Stratton on the Fosse
Priddy
Oldford
Green Ore
Highbury
Great Elm
Mells
Binegar
Gurney Slade
Vestbury-sub-Mendip
Holcombe
Clink
Ashwick
Vobster
Little Green
WOOKEY HOLE CAVES & PAPERMILL
West
Nettlebridge
Coleford
COTSWOLDS
MENDIP HILLS

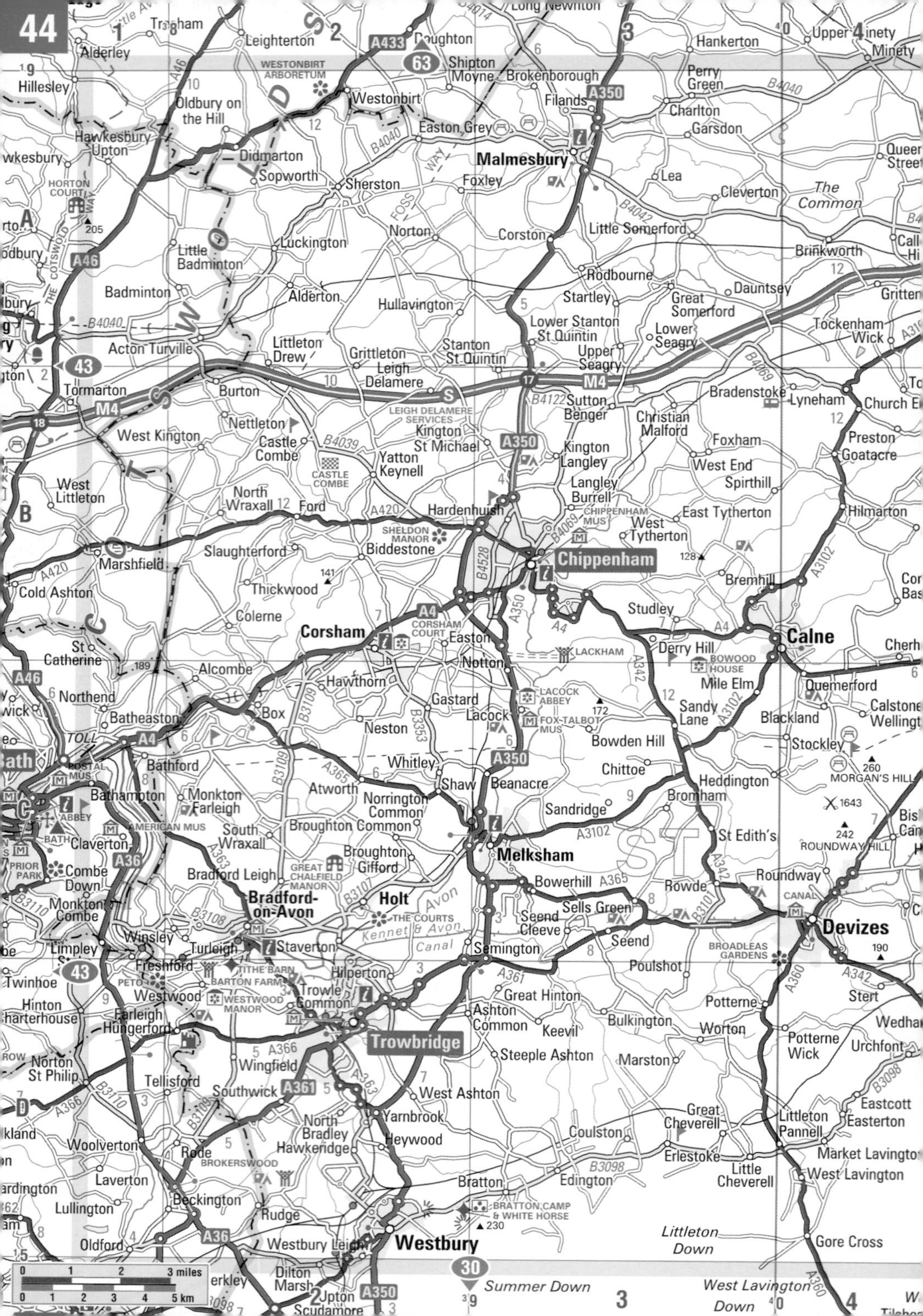
Tresham
Leighterton
Doughton
Long Newnton
Hankerton
Upper Minety
Minety
Alderley
Westonbirt Arboretum
Shipton Moyne
Brokenborough
Perry Green
Hillesley
Oldbury on the Hill
Westonbirt
Filands
Charlton
Hawkesbury Upton
Easton Grey
Garsdon
Didmarton
Malmesbury
Queen Street
Horton Court
Sopworth
Sherston
Foxley
Lea
Cleverton
The Common
Luckington
Norton
Corston
Little Somerford
Little Badminton
Brinkworth
Rodbourne
Badminton
Alderton
Hullavington
Startley
Great Somerford
Dauntsey
Grittenham
Lower Stanton St Quintin
Lower Seagry
Tockenham Wick
Acton Turville
Littleton Drew
Grittleton
Stanton St Quintin
Upper Seagry
Leigh Delamere
Tormarton
Burton
Sutton Benger
Bradenstoke
Lyneham
Church End
Leigh Delamere Services
Christian Malford
West Kington
Nettleton
Castle Combe
Kington St Michael
Kington Langley
Foxham
Preston
Goatacre
Yatton Keynell
West End
Langley Burrell
Spirthill
West Littleton
North Wraxall
Ford
Hardenhuish
Chippenham Mus
East Tytherton
Hilmarton
Sheldon Manor
West Tytherton
Slaughterford
Biddestone
Chippenham
Marshfield
Cold Ashton
Thickwood
Bremhill
Studley
Colerne
Corsham
Corsham Court
Easton
Calne
St Catherine
Derry Hill
Lackham
Alcombe
Notton
Bowood House
Hawthorn
Mile Elm
Quemerford
Northend
Gastard
Lacock Abbey
Batheaston
Box
Lacock
Sandy Lane
Blackland
Calstone Wellington
Fox-Talbot Mus
Neston
Bowden Hill
Stockley
Bath
Bathford
Whitley
Chittoe
Morgan's Hill
Postal Mus
Atworth
Shaw
Beanacre
Heddington
Bathampton
Monkton Farleigh
Norrington Common
Sandridge
Bromham
Abbey
South Wraxall
Broughton Common
St Edith's
Roundway Hill
Claverton
American Mus
Broughton Gifford
Melksham
Prior Park
Combe Down
Bradford Leigh
Great Chalfield Manor
Bowerhill
Rowde
Roundway
Bradford-on-Avon
Holt
The Courts
Sells Green
Canal
Monkton Combe
Seend Cleeve
Devizes
Kennet & Avon Canal
Limpley Stoke
Winsley
Turleigh
Staverton
Seend
Broadleas Gardens
Freshford
Tithe Barn
Barton Farm
Semington
Poulshot
Twinhoe
Peto
Hilperton
Westwood
Trowle Common
Great Hinton
Potterne
Stert
Hinton Charterhouse
Westwood Manor
Farleigh Hungerford
Ashton Common
Keevil
Bulkington
Worton
Potterne Wick
Urchfont
Trowbridge
Norton St Philip
Wingfield
Steeple Ashton
Marston
Tellisford
Southwick
West Ashton
Eastcott
Great Cheverell
Littleton Pannell
Easterton
Yarnbrook
North Bradley
Heywood
Coulston
Woolverton
Rode
Hawkeridge
Erlestoke
Market Lavington
Brokerswood
Little Cheverell
West Lavington
Laverton
Bratton
Edington
Beckington
Bratton Camp & White Horse
Lullington
Rudge
Littleton Down
Oldford
Westbury
Westbury Leigh
Gore Cross
Dilton Marsh
Summer Down
West Lavington Down
Upton Scudamore
Cotswold Way
Foss Way
Cotswolds
M4
A46
A433
A350
A420
A4
A36
A361
A363
A365
A366
A342
A3102
A360
B4040
B4039
B4069
B4122
B4528
B3109
B3108
B3107
B3353
B3110
B3098
B3101
B4042
B4014
A3102
63
43
30
18
17
0 1 2 3 miles
0 1 2 3 4 5 km

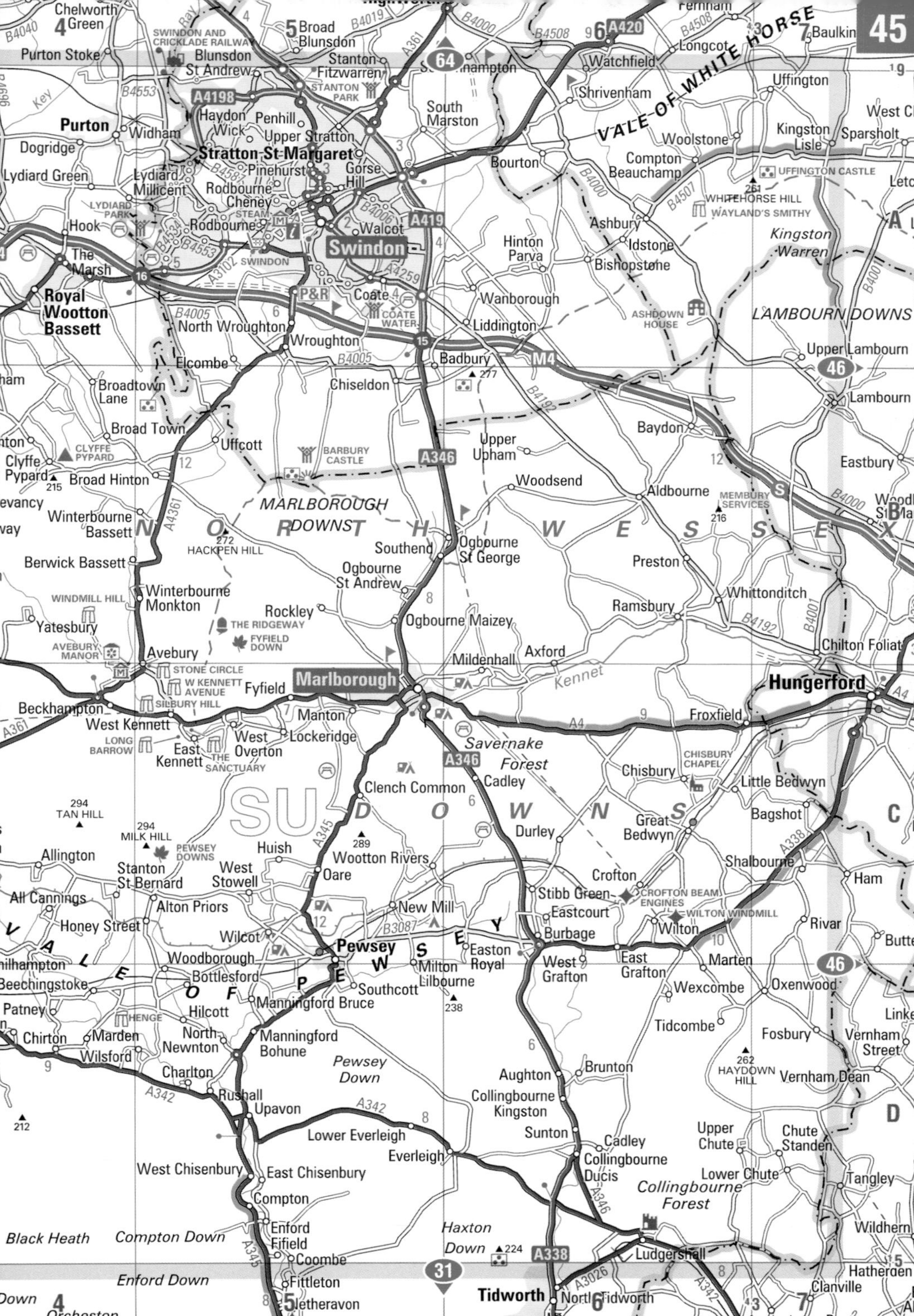

Chelworth Green
Broad Blunsdon
Fernham
Baulking
Purton Stoke
SWINDON AND CRICKLADE RAILWAY
Blunsdon St Andrew
Stanton Fitzwarren
STANTON PARK
Longcot
Watchfield
Shrivenham
Uffington
VALE OF WHITE HORSE
Purton
Widham
Haydon Wick
Penhill
Upper Stratton
South Marston
West Challow
Kingston Lisle
Sparsholt
Dogridge
Stratton St Margaret
Woolstone
Compton Beauchamp
Bourton
Lydiard Green
Lydiard Millicent
Pinehurst
Rodbourne Cheney
Gorse Hill
UFFINGTON CASTLE
Letcombe
LYDIARD PARK
STEAM
WHITEHORSE HILL
WAYLAND'S SMITHY
Hook
Rodbourne
Walcot
Ashbury
Kingston Warren
Idstone
The Marsh
Swindon
SWINDON
Hinton Parva
Bishopstone
Royal Wootton Bassett
P&R
Coate
COATE WATER
Wanborough
ASHDOWN HOUSE
LAMBOURN DOWNS
North Wroughton
Liddington
Wroughton
Upper Lambourn
Elcombe
Badbury
Chiseldon
Broadtown Lane
Lambourn
Broad Town
Baydon
Uffcott
Upper Upham
CLYFFE PYPARD
Clyffe Pypard
Broad Hinton
BARBURY CASTLE
Eastbury
Woodsend
Aldbourne
MEMBURY SERVICES
Woodlands St Mary
MARLBOROUGH DOWNS
Winterbourne Bassett
NORTH WESSEX
HACKPEN HILL
Southend
Ogbourne St George
Berwick Bassett
Preston
Ogbourne St Andrew
WINDMILL HILL
Winterbourne Monkton
Whittonditch
Ramsbury
Rockley
Yatesbury
THE RIDGEWAY
Ogbourne Maizey
FYFIELD DOWN
AVEBURY MANOR
Avebury
Axford
Mildenhall
Chilton Foliat
STONE CIRCLE
Marlborough
Kennet
W KENNETT AVENUE
Fyfield
Hungerford
SILBURY HILL
Beckhampton
Manton
West Kennett
Froxfield
LONG BARROW
West Overton
Lockeridge
Savernake Forest
East Kennett
THE SANCTUARY
CHISBURY CHAPEL
Chisbury
Cadley
Little Bedwyn
Clench Common
TAN HILL
NORTH WESSEX DOWNS
Bagshot
Great Bedwyn
MILK HILL
Durley
PEWSEY DOWNS
Huish
Allington
Wootton Rivers
Stanton St Bernard
West Stowell
Oare
Shalbourne
Crofton
Ham
All Cannings
Alton Priors
Stibb Green
CROFTON BEAM ENGINES
New Mill
Eastcourt
WILTON WINDMILL
Honey Street
Wilton
Rivar
Wilcot
Burbage
Pewsey
Easton Royal
Buttermere
Chilhampton
VALE OF PEWSEY
Woodborough
West Grafton
East Grafton
Marten
Milton Lilbourne
Oxenwood
Beechingstoke
Bottlesford
Southcott
Manningford Bruce
Wexcombe
Patney
Hilcott
Linkenholt
HENGE
Tidcombe
Chirton
Marden
North Newnton
Manningford Bohune
Fosbury
Vernham Street
Wilsford
Pewsey Down
Brunton
HAYDOWN HILL
Vernham Dean
Charlton
Aughton
Rushall
Collingbourne Kingston
Upavon
Lower Everleigh
Upper Chute
Chute Standen
Sunton
Cadley
Everleigh
West Chisenbury
Collingbourne Ducis
East Chisenbury
Lower Chute
Tangley
Collingbourne Forest
Compton
Enford
Haxton Down
Wildhern
Black Heath
Compton Down
Fifield
Ludgershall
Coombe
Hatherden
Enford Down
Fittleton
Clanville
Down
Orcheston
Tidworth
North Tidworth
Netheravon
DOVECOTE
Appleshaw
Penton

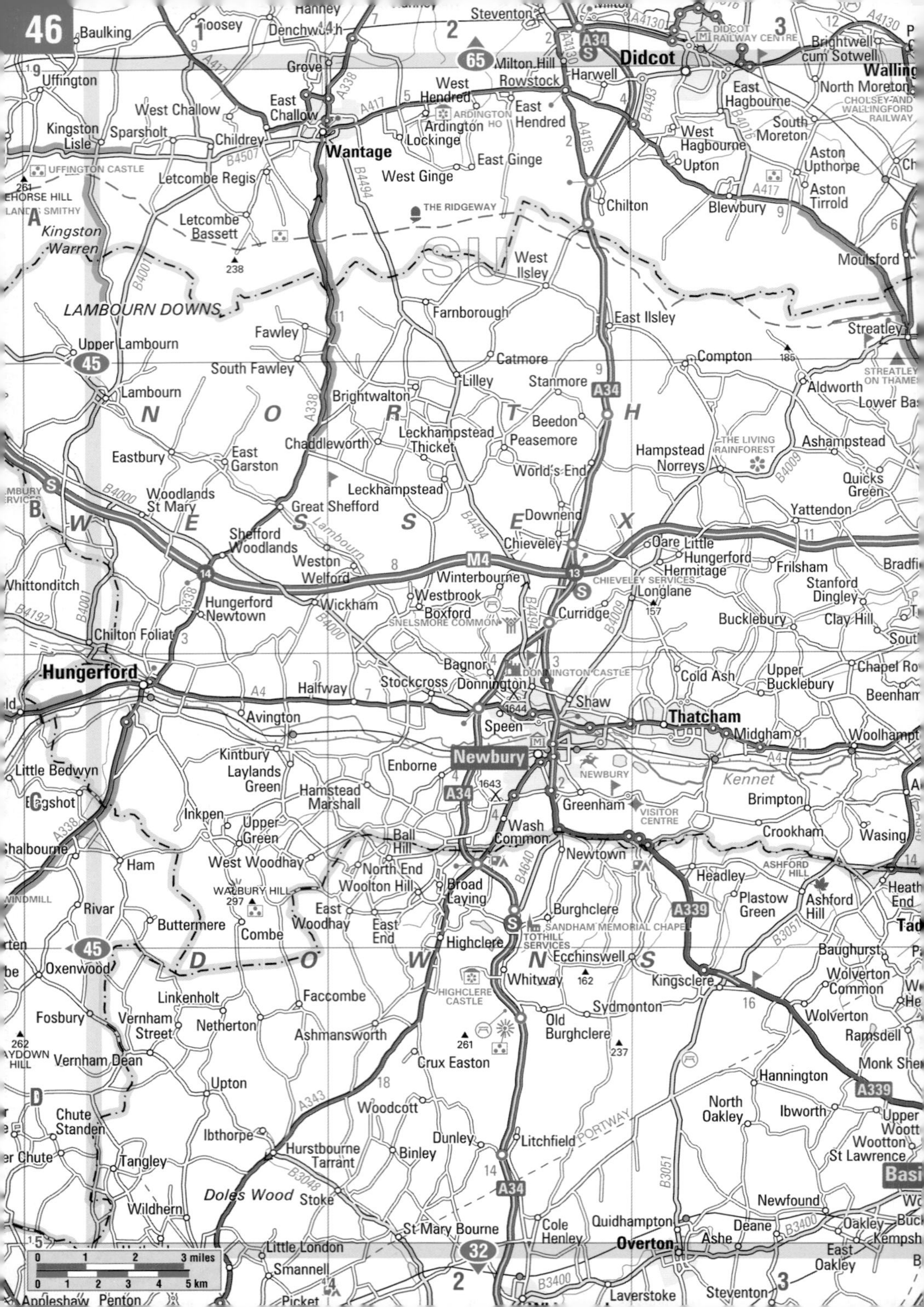

Baulking
Goosey
Denchworth
Hanney
Steventon
Milton
Didcot
DIDCOT RAILWAY CENTRE
Brightwell-cum-Sotwell
Wallingford
Uffington
Grove
Milton Hill
Rowstock
Harwell
West Hendred
East Hendred
ARDINGTON HO
East Hagbourne
North Moreton
CHOLSEY AND WALLINGFORD RAILWAY
South Moreton
West Challow
East Challow
Ardington
Lockinge
Kingston Lisle
Sparsholt
Childrey
Wantage
West Hagbourne
Upton
Aston Upthorpe
Aston Tirrold
UFFINGTON CASTLE
Letcombe Regis
West Ginge
East Ginge
WHITE HORSE HILL
WAYLAND'S SMITHY
THE RIDGEWAY
Chilton
Blewbury
Letcombe Bassett
Kingston Warren
SU
West Ilsley
Moulsford
LAMBOURN DOWNS
Farnborough
East Ilsley
Streatley
Fawley
Upper Lambourn
South Fawley
Catmore
Compton
Lilley
Stanmore
STREATLEY ON THAMES
Aldworth
Lambourn
Brightwalton
Lower Basildon
N O R T H
Leckhampstead Thicket
Beedon
Peasemore
Chaddleworth
THE LIVING RAINFOREST
Ashampstead
Hampstead Norreys
Eastbury
East Garston
World's End
Quicks Green
LAMBOURN SERVICES
Leckhampstead
Woodlands St Mary
Great Shefford
Downend
Yattendon
W E S S E X
Lambourn
Shefford Woodlands
Chieveley
Oare
Little Hungerford
Hermitage
Weston
Frilsham
Bradfield
Welford
Winterbourne
M4
Whittonditch
CHIEVELEY SERVICES
Stanford Dingley
Westbrook
Longlane
Hungerford Newtown
Wickham
Boxford
Curridge
SNELSMORE COMMON
Bucklebury
Clay Hill
Chilton Foliat
Cold Ash
Upper Bucklebury
Chapel Row
Bagnor
DONNINGTON CASTLE
Hungerford
Stockcross
Donnington
Halfway
Shaw
Thatcham
Beenham
Avington
Speen
Midgham
Woolhampton
Kintbury
Newbury
Little Bedwyn
Laylands Green
Enborne
NEWBURY
Kennet
Hamstead Marshall
Greenham
VISITOR CENTRE
Brimpton
Inkpen
Upper Green
Wash Common
Crookham
Wasing
Shalbourne
Ball Hill
Newtown
Ham
West Woodhay
North End
Headley
ASHFORD HILL
Woolton Hill
Broad Laying
Heath End
WALBURY HILL
Plastow Green
Ashford Hill
WINDMILL
Rivar
East Woodhay
Burghclere
Buttermere
Combe
East End
SANDHAM MEMORIAL CHAPEL
Highclere
TOTHILL SERVICES
Ecchinswell
Baughurst
D O W N S
Oxenwood
Whitway
Kingsclere
Wolverton Common
HIGHCLERE CASTLE
Linkenholt
Faccombe
Fosbury
Vernham Street
Netherton
Sydmonton
Wolverton
Old Burghclere
Ramsdell
Ashmansworth
Vernham Dean
Crux Easton
Monk Sherborne
Hannington
Upton
North Oakley
Ibworth
Chute Standen
Woodcott
Upper Wootton
Ibthorpe
Dunley
Litchfield
PORTWAY
Wootton St Lawrence
Hurstbourne Tarrant
Binley
Tangley
Basingstoke
Doles Wood
Stoke
Newfound
Wildhern
St Mary Bourne
Cole Henley
Quidhampton
Deane
Oakley
Overton
Ashe
East Oakley
Little London
Smannell
Laverstoke
Steventon
Appleshaw
Penton
Picket Piece
0 1 2 3 miles
0 1 2 3 4 5 km

Benson
Ewelme
Greenfield
Turville Heath
Turville
Bolter End
Fingest
Lane End
M40
Booker
Cookley Green
Pishill
65
Skirmett
Frieth
WYCOMBE AIR PARK
P&R
A404
Crowmarsh Gifford
Russell's Water
STONOR
Stonor
Flackwell Heath
Little Marlow
Wooburn Green
Marlow Bottom
NUFFIELD PLACE
Park Corner
A4130
Rockwell End
Lower Woodend
Bovingdon Green
Well End
Nuffield
Nettlebed
Fawley
Hambleden
Bourne End
North Stoke
Middle Assendon
Greenlands
Marlow
Cookham Dean
Ipsden
Bix
A4155
Mill End
Bisham
MAHARAJAH'S WELL
Lower Assendon
Medmenham
Cookham
Highmoor Cross
Aston
Stoke Row
GREYS COURT
Remenham
Remenham Hill
Hurley
Park Corner
South Stoke
Checkendon
Satwell
Shepherd's Green
THE THAMES PATH
A4130
Pinkneys Grn.
Furze Platt
Woodcote
Rotherfield Greys
Henley-on-Thames
A321
Burchett's Green
Maidenhead
Cray's Pond
Rotherfield Peppard
Harpsden
RIVER & ROWING MUSEUM
Warren Row
Goring
B4526
Sonning Common
A4074
A4
9B
48
Bray Wick
Goring Heath
Knowl Hill
BARTHOLOMEW'S
BEALE PARK
Cane End
Kidmore End
Lower Shiplake
Shiplake
Littlewick Green
A404(M)
9A
Whitchurch Hill
Binfield Hth.
Wargrave
White Waltham
WHITE WALTHAM
Woodlands Park
8/9
Whitchurch
Mapledurham
Tokers Green
Dunsden Green
Thames
Hare Hatch
Stud Grn.
Holyport
TOLL
MAPLEDURHAM
Sonning Eye
Ruscombe
Waltham St Lawrence
Pangbourne
Purley
Emmer Green
Play Hatch
B478
Charvil
Twyford
B3024
Touchen End
Paley Street
Tidmarsh
A329
Reading
Sonning
Caversham
B3018
Shurlock Row
A340
Sulham
Tilehurst
A4
Woodley
B3030
Whistley Green
M4
Jealott's Hill
Hawthorn Hill
North Street
Englefield
DINTON PASTURES
P&R
Hurst
A3290
Moss End
A3095
Warfield
B3022
Theale
12
Calcot Row
A33
MUS. OF ENGLISH RURAL LIFE
Earley
B3034
Binfield
Newell Grn.
B3034
Whitley
P&R
Winnersh
10
A329(M)
Burleigh
A4
Res
B3031
B3270
Emmbrook
Popeswood
Bullbrook
Ufton Nervet
Sheffield Bottom
READING SERVICES
M4
11
Sindlesham
A329
A329
Sulhamstead
Burghfield
P&R
Shinfield
A327
B3030
WOKINGHAM
Bracknell
Burghfield Hill
Threemile Cross
Arborfield
Arborfield Cross
Eastheath
Easthampstead
Aldermaston Wharf
Burghfield Common
Grazeley
A33
Barkham
Padworth
Wokefield Park
Spencers Wood
Farley Hill
Arborfield Garrison
CALIFORNIA
The Throat
B3430
A322
THE LOOK OUT DISCOVERY CENTRE
Mortimer
Swallowfield
Wick Hill
B3348
Crowthorne
SURREY HILL
Stratfield Mortimer
Beech Hill
Riseley
Finchampstead
A321
A3095
Little Sandhurst
Bagshot
Mortimer West End
WELLINGTON
Pamber Heath
ROMAN TOWN
Stratfield Saye
STRATFIELD SAYE HOUSE
B3349
Eversley
B3348
TRILAKES
48
Sandhurst
A30
Silchester
Bramshill
B3272
West End Green
Eversley Cross
CAMBERLEY
Fair Oak Green
A327
CASTLE BOTTOM
Yateley
Heckfield
Frogmore
York Town
Little London
B3011
Stratfield Turgis
Turgis Green
Hazeley
Bramshill Forest
BLACKBUSHE
YATELEY COMMON
A325
Hound Green
Blackwater
A340
Bramley
Hartley Westpall
Mattingley
Hawley
Frimley
Pamber End
Sherfield on Loddon
Hartfordbridge
B3013
Fox Lane
A327
Farnborough Green
Lyde Green
West Green
Hartley Wintney
FLEET SERVICES
A323
THE VYNE
Church End
M3
4A
Cove
Frimley
Sherborne St John
A33
Rotherwick
Phoenix Green
A30
West Heath
ST MICHAEL'S ABBEY
A331
Chineham
Fleet
Popley
Newnham
Hook
Winchfield
Pondtail
A327
FARNBOROUGH AIRPORT
FARNBOROUGH
Daneshill
Oakridge
Dogmersfield
B3016
B3013
Long Valley
A323
Basingstoke
Old Basing
North Warnborough
Crookham Village
South View
Hatch
Up Nately
South Ham
P&R
Mapledurwell
Greywell
Odiham
A287
Church Crookham
ALDERSHOT
Mill Lane
Ewshot
33
Heath End
Ash
BRICKFIELDS
Badshot Lea
M3
Cliddesden
B3349
Upton Grey
Crondall
Hog Hatch
Upper Hale
Tongham

Loudwater
Beaconsfield
Chalfont St Peter
67
Chalfont Common
Jordans
Forty Green
Northwood
Harefield
Hatch End
Flackwell Heath
Little Marlow
Wooburn Green
Gerrards Cross
Denham Green
Ruislip Common
Pinner
Eastcote
Ruislip
Rayners Lane
Well End
Wooburn
Hedgerley
Tatling End
Cores End
Hedsor
Bourne End
M40
Fulmer
Denham
Ickenham
Cookham Dean
Cookham
Stanley Spencer Gallery
Burnham Beeches
Farnham Common
Stoke Poges
Cliveden
Cookham Rise
Uxbridge
Black Park
Iver Heath
M25
Farnham Royal
Wexham Street
Stoke Green
Park Corner
Burnham
Hillingdon
Furze Platt
Cowley
Yeading
Greenford
Taplow
Langley Park
Maidenhead
George Green
Iver
Yiewsley
Hayes
Southall
SLOUGH
47
West Drayton
Bray Wick
Bray
Dorney
Eton Wick
Richings Park
Langley
A312
Woodlands Park
Upton
Harmondsworth
Harlington
Heston Services
Dorney Court
Eton
M4
Sipson
Cranford
Heston
White Waltham
Stud Grn.
Holyport
Boveney
Windsor Castle
Datchet
Colnbrook
Longford
London Heathrow
Fifield
Poyle
Touchen End
Oakley Green
WINDSOR
Horton
HEATHROW AIRPORT
HOUNSLOW
Paley Street
Household Cavalry Mus
Legoland
Windsor
Old Windsor
Wraysbury
Stanwell Moor
West Bedfont
East Bedfont
Hawthorn Hill
Jealott's Hill
Forest
WINDSOR
GREAT PARK
Stanwell
Maiden's Green
Cranbourne
Hythe End
Runnymede
Moss End
Winkfield
A30
Feltham
Warfield
Englefield Green
EGHAM
Newell Grn.
Winkfield Row
Woodside
Staines-upon-Thames
Ashford
Hanworth
Kempton Park
Burleigh
The Savill Garden
A308
Hampton
Bullbrook
Valley Gdns
Laleham
Littleton
Sunbury-on-Thames
Virginia Water
Thorpe
Ascot
A329
Bracknell
Sunninghill
Wentworth
Thorpe Park
M3
West Molesey
South Ascot
Sunningdale
M3
Shepperton
Broomhall
Lyne
CHERTSEY
Walton-on-Thames
A322
Sandown Park
The Look Out Discovery Centre
Sunningdale
Chobham Common
Addlestone
Crowthorne
Windlesham
WEYBRIDGE
Hersham
Ottershaw
Claremont Landscape Garden
Surrey Hill
Bagshot
Burrowhill
New Haw
47
Lightwater
Fairoaks
Brooklands Mus
Whiteley Village
Chobham
Woodham
Byfleet
West End
A3
CAMBERLEY
Donkey Town
West Byfleet
Cobham
Castle Green
York Town
Chobham Ridges
34
Cheapside
Painshill Park
Stoke D'Abernon
Bisley
Knaphill
Horsell
Wisley
RHS Garden Wisley
Frimley
WOKING
Pyrford
Downside
Deepcut
Brookwood
St John's
Old Woking
Ripley
Martyr's Green
Farnborough Green
Cobham Services
Cove
Frimley Green
Mayford
Send Marsh
Ripley Services
Ockham
West Heath
Mytchett
Basingstoke Canal Centre
Send
Pirbright
Little Bookham
St Michael's Abbey
Fox Corner
Burntcommon
FARNBOROUGH
Sutton Green
Effingham
Farnborough Airport
Worplesdon
East Horsley
West Horsley
Polesden Lacey
Ash Vale
Willey Green
Pitch Place
Slyfield
Burpham
Clandon Park
West Clandon
Tanners Hatch
ALDERSHOT
Wyke
Normandy
Stoughton
P&R
Merrow
East Clandon
Hatchlands Park
Ranmore Common
Wood Street
Dapdune Wharf
Newland's Corner
Wanborough
Hogs Back
Onslow Village
Guildford
Albury
Gomshall
Abinger
North Downs Way
0 1 2 3 miles
0 1 2 3 4 5 km

Edgware
Mill Hill
Wood Green
Woodford
Finchley
Tottenham
Hornsey
Vealdstone
Kingsbury
Hendon
Walthamstow
Wanstead
Barking
Highgate
Golders Green
Leytonstone
Seven Kings
Harrow on the Hill
Hampstead
Stoke Newington
Leyton
Ilford
Wembley
Cricklewood
Willesden
Hackney
Forest Gate
Manor Park
Alperton
Camden
Islington
East Ham
Perivale
Harlesden
Kilburn
Bethnal Green
Stratford
Regents Park
Shoreditch
Finsbury
West Ham
Holborn
Poplar
Beckton
EALING
Paddington
City
Acton
Hanwell
Kensington
Hyde Park
Westminster
Southwark
Bermondsey
Blackwall Tunnel
North Woolwich
Woolwich Ferry
Chiswick
Hammersmith
Chelsea
LAMBETH
Deptford
Greenwich
Woolwich
Charlton
Kew
Kew Br.
Fulham
Battersea
Peckham
Kidbrooke
Camberwell
New Cross
Lewisham
Putney
Mortlake
Clapham
Brixton
Richmond
Dulwich
Hither Green
Eltham
Roehampton
Wandsworth
Catford
New Eltham
Richmond Park
Wimbledon Common
Balham
Grove Park
Mottingham
Twickenham
Streatham
Chislehurst
Ham
Kingston Vale
Upper Tooting
West Norwood
Sydenham
Wimbledon
Merton
Penge
BROMLEY
Raynes Park
South Norwood
Beckenham
Kingston upon Thames
Morden
Mitcham
Thornton Heath
Elmers End
Bickley
Petts Wood
Surbiton
New Malden
Selhurst
Eden Park
West Wickham
St Helier
Addiscombe
Hayes
Bromley Common
Long Ditton
Tolworth
Worcester Park
Hackbridge
Croydon
Shirley
Hook
Carshalton
Beddington
Keston
Chessington
Cheam
Wallington
Addington
Farnborough
Sutton
South Croydon
Ewell
New Addington
Belmont
Selsdon
Leaves Green
Downe
Purley
Sanderstead
EPSOM
Woodmansterne
Hamsey Green
Farleigh
Kenley
Biggin Hill
Wood Field
BANSTEAD
Coulsdon
Great Burgh
Warlingham
Whyteleafe
Ashtead
Burgh Heath
Chipstead
Old Coulsdon
Tatsfield
South Street
Leatherhead
Tadworth
Hooley
Woldingham
Kingswood
Chaldon
Walton on the Hill
CATERHAM
Titsey
Headley
Lower Kingswood
Westerham
Mickleham
Merstham
Limpsfield
Limpsfield Chart
Brewer Street
Godstone
Oxted
Buckland
Church Town
Redhill
Nutfield
Tandridge
Crockham Hill
Pixham
Bletchingley
Betchworth
Earlswood
Brockham
Reigate
South Nutfield
Crowhurst Lane End
Marlpit Hill
Ridge Green
Strood
Doversgreen

Woodford
Woodford Bridge
Hainault
Collier Row
Harold Hill
Ingrave
Herongate
Great Burstead
Dunton Wayletts
Great Warley
Little Warley
Barkingside
Gidea Park
Romford
Harold Wood
Laindon
Wanstead
Newbury Park
Seven Kings
Hornchurch
Cranham
West Horndon
Langdon Hills
Ilford
Becontree
Rush Green
Elm Park
Upminster
Bulphan
Forest Gate
Manor Park
Dagenham
Hacton
Corbets Tey
North Ockendon
Horndon on the Hill
East Ham
Barking
South Hornchurch
West Ham
Beckton
Creekmouth
Rainham
South Ockendon
Baker Street
Orsett
Thames
Thamesmead
Wennington
Aveley
North Stifford
Woolwich Ferry
Belvedere
Thurrock Services
Lakeside
South Stifford
Little Thurrock
Chadwell St Mary
Linford
Woolwich
Plumstead
Abbey Wood
Erith
Purfleet
West Thurrock
Grays
Tilbury
West Tilbury
East Tilbury
Greenwich
Charlton
Dartford Crossing
Welling
Slade Green
Electronic Toll
Swanscombe Skull Site
Bexleyheath
Crayford
Dartford
Stone
Greenhithe
Northfleet
Milton Chantry
Gravesend
Hither Green
Eltham
Bexley
Hall Pl
Bluewater
Darenth
Swanscombe
Chalk
New Eltham
Coldblow
Wilmington
Bean
Perry Street
Secret Cold War Bunker
Grove Park
Mottingham
Sidcup
Foots Cray
North Cray
Darenth
Betsham
Singlewell
Shorne
Chislehurst
Hawley
Beacon Wood
Southfleet
Hextable
Swanley Village
Sutton at Hone
Istead Rise
Thong
Bromley
St John's Jerusalem
Swanley
St Paul's Cray
South Darenth
Longfield
New Barn
Owletts
Bickley
Petts Wood
St Mary Cray
Horton Kirby
Hartley
Sole Street
Cobham
Crockenhill
Meopham Station
Farningham
Bromley Common
Hayes
Orpington
Eynsford
Hook Green
Camer Park
Luddesdown
Lullingstone Roman Villa
Fawkham Green
Meopham
Keston
Chelsfield
Eynsford
New Ash Green
Upper Halling
Farnborough
Well Hill
Maplescombe
Ash
Lullingstone
Brands Hatch
Green St Green
High Elms
Aircraft Museum
West Kingsdown
Culverstone Green
Pratt's Bottom
Badger's Mount
Stansted
Leaves Green
Downe
Shoreham
Fairseat
Vigo Village
Snodland
Darwin Museum
Halstead
Trosley
Birling
Biggin Hill
Trottiscliffe
Ryarsh
Biggin Hill
Cudham
Knockholt Pound
Otford
Wrotham
Knockholt
Kemsing
Heaverham
Addington
South Street
Chevening
Wrotham Heath
West Malling
Tatsfield
North Downs Way
Dunton Green
Seal
Borough Green
Platt
Offham
Chipstead
Ightham
Riverhead
Great Comp
St Leonards Tower
Manor Park
Clacket Lane Services
Stone Street
Crouch
Kent Street
Titsey
Brasted
Sundridge
Sevenoaks
Claygate Cross
Quebec Ho
Knole
Ivy Hatch
Plaxtol
Mereworth
King's Hill
Westerham
Brasted Chart
Ightham Mote
Dunk's Green
Old Soar Manor
Wateringbury
Limpsfield
The Chart
Cross Keys
Limpsfield Chart
Emmetts
Whitley Row
Underriver
Shipbourne
West Peckham
Nettlestead Green
Oxted
Chartwell
Ide Hill
Crockham Hill
Toy's Hill
Sevenoaks Weald
Oakhurst
Coldharbour
Broadview Garden
Pittswood
Hadlow
Hildenborough
Hilden
Higham Wood
East Peckham
Four Elms
Res.
Kent
North
Thorndon
Fairlop Waters
Havering Mus
Hornchurch
Belhus Woods
Grangewaters Outdoor Centre
Orsett Cock Services
London City
Red House
Fort
Darenth
Hale Street
M25
M20
M26
A13
A12
A127
A2
A20
A21
A25
A26
A282
A228
A1089
A406
A205
A1400
3 miles
5 km

Hawkwell
RAYLEIGH
Rochford
North Benfleet
Thundersley
Bowers Gifford
Pitsea
Vange
Hadleigh
Daws Heath
Eastwood
Prittlewell
Great Wakering
Little Wakering
Barling
Potton Island
Havengore Island
South Benfleet
Leigh on Sea
Southchurch
Thorpe Bay
Westcliff-on-Sea
Southend-on-Sea
Shoeburyness
CANVEY ISLAND
Corringham
Fobbing
Coryton
Leigh Beck
Thames Haven
THAMES ESTUARY
TQ
Halstow Marshes
St Mary's Marshes
Allhallows-on-Sea
Allhallows
Grain
Isle of Grain
Cliffe
Cooling
High Halstow
Stoke
Sheerness
Medway
Minster
Queenborough
Eastchurch
Rushenden
Chetney Marshes
ISLE OF SHEPPEY
Hoo St.Werburgh
Chattenden
Upnor
Frindsbury
Strood
ROCHESTER
CHATHAM
Gillingham
Rainham
Upchurch
Iwade
Kemsley
The Swale
SITTINGBOURNE
Milton Regis
Bobbing
Newington
Walderslade
Wouldham
Burham
Bredhurst
Stockbury
Borden
Bapchild
Teynham
Faversham
Conyer
Tunstall
Rodmersham
Eccles
Aylesford
Boxley
Detling
Thurnham
Hucking
Bicknor
Bredgar
Milstead
Doddington
Newnham
Wormshill
Maidstone
Bearsted
Hollingbourne
Eyhorne Street
Leeds
Harrietsham
Lenham
Charing
Loose
Boughton Monchelsea
Langley
Coxheath
Hunton
Linton
Sutton Valence
Kingswood
Ulcombe
Grafty Green
Boughton Malherbe
Westwell
M2
M20
A249
A2
A20
A229

Eastend
Potton Island
FOULNESS ISLAND
1
2
3
71
Barling
Havengore Island
Little Wakering
Great Wakering
MAPLIN SANDS
A1159
Bournes Green
B1017
A13
North Shoebury
Thorpe Bay
A
SEA LIFE ADVENTURE
B1016
Shoeburyness
Cambridge Town
Shoeburyness
51
TQ
Sheerness
B
West Minster
A250
Halfway Houses
Minster
B2008
ABBEY
73
Warden Pt.
Warden
Rushenden
A2500
Eastchurch
B2231
Leysdown-on-Sea
A249
ISLE OF SHEPPEY
ELMLEY
Isle of Harty
THE SWALE
Shell Ness
HERNE BAY
Tankerton
Swalecliffe
WHITSTABLE
MUSEUM & GALLERY
A2990
Greenhill
Chestfield
Seasalter
Kemsley
The Swale
SITTINGBOURNE & KEMSLEY LT RLY
MILTON CREEK
C
Conyer
SITTINGBOURNE
South Street
Uplees
Yorkletts
A290
Barrow Green
Calcott
Bapchild
Teynham
Oare
Graveney
CHART GUNPOWDER MILLS
66
Rodmersham
Faversham
Goodnestone
A299
Dargate
Honey Hill
Broadoak
Tunstall
Highsted
FLEUR DE LIS HERITAGE CENTRE
A291
Lynsted
OSPRINGE MAISON DIEU
Ospringe
Preston
Hernhill
BLEAN WOODS
Blean
Tyler Hill
Sturry
MOUNT EPHRAIM
Hales Place
M2
Boughton Street
Rough Common
P&R
Canterbury
Milstead
Dunkirk
A2
North Street
DODDINGTON PLACE
Newnham
A251
South Street
GATE SERVICES
A257
Frinsted
Harbledown
ST AUGUSTINE'S ABBEY
123
Doddington
Eastling
Sheldwich
Oversland
Chartham Hatch
CANTERBURY TALES
Thanington
ROMAN MUS
CANTERBURY
BELMONT
A2050
Wichling
Throwley
Selling
K
E
N
T
Old Wives Lees
A28
Chartham
West Street
D
Badlesmere
Shottenden
Shalmsford Street
Nackington
Bridge
Chilham
Street End
NORTH DOWNS WAY
Stalisfield Green
Leaveland
Lower Hardres
Warren Street
Garlinge Green
A252
Bishopsbourne
B2068
Lenham
Molash
Petham
Kingston
A20
Upper Hardres Court
M20
Lenham Heath
A252
NORTH DOWNS WAY
Godmersham
Challock
38
Sole Street
Bossingham
Westwell
Oughton Aluph
Crundale
Waltham
ELHAM VALLEY
D
O
W
N
S
0 1 2 3 miles
0 1 2 3 4 5 km

TR
Margate
Cliftonville
Foreness Pt.
Kingsgate
NORTH FORELAND
Northdown
St Peter's
BROADSTAIRS
BLEAK HOUSE
DICKENS HOUSE MUSEUM
Dumpton
Ramsgate
MARITIME MUSEUM
Newington
Northwood
Manston
Isle of Thanet
Westgate on Sea
Birchington
Minnis Bay
RECULVER
RECULVER TOWERS AND ROMAN FORT
Hillborough
St Nicholas at Wade
Boyden Gate
Sarre
Chislet
Monkton
Minster
Acol
Cliffsend
Pegwell
Pegwell Bay
West Stourmouth
East Stourmouth
Grove
Preston
Westmarsh
Ware
Stodmarsh
Elmstone
Hoaden
Great Stonar
Sandwich
Sandwich Bay
Ash
Guilton
Wingham
Ickham
Littlebourne
Bramling
Staple
Marshborough
Woodnesborough
Stone Cross
Worth
Gore
Ham
Eastry
Goodnestone
Finglesham
Knowlton
Chillenden
Aylesham
Betteshanger
Sholden
DEAL
DEAL CASTLE
THE DOWNS
Nonington
Easole Street
Northbourne
Snowdown
Tilmanstone
Elvington
Great Mongeham
Walmer
WALMER CASTLE AND GARDENS
Womenswold
Barfrestone
Eythorne
East Studdal
Sutton
Ringwould
Kingsdown
Woolage Green
West
TURNER CONTEMPORARY
THE SHELL GROTTO
DREAMLAND
LIGHTHOUSE
QUEX HOUSE
SPITFIRE AND HURRICANE MEM
WINDMILL
PEGWELL BAY
SANDWICH & PEGWELL BAY
ST. AUGUSTINE'S CROSS
RICHBOROUGH CASTLE
AMPHITHEATRE
WINGHAM WILDLIFE PARK
STODMARSH
ROYAL ST. GEORGE'S
TOLL
GOODNESTONE PARK
BETTESHANGER
MARITIME AND LOCAL HISTORY MUSEUM
EAST KENT RLY
Stour
A299
A28
A253
A256
A255
A254
A257
A258
B2052
B2190
B2050
B2046
A2
71
39

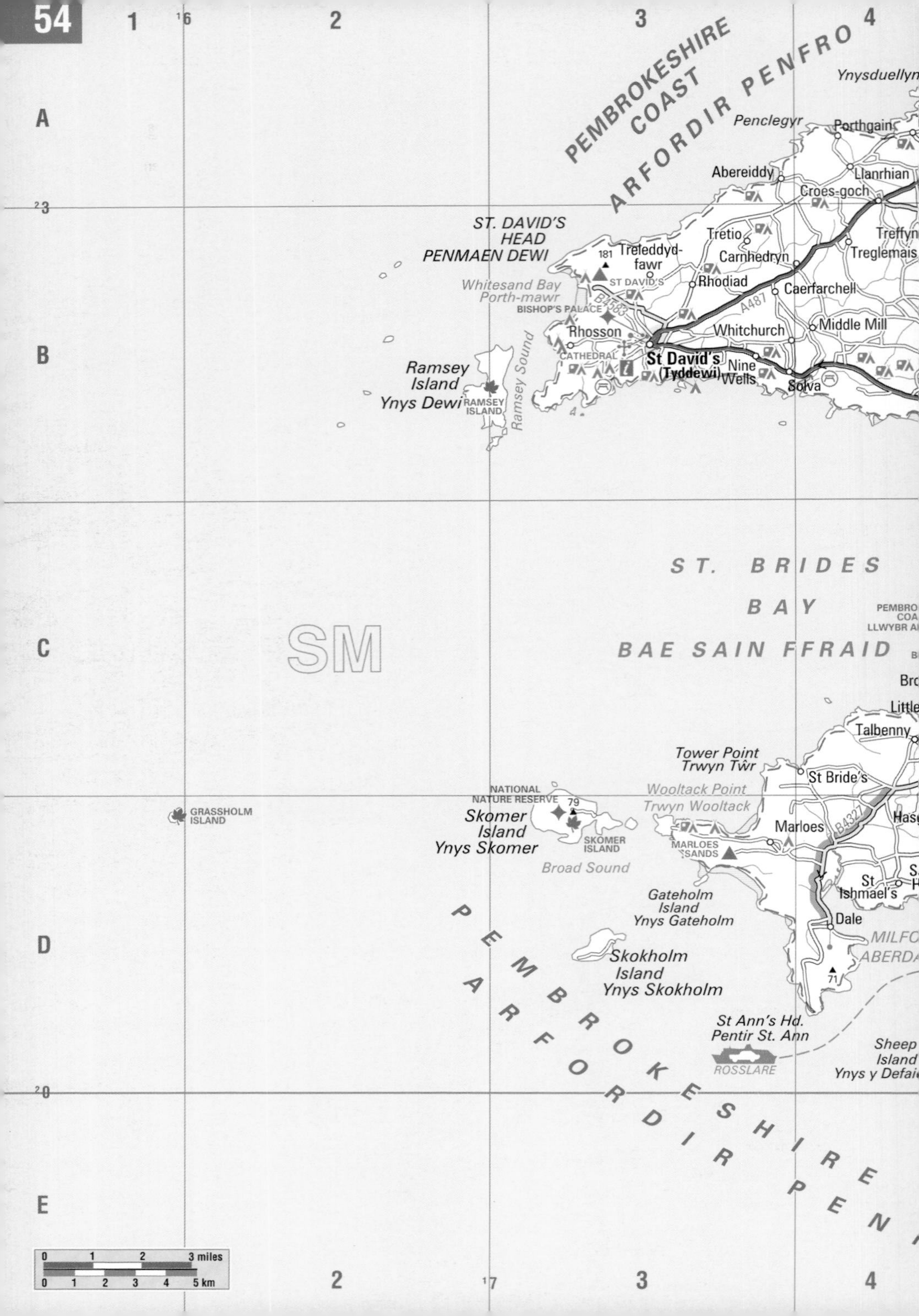
PEMBROKESHIRE COAST
ARFORDIR PENFRO
Ynysduellyn
Penclegyr
Porthgain
Abereiddy
Llanrhian
Croes-goch
ST. DAVID'S HEAD
PENMAEN DEWI
Tretio
Treffyn
Treleddyd-fawr
Carnhedryn
Treglemais
181
Whitesand Bay
Porth-mawr
ST DAVID'S
Rhodiad
Caerfarchell
BISHOP'S PALACE
B4583
A487
Rhosson
Whitchurch
Middle Mill
Ramsey Island
Ynys Dewi
RAMSEY ISLAND
Ramsey Sound
CATHEDRAL
St David's
(Tyddewi)
Nine Wells
Solva
ST. BRIDES BAY
BAE SAIN FFRAID
SM
Talbenny
Tower Point
Trwyn Twr
St Bride's
Wooltack Point
Trwyn Wooltack
NATIONAL NATURE RESERVE
79
GRASSHOLM ISLAND
Skomer Island
Ynys Skomer
SKOMER ISLAND
Marloes
B4327
MARLOES SANDS
Broad Sound
St Ishmael's
Gateholm Island
Ynys Gateholm
Dale
Skokholm Island
Ynys Skokholm
71
St Ann's Hd.
Pentir St. Ann
ROSSLARE
Sheep Island
PEMBROKESHIRE
ARFORDIR PEN
0 1 2 3 miles
0 1 2 3 4 5 km

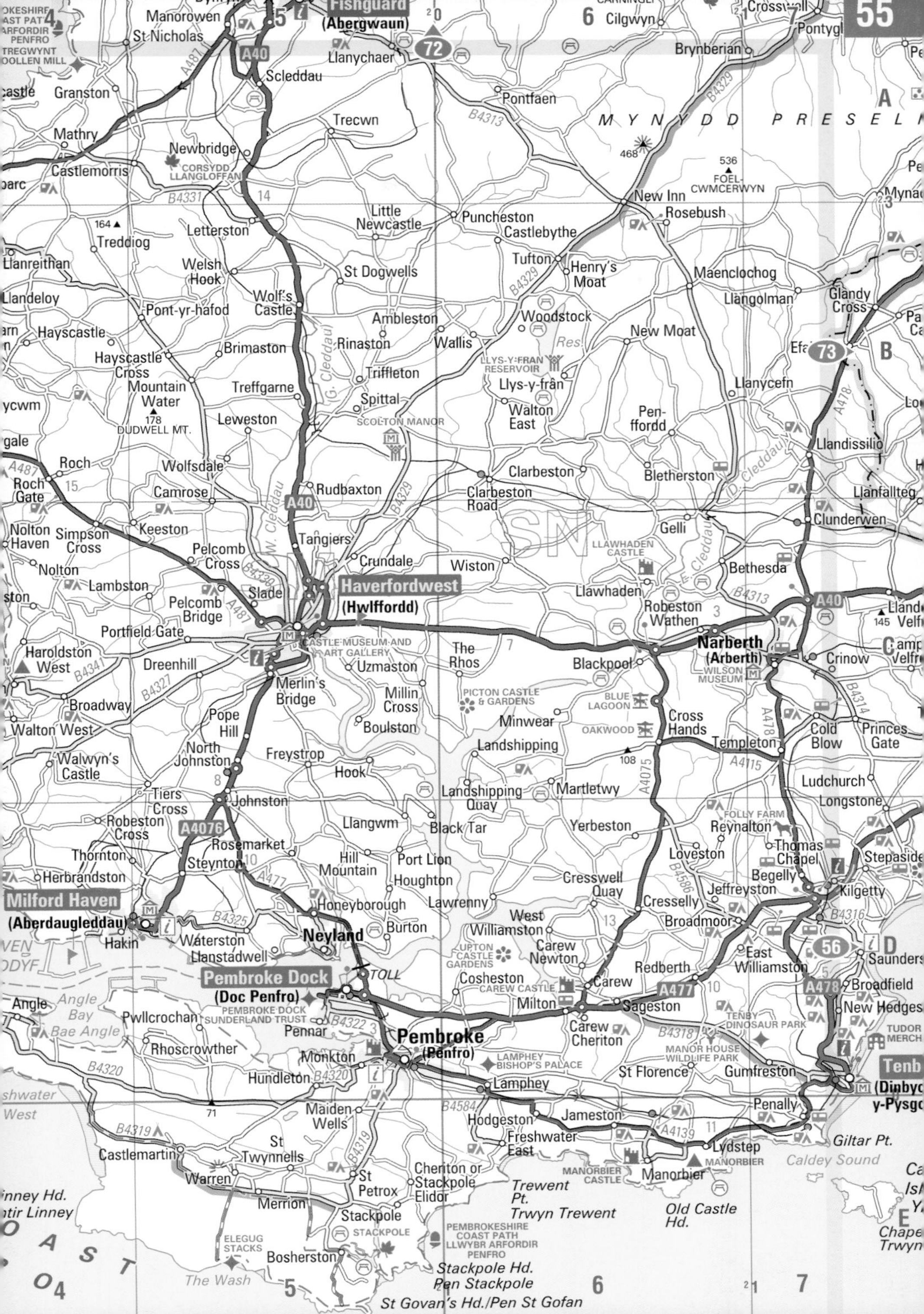
Fishguard
(Abergwaun)
Manorowen
St Nicholas
Llanychaer
72
Cilgwyn
Brynberian
Pontygl
A40
Scleddau
Granston
Pontfaen
B4313
B4329
MYNYDD PRESELI
468
536
FOEL-CWMCERWYN
Trecwn
Mathry
Newbridge
CORSYDD LLANGLOFFAN
Castlemorris
B4331
New Inn
Rosebush
164
Treddiog
Letterston
Little Newcastle
Puncheston
Castlebythe
Llanreithan
Welsh Hook
St Dogwells
Tufton
Henry's Moat
Maenclochog
Llandeloy
Pont-yr-hafod
Wolf's Castle
Ambleston
Woodstock
Llangolman
Glandy Cross
Hayscastle
Rinaston
Wallis
New Moat
Hayscastle Cross
Brimaston
LLYS-Y-FRAN RESERVOIR
Llys-y-frân
Efail
73
Mountain Water
178
DUDWELL MT.
Treffgarne
Triffleton
Spittal
SCOLTON MANOR
Walton East
Llanycefn
Pen-ffordd
A478
Leweston
Llandissilio
Roch
A487
Wolfsdale
Clarbeston
Bletherston
Roch Gate
Camrose
Rudbaxton
Clarbeston Road
Llanfallteg
Nolton Haven
Simpson Cross
Keeston
Tangiers
SN
Gelli
Clunderwen
Nolton
Pelcomb Cross
Crundale
Wiston
LLAWHADEN CASTLE
Bethesda
Lambston
Slade
Haverfordwest
(Hwlffordd)
Llawhaden
Robeston Wathen
B4313
Pelcomb Bridge
Portfield Gate
CASTLE MUSEUM AND ART GALLERY
Narberth
(Arberth)
WILSON MUSEUM
Crinow
Haroldston West
Dreenhill
Uzmaston
The Rhos
Blackpool
B4341
B4327
Merlin's Bridge
Millin Cross
PICTON CASTLE & GARDENS
BLUE LAGOON
B4314
Broadway
Pope Hill
Boulston
Minwear
Cross Hands
Walton West
OAKWOOD
Cold Blow
Princes Gate
Templeton
Landshipping
108
Walwyn's Castle
North Johnston
Freystrop
Hook
A4115
A4075
Ludchurch
Tiers Cross
Johnston
Landshipping Quay
Martletwy
Longstone
Robeston Cross
A4076
Llangwm
Black Tar
Yerbeston
FOLLY FARM
Reynalton
Thomas Chapel
Rosemarket
Thornton
Hill Mountain
Port Lion
Loveston
Stepaside
Steynton
A477
Herbrandston
Houghton
Cresswell Quay
B4586
Begelly
Kilgetty
Jeffreyston
Milford Haven
(Aberdaugleddau)
Honeyborough
Lawrenny
Cresselly
B4325
Hakin
Waterston
Llanstadwell
Neyland
Burton
West Williamston
Broadmoor
B4316
UPTON CASTLE GARDENS
Carew Newton
East Williamston
56
Saunders
TOLL
Pembroke Dock
(Doc Penfro)
Cosheston
Redberth
Carew
CAREW CASTLE
A478
Broadfield
Angle
Angle Bay
Bae Angle
PEMBROKE DOCK SUNDERLAND TRUST
Milton
A477
Sageston
New Hedges
Pwllcrochan
B4322
Pennar
Carew Cheriton
TENBY DINOSAUR PARK
TUDOR MERCH
Rhoscrowther
Pembroke
(Penfro)
B4318
MANOR HOUSE WILDLIFE PARK
Monkton
LAMPHEY BISHOP'S PALACE
Tenb
(Dinbyc y-Pysgo
B4320
Hundleton
St Florence
Gumfreston
Lamphey
Freshwater West
71
B4584
Maiden Wells
Hodgeston
Jameston
Penally
B4319
A4139
St Twynnells
Freshwater East
Lydstep
Giltar Pt.
Castlemartin
Caldey Sound
Cheriton or Stackpole Elidor
MANORBIER CASTLE
Manorbier
MANORBIER
Warren
St Petrox
Trewent Pt.
Trwyn Trewent
Linney Hd.
Trwyn Linney
Merrion
Old Castle Hd.
Stackpole
STACKPOLE
ELEGUG STACKS
PEMBROKESHIRE COAST PATH
LLWYBR ARFORDIR PENFRO
Bosherston
Stackpole Hd.
Pen Stackpole
The Wash
St Govan's Hd./Pen St Gofan
A
B
C
D
E
4
5
6
7

Llandissilio
Hiraeth
Henllan Amgoed
Llanfallteg
Clunderwen
Cwmfelin Boeth
Llangynin
Meidrim
73
Merthyr
Carmarthen (Caerfyrddin)
Sarnau
Llanllwch
Bancyfelin
CORS GOCH, LLANLLWCH
Bethesda
A478
B4313
A40
Whitland
Pwll-trap
B4299
B4298
Llangynog
153
Llangain
Llanddewi Velfrey
145
Trevaughan
Backe
St Clears (Sanclêr)
Afon Cywyn
Afon Taf
Lampeter Velfrey
Crinow
Llwyn-y-brain
Llanddowror
A4066
Morfa Bach
Afon Tywi
B4328
B4314
A477
Tavernspite
Halfpenny Furze
Llanybri
B4312
Cold Blow
Princes Gate
Red Roses
178
Llandawke
DYLAN THOMAS BOATHOUSE
Llansteffan
Templeton
A4115
Ludchurch
Llanteg
12
Laugharne
CASTLE
55
Llansadurnen
Brook
Broadway
Ferryside
FOLLY FARM
Marros
MUSEUM OF SPEED
9
Broadlay
Thomas Chapel
Begelly
Stepaside
COLBY WOODLAND GARDEN
152
Pendine
East Marsh
Llansaint
Kilgetty
Amroth
Pendine Sands
Traeth Pentywyn
B4316
East Williamston
Saundersfoot
ARFORDIR PENFRO
A478
Broadfield
SN
Pembrey Forest
New Hedges
TENBY DINOSAUR PARK
TUDOR MERCHANT'S HOUSE
CARMARTHEN
Gumfreston
Tenby (Dinbych-y-Pysgod)
Penally
BAY
BAE CAERFYRDDIN
Giltar Pt.
Caldey Sound
Caldey Island
Ynys Bŷr
Chapel Pt.
Trwyn Capel
SS
Worms Head
Penrhyn-Gŵyr
Bae Rhossili
A
B
C
D
1
2
3
0 1 2 3 miles
0 1 2 3 4 5 km

White Mill
Pont-ar-gothi
Felindre
Dryslwyn
Cilsan
ABERGLASNEY
Llandeilo
Ffairfach
Nantgaredig
Abergwili
CARMARTHEN
Llanegwad
58
Llanarthne
Afon Tywi
GELLI AUR
Golden Grove
Llangunnor
Capel Dewi
Trapp
CARREG CENNEN CASTLE & FARM
Pensarn
Nantycaws
THE NATIONAL BOTANIC GARDEN OF WALES
Penrhiwgoch
Temple Bar
Milo
Llandyfan
BLACK MOUNTAIN
A48
A40
A483
A476
B4300
B4310
B4297
CARMEL
Carmel
Llanddarog
Maesybont
Pentre-Gwenlais
Llandybie
Dre-fach
Croesyceiliog
Idole
Cwmisfael
Porthyrhyd
LLYN LLECH OWAIN
Bancycapel
Gwendraeth Fach
Foel-gastell
Twynmynydd
Llangendeirne
Cefneithin
Gorslas
B4556
Caer-bryn
Glanaman
Afon Aman
Crwbin
Drefach
Cwm-y-glo
Pen-y-groes
Tir-y-dail
A474
Pontantwn
Bancffosfelen
Cwm-mawr
Cross Hands
Morfa
Saron
Ammanford (Rhydaman)
Pontamman
Garnant
Gwaun-Cae-Gurwen
59
Pontyberem
Tumble
Penybanc
Betws
Pantyffynnon
Meinciau
Pentre
Cwmgwili
Capel Hendre
Tycroes
B4309
B4317
B4306
Four Roads
Pont-Henri
Greynor
Garnswllt
Loughor (Llwchwr)
Mynyddygarreg
Pontyates
Llannon
Mynydd y Gwair
Cynheidre
Llwyn-teg
PONT ABRAHAM SERVICES
Kidwelly (Cydweli)
Sylen
Llanedi
GRAIG FAWR
Carway
FFOS LAS
Five Roads
Horeb
Lliedi Resrs.
Sardis
Pentrebach
Trimsaran
B4308
Fforest
Pontarddulais
Pontardawe
Pinged
Waun-y-clyn
Hendy
Rhyd-y-gwin
Craig-cefn-parc
Cwm-Dulais
Allt
Felindre
Rhyd-y-pandy
Faerdre
Cwmbach
Felinfoel
Llangennech
A4138
Achddu
A484
Furnace
Dafen
Waungron
Clydach
Pembrey
Pwll
Pontlliw
Ynystawe
Burry Port (Porth Tywyn)
Sandy
Bryn
Grovesend
SWANSEA WEST SERVICES
Pant-lasau
M4
MILLENNIUM COASTAL PARK DISCOVERY CENTRE
Llanelli
Llwynhendy
Bynea
Yspitty
Penllergaer
A4240
Llangyfelach
Heol-las
Machynys
Morfa
WILDFOWL AND WETLANDS TRUST
Loughor
Gorseinon
Morriston
Whiteford Pt. Trwyn Whiteford
Llanrhidian Sands Traeth Llanrhidian
Pen-clawdd
Cadle
Llansamlet
WHITEFORD
Gowerton
Fforest-fâch
Landore
Crofty
Blue Anchor
Waunarlwydd
Pentre-chwyth
Cwm
Bon-y-maen
Wernffrwd
Llanmorlais
Three Crosses
Cwmdu
Foxhole
Swansea (Abertawe)
P&R
Cheriton
Dunvant
PLANTASIA
Llanmadoc
Landimore
Killay
Sketty
A4118
Port Tennant
WEOBLEY CASTLE
Brynmill
SWANSEA MUSEUM
Burry Green
Llanrhidian
Llethrid
B4271
B4295
Upper Killay
CLYNE VALLEY
NATIONAL WATERFRONT MUSEUM
40
Llangennith
G O W E R
SWANSEA
Ilston
A4067
Burry
Reynoldston
Mayals
Black Pill
THE BEACON
Lunnon
Bishopston
West Cross
SWANSEA BAY
Llanddewi
GOWER HERITAGE CENTRE
Kittle
Parkmill
Manselfield
LOVESPOON GALLERY
OYSTERMOUTH CASTLE
Knelston
Pennard
Rhossili
Scurlage
Penrice
Nicholaston
Penmaen
Oldway
Newton
The Mumbles (Y Mwmbwls)
BAE ABERTAWE
Middleton
B4247
OXWICH
Southgate
GOWER COAST
Pilton Green
Oxwich Bay Bae Oxwich
Mumbles Hd. Trwyn yr Mwmbwls
Oxwich
OXWICH CASTLE
Pwlldu Hd. Pen Pwlldu
Horton
Overton
Port-Eynon
PORT EYNON
Port Eynon Bay Bae Port Eynon
Port Eynon Pt. Trwyn Port Eynon
A
B
C
D
4
5
6

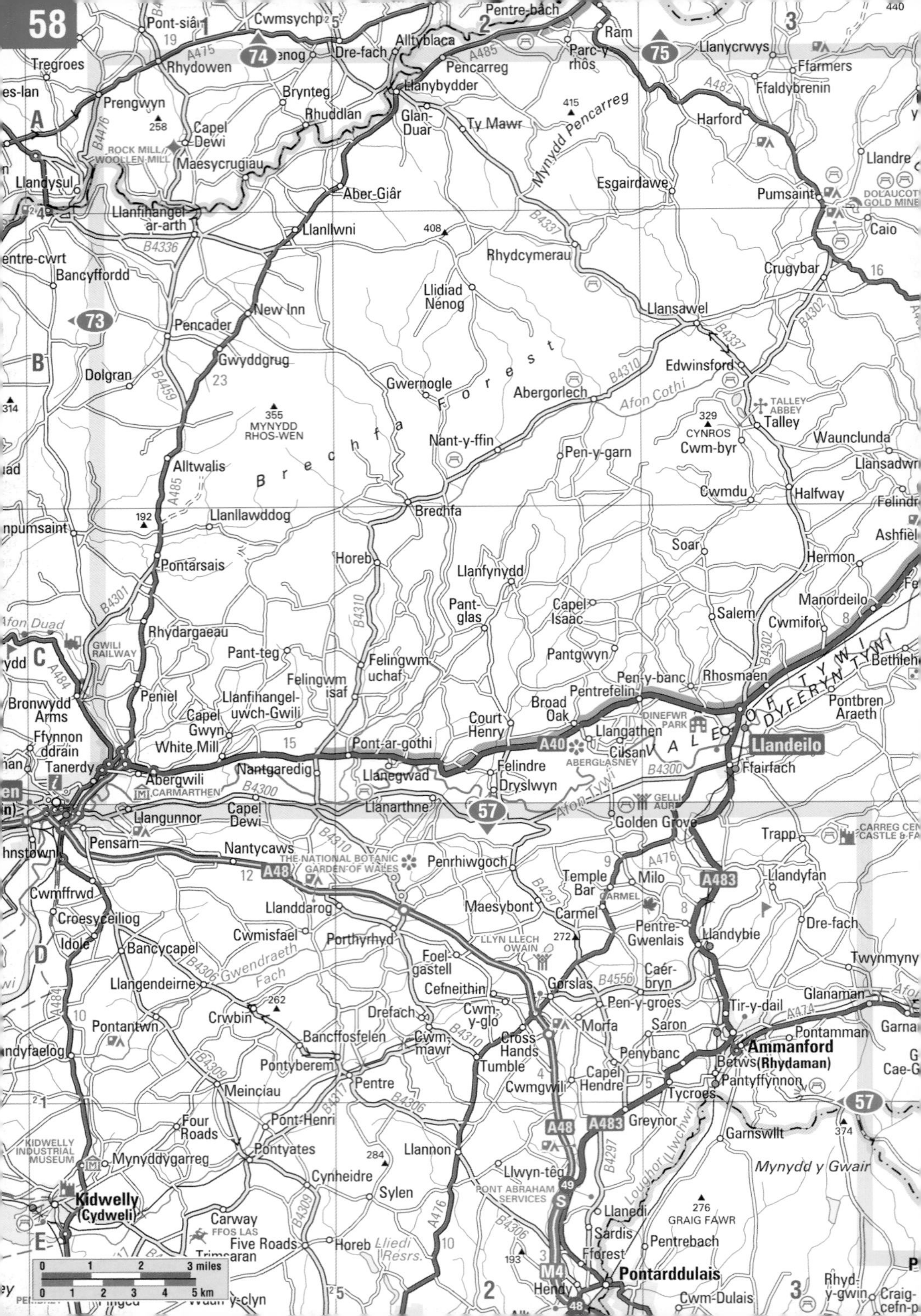

Pont-siân
Cwmsychpant
Pentre-bach
Ram
Llanycrwys
Tregroes
Rhydowen
Dre-fach
Alltyblaca
Pencarreg
Parc-y-rhôs
Ffarmers
Ffaldybrenin
Brynteg
Llanybydder
Prengwyn
Rhuddlan
Glan-Duar
Ty Mawr
Mynydd Pencarreg
Harford
Capel Dewi
ROCK MILL WOOLLEN MILL
Maesycrugiau
Llandre
Llandysul
Aber-Giâr
Esgairdawe
Pumsaint
DOLAUCOTHI GOLD MINES
Llanfihangel-ar-arth
Llanllwni
Caio
Bancyffordd
Rhydcymerau
Crugybar
Llidiad Nenog
New Inn
Pencader
Llansawel
Gwyddgrug
Edwinsford
Dolgran
Gwernogle
Abergorlech
Afon Cothi
MYNYDD RHOS-WEN
Brechfa Forest
TALLEY ABBEY
CYNROS
Talley
Nant-y-ffin
Pen-y-garn
Cwm-byr
Waunclunda
Alltwalis
Llansadwrn
Cwmdu
Halfway
Brechfa
Llanllawddog
Soar
Ashfield
Horeb
Hermon
Pontarsais
Llanfynydd
Pant-glas
Capel Isaac
Salem
Manordeilo
Cwmifor
Afon Duad
Rhydargaeau
GWILI RAILWAY
Pant-teg
Felingwm uchaf
Pantgwyn
Rhosmaen
Pen-y-banc
VALE OF TYWI
DYFFRYN TYWI
Bethlehem
Bronwydd Arms
Felingwm isaf
Peniel
Llanfihangel-uwch-Gwili
Capel Gwyn
Pentrefelin
Broad Oak
Court Henry
DINEFWR PARK
Pontbren Araeth
Ffynnon ddrain
White Mill
Pont-ar-gothi
Llangathen
Cilsan
ABERGLASNEY
Llandeilo
Tanerdy
Nantgaredig
Abergwili
Felindre
Llanegwad
Dryslwyn
Ffairfach
CARMARTHEN
Llangunnor
Capel Dewi
Llanarthne
Afon Tywi
GELLI AUR
Golden Grove
Trapp
CARREG CENNEN CASTLE
Pensarn
Johnstown
Nantycaws
THE NATIONAL BOTANIC GARDEN OF WALES
Penrhiwgoch
Temple Bar
Milo
Llandyfan
Cwmffrwd
Llanddarog
Maesybont
Carmel
CARMEL
Croesyceiliog
Cwmisfael
Porthyrhyd
LLYN LLECH OWAIN
Pentre-Gwenlais
Llandybie
Dre-fach
Idole
Bancycapel
Foel-gastell
Gwendraeth Fach
Llangendeirne
Cefneithin
Gorslas
Caér-bryn
Twynmynydd
Glanaman
Crwbin
Drefach
Cwm-y-glo
Pen-y-groes
Tir-y-dail
Pontantwn
Morfa
Saron
Pontamman
Garnant
Bancffosfelen
Cwm-mawr
Cross Hands
Penybanc
Ammanford
Kidwelly
Pontyberem
Tumble
Betws (Rhydaman)
Meinciau
Pentre
Cwmgwili
Capel Hendre
Tycroes
Pantyffynnon
Cae-Gurwen
Pont-Henri
Four Roads
Greynor
Garnswllt
KIDWELLY INDUSTRIAL MUSEUM
Pontyates
Llannon
Mynyddygarreg
Mynydd y Gwair
Cynheidre
Sylen
Llwyn-têg
PONT ABRAHAM SERVICES
Kidwelly (Cydweli)
Llanedi
GRAIG FAWR
Carway
FFOS LAS
Sardis
Pentrebach
Loughor (Llwchwr)
Five Roads
Horeb
Lliedi Resrs.
Trimsaran
Fforest
Pontarddulais
Hendy
Cwm-Dulais
Rhyd-y-gwin
Craig-cefn-parc
Ponthenry
Waun y clyn
0 1 2 3 miles
0 1 2 3 4 5 km

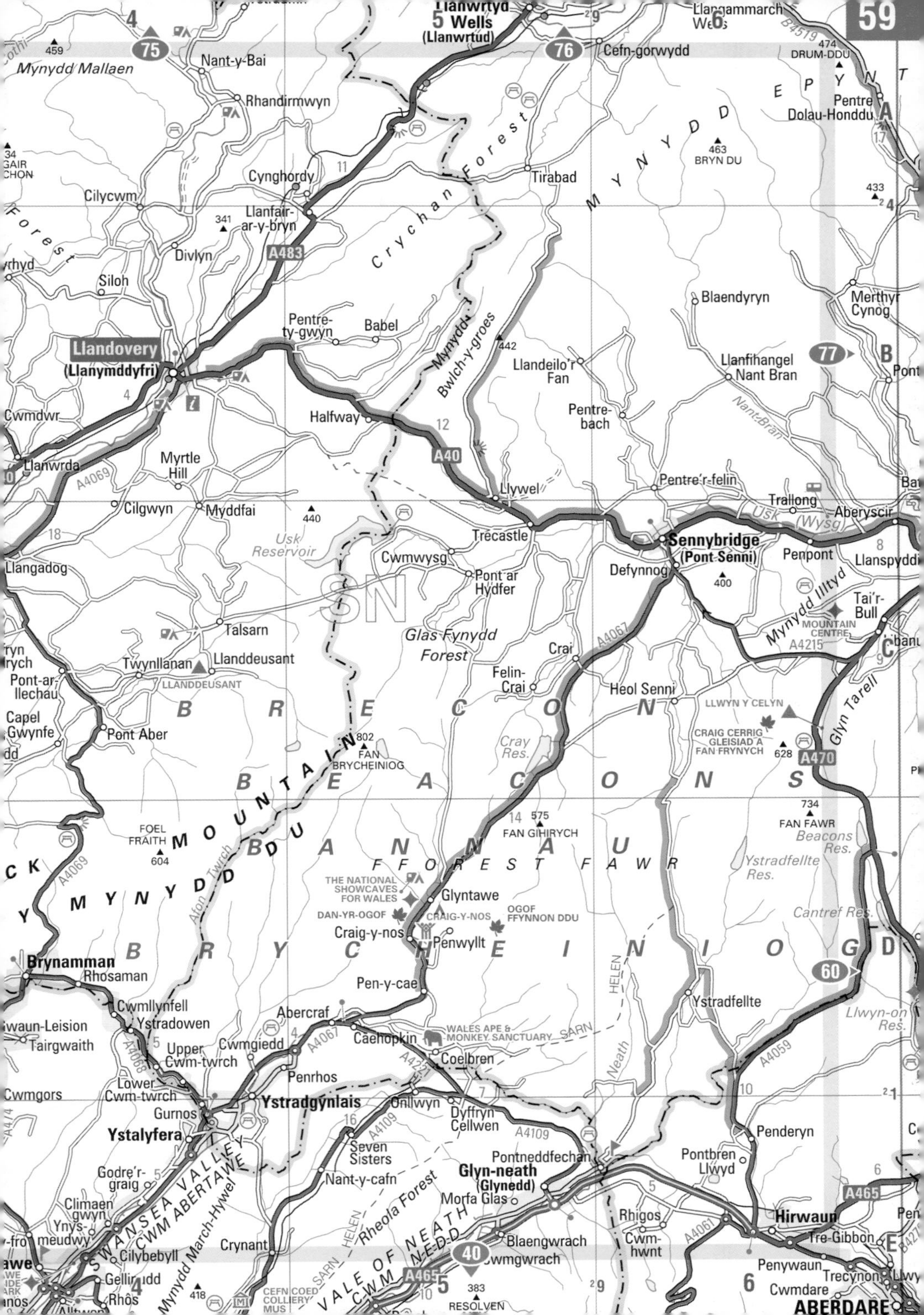
Llanwrtyd Wells (Llanwrtud)
Llangammarch Wells
Cefn-gorwydd
Mynydd Mallaen
Nant-y-Bai
Rhandirmwyn
DRUM-DDU
MYNYDD EPYNT
Pentre
Dolau-Honddu
BRYN DU
Crychan Forest
Cynghordy
Tirabad
Cilycwm
Llanfair-ar-y-bryn
Divlyn
Siloh
Pentre-ty-gwyn
Babel
Blaendyryn
Merthyr Cynog
Llandovery (Llanymddyfri)
Mynydd Bwlch-y-groes
Llandeilo'r Fan
Llanfihangel Nant Bran
Cwmdwr
Halfway
Pentre-bach
Llanwrda
Myrtle Hill
Pentre'r-felin
Trallong
Llywel
Cilgwyn
Myddfai
Aberyscir
Usk Reservoir
Trecastle
Sennybridge (Pont Senni)
Penpont
Llanspyddid
Llangadog
Cwmwysg
Defynnog
Pont ar Hydfer
Mynydd Illtyd
Tai'r-Bull
MOUNTAIN CENTRE
Talsarn
Glas Fynydd Forest
Crai
Twynllanan
Llanddeusant
LLANDDEUSANT
Pont-ar-llechau
Felin-Crai
Heol Senni
LLWYN Y CELYN
Glyn Tarell
Capel Gwynfe
Pont Aber
BRECON BEACONS
FAN BRYCHEINIOG
CRAIG CERRIG GLEISIAD A FAN FRYNYCH
Cray Res.
BLACK MOUNTAIN
FOEL FRAITH
FAN GIHIRYCH
FAN FAWR
Beacons Res.
BANNAU BRYCHEINIOG
FFOREST FAWR
Ystradfellte Res.
THE NATIONAL SHOWCAVES FOR WALES
Glyntawe
DAN-YR-OGOF
CRAIG-Y-NOS
OGOF FFYNNON DDU
Cantref Res.
Afon Twrch
Y MYNYDD DU
Craig-y-nos
Penwyllt
Brynamman
Rhosaman
Pen-y-cae
Ystradfellte
Llwyn-on Res.
Cwmllynfell
Gwaun-Leision
Ystradowen
Abercraf
Tairgwaith
Upper Cwm-twrch
Cwmgiedd
Caehopkin
WALES APE & MONKEY SANCTUARY
Coelbren
SARN HELEN
Penrhos
Lower Cwm-twrch
Cwmgors
Ystradgynlais
Onllwyn
Dyffryn Cellwen
Neath
Gurnos
Ystalyfera
Penderyn
Seven Sisters
Pontneddfechan
Pontbren Llwyd
SWANSEA VALLEY CWM ABERTAWE
Godre'r-graig
Nant-y-cafn
Glyn-neath (Glynedd)
Climaen gwyn
Morfa Glas
Rheola Forest
Hirwaun
Rhigos
Ynys-meudwy
Cwm-hwnt
Tre-Gibbon
Crynant
Blaengwrach
Cilybebyll
VALE OF NEATH CWM NEDD
Cwmgwrach
Penywaun
Mynydd March-Hywel
Trecynon
Gellinudd
CEFN COED COLLIERY MUS
RESOLVEN
Cwmdare
Rhos
ABERDARE
A483
A40
A4069
A4067
A4215
A470
A4068
A4221
A4109
A4059
A4061
A465
B4519
75
76
77
60
40

60
Fach
Llandew
Battle
Trallong
Aberyscir
BRECON GAER ROMAN FORT
CATHEDRAL
Brecon
(Aberhonddu)
SOUTH WALES BORDERERS
Usk (Wysg)
A40
Penpont
Llanspyddid
Llanfaes
Llanywern
BRECON
Llechfaen
Tredomen
Llandefaelog-tre'r-graig
Llanfihangel Tal-y-llyn
Pengenffordd
Mynydd Troed
Llangors
Talyllyn
Llanhamlach
Llangorse Lake
Llangasty Talyllyn
Cathedine
A479
Cwmrhos
Cwmdu
BRECKNOCK MUSEUM AND ART GALLERY
Mynydd Illtyd
Tai'r-Bull
MOUNTAIN CENTRE
Libanus
A4215
Llanfrynach
Pencelli
Scethrog
Llansantffraed
Cross Oak
B4558
Talybont-on-Usk
Bwlch
Gaer
TRETOWER CASTLE & COURT
Tretower
701 PEN CERIG-CALCH
Glyn Tarell
B R E C O N
886 PEN Y FAN
769
Aber Village
B E A C O N S
A470
FAN FAWR
BRECON BEACONS
Neuadd Reservoirs
Talybont Res.
550
Coed-yr-ynys
Llangynidr
Crickhowell
Beacons Res.
Ystradfellte Res.
A N N A U
Abercynafon
Ffawyddog
Llangattock
516 GARN CAWS
Mynydd Llangynidr
CRAIG Y CILAU
LLANGATTOCK
Mynydd Llangattock
B4560
Cantref Res.
Nant-ddu
B B R Y C H E I N I O G
Llanelly
Clydach
GARWNANT VISITOR CENTRE
Pontsticill Reservoir
Trefil
Rassau
Garnlydan
Blackrock
Llwyn-on Res.
BRECON MOUNTAIN RAILWAY
BRYN BACH
A465
A4047
Brynmawr
Llanelly Hill
A4059
Pontsticill
Tafarnau-bach
Dukestown
Beaufort
Nantyglo
460
Vaynor
Princetown
Sirhowy
EBBW VALE (GLYN EBWY)
Coalbrookvale
PONTYPOOL & BLAENAVON RLY
BIG PIT MINING MUSEUM
Penderyn
Cefn-coed-y-cymmer
Llechryd
Tredegar
B4256
Briery Hill
B4486
550
Blaina
Dowlais
Georgetown
Rhymney (Rhymni)
502
Waunlwyd
550 COITY MOUNTAIN
CASTLE MUS. & ART GALL.
A4060
59
Gellideg
Pen-yr-Heolgerrig
Pontlottyn
Abertysswg
A4048
FESTIVAL PARK
East Bank
Cwmtillery
Hirwaun
Tre-Gibbon
B4276
Merthyr Tydfil (Merthyr Tudful)
YNYSFACH ENGINE HOUSE HERITAGE CEN.
Fochriw
A469
New Tredegar (Tredegar Newydd)
Sirhowy
Cwm
A467
Abertillery (Abertyleri)
Penywaun
Trecynon
Llwydcoed
Pentrebach
41
PARC CWM DARRAN
Man-moel
Cwmdare
ABERDARE (ABERDÂR)
Aber-nant
491
Abercanaid
Troedyrhiw
Tirphil
Hollybush
A4046
Aberbeeg
St Illtyd
DARE VALLEY
Cwmbach
A4054
Deri
Bedlinog
Cwmfelin
P&R
Markham
PEN-Y-FAN POND
Brynithel
Llanhilleth (Llanhiledd)
Aberaman
Aberfan
ABERBARGOED GRASSLANDS
Trinant
Cwmaman
MOUNTAIN ASH (ABERPENNAR)
Merthyr Vale
B4255
Bargoed (Bargod)
Argoed
Swffryd
A4059
A470
TAF BARGOED
Gilfach
Pengam
Oakdale
Crumlin (Crymlyn)
A4061
Maerdy
Treorchy (Treorci)
Ferndale
Penrhiwceiber
Treharris
Trelewis
B4254
Blackwood (Coed Duon)
Newbridge
A4233
St Gwynno Forest
B4275
Gelligaer
LLANCAIACH FAWR MANOR
A4049
Pontllanfraith
41
Pentre
RHONDDA
Ynysboeth
Nelson
A472
Ebbw Vale
Llanfach
Ton-Pentre
Ystrad
Tylorstown
Abercynon
Hengoed
Abercarn
Gelli
331
Pont-y-gwaith
Wattstown
Maesycwmmer
Wyllie
Cwmcarn
535 GRAIG Y GEIFRI
Llwynypia
327
Ynysybwl
B4273
Ystrad-mynach
Rhymney Valley
Ynysddu
Pontywaun
Clydach Vale
Trealaw
Ynyshir
CLYDACH VALE
Tonypandy
Porth
RHONDDA HERITAGE PARK
Glyncoch
Cilfynydd
Sirhowy Valley
Cwmfelinfach
B4251
385
Crosskeys
Penygraig
B4278
A4058
Trehafod
A4119
Trebanog
PONTYPRIDD
325
Abertridwr
345
Llanbradach
SIRHOWY VALLEY
Senghenydd
B4263
Glyntaff
Bedwas
A468
Machen
Lower Machen
A4233
Treforest
Tonyrefail
Pen-y-coedcae
Rhydyfelin
Penyrheol
Hendreforgan
B4600
0 1 2 3 miles
0 1 2 3 4 5 km

Llanveynoe
Lower Maes-coed
Bacton
Wormbridge
ABBEY DORE COURT
St Devereux
Kilpeck
Much Dewchurch
Thorn
Little Birch
Much Birch
Abbey Dore
Howton
Wormelow Tump
KILPECK CASTLE (REMS) & CHURCH
A465
A49
A466
B4348
Hoarwithy
Llandinabo
Red Rail
Longtown
Llanthony
PRIORY
Clodock
Ewyas Harold
Pontrilas
Orcop Hill
Llanwarne
Harewood End
OFFA'S DYKE PATH
LLWYBR CLAWDD OFFA
HATTERRALL HILL
531
Rowlestone
Monmouth Cap
Bagwy Llydiart
Pencoyd
Orcop
Kentchurch
Garway Hill
Michaelchurch
Walterstone
Llangua
GROSMONT CASTLE
366
St Owens Cross
Oldcastle
Grosmont
White Rocks
St Weonards
Tretire
B4347
Cwmyoy
Hoaldalbert
A4137
550
Tre-wyn
Pandy
Monnow (Mynwy)
Garway
Three Ashes
Stanton
COED-Y-CERRIG
Broad Oak
B4521
Llangarron
Llanfihangel-Crucorney
Llangattock Lingoed
SKENFRITH CASTLE
Skenfrith
Llancloudy
Cross Ash
Norton
Bont
Marstow
Bettws
LLANFIHANGEL COURT
Upper Green
Crossway
Llanrothal
Llangrove
596
486
Wayne Green
St Maughans
Welsh Newton
WYE VALLEY BUTTERFLY ZOO
Newcastle
Whitchurch
SYMONDS YAT SERVICES
Llantilio Pertholey
Llanvetherine
Llanfaenor
Maypole
Ganarew
Llwyn-du
Mardy
WHITE CASTLE
Llangattock-Vibon-Avel
Buckholt
Symonds Yat
Bryn-y-gwenin
Llantilio Crossenny
HEN GWRT
Onen
Rockfield
LADY PARK WOOD
Abergavenny
(Y Fenni)
B4233
Llanvapley
Llanvihangel-Ystern-Llewern
Dixton
FIDDLER'S ELBOW
Llanfoist
Llanddewi Rhydderch
Wernyrheolydd
Monmouth
(Trefynwy)
NELSON MUS
Wyesham
B4269
B4598
559
BLORENGE
Coed Morgan
Penrhôs
Over Monnow
Llanellen
Llangattock nigh Usk
Llanarth
Pen-yr-heol
Wonastow
Penallt
A40
Bryngwyn
Dingestow
Tregare
Mitcheltroy Common
Mitchel Troy
Redbrook
Blaenavon
Llanover
Llanvihangel Gobion
RAGLAN
HIGHBURY WOOD
Newland
Rhyd-y-meirch
Llanfair Kilgheddin
Raglan
Pen-y-clawdd
Cwmcarvan
Caer Llan
Pen-twyn
OFFA'S DYKE PATH
Hoop
Pen-groes-oped
Cwmavon
Nant-y-derry
Bettws Newydd
Twyn-y-Sheriff
Kingcoed
Llangovan
Whitebrook
448
Goetre
199
Trellech
A4043
Kemeys Commander
Gwehelog
Garndiffaith
Penperlleni
Llandogo
A466
Llandenny
Abersychan
A4042
Little Mill
A472
A449
Llanishen
Parkhouse
Llancayo
Llansoy
Catbrook
Trevethin
PONTYPOOL MUSEUM
Monkswood
Gwernesney
Trelleck Grange
Glascoed
OLD STA.
Tintern Parva
Brockweir
Usk
(Brynbuga)
RURAL LIFE
Llangwm
New Inn
WYE VALLEY CENTRE
TINTERN ABBEY
Llandegfedd Res.
Llanbadoc
Chapel Hill
PONTYPOOL
(PONT-Y-PŴL)
New Inn
Wolvesnewton
Devauden
VEDDW HO
Griffithstown
Coed-y-paen
Llanllowell
Kilgwrrwg Common
284
Chepstow Pk. Wood
Upper Cwmbran
Lowlands
185
Llantrisant
Newchurch
Itton Common
Wye (Gwy)
St Arvans
Croesyceiliog
Llangybi
Gaerllwyd
Pontnewydd
Cwmbran
(Cwmbrân)
Llandegveth
B4235
B4293
Woodcroft
Tredunnock
Pen-y-cae-mawr
Earlswood
CHEPSTOW
LLANYRAFON MANOR HERITAGE CENTRE
Mynydd-bach
309
Oakfield
Llanfrechfa
Newbridge-on-Usk
COOMBE VALLEY WOODS
Llantarnam
B4236
Ponthir
Llanhennock
Llanvair Discoed
Shirenewton
Mounton
Croes-y-mwyalch
Parc-Seymour
Llanvaches
Pwllmeyric
Chepstow
(Cas-gwent)
LEGIONARY MUS.
Caerleon
(Caerllion)
RUNSTON CHAPEL
A48
Cat's Ash
Malpas
CAERLEON BATHS
Llanbeder
Penhow
PENHOW WOODLANDS
Caerwent
Grick
M48
Mathern
Bettws
FOURTEEN LOCKS
Christchurch
Langstone
M4
Magor
St Bride's Netherwent
Highmoor Hill
CALDICOT CASTLE
Maindee
MAGOR SERVICES
Llanwern
Wilcrick
SO
ST

Little Dewchurch
Brockhampton
Falcon
Carey
Ballingham
Court Gardens
Crossway
Lyne Down
Dymock
St Mary's Church
Ryton
Redmarley D'Abitot
Playley Green
A417
Staunton
Fawley Chapel
Penalt
How Caple
Hoarwithy
Llandinabo
Red Rail
King's Caple
Foy
Hole-in-the-Wall
A449
Fishpool
Kempley
M50
B4215
Poolhill
Corse
Brand Green
Leadon
Harewood End
Sellack
Upper Grove Common
Wye
Brampton Abbotts
Phocle Green
Crow Hill
Upton Bishop
B4224
Gorsley
Upleadon
Pencoyd
Ross Spur Services
Rudhall
Linton
B4221
Kilcot
Newent
Michaelchurch
A49
St Owens Cross
Bridstow
Peterstow
Ross-on-Wye
Bromsash
Aston Ingham
The Int Centre for Birds of Prey
Malswick
St Weonards
Tretire
Candlemakers
A4137
Tudorville
A40
Weston under Penyard
Aston Crews
B4222
Clifford's Mesne
Kent's Green
B4215
Highleadon
Three Ashes
Glewstone
Hom Green
B4234
Coughton
203
Penyard
Pontshill
Lea
Tibberton
Taynton
Rudford
Llangarron
Llancloudy
Pencraig
Walford
Glasshouse Hill
Highnam Green
A466
Marstow
Goodrich
Hope Mansell
9
Huntley
Bulley
Highnam
Llangrove
Kerne Bridge
Mitcheldean
A4136
Longhope
Birdwood
A40
Churcham
Wye Valley Butterfly Zoo
Whitchurch
Welsh Bicknor
Ruardean
Drybrook
Oakle Street
Symonds Yat Services
Ganarew
Greater Doward
Lower Lydbrook
Ruardean Woodside
Blaisdon
Elmore Back
Symonds Yat
Upper Lydbrook
Nailbridge
Northwood Green
A48
Lady Park Wood
English Bicknor
A4151
Flaxley
Westbury-on-Severn
Farleys End
Fiddler's Elbow
Brierley
B4227
Cinderford
Elton
Dixton
Christchurch
Edge End
Bilson Green
Littledean
Westbury Court
A4136
Forest of Dean
200
Berry Hill
Five Acres
Littledean Hall
Boxbush
Longney
Wyesham
Staunton
Mile End
Colliery
B4226
Beechenhurst Lodge
Ruspidge
Newnham
Hardwick
Nelson Mus
B4228
Coleford
Broadwell
St Augustines Farm
Rodley
Penallt
Dean Heritage Centre
Arlingham
Mitchel Troy
Redbrook
G W R Museum
Iron Mines
Coalway
Upper Soudley
62
Upper Framilode
Fretherne
Saul
Moreton Valence
Highbury Wood
Newland
Milkwall
B4234
Offa's Dyke Path
Pen-twyn
Caves
Ellwood
Parkend
Awre
Whitminster
Hoop
Clearwell
Yorkley
The Noose
Frampton on Severn
B4071
B4293
Stowe Green
Trow Green
Whitecroft
Pillowell
Viney Hill
Blakeney
River Severn
Whitebrook
The Eaves
M5
Trellech
Offa's Dyke
Bream
Dean Forest Railway & Museum
WWT Slimbridge Wetland Centre
A38
Eastington
St Briavels
Llandogo
St Briavels
B4231
Purton
Purton
Cambridge
Leonard Stanley
Coldharbour
Lydney
Newerne
Slimbridge
Moorend
Catbrook
247
Hewelsfield
Sharpness
Halmore
Gossington
Newtown
Coaley
Tintern Parva
Old Sta.
Brockweir
B4228
Aylburton
Wanswell
Breadstone
A4135
Lower Cam
Tintern Abbey
Netherend
Alvington
B4066
The Quarry
Cam
Uley Tumulus
Chapel Hill
Woolaston
Brookend
Berkeley
Stinchcombe
Berkeley Castle
Tidenham Chase
A48
Ham
Dr Jenner's House
Dursley
Wibdon
Stroat
B4066
Woodmancote
Gwy
Boughspring
Bevington
A4135
St Arvans
Nibley Green
Woodcroft
Tidenham
Woodford Stone
Shepperdine Hill
Michaelwood Services
North Nibley
B4058
Chepstow
Tutshill
B4293
B4235
Sedbury
Rockhampton
Falfield
Tortworth
Mounton
Chepstow (Cas-gwent)
Oldbury-on-Severn
Charfield
B4058
Wotton-under-Edge
Pwllmeyric
B4059
B4060
Whitfield
Kingswood
Abbey Gatehouse
Beachley
M48
B4061
Morton
A38
Mathern
Severn Road Bridge Pont Hafren
Littleton-on-Severn
Milbury Heath
Cromhall
Churchend
Alderley
Severn View Services
Thornbury
Cromhall Common
Hillesley
B4461
Elberton
Alveston
B4058
0 1 2 3 miles
0 1 2 3 4 5 km

Cheltenham
Charlton Kings
Gloucester
Hucclecote
Churchdown
Parton
Bishop's Cleeve
Winchcombe
Stroud
Stonehouse
Nailsworth
Tetbury
Cirencester
Chalford
South Cerney
Cricklade
COTSWOLDS
Walton Cardiff
Fiddington
Oxenton
Dixton
Gretton
Greet
Didbrook
Hailes
Chaceley
Deerhurst
Tredington
Gotherington
Stoke Orchard
Tirley
Apperley
Hasfield
Coombe Hill
Hardwicke
Elmstone Hardwicke
Woodmancote
Cleeve Hill
Ashleworth
Leigh
Swindon
Southam
Norton
Boddington
Uckington
Staverton
Staverton Bridge
Down Hatherley
Golden Valley
Arle
Prestbury
Battledown
Sandhurst
Twigworth
Sandfields
Maisemore
Longford
Longlevens
Lansdown
Up Hatherley
Badgeworth
Leckhampton
Dowdeswell
Andoversford
Shipton
Shipton Solers
Shurdington
Ullenwood
Barnwood
Hempsted
Bentham
Coberley
Cowley
Withington
Compton Abdale
Hazleton
Hampnett
Matson
Brockworth
Great Witcombe
Tuffley
Upton St Leonard's
Whaddon
Cranham
Birdlip
Colesbourne
Cassey Compton
Yanworth
Brimpsfield
Elkstone
Chedworth
Brookthorpe
Sheepscombe
Whiteway
Syde
Fossebridge
Coln St Dennis
Haresfield
Harescombe
Painswick
The Camp
Winstone
Rendcomb
Foss Cross
Woodmancote
Calmsden
Miserden
Pitchcombe
Slad
Sudgrove
Duntisbourne Abbots
Duntisbourne Leer
North Cerney
Whiteshill
Randwick
Bisley
Edgeworth
Duntisbourne Rouse
Bagendon
Arlington
Ebley
Eastcombe
Bournes Green
Daglingworth
Baunton
Barnsley
King's Stanley
Rodborough
Oakley Wood
Stratton
Thrupp
Brownshill
Oakridge
Sapperton
Ampney Crucis
Ampney St Mary
Woodchester
Brimscombe
Frampton Mansell
Littleworth
Amberley
Hyde
Coates
Chesterton
Preston
Ampney St Peter
Windsoredge
Minchinhampton
Box
Tarlton
Siddington
Harnhill
Driffield
Whiteway
Cherington
Source of the Thames
Avening
Rodmarton
Ewen
Horsley
Kemble
Shorncote
Kingscote
Culkerton
Poole Keynes
Cerney Wick
Tetbury Upton
Ashley
Somerford Keynes
Ashton Keynes
Beverston
Chedglow
Chelworth
Crudwell
Oaksey
Eastcourt
Long Newnton
Leigh
Chelworth Green
Leighterton
Doughton
Hankerton
Upper Minety
Minety
Purton Stoke
Shipton Moyne
Brokenborough
Perry Green
Westonbirt
Filands
Charlton
Easton Grey
Garsdon
Purton
Oldbury on the Hill
Alstone
Ford
Farmcote
Charlton Abbots
Guiting Power
Hawling
Brockhampton
Sevenhampton
Whittington
Syreford
Cutsdean

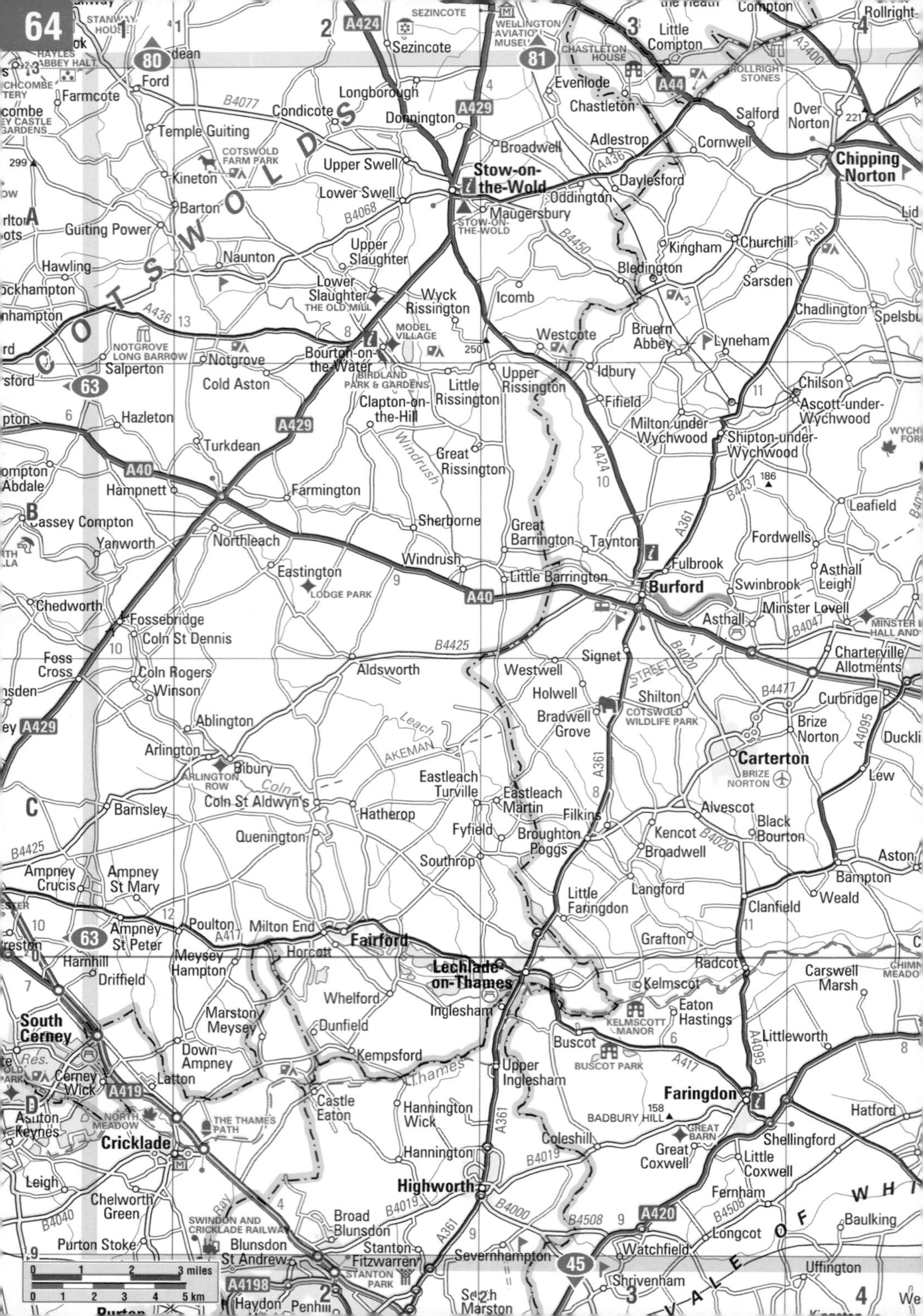

SEZINCOTE
A424
Sezincote
WELLINGTON AVIATION MUSEUM
Little Compton
Compton
Rollright
80
81
Ford
Farmcote
CHASTLETON HOUSE
ROLLRIGHT STONES
A3400
B4077
Longborough
Condicote
Donnington
A429
Evenlode
Chastleton
A44
Salford
Over Norton
Temple Guiting
COTSWOLD FARM PARK
Broadwell
Adlestrop
Cornwell
Chipping Norton
Kineton
Upper Swell
Stow-on-the-Wold
Lower Swell
Daylesford
Oddington
A436
Barton
Maugersbury
STOW-ON-THE-WOLD
Guiting Power
B4068
B4450
Kingham
Churchill
A361
COTSWOLDS
Naunton
Upper Slaughter
Hawling
Bledington
Sarsden
Lower Slaughter
THE OLD MILL
Wyck Rissington
Icomb
Chadlington
Spelsbury
MODEL VILLAGE
Westcote
Bruern Abbey
Lyneham
NOTGROVE LONG BARROW
Notgrove
Salperton
Bourton-on-the-Water
BIRDLAND PARK & GARDENS
Cold Aston
63
Little Rissington
Upper Rissington
Idbury
Fifield
Chilson
Ascott-under-Wychwood
Clapton-on-the-Hill
Hazleton
A429
Milton under Wychwood
Shipton-under-Wychwood
Turkdean
Windrush
Great Rissington
A424
A40
Hampnett
Farmington
B4437
Leafield
Cassey Compton
Sherborne
Great Barrington
Taynton
Fordwells
Yanworth
Northleach
Windrush
Fulbrook
Eastington
LODGE PARK
Little Barrington
Burford
Asthall Leigh
Swinbrook
Chedworth
A40
Minster Lovell
Fossebridge
Asthall
MINSTER HALL AND
Coln St Dennis
B4425
B4047
B4020
Foss Cross
Aldsworth
Signet
Charterville Allotments
Coln Rogers
Westwell
STREET
Winson
Holwell
Shilton
B4477
Curbridge
Ablington
COTSWOLD WILDLIFE PARK
Bradwell Grove
Brize Norton
A429
Leach
A4095
Arlington
AKEMAN
Bibury
ARLINGTON ROW
Carterton
BRIZE NORTON
Coln
Eastleach Turville
Eastleach Martin
Lew
Barnsley
Coln St Aldwyn's
Hatherop
Filkins
Alvescot
Quenington
Fyfield
Broughton Poggs
Kencot
Black Bourton
B4425
Southrop
Broadwell
B4020
Aston
Ampney Crucis
Ampney St Mary
Bampton
Little Faringdon
Langford
Weald
Clanfield
Poulton
Milton End
Ampney St Peter
63
A417
Fairford
Grafton
Horcott
Harnhill
Meysey Hampton
Lechlade-on-Thames
Radcot
Carswell Marsh
Driffield
Kelmscot
Whelford
Inglesham
Eaton Hastings
South Cerney
Marston Meysey
KELMSCOTT MANOR
Dunfield
Buscot
Littleworth
A4095
Down Ampney
Kempsford
BUSCOT PARK
Upper Inglesham
A417
Cerney Wick
Latton
Thames
A419
Castle Eaton
Faringdon
Hatford
Ashton Keynes
NORTH MEADOW
THE THAMES PATH
Hannington Wick
BADBURY HILL
GREAT BARN
Shellingford
A361
Coleshill
Great Coxwell
Cricklade
Hannington
B4019
Little Coxwell
Leigh
Highworth
Fernham
Chelworth Green
B4000
WHI
B4040
Ray
SWINDON AND CRICKLADE RAILWAY
B4019
Broad Blunsdon
B4508
A420
B4508
Baulking
Longcot
Purton Stoke
Blunsdon St Andrew
Stanton Fitzwarren
STANTON PARK
Severnhampton
45
Watchfield
Uffington
Shrivenham
VALE OF
A4198
Haydon
Penhill
South Marston

0 1 2 3 miles
0 1 2 3 4 5 km

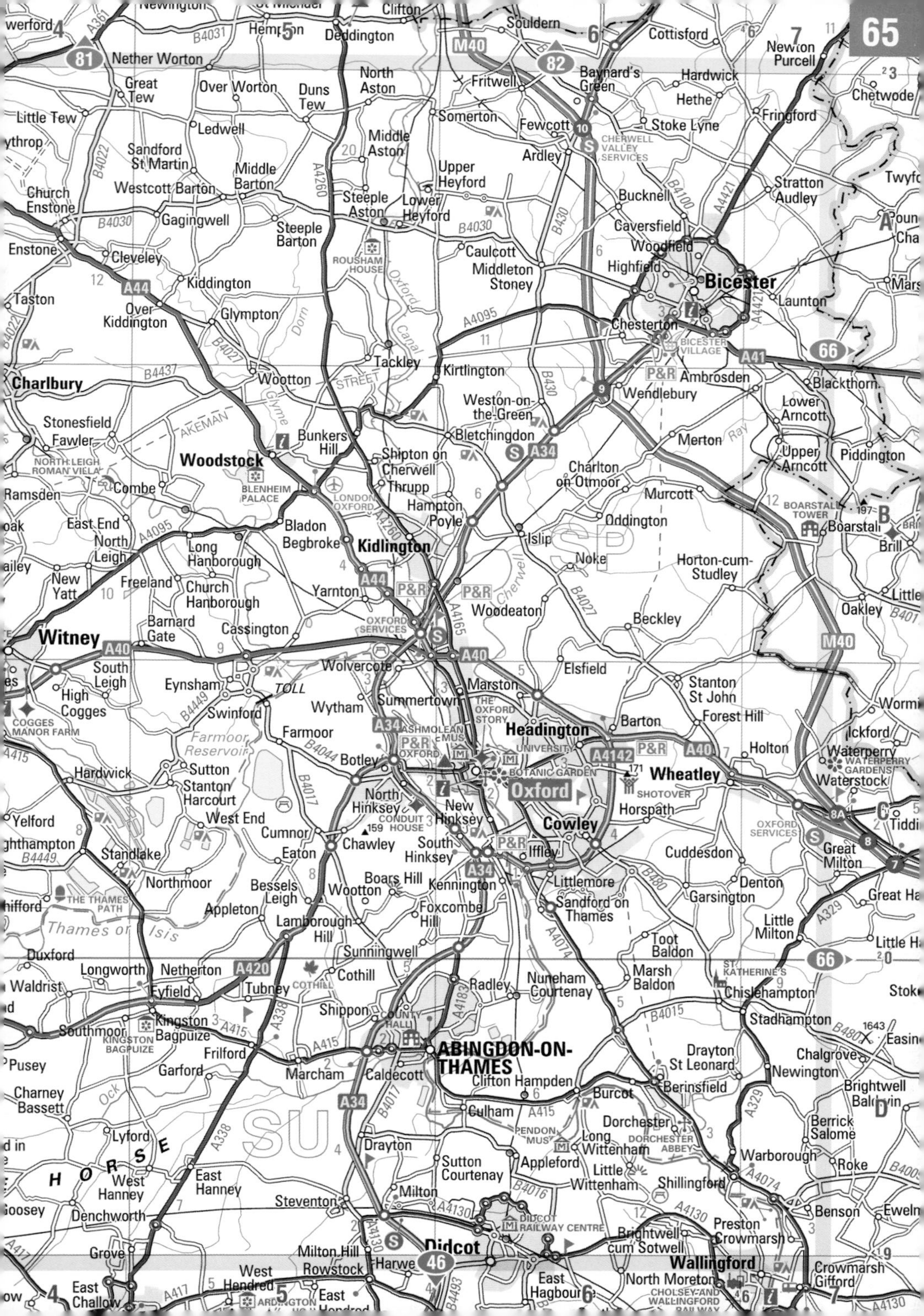
Nether Worton
Hempton
Deddington
Clifton
Souldern
Cottisford
Newton Purcell
Great Tew
Over Worton
North Aston
Duns Tew
Fritwell
Baynard's Green
Hardwick
Hethe
Chetwode
Little Tew
Ledwell
Somerton
Fewcott
Stoke Lyne
Fringford
Sandford St Martin
Middle Aston
Ardley
CHERWELL VALLEY SERVICES
Church Enstone
Westcott Barton
Middle Barton
Upper Heyford
Steeple Aston
Lower Heyford
Bucknell
Stratton Audley
Gagingwell
Steeple Barton
Caversfield
Enstone
Cleveley
ROUSHAM HOUSE
Caulcott
Middleton Stoney
Woodfield
Highfield
Bicester
Launton
Kiddington
Taston
Over Kiddington
Glympton
Chesterton
BICESTER VILLAGE
Tackley
Kirtlington
Charlbury
Wootton
Ambrosden
Blackthorn
Wendlebury
Stonesfield
Fawler
Weston-on-the-Green
Lower Arncott
AKEMAN
STREET
Bunkers Hill
Bletchingdon
Merton
Upper Arncott
Piddington
NORTH LEIGH ROMAN VILLA
Woodstock
Shipton on Cherwell
Charlton on Otmoor
Combe
BLENHEIM PALACE
LONDON OXFORD
Thrupp
Murcott
Ramsden
Hampton Poyle
BOARSTALL TOWER
Boarstall
East End
North Leigh
Bladon
Begbroke
Kidlington
Oddington
Islip
Brill
Long Hanborough
Noke
Horton-cum-Studley
New Yatt
Freeland
Church Hanborough
Yarnton
Woodeaton
Oakley
Barnard Gate
Cassington
OXFORD SERVICES
Beckley
Witney
South Leigh
Eynsham
Wolvercote
Marston
Elsfield
TOLL
High Cogges
COGGES MANOR FARM
Swinford
Wytham
Summertown
THE OXFORD STORY
Headington
Stanton St John
Forest Hill
Barton
Farmoor Reservoir
Farmoor
ASHMOLEAN MUS
Botley
UNIVERSITY
Holton
Ickford
Waterperry
WATERPERRY GARDENS
Hardwick
Sutton
Stanton Harcourt
BOTANIC GARDEN
Oxford
Wheatley
SHOTOVER
Waterstock
Yelford
West End
North Hinksey
CONDUIT HOUSE
New Hinksey
Horspath
Cowley
Cumnor
Chawley
Standlake
Eaton
South Hinksey
Iffley
Cuddesdon
OXFORD SERVICES
Great Milton
Northmoor
Bessels Leigh
Wootton
Boars Hill
Kennington
Littlemore
Denton
THE THAMES PATH
Appleton
Foxcombe Hill
Sandford on Thames
Garsington
Thames or Isis
Lamborough Hill
Little Milton
Duxford
Sunningwell
Toot Baldon
Longworth
Netherton
Cothill
COTHILL
Nuneham Courtenay
Marsh Baldon
ST KATHERINE'S
Chislehampton
Waldrist
Fyfield
Tubney
Radley
Shippon
COUNTY HALL
Southmoor
Kingston Bagpuize
KINGSTON BAGPUIZE
Stadhampton
Frilford
ABINGDON-ON-THAMES
Drayton St Leonard
Chalgrove
Pusey
Garford
Marcham
Caldecott
Clifton Hampden
Berinsfield
Newington
Charney Bassett
Burcot
Brightwell Baldwin
Culham
Dorchester
Lyford
PENDON MUS
Long Wittenham
DORCHESTER ABBEY
Berrick Salome
HORSE
Drayton
West Hanney
East Hanney
Sutton Courtenay
Appleford
Little Wittenham
Warborough
Roke
Milton
Shillingford
Steventon
Denchworth
DIDCOT RAILWAY CENTRE
Benson
Brightwell cum Sotwell
Preston Crowmarsh
Grove
Milton Hill
Rowstock
Harwell
Didcot
Wallingford
West Hendred
East Hagbourne
North Moreton
Crowmarsh Gifford
East Challow
ARDINGTON
East Hendred
CHOLSEY AND WALLINGFORD
SP
SU
M40
A34
A40
A44
A420
A4142
P&R

Gawcott
Singleborough
Barton Hartshorn
Preston Bissett
82
Padbury
Adstock
Great Horwood
Little Horwood
Newton Longville
83
Purcell
Chetwode
Fringford
Hillesden
Addington
A413
B4033
Drayton Parslow
Stoke Hammond
A4146
Mursley
Winslow
Steeple Claydon
Twyford
Swanbourne
B4032
North End
Stratton Audley
Middle Claydon
Claydon House
East Claydon
Stewkley
South End
Poundon
Charndon
Calvert
Botolph Claydon
Granborough
Hoggeston
Dunton
A
Bicester
Launton
Marsh Gibbon
Edgcott
North Marston
Creslow
Wing
Cublington
Grendon Underwood
Quainton Windmill
187
Oving
Whitchurch
A4421
65
A41
Quainton
Pitchcott
Aston Abbotts
A418
Blackthorn
Buckinghamshire Railway Centre
Hardwick
Wingrave
Lower Arncott
Kingswood
17
Weedon
Rowsham
Ray
Ludgershall
Westcott
Waddesdon
Hulcott
Upper Arncott
Piddington
Wotton Underwood
Waddesdon Manor
Akeman Street
Berryfield
A413
1642
Long Marston
B
Boarstall Tower
Boarstall
197
Brill Windmill
Brill
Dorton
147
Bierton
A4157
Puttenham
Aylesbury
Ashendon
Upper Winchendon
Upper Pollicott
Thame
Stone
A41
Buckland
Nether Winchendon House
Lower Winchendon
A418
Southcourt
Weston Turville
Aston Clinton
Little London
Oakley
B4011
Chilton
Cuddington
Dinton
B4443
M40
Easington
Chearsley
Westlington
Stoke Mandeville
Halton
Bishopstone
A413
Townsend
Ford
B4009
Worminghall
Long Crendon
Haddenham
Kimble Wick
North Lee
Terrick
Nash Lee
Wendover
Ickford
Aston Sandford
A4010
Butler's Cross
Holton
Waterperry
Shabbington
Little Kimble
Waterperry Gardens
Kingsey
Owlswick
Meadle
Ellesborough
Waterstock
A4129
Great Kimble
A418
Thame
Ilmer
Askett
C
8A
Rycote Chapel
Towersey
Longwick
Dunsmore
Oxford Services
Tiddington
A329
Moreton
B4012
B4445
Monks Risborough
Great Milton
8
7
Pitch Green
B4009
Manor House
Little Hampden
Denton
A40
Emmington
Henton
Bledlow
Princes Risborough
Great Haseley
Tetsworth
Sydenham
Saunderton
Great Hampden
Little Milton
A329
Chinnor
Loosley Row
Oakley
Little Haseley
Chinnor & Princes Risborough Railway
Prestwood
65
St Katherine's
Postcombe
Crowell
Lacey Green
Speen
Chislehampton
Stoke Talmage
Adwell
Kingston Blount
246
A4128
Great Kingshill
Stadhampton
South Weston
Aston Rowant
Radnage
Bledlow Ridge
Walters Ash
Upper North Dean
1643
B480
Easington
Lewknor
6
Aston Rowant
Cryers Hill
Chalgrove
The City
Bradenham
Naphill
Newington
B4009
Stokenchurch
A4010
Hughenden Valley
187
Pyrton
5
Brightwell Baldwin
Shirburn
A40
West Wycombe
West Wycombe Caves
Hughenden Manor
D
Berrick Salome
Cuxham
255
Beacon's Bottom
Downley
Watlington
Christmas Common
West Wycombe Park
Tylers
Warborough
Roke
The Ridgeway
Ibstone
High Wycombe
A4074
B4009
Britwell Salome
Northend
M40
Greenfield
Cadmore End
Bolter End
Benson
Ewelme
Turville Heath
Turville
Fingest
Lane End
Booker
Preston Crowmarsh
B480
Cookley Green
Wycombe Air Park
P&R
A40
4
Pishill
188
47
Skirmett
Frieth
B482
A404
Flackwell Heath
Russell's Water
Park Corner
Stonor
Marlow Bottom
Little Marlow
0 1 2 3 miles
0 1 2 3 4 5 km
2
3

Tingrith
Barton-le-Clay
Pirton
Great Brickhill
83
Milton Bryan
Harlington
Sharpenhoe
Hexton
84
HITCHIN
KINGS WOOD
STOCKGROVE PARK
Potsgrove
Battlesden
TODDINGTON SERVICES
SUNDON HILLS
Streatley
BARTON HILLS
Toddington
Heath and Reach
Upper Sundon
Charlton
Tebworth
Lower Sundon
Lilley
Great Offley
Gosmore
Hockliffe
Leighton Buzzard
Chalton
187 GALLEY HILL
Wingfield
Eggington
Sundon Park
Limbury
Tilsworth
LEIGHTON BUZZARD RAILWAY
Stanbridge
Houghton Regis
Stopsley
Cockernhoe Green
King's Walden
Leagrave
WARDOWN PARK MUS
Billington
MEAD OPEN FM
Lower End
Dunstable
Biscot
Hart Hill
Beachwood Green
St Paul's Walden
Eaton Green
Totternhoe
THE GUIDED BUSWAY
Luton
Slapton
Church End
PRIORY CHURCH OF ST PETER
Farley Hill
LONDON LUTON
Whitwell
Eaton Bray
DUNSTABLE DOWNS
STOCKWOOD CRAFT MUS
68
Edlesborough
243
Kensworth
Caddington
Peter's Green
Horton
Kimpton
Whipsnade
Slip End
Ivinghoe Aston
Kensworth Common
East Hyde
Codicote
WHIPSNADE WILD ANIMAL PARK
WOODSIDE FARM AND WILDFOWL PARK
Blackmore End
Ayot St Lawrence
Ivinghoe
Kinsbourne Green
Dagnall
Studham
Markyate
Batford
SHAW'S CORNER
Pitstone Green
249
Pitstone
Jockey End
Flamstead
Marshall's Heath
Ringshall
HARPENDEN
Wheathampstead
Trowley Bottom
Tring Wharf
Little Gaddesden
Hatching Green
ASHRIDGE PARK
New Mill
Redbourn
Aldbury
Great Gaddesden
STANBOROUGH PARK
Tring
Water End
Childwick Green
Sandridge
Nettleden
Wigginton
173
Piccotts End
Jersey Farm
Hastoe
Potten End
Northchurch
Townsend
OLD GORHAMBURY HOUSE
BERKHAMSTED CASTLE
Marshalswick
THE GALLERIA
Gadebridge
St Albans
Fleetville
Berkhamsted
ROMAN THEATRE OF VERULAMIUM
Cholesbury
Bourne End
The Camp
Buckland Common
Boxmoor
St. Stephens
Ashley Green
Hemel Hempstead
Sopwell
Colney Heath
Bellingdon
BOURNE END SERVICES
Chiswell Green
London Colney
Lee Clump
Whelpley Hill
Felden
Chartridge
Lye Green
Bovingdon
Bedmond
Primrosehill
Botley
Bovingdon Green
Kings Langley
LEAVESDEN
DE HAVILLAND AIRCRAFT HERITAGE CEN
South Heath
Leyhill
Bricket Wood
Colney Street
Chesham
Chipperfield
Abbots Langley
Shenleybury
Missenden
Flaunden
Radlett
Hyde Heath
WARNER BROS STUDIO TOUR
Shenley
Chesham Bois
Latimer
Sarratt
Aldenham
Little Missenden
Chenies
CHENIES MANOR HO
Letchmore Heath
Amersham
Watford
BOREHAMWOOD
Little Chalfont
Chorleywood
Croxley Green
ALDENHAM
Penn Street
Coleshill
CHILTERN OPEN AIR MUS
Elstree
RICKMANSWORTH
Oxhey
Bushey
Winchmore Hill
Chalfont St Giles
Bushey Heath
Penn
RICKMANSWORTH AQUADROME
South Oxhey
Knotty Green
MILTON'S COTTAGE
Maple Cross
Stanmore
Seer Green
Eastbury
Forty Green
BEKONSCOT MODEL VILLAGE
Jordans
Chalfont Common
Batchworth Heath
Edgware
BISHOP'S WOOD
Harrow Weald
Beaconsfield
Chalfont St Peter
Northwood
Hatch End
Harefield
48
BAYHURST WOOD
RUISLIP WOODS
Pinner
Wealdstone
Ruislip Common
Kingsbury
Gerrards
Denham Green
HARROW
Greenhill

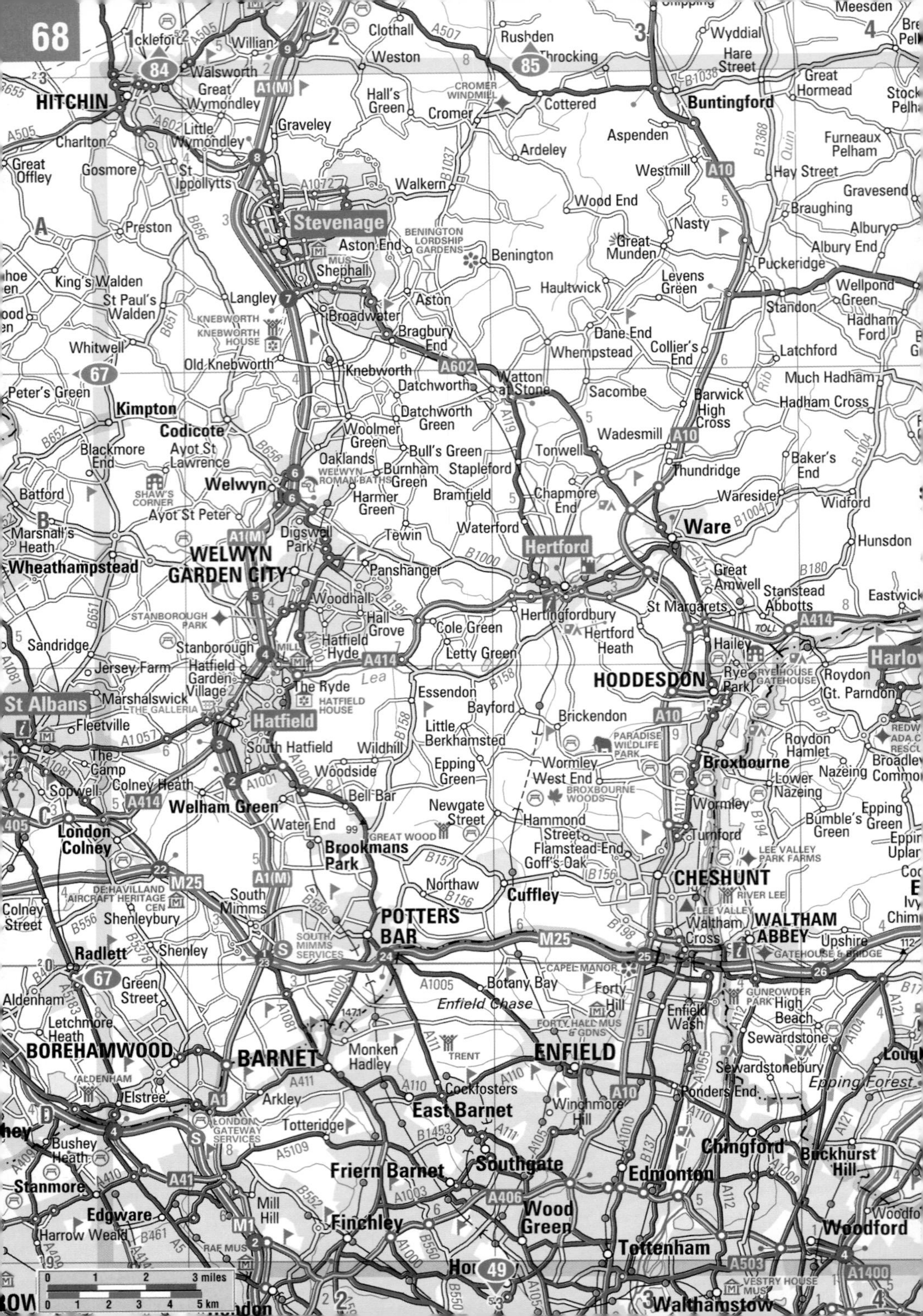

68
HITCHIN
Ickleford
Willian
Walsworth
Great Wymondley
Little Wymondley
Charlton
Great Offley
Gosmore
St Ippollytts
Preston
King's Walden
St Paul's Walden
Langley
Whitwell
Old Knebworth
Peter's Green
Kimpton
Codicote
Blackmore End
Ayot St Lawrence
Welwyn
Batford
Ayot St Peter
Marshall's Heath
Wheathampstead
WELWYN GARDEN CITY
Sandridge
Jersey Farm
Marshalswick
St Albans
Fleetville
The Camp
Sopwell
Colney Heath
London Colney
Colney Street
Radlett
Aldenham
Letchmore Heath
BOREHAMWOOD
Elstree
Bushey Heath
Stanmore
Edgware
Harrow Weald
Clothall
Weston
Graveley
Hall's Green
Cromer
CROMER WINDMILL
Rushden
Throcking
Cottered
Wyddial
Hare Street
Buntingford
Great Hormead
Aspenden
Ardeley
Walkern
Westmill
Wood End
Nasty
Great Munden
Stevenage
Aston End
Shephall
BENINGTON LORDSHIP GARDENS
Benington
Aston
Broadwater
Bragbury End
KNEBWORTH HOUSE
Knebworth
Datchworth
Datchworth Green
Woolmer Green
Oaklands
Bull's Green
Burnham Green
WELWYN ROMAN BATHS
Harmer Green
SHAW'S CORNER
Stapleford
Bramfield
Tewin
Digswell Park
Panshanger
Woodhall
Hall Grove
STANBOROUGH PARK
Stanborough
Hatfield Garden Village
THE GALLERIA
Hatfield Hyde
The Ryde
HATFIELD HOUSE
Hatfield
South Hatfield
Welham Green
Water End
Brookmans Park
Woodside
Bell Bar
DE HAVILLAND AIRCRAFT HERITAGE CEN
South Mimms
SOUTH MIMMS SERVICES
POTTERS BAR
Shenleybury
Shenley
Green Street
BARNET
Monken Hadley
Arkley
Totteridge
LONDON GATEWAY SERVICES
Mill Hill
Friern Barnet
Finchley
RAF MUS
Hendon
East Barnet
Cockfosters
Southgate
Wood Green
Enfield Chase
TRENT
Botany Bay
Watton at Stone
Sacombe
Whempstead
Dane End
Haultwick
Levens Green
Collier's End
Wadesmill
Tonwell
Chapmore End
Waterford
Hertford
Hertingfordbury
Cole Green
Letty Green
Hertford Heath
Essendon
Bayford
Little Berkhamsted
Brickendon
Wildhill
Epping Green
Newgate Street
GREAT WOOD
PARADISE WILDLIFE PARK
Wormley West End
BROXBOURNE WOODS
Hammond Street
Flamstead End
Goff's Oak
Northaw
Cuffley
CAPEL MANOR
Forty Hill
FORTY HALL MUS & GDNS
ENFIELD
Enfield Wash
Winchmore Hill
Edmonton
Tottenham
Ponders End
Meesden
Furneaux Pelham
Hay Street
Gravesend
Braughing
Albury
Albury End
Puckeridge
Wellpond Green
Standon
Hadham Ford
Latchford
Much Hadham
Hadham Cross
Barwick
High Cross
Thundridge
Baker's End
Wareside
Widford
Ware
Hunsdon
Great Amwell
Stanstead Abbotts
Eastwick
St Margarets
Hailey
Rye Park
RYE HOUSE GATEHOUSE
Roydon
Gt. Parndon
HODDESDON
Broxbourne
Roydon Hamlet
Nazeing
Lower Nazeing
Wormley
Turnford
Bumble's Green
LEE VALLEY PARK FARMS
CHESHUNT
RIVER LEE
LEE VALLEY
Waltham Cross
WALTHAM ABBEY
Upshire
GATEHOUSE & BRIDGE
GUNPOWDER PARK
High Beach
Sewardstone
Sewardstonebury
Epping Forest
Chingford
Buckhurst Hill
Woodford
Walthamstow
VESTRY HOUSE MUS
A1(M)
A602
A10
A414
M25
A1
A41
M1
A406
A503
A1400
84
85
67
49
0 1 2 3 miles
0 1 2 3 4 5 km

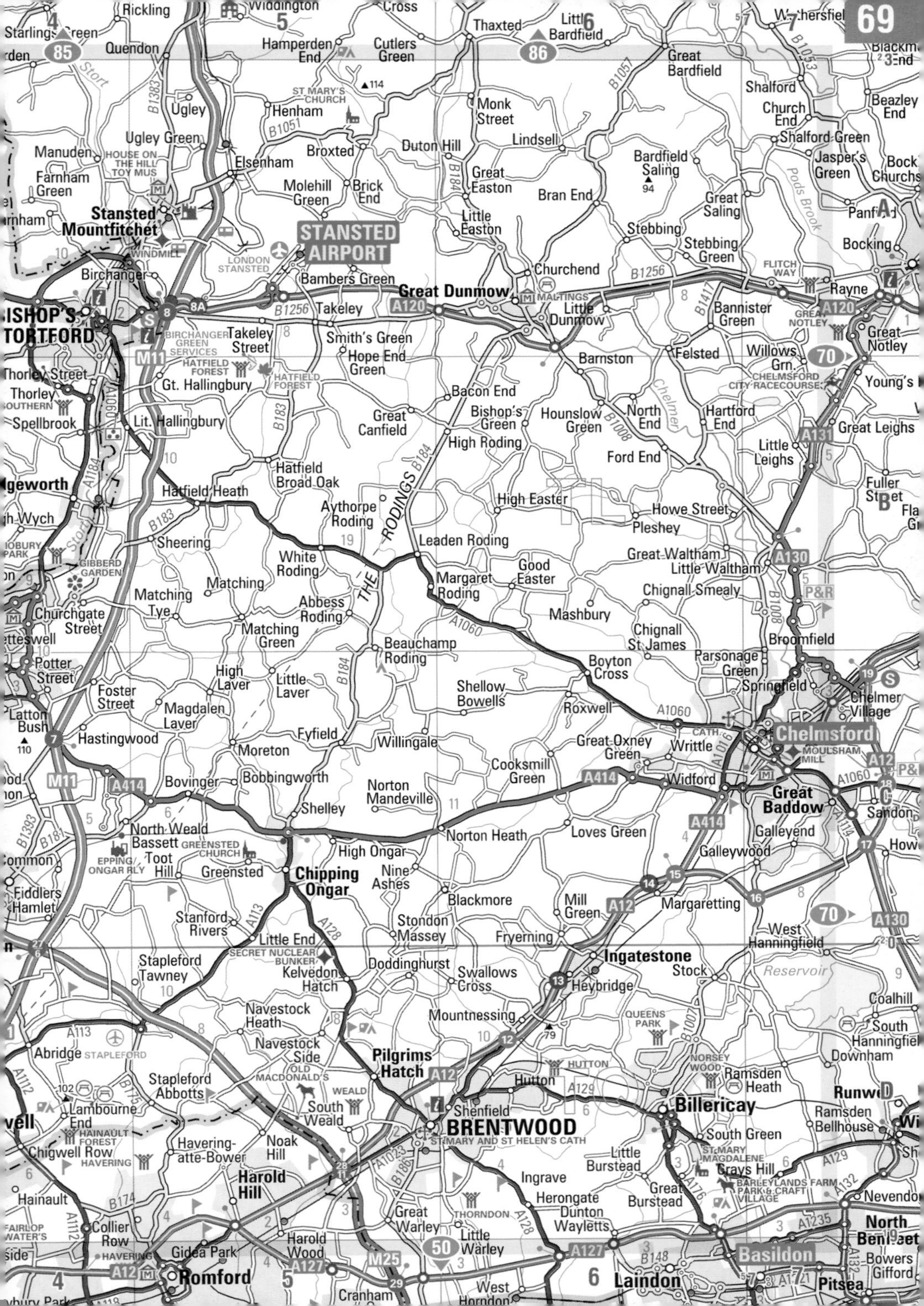
Stansted Mountfitchet
STANSTED AIRPORT
Great Dunmow
BISHOP'S STORTFORD
Thaxted
Great Bardfield
Hatfield Heath
Hatfield Broad Oak
Takeley
Elsenham
Henham
Felsted
Rayne
Great Notley
Pleshey
Great Waltham
Little Waltham
Broomfield
Chelmsford
Springfield
Writtle
Great Baddow
Galleywood
Margaretting
Ingatestone
Stock
Billericay
BRENTWOOD
Shenfield
Chipping Ongar
North Weald Bassett
Abridge
Harold Hill
Romford
Laindon
Basildon
Pitsea
Wickford
Blackmore
Doddinghurst
Kelvedon Hatch
Pilgrims Hatch
Matching Tye
Sheering
High Roding
Leaden Roding
Margaret Roding
Good Easter
High Easter
Barnston
Little Dunmow
Great Canfield
Great Easton
Lindsell
Stebbing
Bocking
Epping
Hutton
Ramsden Heath
Great Burstead
Ingrave
Harold Wood
Gidea Park
Cranham
West Horndon
Little Warley
Great Warley
South Weald
Navestock Side
Stapleford Abbotts
Havering-atte-Bower
Noak Hill
Chigwell Row
Lambourne End
Collier Row
Hainault
Fyfield
Willingale
Shelley
Moreton
Bobbingworth
High Ongar
Norton Heath
Roxwell
Boyton Cross
Mashbury
Chignall Smealy
Chignall St James
Ford End
Little Leighs
Great Leighs
Fuller Street
M11
A120
A130
A12
A414
A1060
A127
M25
A128
A131
B1256
B184
A113
A1023
A129
B1008
B1007
B183
B1051
B1057
B1383
B1417
THE RODINGS
85
86
70
50

Halstead
Colne Engaine
Wakes Colne
Bures
Wormingford
EAST ANGLIAN RAILWAY MUSEUM
Gosfield
Blackmore End
Shalford
Church End
Shalford Green
Beazley End
Jasper's Green
Bocking Churchstreet
High Garrett
Greenstead Green
Earls Colne
Chappel
Fordham
West Bergholt
Horkesley Heath
Great Horkesley
Fordstreet
Eight Ash Green
Aldham
Great Tey
Marks Tey
ST JAMES THE LESS CHURCH
Lexden
Beacon End
Stanway
Shrub End
Panfield
Stisted
Pattiswick
Broad Green
BRAINTREE
Bocking
Rayne
FLITCH WAY
Bradwell
FREEPORT BRAINTREE
Coggeshall
PAYCOCKE'S
GRANGE BARN
Coggeshall Hamlet
Copford Green
Easthorpe
Hardy's Green
Heckfordbridge
Layer de la Haye
COLCHESTER ZOO
Tye Green
Cressing
Great Notley
Black Notley
Silver End
Feering
Gore Pit
Kelvedon
LOCAL HISTORY MUSEUM
CRESSING TEMPLE
Young's End
CHELMSFORD CITY RACECOURSE
White Notley
Great Leighs
Little Leighs
Faulkbourne
Fairstead
Rivenhall End
Inworth
Messing
Smythe's Green
Birch
Birch Green
Layer Marney
Layer Breton
LAYER MARNEY TOWER
Tiptree
Abberton Reservoir
Malting Green
Peldon
Fuller Street
Terling
Flack's Green
Chipping Hill
Witham
Great Braxted
Oxley Green
Paternoster Heath
Great Wigborough
COPT HALL MARSHES
Salcott
Great Totham
Little Totham
Wickham Bishops
Tolleshunt D'Arcy
BLACKWATER ESTUARY
Hatfield Peverel
Nounsley
Boreham
Broomfield
Springfield
Chelmer Village
Chelmer and Blackwater Navigation
Tolleshunt Major
Tollesbury
Broad Street Green
Langford
Goldhanger
Heybridge
Little Baddow
Woodham Walter
Chelmsford
MOULSHAM MILL
COMBINED MILITARY SERVICES MUSEUM
Maldon
HYTHE QUAY
Heybridge Basin
Osea I.
Northey I.
Blackwater
Great Baddow
Sandon
Danbury
Runsell Green
Woodham Mortimer
Ramsey Island
St Lawrence
Galleyend
Howe Green
Cock Clarks
Rudley Green
Mundon
Steeple
Bicknacre
Purleigh
Cold Norton
Latchingdon
Asheldham
Mayland
East Hanningfield
West Hanningfield
HYDE HALL (RHS)
TROPICAL WINGS ZOO
Woodham Ferrers
STOW MARIES GREAT WAR AERODROME
Stow Maries
Althorne
Southminster
Reservoir
Coalhill
Rettendon
South Woodham Ferrers
North Fambridge
Bridgemarsh Island
Ostend
Stoneyhills
MANGAPPS RAILWAY MUS
Burnham-on-Crouch
South Hanningfield
Downham
Rettendon Place
MARSH FARM
South Fambridge
Creeksea
Crouch
Ramsden Heath
Runwell
Ramsden Bellhouse
Wickford
Battlesbridge
Hullbridge
Canewdon
Ashingdon
Paglesham Churchend
WALLASEA WETLANDS
Rawreth
Shotgate
Hockley
Hawkwell
Ballards Gore
Paglesham Eastend
Nevendon
BARLEYLANDS FARM PARK & CRAFT VILLAGE
Great Stambridge
Stroud Green
OLD HOUSE
Potton Island
FOULNE
North Benfleet
RAYLEIGH
CHERRY ORCHARD
Rochford
Thundersley
Eastwood
Barling
Little Wakering
Havengore Island
Daws Heath
0 1 2 3 miles
0 1 2 3 4 5 km

Langham
Lawford
Mistley
Bradfield
Wrabness
Parkeston
Harwich
Redoubt Fort
Manningtree
Ramsey
Upper Dovercourt
Dovercourt
87
88
A12
A137
A120
B1029
B1035
B1352
Ardleigh
Bradfield Heath
Little Bromley
Horsleycross Street
Little Oakley
Horsley Cross
Wix
Fox Street
Crockleford Heath
Great Bromley
Great Oakley
Tendring Green
Stone's Green
B1414
Colchester
Little Bentley
Beaumont
Elmstead Market
Hare Green
Balls Green
Horsey Island
The Naze
Old Heath
Wivenhoe Cross
A133
Tendring
B1035
Thorpe Green
Hamford Water
Bourne Mill
Beth Chatto Gdns
Frating Green
Great Bentley
B1033
Thorpe-le-Soken
Kirby-le-Soken
Maritime Museum
Blackheath
Wivenhoe
Weeley
Rowhedge
Alresford
B1027
Aingers Green
Weeley Heath
B1414
Kirby Cross
B1336
Walton-on-the-Naze
Fingringhoe
Frinton-on-Sea
Thorrington
Row Heath
Clacton Village
Abberton
B1029
Little Clacton
Great Holland
Langenhoe
B1032
St Osyth Heath
Holland Haven
River Colne
Brightlingsea
St Osyth Priory
B1027
Holland-on-Sea
Mersea Island
St Osyth
Great Clacton
East Mersea
Cudmore Grove
Point Clear
Clacton-on-Sea
Blue Row
Colne Estuary
Jaywick
West Mersea
Mersea Island Museum
Colne Pt.
Virley Channel
Sales Pt.
St Peters on the Wall
TM
Dengie
Ray Sand
Montsale
Deal Hall
Foulness Sand
Foulness Pt.
TR
Courtsend
Maplin Sands
A
B
C
D
4
5
6
52
53

SM
Strumble Head
Pen Caer
Dinas Head
Newport Bay
Bae Trefdraeth
Fishguard Bay
Bae Abergwaun
Cemaes Head
Pen Cemaes
ROSSLARE
PEMBROKESHIRE COAST
ARFORDIR PENFRO
PEMBROKESHIRE COAST PATH
LLWYBR ARFORDIR PENFRO
Goodwick
(Wdig)
Fishguard
(Abergwaun)
Newport
(Trefdraeth)
Tresinwen
Llanwnda
Lower Town
Brynhenllan
Dinas Cross
Parrog
Berry Hill
Nevern
Felindre Farchog
CASTELL HENLLYS FORT
Moylgrove
Cippyn
Monington
Glanrhyd
Pontgareg
Trefasser
Penbwchdy
Dyffryn
Manorowen
St Nicholas
TREGWYNT WOOLLEN MILL
Abercastle
Granston
Scleddau
Llanychaer
Pontfaen
Cilgwyn
CARNINGLI
TY CANOL
Crosswell
Pontyglasier
Brynberian
MYNYDD PRESE
FOEL-CWMCERWYN
Trecwn
Mathry
Newbridge
Castlemorris
Penparc
CORSYDD LLANGLOFFAN
Letterston
Little Newcastle
Puncheston
Castlebythe
New Inn
Rosebush
Treddiog
Llanreithan
Welsh Hook
St Dogwells
Tufton
Henry's Moat
Maenclochog
Llangolman
Glandy Cross
Llandeloy
Pont-yr-hafod
Wolf's Castle
Ambleston
Woodstock
Trefgarn Owen
Hayscastle
Brimaston
Rinaston
Wallis
New Moat
Efailwen
Hayscastle Cross
LLYS-Y-FRAN RESERVOIR
Triffleton
Mountain Water
Treffgarne
Llys-y-frân
Llanycefn
Penycwm
Spittal
Walton East
Pen-ffordd
DUDWELL MT.
Leweston
SCOLTON MANOR
Newgale
Roch
Wolfsdale
Clarbeston
Bletherston
Llandissilio
Roch Gate
Camrose
Rudbaxton
Clarbeston Road
Gelli
Clunderwen
Tangiers
Pelcomb Cross
Crundale
LAWHADEN CASTLE
A40
A487
B4313
B4329
B4331
B4330
B4582
A478
W. Cleddau
E. Cleddau
0 1 2 3 miles
0 1 2 3 4 5 km

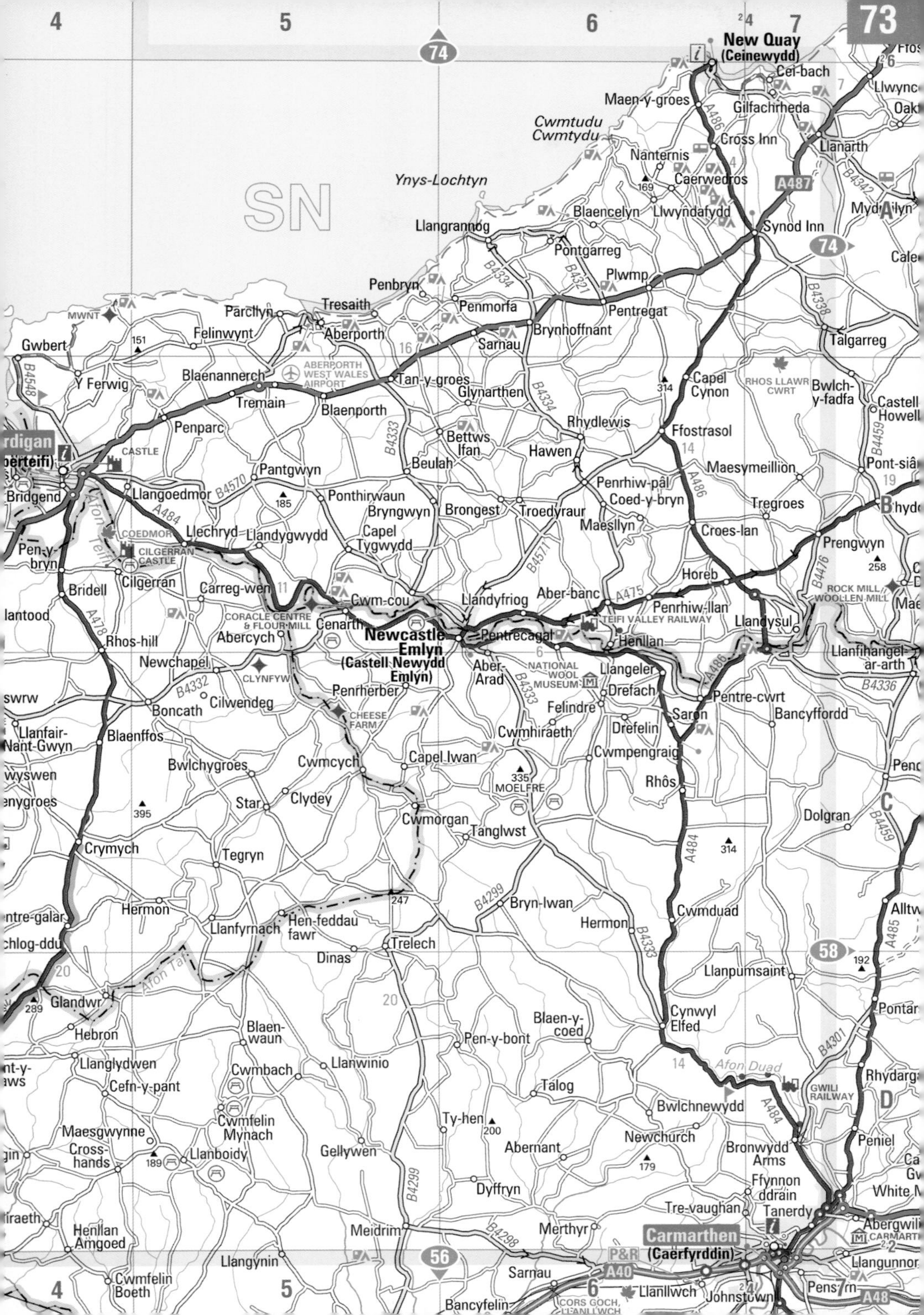
SN
New Quay
(Ceinewydd)
Cei-bach
Maen-y-groes
Gilfachrheda
Cwmtudu
Cwmtydu
Cross Inn
Llanarth
Nanternis
Caerwedros
Ynys-Lochtyn
Blaencelyn
Llwyndafydd
Llangrannog
Synod Inn
Pontgarreg
Plwmp
Penbryn
Penmorfa
Pentregat
Tresaith
Parcllyn
Aberporth
Brynhoffnant
Sarnau
Talgarreg
MWNT
Felinwynt
Gwbert
Y Ferwig
Blaenannerch
ABERPORTH WEST WALES AIRPORT
Tan-y-groes
Glynarthen
Capel Cynon
RHOS LLAWR CWRT
Bwlch-y-fadfa
Tremain
Blaenporth
Penparc
Rhydlewis
Ffostrasol
Bettws Ifan
Hawen
CASTLE
Beulah
Maesymeillion
Pantgwyn
Penrhiw-pâl
Coed-y-bryn
Bridgend
Llangoedmor
Ponthirwaun
Bryngwyn
Brongest
Troedyraur
Tregroes
Maesllyn
Croes-lan
COEDMOR
Llechryd
Llandygwydd
Capel Tygwydd
Prengwyn
CILGERRAN CASTLE
Cilgerran
Horeb
Bridell
Carreg-wen
Cwm-cou
Llandyfriog
Aber-banc
ROCK MILL WOOLLEN MILL
Penrhiw-llan
CORACLE CENTRE & FLOUR MILL
Cenarth
TEIFI VALLEY RAILWAY
Llandysul
Abercych
Newcastle Emlyn
(Castell Newydd Emlyn)
Pentrecagal
Henllan
Rhos-hill
Llanfihangel-ar-arth
Newchapel
CLYNFYW
Aber-Arad
NATIONAL WOOL MUSEUM
Llangeler
Drefach
Pentre-cwrt
Boncath
Cilwendeg
Penrherber
Felindre
Bancyffordd
Saron
CHEESE FARM
Drefelin
Llanfair-Nant-Gwyn
Blaenffos
Cwmhiraeth
Bwlchygroes
Cwmcych
Capel Iwan
Cwmpengraig
MOELFRE
Star
Clydey
Rhôs
Cwmorgan
Tanglwst
Dolgran
Crymych
Tegryn
Hermon
Bryn-Iwan
Hen-feddau fawr
Llanfyrnach
Cwmduad
Hermon
Trelech
Dinas
Afon Taf
Llanpumsaint
Glandwr
Hebron
Blaen-waun
Cynwyl Elfed
Blaen-y-coed
Pen-y-bont
Afon Duad
Llanglydwen
Cwmbach
Llanwinio
Cefn-y-pant
Talog
GWILI RAILWAY
Rhydargaeau
Cwmfelin Mynach
Ty-hen
Bwlchnewydd
Maesgwynne
Cross-hands
Llanboidy
Gellywen
Abernant
Newchurch
Bronwydd Arms
Peniel
Dyffryn
Ffynnon ddrain
Tre-vaughan
Tanerdy
Henllan Amgoed
Meidrim
Merthyr
Carmarthen
(Caerfyrddin)
Llangynin
Sarnau
Llanllwch
Johnstown
Cwmfelin Boeth
Bancyfelin
CORS GOCH, LLANLLWCH
A487
A486
A484
A478
A475
A485
A40
A48
B4334
B4321
B4333
B4570
B4571
B4332
B4299
B4298
B4336
B4476
B4459
B4338
B4342
B4548
B4301
74
56
58
4
5
6
7
A
B
C
D

1
2
3
A
B
C
D
Llansa
Aberarth
Aberaeron
Mon
New Quay
(Ceinewydd)
LLANERC
Ffos-y-ffin
Cei-bach
Gilfachrheda
Maen-y-groes
Llwyncelyn
Oakford
Cili
Aer
73
Cwmtudu
Cwmtydu
Cross Inn
Llanarth
Nanternis
Caerwedros
A487
Dihewyd
169
Ynys-Lochtyn
Blaencelyn
Llwyndafydd
Mydroilyn
B4342
Llangrannog
Synod Inn
Pontgarreg
Caledrhydiau
B4334
B4321
Plwmp
Penbryn
Penmorfa
Pentregat
B4338
Tresaith
Parcllyn
Aberporth
Brynhoffnant
Talgarreg
Gorsgoc
151
Felinwynt
16
Sarnau
B4338
324
ABERPORTH
WEST WALES
AIRPORT
RHOS LLAWR
CWRT
Blaenannerch
Tan-y-groes
Capel
Cynon
314
Bwlch-
y-fadfa
Aber
Glynarthen
Castell-
Howell
A487
Tremain
Blaenporth
B4334
Penparc
B4333
Rhydlewis
Ffostrasol
73
CASTLE
Bettws
Ifan
Hawen
14
B4459
Pont-siân
Cwmsyc
Beulah
Maesymeillion
Pantgwyn
B4570
A486
19
Llangoedmor
Penrhiw-pâl
Llanwenog
185
Ponthirwaun
Coed-y-bryn
A484
Bryngwyn
Brongest
Troedyraur
Tregroes
Rhydo
58
COEDMOR
Llechryd
Llandygwydd
Capel
Tygwydd
Maesllyn
Croes-lan
CILGERRAN
CASTLE
Prengwyn
B4571
Bryn
258
Cilgerran
Carreg-wen
11
Horeb
Capel
Dewi
B4476
ROCK MILL
WOOLLEN MILL
Cwm-cou
Llandyfriog
Aber-banc
A475
Maesycrugiau
CORACLE CENTRE
& FLOUR MILL
Cenarth
Penrhiw-llan
TEIFI VALLEY RAILWAY
Llandysul
Rhos-hill
Abercych
Newcastle
Emlyn
(Castell Newydd
Emlyn)
Pentrecagal
Henllan
Llanfihangel-
ar-arth
6
0
1
2
3 miles
0
1
2
3
4
5 km
Aber-
Arad
NATIONAL
WOOL
MUSEUM
Llangeler
A486
B4336
Penrherber
B4333
Drefach
Pentre-cwrt
Boncath
Cilwendeg
Felindre
Saron
Bancyffordd
CHEESE

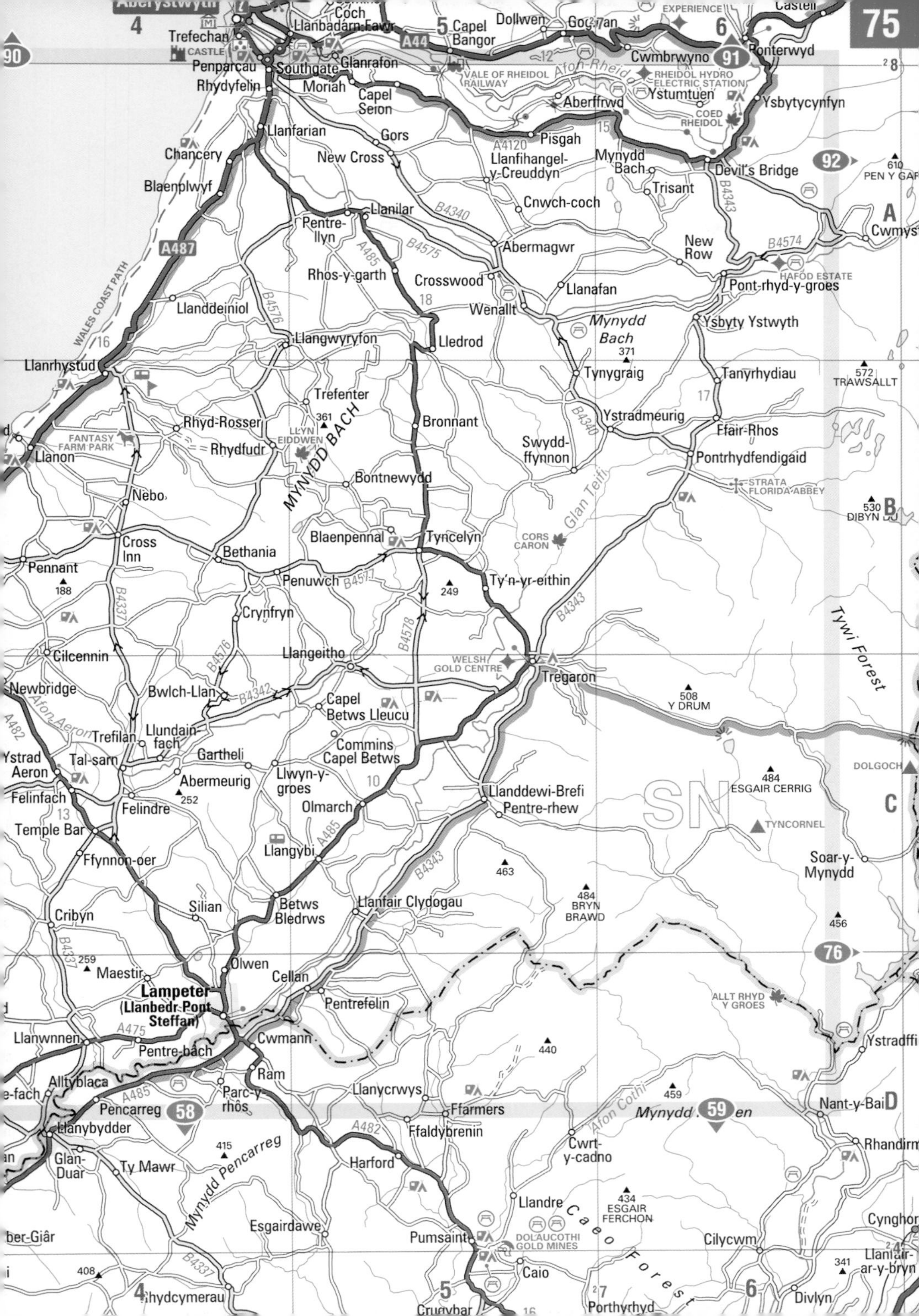

Aberystwyth
Coch
Llanbadarn Fawr
Capel Bangor
Dollwen
Goginan
EXPERIENCE
Castell
Trefechan
CASTLE
Penparcau
Southgate
Glanrafon
Cwmbrwyno
Ponterwyd
Rhydyfelin
Moriah
Capel Seion
VALE OF RHEIDOL RAILWAY
Afon Rheidol
RHEIDOL HYDRO ELECTRIC STATION
Ystumtuen
Ysbytycynfyn
Aberffrwd
COED RHEIDOL
Llanfarian
Gors
A4120
Pisgah
Chancery
New Cross
Llanfihangel-y-Creuddyn
Mynydd Bach
Devil's Bridge
PEN Y GAR
Blaenplwyf
Trisant
Cnwch-coch
B4343
Llanilar
Pentre-llyn
B4340
A485
A487
WALES COAST PATH
B4575
Abermagwr
New Row
Cwmystwyth
B4574
Rhos-y-garth
Crosswood
HAFOD ESTATE
Pont-rhyd-y-groes
Llanafan
Llanddeiniol
B4576
Wenallt
Ysbyty Ystwyth
Llangwyryfon
Lledrod
Mynydd Bach
371
Llanrhystud
Tynygraig
Tanyrhydiau
572 TRAWSALLT
Trefenter
361
LLYN EIDDWEN
MYNYDD BACH
Bronnant
Ystradmeurig
Ffair-Rhos
Rhyd-Rosser
FANTASY FARM PARK
Rhydfudr
Swydd-ffynnon
Pontrhydfendigaid
Llanon
Bontnewydd
STRATA FLORIDA ABBEY
Nebo
Glan Teifi
530 DIBYN DU
Blaenpennal
Tyncelyn
CORS CARON
Cross Inn
Bethania
Pennant
188
Penuwch
B4577
Ty'n-yr-eithin
249
B4337
Crynfryn
B4578
B4343
Tywi Forest
Cilcennin
Llangeitho
WELSH GOLD CENTRE
Tregaron
B4576
Newbridge
Bwlch-Llan
B4342
Capel Betws Lleucu
508 Y DRUM
A482
Afon Aeron
Trefilan
Llundain-fach
Commins Capel Betws
Ystrad Aeron
Tal-sarn
Gartheli
DOLGOCH
Abermeurig
Llwyn-y-groes
484 ESGAIR CERRIG
Felinfach
252
Olmarch
Llanddewi-Brefi
SN
Felindre
Pentre-rhew
Temple Bar
TYNCORNEL
Llangybi
Ffynnon-oer
463
Soar-y-Mynydd
Silian
Betws Bledrws
Llanfair Clydogau
484 BRYN BRAWD
Cribyn
456
259
Maestir
Olwen
Cellan
Lampeter (Llanbedr Pont Steffan)
Pentrefelin
ALLT RHYD Y GROES
A475
Llanwnnen
Cwmann
440
Ystradffin
Pentre-bach
Alltyblaca
Ram
A485
Llanycrwys
459
Afon Cothi
Parc-y-rhôs
Pencarreg
Ffarmers
Nant-y-Bai
Mynydd Mallaen
Llanybydder
A482
Ffaldybrenin
Cwrt-y-cadno
Rhandirmwyn
415
Glan-Duar
Ty Mawr
Mynydd Pencarreg
Harford
Llandre
434 ESGAIR FERCHON
Caeo Forest
Esgairdawe
Pumsaint
DOLAUCOTHI GOLD MINES
Cilycwm
Cynghordy
Llanfair-ar-y-bryn
Aber-Giâr
B4337
408
Caio
341
Rhydcymerau
Crugybar
Porthyrhyd
Divlyn
90
91
92
58
59
76

Rhayader
(Rhaeadr Gwy)
Llansantffraed
Cwmdeuddwr
WELSH ROYAL CRYSTAL
Gaufron
THE GIGRIN FARM RED KITE FEEDING CENTRE
Elan Village
Nant-glas
Llanwrthwl
Argoed
Llanyre
MOEL HYWEL
TRAWSALLT
CLAERWEN
Penygarreg Res.
Garreg-ddu Res.
Claerwen Reservoir
Caban-coch Res.
Afon Claerwen
STRATA FLORIDA ABBEY
DIBYN DU
Tywi Forest
DRUM-DDU
Newbridge on Wye
Disserth
DRYGARN FAWR
BRYN CRWN
DOLGOCH
ESGAIR CERRIG
TYNCORNEL
NANT IRFON
Llanafan-fawr
CORS Y LLYN
Pentre-llwyn-llwyd
Troed-rhiwdalar
Cwmbach
Builth Road
Soar-y-Mynydd
Llyn Brianne Res.
Abergwesyn
Beulah
Cilmery
Llanfechan
Garth
Tyn-y-graig
Cwm Irfon
Mynydd Trawsnant
Maesmynis
Irfon
Llanwrtyd
Ystradffin
Llanwrtyd Wells
(Llanwrtud)
Llangammarch Wells
Cefn-gorwydd
DRUM-DDU
Nant-y-Bai
Rhandirmwyn
MYNYDD EPYNT
Pentre Dolau-Honddu
BRYN DU
Crychan Forest
Tirabad
Cynghordy
Upper Chapel
Llanfair-ar-y-bryn
Divlyn
Myrtle Hill
Blaendyryn
Merthyr Cynog
Pentre-ty-gwyn
Babel
Mynydd Bwlch-y-groes
Llandeilo'r Fan
Llanfihangel Nant Bran
Pont-faen
Pwllgloyw
Sarnau
Lower Chapel
Honddu
Llandovery
(Llanymddyfri)
Halfway
Pentre-bach
Nant Bran
Llywel
Pentre'r-felin
Trallong
Aberyscir
Battle
BRECON GAER ROMAN FORT
CATHEDRAL
Trecastle
Sennybridge
(Pont Senni)
Penpont
Llanspyddid
Usk (Wysg)
Cwmwysg
A470
A44
A483
A40
A4081
B4518
B4358
B4519
B4520
0 1 2 3 miles
0 1 2 3 4 5 km

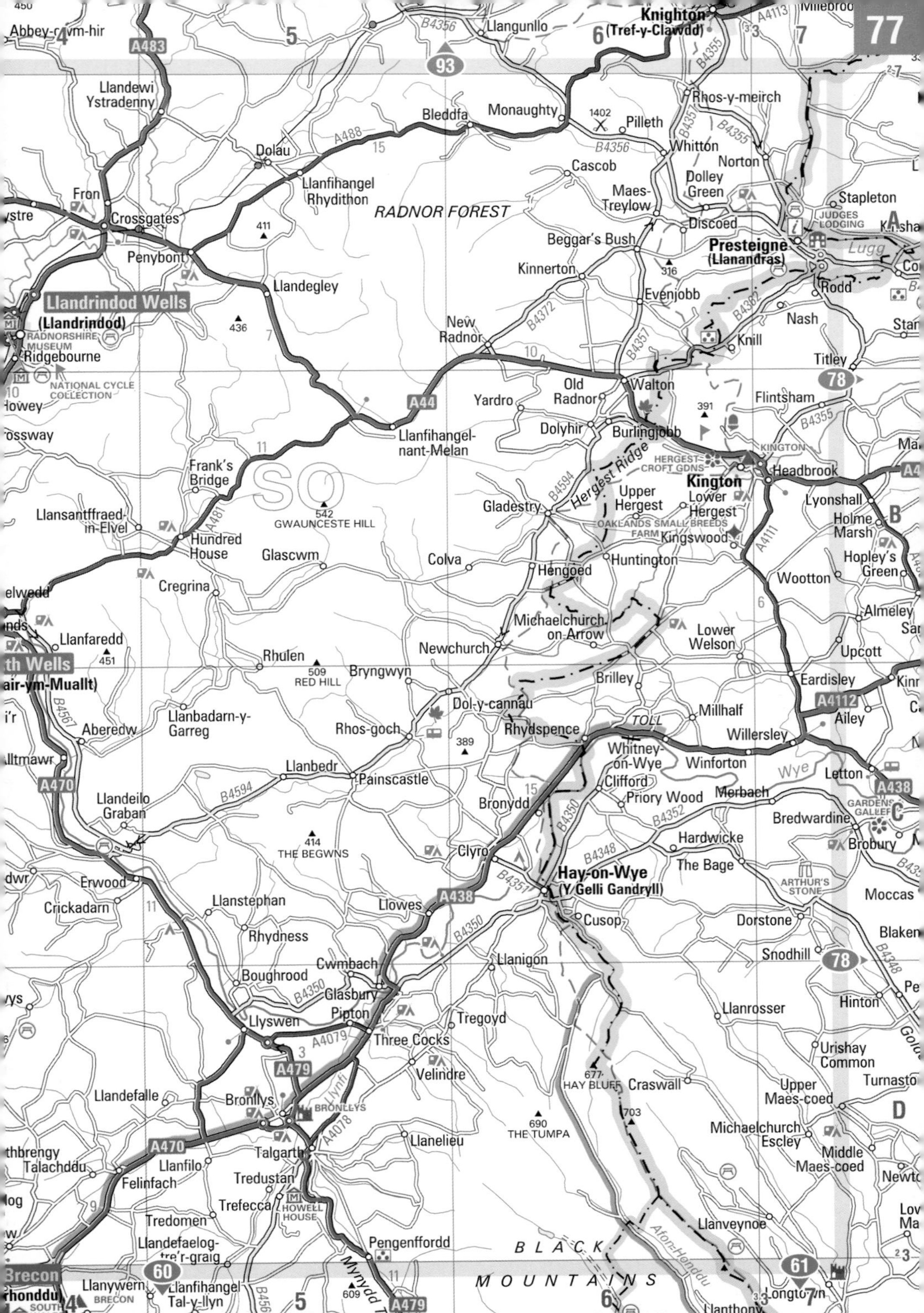
Knighton (Tref-y-Clawdd)
Llangunllo
Abbey-cwm-hir
Llandewi Ystradenny
Bleddfa
Monaughty
Pilleth
Rhos-y-meirch
Whitton
Norton
Dolau
Llanfihangel Rhydithon
RADNOR FOREST
Cascob
Maes-Treylow
Dolley Green
Stapleton
JUDGES LODGING
Fron
Crossgates
Penybont
Discoed
Beggar's Bush
Presteigne (Llanandras)
Lugg
Kinnerton
Llandegley
Rodd
Evenjobb
Llandrindod Wells (Llandrindod)
RADNORSHIRE MUSEUM
Ridgebourne
NATIONAL CYCLE COLLECTION
New Radnor
Nash
Knill
Titley
Walton
Old Radnor
Yardro
Flintsham
Dolyhir
Burlingjobb
Llanfihangel-nant-Melan
Hergest Ridge
HERGEST CROFT GDNS
KINGTON
Kington
Headbrook
Frank's Bridge
Gladestry
Upper Hergest
Lower Hergest
Lyonshall
Llansantffraed-in-Elvel
GWAUNCESTE HILL
OAKLANDS SMALL BREEDS FARM
Kingswood
Holme Marsh
Hundred House
Glascwm
Colva
Hengoed
Huntington
Hopley's Green
Wootton
Cregrina
Michaelchurch-on-Arrow
Almeley
Llanfaredd
Newchurch
Lower Welson
Upcott
Rhulen
RED HILL
Bryngwyn
Brilley
Eardisley
Dol-y-cannau
Millhalf
Aberedw
Llanbadarn-y-Garreg
Rhos-goch
Rhydspence
TOLL
Willersley
Ailey
Alltmawr
Whitney-on-Wye
Winforton
Llanbedr
Painscastle
Clifford
Wye
Letton
Llandeilo Graban
Bronydd
Priory Wood
Merbach
Bredwardine
THE BEGWNS
Hardwicke
Clyro
Hay-on-Wye (Y Gelli Gandryll)
The Bage
Brobury
Erwood
ARTHUR'S STONE
Moccas
Crickadarn
Llanstephan
Llowes
Cusop
Dorstone
Rhydness
Snodhill
Cwmbach
Llanigon
Boughrood
Glasbury
Llanrosser
Hinton
Llyswen
Pipton
Tregoyd
Three Cocks
Urishay Common
Velindre
HAY BLUFF
Craswall
Upper Maes-coed
Llandefalle
Bronllys
BRONLLYS
THE TUMPA
Michaelchurch Escley
Llanelieu
Talgarth
Middle Maes-coed
Talachddu
Llanfilo
Felinfach
Tredustan
Trefecca
HOWELL HOUSE
Tredomen
Llanveynoe
Llandefaelog-tre'r-graig
Pengenffordd
BLACK MOUNTAINS
Afon-Honddu
Brecon
Llanywern
Llanfihangel Tal-y-llyn
Mynydd
Longtown
Llanthony

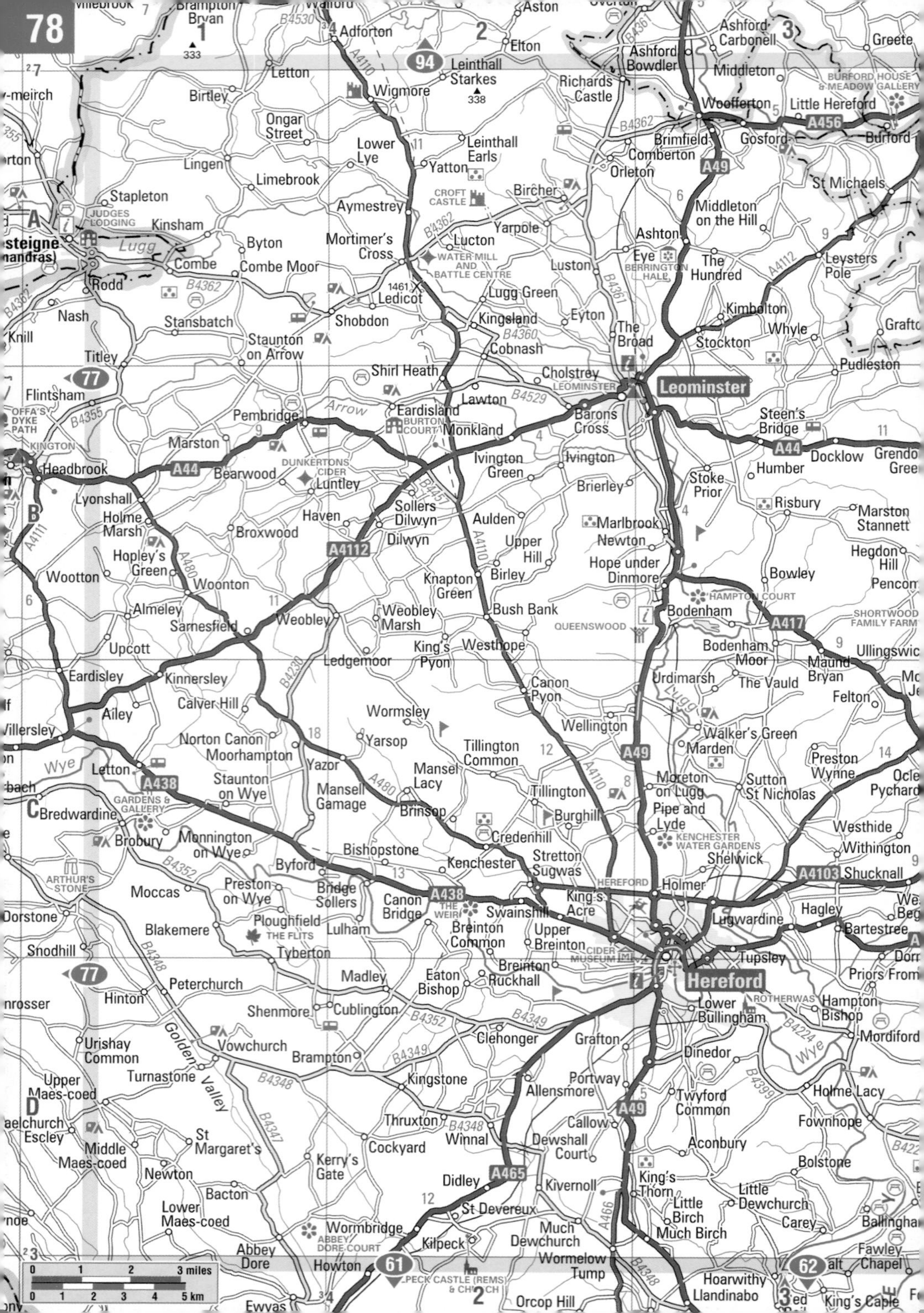
Brampton Bryan
Adforton
Aston
Ashford Carbonell
Greete
Elton
Leinthall Starkes
Ashford Bowdler
Letton
Wigmore
Richards Castle
Middleton
Burford House & Meadow Gallery
Birtley
Woofferton
Little Hereford
Ongar Street
Leinthall Earls
Brimfield
Gosford
Burford
Lower Lye
Comberton
Lingen
Yatton
Orleton
Limebrook
Croft Castle
Bircher
St Michaels
Stapleton
Aymestrey
Middleton on the Hill
Judges Lodging
Kinsham
Yarpole
Ashton
Presteigne
Byton
Mortimer's Cross
Lucton
Eye
Leysters Pole
Lugg
Combe
Combe Moor
Water Mill and Battle Centre
Luston
Berrington Hall
The Hundred
Rodd
Ledicot
Lugg Green
Kimbolton
Nash
Shobdon
Kingsland
Eyton
Stansbatch
The Broad
Whyle
Knill
Staunton on Arrow
Cobnash
Stockton
Titley
Shirl Heath
Cholstrey
Leominster
Pudleston
Flintsham
Lawton
Offa's Dyke Path
Pembridge
Arrow
Eardisland
Burton Court
Monkland
Barons Cross
Steen's Bridge
Kington
Marston
Ivington Green
Ivington
Docklow
Humber
Headbrook
Bearwood
Dunkertons Cider
Luntley
Stoke Prior
Brierley
Risbury
Marston Stannett
Lyonshall
Haven
Sollers Dilwyn
Aulden
Marlbrook
Holme Marsh
Broxwood
Dilwyn
Upper Hill
Newton
Hegdon Hill
Hopley's Green
Hope under Dinmore
Bowley
Wootton
Knapton Green
Birley
Woonton
Hampton Court
Almeley
Weobley Marsh
Bush Bank
Bodenham
Shortwood Family Farm
Sarnesfield
Weobley
Queenswood
Upcott
King's Pyon
Westhope
Bodenham Moor
Maund Bryan
Ullingswick
Eardisley
Kinnersley
Ledgemoor
Urdimarsh
The Vault
Canon Pyon
Felton
Calver Hill
Ailey
Wormsley
Wellington
Walker's Green
Willersley
Norton Canon
Yarsop
Marden
Moorhampton
Tillington Common
Preston Wynne
Letton
Yazor
Mansel Lacy
Moreton on Lugg
Sutton St Nicholas
Wye
Staunton on Wye
Mansell Gamage
Tillington
Pychard
Bredwardine
Gardens & Gallery
Brinsop
Burghill
Pipe and Lyde
Westhide
Brobury
Monnington on Wye
Credenhill
Kenchester Water Gardens
Withington
Arthur's Stone
Bishopstone
Kenchester
Stretton Sugwas
Shelwick
Byford
Shucknall
Moccas
Preston on Wye
Bridge Sollers
Canon Bridge
The Weir
Swainshill
King's Acre
Holmer
Hagley
Dorstone
Ploughfield
Lulham
Breinton Common
Upper Breinton
Lugwardine
Bartestree
Blakemere
The Flits
Tyberton
Cider Museum
Tupsley
Snodhill
Breinton
Ruckhall
Hereford
Priors Frome
Madley
Eaton Bishop
Peterchurch
Hinton
Rotherwas
Hampton Bishop
Shenmore
Cublington
Lower Bullingham
Urishay Common
Vowchurch
Clehonger
Grafton
Mordiford
Golden Valley
Brampton
Dinedor
Turnastone
Kingstone
Portway
Upper Maes-coed
Allensmore
Twyford Common
Holme Lacy
Michaelchurch Escley
Thruxton
Winnal
Callow
Fownhope
St Margaret's
Middle Maes-coed
Cockyard
Dewshall Court
Aconbury
Kerry's Gate
Bolstone
Newton
Didley
Kivernoll
King's Thorn
Little Dewchurch
Bacton
Lower Maes-coed
St Devereux
Little Birch
Carey
Much Birch
Ballingham
Wormbridge
Abbey Dore Court
Much Dewchurch
Kilpeck
Fawley Chapel
Abbey Dore
Howton
Wormelow Tump
Kilpeck Castle (Rems) & Church
Hoarwithy
Llandinabo
Orcop Hill
Ewyas
King's Caple
A4110
B4530
B4361
B4362
A456
A49
A4112
B4360
B4529
B4355
A44
B4457
A4112
A480
A4111
B4230
A417
A438
B4352
A4103
B4348
B4349
B4224
B4399
B4347
A465
A466
B4348
94
77
61
62
333
338
1461
0 1 2 3 miles
0 1 2 3 4 5 km

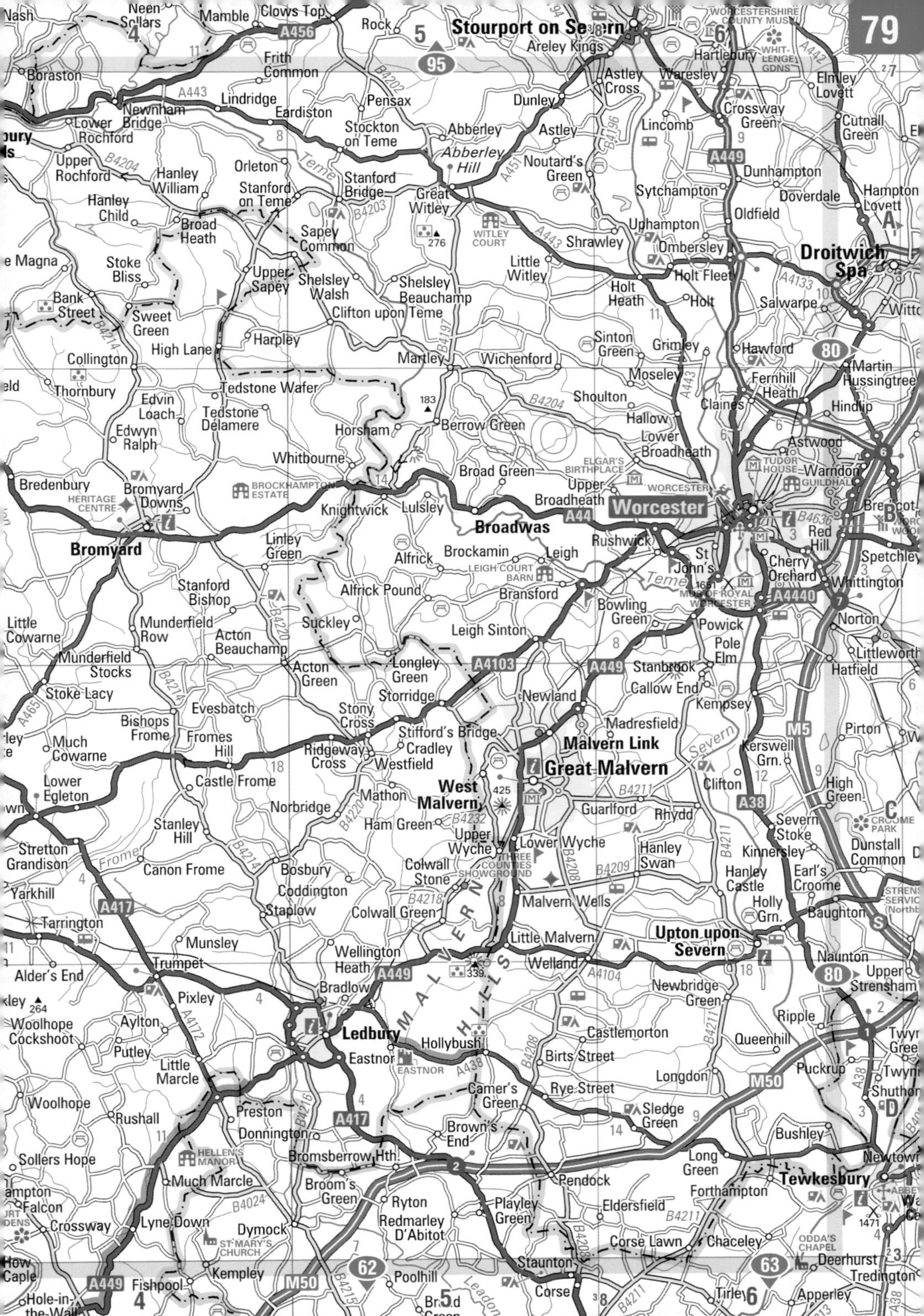
Stourport on Severn
Droitwich Spa
Worcester
Bromyard
Broadwas
Malvern Link
Great Malvern
West Malvern
Upton upon Severn
Ledbury
Tewkesbury
Abberley Hill
Areley Kings
Hartlebury
Astley Cross
Waresley
Dunley
Astley
Lincomb
Crossway Green
Elmley Lovett
Cutnall Green
Noutard's Green
Dunhampton
Sytchampton
Doverdale
Hampton Lovett
Oldfield
Uphampton
Shrawley
Ombersley
Holt Fleet
Holt Heath
Holt
Salwarpe
Little Witley
Great Witley
Witley Court
Sinton Green
Grimley
Hawford
Martin Hussingtree
Fernhill Heath
Hindlip
Claines
Moseley
Shoulton
Hallow
Lower Broadheath
Upper Broadheath
Elgar's Birthplace
Wichenford
Martley
Berrow Green
Broad Green
Horsham
Whitbourne
Knightwick
Lulsley
Brockhampton Estate
Bromyard Downs
Heritage Centre
Bredenbury
Alfrick
Brockamin
Leigh
Leigh Court Barn
Rushwick
St John's
Tudor House
Guildhall
Warndon
Astwood
Red Hill
Cherry Orchard
Whittington
Spetchley
Norton
Littleworth
Hatfield
Bransford
Bowling Green
Powick
Pole Elm
Mus of Royal Worcester
Alfrick Pound
Suckley
Leigh Sinton
Stanbrook
Callow End
Kempsey
Newland
Madresfield
Kerswell Grn.
Pirton
Clifton
High Green
Croome Park
Severn Stoke
Kinnersley
Dunstall Common
Earl's Croome
Hanley Castle
Holly Grn.
Baughton
Naunton
Upper Strensham
Ripple
Queenhill
Puckrup
Twyning
Shuthonger
Bushley
Newtown
Longdon
Rye Street
Birts Street
Castlemorton
Sledge Green
Long Green
Forthampton
Chaceley
Eldersfield
Corse Lawn
Odda's Chapel
Deerhurst
Tredington
Apperley
Tirley
Staunton
Corse
Pendock
Playley Green
Redmarley D'Abitot
Ryton
Poolhill
Broom's Green
Bromsberrow Hth.
Brown's End
Camer's Green
Hollybush
Eastnor
Donnington
Preston
Dymock
Kempley
Fishpool
St Mary's Church
Much Marcle
Hellen's Manor
Lyne Down
Rushall
Woolhope
Sollers Hope
Crossway
Falcon
How Caple
Hole-in-the-Wall
Little Marcle
Putley
Aylton
Pixley
Woolhope Cockshoot
Trumpet
Munsley
Alder's End
Tarrington
Yarkhill
Stretton Grandison
Canon Frome
Bosbury
Coddington
Staplow
Colwall Green
Colwall Stone
Wellington Heath
Bradlow
Welland
Little Malvern
Malvern Wells
Three Counties Showground
Upper Wyche
Lower Wyche
Guarlford
Rhydd
Hanley Swan
Newbridge Green
Ham Green
Mathon
Norbridge
Castle Frome
Westfield
Cradley
Stifford's Bridge
Ridgeway Cross
Storridge
Stony Cross
Longley Green
Acton Green
Acton Beauchamp
Evesbatch
Bishops Frome
Fromes Hill
Stanley Hill
Lower Egleton
Much Cowarne
Stoke Lacy
Munderfield Stocks
Munderfield Row
Little Cowarne
Stanford Bishop
Linley Green
Edwyn Ralph
Edvin Loach
Tedstone Delamere
Tedstone Wafer
Thornbury
Collington
High Lane
Harpley
Sweet Green
Bank Street
Stoke Bliss
Upper Sapey
Shelsley Walsh
Shelsley Beauchamp
Clifton upon Teme
Sapey Common
Broad Heath
Hanley Child
Hanley William
Stanford on Teme
Stanford Bridge
Orleton
Upper Rochford
Lower Rochford
Newnham Bridge
Lindridge
Eardiston
Stockton on Teme
Abberley
Pensax
Frith Common
Boraston
Nash
Neen Sollars
Mamble
Clows Top
Rock
Worcestershire County Mus
Whitlenge Gdns
Malvern Hills
Teme
Severn
Frome
Leadon
A456
A443
A451
B4202
B4196
A449
A4133
A442
B4204
B4203
B4197
B4214
A44
B4636
A4440
A4103
B4220
A465
M5
B4211
A38
B4232
B4218
B4209
B4208
A417
A4172
A4104
M50
B4216
B4024
B4215
95
80
62
63
2
1
6
7
3
Eastnor
276
183
425
339
264
1651
1471

Rushock
Sidemoor
Bromsgrove
96
Alvechurch
Rowney Green
Portway
Branson's Cross
Wood End
Umberslade Farm
Tanworth-in-Arden
A448
A441
A435
Elmley Lovett
Charford
Finstall
Tardebigge
Beoley
B4101
Holt End
Forge Mill Needle Mus
Crossway Green
M5
Aston Fields
Avoncroft Mus of Historic Buildings
A448
Redditch
A4023
Gorcott Hill
Cutnall Green
Elmbridge
Arrow Valley
Ullenhall
Upton Warren
Stoke Prior
Woodgate
Webheath
Ipsley
A4189
Oldberrow
Dunhampton
Hampton Lovett
Bentley
Headless Cross
Mappleborough Green
Doverdale
Wychbold
Fosters Green Meadows
Morton Bagot
Oldfield
A38
Crabbs Cross
B4091
Hanbury Hall
Droitwich Spa
Woolmere Green
Hanbury
Ham Green
Hunt End
A441
A448
Studley
A4133
B4092
Salwarpe
Hadzor
B4090
Witton
Astwood Bank
Sambourne
Shelfield
Coughton Court
Little Alne
Hawford
Shernal Green
Bradley Green
Feckenham
Coughton
Great Alne
B4089
79
Martin Hussingtree
New End
Fernhill Heath
Oddingley
Stock Wood
B4092
Holberrow Green
B4090
King's Coughton
Hindlip
Sale Green
Himbleton
Stock Green
Cookhill
Alcester
Walcot
A422
Astwood
Tibberton
Huddington
Dormston
Oversley Green
Haselor
Tudor House
Warndon
Inkberrow
A435
A46
Billesley
Guildhall
Crowle
Grafton Flyford
Arrow
Kington
Abbots Morton
Exhall
Bredicot
Broughton Hackett
Ragley Hall
Weethley Gate
Wixford
Temple Grafton
B4636
Worcester Woods
A422
16
Flyford Flavell
Red Hill
North Piddle
Ardens Grafton
Spetchley
Upton Snodsbury
Rous Lench
Dunnington
Cherry Orchard
Churchill
Abberton
Iron Cross
Broom
Whittington
White Ladies Aston
A46
A4440
7
Naunton Beauchamp
Ab Lench
Church Lench
Bidford-on-Avon
B4082
B4088
Salford Priors
Norton
Egdon
Bishampton
Barton
A44
Peopleton
Atch Lench
Abbots Salford
Marlcliff
Littleworth
Stoulton
Hatfield
Pinvin
Throckmorton
Harvington Cross
Harvington
Cleeve Prior
Drake's Broughton
Avon
B4084
14
Norton
Lenchwick
B4510
North Littleton
Pirton
Wadborough
Wyre Piddle
Lower Moor
A44
Pebworth
Kerswell Grn.
M5
The Valley
10
Middle Littleton
Fladbury
Pershore
Offenham
Broad Marston
High Green
Abbey
Wick
Charlton
B4085
South Littleton
Besford
Cropthorne
1265
A46
A4104
A4184
Severn Stoke
Croome Park
B4084
Evesham
All Things Wild Nature Centre
Honeybourne
Aldington
Kinnersley
Avon
Dunstall Common
Little Comberton
Bretforton
Hanley Castle
Earl's Croome
Defford
B4080
Birlingham
B4084
Bengeworth
B4035
The Fleece Inn
Hampton
Fairfield
Badsey
Strensham Services (Northbound Only)
Great Comberton
Bricklehampton
Holly Grn.
Baughton
Eckington
Netherton
Wickhamford
Vale of Evesham
Lower Strensham
Elmley Castle
A44
Bredon Hill
293
Bredon Hill
B4632
West sub-Edge
Strensham Services (Southbound Only)
Naunton
Kersoe
Hinton on the Green
Upper Strensham
Bredon's Norton
Ashton under Hill
Childswickham
Willersey
Saintbury
79
8
Sedgeberrow
Ripple
Bredon Barn
Overbury
A46
Kemerton
Queenhill
Conderton Pottery
Aston Somerville
Twyning Green
Conderton
Broadway
Bredon
Puckrup
Twyning
Silk Centre
Buckland
M50
A38
Shuthonger
Kinsham
Dumbleton
Wormington
Beckford
Alderton Hill
205
Laverton
B4079
B4078
Broadway Tower
B4080
316
Northway
A46
Great Washbourne
Isbourne
B4632
Snowshill Manor
Bushley
Stanton
Snowshill Lavender
Cotswolds
A438
11
Aston Cross
Alderton
Snowshill
Newtown
9
Teddington
Toddington
Gloucestershire Warwickshire Steam Railway
Tewkesbury
Ashchurch
A435
Stanway
Abbey
Walton Cardiff
Alstone
B4077
Stanway House
1471
Fiddington
Oxenton
B4632
Odda's Chapel
Dixton
Didbrook
Deerhurst
M5
Greet
Hayles Abbey Halt
Cutsdean
Gretton
63
Hailes
64
Gotherington
Ford
274
Winchcombe Pottery
Stoke Orchard
Bishop's Cleeve
Langley Hill
Winchcombe
Farmcote
B4077
279
Sudeley Castle
0 1 2 3 miles
0 1 2 3 4 5 km

Baddesley Clinton
Wroxall
Kingswood
Lapworth
Beausale
Kenilworth
National Agricultural Centre
Ryton Pools
Stretton-on-Dunsmore
Ashow
Stareton
Princethorpe
97
Rowington
A4177
A452
Weston under Wetherley
Wappenbury
Frankton
Draycote
Marton
Leek Wootton
Eathorpe
B4453
Birdingbury
Lowsonford
M40
Shrewley
Old Milverton
Cubbington
Hunningham
Haseley
Hatton Country World
Lillington
Leamington Hastings
A46
Hatton
Milverton
Royal Leamington Spa
A423
A426
Henley-in-Arden
Preston Bagot
Budbrooke
P&R
Jephson Gardens
Offchurch
Claverdon
Hampton on the Hill
St Mary's
Warwick Castle
Long Itchington
A4189
Warwick
Grand Union Canal
Radford Semele
Stockton
Wootton Wawen
Longbridge
Bascote
Langley
Norton Lindsey
Whitnash
Edstone
A425
Southam
Wolverton
Ufton
Heath End
Sherbourne
Bishop's Tachbrook
Bearley
Barford
Chapel Green
Harbury
82
Snitterfield
Chesterton Windmill
Ladbroke
A3400
Wasperton
Chesterton
Warwick Services
Wilmcote
Ingon
Hampton Lucy
Newbold Pacey
Ashorne
Marston Doles
Bishopton
Stratford-upon-Avon
Cross Green
Bishop's Itchington
Alveston
Moreton Morrell
Charlecote Park
Charlecote
B4100
Priors Hardwick
Shakespeare's Birthplace
Tiddington
B4086
Wellesbourne
M40
Shottery
Anne Hathaway's Cottage
Lighthorne
British Motor Museum
Knightcote
Oxford Canal
Stratford-upon-Avon
Wellesbourne Watermill
Gaydon
A423
Stratford
Compton Verney
Chadshunt
Avon
Walton
Northend
Burton Dassett Hills
Loxley
Clifford Chambers
A429
B4455
Temple Herdewyke
Fenny Compton
Combrook
Kineton
Atherstone on Stour
Ailstone
Burton Dassett
A422
Little Kineton
Claydon
Preston on Stour
Butlers Marston
Avon Dassett
Farnborough
Ettington
Radway
Wimpstone
Alderminster
Warmington
Lower Quinton
Pillerton Hersey
Mollington
Stour
Pillerton Priors
Edge Hill
Ratley
Newbold on Stour
Upper Quinton
Admington
Oxhill
Cropredy
Halford
Upton House
Shotteswell
Meon Hill
Armscote
Lower Tysoe
Hornton
Idlicote
Whatcote
Middle Tysoe
Kiftsgate Court Garden
Ilmington
Blackwell
Upper Tysoe
Horley
Hidcote Manor Garden
Tredington
Honington Hall
Alkerton
Hanwell
Hidcote Boyce
Darlingscott
Honington
Shenington
Wroxton
Drayton
Shipston-on-Stour
Winderton
Balscote
Neithrop
Ebrington
Barcheston
Upper Brailes
Epwell
Shutford
Banbury
Charingworth
B4035
Willington
Lower Brailes
North Newington
Easington
Chipping Campden
Stretton-on-Fosse
Tidmington
Sibford Gower
Swalcliffe Barn
Broughton Castle
Paxford
Burmington
Sutton under Brailes
Swalcliffe
Tadmarton
Broughton
Bodicote
Sibford Ferris
Sor Brook
Todenham
Cherington
Stourton
Aston Magna
Bloxham
West Adderbury
Draycott
Little Wolford
Lower Lemington
Ascott
Milcombe
Milton
Arboretum
Batsford
Falconry Ctr
Great Wolford
Whichford
Hook Norton Brewery Visitors Centre
Barford St John
Bourton on the Hill
Moreton-in-Marsh
Barton on the Heath
Long Compton
Hook Norton
Wigginton
South Newington
Barford St Michael
Sezincote
Wellington Aviation Museum
Great Rollright
Swerford
Hempton
Little Compton
Chastleton House
Nether Worton
Rollright Stones
64
65
Evenlode
A44
Great Tew
Over Worton
Chastleton
Salford
Over Norton
A361
Little Tew
Donnington

Bourton on Dunsmore
Thurlaston
Dunchurch
Kilsby
Crick
West Haddon
Coton
COTON MANOR
Ravensthorpe
Res.
M45
Barby
98
Frankton
Draycote
Draycote Water
DRAYCOTE WATER
Marton
Kites Hardwick
Birdingbury
Leam
A45
Watford
WATFORD GAP SERVICES
B5385
East Haddon
Holdenby
Ashby St Ledgers
A361
Woolscott
Long Buckby
Leamington Hastings
Willoughby
A423
A426
Grandborough
Braunston
Welton
A5
M1
Broadwell
Sawbridge
Great Brington
Long Itchington
Stockton
Nethercote
DAVENTRY
Daventry Res.
Whilton
Little Brington
Flecknoe
Lower Shuckburgh
Norton
Brockhall
Nobottle
Southam
A425
Napton on the Hill
Staverton
DAVENTRY MUS
Daventry
Harpole
Dodford
Flore
141
Chapel Green
81
Upper Catesby
B4037
A45
Upper Weedon
Newnham
Badby
Upper Heyford
Nether Heyford
Ladbroke
Nene
Weedon Bec
Church Stowe
Marston Doles
Hellidon
Everdon
Bishop's Itchington
Priors Marston
OLD DAIRY FARM COUNTRY SHOPPING & CRAFT CENTRE
Upper Stowe
Priors Hardwick
Charwelton
222
Oxford Canal
Preston Capes
Farthingstone
Litchborough
Pattishall
Grimscote
A423
Wormleighton
Upper Boddington
Byfield
Cold Higham
Maidford
BURTON DASSETT HILLS
Boddington Reservoir
Hinton
Woodford Halse
Fenny Compton
Lower Boddington
203
Burton Dassett
CANONS ASHBY HOUSE
Adstone
Blakesley
Duncote
Aston le Walls
Eydon
Canons Ashby
Claydon
Avon Dassett
Farnborough
FARNBOROUGH HALL
Moreton Pinkney
Cherwell
Woodend
Greens Norton
Chipping Warden
CATANGER LLAMA TREKKING
Woodend Green
Bradden
Warmington
Mollington
Weston
Slapton
1469
Culworth
182
Cropredy
1644
Wardington
Weedon Lois
Abthorpe
Shotteswell
A361
Upper Wardington
Sulgrave
SULGRAVE MANOR
Wappenham
Great Bourton
B4100
Williamscott
Thorpe Mandeville
Horley
Silverstone
A413
Hanwell
Chacombe
Helmdon
Middleton Cheney
Marston St Lawrence
B4525
SILVERSTONE
A422
Wroxton
Greatworth
Syresham
A43
Drayton
Thenford
Balscote
Neithrop
Grimsbury
Overthorpe
Crowfield
Halse
Radstone
Banbury
Warkworth
A422
Biddlesden
Whitfield
North Newington
Farthinghoe
Easington
BROUGHTON CASTLE
Tadmarton
Broughton
M40
Turweston
Dadford
STOWE SCHOOL AND GARDENS
Upper Astrop
Bodicote
Sor Brook
A4260
Brackley
Newbottle
Shalstone
Bloxham
West Adderbury
Astrop
Hinton-in-the-Hedges
A422
Buffler's Holt
King's Sutton
Charlton
Great Ouse
Westbury
East Adderbury
Milcombe
Milton
Evenley
Water Stratford
Radclive
Barford St John
B4100
Croughton
A43
Mixbury
A421
Finmere
B4031
Barford St Michael
Aynho
Tingewick
South Newington
Clifton
Souldern
Cottisford
A4421
Barton Hartshorn
B4031
Hempton
Deddington
Newton Purcell
Nether Worton
North Aston
65
Fritwell
B4100
Baynard's Green
Hardwick
Hethe
Chetwode
66
Preston Bissett
Somerton
Fewcott
Stoke Lyne
Fringford
0 1 2 3 miles
0 1 2 3 4 5 km

Northampton
Wellingborough
Irthlingborough
Higham Ferrers
Rushden
Milton Keynes
Newport Pagnell
Olney
Bletchley
Wolverton
Stony Stratford
Cranfield
Finedon
Walgrave
Hannington
Little Harrowden
Great Harrowden
Hardwick
Holcot
Brixworth
Spratton
Pitsford Reservoir
Pitsford
Sywell
Mears Ashby
Moulton
Overstone
Sywell Reservoir
Wilby
Boughton
Boothville
Harlestone
Kingsthorpe
Kingsley Park
Queen's Park
Weston Favell
Ecton
Earls Barton
Great Billing
Little Billing
New Barton
Great Doddington
Little Irchester
Irchester
Knuston
Little Wymington
Wymington
Newton Bromswold
Chelveston
Caldecott
Warmonds Hill
Farndish
Podington
Souldrop
Wollaston
Strixton
Hinwick
Santa Pod Raceway
Sharnbrook
Whiston
Grendon
Cogenhoe
Little Houghton
Brafield-on-the-Green
Castle Ashby
Bozeat
Easton Maudit
Great Houghton
Denton
Yardley Hastings
Odell
Harrold
Felmersham
Chellington
Pavenham
Carlton
Hardingstone
Wootton
Collingtree
Milton Malsor
Hackleton
Yardley Chase
Quinton
Piddington
Horton
Warrington
Lavendon
Cold Brayfield
West End
Stevington
Oakley
Blisworth
Courteenhall
Salcey Forest
Roade
Grand Union Canal
Eakley Lanes
Weston Underwood
Turvey
Bromham
Clifton Reynes
Newton Blossomville
Hartwell
Ravenstone
Emberton
Stoke Bruerne
Ashton
Stoke Goldington
Towcester
Box End
Stagsden
Long Street
Filgrave
Tyringham
Alderton
Grafton Regis
Hanslope
Tathall End
Gayhurst
Sherington
Hardmead
Astwood
Chicheley
Chicheley Hall
North Crawley
Paulerspury
Yardley Gobion
Castlethorpe
Lathbury
Bourne End
Upper Shelton
Potterspury
Haversham
Broad Green
Lower Shelton
Great Linford
Gullivers Land
Cosgrove
New Bradwell
Willen
Moulsoe
Whittlewood Forest
Old Stratford
Marston Moretaine
Deanshanger
Passenham
Bradwell
Broughton
Salford
Lidlington
Wicken
Calverton
Woolstone
Milton Keynes Village
Leckhampstead
Upper Weald
Woughton-on-the-Green
Brogborough
Beachampton
Loughton
Shenley Church End
Simpson
Walton
Wavendon
Aspley Guise
Thornton
Shenley Brook End
Woburn Sands
Bow Brickhill
Aspley Heath
Ridgmont
Husborne Crawley
Woburn Safari Park
Whaddon
Nash
Fenny Stratford
Woburn
Eversholt
Church End
Woburn Abbey
Tattenhoe
Bletchley Park
Far Bletchley
Thornborough
Singleborough
Little Brickhill
Great Brickhill
Padbury
Adstock
Great Horwood
Little Horwood
Newton Longville
Milton Bryan
Potsgrove
Battlesden
Toddington
Tingrith
Addington
Drayton Parslow
Stoke Hammond
Mursley
Whaddon Chase
Great Ouse
Ouse
Tove
A508
A43
A45
A509
A428
A5
A422
A421
A4146
A6
A5076
A5123
A4500
A510
A5199
A413
A507
M1
B526
B5388
B565
B4034
B4033
B5704
B571
B574
99
84
66
67
SP

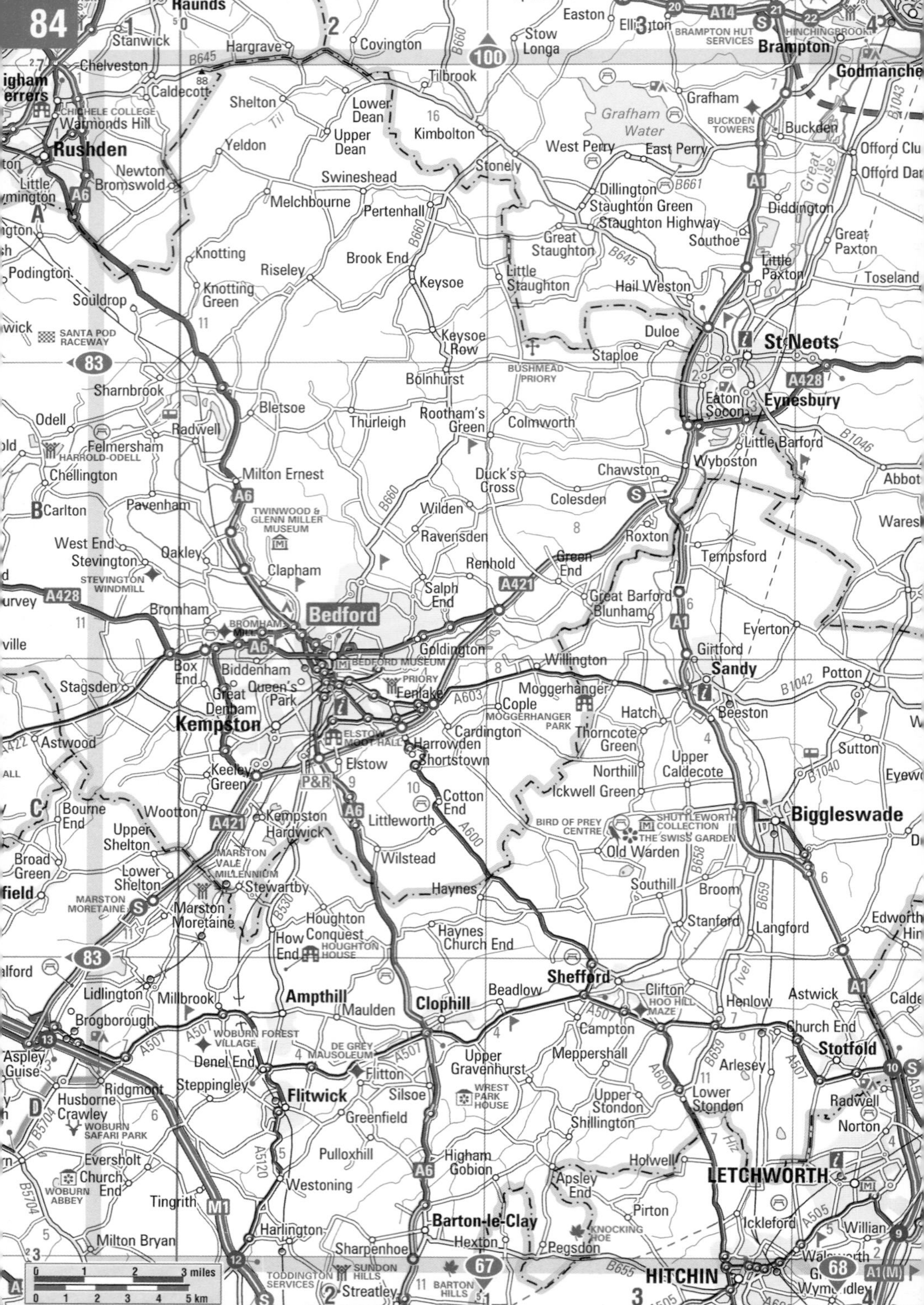
Raunds
Stanwick
Hargrave
Covington
Easton
Ellington
Stow Longa
Brampton
Godmanchester
BRAMPTON HUT SERVICES
HINCHINGBROOKE
A14
100
Chelveston
Higham Ferrers
Caldecott
Tilbrook
Shelton
Lower Dean
Upper Dean
Kimbolton
Grafham
Grafham Water
BUCKDEN TOWERS
Buckden
CHICHELE COLLEGE
Wymington
Rushden
Yeldon
Newton Bromswold
West Perry
East Perry
Offord Cluny
Offord Darcy
Great Ouse
Little Irchester
Swineshead
Melchbourne
Pertenhall
Stonely
Dillington
B661
Staughton Green
Staughton Highway
Diddington
Southoe
Great Paxton
Great Staughton
B645
Podington
Knotting
Riseley
Brook End
Keysoe
Little Staughton
Hail Weston
Little Paxton
Toseland
Souldrop
Knotting Green
SANTA POD RACEWAY
Keysoe Row
Duloe
Staploe
St Neots
83
Sharnbrook
Bolnhurst
BUSHMEAD PRIORY
A428
Eaton Socon
Eynesbury
Odell
Bletsoe
Radwell
Thurleigh
Rootham's Green
Colmworth
Little Barford
B1046
Felmersham
HARROLD-ODELL
Chellington
Milton Ernest
Duck's Cross
Chawston
Wyboston
Abbotsley
Carlton
Pavenham
A6
TWINWOOD & GLENN MILLER MUSEUM
Wilden
Colesden
West End
Stevington
Oakley
Ravensden
Roxton
Tempsford
Waresley
STEVINGTON WINDMILL
Clapham
Renhold
Green End
Salph End
A421
Great Barford
Blunham
Turvey
Bromham
Bedford
BROMHAM MILL
Goldington
Everton
Gamlingay
Box End
Biddenham
BEDFORD MUSEUM
Willington
Girtford
Sandy
Potton
Stagsden
Queen's Park
PRIORY
Fenlake
Moggerhanger
Great Denham
Kempston
Cople
MOGGERHANGER PARK
Hatch
Beeston
B1042
Astwood
ELSTOW MOOT HALL
Cardington
Thorncote Green
Harrowden
Shortstown
Elstow
Upper Caldecote
Sutton
Northill
Keeley Green
P&R
Cotton End
Ickwell Green
B1040
Eyeworth
Bourne End
Wootton
Kempston Hardwick
Littleworth
BIRD OF PREY CENTRE
SHUTTLEWORTH COLLECTION
THE SWISS GARDEN
Biggleswade
Upper Shelton
Old Warden
MARSTON VALE MILLENNIUM
Wilstead
Broad Green
Lower Shelton
Southill
Broom
B658
B659
Cranfield
MARSTON MORETAINE
Stewartby
Haynes
Marston Moretaine
B530
Houghton Conquest
Stanford
Langford
Edworth
How End
HOUGHTON HOUSE
Haynes Church End
Salford
Lidlington
Millbrook
Ampthill
Maulden
Clophill
Beadlow
Shefford
Clifton
Henlow
Astwick
Brogborough
HOO HILL MAZE
Ivel
WOBURN FOREST VILLAGE
A507
Campton
Church End
Stotfold
Aspley Guise
DE GREY MAUSOLEUM
Upper Gravenhurst
Meppershall
Arlesey
Denel End
Flitton
Ridgmont
Steppingley
Flitwick
Silsoe
WREST PARK HOUSE
Upper Stondon
Lower Stondon
Radwell
Husborne Crawley
Greenfield
Shillington
Norton
WOBURN SAFARI PARK
B5704
Eversholt
Pulloxhill
Higham Gobion
Holwell
LETCHWORTH
Church End
WOBURN ABBEY
A5120
Westoning
Apsley End
Tingrith
M1
Pirton
Harlington
Barton-le-Clay
KNOCKING HOE
Ickleford
A505
Willian
Milton Bryan
Hexton
Pegsdon
Sharpenhoe
Walsworth
67
68
TODDINGTON SERVICES
SUNDON HILLS
BARTON HILLS
B655
HITCHIN
Great Wymondley
Streatley
A1(M)
A1
A600
A603
A5
3 miles
5 km

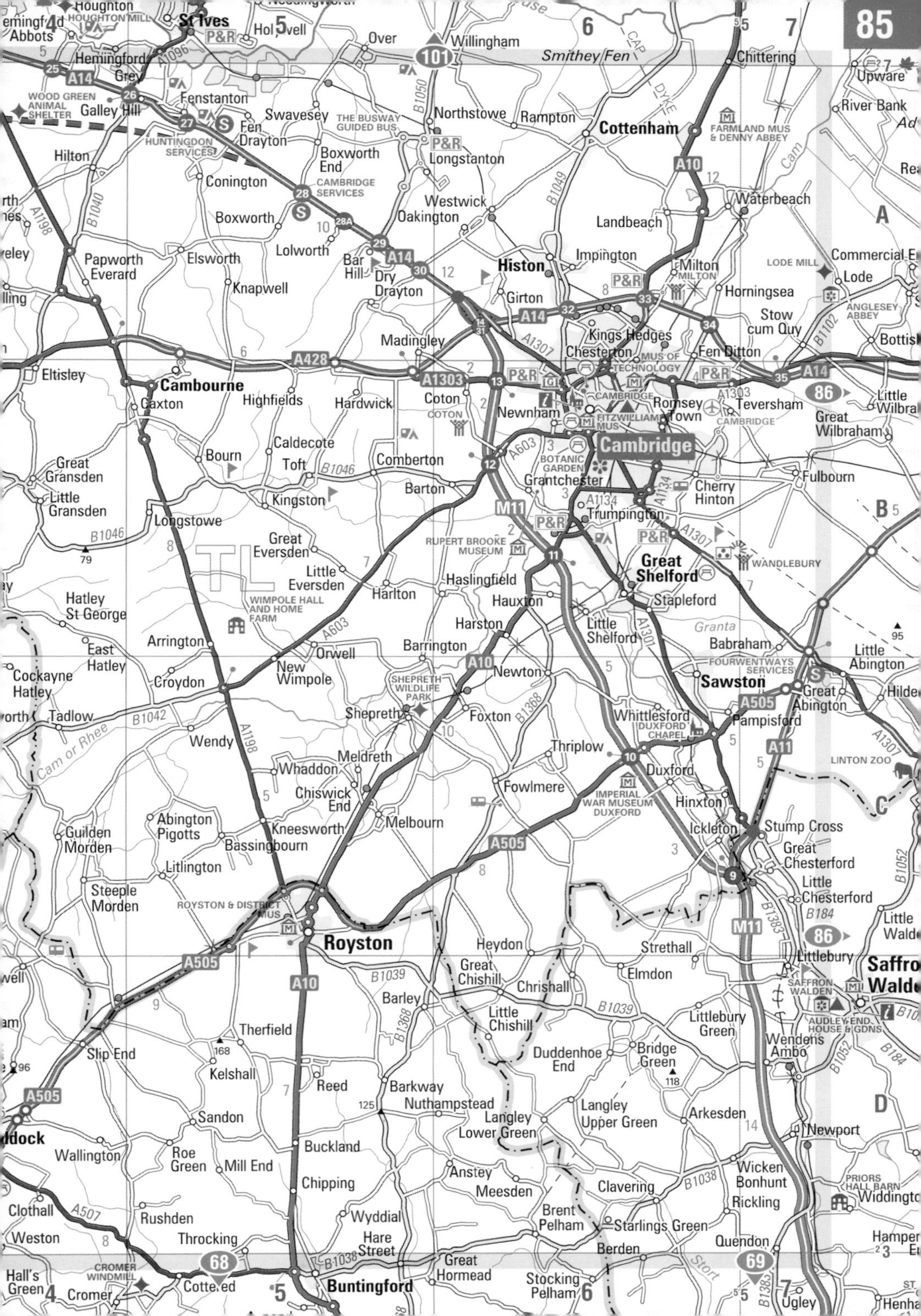
Houghton
Hemingford Abbots
HOUGHTON MILL
St Ives
P&R
Holywell
Over
Willingham
101
Smithey Fen
CAR DYKE
Chittering
Upware
Hemingford Grey
A1096
A14
25
26
27
28
28A
29
30
WOOD GREEN ANIMAL SHELTER
Galley Hill
Fenstanton
Fen Drayton
Swavesey
THE BUSWAY GUIDED BUS
B1050
Northstowe
Rampton
Cottenham
A10
FARMLAND MUS & DENNY ABBEY
River Bank
HUNTINGDON SERVICES
Hilton
Boxworth End
Longstanton
Conington
CAMBRIDGE SERVICES
Westwick
Oakington
B1049
Waterbeach
Landbeach
Cam
A1198
B1040
Boxworth
Lolworth
Bar Hill
Dry Drayton
Histon
Impington
Milton
MILTON
Horningsea
LODE MILL
Commercial End
Lode
ANGLESEY ABBEY
Papworth Everard
Elsworth
Knapwell
Girton
32
33
34
Stow cum Quy
B1102
Bottisham
Madingley
14/31
A1307
Kings Hedges
Chesterton
MUS OF TECHNOLOGY
Fen Ditton
A428
Eltisley
Cambourne
Caxton
A1303
13
CAMBRIDGE
Romsey Town
Teversham
35
86
Little Wilbraham
Great Wilbraham
Highfields
Hardwick
Coton
COTON
Newnham
FITZWILLIAM MUS
CAMBRIDGE
Cambridge
A603
BOTANIC GARDEN
Caldecote
Bourn
Toft
B1046
Comberton
12
Great Gransden
Little Gransden
Barton
Grantchester
A1134
Cherry Hinton
Fulbourn
Kingston
Longstowe
M11
Trumpington
B1046
79
TL
Great Eversden
RUPERT BROOKE MUSEUM
Little Eversden
Harlton
Haslingfield
Hauxton
11
Great Shelford
WANDLEBURY
Stapleford
Hatley St George
WIMPOLE HALL AND HOME FARM
Arrington
East Hatley
Cockayne Hatley
Croydon
Orwell
New Wimpole
Barrington
Harston
Little Shelford
A1301
Granta
Babraham
95
Little Abington
Newton
FOURWENTWAYS SERVICES
Sawston
Great Abington
Hildersham
Tadlow
B1042
Wendy
SHEPRETH WILDLIFE PARK
Shepreth
Foxton
B1368
Whittlesford
DUXFORD CHAPEL
A505
Pampisford
A11
Cam or Rhee
Meldreth
Whaddon
Thriplow
10
Duxford
LINTON ZOO
Chiswick End
Fowlmere
IMPERIAL WAR MUSEUM DUXFORD
Hinxton
Guilden Morden
Abington Pigotts
Kneesworth
Melbourn
Bassingbourn
Ickleton
Stump Cross
Great Chesterford
Litlington
Steeple Morden
ROYSTON & DISTRICT MUS
Royston
9
Little Chesterford
B1383
B184
B1052
Little Walden
Heydon
Strethall
Littlebury
Saffron Walden
SAFFRON WALDEN
Great Chishill
Chrishall
Elmdon
B1039
Barley
Little Chishill
Littlebury Green
AUDLEY END HOUSE & GDNS
Therfield
168
Slip End
Kelshall
Duddenhoe End
Bridge Green
118
Wendens Ambo
Reed
Barkway
125
Nuthampstead
Langley Lower Green
Langley Upper Green
Arkesden
Sandon
Baldock
Wallington
Roe Green
Mill End
Buckland
Anstey
Newport
Meesden
Clavering
B1038
Wicken Bonhunt
PRIORS HALL BARN
Widdington
Clothall
A507
Chipping
Rickling
Rushden
Wyddial
Brent Pelham
Starlings Green
Weston
Throcking
Hare Street
Quendon
Berden
Hamperden End
CROMER WINDMILL
68
Great Hormead
Stocking Pelham
Stort
69
Hall's Green
Cromer
Cottered
Buntingford
Ugley
Henham

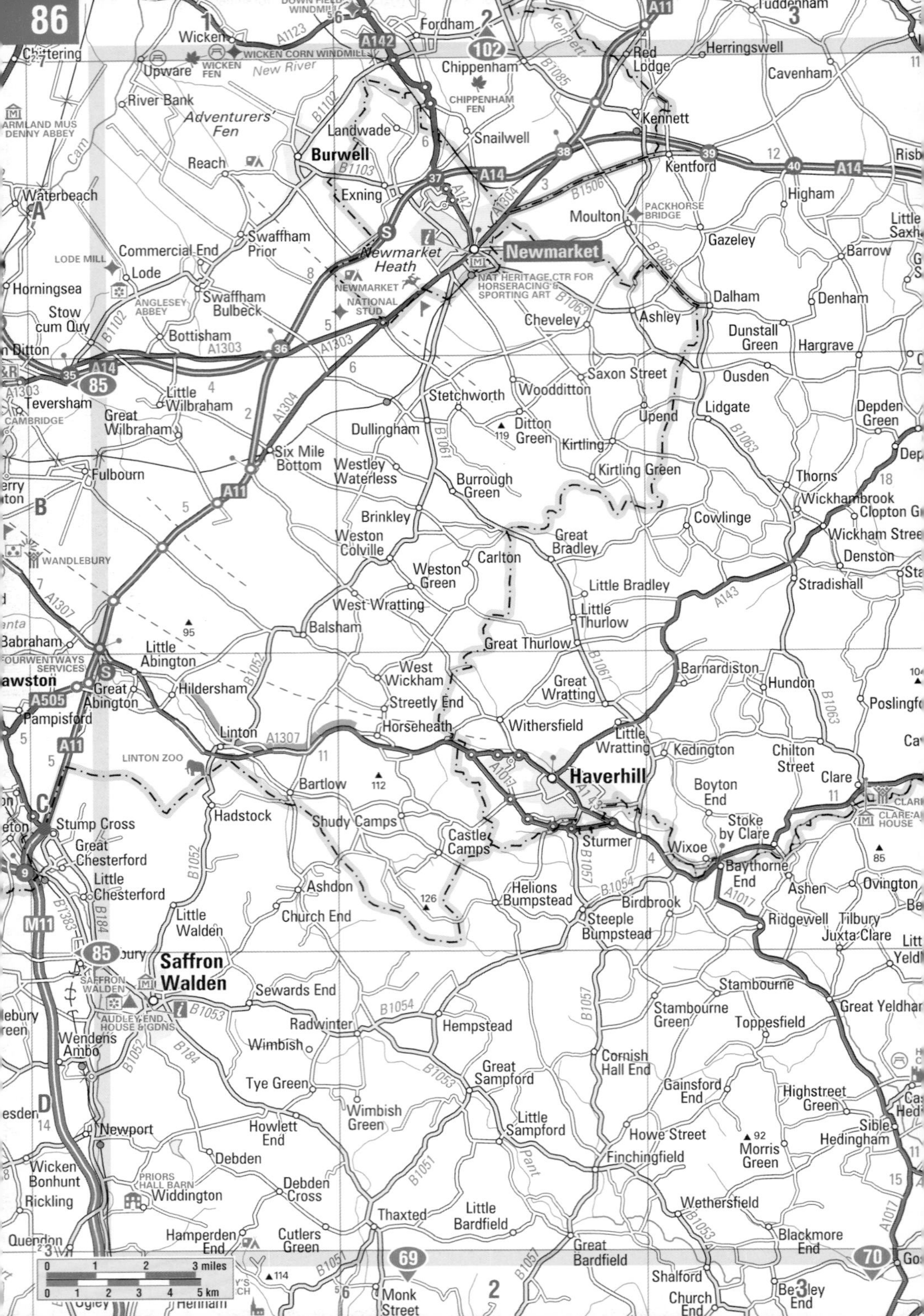
Wicken
Chittering
Upware
WICKEN CORN WINDMILL
New River
Fordham
Tuddenham
Red Lodge
Herringswell
Chippenham
CHIPPENHAM FEN
Cavenham
River Bank
Adventurers' Fen
Landwade
Kennett
Snailwell
Burwell
Reach
Kentford
Exning
Waterbeach
Higham
Moulton
PACKHORSE BRIDGE
Swaffham Prior
Newmarket
Newmarket Heath
Commercial End
Lode
LODE MILL
Horningsea
Gazeley
Barrow
NAT HERITAGE CTR FOR HORSERACING & SPORTING ART
NEWMARKET NATIONAL STUD
Dalham
Denham
Swaffham Bulbeck
ANGLESEY ABBEY
Stow cum Quy
Ashley
Cheveley
Dunstall Green
Hargrave
Bottisham
Ditton
Saxon Street
Ousden
Teversham
Little Wilbraham
Great Wilbraham
Stetchworth
Wooditton
Lidgate
Depden Green
Upend
Dullingham
Ditton Green
Kirtling
Six Mile Bottom
Fulbourn
Westley Waterless
Burrough Green
Kirtling Green
Thorns
Wickhambrook
Clopton Green
Brinkley
Cowlinge
Weston Colville
Great Bradley
Wickham Street
Carlton
Weston Green
Denston
WANDLEBURY
Stradishall
Little Bradley
West Wratting
Little Thurlow
Balsham
Babraham
Great Thurlow
Little Abington
FOURWENTWAYS SERVICES
West Wickham
Barnardiston
Hundon
Great Abington
Hildersham
Great Wratting
Poslingford
Pampisford
Streetly End
Horseheath
Withersfield
Linton
Little Wratting
Kedington
Chilton Street
Clare
LINTON ZOO
Haverhill
Boyton End
Bartlow
Hadstock
Stoke by Clare
Stump Cross
Shudy Camps
Castle Camps
CLARE
Great Chesterford
Sturmer
Wixoe
Baythorne End
Little Chesterford
Ashdon
Helions Bumpstead
Ashen
Ovington
Birdbrook
Church End
Steeple Bumpstead
Little Walden
Ridgewell
Tilbury Juxta Clare
Saffron Walden
SAFFRON WALDEN
Sewards End
Stambourne
AUDLEY END HOUSE & GDNS
Radwinter
Hempstead
Stambourne Green
Toppesfield
Great Yeldham
Wendens Ambo
Wimbish
Cornish Hall End
Tye Green
Great Sampford
Gainsford End
Highstreet Green
Wimbish Green
Newport
Howlett End
Little Sampford
Sible Hedingham
Howe Street
Morris Green
Debden
Finchingfield
Wicken Bonhunt
PRIORS HALL BARN
Widdington
Debden Cross
Rickling
Wethersfield
Thaxted
Little Bardfield
Quendon
Hamperden End
Cutlers Green
Blackmore End
Great Bardfield
Shalford
Monk Street
Church End
Beazley End
A11
A14
A142
A1304
A1303
A1307
A143
A1017
A505
M11
B1085
B1506
B1063
B1061
B1052
B1053
B1054
B1057
B1051
B1383
B184
B1102
B1103
0 1 2 3 miles
0 1 2 3 4 5 km

Bury St Edmunds
Stowmarket
Needham Market
Sudbury
Hadleigh
Halstead
Capel St Mary
East Bergholt
Lawford
Lavenham
Long Melford
Ixworth
Woolpit
Elmswell
Haughley
Nayland
Dedham
Bures
DEDHAM VALE
A14
A134
A143
A1141
A1071
A131
A12
A120
88
70
71
103

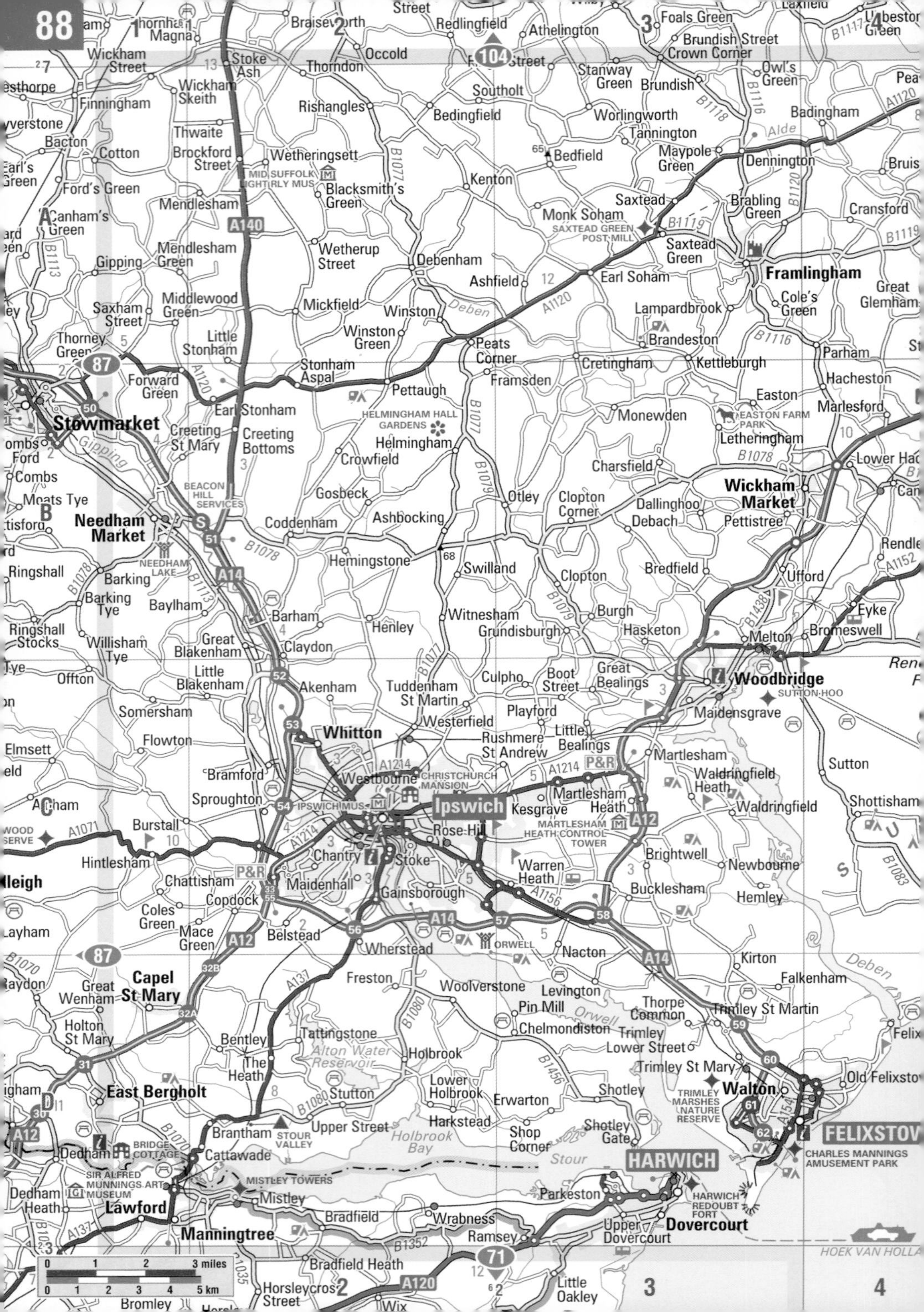
1
Thornham Magna
2
Braiseworth
Redlingfield
Athelington
3
Foals Green
4
Ubbeston Green
Wickham Street
Stoke Ash
Occold
104
Brundish Street
Crown Corner
Thorndon
Stanway Green
Brundish
Owl's Green
Westhorpe
Wickham Skeith
Southolt
Finningham
Rishangles
Bedingfield
Worlingworth
Badingham
Wyverstone
Thwaite
Tannington
Alde
Bacton
Cotton
Brockford Street
Wetheringsett
Bedfield
Maypole Green
Dennington
Bruisyard
Earl's Green
MID SUFFOLK LIGHT RLY MUS
Ford's Green
Blacksmith's Green
Kenton
Mendlesham
Saxtead
Brabling Green
Cransford
A
Canham's Green
A140
Monk Soham
SAXTEAD GREEN POST MILL
B1119
Saxtead Green
B1113
Mendlesham Green
Wetherup Street
Debenham
Framlingham
Gipping
Ashfield
Earl Soham
Great Glemham
Middlewood Green
Saxham Street
Mickfield
Winston
Deben
A1120
Lampardbrook
Cole's Green
Thorney Green
Little Stonham
Winston Green
Peats Corner
Brandeston
B1116
Parham
87
Forward Green
Stonham Aspal
Cretingham
Kettleburgh
Framsden
Hacheston
Pettaugh
Easton
Stowmarket
50
Earl Stonham
HELMINGHAM HALL GARDENS
Monewden
EASTON FARM PARK
Marlesford
Creeting St Mary
Creeting Bottoms
Helmingham
Letheringham
Combs Ford
Gipping
Crowfield
B1078
Combs
B1077
B1079
Charsfield
Lower Hacheston
BEACON HILL SERVICES
Wickham Market
Moats Tye
Gosbeck
Otley
Clopton Corner
Dallinghoo
Campsea Ashe
B
Needham Market
Coddenham
Ashbocking
Debach
Pettistree
51
Hemingstone
Rendlesham
Ringshall
NEEDHAM LAKE
Barking
A14
Swilland
Clopton
Bredfield
Ufford
A1152
Barking Tye
Baylham
Witnesham
Burgh
Eyke
Ringshall Stocks
Willisham Tye
Barham
Henley
Grundisburgh
Hasketon
Melton
Bromeswell
Great Blakenham
Claydon
Offton
Little Blakenham
52
Akenham
Tuddenham St Martin
Culpho
Boot Street
Great Bealings
Woodbridge
SUTTON HOO
Somersham
53
Whitton
Westerfield
Playford
Maidensgrave
Flowton
Rushmere St Andrew
Little Bealings
Elmsett
Martlesham
Sutton
Bramford
Westbourne
CHRISTCHURCH MANSION
A1214
P&R
Waldringfield Heath
Sproughton
IPSWICH MUS
Ipswich
Martlesham Heath
Waldringfield
Shottisham
C
Aldham
54
Kesgrave
A12
Burstall
Rose Hill
MARTLESHAM HEATH CONTROL TOWER
A1071
Hintlesham
Chantry
Stoke
Warren Heath
Brightwell
Newbourne
Hadleigh
Chattisham
Maidenhall
Gainsborough
Bucklesham
Hemley
Coles Green
Copdock
A1156
58
B1083
Layham
Mace Green
Belstead
56
57
Wherstead
ORWELL
Nacton
87
Kirton
Raydon
Capel St Mary
Great Wenham
A137
Freston
Woolverstone
Levington
Falkenham
Pin Mill
Orwell
Thorpe Common
Trimley St Martin
Holton St Mary
32A
32B
Chelmondiston
Trimley Lower Street
59
Felixstowe Ferry
Bentley
Tattingstone
Alton Water Reservoir
Holbrook
B1080
B1456
60
31
The Heath
Trimley St Mary
Old Felixstowe
Lower Holbrook
Shotley
TRIMLEY MARSHES NATURE RESERVE
Walton
East Bergholt
Stutton
Erwarton
61
D
30
Brantham
STOUR VALLEY
Upper Street
Harkstead
Shop Corner
Shotley Gate
62
FELIXSTOWE
BRIDGE COTTAGE
Dedham
Cattawade
Holbrook Bay
Stour
HARWICH
CHARLES MANNINGS AMUSEMENT PARK
SIR ALFRED MUNNINGS ART MUSEUM
MISTLEY TOWERS
Dedham Heath
Lawford
Mistley
Parkeston
HARWICH REDOUBT FORT
Bradfield
Wrabness
Manningtree
Upper Dovercourt
Dovercourt
Ramsey
B1352
HOEK VAN HOLLAND
71
Bradfield Heath
A120
Horsleycross Street
Little Oakley
Bromley
Wix
3
4
0 1 2 3 miles
0 1 2 3 4 5 km

Dunwich
Dunwich Forest
DUNWICH UNDERWATER EXPLORATION EXHIBITION
105
High Street
Hemp Green
Sibton
Darsham
Yoxford
Middleton Moor
Westleton
WESTLETON HEATH
MINSMERE RSPB NATURE RESERVE
Rotten End
A12
B1122
North Green
Middleton
Theberton
Curlew Green
Kelsale
Eastbridge
LEISTON ABBEY
B1121
Carlton
Saxmundham
B1119
Leiston
Sizewell
Knodishall
LONG SHOP MUS
Benhall Street
Sternfield
Aldringham
Benhall Green
Coldfair Green
B1069
B1353
Friston
Farnham
Thorpeness
Gromford
A1094
B1122
SNAPE MALTINGS
Snape
NORTH WARREN RSPB NATURE RESERVE
Blaxhall
Aldeburgh
Iken
Aldeburgh Bay
High Street
Tunstall
Tunstall Forest
B1078
Sudbourne
Alde
Chillesford
B1084
ORFORD CASTLE
Orford
Orford Ness
ORFORDNESS-HAVERGATE
Butley High Corner
Boyton
Hollesley Bay
Shingle Street
SUFFOLK COAST & HEATHS
TM
A
B
C
D
4
5
6
7

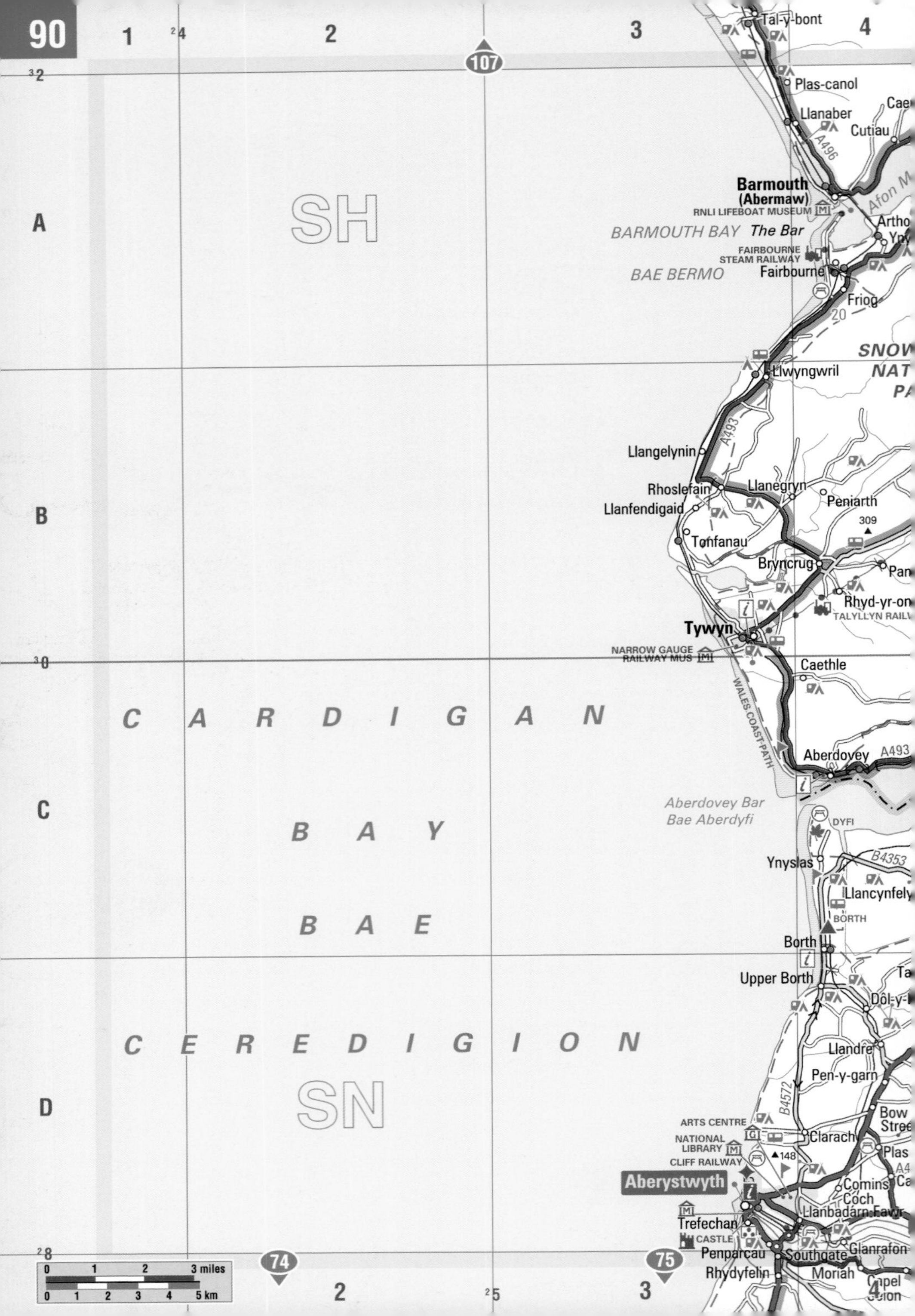
1
2
3
4
107
Tal-y-bont
Plas-canol
Llanaber
Cutiau
A496
Barmouth
(Abermaw)
RNLI LIFEBOAT MUSEUM
BARMOUTH BAY
The Bar
BAE BERMO
FAIRBOURNE
STEAM RAILWAY
Fairbourne
Friog
SNOW
NAT
Llwyngwril
A493
Llangelynin
Rhoslefain
Llanegryn
Llanfendigaid
Peniarth
309
Tonfanau
Bryncrug
Rhyd-yr-on
TALYLLYN RAILW
Tywyn
NARROW GAUGE
RAILWAY MUS
Caethle
WALES COAST PATH
Aberdovey
A493
SH
A
B
C
D
CARDIGAN
BAY
BAE
CEREDIGION
SN
Aberdovey Bar
Bae Aberdyfi
DYFI
Ynyslas
B4353
Llancynfely
BORTH
Borth
Upper Borth
Dôl-y-
Llandre
Pen-y-garn
B4572
ARTS CENTRE
NATIONAL
LIBRARY
CLIFF RAILWAY
Clarach
148
Bow
Stree
Plas
Aberystwyth
Comins
Coch
Llanbadarn Fawr
Trefechan
CASTLE
Penparcau
Southgate
Glanrafon
Rhydyfelin
Moriah
Capel
Seion
74
75
0
1
2
3 miles
3
4
5 km

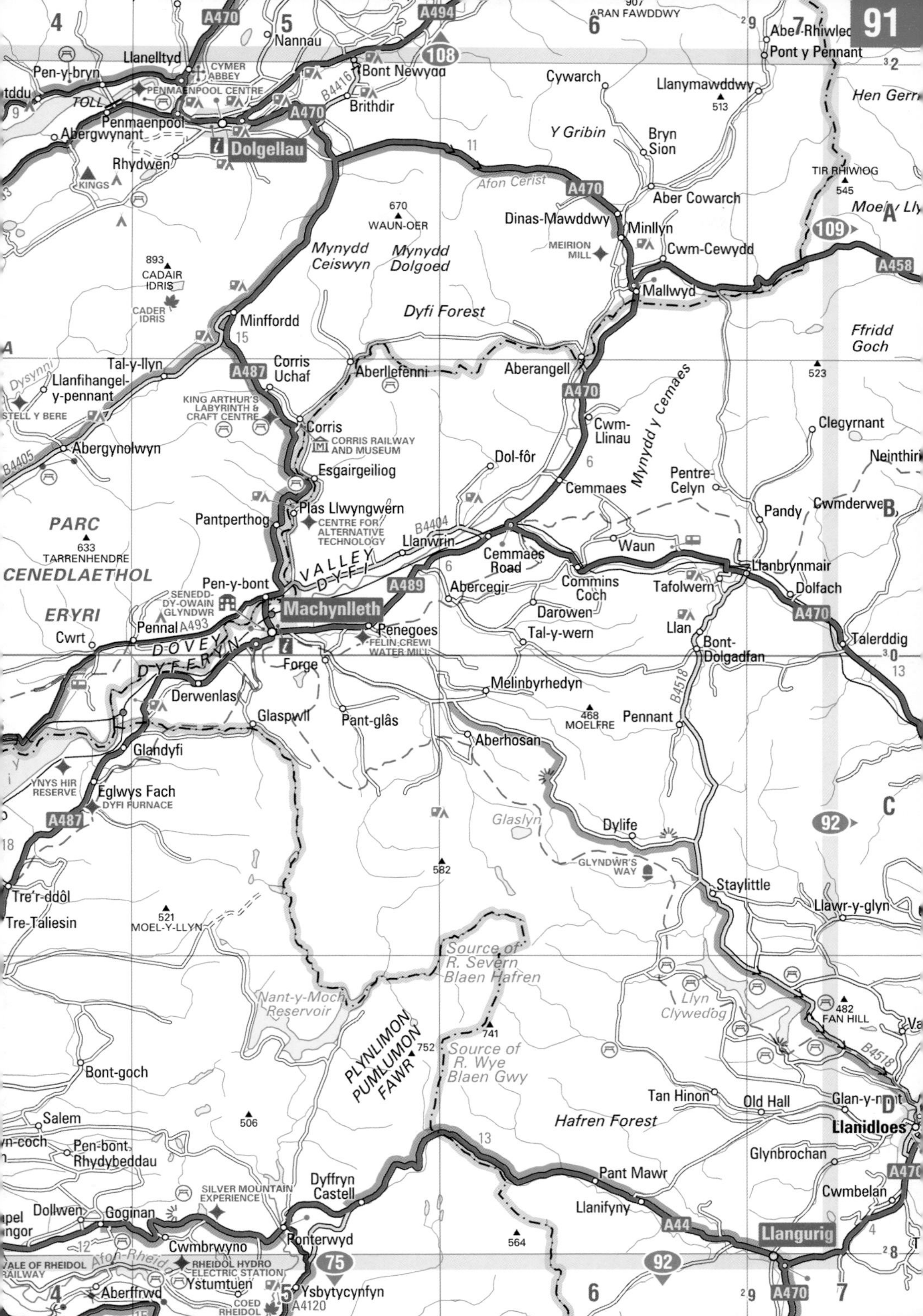

Nannau
Llanelltyd
Pen-y-bryn
CYMER ABBEY
PENMAENPOOL CENTRE
Bont Newydd
Brithdir
Penmaenpool
Abergwynant
Dolgellau
Rhydwen
KINGS
Cywarch
Llanymawddwy
Y Gribin
Bryn Sion
ARAN FAWDDWY
Abe-Rhiwlech
Pont y Pennant
Hen Gerr
TIR RHIWIOG
Aber Cowarch
Afon Cerist
WAUN-OER
Dinas-Mawddwy
Minllyn
MEIRION MILL
Cwm-Cewydd
Moel y Ll
Mallwyd
Mynydd Ceiswyn
Mynydd Dolgoed
CADAIR IDRIS
CADER IDRIS
Dyfi Forest
Minffordd
Ffridd Goch
Tal-y-llyn
Corris Uchaf
Aberllefenni
Aberangell
Dysynni
Llanfihangel-y-pennant
KING ARTHUR'S LABYRINTH & CRAFT CENTRE
CASTELL Y BERE
Corris
Mynydd y Cemaes
Cwm-Llinau
Clegyrnant
CORRIS RAILWAY AND MUSEUM
Abergynolwyn
Dol-fôr
Neinthirion
Esgairgeiliog
Pentre-Celyn
Cemmaes
Plas Llwyngwern
CENTRE FOR ALTERNATIVE TECHNOLOGY
Pantperthog
Pandy
Cwmderwen
PARC CENEDLAETHOL ERYRI
TARRENHENDRE
Llanwrin
DYFI VALLEY
Cemmaes Road
Waun
Llanbrynmair
Commins Coch
Tafolwern
Dolfach
Pen-y-bont
SENEDD-DY-OWAIN GLYNDWR
Machynlleth
Abercegir
Darowen
Pennal
Cwrt
Penegoes
FELIN CREWI WATER MILL
Tal-y-wern
Llan
Bont-Dolgadfan
Talerddig
DOVEY
DYFFRYN
Forge
Melinbyrhedyn
Derwenlas
Glaspwll
Pant-glâs
MOELFRE
Pennant
Aberhosan
Glandyfi
YNYS HIR RESERVE
Eglwys Fach
DYFI FURNACE
Glaslyn
Dylife
GLYNDWR'S WAY
Staylittle
Tre'r-ddôl
Tre-Taliesin
MOEL-Y-LLYN
Llawr-y-glyn
Source of R. Severn Blaen Hafren
Nant-y-Moch Reservoir
PLYNLIMON PUMLUMON FAWR
Llyn Clywedog
FAN HILL
Source of R. Wye Blaen Gwy
Bont-goch
Tan Hinon
Old Hall
Glan-y-nant
Salem
Hafren Forest
Llanidloes
Pen-bont Rhydybeddau
Glynbrochan
Dyffryn Castell
Pant Mawr
Cwmbelan
SILVER MOUNTAIN EXPERIENCE
Llanifyny
Dollwen
Goginan
Ponterwyd
Llangurig
Cwmbrwyno
VALE OF RHEIDOL RAILWAY
Afon Rheidol
RHEIDOL HYDRO ELECTRIC STATION
Ystumtuen
Ysbytycynfyn
Aberffrwd
COED RHEIDOL
A470
A494
A487
A489
A493
A458
A44
A4120
B4416
B4404
B4405
B4518
108
109
92
75

Dyfi Forest
Corris Uchaf
Aberllefenni
Aberangell
A470
SH
Cwm-Llinau
Mynydd y Cemaes
Corris
CORRIS RAILWAY AND MUSEUM
Dol-fôr
Esgairgeiliog
Cemmaes
Pentre-Celyn
Plas Llwyngwern
CENTRE FOR ALTERNATIVE TECHNOLOGY
B4404
Llanwrin
Cemmaes Road
Waun
Pandy
Cwmderwen
Llanbrynmair
DYFI VALLEY
A489
Abercegir
Commins Coch
Tafolwern
Dolfach
Machynlleth
Darowen
Llan
A470
Penegoes
FELIN CREWI WATER MILL
Tal-y-wern
Bont-Dolgadfan
Talerddig
Forge
Melinbyrhedyn
B4518
Pennant
468 MOELFRE
Pant-glâs
Aberhosan
91
Glaslyn
Dylife
GLYNDWR'S WAY
582
Staylittle
Source of R. Severn Blaen Hafren
Nant-y-Moch Reservoir
Llyn Clywedog
PLYNLIMON PUMLUMON FAWR
741
752
Source of R. Wye Blaen Gwy
SN
Tan Hinon
Hafren Forest
Old Hall
Ffridd Goch
523
Foel
109
Llangadfan
Llanerfyl
Pen Coed
GLYNDWR'S WAY
Clegyrnant
Dolwen
Sychtyn
Neinthirion
Melin-y-
Mynydd Waun Fawr
440
Rhyd
Carno
458
Clatter
398
Llanwnog
Caersws
Llawr-y-glyn
Gleiniant
B4569
Trefeglwys
482 FAN HILL
Van
Oakley Park
307
Severn (Hafren)
B4518
A470
Glan-y-nant
Llanidloes
Glynbrochan
Newchapel
Cwmbelan
GLYNDWR'S WAY
584
13
Dyffryn Castell
Pant Mawr
Llanifyny
A44
Llangurig
Tylwch
Ponterwyd
564
91
Ysbytycynfyn
A4120
75
Devil's Bridge
610 PEN Y GARN
Blaenycwm
Nantgwyn
B4518
Pant-y-dwr
A470
Cwmystwyth
B4574
Bwlch-y-sarnau
HAFOD ESTATE
498
Wye (Gwy)
St Harmon
Pont-rhyd-y-groes
571 GEIFAS
505 MOEL HYWEL
Ysbyty Ystwyth
Craig-goch Res.
76
0 1 2 3 miles
0 1 2 3 4 5 km
CLAERWEN
WELSH ROYAL CRYSTAL
Rhayader
Penygarreg Res.
Caufron

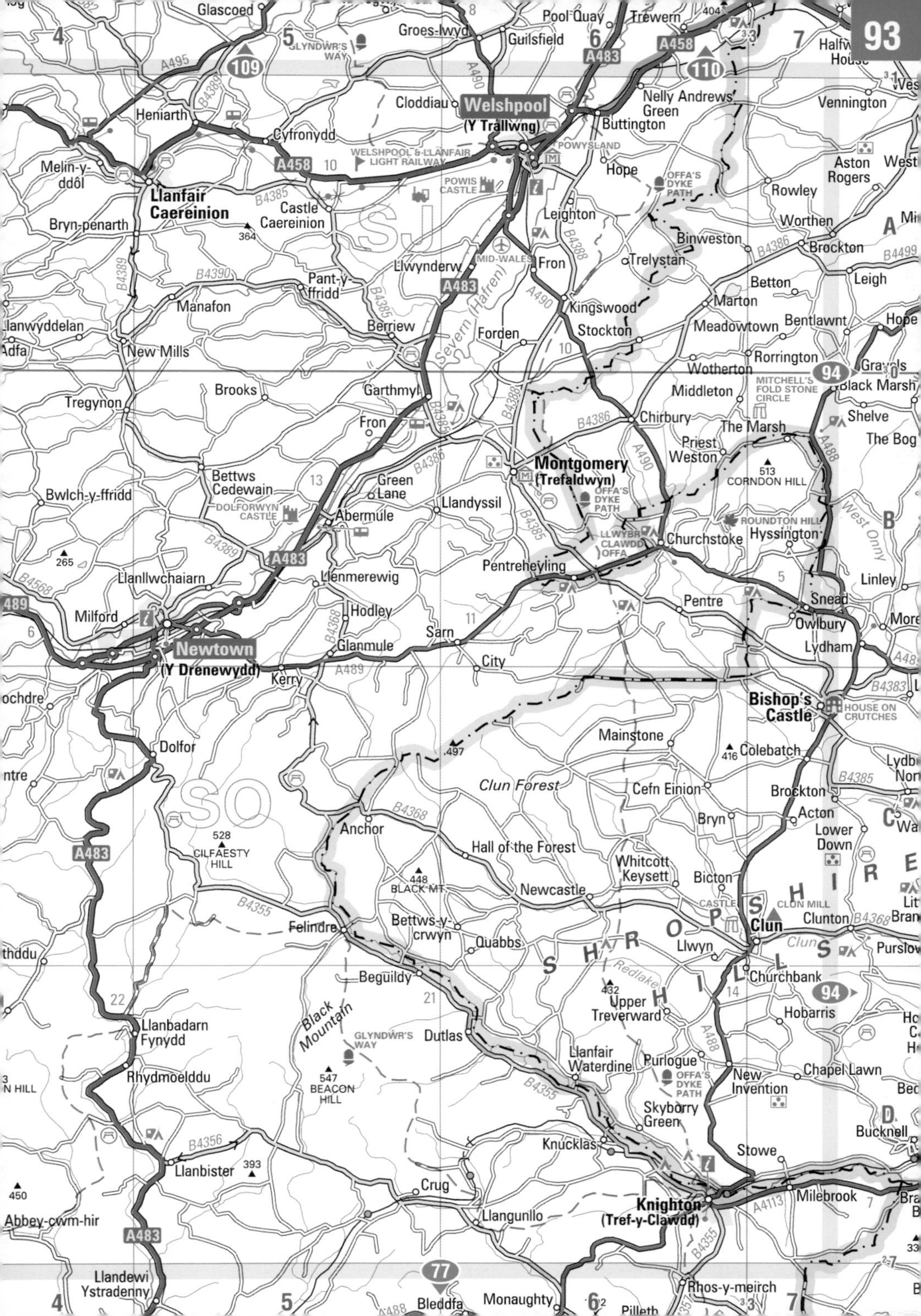

Glascoed
Groes-lwyd
Pool Quay
Trewern
Guilsfield
GLYNDWR'S WAY
109
110
A495
A458
A483
A490
Halfway House
Cloddiau
Welshpool
(Y Trallwng)
Nelly Andrews Green
Buttington
Vennington
Heniarth
Cyfronydd
Melin-y-ddôl
Llanfair Caereinion
WELSHPOOL & LLANFAIR LIGHT RAILWAY
POWYSLAND
Hope
OFFA'S DYKE PATH
Aston Rogers
Rowley
POWIS CASTLE
B4385
Castle Caereinion
Bryn-penarth
364
SJ
Leighton
Worthen
Brockton
Binweston
B4386
B4499
Trelystan
Fron
MID-WALES
Llwynderw
Pant-y-ffridd
B4390
B4389
B4388
Manafon
Betton
Leigh
Kingswood
Marton
Llanwyddelan
Adfa
New Mills
Berriew
Severn (Hafren)
Forden
Stockton
Meadowtown
Bentlawnt
Rorrington
Wotherton
94
Black Marsh
Brooks
Garthmyl
Middleton
MITCHELL'S FOLD STONE CIRCLE
Tregynon
Chirbury
Shelve
Fron
The Marsh
The Bog
Priest Weston
Montgomery
(Trefaldwyn)
513
CORNDON HILL
Bettws Cedewain
Green Lane
Llandyssil
Bwlch-y-ffridd
DOLFORWYN CASTLE
Abermule
ROUNDTON HILL
Hyssington
LLWYBR CLAWDD OFFA
Churchstoke
West Onny
265
A483
Pentreheyling
Llanllwchaiarn
Llanmerewig
Linley
Milford
Hodley
Pentre
Snead
Owlbury
B4568
Sarn
Lydham
Newtown
(Y Drenewydd)
Glanmule
City
Kerry
A489
B4368
B4383
Bishop's Castle
HOUSE ON CRUTCHES
Mainstone
Colebatch
416
Dolfor
497
Clun Forest
Cefn Einion
B4385
Brockton
Acton
Bryn
Anchor
SO
Lower Down
528
CILFAESTY HILL
Hall of the Forest
Whitcott Keysett
448
BLACK MT
Bicton
Newcastle
B4355
CASTLE
CLUN MILL
SHROPSHIRE
Clun
Clunton
B4368
Felindre
Bettws-y-crwyn
Quabbs
Llwyn
Purslow
Beguildy
Churchbank
Redlake
432
Upper Treverward
Hobarris
Black Mountain
Llanbadarn Fynydd
Dutlas
GLYNDWR'S WAY
Llanfair Waterdine
Purlogue
A488
Rhydmoelddu
547
BEACON HILL
New Invention
Chapel Lawn
Skyborry Green
B4356
Knucklas
Stowe
Bucknell
Llanbister
393
Crug
Milebrook
A4113
450
Knighton
(Tref-y-Clawdd)
Abbey-cwm-hir
Llangunllo
Llandewi Ystradenny
77
Bleddfa
Monaughty
Rhos-y-meirch
Pilleth

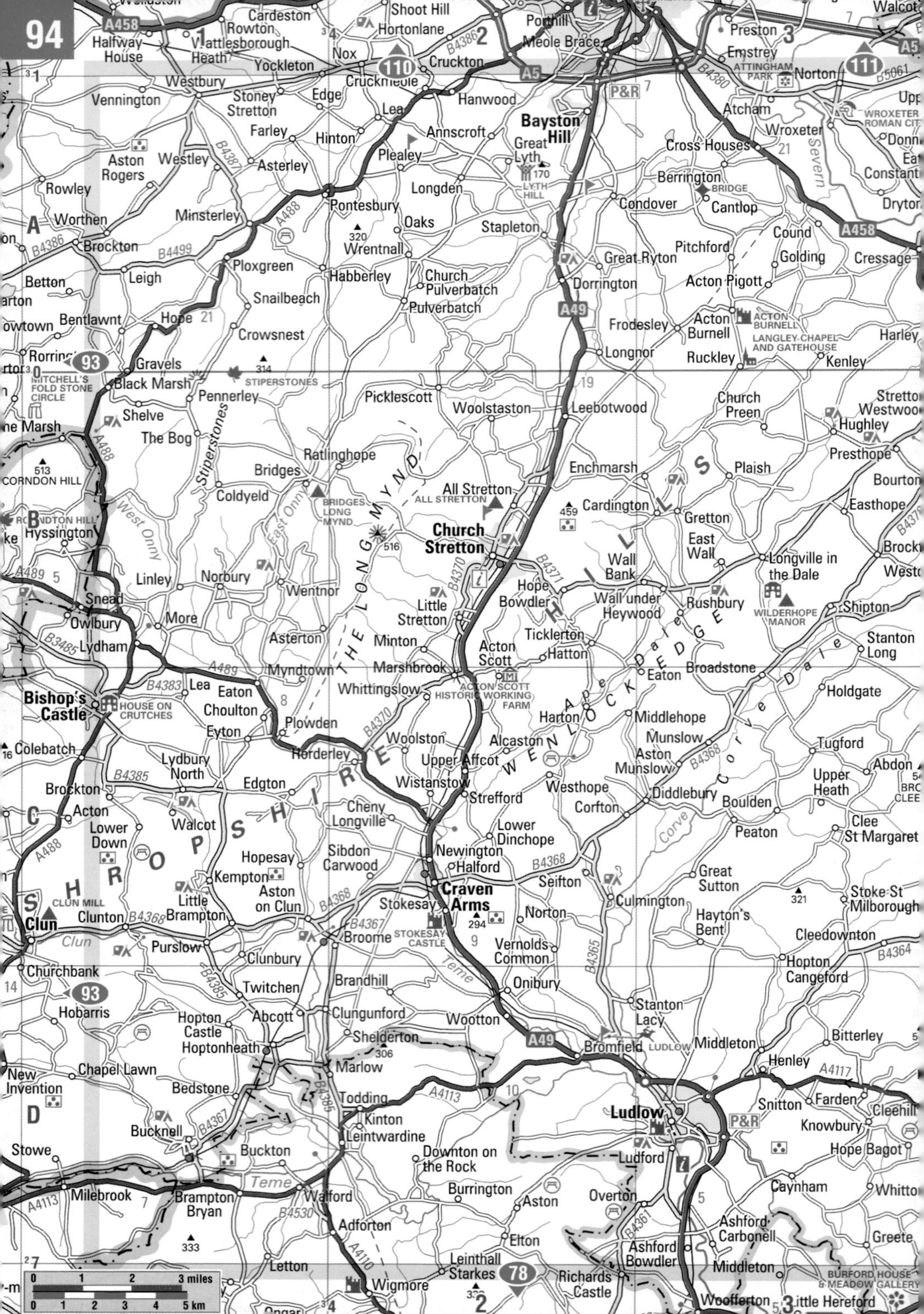

Shoot Hill
Cardeston
Rowton
Wattlesborough Heath
Halfway House
Nox
Hortonlane
Cruckton
Yockleton
Cruckmeole
Westbury
Vennington
Stoney Stretton
Edge
Lea
Hanwood
Porthill
Meole Brace
Bayston Hill
Preston
Emstrey
ATTINGHAM PARK
Norton
Atcham
Wroxeter
WROXETER ROMAN CITY
Farley
Hinton
Annscroft
Great Lyth
LYTH HILL
Cross Houses
Severn
Aston Rogers
Westley
Asterley
Plealey
Longden
Berrington
BRIDGE
Cantlop
Condover
Rowley
Worthen
Minsterley
Pontesbury
Oaks
Stapleton
Cound
Golding
Cressage
Brockton
Wrentnall
Pitchford
Great Ryton
Betton
Leigh
Ploxgreen
Habberley
Church Pulverbatch
Pulverbatch
Dorrington
Acton Pigott
Snailbeach
Bentlawnt
Hope
Crowsnest
Frodesley
Acton Burnell
ACTON BURNELL
LANGLEY CHAPEL AND GATEHOUSE
Harley
Rorrington
Gravels
Black Marsh
MITCHELL'S FOLD STONE CIRCLE
STIPERSTONES
Longnor
Ruckley
Kenley
Pennerley
Picklescott
Shelve
Woolstaston
Leebotwood
Church Preen
Hughley
The Bog
Stiperstones
Ratlinghope
Presthope
CORNDON HILL
Bridges
Enchmarsh
Plaish
Coldyeld
BRIDGES LONG MYND
THE LONG MYND
All Stretton
ALL STRETTON
Cardington
Gretton
Easthope
RODNTON HILL
Hyssington
West Onny
East Onny
Church Stretton
East Wall
Wall Bank
Longville in the Dale
Linley
Norbury
Wentnor
Little Stretton
Hope Bowdler
Wall under Heywood
Rushbury
WILDERHOPE MANOR
Shipton
Snead
Owlbury
More
Minton
Ticklerton
Hatton
Acton Scott
Stanton Long
Lydham
Asterton
Myndtown
Marshbrook
Eaton
Broadstone
Holdgate
Bishop's Castle
HOUSE ON CRUTCHES
Lea
Eaton
Choulton
Whittingslow
ACTON SCOTT HISTORIC WORKING FARM
Harton
Middlehope
Plowden
Eyton
Woolston
Alcaston
Munslow
Aston Munslow
Tugford
Colebatch
Lydbury North
Horderley
Upper Affcot
Abdon
Brockton
Edgton
Wistanstow
Westhope
Strefford
Diddlebury
Corfton
Boulden
Upper Heath
Acton
Walcot
Cheny Longville
Lower Dinchope
Peaton
Clee St Margaret
Lower Down
Hopesay
Sibdon Carwood
Newington
Halford
Craven Arms
Seifton
Great Sutton
Kempton
Aston on Clun
Culmington
Stoke St Milborough
Clun
CLUN MILL
Clunton
Little Brampton
Stokesay
Norton
Hayton's Bent
Broome
STOKESAY CASTLE
Vernolds Common
Cleedownton
Purslow
Clunbury
Hopton Cangeford
Churchbank
Brandhill
Onibury
Twitchen
Teme
Hobarris
Hopton Castle
Abcott
Clungunford
Wootton
Stanton Lacy
Hoptonheath
Shelderton
Bromfield
LUDLOW
Middleton
Bitterley
Henley
New Invention
Chapel Lawn
Marlow
Bedstone
Todding
Kinton
Leintwardine
Ludlow
Snitton
Farden
Cleehill
Knowbury
Bucknell
Stowe
Buckton
Downton on the Rock
Ludford
Hope Bagot
Milebrook
Brampton Bryan
Walford
Burrington
Aston
Overton
Caynham
Adforton
Ashford Carbonell
Elton
Ashford Bowdler
Greete
Letton
Leinthall Starkes
Richards Castle
Middleton
Wigmore
BURFORD HOUSE & MEADOW GALLERY
Woofferton
Little Hereford
A458
A5
A49
A488
A489
A4113
A4110
A4117
B4386
B4380
B4387
B4499
B4370
B4371
B4383
B4385
B4368
B4367
B4365
B4364
B4361
B4530
B3485
0 1 2 3 miles
0 1 2 3 4 5 km

Stretton
Gailey
Oldfallow
Littleworth
Gentleshaw
Farewell
Elmhurst
Wimblebury
Chorley
Hatherton
Horsebrook
Heath Hayes
Kiddemore Green
Cannock
Burntwood
Lichfield
Norton Canes
Norton East
Samuel Johnson Birthplace Mus
Leomansley
Brewood
Bridgtown
Chasetown
Norton Canes Services
Chasewater Rly
Hammerwich
Standeford
Churchbridge
Toll
Great Wyrley
Muckley Corner
Wall (Letocetum)
Wall
Chillington Hall
Coven
Shareshill
Cheslyn Hay
Little Wyrley
Brownhills
Featherstone
Hilton Park Services
Springhill
Clayhanger
Shenstone
Kingswood
Essington
Pelsall
Walsall Wood
Stonnall
Moseley Old Hall
Codsall
Fordhouses
Oaken
Northycote Farm
Bushbury
Oxley
Bloxwich
Shelfield
Leighswood
Little Hay
New Invention
Wood Hayes
Harden
Rushall
Aldridge
Watford Gap
Short Heath
Wergs
Wednesfield
Little Aston
Tettenhall
Bantock House
Wolverhampton
Heath Town
Roughwood
Hill
Roughley
Wightwick Manor
Willenhall
Arboretum
Hardwick
Streetly
Four Oaks
Mere Grn.
Perton
Wolverhampton
Moseley
Walsall
Gal & Mus
Palfrey
Bradmore
Bilston
Darlaston
SUTTON COLDFIELD
Lower Penn
Penn
Blakenhall
Ettingshall
Great Barr
Sutton Park
Kingstanding
Moxley
Wylde Green
Bradley
Wednesbury
Coseley
Sedgley
Hill Top
Grove Vale
New Oscott
Walmley
Wombourne
Toll End
Sandwell Valley
Hamstead
Baggeridge
Tipton
Upper Witton
Blakeley
Himley Hall
Upper Gornal
Gt. Bridge
Churchfield
Erdington
Himley
Gornalwood
Wrens Nest
BCLM
West Bromwich
Perry Barr
Dudley Zoo & Castle
Dudley Port
Gravelly Hill
Swindon
Tividale
Wall Heath
Dudley
Handsworth
Aston
Sandwell
Winson Grn.
Aston Hall
Castle Bromwich Hall
Oldbury
Kingswinford
Bromley
Netherton
Rowley Regis
Nat. Sea Life
Birmingham
SMETHWICK
Ward End
Brierley Hill
Old Hill
BIRMINGHAM
Bearwood
Wordsley
Red House Glass Cone
Blackheath
Stourton
Amblecote
Quarry Bank
Cradley Heath
Quinton
Chad Valley
Blakesley Hall
Yardley
Wollescote
Botanical Gdns
Lye
Woodgate Valley
Harborne
Edgbaston
Balsall Hth.
Tyseley Locomotive Works
Acock's Green
Stourbridge
HALESOWEN
Sparkhill
Hasbury
Bartley Green
Selly Oak
Moseley
Whittington
Pedmore
Woodgate
Selly Manor
King's Heath
Springfield
Olton
Illey
Bartley Res.
Bournville
Sarehole Mill
Hall Green
Caunsall
Frankley Services
Cadbury World
West Hagley
Hagley
Clent Hills
Frankley
Churchill
Clent
Romsley
Cotteridge
Shirley
Broome
Northfield
Solihull
Blakedown
Holy Cross
Longbridge
King's Norton
Hollywood
Kidderminster
Bell End
Waseley Hills
Rubery
Drakes Cross
Whitlock's End
Belbroughton
Monkspath
Drayton
Stone
Wildmoor
Lickey Hills
Cofton Hackett
Hopwood
Wythall
Harvington Hall
Fairfield
Lickey
Earlswood Lakes Craft Centre
Cottage Garden
Mustow Green
Bluntington
Marlbrook
The Transport Mus
Chaddesley Corbett
Bournheath
Barnt Green
Hopwood Park Services
Earlswood
Shenstone
Chaddesley Woods
Catshill
Dodford
Lickey End
Blackwell
Alvechurch
Portway
Worcestershire County Mus
Sidemoor
Rowney Green
Rushock
Bromsgrove
Branson's Cross
Wood End
Umberslade Farm
Whitlenge Gdns
Tutnall
Tanworth-in-Arden
Charford
Finstall
Tardebigge
Beoley
Aston Fields
Holt End
Forge Mill Needle Mus
Redditch
Gorcott Hill
Avoncroft Mus of
Elmbridge
0 1 2 3 miles
0 1 2 3 4 5 km
M6
M54
M5
M42
M6 Toll
A5
A449
A34
A452
A461
A4148
A4041
A38
A41
A4123
A456
A458
A45
A435
A491
A448
A441
112
113
95
80

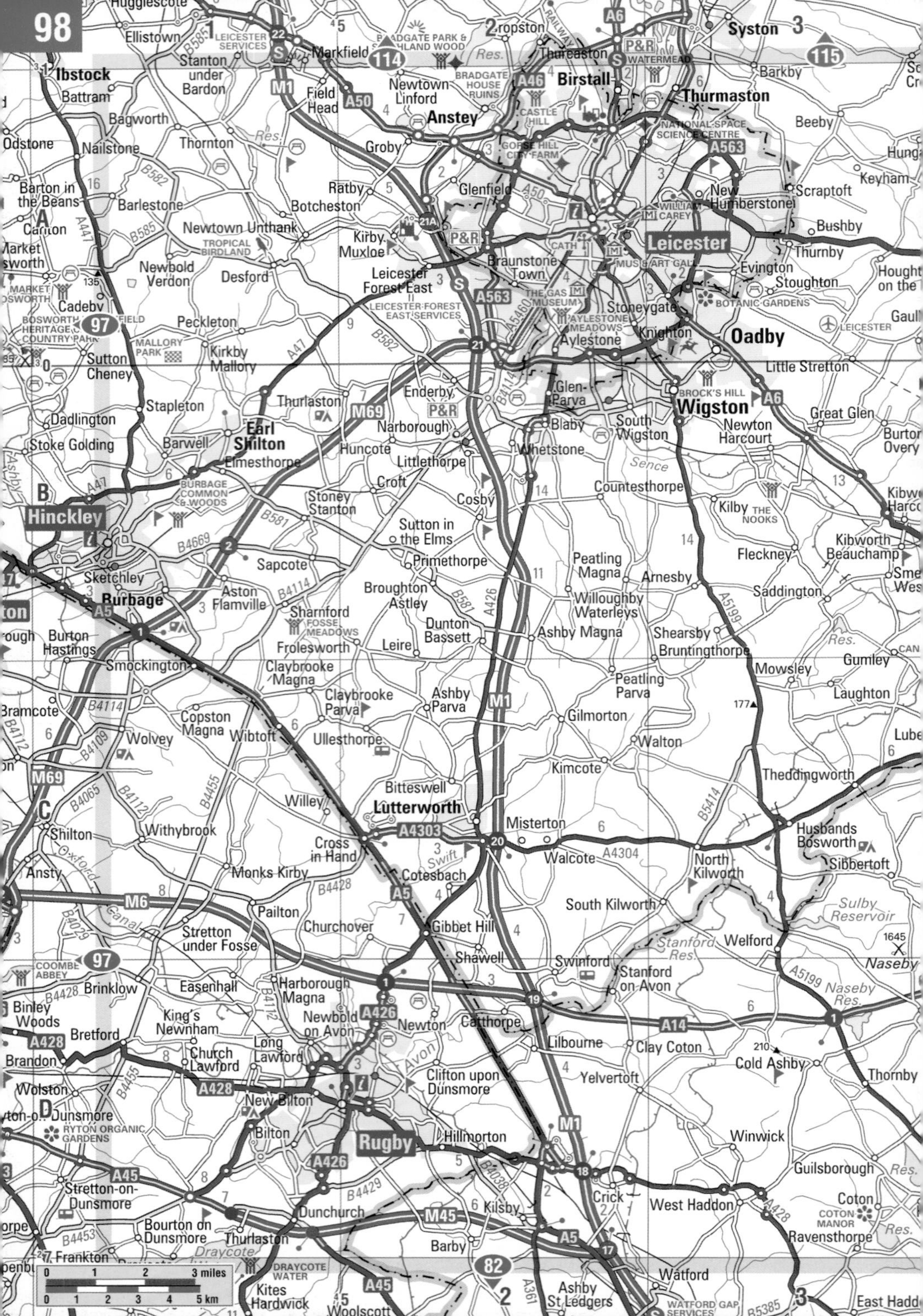
Hugglescote
Ellistown
Leicester Services
Stanton under Bardon
Markfield
Bradgate Park & Swithland Wood
114
Cropston
Thurcaston
Syston
115
Ibstock
Battram
Field Head
Newtown Linford
Bradgate House Ruins
Birstall
Watermead
Barkby
Thurmaston
Bagworth
Anstey
Castle Hill
National Space Science Centre
Beeby
Odstone
Nailstone
Thornton
Groby
Gorse Hill City Farm
Barton in the Beans
Barlestone
Ratby
Glenfield
New Humberstone
Scraptoft
Keyham
Botcheston
William Carey
Bushby
Carlton
Market Bosworth
Newtown Unthank
Tropical Birdland
Kirby Muxloe
Leicester
Thurnby
Cath
Mus & Art Gall
Newbold Verdon
Desford
Braunstone Town
Evington
Houghton on the Hill
Leicester Forest East
Stoughton
Cadeby
Bosworth Heritage & Country Park
Leicester Forest East Services
The Gas Museum
Stoneygate
Botanic Gardens
97
Peckleton
Aylestone Meadows
Oadby
Leicester
Gaulby
Mallory Park
Kirkby Mallory
Aylestone
Knighton
Sutton Cheney
Little Stretton
Stapleton
Thurlaston
Enderby
Glen Parva
Brock's Hill
Wigston
Dadlington
P&R
Narborough
Blaby
South Wigston
Great Glen
Newton Harcourt
Burton Overy
Stoke Golding
Barwell
Earl Shilton
Huncote
Whetstone
Elmesthorpe
Littlethorpe
Sence
Croft
Countesthorpe
Burbage Common & Woods
Stoney Stanton
Cosby
Kilby
The Nooks
Kibworth Harcourt
Hinckley
Sutton in the Elms
Kibworth Beauchamp
Sapcote
Primethorpe
Peatling Magna
Fleckney
Sketchley
Arnesby
Smeeton Westerby
Aston Flamville
Broughton Astley
Willoughby Waterleys
Saddington
Burbage
Sharnford
Fosse Meadows
Dunton Bassett
Ashby Magna
Shearsby
Burton Hastings
Frolesworth
Leire
Bruntingthorpe
Gumley
Smockington
Claybrooke Magna
Mowsley
Peatling Parva
Laughton
Bramcote
Claybrooke Parva
Ashby Parva
Gilmorton
Copston Magna
Wolvey
Wibtoft
Ullesthorpe
Walton
Kimcote
Theddingworth
Bitteswell
Willey
Lutterworth
Shilton
Withybrook
Misterton
Husbands Bosworth
Cross in Hand
Walcote
Sibbertoft
Ansty
Swift
North Kilworth
Monks Kirby
Cotesbach
Oxford Canal
Pailton
South Kilworth
Sulby Reservoir
Stretton under Fosse
Churchover
Gibbet Hill
Welford
Stanford Res.
Shawell
Naseby
Coombe Abbey
97
Swinford
Stanford on Avon
Easenhall
Harborough Magna
Naseby Res.
Brinklow
Binley Woods
King's Newnham
Newbold on Avon
Newton
Catthorpe
Bretford
Long Lawford
Lilbourne
Clay Coton
Brandon
Church Lawford
Cold Ashby
Clifton upon Dunsmore
Yelvertoft
Thornby
Wolston
New Bilton
Dunsmore
Ryton Organic Gardens
Bilton
Rugby
Hillmorton
Winwick
Guilsborough
Stretton-on-Dunsmore
Crick
West Haddon
Coton
Coton Manor
Bourton on Dunsmore
Dunchurch
Kilsby
Ravensthorpe
Thurlaston
Barby
Frankton
Draycote
Draycote Water
82
Watford
Kites Hardwick
Woolscott
Ashby St Ledgers
Watford Gap Services
East Haddon
A6
A46
A50
A563
A447
A47
M1
M69
A5
A5199
A426
A4303
A4304
B5414
M6
A14
A428
A45
M45
A361
B5385
B585
B582
B581
B4669
B4114
B4109
B4112
B4065
B4455
B4428
B4029
B4429
B4453
B4038
A5460
B4114
Res.
0 1 2 3 miles
0 1 2 3 4 5 km

Satchville
Burrough Hill
Pickwell
Cold Overton
A606
Langham
Exton
Barnsdale Gardens
116
115
Bloody Oaks Services
A1
Twyford
Burrough on the Hill
B6047
Burley
Falconry Centre
Tickencote
Barleythorpe
Oakham
Whitwell
Empingham
Marefield
Knossington
Upper Hambleton
A606
Owston
Egleton
Rutland Water
Cold Newton
Tinwell
Braunston-in-Rutland
Brooke
Rutland Water
Normanton
Tilton on the Hill
Halstead
SK
Manton
Edith Weston
Ketton
226
Lyndon
North Luffenham
Chater
A6121
17
A6003
Pilton
Skeffington
Loddington
Ridlington
Preston
Wing
South Luffenham
Belton in Rutland
A47
Ayston
Tugby
East Norton
Morcott
Glaston
A47
Rolleston
Allexton
Wardley
Barrowden
Tixover
Duddington
Uppingham
100
163
Bisbrooke
Welland
Wakerley
Noseley
Goadby
Seaton
Horninghold
Stockerston
Stoke Dry
Lyddington
Harringworth
B6047
Hallaton
Bede House
Laxton
A43
Blatherwycke
Glooston
Blaston
Eyebrook Reservoir
B672
Thorpe by Water
Stonton Wyville
Cranoe
A6003
B
B664
Slawston
Gretton
Bulwick
Church Langton
Great Easton
Caldecott
Medbourne
Kirby Hall
Welham
East Langton
Drayton
Bringhurst
Deene
Deenethorpe
Thorpe Langton
Rockingham
Rockingham Castle
Rockingham
Deene Park
Weston by Welland
A6
Ashley
Cottingham
A6116
Little Weldon
Foxton Locks
Sutton Bassett
Middleton
B670
Corby
Great Bowden
East Carlton
Weldon
A427
Market Harborough
Stoke Albany
Wilbarston
East Carlton
123
Great Weldon
Upper Benefield
Lower Benefield
Dingley
A427
Brampton Ash
Stanion
Rockingham Forest
A427
A6014
Little Bowden
B669
Pipewell
Great Oakley
A43
Harper's Brook
East Farndon
SP
Little Oakley
Brigstock
Lyveden New Bield
C
Braybrooke
A6
A6003
Fermyn Woods
Wadenhoe
Great Oxendon
Desborough
Rushton Triangular Lodge
Rushton
Newton
Geddington
Eleanor Cross
A6116
B576
Sudborough
Aldwincle
Clipston
Arthingworth
Rothwell
A4300
Boughton House
A508
Harrington
Weekley
Warkton
Grafton Underwood
Lowick
A43
Ise
100
Kelmarsh
Orton
Kettering
Slipton
Islip
A14
Loddington
Thorpe Malsor
Barton Seagrave
Cranford St Andrew
Cranford St John
Twywell
A14
A6003
Thrapston
Haselbech
Woodford
Maidwell
Draughton
Great Cransley
A14
Wicksteed Park
Denford
Mawsley
Broughton
Burton Latimer
Great Addington
Ringstead
A510
Lamport
Lamport Hall
Pytchley
Isham
Cottesbrooke
Cottesbrooke Hall and Gdns.
Old
Little Addington
A45
A509
A6
Scaldwell
Orlingbury
Finedon
Creaton
A508
Walgrave
B574
Stanwick Lakes
Little Harrowden
Hannington
Irthlingborough
Stanwick
Great Harrowden
A510
Chelveston
Brixworth
Spratton
Holcot
83
Wellingborough
B571
Higham Ferrers
A5199
Pitsford Reservoir
Brixworth
Sywell
Rushden Lakes
Chichele College
Caldecott
A510

TOLETHORPE HALL RUTLAND OPEN AIR THEATRE
Ryhall
Barholm
Towngate
Market Deeping
Frognall
116
117
Crowland
BLOODY OAKS SERVICES
Little Casterton
Tickencote
Great Casterton
Belmesthorpe
Deeping St James
Deeping Gate
Empingham
A606
Northfields
Uffington
Tallington
West Deeping
Maxey
Northborough
A16
Stamford
BURGHLEY
B1443
Etton
Peakirk
Newborough
Tinwell
Pilsgate
Bainton
Glinton
Ketton
Easton on the Hill
Barnack
Helpston
Bedford Level (North)
Ufford
A15
Eye Green
BARNACK HILLS AND HOLES
Southorpe
Werrington
Gunthorpe
A43
South Luffenham
Collyweston
Wittering
Marholm
Walton
Eye
COLLYWESTON GREAT WOOD
A1
SACREWELL FARM & COUNTRY CENTRE
CASTOR HANGLANDS
Dogsthorpe
Newark
Duddington
Thornhaugh
Upton
A47
A1139
99
BEDFORD PURLIEUS
Wansford
LONGTHORPE TOWER
Peterborough
Wakerley
Stibbington
Ailsworth
Longthorpe
CATH.
Fengate
Sutton
Castor
FERRY MEADOWS
NENE VALLEY RAILWAY
RAILWORLD
FLAG FEN BRONZE AGE EXCAVATION
Old Fletton
King's Cliffe
Yarwell
Water Newton
Orton Longueville
Stanground
Sibson
A605
B671
SIBSON
Alwalton
Blatherwycke
Nassington
Orton Waterville
Apethorpe
Chesterton
CROWN LAKES
Farcet
Bulwick
Woodnewton
Fotheringhay
ELTON HALL
Elton
PETERBOROUGH SERVICES
Haddon
B1091
SOUTHWICK HALL
Deenethorpe
Southwick
CASTLE SITE
Eaglethorpe
Warmington
Morborne
Farcet Fen
Yaxley
Whittlesey Mere
Rockingham Forest
Tansor
Glapthorn
Cotterstock
Folksworth
Norman Cross
A427
Upper Benefield
Lower Benefield
Oundle
Ashton
Caldecote
Stilton
HOLME FEN
BARNWELL
Polebrook
Lutton
Denton
Holme
B660
Stoke Doyle
Nene
Conington
Glatton
LYVEDEN NEW BIELD
Barnwell St Andrew
Hemington
A1(M)
WOODWALTON FEN
FERMYN WOODS
Pilton
Sawtry
A6116
Wadenhoe
Barnwell All Saints
Luddington in the Brook
Church End
Achurch
Wigsthorpe
Thurning
Great Gidding
B1043
Little Gidding
Aldwincle
Wood Walton
Thorpe Waterville
B662
Steeple Gidding
Lowick
A605
Clopton
Winwick
HAMERTON ZOO PARK
Coppingford
MONKS WOOD
Slipton
Titchmarsh
Hamerton
Islip
Twywell
Thrapston
Upton
Wennington
Old Weston
Alconbury Weston
Abbots Ripton
Woodford
A14
Buckworth
Denford
Bythorn
Brington
Little Stukeley
Keyston
Molesworth
Alconbury
Great Stukeley
Barham
Ringstead
Leighton Bromswold
Woolley
Little Addington
A45
B663
Catworth
A141
Huntingdon
STANWICK LAKES
Raunds
Spaldwick
HUNTINGDON
Easton
Ellington
HINCHINGBROOKE
Stanwick
Hargrave
Covington
Stow Longa
BRAMPTON HUT SERVICES
Brampton
Chelveston
B645
B660
Tilbrook
84
Godmanchester
0 1 2 3 miles
0 1 2 3 4 5 km
Shelton
Lower Dean
Grafham
Grafham
BUCKDEN

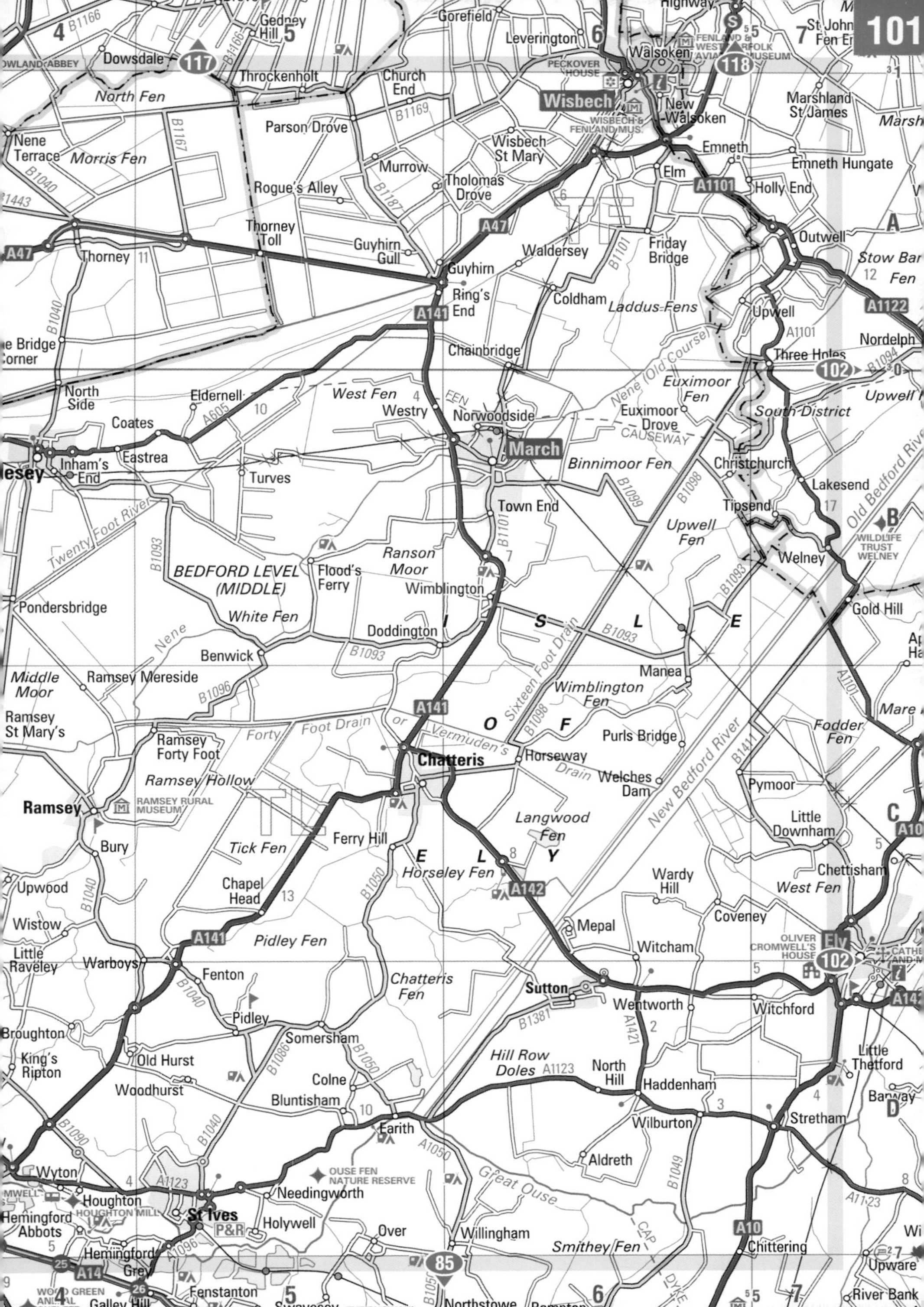
Gedney Hill
Dowsdale
Gorefield
Leverington
Walsoken
Fenland & West Norfolk Aviation Museum
Peckover House
Wisbech
Wisbech & Fenland Mus.
New Walsoken
Marshland St James
Throckenholt
Church End
North Fen
Parson Drove
Wisbech St Mary
Emneth
Emneth Hungate
Nene Terrace
Morris Fen
Murrow
Tholomas Drove
Elm
Holly End
Rogue's Alley
Thorney Toll
Guyhirn Gull
Friday Bridge
Outwell
Thorney
Waldersey
Guyhirn
Ring's End
Coldham
Laddus Fens
Stow Bardolph Fen
Upwell
Chainbridge
Nordelph
Three Holes
Euximoor Fen
Upwell Fen
North Side
Eldernell
West Fen
Westry
Norwoodside
Euximoor Drove
South District
Coates
March
Causeway
Eastrea
Inham's End
Turves
Binnimoor Fen
Christchurch
Lakesend
Old Bedford River
Town End
Tipsend
Twenty Foot River
Upwell Fen
Welney
Wildlife Trust Welney
Ranson Moor
Bedford Level (Middle)
Flood's Ferry
Wimblington
Gold Hill
Pondersbridge
White Fen
Doddington
Isle of Ely
Nene
Benwick
Manea
Middle Moor
Ramsey Mereside
Wimblington Fen
Sixteen Foot Drain
Ramsey St Mary's
Forty Foot Drain or Vermuden's Drain
Purls Bridge
Fodder Fen
Ramsey Forty Foot
Chatteris
Horseway
Welches Dam
Pymoor
Ramsey Hollow
New Bedford River
Ramsey
Ramsey Rural Museum
Langwood Fen
Little Downham
Bury
Tick Fen
Ferry Hill
Chettisham
Horseley Fen
Wardy Hill
West Fen
Upwood
Chapel Head
Coveney
Mepal
Wistow
Pidley Fen
Witcham
Oliver Cromwell's House
Ely
Little Raveley
Warboys
Fenton
Chatteris Fen
Sutton
Wentworth
Witchford
Pidley
Broughton
Somersham
Hill Row Doles
North Hill
Little Thetford
King's Ripton
Old Hurst
Haddenham
Colne
Woodhurst
Bluntisham
Barway
Wilburton
Stretham
Earith
Aldreth
Wyton
Ouse Fen Nature Reserve
Great Ouse
Houghton
Needingworth
Houghton Mill
Hemingford Abbots
St Ives
Holywell
Over
Willingham
Smithey Fen
Chittering
Hemingford Grey
Upware
Wood Green Animal Shelter
Fenstanton
River Bank
Galley Hill
Swavesey
Northstowe
Rampton
Cap Dyke
A47
A141
A605
A1101
A1122
A142
A10
A1123
A14
A1096
A1421
B1166
B1167
B1169
B1187
B1040
B1101
B1093
B1099
B1098
B1411
B1096
B1050
B1381
B1086
B1090
B1049
B1094
117
118
102
85
25
26
TF
TL
4
5
6
7
A
B
C
D

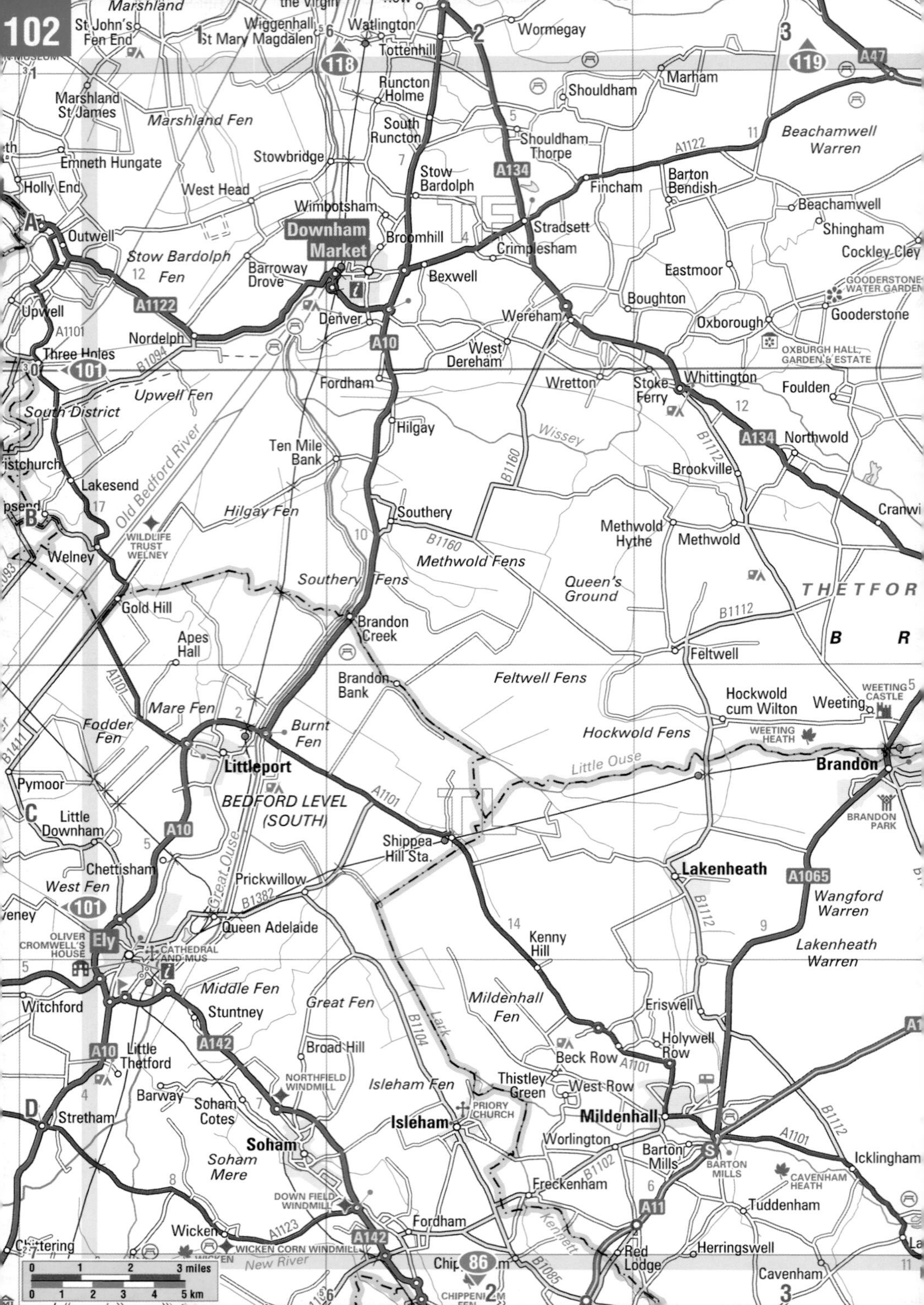

Marshland
St John's Fen End
Wiggenhall St Mary Magdalen
Watlington
Tottenhill
Wormegay
Marham
Shouldham
Runcton Holme
South Runcton
Marshland St James
Marshland Fen
Shouldham Thorpe
Beachamwell Warren
Emneth Hungate
Stowbridge
Stow Bardolph
Fincham
Barton Bendish
Holly End
West Head
Wimbotsham
Beachamwell
Shingham
Downham Market
Broomhill
Stradsett
Crimplesham
Cockley Cley
Outwell
Stow Bardolph Fen
Barroway Drove
Bexwell
Eastmoor
Upwell
Denver
Wereham
Boughton
Gooderstone Water Gardens
Gooderstone
Oxborough
Oxburgh Hall, Garden & Estate
Nordelph
West Dereham
Three Holes
Upwell Fen
Fordham
Wretton
Stoke Ferry
Whittington
Foulden
South District
Hilgay
Wissey
Northwold
Ten Mile Bank
Old Bedford River
Lakesend
Brookville
Hilgay Fen
Southery
Methwold Hythe
Methwold
Cranwi
Wildlife Trust Welney
Welney
Methwold Fens
Southery Fens
Queen's Ground
THETFOR
Gold Hill
Brandon Creek
Apes Hall
Feltwell
B
R
Brandon Bank
Feltwell Fens
Weeting Castle
Hockwold cum Wilton
Weeting
Mare Fen
Burnt Fen
Hockwold Fens
Weeting Heath
Fodder Fen
Littleport
Little Ouse
Brandon
Pymoor
Bedford Level (South)
Little Downham
Brandon Park
Shippea Hill Sta.
Chettisham
Great Ouse
Prickwillow
Lakenheath
West Fen
Wangford Warren
Queen Adelaide
Kenny Hill
Lakenheath Warren
Oliver Cromwell's House
Ely
Cathedral and Mus
Middle Fen
Witchford
Great Fen
Mildenhall Fen
Eriswell
Stuntney
Lark
Broad Hill
Holywell Row
Little Thetford
Beck Row
Northfield Windmill
Isleham Fen
Thistley Green
West Row
Barway
Soham Cotes
Priory Church
Stretham
Isleham
Mildenhall
Soham
Worlington
Barton Mills
Icklingham
Soham Mere
Cavenham Heath
Freckenham
Down Field Windmill
Tuddenham
Fordham
Wicken
Kennett
Chittering
Wicken Corn Windmill
Red Lodge
Herringswell
New River
Cavenham
Chippenham Fen
A47
A1122
A134
A10
A1101
B1094
B1160
B1112
A1065
B1382
A142
B1104
B1102
A11
A1123
B1085
B1411
118
119
101
86
0 1 2 3 miles
0 1 2 3 4 5 km

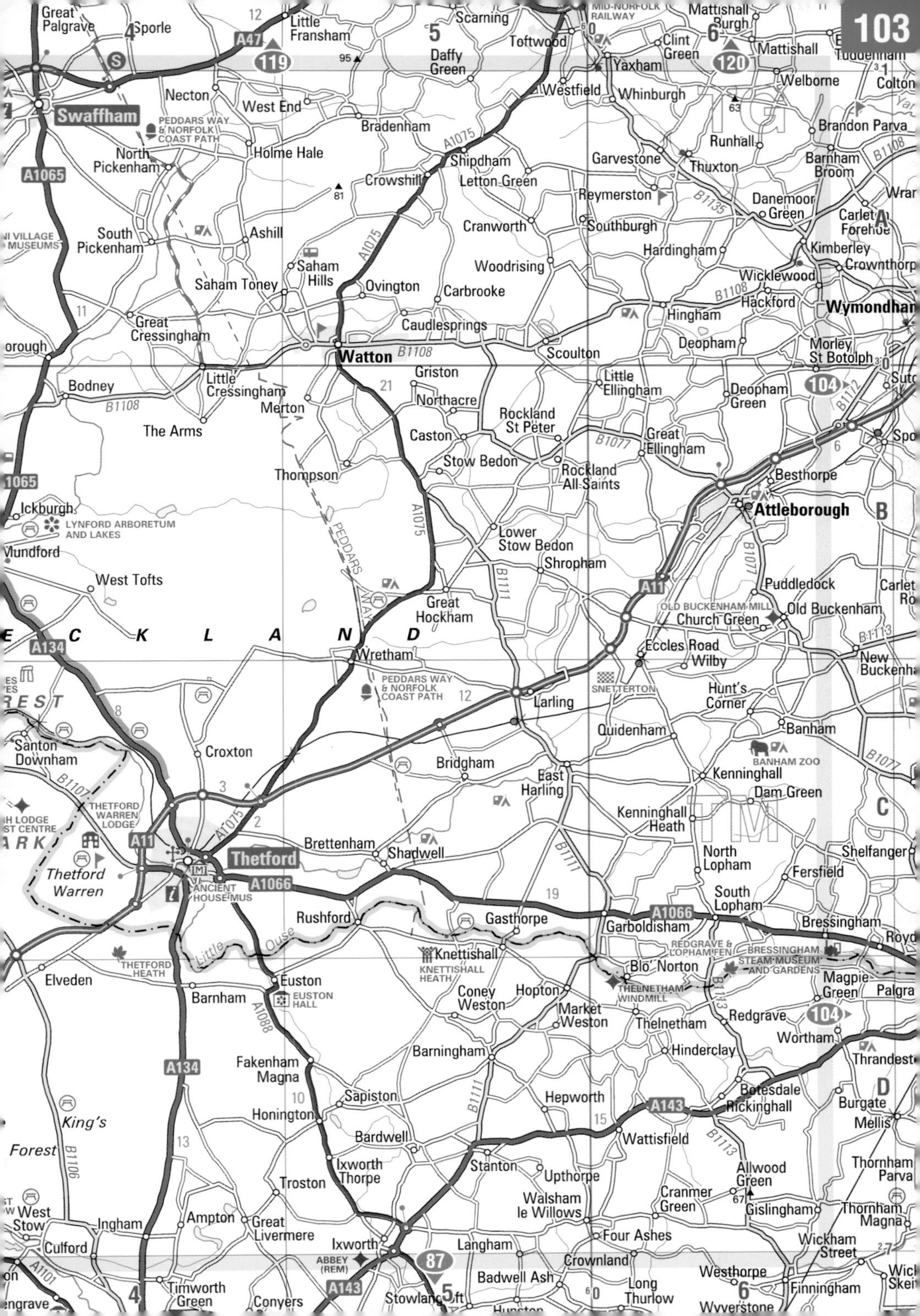
Swaffham
Watton
Thetford
Attleborough
Wymondham
Great Palgrave
Sporle
Little Fransham
Scarning
Toftwood
Yaxham
Mattishall Burgh
Mattishall
Clint Green
Daffy Green
Necton
West End
Bradenham
Westfield
Whinburgh
Welborne
Colton
North Pickenham
Holme Hale
Shipdham
Crowshill
Letton Green
Garvestone
Thuxton
Runhall
Brandon Parva
Barnham Broom
Reymerston
Southburgh
Cranworth
Danemoor Green
South Pickenham
Ashill
Saham Hills
Saham Toney
Ovington
Carbrooke
Woodrising
Hardingham
Kimberley
Wicklewood
Crownthorpe
Hackford
Hingham
Great Cressingham
Caudlesprings
Scoulton
Deopham
Morley St Botolph
Little Cressingham
Bodney
Griston
Northacre
Merton
Little Ellingham
Deopham Green
Rockland St Peter
The Arms
Caston
Great Ellingham
Stow Bedon
Thompson
Rockland All Saints
Besthorpe
Ickburgh
LYNFORD ARBORETUM AND LAKES
Mundford
Lower Stow Bedon
Shropham
West Tofts
Puddledock
Great Hockham
OLD BUCKENHAM MILL
Church Green
Old Buckenham
Eccles Road
Wilby
New Buckenham
Wretham
PEDDARS WAY & NORFOLK COAST PATH
SNETTERTON
Larling
Hunt's Corner
Quidenham
Banham
BANHAM ZOO
Santon Downham
Croxton
Bridgham
East Harling
Kenninghall
Dam Green
THETFORD WARREN LODGE
Kenninghall Heath
Brettenham
Shadwell
North Lopham
Shelfanger
Fersfield
Thetford Warren
ANCIENT HOUSE MUS
South Lopham
Rushford
Gasthorpe
Garboldisham
Bressingham
REDGRAVE & LOPHAM FEN
BRESSINGHAM STEAM MUSEUM AND GARDENS
Knettishall
KNETTISHALL HEATH
THETFORD HEATH
Elveden
Euston
EUSTON HALL
Barnham
Blo' Norton
THELNETHAM WINDMILL
Coney Weston
Hopton
Market Weston
Thelnetham
Redgrave
Magpie Green
Wortham
Barningham
Hinderclay
Fakenham Magna
Thrandeston
Botesdale
Rickinghall
Burgate
Mellis
Sapiston
Hepworth
Honington
King's Forest
Bardwell
Wattisfield
Ixworth Thorpe
Stanton
Upthorpe
Allwood Green
Thornham Parva
Troston
Walsham le Willows
Cranmer Green
Gislingham
Thornham Magna
West Stow
Ingham
Ampton
Great Livermere
Four Ashes
Culford
Ixworth
Langham
Wickham Street
ABBEY (REM)
Crownland
Westhorpe
Timworth Green
Badwell Ash
Long Thurlow
Finningham
Conyers
Stowlangtoft
Wyverstone
MID-NORFOLK RAILWAY
A47
A1065
A1075
A134
A11
A1066
A1088
A143
A1101
B1108
B1077
B1111
B1113
B1135
B1107
B1106
B1172
119
120
104
87
TG
TM
BRECKLAND
A
B
C
D
4
5
6

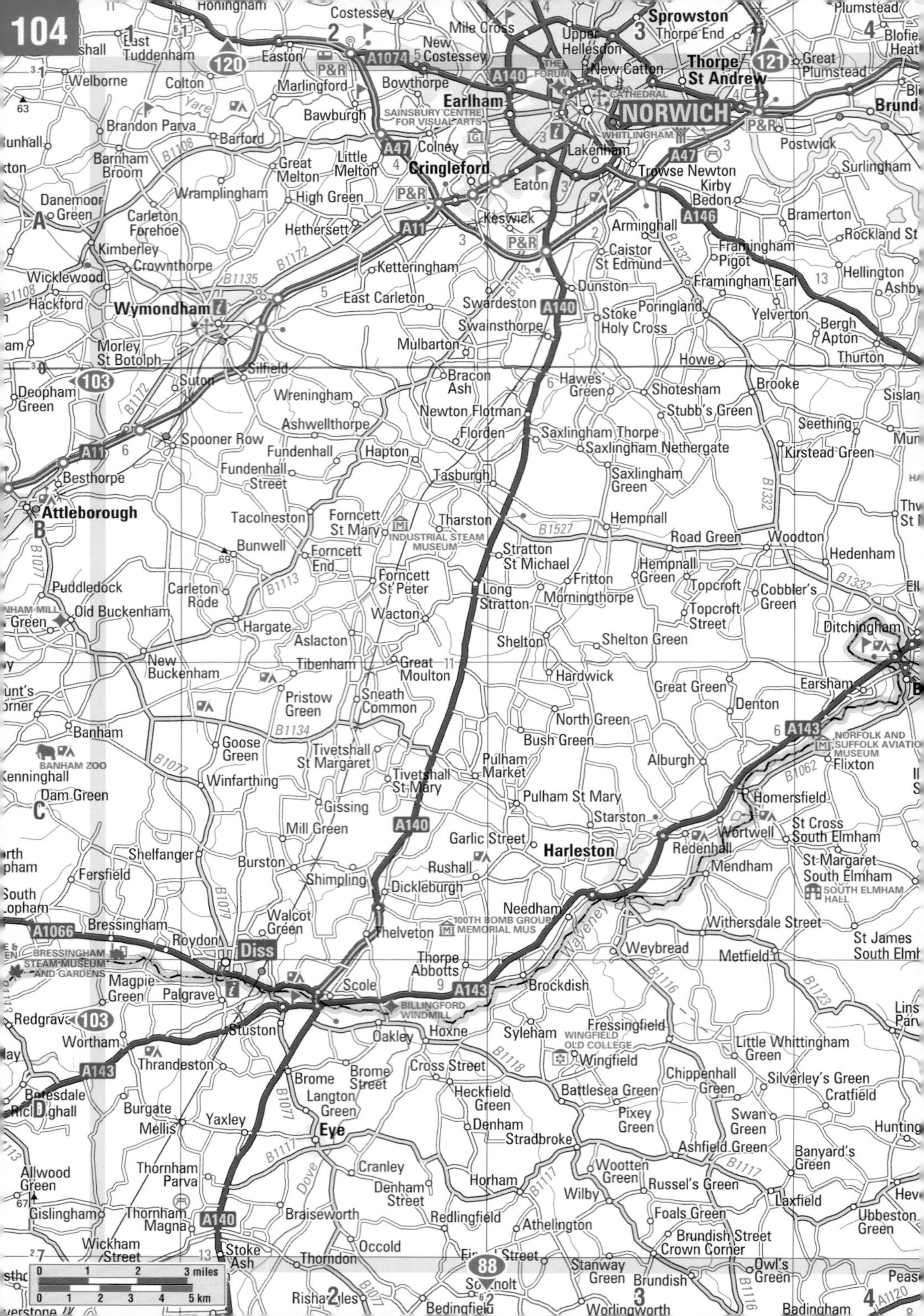
104
Honingham
Costessey
Mile Cross
Sprowston
Thorpe End
Plumstead
East Tuddenham
Easton
A1074
New Costessey
Upper Hellesdon
120
121
Great Plumstead
Welborne
Colton
Yare
Marlingford
Bowthorpe
A140
THE FORUM
New Catton
Thorpe St Andrew
CATHEDRAL
Earlham
NORWICH
Brandon Parva
Bawburgh
SAINSBURY CENTRE FOR VISUAL ARTS
WHITLINGHAM
Barford
B1108
Colney
Lakenham
A47
Postwick
Barnham Broom
Great Melton
Little Melton
Cringleford
Trowse Newton
Surlingham
Wramplingham
Eaton
Kirby Bedon
Danemoor Green
High Green
P&R
Bramerton
Carleton Forehoe
Keswick
A146
Arminghall
Rockland St
Hethersett
A11
Kimberley
Caistor St Edmund
B1332
Framingham Pigot
Crownthorpe
B1172
Ketteringham
Wicklewood
B1135
Hellington
Framingham Earl
Dunston
Ashby
Hackford
East Carleton
Swardeston
B1113
Poringland
Wymondham
Stoke Holy Cross
Yelverton
Swainsthorpe
Bergh Apton
Morley St Botolph
Mulbarton
Howe
Thurton
103
Silfield
Bracon Ash
Suton
Hawes' Green
Shotesham
Brooke
Deopham Green
Wreningham
Newton Flotman
Stubb's Green
Ashwellthorpe
Seething
Florden
Saxlingham Thorpe
Spooner Row
Saxlingham Nethergate
Fundenhall
Hapton
Kirstead Green
Besthorpe
Fundenhall Street
Tasburgh
Saxlingham Green
Attleborough
Tacolneston
Forncett St Mary
Tharston
Hempnall
INDUSTRIAL STEAM MUSEUM
B1527
Road Green
Woodton
Bunwell
Forncett End
Stratton St Michael
Hedenham
B1077
Hempnall Green
Fritton
Puddledock
Carleton Rode
Forncett St Peter
B1113
Topcroft
Cobbler's Green
Long Stratton
Morningthorpe
Topcroft Street
Old Buckenham
Wacton
Hargate
Ditchingham
Aslacton
Shelton
Shelton Green
New Buckenham
Tibenham
Great Moulton
Hardwick
Pristow Green
Sneath Common
Great Green
Earsham
Denton
Banham
North Green
B1134
Bush Green
A143
Goose Green
NORFOLK AND SUFFOLK AVIATION MUSEUM
BANHAM ZOO
Tivetshall St Margaret
Pulham Market
Alburgh
Flixton
Kenninghall
Winfarthing
Tivetshall St Mary
B1062
Dam Green
Pulham St Mary
Homersfield
Gissing
Starston
St Cross South Elmham
Mill Green
Garlic Street
Wortwell
Shelfanger
Harleston
Redenhall
Burston
Rushall
Mendham
St Margaret South Elmham
Fersfield
Shimpling
Dickleburgh
SOUTH ELMHAM HALL
South Lopham
Needham
Waveney
Walcot Green
Withersdale Street
Bressingham
100TH BOMB GROUP MEMORIAL MUS
St James South Elmham
A1066
Roydon
Thelveton
Weybread
Diss
BRESSINGHAM STEAM MUSEUM AND GARDENS
Thorpe Abbotts
Metfield
Magpie Green
Scole
Palgrave
Brockdish
B1116
B1123
BILLINGFORD WINDMILL
Redgrave
Stuston
Fressingfield
Wortham
Oakley
Hoxne
Syleham
WINGFIELD OLD COLLEGE
Little Whittingham Green
Thrandeston
Wingfield
B1118
Cross Street
Brome
Brome Street
Chippenhall Green
Silverley's Green
Botesdale
Heckfield Green
Battlesea Green
Cratfield
Langton Green
Burgate
Pixey Green
Swan Green
Mellis
Yaxley
Denham
Eye
Stradbroke
Ashfield Green
B1117
Banyard's Green
Dove
Allwood Green
Thornham Parva
Cranley
Wootten Green
Russel's Green
Denham Street
Horham
Wilby
Laxfield
Gislingham
Thornham Magna
Braiseworth
Redlingfield
Athelington
Foals Green
Ubbeston Green
Brundish Street
Wickham Street
Occold
Crown Corner
Stoke Ash
Thorndon
Stanway Green
Owl's Green
88
Brundish
Badingham
Bedingfield
Worlingworth
0 1 2 3 miles
0 1 2 3 4 5 km

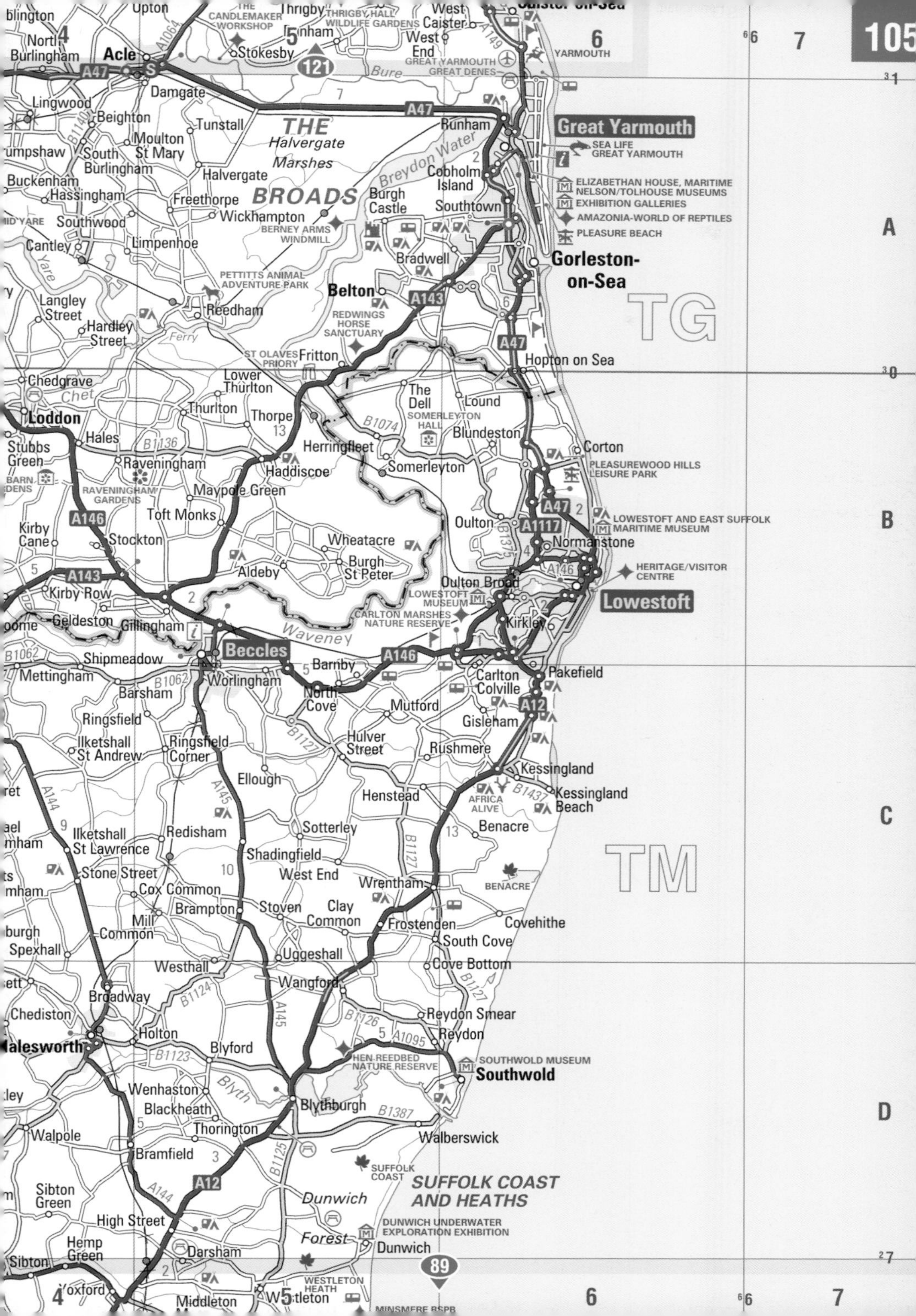
Great Yarmouth
Lowestoft
Beccles
Gorleston-on-Sea
Southwold
THE BROADS
Halvergate Marshes
SUFFOLK COAST AND HEATHS
TG
TM
Acle
Loddon
Halesworth
Belton
Hopton on Sea
Kessingland
Kessingland Beach
Oulton Broad
Blythburgh
Walberswick
Dunwich
Wrentham
Reydon
Bungay
SEA LIFE GREAT YARMOUTH
ELIZABETHAN HOUSE, MARITIME NELSON/TOLHOUSE MUSEUMS
EXHIBITION GALLERIES
AMAZONIA-WORLD OF REPTILES
PLEASURE BEACH
PLEASUREWOOD HILLS LEISURE PARK
LOWESTOFT AND EAST SUFFOLK MARITIME MUSEUM
HERITAGE/VISITOR CENTRE
SOUTHWOLD MUSEUM
DUNWICH UNDERWATER EXPLORATION EXHIBITION
AFRICA ALIVE
BENACRE
HEN REEDBED NATURE RESERVE
CARLTON MARSHES NATURE RESERVE
REDWINGS HORSE SANCTUARY
PETTITTS ANIMAL ADVENTURE PARK
BERNEY ARMS WINDMILL
SOMERLEYTON HALL
RAVENINGHAM GARDENS
A47
A143
A146
A12
A144
A145
A1117
121
89

Ynys Llanddwyn
1
2
3
122
A
B
C
D
CAERNARFON BAY
BAE CAERNARFON
SH
LLEYN
PENRHYN LLYN
Clynnog
Gyrn-goch
Bryn-yr-eryr
Trefor
564 YR EIFL
WALES COAST PATH
B4417
Llithfaen
Carreg Ddu
Porth Dinllaen
Pistyll
Llwyndyrys
Morfa Nefyn
Nefyn
LLEYN MARITIME MUSEUM
Fron
Edern
Tan-y-graig
Rhos-fawr
Porth Ysgadan
B4417
Glanrhyd
Rhos-y-llan
CORS GEIRCH
Boduan
A497
Llannor
Tudweiliog
A499
Efailnewydd
Dinas
Rhyd-y-clafdy
Denio
Pwllheli
Porth Golmon
Garnfadryn
B4415
South Beach
Bryn-mawr
Llaniestyn
Penrhos
Pen-y-graig
Llangwnnadl
Rhedyn
Sarn Meyllteyrn
Penrhyn Mawr
B4413
Llanbedrog
Pen-y-groeslon
Ty-hen
Botwnnog
Nanhoron
Bryncroes
Mynytho
Trwyn Llanbedrog
Methlem
Rhydlios
Llandegwning
304 MYNYDD RHIW
PLAS-YN-RHIW
St Tudwal's Road
Angorfa St Tudwal
Rhoshirwaun
Llawrdref Bellaf
Capel Carmel
Llangian
A499
Rhiw
Abersoch
B4413
191
Porth Neigwl or Hell's Mouth
Llanengan
St Tudwal's Island East
Ynys St Tudwal Dwyrain
Uwchmynydd
Sarn Bach
Aberdaron
Llanfaelrhys
Bwlchtocyn
Marchroes
St Tudwal's Island West
Ynys St Tudwal Gorllewin
Bodermid
Bardsey Sound
Swnt Enlli
Pen-y-cil
Cilan Uchaf
Trwyn Cilan
167
Bardsey Island
Ynys Enlli
YNYS ENLLI
0 1 2 3 miles
0 1 2 3 4 5 km

123
124
108
90

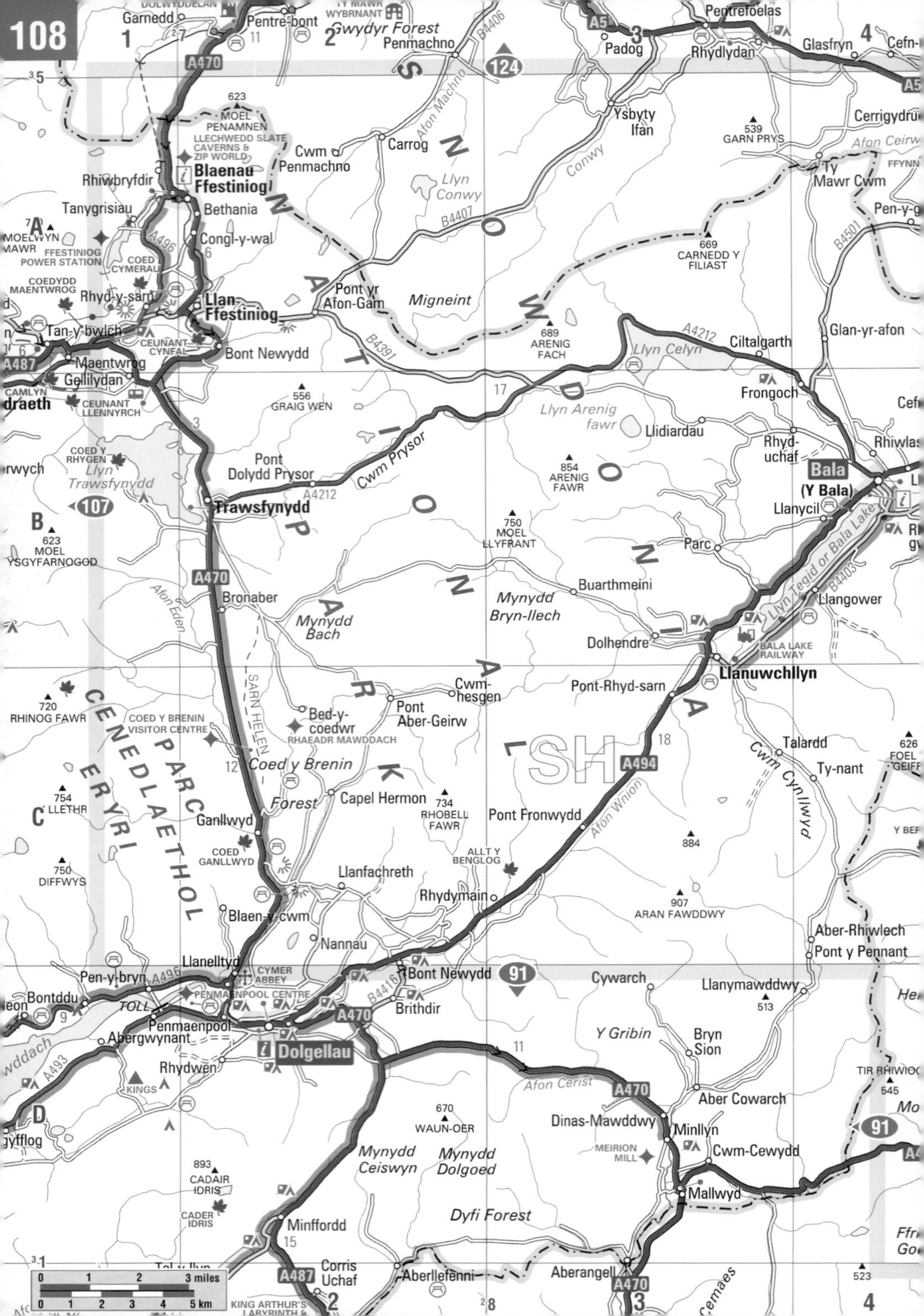
Garnedd
Pentre-bont
Gwydyr Forest
Penmachno
B4406
124
A5
Padog
Pentrefoelas
Rhydlydan
Glasfryn
Cefn-
A470
623
MOEL PENAMNEN
LLECHWEDD SLATE CAVERNS & ZIP WORLD
Blaenau Ffestiniog
Rhiwbryfdir
Tanygrisiau
Bethania
Congl-y-wal
MOELWYN MAWR
FFESTINIOG POWER STATION
COED CYMERAU
A496
COEDYDD MAENTWROG
Rhyd-y-sarn
Llan-Ffestiniog
Tan-y-bwlch
CEUNANT CYNFAL
Bont Newydd
A487
Maentwrog
Gellilydan
CAMLYN
draeth
CEUNANT LLENNYRCH
Cwm Penmachno
Carrog
Afon Machno
Llyn Conwy
Conwy
B4407
Ysbyty Ifan
539
GARN PRYS
Cerrigydrud
Afon Ceirw
Ty Mawr Cwm
FFYNN
Pen-y-g
B4501
669
CARNEDD Y FILIAST
Pont yr Afon-Gam
Migneint
B4391
689
ARENIG FACH
Llyn Celyn
A4212
Ciltalgarth
Glan-yr-afon
Frongoch
556
GRAIG WEN
17
Llyn Arenig fawr
Llidiardau
Rhyd-uchaf
Rhiwlas
Bala
(Y Bala)
Llanycil
COED Y RHYGEN
Llyn Trawsfynydd
rwych
Pont Dolydd Prysor
Cwm Prysor
A4212
854
ARENIG FAWR
107
Trawsfynydd
B
623
MOEL YSGYFARNOGOD
750
MOEL LLYFRANT
Parc
Llyn Tegid or Bala Lake
B4403
Afon Eden
Bronaber
Mynydd Bach
Buarthmeini
Mynydd Bryn-llech
Llangower
Dolhendre
BALA LAKE RAILWAY
Llanuwchllyn
SARN HELEN
720
RHINOG FAWR
COED Y BRENIN VISITOR CENTRE
Bed-y-coedwr
Pont Aber-Geirw
Cwm-hesgen
Pont-Rhyd-sarn
RHAEADR MAWDDACH
Coed y Brenin
Forest
12
18
SH
A494
Talardd
Cwm Cynllwyd
Ty-nant
626
FOEL Y GEIFR
754
LLETHR
C
Capel Hermon
734
RHOBELL FAWR
Pont Fronwydd
Afon Wnion
Ganllwyd
COED GANLLWYD
884
750
DIFFWYS
ALLT Y BENGLOG
Llanfachreth
Rhydymain
907
ARAN FAWDDWY
Blaen-y-cwm
Nannau
Aber-Rhiwlech
Pont y Pennant
Llanelltyd
CYMER ABBEY
Bont Newydd
91
Cywarch
Llanymawddwy
513
Pen-y-bryn
PENMAENPOOL CENTRE
Bontddu
TOLL
9
Penmaenpool
B4416
Brithdir
Abergwynant
Dolgellau
A493
Rhydwen
KINGS
Y Gribin
Bryn Sion
11
Afon Cerist
TIR RHIWIOG
545
D
670
WAUN-OER
Aber Cowarch
Dinas-Mawddwy
Minllyn
91
MEIRION MILL
Cwm-Cewydd
Mynydd Ceiswyn
Mynydd Dolgoed
893
CADAIR IDRIS
CADER IDRIS
Mallwyd
Dyfi Forest
Minffordd
15
Corris Uchaf
A487
Aberllefenni
Aberangell
A470
523
KING ARTHUR'S LABYRINTH
0 1 2 3 miles
0 1 2 3 4 5 km
1
2
3
4
A
5
6

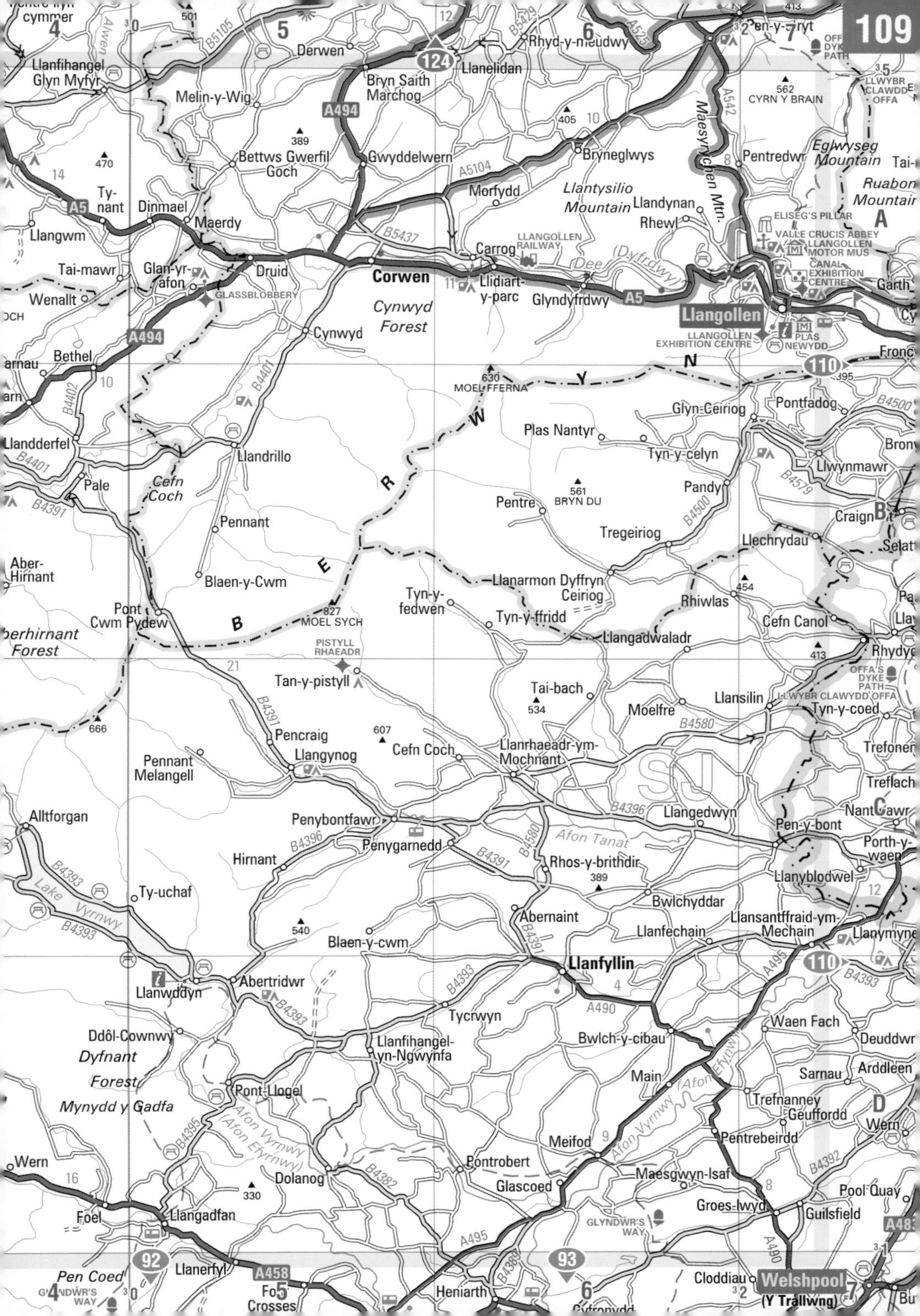
Derwen
Rhyd-y-meudwy
Pen-y-stryt
OFFA'S DYKE PATH
Llanfihangel Glyn Myfyr
Llanelidan
Bryn Saith Marchog
Melin-y-Wig
CYRN Y BRAIN
LLWYBR CLAWDD OFFA
Bettws Gwerfil Goch
Gwyddelwern
Bryneglwys
Pentredwr
Eglwyseg Mountain
Maesyrychen Mtn.
Llantysilio Mountain
Ruabon Mountain
Ty-nant
Dinmael
Morfydd
Llandynan
Maerdy
Rhewl
Llangwm
ELISEG'S PILLAR
VALLE CRUCIS ABBEY
LLANGOLLEN MOTOR MUS
LLANGOLLEN RAILWAY
Carrog
Tai-mawr
Glan-yr-afon
Druid
Corwen
Llidiart-y-parc
Glyndyfrdwy
Dee (Dyfrdwy)
CANAL EXHIBITION CENTRE
Garth
Wenallt
GLASSBLOBBERY
Cynwyd Forest
Llangollen
LLANGOLLEN EXHIBITION CENTRE
PLAS NEWYDD
Cynwyd
Bethel
MOEL FFERNA
BERWYN
Glyn-Ceiriog
Pontfadog
Plas Nantyr
Llandderfel
Llandrillo
Tyn-y-celyn
Llwynmawr
Pale
Cefn Coch
Pandy
Pentre
BRYN DU
Craignant
Pennant
Tregeiriog
Llechrydau
Selattyn
Aber-Hirnant
Blaen-y-Cwm
Llanarmon Dyffryn Ceiriog
Rhiwlas
Tyn-y-fedwen
Pont Cwm Pydew
MOEL SYCH
Tyn-y-ffridd
Cefn Canol
Penybontfawr
Hirnant
Penygarnedd
Afon Tanat
Rhos-y-brithdir
Bwlchyddar
Llanyblodwel
Ty-uchaf
Lake Vyrnwy
Abernaint
Blaen-y-cwm
Llanfechain
Llansantffraid-ym-Mechain
Llanymynech
Llanfyllin
Llanwddyn
Abertridwr
Tycrwyn
Waen Fach
Deuddwr
Ddôl-Cownwy
Dyfnant Forest
Llanfihangel-yn-Ngwynfa
Bwlch-y-cibau
Sarnau
Arddleen
Main
Pont-Llogel
Mynydd y Gadfa
Trefnanney
Geuffordd
Afon Vyrnwy (Afon Efyrnwy)
Pentrebeirdd
Wern
Meifod
Pontrobert
Maesgwyn-Isaf
Dolanog
Glascoed
Pool Quay
Groes-lwyd
Guilsfield
Foel
Llangadfan
GLYNDŴR'S WAY
Llanerfyl
Pen Coed
Cloddiau
Welshpool (Y Trallwng)
Heniarth
Fo Crosses
Cyfronydd
Bu
Rhydycroesau
PISTYLL RHAEADR
Tan-y-pistyll
Tai-bach
Llangadwaladr
Moelfre
Llansilin
Tyn-y-coed
Trefonen
Pencraig
Llangynog
Cefn Coch
Llanrhaeadr-ym-Mochnant
Treflach
Pennant Melangell
Nant Mawr
Alltforgan
Llangedwyn
Pen-y-bont
Porth-y-waen
Llandderfel
Berhirnant Forest
Alwen
Tai-

Wrexham
(Wrecsam)
Coedpoeth
Broughton
Acton
Rhosnesni
Llan-y-pwll
Ridleywood
Tilston
Edge Green
Castletown
Horton Green
Isycoed
126
127
LEAD MINES
Minera
MOSS VALLEY
OFFA'S DYKE PATH
Bersham
ESCLUSHAM MOUNTAIN
LLWYBR CLAWDD OFFA
562
CYRN Y BRAIN
456
Rhostyllen
King's Mills
Wrexham Industrial Estate
Bowling Bank
Shocklach
Chorlton Lane
Malpas
Talwrn
ERDDIG
Marchwiel
Sontley
Cross Lanes
Worthenbury
Cuddington Heath
Threapwood
Pentredwr
Eglwyseg Mountain
Tai-nant
Johnstown
Rhosllanerchrugog
Ruabon Mountain
Stryt-issa
Penycae
Gyfelia
Eyton
Cock Bank
Bangor-is-y-coed
BANGOR
Tallarn Green
ELISEG'S PILLAR
VALLE CRUCIS ABBEY
LLANGOLLEN MOTOR MUS
CANAL EXHIBITION CENTRE
Acrefair
PONTCYSYLLTE AQUEDUCT
Garth
Cefn-mawr
Ruabon
(Rhiwabon)
Overton Bridge
Cloy
Overton
(Owrtyn)
Llangollen
Pont Cysyllte
New Bridge
Rhos-y-Madoc
Erbistock
Lightwood Green
Horseman's Green
Eglwys Cross
The Chequer
TY MAWR
PLAS NEWYDD
Froncysyllte
Pentre
Halton
Dee (Dyfrdwy)
Sandy Lane
Penley
Hanmer
Street Lydan
Arowry
109
395
Pontfadog
CHIRK CASTLE
Chirk
(Y Waun)
Dudleston
Knolton Bryn
Knolton
Street Dinas
Ifton Heath
Dudleston Heath
FENN'S, WHIXALL & BETTISFIELD
Bronygarth
Chirk Bank
Llwynmawr
Preesgweene
St Martin's
Breaden Heath
Weston Rhyn
New Marton
Elson
Welshampton
Ellesmere
THE MERE
Llangollen
Bettisfield
Craignant
Perthy
Balmer Heath
WEM MOSS
Llechrydau
Selattyn
Hengoed
Gobowen
COLEMERE
Lyneal
Northwood
454
Hindford
Welsh Frankton
Tetchill
Lee
Colemere
Pant-glas
WHITTINGTON CASTLE
Lower Frankton
Wolverley
Cefn Canol
Llawnt
OLD OSWESTRY HILL FORT
Whittington
Hordley
English Frankton
413
Rhydycroesau
CAMBRIAN RAILWAY MUS
Babbinswood
Kenwick
OFFA'S DYKE PATH
Oswestry
Middleton
Lower Hordley
Cockshutt
Loppington
Llansilin
LLWYBR CLAWDD OFFA
Tyn-y-coed
Wootton
Rednal
Stanwardine in the Wood
Noneley
MILE END
Morda
Queen's Head
Haughton
Bagley
Trefonen
Ball
Grimpo
Petton
Burlton
Maesbury
Weston Lullingfields
Westoncommon
Treflach
Maesbury Marsh
West Felton
Nantmawr
Morton
Eardiston
Wykey
Marton
Myddle
Alderton
Pen-y-bont
Woolston
131
Stanwardine in the Fields
Porth-y-waen
Llynclys
Crickheath
Osbaston
Shotatton
Llanyblodwel
Knockin
Brownhill
Pant
CAMBRIAN HERITAGE RAILWAYS
Maesbrook
Ruyton-XI-Towns
Baschurch
Llansantffraid-ym-Mechain
Kinnerley
Dovaston
Prescott
Merrington
Llanymynech
Kynaston
Hopton
Little Ness
Walford
Walford Heath
Bomere Heath
Kinton
Nesscliffe
NESSCLIFFE
Yeaton
Llandysilio
Crosslanes
Wilcott
Great Ness
Grafton
Leaton
Four Crosses
Melverley Green
Pentre
Felton Butler
Albrighton
Waen Fach
Deuddwr
Forton Heath
Fitz
Llandrinio
Ensdon
Forton
Mytton
Sarnau
Arddleen
Melverley
Shrawardine
Montford Bridge
Trefnanney
Geuffordd
Criggion
Coedway
Bicton
Crewgreen
Alberbury
Montford
Dithe
Wern
Ford
P&R
Coton Hill
Pentrebeirdd
MUS & ART GALL
Shelton
Middletown
Copthorne
Shoot Hill
Wollaston
Cardeston
Pool Quay
Trewern
404
Rowton
Hortonlane
Porthill
Guilsfield
Halfway House
Wattlesborough Heath
Meole Brace
Nox
Cruckton
Yockleton
Westbury
Cruckmeole
Nelly Andrews Green
Vennington
Stoney Stretton
Edge
Hanwood
Bayston Hill
Farley
Annscroft
93
94
Severn (Hafren)
Severn
Perry
Efyrnwy
0 1 2 3 miles
0 1 2 3 4 5 km
A525
A542
A483
A539
A528
A5
B5426
B5130
B5069
B5070
B4500
B4579
B5068
A495
B5063
B4397
B5009
B4580
B4396
B4398
B4393
B4392
A490
A458
B4386
B4473
B4380
B5067

111
CHOLMONDELEY CASTLE GDNS
Chorley
Larden Green
Nantwich
Shavington
Barthomley
Englesea-brook
Butt Green
Hough
Gorsteyhill
Ravensmoor
Stapeley
Balterley
Wybunbury
Betley
Halmer End
Bickley Moss
Walgherton
Sound
Wrenbury
Broomhall
Sound Heath
Norbury
Hatherton
Blakenhall
Wrinehill
Aston
Hunsterson
Madeley Heath
Marbury
Marley Green
Newhall
Hankelow
Checkley
Keele
Madeley
Wirswall
Audlem
Buerton
Whitchurch
Burleydam
Lightwood Green
Kinsey Heath
Woore
Onneley
Madeley Park
Brooklands
Chemistry
Coxbank
Ireland's Cross
Pipe Gate
Aston
Whitmore
Redbrook
Waymills
Broughall
Wilkesley
Adderley
Knighton
Willoughbridge
THE DOROTHY CLIVE GARDEN
Ash Magna
Bearstone
Alkington
Blackbrook
Ightfield
Newstreet Lane
Norton in Hales
Prees Heath
Maer
Tilstock
Calverhall
Betton
Mucklestone
Ashley Heath
Ashley
Hollinwood
Prees Higher Heath
Loggerheads
Welsh End
Podmore
Moreton Say
Hookgate
Almington
Sandford
Longford
Market Drayton
Chatcull
Prees
Quina Brook
Prees Lower Heath
Darliston
Fauls
Bletchley
Hales
Wetwood
Fairoak
Croxtonbank
Croxton
Edstaston
Ternhill
The Four Alls
Prees Green
Lostford
Sutton
Woodseaves
Chipnall
Rosehill
Cheswardine
Bishop's Offley
WOLLERTON OLD HALL
Wollerton
HAWKSTONE PARK
Stoke Heath
Marchamley
Weston
Aston
Wixhill
Hodnet
Wistanswick
Soudley
HODNET HALL
Lee Brockhurst
Mill Green
Lockleywood
Adbaston
Stoke on Tern
Hinstock
Knighton
Moston
Hopton
High Offley
Preston Brockhurst
High Hatton
Ollerton
Child's Ercall
Ellerton
Shebdon
Woodseaves
Stanton upon Hine Heath
Radmoor
Weston Jones
Sambrook
Norbury
Grinshill
Moreton Corbet
MORETON CORBET
Howle
Eaton on Tern
Pickstock
Ellerdine Heath
Sutton
Puleston
Shawbury
Great Bolas
Edgebolton
Forton
Muckleton
Cold Hatton
Meese
Tibberton
Edgmond Marsh
Aqualate Mere
Cherrington
Hadnall
Great Wytheford
Rowton
Waters Upton
Edgmond
Astley
Walton
Newport
Poynton Green
Crudgington
Adeney
Longford
Outwoods
Bings Heath
Church Aston
High Ercall
Chetwynd Aston
Haughton
Roden
Kynnersley
Brockton
HAUGHMOND ABBEY
Sleapford
Preston upon the Weald Moors
Lilleshall
Longdon on Tern
Eyton upon the Weald Moors
HOO FARM ANIMAL KINGDOM
LILLESHALL ABBEY
Rodington
Muxton
Uffington
Bratton
Heath Hill
Donnington
Shrewsbury
Withington
Admaston
Upton Magna
Trench
Donnington Wood
Lilyhurst
Weston Heath
Sheriffhales
Wrockwardine
Hadley
Walcot
GRANVILLE
Preston
Wellington
Ketley
Oakengates
Charlton
Arleston
Ketley Bank
Crackleybank
Emstrey
Priorslee
TELFORD SERVICES
ATTINGHAM PARK
Norton
Aston
Uppington
Atcham
WROXETER ROMAN CITY
Rushton
Lawley
Telford
Haughton
Shifnal
Weaver
Tern
Roden
SJ

Ashbourne
Belper
Derby
Uttoxeter
Burton upon Trent
Swadlincote
Lichfield
Ashby-de-la-Zouch
Alton
Duffield
Allestree
Mickleover
Normanton
Tutbury
Horninglow
Newhall
Woodville
Willington
Repton
Abbots Bromley
Barton-under-Needwood
NEEDWOOD FOREST
THE NATIONAL FOREST
Measham
Waterfall
Waterhouses
Ilam
Thorpe
Fenny Bentley
Kniveton
Hognaston
Carsington Res.
Kirk Ireton
Biggin
Hulland Ward
Hulland
Bradley
Atlow
Mapleton
Swinscoe
Blore
Calton
Cauldon
Cotton
Weaver Hills
Stanton
Mayfield
Church Mayfield
Clifton
Ramshorn
Wootton
Farley
Ellastone
Snelston
Osmaston
Wyaston
Norbury
Quixhill
Denstone
Roston
Rocester
Croxden
Shirley
Ednaston
Brailsford
Mugginton
Weston Underwood
Yeaveley
Rodsley
Hollington
Alkmonton
Great Cubley
Cubley Common
Hollington Grove
Kirk Langley
Thurvaston
Longlane
Longford
Mackworth
Langley Common
Lees
Radbourne
Longfordlane
Boylestone
Trusley
Dalbury
Sutton on the Hill
Church Broughton
Foston
Etwall
Burnaston
Littleover
Marston Montgomery
Waldley
Combridge
Beamhurst
Crakemarsh
Stramshall
Somersal Herbert
Doveridge
Oaks Green
Sudbury
Marchington
Scropton
Hatton
Hilton
Marston on Dove
Egginton
Findern
Stenson
Twyford
Barrow upon Trent
Ingleby
Milton
Newton Solney
Kingstone
Gorsty Hill
Marchington Woodlands
Draycott in the Clay
Hanbury
Hanbury Woodend
Anslow Gate
Anslow
Rolleston-on-Dove
Stretton
Newborough
Needwood
Hoar Cross
Newchurch
Rangemore
Shobnall
Winshill
Bretby
Foremark Res.
Tatenhill
Stapenhill
Upper Midway
Lower Midway
Hartshorne
Branston
Hadley End
Woodlane
Dunstall
Blithbury
Hamstall Ridware
Hill Ridware
Morrey
Yoxall
Woodhouses
Walton-on-Trent
Church Gresley
Castle Gresley
Caldwell
Mount Pleasant
Blackfordby
Norris Hill
Rosliston
Linton
Armitage
Handsacre
King's Bromley
Orgreave
Alrewas
Longdon
Rileyhill
Fradley
Croxall
Coton in the Elms
Overseal
Moira
Donisthorpe
Oakthorpe
Edingale
Lullington
Netherseal
Elmhurst
Farewell
Chorley
Streethay
Elford
Harlaston
Haunton
Clifton Campville
Chilcote
No Man's Heath
Appleby Magna
Appleby Parva
Snarestone
Whittington
Thorpe Constantine
Leomansley
Beighton Hill
Shottle
Idridgehay
Hillcliffane
Blackbrook
Shottlegate
Cowers Lane
Turnditch
Cross o' th' hands
Windley
Hazelwood
Belper Lane End
Mount Pleasant
Kedleston
Quarndon
Flaxholme
Kedleston Hall
Alton Towers
Darley Moor
Sudbury Hall
Uttoxeter
Derby & Burton Services
City Mus & Art Gall
Bass Mus
National Memorial Arboretum
Conkers Nat Forest Discovery Ctr
Derwent Valley Visitor Cen
Samuel Johnson Birthplace Mus
Ilam Hall
Dovedale
Heritage Centre
A523
A52
A515
A517
A50
A516
A38
A511
A5132
A513
A51
A444
A42
A6
B5035
B5032
B5033
B5031
B5030
B5013
B5017
B5234
B5016
B5014
B5020
B5008
B5023
B5493
129
130
114
96
97

Ambergate
Toadmoor
Heage
Net Heage
130
Ironville
Jacksdale
Bagthorpe
FELLEY PRIORY
Newstead
Linby
Papplewick
A617
PAPPLEWICK PUMPING
MIDLAND RAILWAY BUTTERLEY
RIPLEY
Codnor
New Brinsley
Underwood
M1
131
Belper Lane End
Shottle
DERWENT VALLEY VISITOR CEN
Broadholme
Marehay
Cross Hill
Brinsley
HUCKNALL
Mount Pleasant
Far Laund
A38
A6007
B600
BESTWOOD
Westville
Blackbrook
Openwoodgate
Loscoe
Aldercar
Moorgreen
Bestwood Village
A60
Shottlegate
Cowers Lane
Belper
DE BRADELEI
Denby
HEANOR
Eastwood
Kilburn
Milford
Hazelwood
Horsley Woodhouse
Marlpool
Watnall
A610
Bulwell
Bestwood
Nuthall
Holbrook
A609
Smalley
Shipley
SHIPLEY
Kimberley
Awsworth
Old Basford
B5023
Horsley
Cotmanhay
Swingate
Weston Underwood
Duffield
Coxbench
Mapperley
EREWASH MUSEUM
Cossall
Bilborough
Mapperley Park
Little Eaton
Flaxholme
Stanley Common
West Hallam
ILKESTON
Strelley
CASTLE MUSEUM & GALLERY
THE TALES OF ROBIN HOOD
Kedleston
A6
Morley
TROWELL SERVICES
A609
Quarndon
Breadsall
Stanley
Kirk Hallam
Trowell
Wollaton
KEDLESTON HALL
113
Allestree
A61
126
A6096
Dale Abbey
Stanton-by-Dale
WOLLATON HALL
Lenton
A52
Mackworth
Chaddesden
Bramcote
A52
TRENT BRIDGE CRICKET
Langley Common
CATH
Sandiacre
Stapleford
BEESTON
WEST BRIDGFORD
Spondon
Ockbrook
Risley
P&R
Chilwell
A6005
Wilford
B5020
CITY MUS & ART GALL
Derby
A52
Attenborough
Toton
Borrowash
Breaston
Barton in Fabis
Clifton
Littleover
A6005
Mickleover
Normanton
A5111
Osmaston
ELVASTON CASTLE
Elvaston
Draycott
LONG EATON
Ruddington
FRAMEWORK KNITTERS MUS
Alvaston
Thulston
Thrumpton
A453
A38
Allenton
A514
Shardlow
M1
Sawley
GREAT CENTRAL RLY (NOTT'M)
Bradmore
Findern
Chellaston
Cavendish Bridge
98
Gotham
Stenson
A50
Aston-on-Trent
DERBY SOUTH (SHARDLOW) SERVICES
Ratcliffe on Soar
Bunny
A5132
Twyford
Barrow upon Trent
Swarkestone
Lockington
24A
New Kingston
Willington
Canal
Weston-on-Trent
Hemington
Castle Donington
24
Kingston on Soar
West Leake
East Leake
A60
Repton
Ingleby
Stanton by Bridge
King's Newton
DONINGTON PARK
Kegworth
Costock
Milton
GRAND PRIX RACING CARS
EAST MIDLANDS
DONINGTON PARK SERVICES
MANOR FARM
Newton Solney
Melbourne
MELBOURNE HALL
Isley Walton
A453
Sutton Bonington
Wilson
Diseworth
Long Whatton
A6006
Bretby
Foremark Res.
Ticknall
CALKE
Res.
B587
Soar
A514
Tonge
A42
Normanton on Soar
Hathern
Breedon on the Hill
CALKE ABBEY
Hoton
Lower Midway
Hartshorne
Calke
B5324
THE OLD RECTORY MUSEUM
Stanford on Soar
113
B5006
FERRERS CENTRE FOR ARTS & CRAFTS
Worthington
Belton
A6
CHARNWOOD MUSEUM
Cotes
THE BELL FOUNDRY MUSEUM
Woodville
ARBORETUM
Lount
Shepshed
Thorpe Acre
Loughborough
Smisby
Osgathorpe
A512
Newbold
Thringstone
Shelthorpe
MUSEUM
Coleorton
Blackfordby
Woodthorpe
Norris Hill
Ashby-de-la-Zouch
Res.
Nanpantan
Quorndon
Swannington
CHARNWOOD LODGE
Moira
A511
Whitwick
Woodhouse
248
BEACON HILL
CONKERS NAT. FOREST DISCOVERY CTR
THE
COALVILLE
Charnwood
Forest
Mountsorrel
A444
Donisthorpe
Packington
Greenhill
B591
Woodhouse Eaves
Oakthorpe
Ravenstone
NATIONAL
278
BROOMBRIGGS FARM
Swithland
Rothley
Measham
Bardon
Copt Oak
GREAT CENTRAL RAILWAY
Normanton le Heath
THE MANOR HOUSE
Hugglescote
A42
FOREST
Ellistown
Cropston
B585
LEICESTER SERVICES
BRADGATE PARK & SWITHLAND WOOD
Swepstone
Heather
Markfield
Res.
Thurcaston
Appleby
Stanton under Bardon
97
Ibstock
98
Newtown Linford
BRADGATE HOUSE RUINS
A46
Birstall
Battram
Field Head
A50
Anstey
Newton Burgoland
Bagworth
0 1 2 3 miles
0 1 2 3 4 5 km

Farndon
Balderton
Barnby in the Willows
Halloughton
Park Hill
Morton
Fiskerton
Oxton
Hawton
Fenton
Claypole
Thurgarton
Bleasby
East Stoke
Thorpe
Stubton
Epperstone
Elston
Gonalston
Syerston
Cotham
Dry Doddington
Lowdham
Hoveringham
Flintham
Kneeton
Caythorpe
Sibthorpe
Long Bennington
Lambley
Shelton
Hougham
Burton Joyce
Bulcote
Gunthorpe
Screveton
Staunton in the Vale
Westborough
East Bridgford
Hawksworth
Flawborough
Marston
Gedling
Thoroton
Kilvington
Foston
Car Colston
Shelford
Alverton
Carlton
Newton
Scarrington
Stoke Bardolph
Orston
Normanton
Colwick
Radcliffe on Trent
Saxondale
Bingham
Aslockton
Allington
Holme Pierrepont
Harlequin
Upper Saxondale
Whatton
Bottesford
Great Gonerby
Elton
Easthorpe
Sedgebrook
Cropwell Butler
Sutton
Muston
Bassingfield
Tithby
Granby
Barrowby
Barnstone
Redmile
Stenwith
Earlsfield
Cotgrave
Cropwell Bishop
Vale of Belvoir
Barkestone-le-Vale
Langar
Woolsthorpe by Belvoir
Owthorpe
Plungar
Belvoir
Normanton-on-the-Wolds
Colston Bassett
Belvoir Castle
Denton
Harston
Harlaxton
Stathern
Kinoulton
Knipton
Stroxton
Harby
Hose
Eaton
Branston
Hungerton
Hickling
Croxton Kerrial
Wyville
Eastwell
Widmerpool
Upper Broughton
Long Clawson
Goadby Marwood
Stoke Rochford
Saltby
Willoughby-on-the-Wolds
Skillington
Waltham on the Wolds
Nether Broughton
Wycomb
Chadwell
Stonesby
Holwell
Scalford
Sproxton
Old Dalby
Wartnaby
Ab Kettleby
Buckminster
Grimston
Coston
Saxelbye
Thorpe Arnold
Sewstern
Gunby
Six Hills
Melton Mowbray
Freeby
Garthorpe
Ragdale
Shoby
Saxby
Wymondham
Asfordby
Asfordby Hill
Wyfordby
Brentingby
Seagrave
Hoby
Frisby on the Wreake
Burton Lazars
Stapleford
Edmondthorpe
Kirby Bellars
Thrussington
Rotherby
Market Overton
Teigh
Ratcliffe on the Wreake
Barrow
Great Dalby
Rearsby
Little Dalby
Whissendine
East Goscote
Ashwell
Gaddesby
Queniborough
Ashby Folville
Thorpe Satchville
Pickwell
Cold Overton
Syston
Barsby
Burrough Hill
Langham
Twyford
Burrough on the Hill
Somerby
Burley
Barkby
South Croxton
Barleythorpe
Oakham
Thurmaston
Marefield
A6097
A46
A52
A606
A607
A612
B6386
B692
B676
B668
B6047
A1
131
132
116
98
99

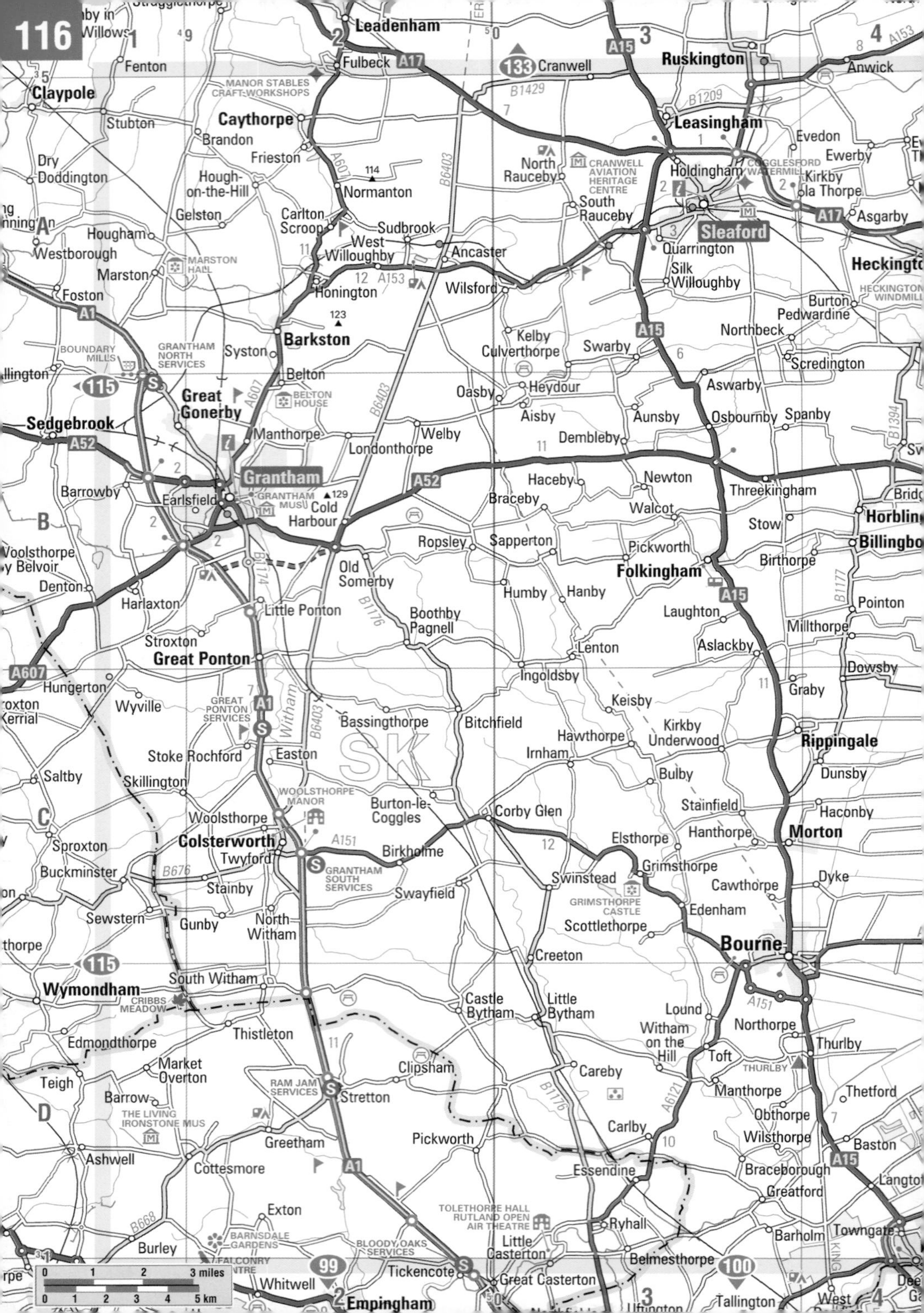
1
2
3
4
A
B
C
D
SK
Leadenham
Fulbeck
A17
133
Cranwell
A15
Ruskington
Anwick
A153
Fenton
Claypole
MANOR STABLES CRAFT WORKSHOPS
B1429
B1209
Stubton
Caythorpe
Brandon
Leasingham
Evedon
Ewerby
Dry Doddington
Frieston
A607
B6403
114
Normanton
North Rauceby
CRANWELL AVIATION HERITAGE CENTRE
Holdingham
COGGLESFORD WATERMILL
Kirkby la Thorpe
Hough-on-the-Hill
South Rauceby
Asgarby
Gelston
Carlton Scroop
Sudbrook
Sleaford
Hougham
West Willoughby
Ancaster
Quarrington
Heckington
Westborough
MARSTON HALL
Marston
A153
Silk Willoughby
Foston
Honington
Wilsford
HECKINGTON WINDMILL
Burton Pedwardine
A1
123
Northbeck
Barkston
Kelby
Culverthorpe
Swarby
BOUNDARY MILLS
GRANTHAM NORTH SERVICES
Syston
Scredington
115
Belton
BELTON HOUSE
Oasby
Heydour
Aswarby
Great Gonerby
Aisby
Aunsby
Osbournby
Spanby
B1394
Sedgebrook
Manthorpe
Welby
Dembleby
A52
Londonthorpe
Grantham
Haceby
Newton
Threekingham
Barrowby
Earlsfield
GRANTHAM MUS
129
Cold Harbour
Braceby
Walcot
Stow
Horbling
Ropsley
Sapperton
Pickworth
Billingborough
Woolsthorpe by Belvoir
Old Somerby
Folkingham
Birthorpe
B1174
B1176
Humby
Hanby
B1177
Denton
Harlaxton
Little Ponton
Boothby Pagnell
Laughton
Pointon
Millthorpe
Stroxton
Lenton
Aslackby
Great Ponton
Ingoldsby
Dowsby
A607
Hungerton
Graby
Croxton Kerrial
Wyville
GREAT PONTON SERVICES
Witham
Keisby
Bassingthorpe
Bitchfield
Kirkby Underwood
Hawthorpe
Rippingale
Irnham
Stoke Rochford
Easton
Saltby
Skillington
Bulby
Dunsby
WOOLSTHORPE MANOR
Burton-le-Coggles
Stainfield
Corby Glen
Haconby
Woolsthorpe
Elsthorpe
Hanthorpe
Morton
Sproxton
Colsterworth
A151
Birkholme
Grimsthorpe
Twyford
Buckminster
GRANTHAM SOUTH SERVICES
Dyke
B676
Swinstead
Cawthorpe
Stainby
Swayfield
GRIMSTHORPE CASTLE
Edenham
Sewstern
Gunby
North Witham
Scottlethorpe
Bourne
Creeton
Wymondham
South Witham
CRIBBS MEADOW
Castle Bytham
Little Bytham
Lound
Northorpe
Edmondthorpe
Thistleton
Witham on the Hill
Thurlby
Market Overton
Clipsham
Toft
THURLBY
Teigh
Careby
Thetford
RAM JAM SERVICES
Stretton
Manthorpe
Barrow
THE LIVING IRONSTONE MUS
Obthorpe
A6121
Carlby
Pickworth
Wilsthorpe
Greetham
Baston
Ashwell
Cottesmore
Essendine
Braceborough
Langtoft
Greatford
Exton
TOLETHORPE HALL RUTLAND OPEN AIR THEATRE
Ryhall
B668
Barholm
Towngate
KING
BARNSDALE GARDENS
Burley
Little Casterton
BLOODY OAKS SERVICES
Belmesthorpe
FALCONRY CENTRE
99
100
Whitwell
Tickencote
Great Casterton
Empingham
Uffington
Tallington
West Deeping
0 1 2 3 miles
0 1 2 3 4 5 km

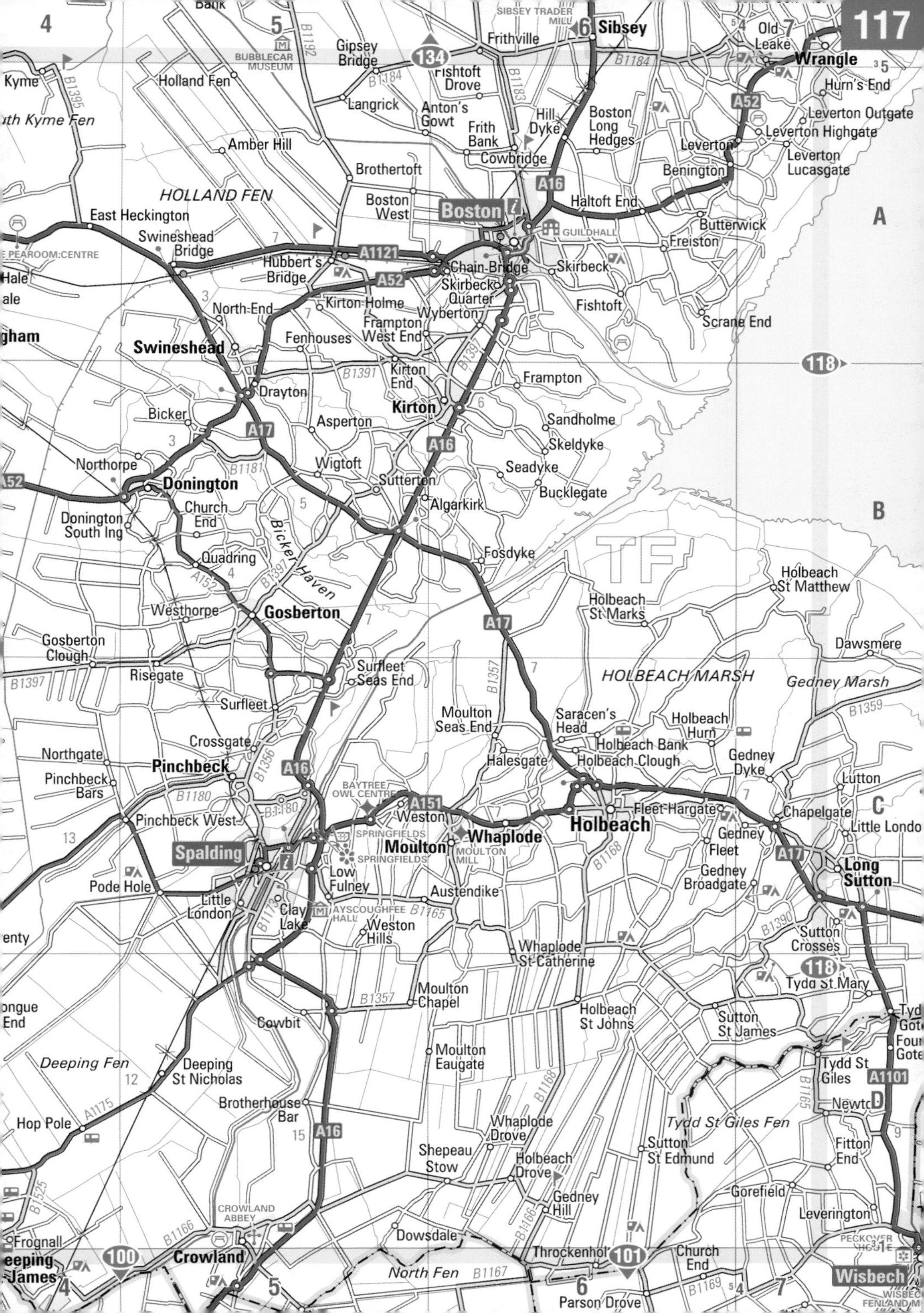
Sibsey
Wrangle
Boston
Kirton
Donington
Swineshead
Gosberton
Pinchbeck
Spalding
Moulton
Whaplode
Holbeach
Long Sutton
Crowland
Wisbech
HOLLAND FEN
HOLBEACH MARSH
Gedney Marsh
Deeping Fen
Tydd St Giles Fen
North Fen
TF
Frithville
Gipsey Bridge
Fishtoft Drove
Langrick
Anton's Gowt
Frith Bank
Hill Dyke
Boston Long Hedges
Amber Hill
Brothertoft
Cowbridge
Leverton
Benington
Leverton Outgate
Leverton Highgate
Leverton Lucasgate
Hurn's End
Old Leake
Haltoft End
Boston West
East Heckington
Swineshead Bridge
Hubbert's Bridge
Chain Bridge
Skirbeck
Skirbeck Quarter
Butterwick
Freiston
Fishtoft
Scrane End
Kirton Holme
North End
Wyberton
Frampton West End
Fenhouses
Kirton End
Frampton
Drayton
Bicker
Asperton
Sandholme
Skeldyke
Seadyke
Bucklegate
Northorpe
Wigtoft
Sutterton
Algarkirk
Church End
Donington South Ing
Quadring
Bicker Haven
Fosdyke
Westhorpe
Holbeach St Marks
Holbeach St Matthew
Dawsmere
Gosberton Clough
Risegate
Surfleet
Surfleet Seas End
Moulton Seas End
Saracen's Head
Holbeach Hurn
Holbeach Bank
Holbeach Clough
Gedney Dyke
Crossgate
Northgate
Halesgate
Lutton
Pinchbeck Bars
Pinchbeck West
Weston
Fleet Hargate
Chapelgate
Gedney
Fleet
Little London
Pode Hole
Low Fulney
Austendike
Gedney Broadgate
Little London
Clay Lake
Weston Hills
Whaplode St Catherine
Sutton Crosses
Tydd St Mary
Moulton Chapel
Holbeach St Johns
Sutton St James
Cowbit
Moulton Eaugate
Tydd St Giles
Deeping St Nicholas
Newton
Brotherhouse Bar
Hop Pole
Whaplode Drove
Sutton St Edmund
Fitton End
Shepeau Stow
Holbeach Drove
Gedney Hill
Gorefield
Leverington
Dowsdale
Throckenholt
Church End
Frognall
Parson Drove
Kyme
Holland Fen
Bank
BUBBLECAR MUSEUM
SIBSEY TRADER MILL
GUILDHALL
PEAROOM CENTRE
BAYTREE OWL CENTRE
SPRINGFIELDS
MOULTON MILL
AYSCOUGHFEE HALL
CROWLAND ABBEY
PECKOVER HOUSE
WISBECH FENLAND M
A16
A17
A52
A151
A1121
A1101
A1175
A152
B1184
B1183
B1192
B1395
B1391
B1397
B1181
B1357
B1356
B1180
B1168
B1165
B1166
B1359
B1390
B1173
B1167
B1169
B1525
134
118
100
101
A
B
C
D
4
5
6
7

Wrangle
Lowgate
Friskney Flats
Hurn's End
Leverton Outgate
Leverton Highgate
Leverton Lucasgate
BOSTON DEEPS
LYNN DEEPS
THE WASH
NORFOLK
Holbeach St Matthew
Lynn Channel
Dawsmere
Gedney Marsh
Gedney Drove End
B1359
THE WASH
Gedney Dyke
Lutton
Guy's Head
Terrington Marsh
Ongar Hill
Chapelgate
Little London
Gedney
Long Sutton
Sutton Bridge
Orange Row
Clenchwarton
Sutton Crosses
Walpole Cross Keys
Terrington St Clement
Tydd St Mary
Walpole St Andrew
Hay Green
Tilney High End
Tilney All Saints
Sutton St James
Tydd Gote
Four Gotes
Walpole Marsh
Walpole St Peter
Tydd St Giles
Newton
St Giles Fen
Ingleborough
St John's Highway
Terrington St John
Tilney St Lawrence
West Walton
Fitton End
Walpole Highway
West Walton Highway
Marshland
Gorefield
Leverington
St John's Fen End
Wiggenhall St Mary Magdalen
Walsoken
PECKOVER HOUSE
FENLAND & WEST NORFOLK AVIATION MUSEUM
New Walsoken
Marshland St James
Marshland Fen
FENLAND MUS.
HOLME B OBSERVAT
Old Hunstanton
Hunstanton
SEA LIFE SANCTUARY
Heacham
SNETTISHAM NATURE RESERVE
Shepherd's Port
DERSINGHAM BOG
SANDRINGHAM
Wolferton
Castle Rising
CASTLE RISING
North Wootton
South Wootton
King's Lynn
MARITIME EXHIBITION
GUILDHALL
Gaywood
ROYDON COMMON
West Lynn
Fairstead
Hardwick
Fair Green
Tower End
Middleton
Saddle Bow
West Winch
North Runcton
Wiggenhall St Germans
Blackborough End
Setchey
Wiggenhall St Mary the Virgin
Tottenhill Row
Watlington
Wormegay
Tottenhill
Runcton Holme
South
A52
A17
A1101
B1165
B1390
A47
A10
A134
A149
A148
A1078
135
117
101
102
0 1 2 3 miles
0 1 2 3 4 5 km

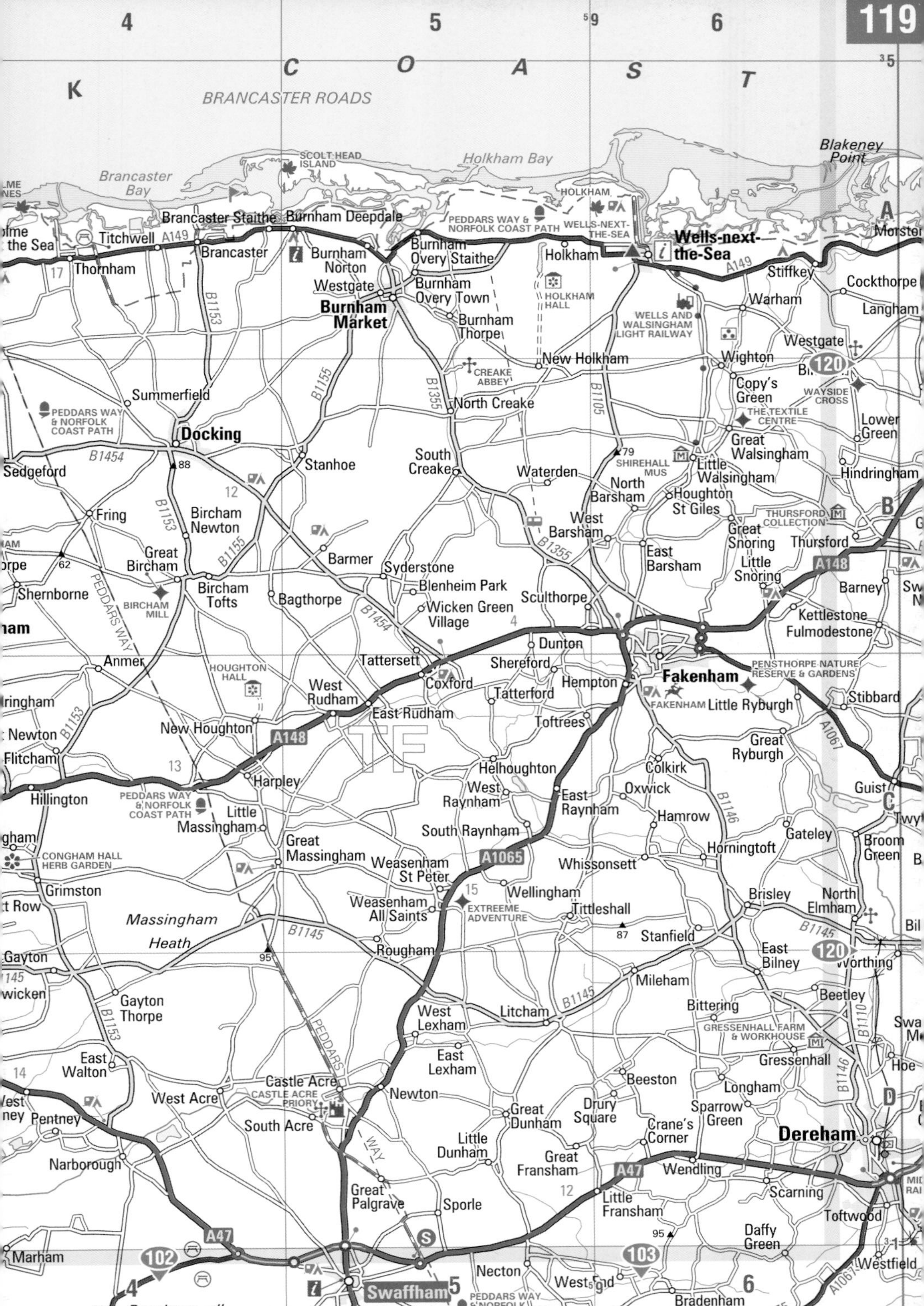
COAST
BRANCASTER ROADS
Brancaster Bay
SCOLT HEAD ISLAND
Holkham Bay
Blakeney Point
HOLKHAM
PEDDARS WAY & NORFOLK COAST PATH
WELLS-NEXT-THE-SEA
Brancaster Staithe
Burnham Deepdale
Titchwell
Brancaster
Thornham
Burnham Norton
Burnham Overy Staithe
Holkham
Wells-next-the-Sea
Morston
Stiffkey
Cockthorpe
Westgate
Burnham Market
Burnham Overy Town
Burnham Thorpe
HOLKHAM HALL
WELLS AND WALSINGHAM LIGHT RAILWAY
Warham
Langham
Wighton
Copy's Green
New Holkham
CREAKE ABBEY
North Creake
Summerfield
PEDDARS WAY & NORFOLK COAST PATH
Docking
WAYSIDE CROSS
THE TEXTILE CENTRE
Lower Green
Great Walsingham
Little Walsingham
SHIREHALL MUS
Hindringham
Sedgeford
Stanhoe
South Creake
Waterden
North Barsham
Houghton St Giles
Fring
Bircham Newton
West Barsham
Great Snoring
THURSFORD COLLECTION
Thursford
Great Bircham
Barmer
Syderstone
East Barsham
Little Snoring
Shernborne
Bircham Tofts
Bagthorpe
Blenheim Park
Wicken Green Village
Sculthorpe
Barney
BIRCHAM MILL
PEDDARS WAY
Kettlestone
Fulmodestone
Anmer
HOUGHTON HALL
Tattersett
Dunton
Shereford
Fakenham
PENSTHORPE NATURE RESERVE & GARDENS
West Rudham
Coxford
Hempton
Tatterford
FAKENHAM
Little Ryburgh
Stibbard
East Rudham
Toftrees
New Houghton
Great Ryburgh
Flitcham
TF
Helhoughton
Colkirk
Hillington
Harpley
West Raynham
East Raynham
Oxwick
Guist
PEDDARS WAY & NORFOLK COAST PATH
Little Massingham
South Raynham
Hamrow
Great Massingham
Horningtoft
Gateley
Broom Green
CONGHAM HALL HERB GARDEN
Weasenham St Peter
Whissonsett
Grimston
Wellingham
Brisley
North Elmham
Weasenham All Saints
EXTREEME ADVENTURE
Tittleshall
Massingham Heath
Stanfield
Rougham
Gayton
East Bilney
Worthing
Mileham
Beetley
Gayton Thorpe
West Lexham
Litcham
Bittering
GRESSENHALL FARM & WORKHOUSE
East Lexham
Gressenhall
East Walton
Hoe
Castle Acre
CASTLE ACRE PRIORY
Beeston
Longham
West Acre
Newton
Pentney
Great Dunham
Drury Square
Sparrow Green
South Acre
Crane's Corner
Dereham
Little Dunham
Narborough
Great Fransham
Wendling
Great Palgrave
Sporle
Little Fransham
Scarning
Toftwood
Daffy Green
Marham
Necton
West End
Westfield
Swaffham
Bradenham
A149
A148
A1065
A1067
A47
B1153
B1155
B1355
B1105
B1454
B1145
B1146
B1110
120
102
103

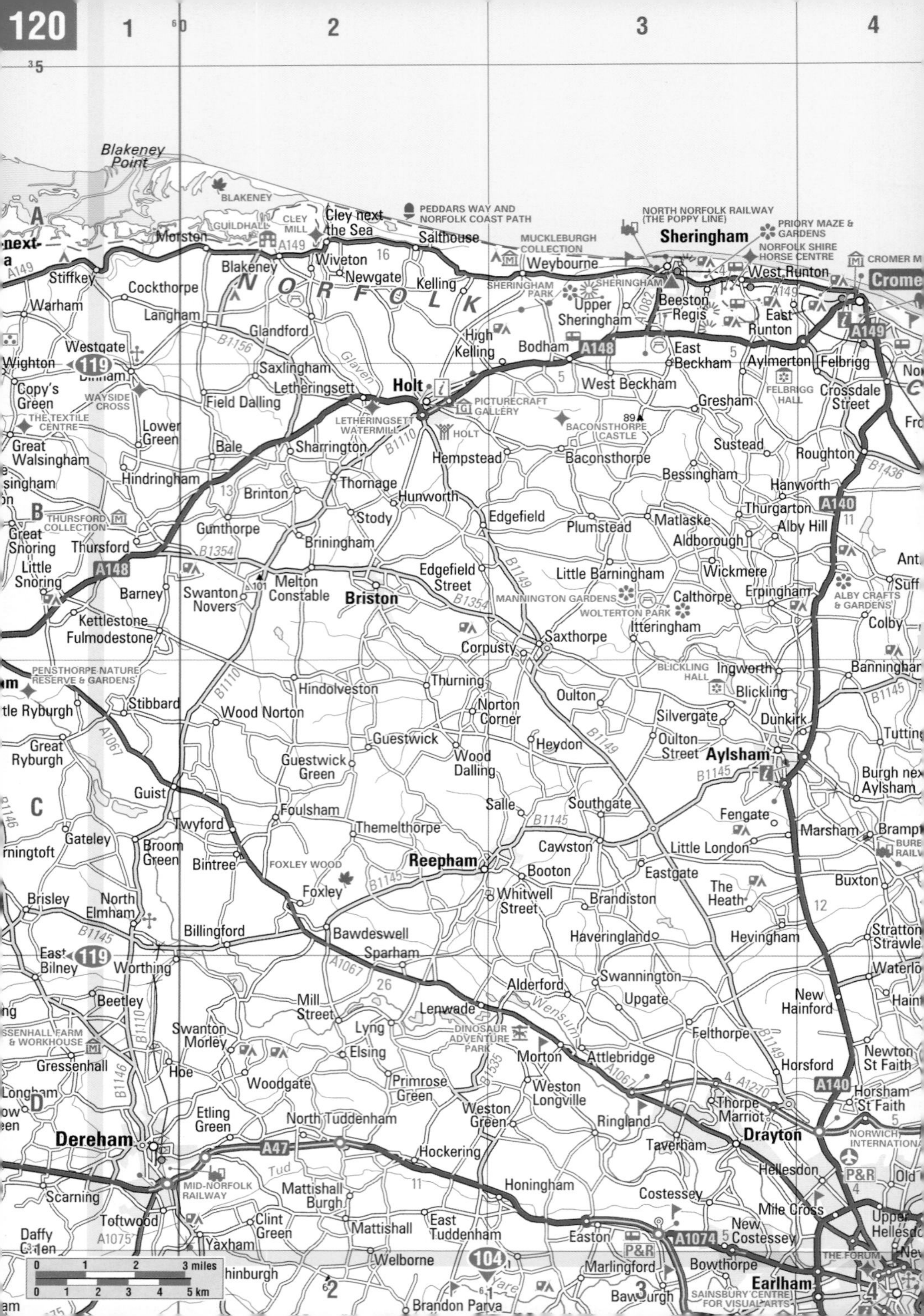

Blakeney Point
BLAKENEY
GUILDHALL
CLEY MILL
Cley next the Sea
PEDDARS WAY AND NORFOLK COAST PATH
NORTH NORFOLK RAILWAY (THE POPPY LINE)
PRIORY MAZE & GARDENS
MUCKLEBURGH COLLECTION
NORFOLK SHIRE HORSE CENTRE
CROMER M
Cromer
Sheringham
Morston
Salthouse
Stiffkey
Blakeney
Wiveton
Newgate
Kelling
Weybourne
West Runton
SHERINGHAM PARK
SHERINGHAM
Upper Sheringham
Beeston Regis
East Runton
Warham
Cockthorpe
Langham
Glandford
High Kelling
Bodham
East Beckham
Aylmerton
Felbrigg
Westgate
Wighton
Binham
Saxlingham
Letheringsett
Holt
Glaven
West Beckham
FELBRIGG HALL
Crossdale Street
Copy's Green
WAYSIDE CROSS
Field Dalling
THE TEXTILE CENTRE
LETHERINGSETT WATERMILL
PICTURECRAFT GALLERY
HOLT
Gresham
BACONSTHORPE CASTLE
Lower Green
Great Walsingham
Bale
Sharrington
Hempstead
Baconsthorpe
Sustead
Roughton
Hindringham
Brinton
Thornage
Hunworth
Bessingham
Hanworth
THURSFORD COLLECTION
Thurgarton
Great Snoring
Thursford
Gunthorpe
Stody
Edgefield
Plumstead
Matlaske
Alby Hill
Aldborough
Little Snoring
Briningham
Barney
Swanton Novers
Melton Constable
Briston
Edgefield Street
Little Barningham
Wickmere
MANNINGTON GARDENS
Calthorpe
Erpingham
ALBY CRAFTS & GARDENS
WOLTERTON PARK
Kettlestone
Fulmodestone
Corpusty
Saxthorpe
Itteringham
Colby
PENSTHORPE NATURE RESERVE & GARDENS
Hindolveston
Thurning
BLICKLING HALL
Ingworth
Banningham
Stibbard
Little Ryburgh
Oulton
Blickling
Wood Norton
Norton Corner
Silvergate
Dunkirk
Great Ryburgh
Guestwick
Heydon
Oulton Street
Aylsham
Guestwick Green
Wood Dalling
Burgh next Aylsham
Guist
Salle
Southgate
Fengate
Foulsham
Twyford
Themelthorpe
Marsham
Gateley
Broom Green
Cawston
Little London
Bintree
FOXLEY WOOD
Reepham
Booton
Eastgate
The Heath
Buxton
Brisley
North Elmham
Foxley
Whitwell Street
Brandiston
Billingford
Bawdeswell
Haveringland
Hevingham
East Bilney
Worthing
Sparham
Swannington
Alderford
New Hainford
Beetley
Mill Street
Lenwade
Upgate
Swanton Morley
Lyng
DINOSAUR ADVENTURE PARK
Wensum
Felthorpe
GRESSENHALL FARM & WORKHOUSE
Elsing
Morton
Attlebridge
Horsford
Newton St Faith
Gressenhall
Hoe
Woodgate
Primrose Green
Weston Longville
Thorpe Marriot
Horsham St Faith
Etling Green
North Tuddenham
Weston Green
Ringland
Drayton
Dereham
Hockering
Taverham
NORWICH INTERNATIONAL
MID-NORFOLK RAILWAY
Tud
Mattishall Burgh
Honingham
Hellesdon
Scarning
Costessey
Mile Cross
Toftwood
Clint Green
Mattishall
East Tuddenham
Easton
New Costessey
Upper Hellesdon
Daffy Green
Yaxham
Welborne
Marlingford
Bowthorpe
THE FORUM
Earlham
Brandon Parva
Bawburgh
SAINSBURY CENTRE FOR VISUAL ARTS
Yare
Whinburgh
N O R F O L K
A149
A148
A1082
B1156
B1110
B1354
B1149
B1436
A140
B1145
A1067
B1146
A1270
A47
A1075
A1074
B1535
119
104
P&R
0 1 2 3 miles
0 1 2 3 4 5 km
1
2
3
4
A
B
C
D

4
5
6
7
A
B
C
D
TG
Mundesley
STOW WINDMILL
ENGLAND COAST PATH
Sidestrand
Trimingham
Gimingham
Trunch
Paston
Knapton
Bacton
Keswick
Walcott
Broomholm
Bradfield
Swafield
Edingthorpe
Edingthorpe Green
Witton Bridge
Ridlington
Happisburgh
Spa Common
Crostwight
Whimpwell Green
Eccles on Sea
Happisburgh Common
EAST RUSTON OLD VICARAGE GARDEN
Honing
Lessingham
Hempstead
Sea Palling
Ingham Corner
East Ruston
Bengate
Worstead
WAXHAM GREAT BARN
Waxham
Ingham
Sloley
Dilham
Stalham
Stalham Green
Smallburgh
NORFOLK COAST
MUSEUM OF THE BROADS
Hickling
Sutton
Hickling Green
Scottow
Pennygate
Barton Turf
Hickling Heath
Horsey
Tunstead
Wood Street
ANT BROADS AND MARSHES
Hickling Broad
HORSEY WINDMILL
WINTERTON DUNES
Sco Ruston
Neatishead
Catfield
Barton Broad
WROXHAM BARNS
Ashmanhaugh
MARTHAM BROAD
East Somerton
Coltishall
Irstead
Sharp Street
Potter Heigham
West Somerton
Winterton-on-Sea
Threehammer Common
Hoveton
THE BROADS
Belaugh
Wroxham
Lower Street
Ludham
Bastwick
Martham
Upper Street
Horning
LUDHAM MARSHES
Repps
Rollesby
Hemsby
Newport
Wroxham Broad
BURE MARSHES
Thurne
Ormesby St Michael
Scratby
California
Crostwick
Woodbastwick
Ranworth
Rackheath
Salhouse
FAIRHAVEN WOODLAND & WATER GARDEN
Clippesby
Filby Broad
Ormesby St Margaret
Panxworth
South Walsham
Billockby
Burgh St Margaret
Filby
CAISTER ROMAN TOWN
New Rackheath
Little Plumstead
Upton
THE CANDLEMAKER WORKSHOP
Thrigby
THRIGBY HALL WILDLIFE GARDENS
Mautby
West Caister
Caister-on-Sea
Hemblington
Runham
West End
Thorpe St Andrew
Great Plumstead
Blofield Heath
North Burlingham
Acle
Stokesby
GREAT YARMOUTH GREAT DENES
YARMOUTH
Blofield
Brundall
Lingwood
Beighton
Damgate
Tunstall
Great Yarmouth
A149
A1151
A1062
A1064
A47
A140
B1145
B1159
B1150
B1354
B1140
B1152
105
Bure
Thurne
Ant

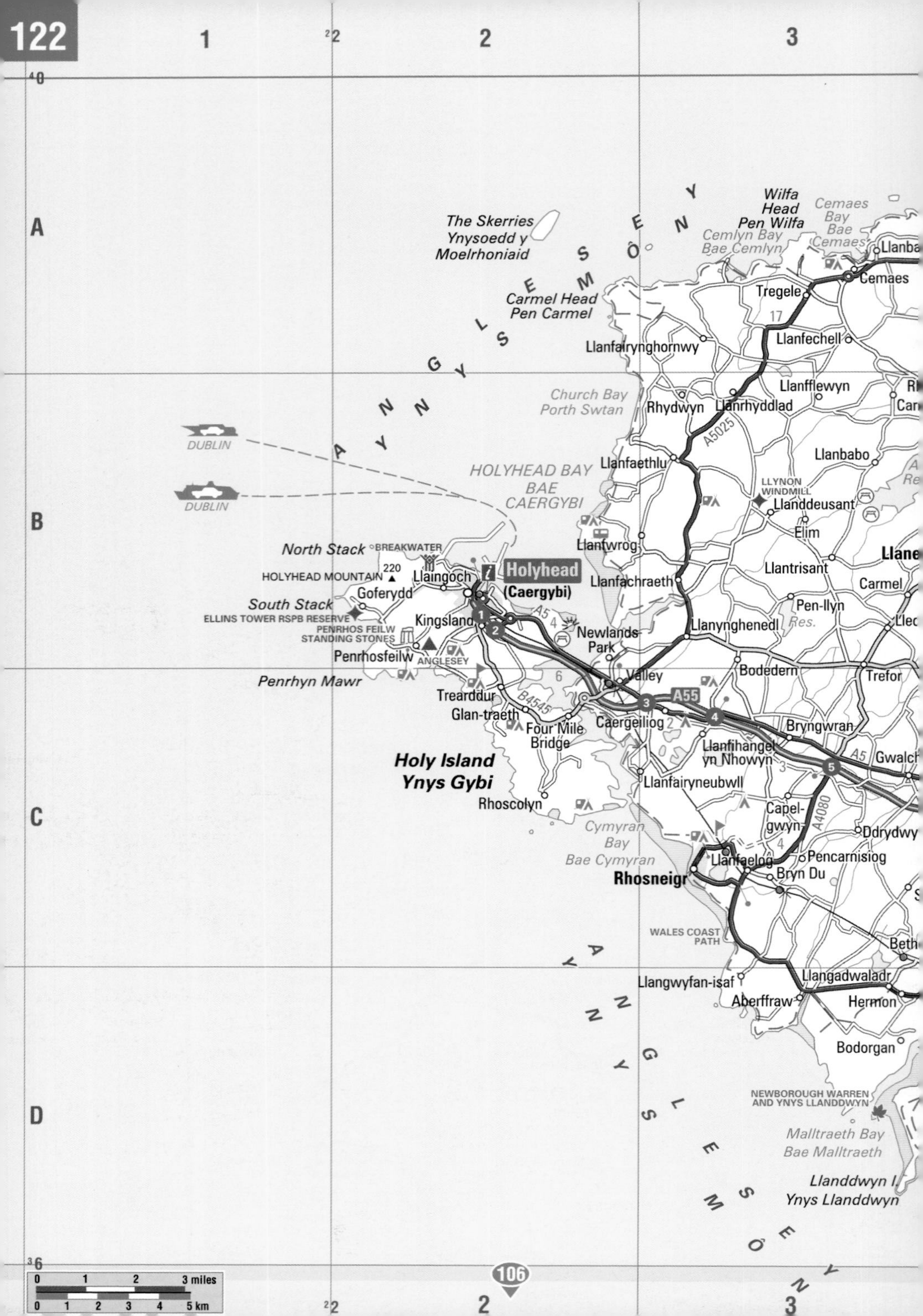

1
2
3
A
B
C
D
The Skerries
Ynysoedd y Moelrhoniaid
Carmel Head
Pen Carmel
Wilfa Head
Pen Wilfa
Cemlyn Bay
Bae Cemlyn
Cemaes Bay
Bae Cemaes
Cemaes
Tregele
Llanfechell
Llanfairynghornwy
Llanfflewyn
Church Bay
Porth Swtan
Rhydwyn
Llanrhyddlad
A5025
Llanfaethlu
Llanbabo
LLYNON WINDMILL
Llanddeusant
Elim
HOLYHEAD BAY
BAE CAERGYBI
DUBLIN
DUBLIN
ANGLESEY
YNYS MÔN
North Stack
BREAKWATER
HOLYHEAD MOUNTAIN
220
Llaingoch
Holyhead
(Caergybi)
Goferydd
South Stack
ELLINS TOWER RSPB RESERVE
Kingsland
PENRHOS FEILW STANDING STONES
Penrhosfeilw
Penrhyn Mawr
Llanfwrog
Llanfachraeth
Llantrisant
Carmel
Pen-llyn
Res.
Newlands Park
Llanynghenedl
Valley
Bodedern
Trefor
A5
A55
B4545
Trearddur
Glan-traeth
Four Mile Bridge
Caergeiliog
Bryngwran
Llanfihangel yn Nhowyn
Gwalch
Holy Island
Ynys Gybi
Llanfairyneubwll
Rhoscolyn
Capel-gwyn
A4080
Ddrydwy
Cymyran Bay
Bae Cymyran
Llanfaelog
Pencarnisiog
Rhosneigr
Bryn Du
WALES COAST PATH
Llangwyfan-isaf
Llangadwaladr
Aberffraw
Hermon
Bodorgan
NEWBOROUGH WARREN AND YNYS LLANDDWYN
Malltraeth Bay
Bae Malltraeth
Llanddwyn I.
Ynys Llanddwyn
0 1 2 3 miles
0 1 2 3 4 5 km

106

4
5
6
A
B
C
D
SH
YSGLS MÔN
ANGLESEY
Bull Bay
Porth Llechog
Amlwch Port
Amlwch
Point Lynas
Trwyn Eilian
Llaneilian
Pengorffwysfa
Penysarn
Nebo
Dulas
Dulas Bay
Bae Dulas
Rhosybol
Tyn-y-pwll
City Dulas
Brynrefail
Moelfre
Ty-mawr
Llandyfrydog
Llanallgo
Hebron
Mynydd Bodafon
Marianglas
Bachau
Maenaddwyn
Tynygongl
Brynteg
Benllech
Capel Coch
CORS ERDDREINIOG
Red Wharf Bay
Traeth-coch
CORS GOCH
Red Wharf Bay
Llanbedrgoch
Tregaian
Tan-y-graig
Llangwyllog
Llanddyfnan
Pentraeth
Glan Gors
THE STONE SCIENCE
CORS BODEILIO
Rhosmeirch
Res.
ORIEL YNYS MON
Talwrn
Pen-y-garnedd
Rhoscefnhir
Heneglwys
Llangefni
Ceint
Penmynydd
Mariandyrys
Glan-yr-afon
Caim
Penmon
Puffin Island
Ynys Seiriol
Llanddona
Llangoed
Llanfaes
Llansadwrn
GAOL AND COURTHOUSE
Beaumaris
Lavan Sands
Traeth Lafan
Llandegfan
Menai Bridge
(Porthaethwy)
JAMES PRINGLE WEAVERS
PILI PALAS
Llangristiolus
HENBLAS COUNTRY PARK
Capel Mawr
Pentre Berw
Gaerwen
Llanfairpwll -gwyngyll
Afon Cefni
Llanddaniel Fab
PLAS NEWYDD
Capel-y-graig
Garth
TEGFRYN
Hirael
PENRHYN
BANGOR
Coed Mawr
Bangor
Glan Adda
Minffordd
Llandegai
Tal-y-bont
Crymlyn
Abergwyngregyn
Penmaenmawr
Llanfairfechan
Nant-y-pandy
COEDYDD ABER
Aber Falls
Rhaeadr Aber
COCHWILLAN OLD HALL
Llanllechid
Rachub
SNOWDONIA NATIONAL PARK
PARC CENEDLAETHOL ERYRI
942 FOEL FRAS
Glasinfryn
BANGOR SERVICES
Tregarth
Malltraeth
Llangaffo
Brynsiencyn
ACLA TAID MUSEUM
GREENWOOD CENTRE
Seion
Pentir
Sling
Bethesda
Gerlan
Braichmelyn
Dwyran
SEA ZOO
Y Felinheli
Saron
Llanddeiniolen
Rhiwlas
ZIP WORLD PENRHYN QUARRY
Pen-lon
MODEL VILLAGE
FOEL FARM PARK
MENAI STRAIT AFON MENAI
Bethel
Penisarwaun
Ty'n-y-maes
1064 CARNEDD LLYWELYN
Waterloo Port
Llanrug
BRYN BRAS CASTLE
Deiniolen
Marchlyn Mawr Res.
CASTLE & REGIMENTAL MUS
Pont-rug
SEGONTIUM FORT
Clwt-y-bont
1044 CARNEDD DAFYDD
Caernarfon
Cwm-y-glo
Brynrefail
Llyn Padarn
Dinorwic
Caeathro
POWER OF WALES
LLANBERIS LAKE RAILWAY
PADARN
Abermenai Pt.
Trwyn Abermenai
WELSH HIGHLAND RAILWAY
Ceunant
Llyn Ogwen
Pont Rhyd-goch
Pont Pen-y-benglog
Llanfaglan
Croesywaun
Groeslon
Llanberis
SLATE MUS
IDWAL COTTAGE
Llyn Peris
Waunfawr
107
CAERNARFON AIR MUSEUM
Saron
Bontnewydd
DOLBADARN
Glan-rhyd
Nant Peris
CWM IDWAL
Capel
124
A55
A5
A5025
A5114
A545
A487
A4080
A4244
B5111
B5110
B5108
B5109
B5420
B4419
B4421
B4366
B4409
B4547

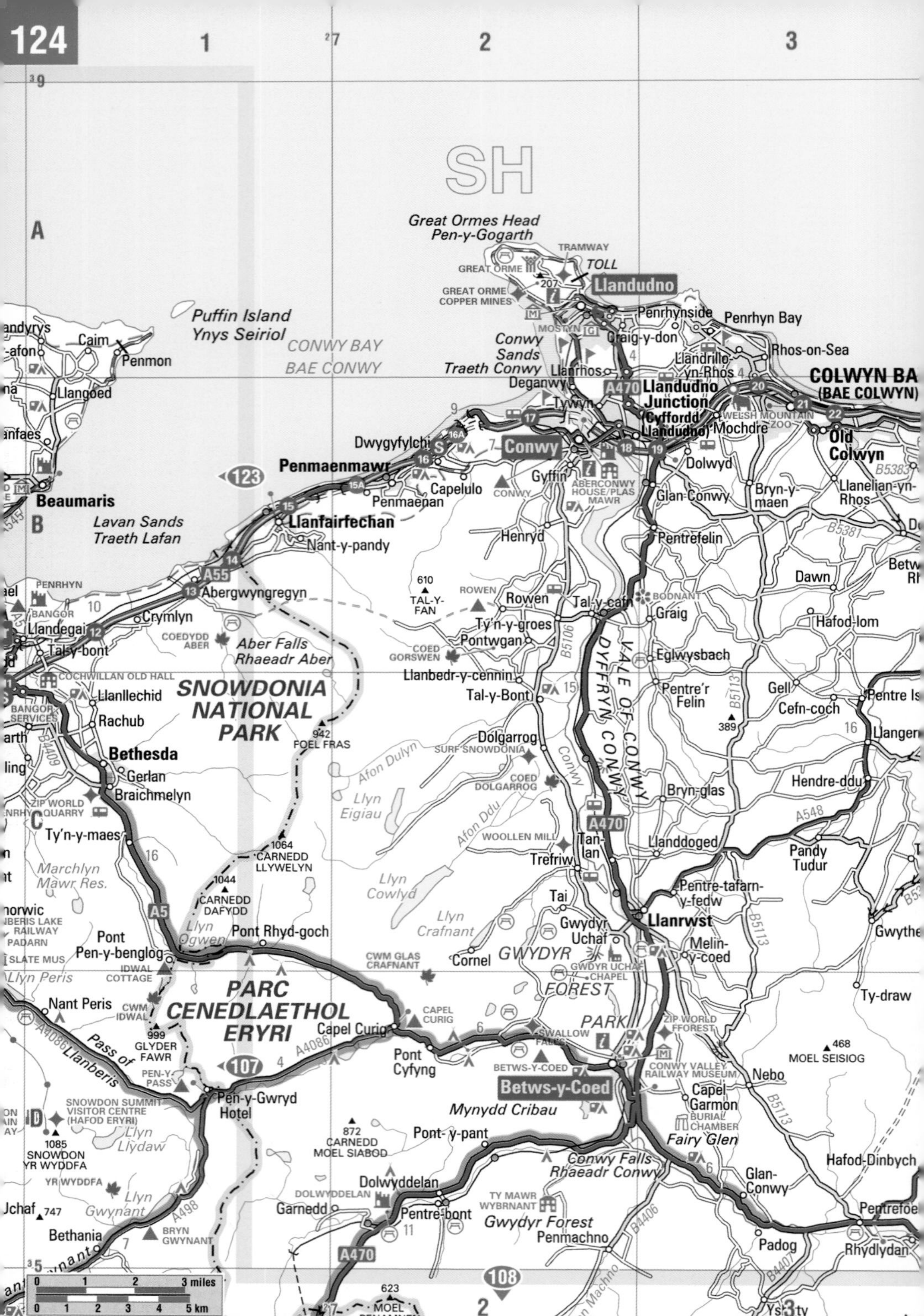

SH
Great Ormes Head
Pen-y-Gogarth
Llandudno
Puffin Island
Ynys Seiriol
CONWY BAY
BAE CONWY
Conwy Sands
Traeth Conwy
Penrhynside
Penrhyn Bay
Craig-y-don
Rhos-on-Sea
Llandrillo-yn-Rhos
Llanrhos
Deganwy
COLWYN BAY (BAE COLWYN)
Llandudno Junction (Cyffordd Llandudno)
Mochdre
WELSH MOUNTAIN ZOO
Old Colwyn
Caim
Penmon
Llangoed
Beaumaris
Dwygyfylchi
Penmaenmawr
Conwy
Gyffin
ABERCONWY HOUSE/PLAS MAWR
Capelulo
Penmaenan
Llanfairfechan
Lavan Sands
Traeth Lafan
Nant-y-pandy
Glan-Conwy
Bryn-y-maen
Llanelian-yn-Rhos
Henryd
Pentrefelin
Dawn
PENRHYN
BANGOR
Abergwyngregyn
Crymlyn
Llandegai
Tal-y-bont
COEDYDD ABER
Aber Falls
Rhaeadr Aber
610 TAL-Y-FAN
ROWEN
Rowen
Tal-y-cafn
BODNANT
Graig
Ty'n-y-groes
Pontwgan
Hafod-lom
COED GORSWEN
Eglwysbach
Llanbedr-y-cennin
COCHWILLAN OLD HALL
Llanllechid
SNOWDONIA NATIONAL PARK
BANGOR SERVICES
Rachub
Tal-y-Bont
VALE OF CONWY
DYFFRYN CONWY
Pentre'r Felin
Gell
Pentre Isa
Cefn-coch
942 FOEL FRAS
389
Llangernyw
Bethesda
Gerlan
Braichmelyn
Dolgarrog
SURF SNOWDONIA
Afon Dulyn
COED DOLGARROG
Llyn Eigiau
Bryn-glas
Hendre-ddu
ZIP WORLD QUARRY
Ty'n-y-maes
Afon Ddu
WOOLLEN MILL
Tan-lan
Llanddoged
Pandy Tudur
Marchlyn Mawr Res.
1064 CARNEDD LLYWELYN
Trefriw
1044 CARNEDD DAFYDD
Llyn Cowlyd
Pentre-tafarn-y-fedw
Tai
LLANBERIS LAKE RAILWAY PADARN
Llyn Ogwen
Pont Rhyd-goch
Llyn Crafnant
Gwydyr Uchaf
Llanrwst
Gwytherin
Pont Pen-y-benglog
SLATE MUS
IDWAL COTTAGE
Llyn Peris
CWM GLAS CRAFNANT
Cornel
GWYDYR FOREST PARK
GWDYR UCHAF CHAPEL
Melin-y-coed
Ty-draw
Nant Peris
PARC CENEDLAETHOL ERYRI
CWM IDWAL
999 GLYDER FAWR
Capel Curig
CAPEL CURIG
SWALLOW FALLS
ZIP WORLD FFOREST
Pass of Llanberis
Pont Cyfyng
BETWS-Y-COED
CONWY VALLEY RAILWAY MUSEUM
468 MOEL SEISIOG
Nebo
PEN-Y-PASS
Pen-y-Gwryd Hotel
Betws-y-Coed
Capel Garmon
SNOWDON SUMMIT VISITOR CENTRE (HAFOD ERYRI)
Mynydd Cribau
BURIAL CHAMBER
1085 SNOWDON YR WYDDFA
Llyn Llydaw
872 CARNEDD MOEL SIABOD
Pont-y-pant
Fairy Glen
Conwy Falls
Rhaeadr Conwy
Hafod-Dinbych
Glan-Conwy
YR WYDDFA
Llyn Gwynant
Dolwyddelan
DOLWYDDELAN
TY MAWR WYBRNANT
Garnedd
Pentre-bont
Gwydyr Forest
Pentrefoelas
747
Bethania
BRYN GWYNANT
Penmachno
Padog
Rhydlydan
623 MOEL
0 1 2 3 miles
0 1 2 3 4 5 km

123
107
108

SJ
West Hoyle Bank
Hilbre I.
West Kirk
Welsh Channel
Point of Ayr
Yr Parlwr Du
River Dee
Afon Dyfrdwy
Talacre
Gwespyr
Gronant
Ffynnongroyw
Y-Ffrith
SEAQUARIUM
RHYL
(Y RHYL)
Prestatyn
Gwaenysgor
Picton
Meliden
Llanasa
Mostyn Quay
Mostyn
OFFA'S DYKE PATH
LLWYBR CLAWDD OFFA
Kinmel Bay
Axton
Trelogan
Abergele Roads
Angorfa
Abergele
COLWYN BAY
Towyn
Trelawnyd
Glan-y-don
Rhuddlan
Dyserth
Pensarn
Whitford
Abergele
Cwm
Greenfield
Carmel
Pant-y-Wacco
Gorsedd
Bodelwyddan
Holywell
(Treffynnon)
St George
Rhuallt
BODELWYDDAN
St Asaph
(Llanelwy)
Pen-y-cefn
Brynford
Glascoed
Groesffordd Marli
ST. ASAPH CATHEDRAL
Waen
Goleugoed
Tremeirchion
Babell
Caerwys
MOELFRE ISAF
VALE OF CLWYD
DYFFRYN CLWYD
Graig
AFON-WEN CRAFT AND ANTIQUE CENTRE
Pentre Halkyn
Plas-yn-Cefn
Afon-wen
Ysceifiog
Lixwm
Llanfair Talhaiarn
Llannefydd
Bont-newydd
Trefnant
Bodfari
Halkyn Mountain
Rhes-y-cae
Nannerch
Bryn-nantllech
Cefn Berain
Green
Castell
Rhosesmor
Bryn Rhyd-yr-Arian
Henllan
Hendre
Denbigh
(Dinbych)
Fron
CLWYDIAN RANGE
BRYNIAU CLWYD
Llansannan
Waen
Llangwyfan
Cilcain
CASTLE & TOWN WALLS
Llandyrnog
MOEL LLYS-Y-COED
Pantymwyn
Gwernaffield
Tan-y-fron
Groes
Llangynhafal
LOGGERHEADS
Clwt-grugoer
Llanrhaeadr
MOEL FAMAU
isaf
Bylchau
Waen
Peniel
Prion
Pentre Llanrhaeadr
Llanynys
Gellifor
Tafarn-y-gelyn
Nantglyn
Saron
Hirwaen
Rhewl
Llanferres
BRYN TRILLYN
GORSEDD BRAN
Meifod
Llanbedr-Dyffryn-Clwyd
CRAFT CENTRE
Llanfwrog
Cyffylliog
Bontuchel
Ruthin
(Rhuthun)
Tai-Ucha
Mynydd Hiraethog
Brenig Res.
Llanarmon-yn-Ial
Graig
Nant Uchaf
Efenechtyd
Llanfair-Dyffryn-Clwyd
Alwen Reservoir
HAFOD ELWY MOOR
Nilig
Pennant
Pwll-glas
LLYN BRENIG VISITOR CENTRE
Clocaenog
Graig-fechan
Mwdwl-eithin
Clocaenog Forest
Pentre-celyn
Clawdd-newydd
Llandegla
Pentre-llyn cymmer
Afon Alwen
Rhyd-y-meudwy
Hafod Cefn-brith
Derwen
Llanelidan
Llanfihangel Glyn Myfyr
Bryn Saith Marchog
Cerrigydrudion
Melin-y-Wig
Mae
Elwy
Clwyd
A55
A548
A547
A525
A5151
B5119
B5429
A5026
B5122
B5121
A541
B5381
A543
B5428
B5382
A544
B5429
A525
B4501
B5435
A494
B5430
B5431
A5
B5105
A5104
A542
109
126

HOYLAKE
West Hoyle Bank
Hilbre I.
Meols
Moreton
Wallasey
Seacombe
Poulton
Bidston
LIVERPOOL
Edge Hill
Claughton
Birkenhead
Toxteth
Mossley Hill
Dingle
Upton
Greasby
Grange
West Kirby
Woodchurch
Frankby
Tranmere
Rock Ferry
Prenton
Aigburth
New Ferry
Grassendale
Port Sunlight
BEBINGTON
Storeton
Thingwall
Caldy
Thurstaston
Irby
Pensby
Barnston
Brimstage
Bromborough
Eastham Ferry
Eastham
Heswall
Thornton Hough
Gayton
Raby
Dawpool Bank
Parkgate
Hinderton
Willaston
Hooton
Childer Thornton
Neston
Gayton Sands
Little Neston
Ness
Little Sutton
Great Sutton
Burton
Ledsham
Two Mills
Puddington
Capenhurst
Backford Cross
Shotwick
Saughall
Mollington
Sealand
Blacon
Welsh Channel
Point of Ayr
Yr Parlwr Du
River Dee
Afon Dyfrdwy
Talacre
Gwespyr
Ffynnongroyw
Picton
Llanasa
Mostyn Quay
Mostyn
Axton
Trelogan
Glan-y-don
WALES COAST PATH
Whitford
Greenfield
Carmel
Holywell Bank
GREENFIELD VALLEY HERITAGE PARK
Walwen
Pant-y-Wacco
Gorsedd
Holywell (Treffynnon)
Bagillt
Ben-y-cefn
Brynford
Dolphin
Babell
Caerwys
Flint (Y Fflint)
Pentre Halkyn
Mount Pleasant
AFON-WEN CRAFT AND ANTIQUE CENTRE
Ysceifiog
Afon-wen
Lixwm
Oakenholt
Halkyn Mountain
Halkyn
Rhes-y-cae
Flint Mountain
Connah's Quay
Garden City
Nannerch
Castell
OFFA'S DYKE PATH
LLWYBR CLAWDD OFFA
Rhosesmor
Northop
Northop Hall
Shotton
Hendre
Rhydymwyn
WEPRE
Queensferry
Sandycroft
Ewloe Grn.
Mancot
GREENACRES
Ewloe
Hawarden (Penarlâg)
Chester
Waen
Llangwyfan
Soughton
New Brighton
Cilcain
465
MOEL LLYS-Y-COED
Pantymwyn
Gwernaffield
Mold (Yr Wyddgrug)
Buckley (Bwcle)
Drury
HAWARDEN
Saltney
Llangynhafal
MOEL FAMAU 554
LOGGERHEADS
Cadole
Mynydd Isa
Llong
Spon Green
Broughton
Bretton
Llanynys
Gellifor
Tafarn-y-gelyn
Gwernymynydd
Lower Kinnerton
Balderton
Hirwaen
Maeshafn
Nercwys
Penyffordd
Dodleston
Higher Kinnerton
Rhewl
Llanbedr-Dyffryn-Clwyd
Llanferres
Pontblyddyn
Leeswood
Coed-Talon
Alyn
Hope (Yr Hôb)
Burton Green
Pulford
Lavister
CRAFT CENTRE
Ruthin (Rhuthun)
Llanfwrog
Eryrys
Treuddyn
WAUN-Y-LLYN
Caergwrle
Rossett
467
Llanfynydd
330
Cefn-y-bedd
Llay
Marford
Llanarmon-yn-Ial
Graianrhyd
Llanfair-Dyffryn-Clwyd
Rhydtalog
378
Ffrith
Gresford
Graig-fechan
Brymbo
ALYN WATERS
Moss
Gwersyllt
Four Crosses
Bwlchgwyn
Borras Head
Pentre-celyn
Llandegla
Rhosrobin
Garden Village
Gwynfryn
LEAD MINES
Minera
MOSS VALLEY
Acton
Llan-y-pwll
Pen-y-stryt
413
OFFA'S DYKE PATH
Coedpoeth
New Broughton
Rhosnesni
Rhyd-y-meudwy
Llanelidan
Wrexham (Wrecsam)
562
CYRN Y BRAIN
LLWYBR CLAWDD OFFA
ESCLUSHAM MOUNTAIN
Bersham
Rhostyllen
King's Mills
Wrexham Industrial Estate
CLWYDIAN RANGE
BRYNIAU CLWYD
0 1 2 3 miles
0 1 2 3 4 5 km

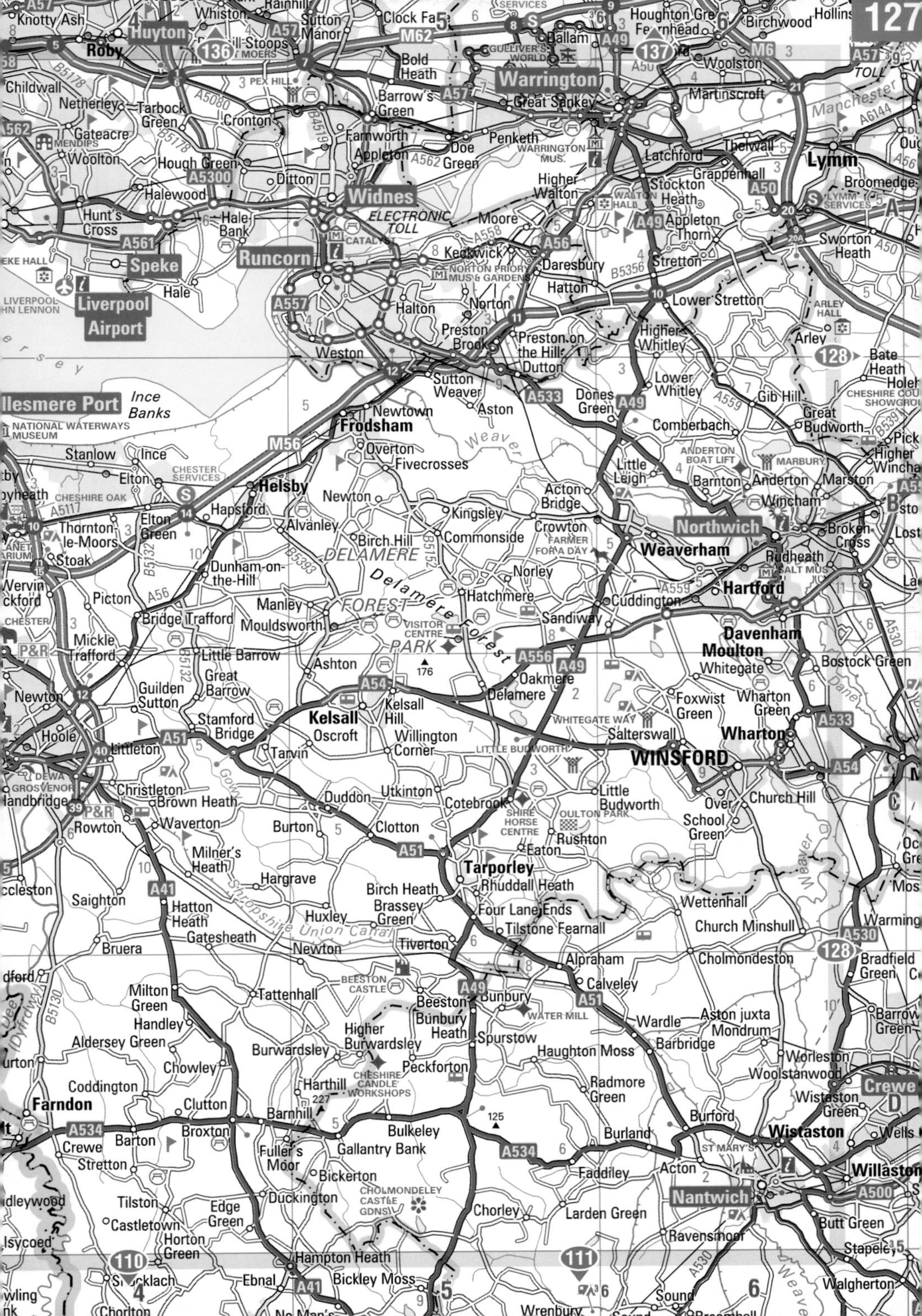
Knotty Ash
Huyton
Roby
Whiston
Rainhill
Sutton Manor
Clock Face
Rainhill Stoops
St Helens
M62
Gulliver's World
Dallam
Houghton Green
Fearnhead
Birchwood
Hollins
Warrington
Woolston
M6
A57
Toll
Childwall
Netherley
Tarbock Green
Pex Hill
Bold Heath
Barrow's Green
Great Sankey
Martinscroft
Manchester
Gateacre
Cronton
Farnworth
Penketh
Doe Green
Warrington Mus.
Latchford
Thelwall
Lymm
Mendips
Woolton
Hough Green
Appleton
A562
Grappenhall
Ditton
Halewood
A5300
Widnes
Higher Walton
Walton Hall
Stockton Heath
Broomedge
Lymm Services
Electronic Toll
Hunt's Cross
Hale Bank
Moore
Appleton Thorn
Swarton Heath
Catalyst
A561
A558
A56
A49
A50
Speke Hall
Speke
Runcorn
Keckwick
Norton Priory Mus & Gardens
Daresbury
Stretton
Liverpool John Lennon
Liverpool Airport
Hale
B5356
Hatton
A557
Halton
Norton
Lower Stretton
Arley Hall
Preston Brook
Preston on the Hill
Higher Whitley
Arley
Bate Heath
Weston
Dutton
Mersey
Sutton Weaver
Lower Whitley
Holeh
Aston
A533
Dones Green
Gib Hill
A559
Cheshire County Showground
Ellesmere Port
Ince Banks
Newtown
Frodsham
Comberbach
Great Budworth
B5391
Pickmere
National Waterways Museum
M56
Overton
Fivecrosses
Weaver
Stanlow
Ince
Elton
Chester Services
Little Leigh
Anderton Boat Lift
Marbury
Higher Wincham
Barnton
Anderton
Marston
Helsby
Newton
Acton Bridge
Wincham
Cheshire Oaks
A5117
Hapsford
Kingsley
Crowton
Farmer for a Day
Northwich
Broken Cross
Thornton-le-Moors
Elton Green
Alvanley
Birch Hill
Commonside
Weaverham
Stoak
Delamere
B5393
B5152
Norley
Rudheath
Salt Mus
Dunham-on-the-Hill
B5132
Delamere Forest
Hatchmere
Cuddington
Hartford
Picton
A56
Manley
Forest
Sandiway
Bridge Trafford
Mouldsworth
Visitor Centre
Davenham
Mickle Trafford
Park
Moulton
A530
P&R
Little Barrow
Ashton
A556
Bostock Green
Great Barrow
176
Oakmere
Whitegate
Guilden Sutton
A54
Kelsall Hill
Delamere
Foxwist Green
Wharton Green
Kelsall
Whitegate Way
Dane
Stamford Bridge
Oscroft
Willington Corner
Salterswall
Wharton
Hoole
A51
Tarvin
Little Budworth
Winsford
Littleton
Christleton
Brown Heath
Duddon
Utkinton
Cotebrook
Little Budworth
Church Hill
Dewa Grosvenor
Handbridge
Over
School Green
Rowton
Waverton
Shire Horse Centre
Oulton Park
Burton
Clotton
Eaton
Rushton
Milner's Heath
Tarporley
Weaver
Eccleston
Hargrave
Rhuddall Heath
Saighton
A41
Hatton Heath
Birch Heath
Wettenhall
Brassey Green
Four Lane Ends
Huxley
Tilstone Fearnall
Church Minshull
Warmingham
Shropshire Union Canal
Gatesheath
Tiverton
Bruera
Newton
Alpraham
Cholmondeston
A530
Bradfield Green
Beeston Castle
Calveley
Milton Green
Tattenhall
Bunbury
Beeston
Bunbury Heath
Water Mill
Handley
Aston juxta Mondrum
Wardle
Barrow Green
Higher Burwardsley
Aldersey Green
Spurstow
Barbridge
Burwardsley
Haughton Moss
Worleston
Chowley
Peckforton
Woolstanwood
Cheshire Candle Workshops
Harthill
Radmore Green
Crewe
Coddington
Wistaston Green
Farndon
Clutton
227
Barnhill
125
Burford
Wistaston
Wells Green
A534
Barton
Broxton
Bulkeley
Burland
Crewe
Fuller's Moor
Gallantry Bank
St Mary's
Willaston
Stretton
Bickerton
Acton
Faddiley
Cholmondeley Castle Gdns
Nantwich
A500
Duckington
Tilston
Edge Green
Chorley
Larden Green
Butt Green
Castletown
Horton Green
Ravensmoor
Stapeley
Isycoed
Hampton Heath
Ebnal
Bickley Moss
Sound
Walgherton
Shocklach
Chorlton
No Man's Heath
Wrenbury
Broomhall
136
137
128
110
111

Hollins Green
Partington
upon Mersey
SALE
Heaton Moor
Orford
Woolston
Warburton
Mossbrow
Broadheath
Timperley
Brooklands
Northenden
Cheadle Heath
Martinscroft
Manchester Ship Canal
Heatley
Dunham Town
Wythenshawe
GATLEY
Cheadle
Latchford
Thelwall
Oughtrington
DUNHAM MASSEY
Altrincham
Hale
Woodhouse Park
Cheadle Hulme
Grappenhall
Lymm
Little Bollington
Bowdon
Bowgreen
Hale Barns
Stockton Heath
Broomedge
LYMM SERVICES
MANCHESTER
Heald Green
WALTON HALL
Appleton Thorn
High Legh
ROSTHERNE MERE
Rostherne
Ashley
Thorns Green
Manchester Airport
Styal
Handforth
Woodford
Stretton
Swarton Heath
Bucklow Hill
QUARRY BANK MILL
Lower Stretton
Hoo Green
Mere
New Mills
TATTON HOUSE
Morley Green
ARLEY HALL
Higher Whitley
Arley
Over Tabley
WILMSLOW
Dean Row
Bate Heath
Holehouses
Davenport Green
Lower Whitley
Mobberley
Knolls Green
Hough
Dones Green
Gib Hill
CHESHIRE COUNTY SHOWGROUND
Knutsford
Alderley Edge
Mottram St Andrew
Great Budworth
Over Knutsford
KNUTSFORD SERVICES
Comberbach
Pickmere
TABLEY
Ollerton
ANDERTON BOAT LIFT
MARBURY
Higher Wincham
Marthall
Nether Alderley
NETHER ALDERLEY MILL
Little Leigh
Barnton
Anderton
Marston
Plumley
Smithy Green
Wincham
Lostock Gralam
Over Peover
Chelford
Monks Heath
Northwich
Broken Cross
Lostock Green
Lower Peover
Henbury
Weaverham
Rudheath
Swan Green
Peover Heath
SALT MUS
PEOVER HALL
Hartford
Lach Dennis
CAPESTHORNE HALL
Lower Pexhill
Cuddington
JODRELL BANK VISITOR CENTRE
Davenham
Blackden Heath
Withington Green
Siddington
Warren
Moulton
Puddinglake
Goostrey
Gawsworth
Whitegate
Bostock Green
Byley
Twemlow Green
Lower Withington
Highlane
Foxwist Green
Wharton Green
Cranage
Marton
Sproston Green
Holmes Chapel
Gleadsmoss
Salterswall
Wharton
Swettenham
Rodeheath
WINSFORD
Sandlow Green
Newsbank
Middlewich
Little Budworth
Over
Church Hill
Hulme Walfield
Brereton Green
Brereton Heath
Eaton
School Green
BRERETON HEATH
Lower Heath
Buglawton
Occlestone Green
Bradwall Green
West Heath
Congleton
Hightown
Moston Green
Elworth
Arclid
Wettenhall
SANDBACH CROSSES
Brownlow
Warmingham
Astbury
Mossley
Church Minshull
Sandbach
Brookhouse Green
Brownlow Heath
SANDBACH SERVICES
Cholmondeston
Bradfield Green
Coppenhall Moss
Fourlanes End
Calveley
Wheelock
LITTLE MORETON HALL
Marsh Green
Hassall Green
Wardle
Aston juxta Mondrum
Barrows Green
Maw Green
Wheelock Heath
Gillow Heath
Barbridge
Winterley
Hassall
Thurlwood
Rode Heath
Scholar Green
Mow Cop
MOW COP CASTLE
Worleston
Haslington
Church Lawton
Mount Pleasant
Radmore Green
Woolstanwood
Crewe
Wistaston Green
Alsager
Kidsgrove
Burford
Wistaston
Wells Green
Radway Green
Newchapel
Burland
Gresty Green
CREWE SERVICES
Talke
Goldenhill
ST MARY'S
Acton
Willaston
Weston
FREEPORT TALKE
Nantwich
Shavington
Barthomley
Sandyford
Tunstall
Bradeley
Ravensmoor
Butt Green
Englesea-brook
Hough
Red Street
Stapeley
Gorsteyhill
Audley
Chesterton
Burslem
Balterley
Walgherton
Alsagers Bank
Bradwell
Halmer End
Wolstanton
0 1 2 3 miles
0 1 2 3 4 5 km

PEAK DISTRICT NATIONAL PARK
HIGH PEAK
Bredbury
Romiley
Compstall
Marple
Marple Bridge
Stockport
Hawk Green
Mellor
HAZEL GROVE
Thornsett
Strines
Windlehurst
Birch Vale
Hayfield
Little Hayfield
Chunal
High Lane
Disley
New Mills
Low Leighton
Newtown
Poynton
Furness Vale
Chinley Head
Chinley
Chapel Milton
Malcoff
Buxworth
Whitehough
Whaley Bridge
Chapel-en-le-Frith
Slackhall
Perryfoot
Sparrowpit
Bridgemont
Wood Lanes
Horwich End
Lower Crossings
Peak Forest
Kettleshume
Taxal
Whiteley Green
Pott Shrigley
Bollington
Fernilee
Combs
Dove Holes
Bollington Cross
Rainow
Peak Dale
Upper End
Wheston
Tideswell
Hurdsfield
Walker Barn
Tunstead
Hargatewall
Buxton
Fairfield
Burbage
Wormhill
Miller's Dale
Blackwell
Gurnett
Langley
Macclesfield Forest
Cowdale
King Sterndale
Canholes
Harpur Hill
Chelmorton
Taddington
Sutton Lane Ends
Oakgrove
Haddon
Wildboarclough
Sterndale Moor
Flagg
Sheldon
Flash
Allgreave
Earl Sterndale
Hollinsclough
Glutton Bridge
Monyash
Wincle
Danebridge
Longnor
Crowdicote
Fawfieldhead
Newtown
Pilsbury
Parsley Hay
Rushton Spencer
Heaton
Upper Hulme
Brund
Sheen
Hartington
Ryecroft Gate
Meerbrook
Hulme End
Heathcote
Newhaven
Biddulph Moor
Rudyard
Poolend
Ball Haye Green
Thorncliffe
Upper Elkstone
Lower Elkstone
Warslow
Biggin
Pikehall
Horton
Leek
Blackwood Hill
Dunwood
Lowe Hill
Bradnop
Butterton
Wetton
Alstonefield
Alsop en le Dale
Grindonmoor Gate
Onecote
Ford
Grindon
Hope
Milldale
Parwich
Endon Bank
Longsdon
Horse Bridge
Leekbrook
Endon
Stanley
Cheddleton
Bottom House
New Street
Waterfall
Tissington
Baddeley Green
Basford Green
Winkhill
Waterhouses
Ilam
Thorpe
Fenny Bentley
Bagnall
Ipstones
Calton
Wetley Rocks
Cauldon
Foxt
Blore
Abbey Hulton
Edale
Nether Booth
Barber Booth
Hope
Aston
Castleton
Thornhill
Brough
Bradwell
Coplow Dale
Great Hucklow
Little Hucklow
Grindlow
Lane Head
Foolow
Litton
Wardlow
Cressbrook
Little Longstone
Ashford in the Water
Middleton
Youlgrave
Axe Edge
Brand Side
Dove Dale
Ladybower Res.
Tittesworth Res.
Rudyard Res.
Fernilee Res.
KINDER SCOUT
MAM TOR
SHINING TOR 559
SHUTLINGSLOE 506
THE PENNINE BRIDLEWAY
PENNINE WAY
BUXTON MUS & ART GALLERY
POOLE'S CAVERN
ARBOR LOW HENGE
PEAK CAVERN
SPEEDWELL CAVERN
BLUE JOHN CAVERN
TREAK CLIFF CAVERN
THE MOORLAND CENTRE
CHURNET VALLEY RLY
CHEDDLETON RAILWAY CENTRE
PEAK WILDLIFE PARK
BRINDLEY'S MILL AND MUS
LYME PARK
TEGG'S NOSE
PARADISE MILL
DEEP HAYES
FLINT MILL
A6
A53
A54
A515
A523
A537
A623
A5004
B5470
B5053
B5054
B5055
A6187
A6015
A520
A555
138
139
130
112
113
SK

PEAK DISTRICT NATIONAL PARK
Sheffield
Dronfield
Chesterfield
Matlock
Bakewell
Hathersage
Baslow
Tideswell
Ashford in the Water
Youlgrave
Wirksworth
Cromford
Clay Cross
Edale
Castleton
Hope
Bamford
Eyam
Grindleford
Froggatt
Curbar
Calver
Stoney Middleton
Rowsley
Darley Bridge
Two Dales
Tansley
Matlock Bath
Bonsall
Winster
Elton
Birchover
Hartington
Monyash
Flagg
Sheldon
Taddington
Chelmorton
Blackwell
Wardlow
Litton
Foolow
Great Longstone
Little Longstone
Hassop
Pilsley
Edensor
Beeley
Holymoorside
Walton
Brampton
Wadshelf
Ashover
Kelstedge
Crich
Whatstandwell
Ambergate
Alderwasley
Carsington
Brassington
Bradbourne
Tissington
Parwich
Alstonefield
Ilam
Longcliffe
Aldwark
Grangemill
Ible
Middleton
Parsley Hay
Pilsbury
Crowdicote
Sheen
Biggin
Newhaven
Heathcote
Pikehall
Ladybower Res.
Carsington Res.
Derwent
Wye
Dove
Dove Dale
Manifold
Noe
Moors
Reservoirs
East Moor
A6
A57
A61
A515
A619
A623
A625
A621
A632
A615
A5012
A6020
A6102
A6187
B5057
B5055
B5056
B5035
B5023
B6001
B6012
B6049
B6465
B6054
B6051
B6050
B6056
B6057
B6077
B6076
A6101
A6013
A5270
B5054
B6014
B6036
CHATSWORTH
HADDON HALL
PEAK VILLAGE
CAUDWELL'S MILL
NINE LADIES STONE CIRCLE
ARBOR LOW HENGE
THE PENNINE BRIDLEWAY
MATLOCK PARKS
GULLIVER'S KINGDOM
ARKWRIGHT'S CROMFORD MILL
MASSON MILLS
NATIONAL STONE CEN
MIDDLETON TOP ENGINE HOUSE
LEAWOOD PUMPHOUSE
THE NATIONAL TRAMWAY MUS
WINGFIELD MANOR
ECCLESBOURNE VALLEY RLY
DERWENT VALLEY VISITOR
HOB HURSTS HOUSE
EYAM HALL
LONGSHAW
UPPER DERWENT VISITOR CENTRE
BOTANICAL GARDENS
KELHAM ISLAND MUSEUM
HEELEY CITY FARM
BISHOPS HOUSE
PEAK CAVERN
SPEEDWELL CAVERN
TREAK CLIFF CAVERN
BLUE JOHN CAVERN
MAM TOR
PEVERIL
THE MOORLAND CENTRE
DERBYSHIRE DALES
RAVENSTOR
BIGGIN DALE
DOVEDALE
ILAM HALL
HARTINGTON HALL
PEAK RAIL
ST MARY & ALL SAINTS
HIGH NEB 458
0 1 2 3 miles
0 1 2 3 4 5 km

Maltby
Tickhill
Harworth
Bircotes
Scaftworth
Scrooby
Wickersley
Hooton Levitt
Stone
Styrrup
Brinsworth
Whiston
Thurcroft
Carr
ROCHE ABBEY
Firbeck
Oldcotes
Serlby
BLYTH SERVICES
Ranskill
Mattersey Thorpe
Mattersey
Catcliffe
Treeton
ULLEY
Ulley
Brampton en le Morthen
Laughton en le Morthen
Langold
Blyth
Torworth
Handsworth
Aughton
Aston
Laughton Common
Dinnington
Letwell
LANGOLD
Gildingwells
Lound
Woodhouse
Swallownest
Beighton
Todwick
Kiveton Park
North Anston
Carlton in Lindrick
Barnby Moor
Sutton
ROTHER VALLEY
Hackenthorpe
Wales
South Anston
Woodsetts
Wigthorpe
Holbrook
Norwood
Thorpe Salvin
Gateford
West Retford
Killamarsh
Harthill
Netherthorpe
Shireoaks
Scofton
Ranby
Babworth
WOODALL SERVICES
Rhodesia
Kilton
Spinkhill
Darfoulds
Manton
NISHAW HALL GARDENS
Renishaw
Barlborough
Worksop
Middle Handley
Handley
BARROW HILL ROUNDHOUSE
Mastin Moor
Whitwell
Hodthorpe
Staveley
Clowne
SK
CLUMBER PARK
Elkesley
Creswell
Hardwick Village
Woodthorpe
CRESWELL CRAGS MUSEUM
Poulter
West Drayton
Stanfree
Poolsbrook
Holbeck
Great Lake
Bothamsall
Elmton
Carburton
Haughton
Duckmanton
Shuttlewood
Holbeck Woodhouse
Norton
Bevercotes
Whaley
POULTER
Whaley Thorns
Perlethorpe
Walesby
BOLSOVER CASTLE
Bolsover
Cuckney
Arkwright Town
Nether Langwith
HAMLYN LODGE COTTAGE INDUSTRY
Sutton Scarsdale
Scarcliffe
Langwith
Meden Vale
Budby
Kirton
Langwith Junction
Church Warsop
SHERWOOD FOREST
Market Warsop
New Ollerton
Palterton
Shirebrook
VISITORS CENTRE
Boughton
GRASSMOOR
Heath
Glapwell
Edwinstowe
Ollerton
Holmewood
New Houghton
Lidgett
Wellow
THE NATIONAL HOLOCAUST CENTRE & MUSEUM
Doe Lea
Stainsby
PLEASLEY PIT
Old Clipstone
RUFFORD
Ompton
North Wingfield
Pleasley
MANSFIELD WOODHOUSE
Kneesall
Parkhouse Green
HARDWICK HALL
Radmanthwaite
SHERWOOD
Hardstoft
Pilsley
Teversal
Clipstone
PINES
Skegby
Forest Town
FOREST
Eakring
Tibshelf
Mansfield
TIBSHELF SERVICES
PARK
Bilsthorpe
Morton
Stanton Hill
Maplebeck
Stonebroom
BRIERLEY
Bilsthorpe Moor
Newton
Huthwaite
SUTTON IN ASHFIELD
Rainworth
Blackwell
Hilcote
WHITE POST FARM CENTRE
South Normanton
KIRKBY IN ASHFIELD
WHEELGATE PARK
Kirklington
ALFRETON
Cox Moor
White Post
Farnsfield
ASHFIELD
Blidworth
Pinxton
EAST MIDLANDS
Ravenshead
Haywood Oaks
Edingley
Normanton
PORTLAND PARK
NEWSTEAD ABBEY
Somercotes
Nuncargate
Halam
Southwell
Selston
Annesley
Leabrooks
Annesley Woodhouse
Newstead
SOUTHWELL MINSTER
Jacksdale
Halloughton
Ironville
Bagthorpe
FELLEY PRIORY
PAPPLEWICK PUMPING STATION
MIDLAND RAILWAY BUTTERLEY
New Brinsley
Linby
BURNSTUMP
Oxton
Underwood
Papplewick
Codnor
Brinsley
Calverton
Thurgarton
HUCKNALL
M1
M18
A1(M)
A1
A57
A60
A614
A617
A619
A616
A631
A632
A38
A610
A620
A634
A638
A6075
A6117
A611
B6059
B6463
B6045
B6079
B6420
B6034
B6035
B6030
B6417
B6407
B6418
B6419
B6014
B6028
B6026
B6139
B6020
B6018
B6011
B6386
B683
132
140
114
115

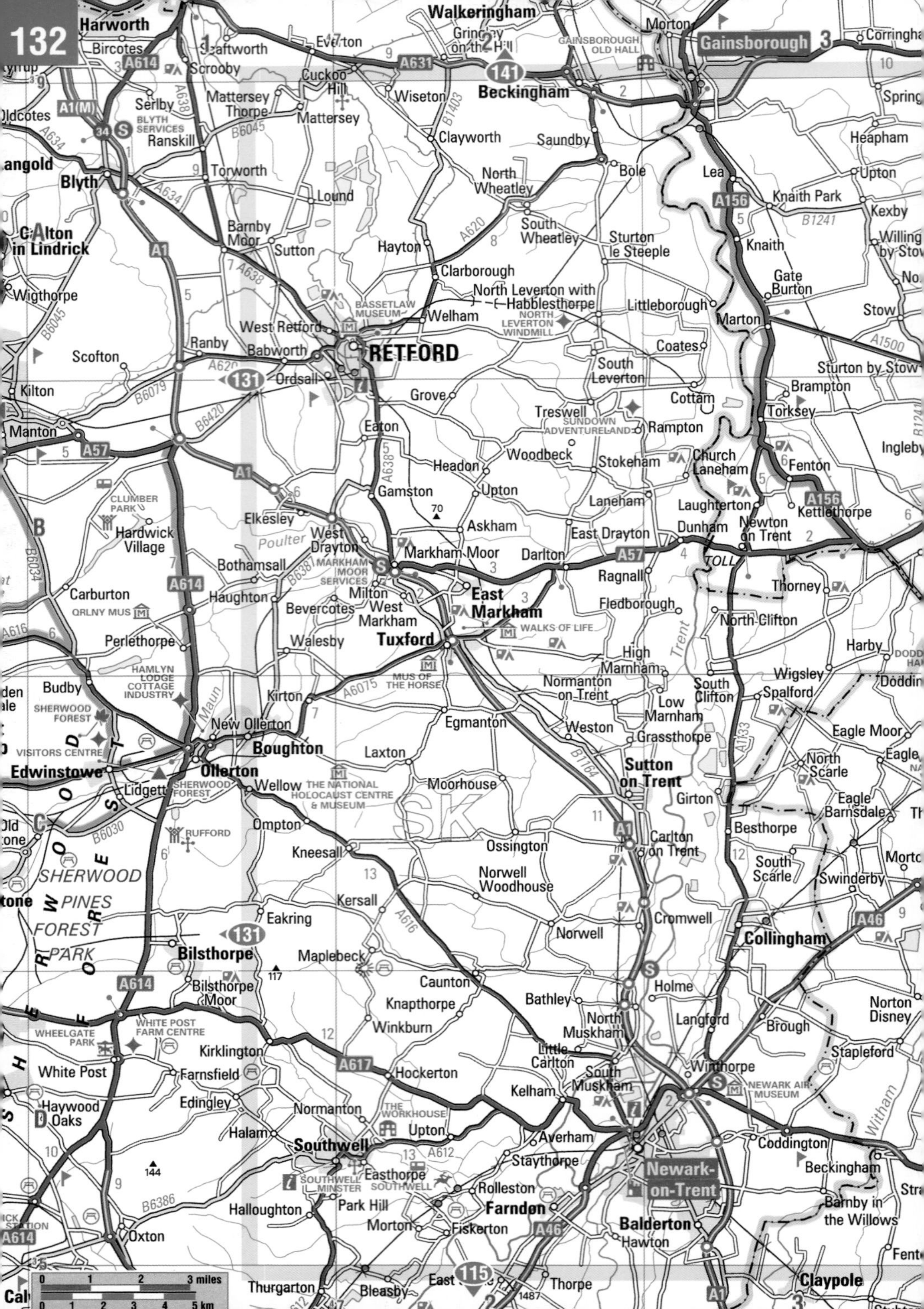
Harworth
Bircotes
Walkeringham
Everton
Gringley on the Hill
Morton
Gainsborough
Corringham
GAINSBOROUGH OLD HALL
Scaftworth
Scrooby
A614
A631
141
Beckingham
Cuckoo Hill
Wiseton
Serlby
Mattersey Thorpe
Mattersey
B1403
Spring
A1(M)
BLYTH SERVICES
Ranskill
B6045
Clayworth
Saundby
Heapham
A634
Blyth
Torworth
Lound
North Wheatley
Bole
Lea
Upton
A156
Knaith Park
Kexby
B1241
Carlton in Lindrick
A1
Barnby Moor
Sutton
Hayton
A620
South Wheatley
Sturton le Steeple
Knaith
Willingham by Stow
A638
Clarborough
Gate Burton
Wigthorpe
B6045
BASSETLAW MUSEUM
North Leverton with Habblesthorpe
Littleborough
Marton
Stow
Welham
NORTH LEVERTON WINDMILL
West Retford
A1500
Scofton
Ranby
Babworth
RETFORD
Coates
South Leverton
Sturton by Stow
131
Ordsall
Cottam
Brampton
Kilton
B6079
B6420
Grove
Torksey
Manton
Treswell
SUNDOWN ADVENTURELAND
Rampton
A57
Eaton
Ingleby
Woodbeck
Stokeham
Church Laneham
Fenton
Headon
CLUMBER PARK
Gamston
Upton
Laneham
Laughterton
A156
Kettlethorpe
70
Elkesley
Askham
Newton on Trent
Hardwick Village
Poulter
West Drayton
East Drayton
Dunham
Markham Moor
Darlton
A57
TOLL
MARKHAM MOOR SERVICES
B6387
Bothamsall
B6034
Ragnall
Thorney
Carburton
A614
Haughton
Milton
East Markham
Fledborough
QRLNY MUS
Bevercotes
West Markham
North Clifton
A616
WALKS OF LIFE
Perlethorpe
Walesby
Tuxford
Trent
Harby
High Marnham
HAMLYN LODGE COTTAGE INDUSTRY
MUS OF THE HORSE
Normanton on Trent
South Clifton
Wigsley
Budby
A6075
Kirton
Low Marnham
Spalford
Doddington
SHERWOOD FOREST VISITORS CENTRE
Maun
New Ollerton
Egmanton
Weston
Grassthorpe
Eagle Moor
Boughton
Laxton
Sutton on Trent
A1133
North Scarle
Eagle
Edwinstowe
Ollerton
Wellow
THE NATIONAL HOLOCAUST CENTRE & MUSEUM
Moorhouse
B1164
Girton
Eagle Barnsdale
Lidgett
SHERWOOD FOREST
SK
Besthorpe
B6030
RUFFORD
Ompton
A1
Carlton on Trent
SHERWOOD PINES FOREST PARK
Kneesall
Ossington
South Scarle
Swinderby
Norwell Woodhouse
Morton
Kersall
A616
Cromwell
A46
Eakring
131
Norwell
Collingham
Bilsthorpe
Maplebeck
117
Caunton
Holme
A614
Bilsthorpe Moor
Bathley
Knapthorpe
Norton Disney
North Muskham
Langford
Brough
WHITE POST FARM CENTRE
WHEELGATE PARK
Winkburn
Kirklington
Little Carlton
Stapleford
White Post
Farnsfield
A617
Hockerton
South Muskham
Winthorpe
NEWARK AIR MUSEUM
Haywood Oaks
Edingley
Kelham
Normanton
THE WORKHOUSE
Witham
Halam
Upton
Averham
Coddington
Southwell
A612
Staythorpe
Newark-on-Trent
Beckingham
144
SOUTHWELL MINSTER
Easthorpe
SOUTHWELL
Rolleston
B6386
Park Hill
Farndon
Barnby in the Willows
Halloughton
Morton
Fiskerton
A46
Balderton
Hawton
Oxton
A614
115
Thorpe
Claypole
1487
Thurgarton
Bleasby
East Stoke
A1
0 1 2 3 miles
0 1 2 3 4 5 km

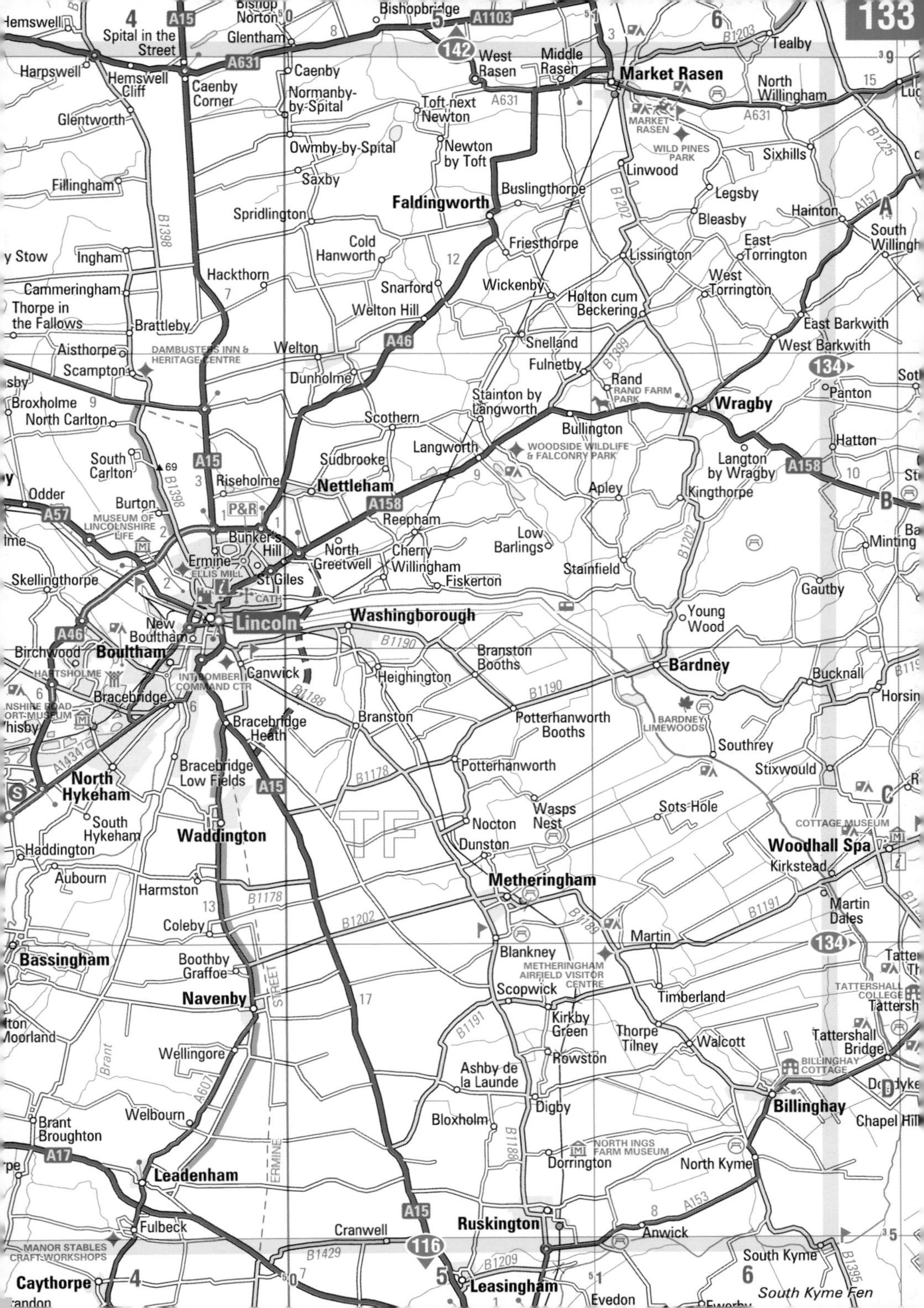

Hemswell
Bishop Norton
Bishopbridge
A1103
A15
Spital in the Street
Glentham
142
West Rasen
Middle Rasen
Market Rasen
Tealby
Harpswell
Hemswell Cliff
A631
Caenby
Caenby Corner
Normanby-by-Spital
Toft next Newton
North Willingham
Glentworth
MARKET RASEN
WILD PINES PARK
Ownby-by-Spital
Newton by Toft
Linwood
Sixhills
B1225
Fillingham
Saxby
Legsby
Buslingthorpe
Faldingworth
Spridlington
B1202
Bleasby
Hainton
A157
South Willingham
B1398
Cold Hanworth
Friesthorpe
Lissington
East Torrington
Stow
Ingham
Hackthorn
Snarford
Wickenby
West Torrington
Cammeringham
Holton cum Beckering
Thorpe in the Fallows
Welton Hill
Brattleby
East Barkwith
West Barkwith
A46
Snelland
Aisthorpe
DAMBUSTERS INN & HERITAGE CENTRE
Welton
B1399
Fulnetby
134
Scampton
Dunholme
Rand
RAND FARM PARK
Panton
Broxholme
Stainton by Langworth
Wragby
North Carlton
Scothern
Bullington
Langworth
WOODSIDE WILDLIFE & FALCONRY PARK
Hatton
South Carlton
Sudbrooke
Langton by Wragby
A158
Riseholme
Nettleham
Apley
Kingthorpe
Odder
Burton
P&R
A57
MUSEUM OF LINCOLNSHIRE LIFE
Reepham
Low Barlings
Minting
Bunker's Hill
Ermine
ELLIS MILL
North Greetwell
Cherry Willingham
Stainfield
Skellingthorpe
St Giles
Fiskerton
Gautby
CATH
Young Wood
New Boultham
Lincoln
Washingborough
A46
Birchwood
Boultham
B1190
Branston Booths
Bardney
Canwick
Heighington
Bucknall
HARTSHOLME
INT. BOMBER COMMAND CTR
B1188
Horsington
Bracebridge
LINCOLNSHIRE ROAD TRANSPORT MUSEUM
Branston
Potterhanworth Booths
BARDNEY LIMEWOODS
Whisby
Bracebridge Heath
Southrey
A1434
Bracebridge Low Fields
B1178
Potterhanworth
Stixwould
North Hykeham
Wasps Nest
Sots Hole
TF
Nocton
COTTAGE MUSEUM
South Hykeham
Waddington
Dunston
Woodhall Spa
Haddington
Kirkstead
Aubourn
Harmston
Metheringham
Martin Dales
B1202
B1191
B1189
Coleby
Martin
Bassingham
Blankney
Boothby Graffoe
METHERINGHAM AIRFIELD VISITOR CENTRE
TATTERSHALL COLLEGE
Tattershall
Navenby
STREET
Scopwick
Timberland
Kirkby Green
Thorpe Tilney
Moorland
Walcott
Tattershall Bridge
Wellingore
Rowston
Brant
Ashby de la Launde
BILLINGHAY COTTAGE
A607
Dogdyke
Billinghay
Welbourn
Digby
Bloxholm
Brant Broughton
Chapel Hill
B1188
NORTH INGS FARM MUSEUM
A17
ERMINE
Dorrington
North Kyme
Leadenham
A153
A15
Ruskington
Fulbeck
Cranwell
Anwick
MANOR STABLES CRAFT WORKSHOPS
116
South Kyme
B1429
B1209
B1395
Caythorpe
Leasingham
Evedon
South Kyme Fen

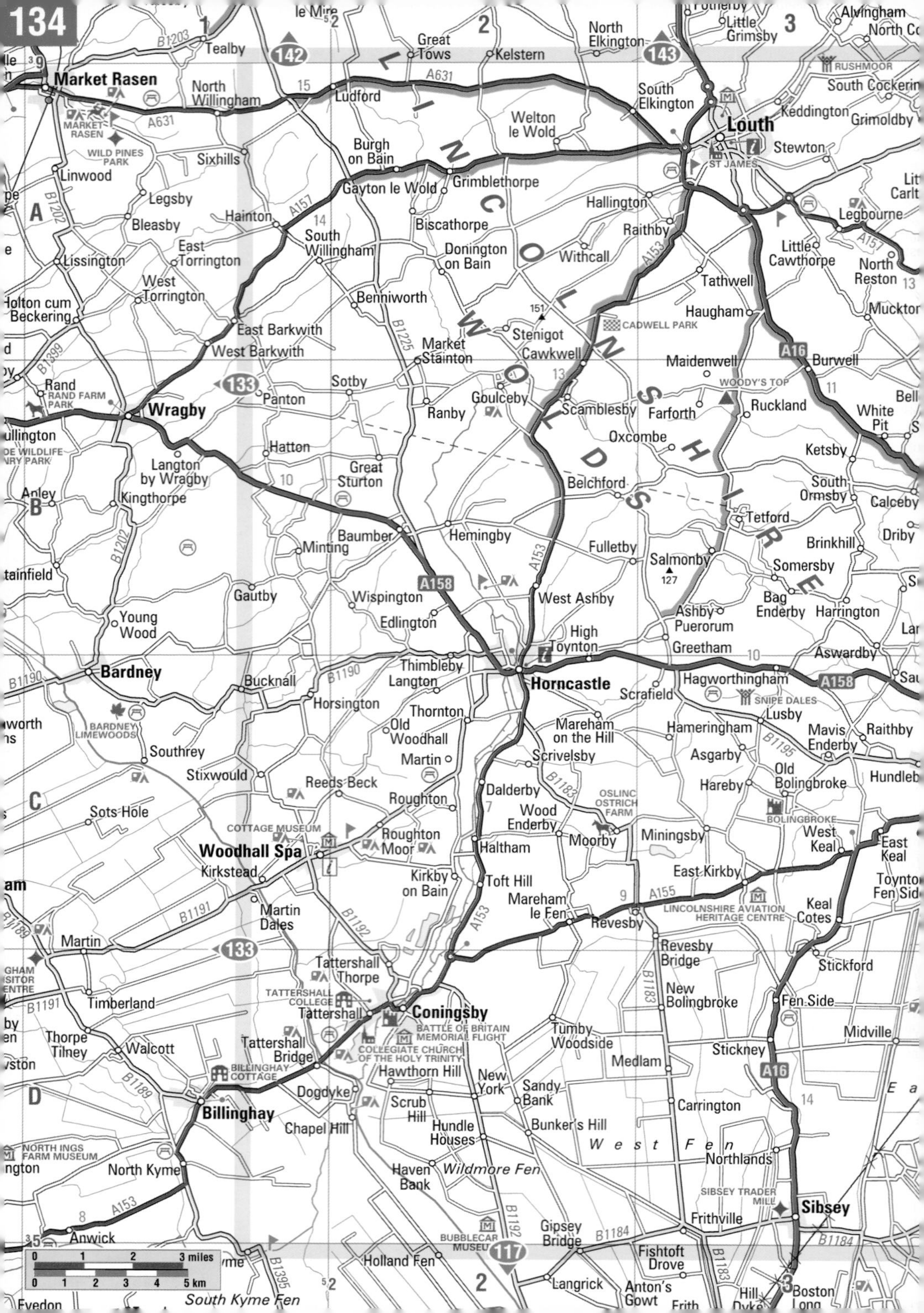
Market Rasen
Tealby
le Mire
Great Tows
Kelstern
North Elkington
Little Grimsby
Alvingham
North Cockerington
RUSHMOOR
South Cockerington
142
143
A631
15
North Willingham
Ludford
South Elkington
Louth
Keddington
Grimoldby
MARKET RASEN
WILD PINES PARK
Sixhills
Welton le Wold
Burgh on Bain
Stewton
ST JAMES
Linwood
Gayton le Wold
Grimblethorpe
Little Carlton
Legsby
Hallington
Legbourne
B1202
A157
Hainton
Biscathorpe
Raithby
Bleasby
14
South Willingham
Donington on Bain
Withcall
Little Cawthorpe
North Reston
East Torrington
Lissington
A153
Tathwell
West Torrington
Benniworth
Holton cum Beckering
151
Haugham
Muckton
LINCOLNSHIRE WOLDS
East Barkwith
B1225
Stenigot
CADWELL PARK
West Barkwith
Market Stainton
Cawkwell
Maidenwell
A16
Burwell
B1399
13
133
Rand
RAND FARM PARK
Sotby
Panton
Goulceby
Scamblesby
Farforth
WOODY'S TOP
Ruckland
11
Wragby
Ranby
White Pit
Oxcombe
Hatton
Langton by Wragby
Great Sturton
Belchford
Ketsby
10
South Ormsby
Calceby
Apley
Kingthorpe
Tetford
Baumber
Hemingby
Minting
Brinkhill
Driby
Fulletby
Salmonby
Somersby
127
A158
Gautby
Wispington
West Ashby
Bag Enderby
Harrington
Young Wood
Edlington
Ashby Puerorum
High Toynton
Greetham
Aswardby
Bardney
B1190
Bucknall
Thimbleby
Langton
Horncastle
Scrafield
Hagworthingham
SNIPE DALES
Horsington
BARDNEY LIMEWOODS
Thornton
Old Woodhall
Mareham on the Hill
Hameringham
Lusby
Mavis Enderby
Raithby
Southrey
Martin
Scrivelsby
Asgarby
B1195
Old Bolingbroke
Stixwould
Reeds Beck
Hareby
Hundleby
Dalderby
B1183
OSLINC OSTRICH FARM
Roughton
BOLINGBROKE
Sots Hole
Wood Enderby
7
COTTAGE MUSEUM
Roughton Moor
Moorby
Miningsby
West Keal
East Keal
Woodhall Spa
Haltham
Kirkstead
Kirkby on Bain
Toft Hill
East Kirkby
Toynton Fen Side
Martin Dales
B1191
Mareham le Fen
9
A155
LINCOLNSHIRE AVIATION HERITAGE CENTRE
Revesby
Keal Cotes
B1192
Martin
Revesby Bridge
Stickford
Tattershall Thorpe
TATTERSHALL COLLEGE
New Bolingbroke
Fen Side
Timberland
Tattershall
Coningsby
BATTLE OF BRITAIN MEMORIAL FLIGHT
Tumby Woodside
Midville
Thorpe Tilney
Walcott
Tattershall Bridge
COLLEGIATE CHURCH OF THE HOLY TRINITY
Stickney
Medlam
BILLINGHAY COTTAGE
Hawthorn Hill
New York
Sandy Bank
B1189
Dogdyke
Scrub Hill
Carrington
Billinghay
Chapel Hill
Hundle Houses
Bunker's Hill
West Fen
NORTH INGS FARM MUSEUM
Northlands
North Kyme
Haven Bank
Wildmore Fen
SIBSEY TRADER MILL
Sibsey
A153
8
Gipsey Bridge
Frithville
Anwick
B1184
BUBBLECAR MUSEUM
B1395
Holland Fen
117
Fishtoft Drove
Langrick
Anton's Gowt
Boston
South Kyme Fen
0 1 2 3 miles
0 1 2 3 4 5 km

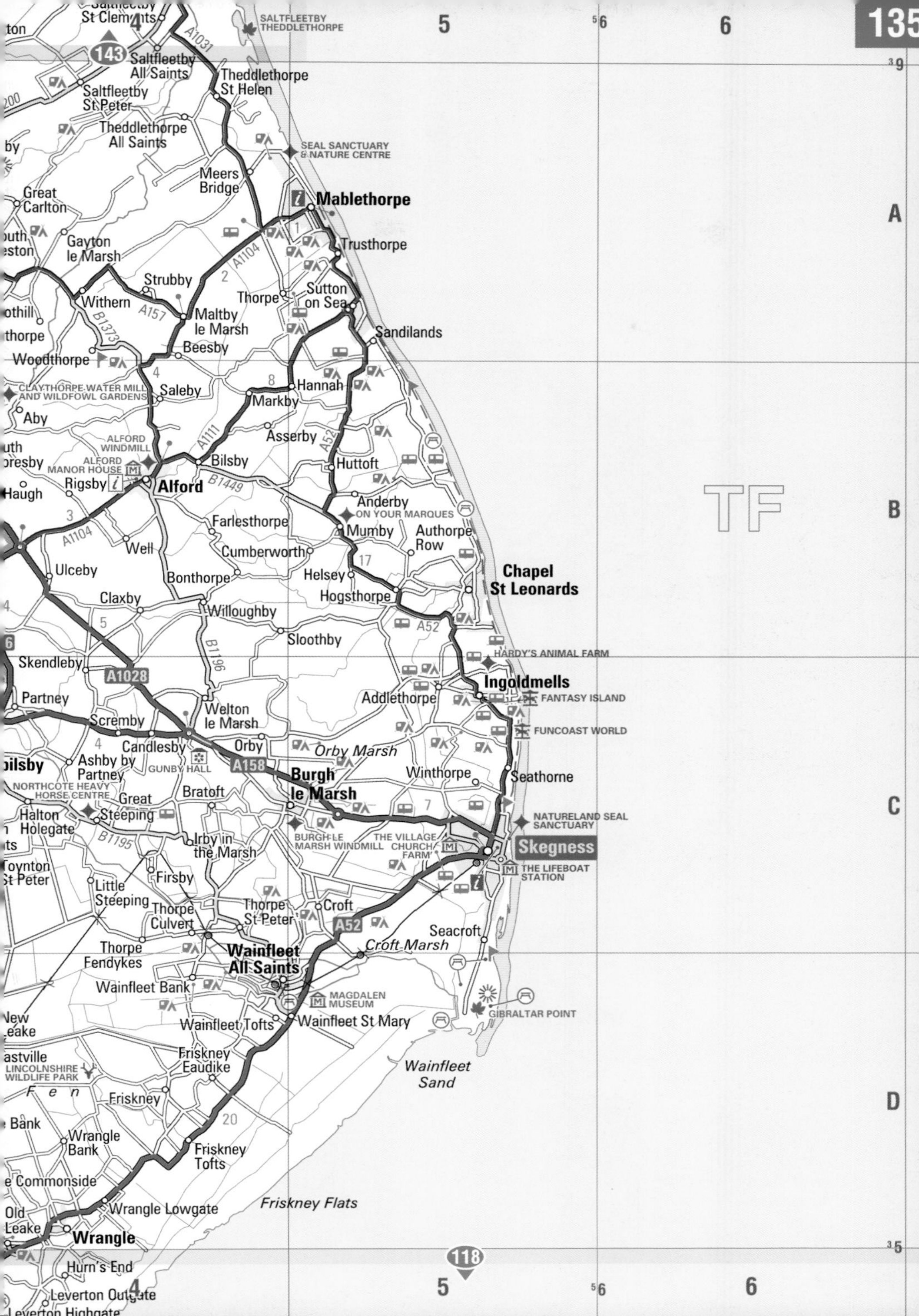

Saltfleetby St Clements
143
Saltfleetby All Saints
Saltfleetby St Peter
SALTFLEETBY THEDDLETHORPE
Theddlethorpe St Helen
Theddlethorpe All Saints
SEAL SANCTUARY & NATURE CENTRE
Meers Bridge
Great Carlton
Mablethorpe
Gayton le Marsh
Trusthorpe
Strubby
Thorpe
Sutton on Sea
Withern
Maltby le Marsh
Sandilands
Woodthorpe
Beesby
CLAYTHORPE WATER MILL AND WILDFOWL GARDENS
Saleby
Hannah
Markby
Aby
Asserby
ALFORD WINDMILL
ALFORD MANOR HOUSE
Bilsby
Huttoft
Rigsby
Alford
Haugh
Anderby
ON YOUR MARQUES
Farlesthorpe
Mumby
Authorpe Row
Well
Cumberworth
Ulceby
Helsey
Chapel St Leonards
Bonthorpe
Hogsthorpe
Claxby
Willoughby
Sloothby
HARDY'S ANIMAL FARM
Skendleby
Ingoldmells
FANTASY ISLAND
Addlethorpe
Partney
Welton le Marsh
Scremby
FUNCOAST WORLD
Candlesby
Orby
Orby Marsh
Ashby by Partney
GUNBY HALL
Burgh le Marsh
Winthorpe
Seathorne
NORTHCOTE HEAVY HORSE CENTRE
Great Steeping
Bratoft
Halton Holegate
NATURELAND SEAL SANCTUARY
BURGH LE MARSH WINDMILL
THE VILLAGE CHURCH FARM
Irby in the Marsh
Skegness
THE LIFEBOAT STATION
Toynton St Peter
Little Steeping
Firsby
Thorpe Culvert
Thorpe St Peter
Croft
Seacroft
Thorpe Fendykes
Croft Marsh
Wainfleet All Saints
Wainfleet Bank
MAGDALEN MUSEUM
GIBRALTAR POINT
New Leake
Wainfleet Tofts
Wainfleet St Mary
Friskney Eaudike
Wainfleet Sand
LINCOLNSHIRE WILDLIFE PARK
Friskney
Wrangle Bank
Friskney Tofts
Friskney Flats
Wrangle Lowgate
Old Leake
Wrangle
Hurn's End
Leverton Outgate
Leverton Highgate
118
TF
A1031
A1104
A157
B1373
A1111
A52
B1449
A1028
B1196
A158
B1195
A
B
C
D
4
5
6

1
A
B
C
D
Squires Gate
BLACKPOOL
Westby
Moss Side
Wrea Green
Newton
Scales
Lea Town
Ingol
Cadley
Higher Ballam
144
145
Preston
Clifton
ROYAL LYTHAM & ST ANNES
LYTHAM HALL
Ansdell
Lytham
St Annes
Lytham St Anne's
Fairhaven
Salters Bank
Warton
Freckleton
A584
RIBBLE STEAM RAILWAY
Higher Penwortham
Bottom of Hutton
Hutton
Ribble
Longton
A582
A59
New Longton
Banks Sands
RIBBLE MARSHES
WEST LANCASHIRE LIGHT RAILWAY
Walmer Bridge
Hesketh Bank
Great Bank
Midge Hall
BRITISH COMMERCIAL VEHICLE MUSEUM
Much Hoole
Becconsall
LEYLAND
Hundred End
Banks
Tarleton
B5248
Broadfield
SOUTH RIBBLE MUSEUM & EXHIBITION CENTRE
Horse Bank
Bretherton
B5247
Crossens
A565
Sollom
Croston
B5249
Ulnes Walton
Shaw Green
P&R
Marshside
ECO VISITOR CENTRE
Southport
Churchtown
Mere Brow
A581
Yarrow
Eccleston
Holmeswood
B5246
RUFFORD OLD HALL
Blowick
WINDMILL ANIMAL FARM
Rufford
MARTIN MERE WILDFOWL AND WETLAND CENTRE
Birkdale
Brown Edge
Tarlscough
Mawdesley
Heskin Green
Snape Green
Bescar
B5243
Hillside
ROYAL BIRKDALE
Scarisbrick
New Lane
Douglas
Canal
Bispham Green
Wrightington Bar
Ainsdale-on-Sea
Ainsdale
Shirdley Hill
ECCLES FARM CRAFT CENTRE
Hill Dale
Mossy Lea
Pinfold
Liverpool
Burscough Bridge
Dangerous Corner
Woodvale
Burscough
Parbold
B5242
A570
A5209
Newburgh
Formby Hills
AINSDALE SAND DUNES
Halsall
A5147
Leeds and
Appley Bridge
B5240
Freshfield
Barton
Haskayne
ORMSKIRK
A577
Westhead
Dalton
BEACON
Roby Mill
Formby
Formby Pt.
Downholland Cross
Stanley
Little Altcar
Aughton Park
Blaguegate
Skelmersdale
Orrell
Great Altcar
B5195
Stanley Gate
Digmoor
Up Holland
CABIN HILL
Aughton
Royal Oak
A5061
M58
Hightown
A565
Ince Blundell
Lydiate
Bickerstaffe
Rainford Junction
Higher End
B5206
A59
Maghull
Barrow Nook
Crawford
B5193
Lunt
B5422
Longshaw
Little Crosby
M58
Melling Mount
Rainford
A5758
Sefton
Thornton
Netherton
Billinge
B5205
Great Crosby
Melling
Kirkby
Crank
BELFAST
Crosby Channel
A565
AINTREE
Aintree
B5203
Moss Bank
LITHERLAND
Southdene
Waterloo
A506
Seaforth
Orrell
A59
DOUGLAS (Nov-March)
DUBLIN
A580
Fazakerley
Denton's Green
Knowsley
Bootle
Gillar's Green
St Helens
Eccleston
Peasley Cross
DOUGLAS (March-Nov)
New Brighton
M57
Norris Green
NEW PALACE
Walton
CROXTETH
KNOWSLEY SAFARI PARK
A58
Kirkdale
Thatto Heath
Liscard
Egremont
Anfield
West Derby
Longview
Prescot
Eccleston Park
WALKER GALL
Everton
A570
Rainhill
Wallasey
A57
Whiston
Leasowe
Seacombe
Knotty Ash
LIVERPOOL
Huyton
A57
Sutton Manor
Moreton
Poulton
MARITIME MUS
Edge Hill
Roby
Rainhill Stoops
STADT MOERS
Bidston
126
127
A5058
B5178
PEX HILL
TOLL
TATE
Wavertree
Childwall
A5080
Barrow Green
Toxteth
A562
Netherley
Tarbock
ALBERT
Mossley
0 1 2 3 miles
0 1 2 3 4 5 km

Brockholes Nature Res
Samlesbury
Mellor Brook
Osbaldeston
Mellor
Brownhill
Rishton
Clayton-le-Moors
Huncoat
Ends
Pleckgate
Beardwood
Samlesbury Bottoms
Higher Walton
Coup Green
Hoghton Tower
Blackburn
Blackburn Mus. & Art Gallery
West End
Church
Milnshaw
ACCRINGTON
Scaitcliffe
Oswaldtwistle
Clow Bridge
Dunnockshaw
Love Clough
Gregson Lane
Pleasington
Feniscliffe
Witton
Shadsworth
Guide
Baxenden
Forest of Rossendale
Goodshaw
Goodshaw Chapel
Water
Hoghton
Riley Green
Ewood
Lower Darwen
Feniscowles
Earcroft
Rising Bridge
Acre
Crawshawbooth
Whitewell Bottom
Clayton Green
Brindle
Higher Wheelton
Abbey Village
Tockholes
Blackburn with Darwen Services
Belthorn
Waterside
Haslingden
Rossendale Museum
Lane Side
RAWTENSTALL
Edgeside
Clayton-le-Woods
Whittle-le-Woods
Withnell
Sunnyhurst
Ryal Fold
Hoddlesden
DARWEN
Bent Gate
Waterfoot
Wheelton
Brinscall
Whitehall
Helmshore
Cowpe
Whittlestone Head
Edenfield
Turton Moor
White Coppice
Anglezarke Moor
Cadshaw
Stubbins
Turn
CHORLEY
Anglezarke Reservoir
Res.
Ramsbottom
Cowling
Edgworth
Weld Bank
Belmont
Chapeltown
Turton Bottoms
Woodhey
Turton Tower
Rivington
Yarrow Valley
Egerton
Summerseat
Burrs
Norden
Coppull
Rivington
Winter Hill
Greenmount
Jumbles
Toppings
Adlington
Grimeford Village
Smithills Hall
Astley Bridge
Tottington
Walmersley
Limefield
East Lancashire Railway
Bamford
Coppull Moor
Horwich
Rivington Services
Bradshaw
Bury
Walshaw
HEYWOOD
Standish
Blackrod
Bottom o' th' Moor
Halliwell
Harwood
Lancs Fusiliers Regimental Mus
Ainsworth
Bolton
Breightmet
Broadfield
Red Rock
Haigh
Lostock Junction
Darcy Lever
Redvales
Black Lane
Birch Services
Hollins
Beech Hill
Haigh Hall
Aspull
Deane
Moses Gate
Marylebone
Wingates
Daubhill
Great Lever
Little Lever
Radcliffe
WESTHOUGHTON
Hart Common
Highfield
FARNWORTH
Whitefield
Middleton
Wigan
Water's Nook
Over Hulton
Kearsley
Stand
Rhodes
Clifton
Daisy Hill
Hindley
Hindley Green
Blackleach
Heaton Hall
Ince in Makerfield
Platt Bridge
ATHERTON
Tyldesley
Little Hulton
Walkden
Clifton Green
PRESTWICH
Bickershaw
Howe Bridge
Swinton
Pendlebury
Crumpsall
Bryn Gates
Abram
Westleigh
Worsley
Broughton Park
Mus of Transport
Bryn
Crank Wood
Leigh, Guided Busway
Leigh
Lancashire Mining Mus
Charlestown
ASHTON-IN-MAKERFIELD
Pennington Flash
Plank Lane
Pennington
Astley Green
SALFORD
Lowton Common
Haydock Park
Lately Common
Barton
Eccles
Golborne
Lowton
Imp War Mus North
The Lowry
Haydock
Twiss Green
Glazebury
The Trafford Centre
Trafford Park
Hulme
Lane Head
Chat Moss
Old Trafford
Fowley Common
Davyhulme
Newton-le-Willows
New Lane End
Culcheth
Irlam
URMSTON
Stretford
Croft
Flixton
Burtonwood
Glazebrook
Chorlton cum Hardy
Withington
Winwick
Risley
Cadishead
Carrington
Ashton upon Mersey
West Didsbury
Burtonwood Services
Hollins Green
SALE
Houghton Green
Fearnhead
Birchwood
Partington
Dallam
Gulliver's World
Orford
Woolston
Brooklands
Northenden
Warburton
Broadheath
Timperley
Warrington
Martinscroft
Mossbrow
Dunham Town
Great Sankey
Manchester Ship Canal
Heatley
Wythenshawe
Gatley
Toll
M6
M61
M65
M66
M60
M62
M602
A59
A677
A666
A56
A58
A6027
A676
A579
A580
A49
A57
A560
A510
A6010
SD
SJ
145
146
138
127
128
137

Rose Hill
Walk Mill
Hurstwood
Mereclough
146
Heptonstall Moor
Towneley Hall
Clow Bridge
Holme Chapel
Colden
Pecket Well
Blackshaw Head
Heptonstall
Hebden Bridge
Mytholm
Chiserley
Wainstalls
Mount Tabor
Booth
Ovenden
Midgley
Wheatley
Illingworth
Queensbury
147
Causeway Foot
Dean Head Res.
A6033
A646
A629
Forest of Rossendale
Thieveley Pike
449
Goodshaw Chapel
Water
Crawshawbooth
Portsmouth
Cornholme
Lydgate
Charlestown
Walkley Clogs
Mytholmroyd
Luddenden
Luddenden Foot
Pellon
Eastwood
Weir
Whitewell Bottom
Clough Foot
Todmorden
Mankinholes
Greave
Bacup
Rawtenstall
Edgeside
A681
Shade
Walsden
Cragg Vale
Sowerby
Triangle
Sowerby Bridge
Lumb
Mill Bank
Waterfoot
Nun Hills
A6066
Shawforth
Britannia
Cowpe
Reservoirs
B6138
Warland
Greetland
A672
B6113
B6114
137
Edenfield
The Mary Towneley Loop
Facit
Whitworth
Pennine Way
Soyland Moor
Ripponden
Barkisland
Stainland
Turn
468
Calderbrook
A58
Rishworth
Sowood
Outlane
B6112
SD
Broadley
Healey
Healey Dell
Wardle
Rishworth Moor
472
Booth Wood
Littleborough
Hollingworth Lake
Rakewood
Colne Valley Museum
A680
Syke
Smallbridge
Norden
Cutgate
Rochdale
M62
22
Moss Moor
453
Bradshaw
A640
Wilberlee
Slaithwaite
Bamford
Firgrove
Milnrow
466
Standedge Visitor Centre
Lingards Wood
Marsden
Walmersley
East Lancashire Railway
B6222
Marland
Lower Place
Haugh
Newhey
Heywood
A58
Castleton
21
Denshaw
A62
Res.
Meltham
M66
Broadfield
Hopwood
20
Summit
B6194
B6197
Bleak Hey Nook
Slattocks
Birch Services
Tandle Hill
Shaw
Hollins
Royton
Heyside
Diggle
Wessenden Moor
Top of Hebers
Birch
A627(M)
Long Sight
Moorside
Delph
Dobcross
A635
Whitefield
18
Middleton
Chadderton Fold
Rhodes
A62
Uppermill
Saddleworth Moor
17
Heaton Hall
19
Chadderton
Oldham
A669
Lees
Grasscroft
Greenfield
Tunstead
582
Black Hill
A664
M60
A6104
Prestwich
Blackley
Hathershaw
308
A670
Dove Stone Res.
Pennine Way
Crumpsall
Moston
A56
Broughton Park
Mus of Transport
Harpurhey
A663
Hollinwood
A627
Mossley
469
The Pennine Bridleway
Chew Res.
Failsworth
Daisy Nook
Waterloo
Ashton-under-Lyne
Hazelhurst
B6175
Charlestown
Newton Heath
Manchester
Mus of the Manchesters
Stalybridge
Crowden
A628
Salford
National Squash
Manchester Velodrome
Astley Cheetham
Droylsden
Longdendale
Reservoirs
Lowry
A635
Audenshaw
Dukinfield
Tintwistle
B6105
Hulme
Ardwick
Newton
Mottram in Longdendale
A6018
Hadfield
Padfield
Old Trafford
Whitworth
Rusholme
Gorton
1A
A57
24
M67
Hollingworth
Pennine Way
Bleaklow
Stretford
A5103
Denton
Hyde
Godley
Warhill
Gamesley
Old Glossop
A6010
Levenshulme
M60
Broadbottom
A560
Reddish Vale
Reddish
Glossop
Shelf Moor
Chorlton cum Hardy
Withington
Fallowfield
Highfield
Haughton Grn.
Gee Cross
Werneth Low
Simmondley
Charlestown
A57
West Didsbury
A6
Woodley
Chisworth
Charlesworth
Sale
A34
Heaton Moor
Etherow
Bredbury
Didsbury
A5145
Chunal
A624
Romiley
Compstall
Brooklands
Northenden
Stockport
Chadkirk Country Estate
National
128
129
Cheadle Heath
Heaviley
Marple
Marple Bridge
Little Hayfield
Stepping Hill
Wythenshawe
Gatley
Cheadle
Hawk Green
Mellor
0 1 2 3 miles
0 1 2 3 4 5 km

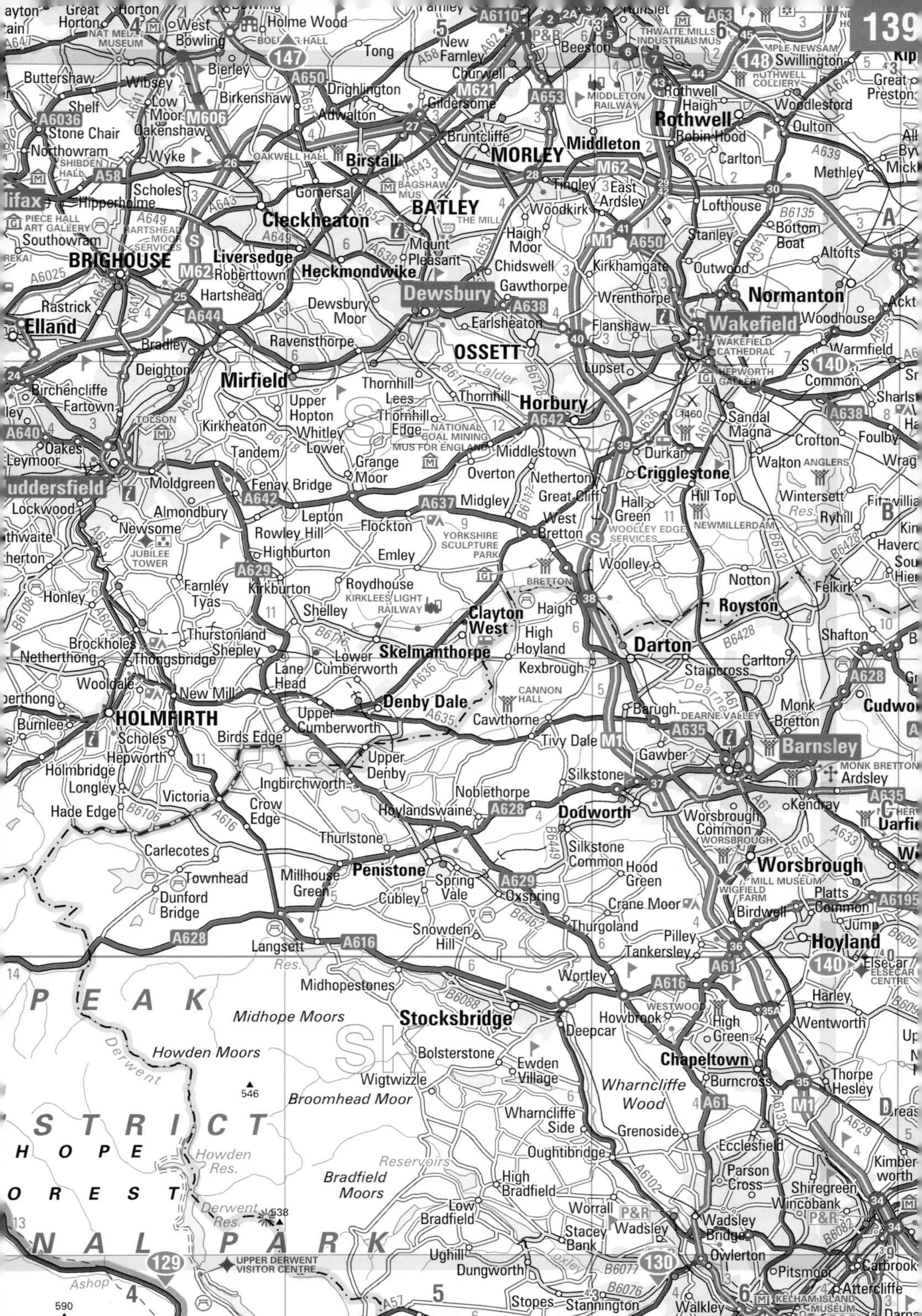
Great Horton
West Bowling
Holme Wood
Tong
New Farnley
Beeston
Swillington
Buttershaw
Wibsey
Bierley
Birkenshaw
Drighlington
Churwell
Gildersome
Rothwell
Woodlesford
Shelf
Low Moor
Oakenshaw
Adwalton
Bruntcliffe
Middleton
Oulton
Stone Chair
Northowram
Wyke
Birstall
MORLEY
Robin Hood
Carlton
Methley
Scholes
Hipperholme
Gomersal
BATLEY
Tingley
East Ardsley
Lofthouse
Cleckheaton
Woodkirk
Southowram
BRIGHOUSE
Liversedge
Heckmondwike
Mount Pleasant
Haigh Moor
Chidswell
Stanley
Kirkhamgate
Outwood
Altofts
Normanton
Rastrick
Elland
Hartshead
Dewsbury
Dewsbury Moor
Gawthorpe
Wrenthorpe
Wakefield
Earlsheaton
Flanshaw
Bradley
Ravensthorpe
OSSETT
Warmfield
Deighton
Mirfield
Lupset
Birchencliffe
Fartown
Thornhill
Lees
Horbury
Upper Hopton
Sandal Magna
Kirkheaton
Whitley Lower
Thornhill Edge
Oakes
Tandem
Grange Moor
Middlestown
Durkar
Crofton
Walton
Huddersfield
Moldgreen
Fenay Bridge
Overton
Netherton
Crigglestone
Lockwood
Almondbury
Lepton
Midgley
Great Cliff
Hall Green
Hill Top
Wintersett
Newsome
Rowley Hill
Flockton
West Bretton
Ryhill
Highburton
Emley
Woolley
Honley
Farnley Tyas
Kirkburton
Roydhouse
Notton
Felkirk
Royston
Shelley
Clayton West
Haigh
Brockholes
Thurstonland
Shepley
High Hoyland
Darton
Shafton
Netherthong
Thongsbridge
Lane Head
Lower Cumberworth
Skelmanthorpe
Kexbrough
Staincross
Carlton
Wooldale
New Mill
Denby Dale
Barugh
Monk Bretton
Cudworth
HOLMFIRTH
Upper Cumberworth
Cawthorne
Burnlee
Scholes
Birds Edge
Tivy Dale
Barnsley
Hepworth
Upper Denby
Gawber
Silkstone
Holmbridge
Longley
Victoria
Ingbirchworth
Noblethorpe
Ardsley
Crow Edge
Hoylandswaine
Dodworth
Kendray
Hade Edge
Worsbrough Common
Thurlstone
Silkstone Common
Carlecotes
Penistone
Hood Green
Worsbrough
Townhead
Millhouse Green
Spring Vale
Oxspring
Dunford Bridge
Cubley
Crane Moor
Platts Common
Birdwell
Snowden Hill
Thurgoland
Pilley
Langsett
Tankersley
Jump
Hoyland
Elsecar
Midhopestones
Wortley
Harley
PEAK
Midhope Moors
Stockbridge
Deepcar
Howbrook
High Green
Wentworth
Howden Moors
Bolsterstone
Ewden Village
Chapeltown
Wigtwizzle
Wharncliffe Wood
Burncross
Thorpe Hesley
Broomhead Moor
Wharncliffe Side
STRICT
Grenoside
HOPE
Oughtibridge
Ecclesfield
Kimberworth
Howden Res.
Reservoirs
Parson Cross
OREST
Bradfield Moors
High Bradfield
Shiregreen
Wincobank
Derwent Res.
Low Bradfield
Worrall
Wadsley
Wadsley Bridge
NAL PARK
Stacey Bank
Owlerton
Ughill
Dungworth
Pitsmoor
Carbrook
Attercliffe
Ashop
Stopes
Stannington
Walkley
Derwent
Loxley
Dearne
Calder
Res.
UPPER DERWENT VISITOR CENTRE
KELHAM ISLAND MUSEUM
WIGFIELD FARM
MILL MUSEUM
WORSBROUGH
DEARNE VALLEY
CANNON HALL
KIRKLEES LIGHT RAILWAY
BRETTON
YORKSHIRE SCULPTURE PARK
WOOLLEY EDGE SERVICES
NEWMILLERDAM
JUBILEE TOWER
NATIONAL COAL MINING MUS FOR ENGLAND
TOLSON
HEPWORTH GALLERY
WAKEFIELD CATHEDRAL
THE MILL
BAGSHAW MUS
OAKWELL HALL
PIECE HALL ART GALLERY
HARTSHEAD MOOR SERVICES
SHIBDEN HALL
MIDDLETON RAILWAY
THWAITE MILLS INDUSTRIAL MUS
TEMPLE NEWSAM
ROTHWELL COLLIERY
MONK BRETTON
ANGLERS
WESTWOOD
ELSECAR CENTRE
NAT MEDIA MUSEUM
BOLLING HALL
M62
M606
M621
M1
A650
A653
A6110
A58
A62
A638
A642
A644
A649
A643
A6036
A640
A637
A629
A636
A635
A628
A616
A61
A6195
A633
A655
A639
A652
A651
A641
A6025
A6024
A6102
A6135
A629
A57
B6135
B6132
B6428
B6108
B6106
B6118
B6116
B6449
B6462
B6088
B6077
B6076
B6100
B6082
B6128
B6117
B6111
147
148
140
129
130
546
538
590
1460

NEWSAM HOUSE
Swillington
ROTHWELL COLLIERY
Kippax
Ledston Luck
148
South Milford
Lumby
Ledsham
Hambleton
Willoughby
Monk Fryston
Braytor
149
Great Preston
Woodlesford
Oulton
Ledston
FAIRBURN INGS RSPB RESERVE
Fairburn
A1(M)
Hillam
Selby Canal
Gateforth
Burn
Allerton Bywater
Mickletown
Methley
Burton Salmon
Birkin
West Haddlesey
Chapel Haddlesey
New Fryston
Brotherton
CASTLEFORD
Ferrybridge
Beal
Kellington
Temple Hirst
Sutton
Hirst Courtney
Bottom Boat
Altofts
Whitwood
JUNCTION 32
M62
Kellingley
Eggborough
Hensall
Knottingley
North Featherstone
PONTEFRACT
Normanton
Ackton
Woodhouse
Pontefract
Featherstone
A628
Chequerfield
FERRYBRIDGE SERVICES
Cridling Stubbs
High Eggborough
Whitley
Great Heck
Gowdall
Snaith
Wakefield
WAKEFIELD CATHEDRAL
Warmfield
Sharlston Common
Snydale
Darrington
Purston Jaglin
Womersley
Pollington
Balne
Aire and Calder Navigation
Sandal Magna
139
A638
Sharlston
West Hardwick
East Hardwick
Went
Crofton
Foulby
High Ackworth
Wentbridge
Little Smeaton
Walden Stubbs
Sykehouse
Walton
ANGLERS
Wragby
NOSTELL PRIORY
Low Ackworth
Kirk Smeaton
Fenwick
Wintersett
Fitzwilliam
Ackworth Moor Top
Thorpe Audlin
A1
BARNSDALE BAR SERVICES
Ryhill
Kinsley
Havercroft
FITZWILLIAM
A638
Badsworth
Norton
Campsall
CAMPSALL
Moss
Fosterhouses
South Hiendley
Upton
Wrangbrook
Instoneville
Askern
Far Banks
Notton
Felkirk
Hemsworth
North Elmshall
Sutton
Haywood
Braithwaite
Royston
Burghwallis
Skelbrooke
A19
Moorthorpe
Owston
Thorpe in Balne
Kirk Bramwith
Shafton
Brierley
South Kirkby
South Elmsall
Hampole
Skellow
Carcroft
Carlton
A628
Grimethorpe
Adwick le Street
Barnby Dun
Monk Bretton
Cudworth
HOWELL WOOD
Clayton
Hooton Pagnell
Almholme
Kirk Sandall
A6195
Woodlands
Toll Bar
Barnsley
Brodsworth
Great Houghton
HIGHFIELDS
A638
Arksey
Edenthorpe
MONK BRETTON PRIORY
Ardsley
Thurnscoe
Thurnscoe East
BRODSWORTH HALL
A1(M)
P&R
Bentley
A630
Kendray
A635
Little Houghton
A635
Scawsby
MUSEUM & ART GALLERY
Armthorpe
Darfield
Billingley
Hickleton
Marr
CUSWORTH
Wheatley
Nutwell
Goldthorpe
MELTON WOOD
Newton
Intake
DONCASTER
Worsbrough
MILL MUSEUM
Wombwell
Bolton upon Dearne
Barnburgh
CUSWORTH HALL MUSEUM
Doncaster
Cantley
Platts Common
A6195
Broomhill
Harlington
Sprotbrough
Hyde Park
Bessacarr
Birdwell
Adwick upon Dearne
High Melton
Balby
LAKESIDE VILLAGE
A6182
AEROVENTURE
Hoyland
Jump
Brampton
Cadeby
Mexborough
139
Wath upon Dearne
Warmsworth
Elsecar
ELSECAR HERITAGE CENTRE
Swinton
Denaby Main
New Edlington
A6182
Rossington
Harley
Old Denaby
Conisbrough
Loversall
P&R
Wentworth
CONISBROUGH/IVANHOE
New Rossington
Upper Haugh
Kilnhurst
Old Edlington
ST LEGER HORSE PARK
Nether Haugh
Rawmarsh
Hooton Roberts
Clifton
Wadworth
Thorpe Hesley
Thrybergh
THRYBERGH
Ravenfield
M1
Greasbrough
Dalton
Micklebring
Braithwell
A1(M)
Spital Hill
Ecclesfield
Kimberworth
Rotherham
M18
Stainton
Parson Cross
Shiregreen
MAGNA SCIENCE ADVENTURE CENTRE
CLIFTON PARK
Bramley
Hellaby
Maltby
A631
Tickhill
Harworth
Wincobank
Broom
A631
P&R
Moorgate
Wickersley
Hooton Levitt
Styrrup
Bircotes
Tinsley
Brinsworth
Whiston
131
Stone
Maltby
ROCHE ABBEY
Letwell
Oldcotes
Catcliffe
ULLEY
Brampton en le Morthen
Laughton en le Morthen
0 1 2 3 miles
0 1 2 3 4 5 km

Wressle
North Howden
Portington
Hive
Everthorpe
West End
Newsholme
Cavil
Sandholme
Scalby
Newport
HOWDEN MINSTER
Eastrington
Gilberdyke
Ellerker
Barmby on the Marsh
Howden
Staddlethorpe
Long Drax
Asselby
Knedlington
Kilpin Pike
Kilpin
Balkholme
Elloughton
Drax
Boothferry
Broomfleet
Newland
Airmyn
Hook
Skelton
Laxton
Saltmarshe
Yokefleet
Blacktoft
Faxfleet
Whitton
Goole
Rawcliffe
Rawcliffe Bridge
East Cowick
Old Goole
THE YORKSHIRE WATERWAYS MUSEUM
Reedness
Swinefleet
Whitgift
Little Reedness
Ousefleet
BLACKTOFT SANDS RSPB
JULIAN'S BOWER (TURF MAZE)
Alkborough
Winteringham
West Halton
Walcot
Adlingfleet
Goole Fields
Fockerby
Garthorpe
Coleby
Winterton
Burton Stather
Burton upon Stather
Thealby
Goole Moors
Luddington
Normanby
NORMANBY HALL
Roxby
Eastoft
Moorends
HUMBERHEAD PEATLANDS
Thorne Waste or Moors
Amcotts
Flixborough
Flixborough Stather
Appleby
Dragonby
Crowle
Thorne
Windsor
Canal Side
Wike Well End
Stainforth & Keadby Canal
Ealand
Keadby
Gunness
Crosby
Santon
APPLEBY FRODINGHAM RLY PRESERVATION SOC
Frodingham
NORTH LINCOLNSHIRE MUSEUM
Scunthorpe
Hatfield Chase
Althorpe
Burringham
Brumby
Hatfield Woodhouse
Sandtoft
THE TROLLEYBUS MUSEUM AT SANDTOFT
Woodhouse
Derrythorpe
Ashby
Broughton
West End
Grey Green
Westgate
Belton
Beltoft
Yaddlethorpe
Bottesford
Hatfield Moors
Church Town
West Butterwick
East Butterwick
ISLE OF AXHOLME
Epworth
OLD RECTORY
Messingham
Wroot
Epworth Turbary
Manton
Low Burnham
Kelfield
Susworth
Scotterthorpe
GAINSTHORPE DESERTED MEDIEVAL VILLAGE
Blaxton
Upperthorpe
Owston Ferry
Scotter
Finningley
Westwoodside
Haxey
East Lound
East Ferry
Laughton Woods
Scotton
Kirton in Lindsey
Craiselound
Wildsworth
Laughton
Northorpe
Grayingham
Misson
Misterton
West Stockwith
Blyton
Austerfield
Newington
East Stockwith
Pilham
Blyborough
Aisby
Willoughton
Walkerith
Walkeringham
Gringley on the Hill
Morton
Gainsborough
GAINSBOROUGH OLD HALL
Corringham
Hemswell
Everton
Scaftworth
Cuckoo Hill
Wiseton
Beckingham
Springthorpe
Harpswell
Mattersey Thorpe
Mattersey
Sawtry
SE
SK

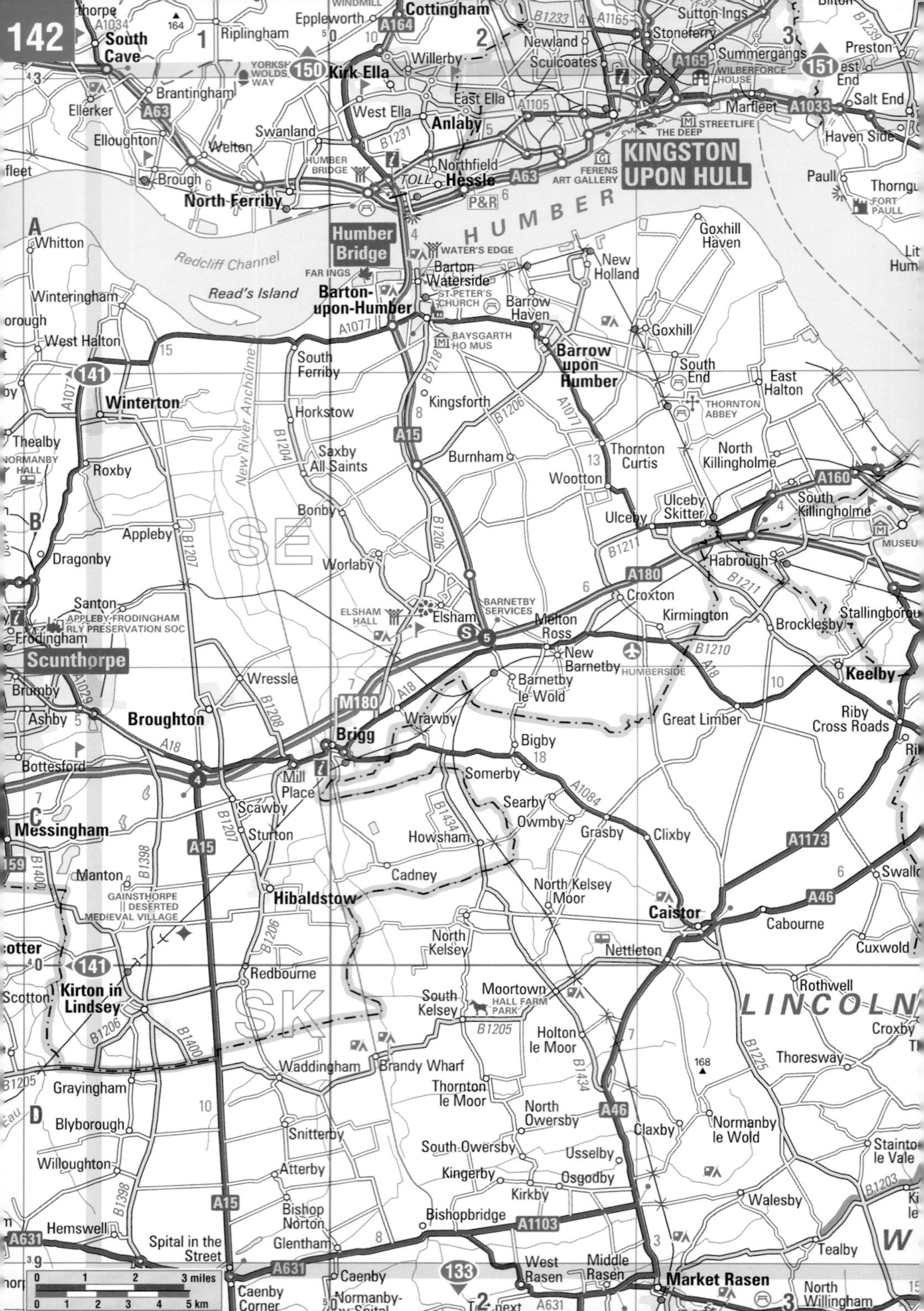

South Cave
Riplingham
Eppleworth
Cottingham
Newland
Sutton Ings
Stoneferry
Sculcoates
Summergangs
Preston
Kirk Ella
Willerby
YORKSHIRE WOLDS WAY
WILBERFORCE HOUSE
Brantingham
Ellerker
East Ella
Marfleet
Salt End
West Ella
Anlaby
STREETLIFE
THE DEEP
Haven Side
Elloughton
Swanland
Welton
KINGSTON UPON HULL
HUMBER BRIDGE
Northfield
FERENS ART GALLERY
Paull
Brough
TOLL
Hessle
P&R
FORT PAULL
North Ferriby
HUMBER
Humber Bridge
Whitton
WATER'S EDGE
Goxhill Haven
Redcliff Channel
FAR INGS
Barton Waterside
New Holland
Read's Island
Barton-upon-Humber
ST PETER'S CHURCH
Barrow Haven
Winteringham
Goxhill
West Halton
BAYSGARTH HO MUS
Barrow upon Humber
South Ferriby
South End
East Halton
Winterton
New River Ancholme
Horkstow
Kingsforth
THORNTON ABBEY
Thealby
NORMANBY HALL
Roxby
Saxby All Saints
Burnham
Thornton Curtis
North Killingholme
Wootton
Bonby
Ulceby Skitter
South Killingholme
Ulceby
MUSEUM
Appleby
SE
Dragonby
Worlaby
Habrough
Croxton
Santon
ELSHAM HALL
Elsham
BARNETBY SERVICES
Melton Ross
Kirmington
Stallingborough
Brocklesby
APPLEBY-FRODINGHAM RLY PRESERVATION SOC
Frodingham
New Barnetby
HUMBERSIDE
Scunthorpe
Keelby
Brumby
Wressle
Barnetby le Wold
Ashby
Broughton
Wrawby
Great Limber
Riby Cross Roads
Brigg
Bigby
Bottesford
Somerby
Mill Place
Searby
Scawby
Ownby
Grasby
Clixby
Messingham
Sturton
Howsham
Manton
Cadney
Swallow
GAINSTHORPE DESERTED MEDIEVAL VILLAGE
North Kelsey Moor
Hibaldstow
Caistor
Cabourne
Scotter
North Kelsey
Nettleton
Cuxwold
Redbourne
Rothwell
Kirton in Lindsey
Scotton
South Kelsey
Moortown
HALL FARM PARK
LINCOLN
Croxby
Holton le Moor
Thoresway
Waddingham
Brandy Wharf
Grayingham
Thornton le Moor
Blyborough
North Owersby
Claxby
Normanby le Wold
Snitterby
South Owersby
Usselby
Stainton le Vale
Willoughton
Atterby
Kingerby
Osgodby
Kirkby
Walesby
Bishop Norton
Bishopbridge
Hemswell
Spital in the Street
Glentham
Tealby
West Rasen
Middle Rasen
Market Rasen
Caenby
Caenby Corner
Normanby-by-Spital
North Willingham
SK
A1034
A164
B1233
A1165
A165
B1239
A63
A1105
B1231
A1033
A1077
B1218
A107
B1204
A15
B1206
A1077
A160
B1211
B1207
A180
A18
A1029
M180
B1208
B1210
B1398
B1400
B1205
B1434
A1084
A1173
A46
B1225
A631
A1103
B1203
A631
141
150
151
133
159
0 1 2 3 miles
0 1 2 3 4 5 km

Elstronwick
Tunstall
Burton Pidsea
Roos
North End
151
B1242
Waxholme
Owthorne
Rimswell
Withernsea
Burstwick
B1362
Halsham
East End
Camerton
Keyingham
Ryehill
18
Ottringham
Hollym
Winestead
A1033
Holmpton
Patrington
B1445
Out Newton
Welwick
Weeton
Sunk Island
Skeffling
Easington
Kilnsea
SPURN DISCOVERY CENTRE
TA
SPURN
ROTTERDAM EUROPOORT ZEEBRUGGE
SPURN HEAD
A180
Pyewipe
Grimsby
Healing
West Marsh
Great Coates
FISHING HERITAGE CENTRE
Old Clee
CLEETHORPES
MOUTH OF THE HUMBER
CLEETHORPES COAST LIGHT RAILWAY
Freshney
A46
Nunsthorpe
A16
Bradley
Scartho
A1098
CLEETHORPES
Humberston
B1219
Waltham
New Waltham
Barnoldby le Beck
A18
WALTHAM WINDMILL
Holton le Clay
A1031
Tetney Lock
Brigsley
Beelsby
B1203
Ashby cum Fenby
North Cotes
Hatcliffe
Tetney
Waithe
East Ravendale
Grainsby
Marshchapel
Donna Nook
B1201
Eskham
TF
Wragholme
North Thoresby
Grainthorpe
Wold Newton
Fulstow
North Somercotes
A16
LINCOLNSHIRE WOLDS RLY
DONNA NOOK
Ludborough
Covenham St Bartholomew
Conisholme
Skidbrooke North End
South Somercotes
A1031
Saltfleet
North Ormsby
Binbrook
Utterby
Covenham St Mary
Yarburgh
Skidbrooke
Fotherby
Little Grimsby
Alvingham
Saltfleetby St Clements
North Elkington
North Cockerington
Great Tows
Kelstern
SALTFLEETBY THEDDLETHORPE
134
A16
RUSHMOOR
135
Saltfleetby All Saints
Theddlethorpe St Helen
A631
South Elkington
South Cockerington
Saltfleetby St Peter
B1200
Keddington
A
B
C
D
4
5
6

Barrow-in-Furness
North Scale
Vickerstown
Barrow Island
Biggar
Isle of Walney
South End
Piel Island
Roa Island
Foulney Island
Rampside
Roosebeck
Leece
Newbiggin
Yarlside
Dendron
Newbarns
Hawcoat
Baycliff
Aldingham
South End Point
South Channel
MORECAMBE
BAY
Morecambe
Sandylands
Heysham
DOUGLAS
Sunderland Pt.
Shoulder of Lune
Cockerham Sands
Knott End-on-Sea
Fleetwood
Rossall Point
Preesall
Pilling Lane
Pilling
Dam Side
Stake Pool
Eagland Hill
Stalmine
Staynall
Hambleton
Cleveleys
Thornton
Anchorsholme
Norbreck
Bispham
Carleton
Skippool
Little Singleton
Singleton
Poulton-le-Fylde
Out Rawcliffe
Little Eccleston
Warbreck
North Shore
Queenstown
Blackpool
Normoss
Layton
Staining
Great Marton
Weeton
Thistleton
Esprick
Elswick
Corner Row
Mereside
Hawes Side
South Shore
Little Plumpton
Great Plumpton
Wesham
Common Edge
Squires Gate
Westby
Wrea Green
Moss Side
Higher Ballam
Kirkham
BLACKPOOL TOWER
SEA LIFE CENTRE
MADAME TUSSAUD'S BLACKPOOL
BLACKPOOL PLEASURE BEACH
BLACKPOOL ZOO
FREEPORT FLEETWOOD
MARSH MILL-IN-WYRE
WYRE ESTUARY
THE DOCK MUSEUM
A5087
A589
A683
A588
B5270
A587
A584
A586
B5266
B5260
A585
M55
A583
B5140
B5261
B5259
153
154
136
0 1 2 3 miles
0 1 2 3 4 5 km

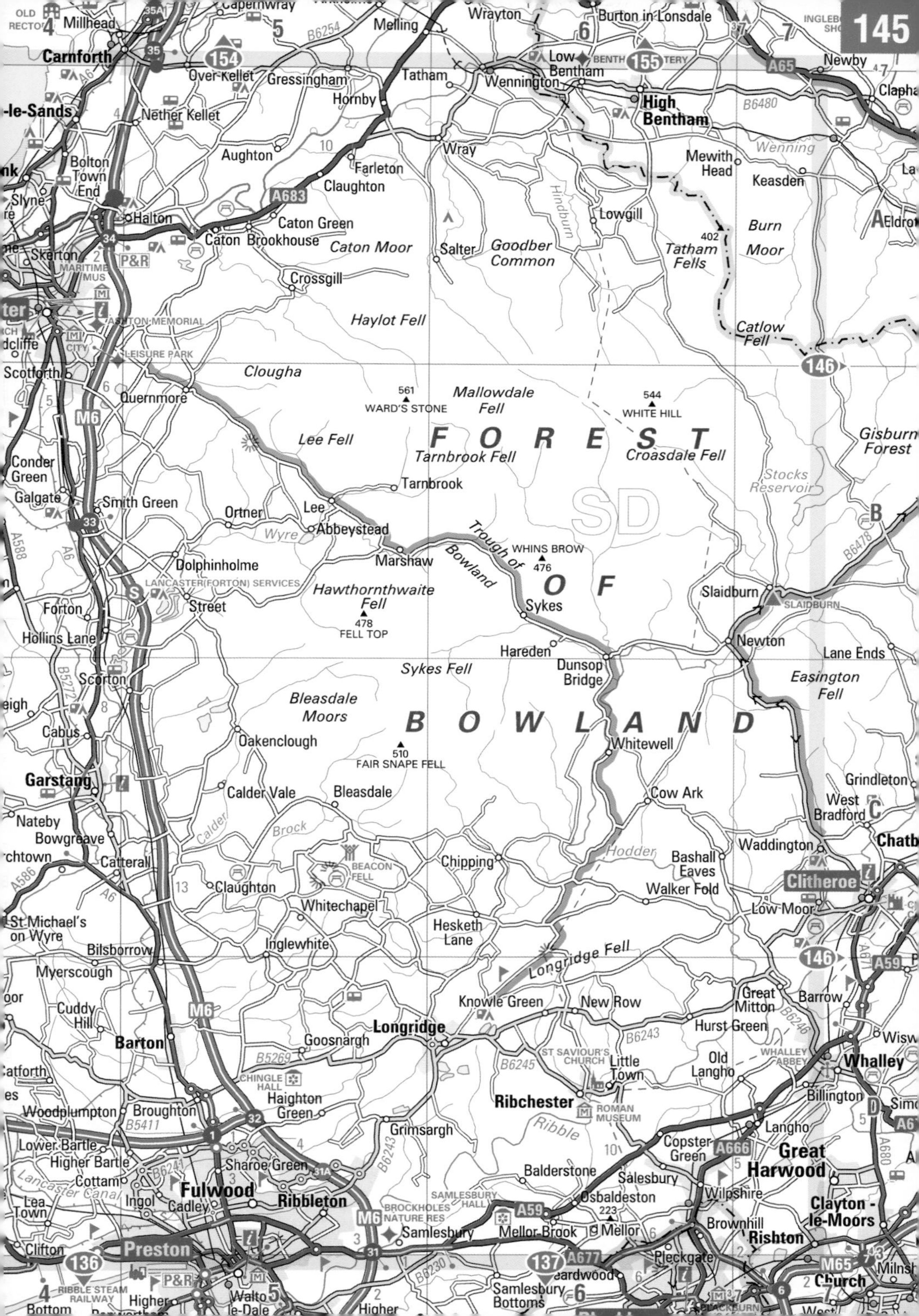
Carnforth
Millhead
Over Kellet
Gressingham
Melling
Wrayton
Burton in Lonsdale
Tatham
Wennington
Low Bentham
High Bentham
Newby
Clapham
Hornby
Nether Kellet
Bolton Town End
Aughton
Farleton
Claughton
Wray
Mewith Head
Keasden
Wenning
Halton
Caton Green
Caton
Brookhouse
Caton Moor
Salter
Goodber Common
Lowgill
Tatham Fells
Burn Moor
Skerton
Crossgill
Haylot Fell
Catlow Fell
Scotforth
Clougha
Quernmore
Ward's Stone
Mallowdale Fell
White Hill
Lee Fell
Tarnbrook Fell
Croasdale Fell
Gisburn Forest
Stocks Reservoir
Conder Green
Galgate
Smith Green
Tarnbrook
Ortner
Lee
Abbeystead
Wyre
Marshaw
Dolphinholme
Trough of Bowland
Whins Brow
FOREST OF BOWLAND
Lancaster (Forton) Services
Forton
Street
Hawthornthwaite Fell
Fell Top
Sykes
Slaidburn
Hollins Lane
Hareden
Newton
Lane Ends
Dunsop Bridge
Sykes Fell
Easington Fell
Scorton
Bleasdale Moors
Cabus
Oakenclough
Fair Snape Fell
Whitewell
Garstang
Calder Vale
Bleasdale
Cow Ark
Grindleton
West Bradford
Nateby
Bowgreave
Catterall
Beacon Fell
Chipping
Hodder
Bashall Eaves
Waddington
Walker Fold
Clitheroe
Claughton
Whitechapel
Low Moor
St Michael's on Wyre
Hesketh Lane
Bilsborrow
Inglewhite
Longridge Fell
Myerscough
Knowle Green
New Row
Great Mitton
Barrow
Cuddy Hill
Longridge
Hurst Green
Barton
Goosnargh
Little Town
St Saviour's Church
Old Langho
Whalley Abbey
Whalley
Billington
Haighton Green
Chingle Hall
Woodplumpton
Broughton
Ribchester
Roman Museum
Grimsargh
Ribble
Langho
Lower Bartle
Higher Bartle
Sharoe Green
Copster Green
Great Harwood
Cottam
Balderstone
Salesbury
Lancaster Canal
Ingol
Fulwood
Cadley
Ribbleton
Samlesbury Hall
Osbaldeston
Wilpshire
Clayton-le-Moors
Lea Town
Brockholes Nature Res
Mellor Brook
Mellor
Brownhill
Rishton
Clifton
Preston
Samlesbury
Pleckgate
Ribble Steam Railway
Samlesbury Bottoms
Church
Walton-le-Dale
Higher
Bottom
M6
M65
A6
A65
A683
A59
A666
A677
A588
A586
B6254
B6480
B6478
B5272
B5269
B6245
B6243
B6246
B5411
B6241
B6230
SD
154
155
146
136
137

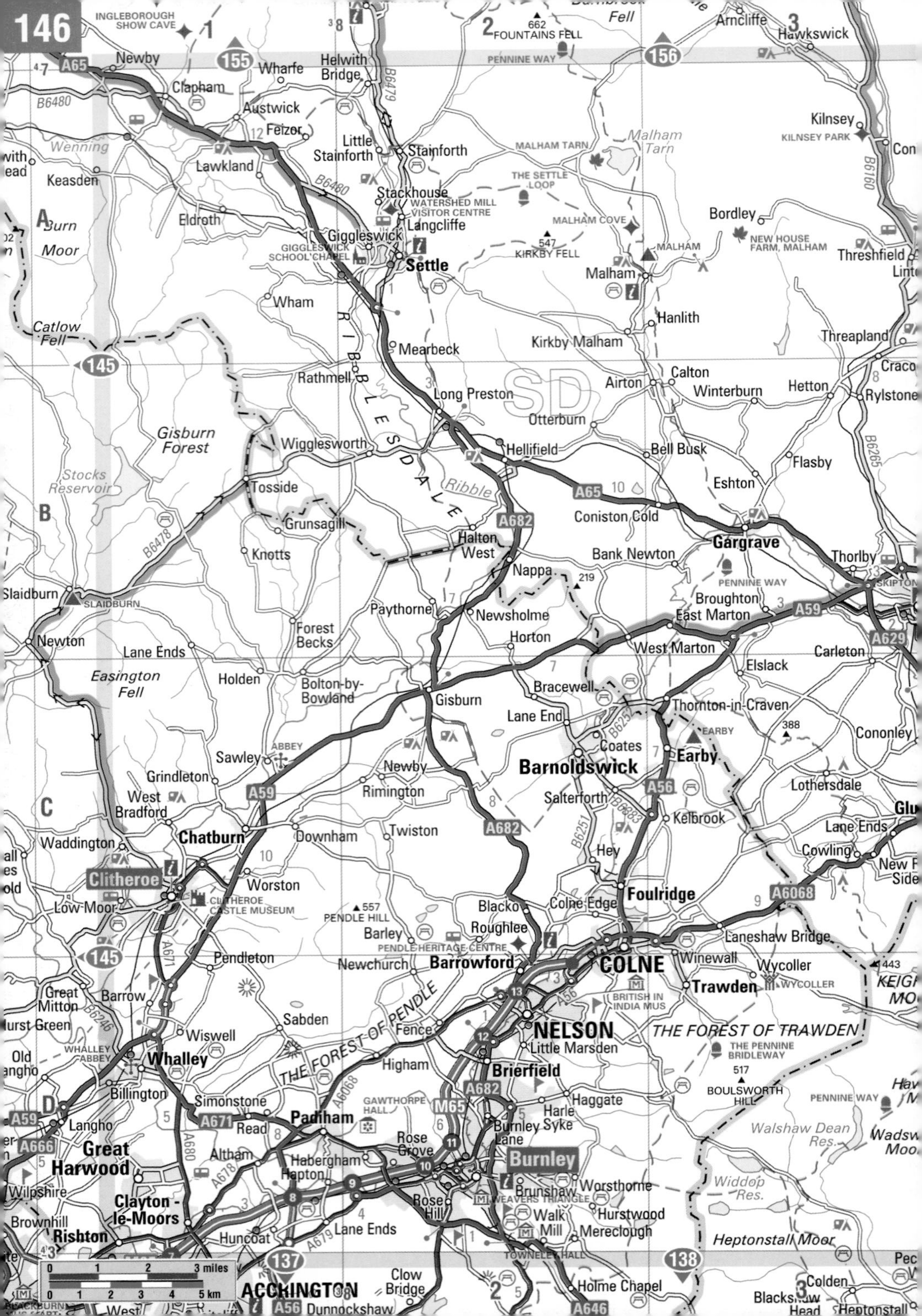

INGLEBOROUGH SHOW CAVE
FOUNTAINS FELL
Arncliffe
Hawkswick
155
156
PENNINE WAY
Newby
Wharfe
Helwith Bridge
Clapham
Austwick
Feizor
Little Stainforth
Stainforth
MALHAM TARN
Malham Tarn
Kilnsey
KILNSEY PARK
Wenning
Lawkland
Keasden
THE SETTLE LOOP
Stackhouse
WATERSHED MILL VISITOR CENTRE
Langcliffe
Eldroth
MALHAM COVE
Bordley
NEW HOUSE FARM, MALHAM
Burn Moor
Giggleswick
GIGGLESWICK SCHOOL CHAPEL
Settle
KIRKBY FELL
MALHAM
Malham
Threshfield
Wham
Hanlith
Catlow Fell
Mearbeck
Kirkby Malham
Threapland
145
Rathmell
RIBBLESDALE
Long Preston
SD
Airton
Calton
Winterburn
Hetton
Rylstone
Otterburn
Gisburn Forest
Wigglesworth
Hellifield
Bell Busk
Flasby
Stocks Reservoir
Tosside
Ribble
A65
Eshton
Coniston Cold
Grunsagill
Gargrave
Halton West
Bank Newton
Knotts
Nappa
Thorlby
PENNINE WAY
SKIPTON
Slaidburn
SLAIDBURN
Broughton
Paythorne
Newsholme
East Marton
A59
Newton
Forest Becks
Horton
West Marton
Carleton
A629
Lane Ends
Elslack
Easington Fell
Holden
Bolton-by-Bowland
Bracewell
Gisburn
Lane End
Thornton-in-Craven
EARBY
Cononley
ABBEY
Coates
Sawley
Earby
Barnoldswick
Newby
Grindleton
Rimington
A56
Lothersdale
West Bradford
Salterforth
Kelbrook
Lane Ends
Chatburn
Downham
Twiston
A682
Waddington
Hey
Cowling
Worston
New Side
Clitheroe
Foulridge
A6068
CLITHEROE CASTLE MUSEUM
PENDLE HILL
Blacko
Colne Edge
Low Moor
Barley
Roughlee
Laneshaw Bridge
PENDLE HERITAGE CENTRE
Pendleton
Newchurch
Barrowford
COLNE
Winewall
Wycoller
WYCOLLER
Trawden
BRITISH IN INDIA MUS
Great Mitton
Barrow
THE FOREST OF PENDLE
Fence
Sabden
Hurst Green
NELSON
THE FOREST OF TRAWDEN
Wiswell
Little Marsden
THE PENNINE BRIDLEWAY
WHALLEY ABBEY
Whalley
Higham
Brierfield
BOULSWORTH HILL
Billington
GAWTHORPE HALL
Haggate
Harle Syke
PENNINE WAY
Simonstone
Padiham
M65
Langho
A671
Read
Burnley Lane
Walshaw Dean Res.
Great Harwood
Altham
Rose Grove
Habergham
Hapton
Burnley
Wilpshire
Brunshaw
Worsthorne
Widdop Res.
WEAVERS TRIANGLE
Clayton-le-Moors
Walk Mill
Hurstwood
Brownhill
Rose Hill
Lane Ends
Mereclough
Rishton
Huncoat
Heptonstall Moor
TOWNELEY HALL
137
138
Clow Bridge
Holme Chapel
Colden
ACCRINGTON
Dunnockshaw
A646
Blackshaw Head
Heptonstall
0 1 2 3 miles
0 1 2 3 4 5 km

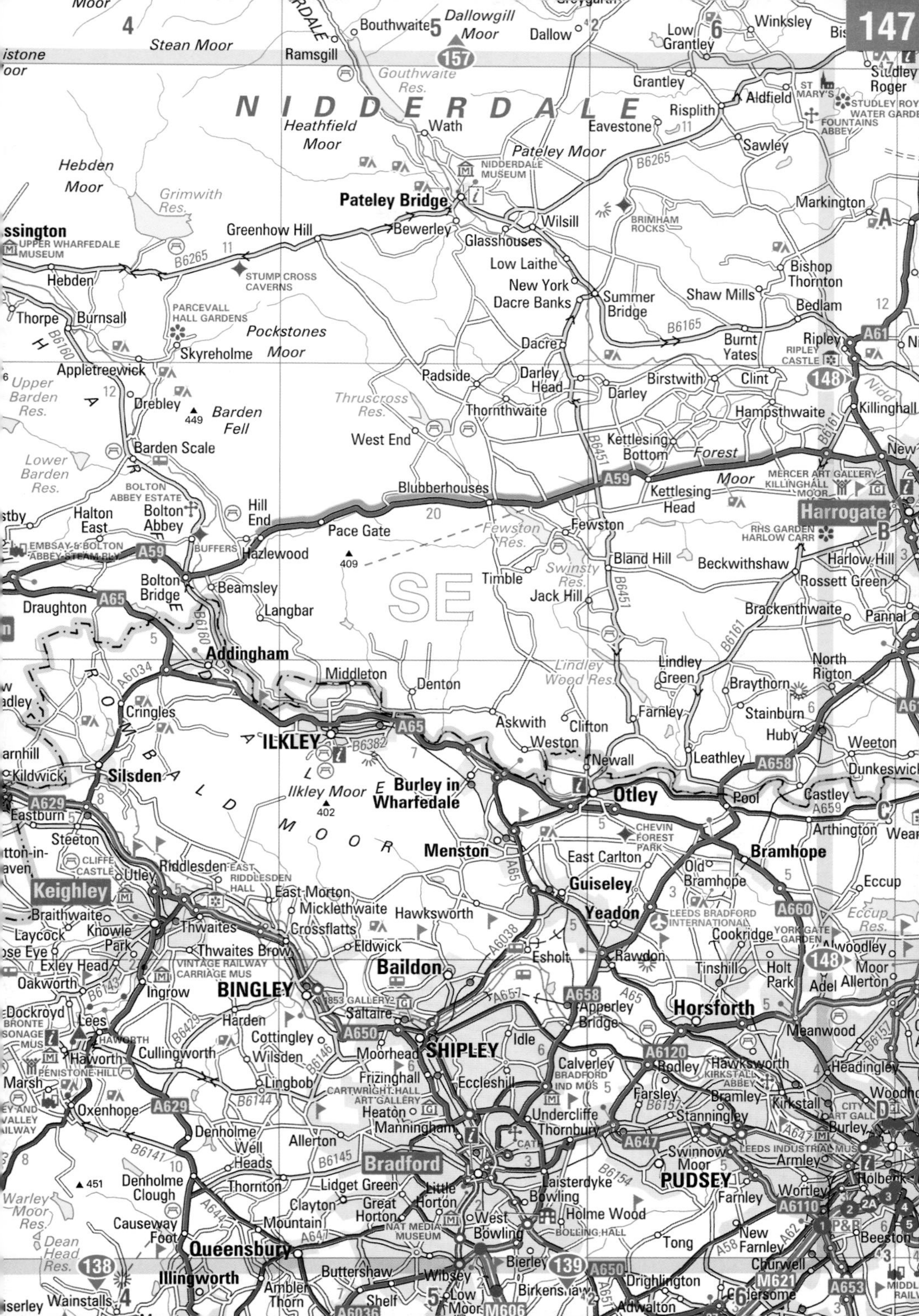
NIDDERDALE
Pateley Bridge
Harrogate
ILKLEY
Otley
Keighley
BINGLEY
SHIPLEY
Bradford
PUDSEY
Horsforth
Queensbury
Baildon
Ilkley Moor
Addingham
Silsden
Guiseley
Yeadon
Menston
Bramhope
Burley in Wharfedale
Fewston
Blubberhouses
Thruscross Res.
Grimwith Res.
Gouthwaite Res.
Ramsgill
Wath
Hebden
Burnsall
Appletreewick
Bolton Abbey
Bolton Bridge
Draughton
Steeton
Riddlesden
Haworth
Oxenhope
Denholme
Thornton
Illingworth
Wibsey
Farnley
Armley
Beeston
Headingley
Kirkstall
Bramley
Rawdon
Cookridge
Pool
Castley
Ripley
Killinghall
Pannal
Beckwithshaw
Hampsthwaite
Darley
Birstwith
Markington
Sawley
Aldfield
Winksley
Dallow
Bewerley
Greenhow Hill
Summer Bridge
Dacre Banks
Glasshouses
Timble
Askwith
Denton
Middleton
Langbar
Beamsley
Hazlewood
Pace Gate
Cringles
Crossflatts
Eldwick
Micklethwaite
Hawksworth
Esholt
Idle
Calverley
Eccleshill
Saltaire
Cottingley
Wilsden
Cullingworth
Harden
Allerton
Clayton
Great Horton
Little Horton
Bowling
Holme Wood
Tong
Drighlington
Bierley
Low Moor
Adwalton
Shelf
Buttershaw
Wainstalls
Causeway Foot
A59
A65
A61
A660
A658
A629
A650
A6120
A647
A6110
A62
A58
M621
M606
A653
A651
B6265
B6165
B6451
B6161
A6034
B6160
A6038
A657
B6382
B6429
B6146
B6144
B6145
B6141
B6154
B6157
A644
A6036
157
148
138
139
SE

Ripon
Bishopton
Studley Roger
Copt Hewick
Bridge Hewick
Marton-le-Moor
Norton-le-Clay
Brafferton
Helperby
Raskelf
Easingwold
Aldfield
Studley Royal Water Garden
Fountains Abbey
Littlethorpe
Skelton-on-Ure
Newby Hall
Kirby Hill
Langthorpe
Boroughbridge
Aldborough Roman Town
Aldborough
Tholthorpe
Myton-on-Swale
Flawith
Alne
Sawley
Park Hill
Roecliffe
Bishop Monkton
Minskip
Lower Dunsforth
Markington
Wormald Green
Burton Leonard
Copgrove
Grafton
Upper Dunsforth
Aldwark
Tollerton
Youlton
Bishop Thornton
South Stainley
Staveley
Marton
Great Ouseburn
Linton-on-Ouse
Bedlam
Ripley
Ripley Castle
Brearton
Nidd
Ferrensby
Farnham
Arkendale
Little Ouseburn
Burnt Yates
Clint
Hampsthwaite
Killinghall
Scotton
Scriven
Coneythorpe
Allerton Castle
Flaxby
Allerton Mauleverer
Thorpe Underwood
Newton on Ouse
Nun Monkton
Beningbrough Hall
Whixley
Green Hammerton
Knaresborough
Knaresborough Castle & Courthouse Museum
New Park
Starbeck
Mercer Art Gallery
Killinghall Moor
Harrogate
RHS Garden Harlow Carr
Forest Lane Head
Mother Shipton's Cave
Goldsborough
Hopperton
Moor Monkton
Kirk Hammerton
Woodlands
Plumpton Rocks
Walshford
Cattal
Marston Moor
Harlow Hill
Oatlands
Little Ribston
Hunsingore
Tockwith
Hessay
Rossett Green
Follifoot
Cowthorpe
Long Marston
Brackenthwaite
Pannal
Spofforth Castle
Spofforth
North Deighton
Bickerton
Hutton Wandesley
Spacey Houses
Kirk Deighton
Wetherby Services
North Rigton
Braythorn
Kirkby Overflow
Sicklinghall
Bilton in Ainsty
Stainburn
Huby
Wetherby
Walton
Angram
Weeton
Netherby
Chapel Hill
Linton
Wighill
Healaugh
Dunkeswick
Collingham
Bilbrough
Castley
Harewood
Boston Spa
Thorp Arch
Catterton
Harewood House
Arthington
Weardley
East Keswick
Newton Kyme
Bramhope
Clifford
Bardsey
East Rigton
Bramham
Tadcaster
Eccup
Wike
Scarcroft
Bramham Park
Stutton
Kirkby Wharfe
Bolton Percy
Cookridge
York Gate Garden
Alwoodley
Eccup Res.
Scarcroft Hill
Shadwell
Thorner
Ulleskelf
Holt Park
Adel
Moor Allerton
Tropical World
Towton
Roundhay
Potterton
Meanwood
Chapel Allerton
Wellington Hill
Barwick in-Elmet
Scholes
Church Fenton
Hawksworth
Headingley
Potternewton
Aberford
Saxton
Seacroft
Lotherton Hall
Barkston
Kirkstall Abbey
Bramley
Kirkstall
Woodhouse
Harehills
Manston
City Art Gallery
Burley
Sheepscar
Whitkirk
Old Micklefield
Micklefield
Garden Village
Sherburn in Elmet
Little Fenton
Leeds Industrial Mus
Armley
Halton
Garforth
Home Farm
Colton
Newthorpe
Steeton Hall Gateway
Leeds
Temple Newsam House
New Micklefield
Wortley
Farnley
Holbeck
Hunslet
South Milford
Thwaite Mills Industrial Mus
Monk Fryston
New Farnley
Beeston
Temple Newsam
Swillington
Kippax
Ledston Luck
Lumby
Rothwell Colliery
Great Preston
Ledsham
Haigh
Woodlesford
Rothwell
Fairburn Ings
Hillam
Oulton
A61
A19
A59
A658
A661
A168
A1(M)
A6055
A659
A660
A58
A6120
A64
A63
A162
A1246
A656
A642
A6110
A62
A647
A657
B6265
B6165
B6161
B6164
B1224
B1217
B1222
M1
Dere Street
Nidd
Ouse
Wharfe
TOLL
1644
1461
147
158
139
140
0 1 2 3 miles
0 1 2 3 4 5 km

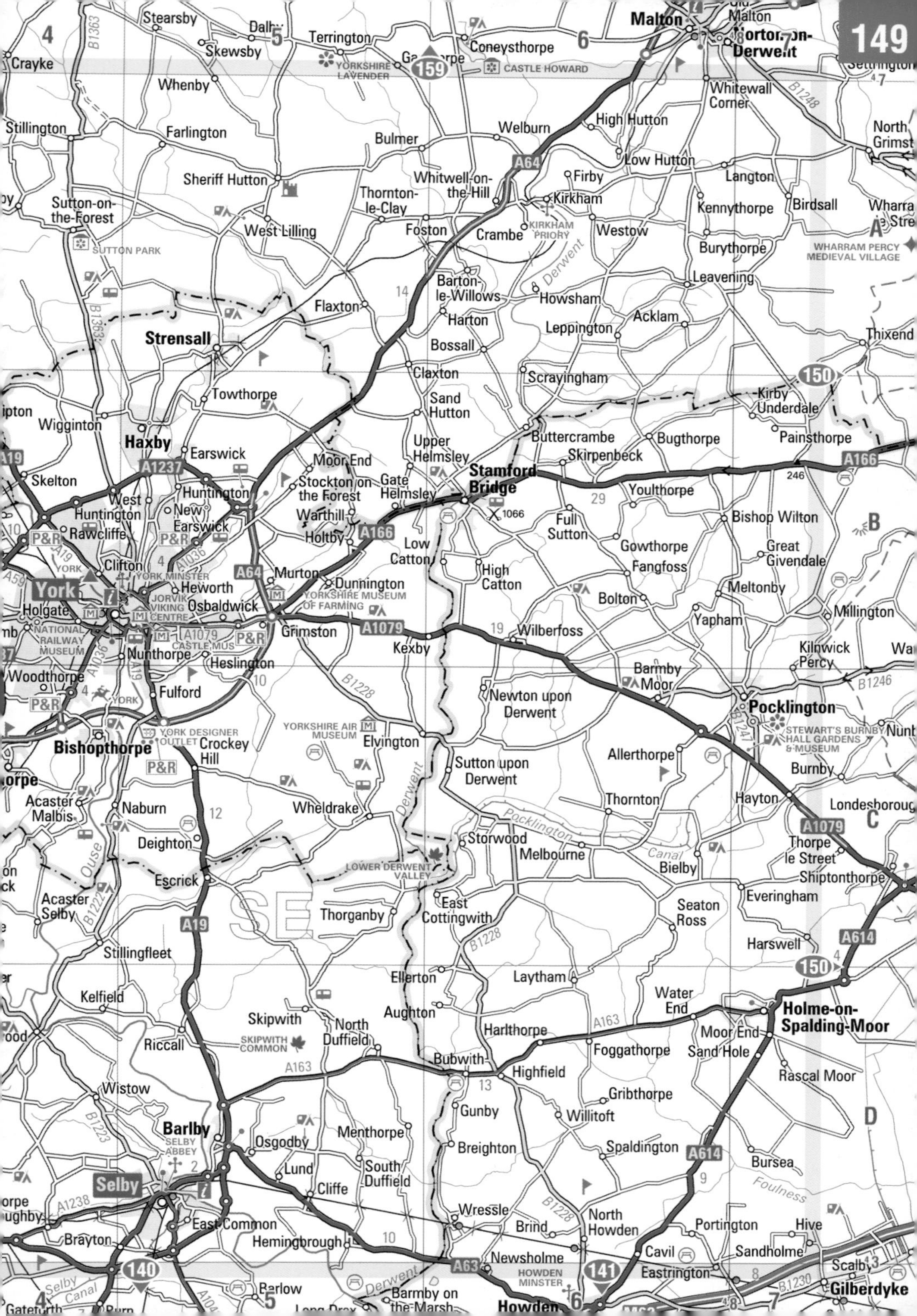

Malton
Old Malton
Norton-on-Derwent
Stearsby
Dalby
Skewsby
Terrington
Coneysthorpe
YORKSHIRE LAVENDER
CASTLE HOWARD
Crayke
Whenby
Whitewall Corner
Stillington
Farlington
Bulmer
Welburn
High Hutton
North Grimston
Sheriff Hutton
Whitwell-on-the-Hill
Low Hutton
Langton
Firby
Sutton-on-the-Forest
Thornton-le-Clay
Kirkham
Kennythorpe
Birdsall
West Lilling
Foston
Crambe
KIRKHAM PRIORY
Westow
Burythorpe
SUTTON PARK
WHARRAM PERCY MEDIEVAL VILLAGE
Barton-le-Willows
Howsham
Leavening
Flaxton
Harton
Acklam
Strensall
Leppington
Thixendale
Bossall
Claxton
Scrayingham
Towthorpe
Sand Hutton
Kirby Underdale
Wigginton
Haxby
Upper Helmsley
Buttercrambe
Bugthorpe
Painsthorpe
Earswick
Moor End
Skirpenbeck
Skelton
Stockton on the Forest
Gate Helmsley
Stamford Bridge
Youlthorpe
West Huntington
Huntington
Warthill
New Earswick
Full Sutton
Bishop Wilton
Rawcliffe
Holtby
Low Catton
Gowthorpe
Great Givendale
Clifton
YORK MINSTER
Murton
High Catton
Fangfoss
York
Heworth
Dunnington
Meltonby
JORVIK VIKING CENTRE
Osbaldwick
YORKSHIRE MUSEUM OF FARMING
Bolton
Millington
Holgate
Grimston
Wilberfoss
Yapham
NATIONAL RAILWAY MUSEUM
CASTLE MUS
Kexby
Kilnwick Percy
Nunthorpe
Heslington
Barmby Moor
Woodthorpe
Fulford
Newton upon Derwent
Pocklington
STEWART'S BURNBY HALL GARDENS & MUSEUM
Bishopthorpe
YORK DESIGNER OUTLET
Crockey Hill
YORKSHIRE AIR MUSEUM
Elvington
Allerthorpe
Burnby
Sutton upon Derwent
Acaster Malbis
Naburn
Wheldrake
Thornton
Hayton
Londesborough
Deighton
Storwood
Pocklington Canal
Melbourne
Thorpe le Street
Bielby
Shiptonthorpe
LOWER DERWENT VALLEY
Escrick
Acaster Selby
East Cottingwith
Everingham
Seaton Ross
Thorganby
Harswell
Stillingfleet
Ellerton
Laytham
Kelfield
Water End
Aughton
Holme-on-Spalding-Moor
Skipwith
North Duffield
Harlthorpe
Moor End
SKIPWITH COMMON
Riccall
Foggathorpe
Sand Hole
Bubwith
Highfield
Rascal Moor
Wistow
Gribthorpe
Gunby
Willitoft
Barlby
Menthorpe
SELBY ABBEY
Osgodby
Breighton
Spaldington
Bursea
Lund
South Duffield
Selby
Cliffe
Foulness
Wressle
North Howden
East Common
Brind
Portington
Hive
Brayton
Hemingbrough
Cavil
Sandholme
Newsholme
HOWDEN MINSTER
Eastrington
Scalby
Selby Canal
Barlow
Barmby on the Marsh
Howden
Gilberdyke
Derwent
Ouse
A64
A166
A1079
A1237
A19
A1036
A59
A163
A614
A63
A1238
B1363
B1248
B1228
B1246
B1247
B1222
B1223
B1230
SE
1066

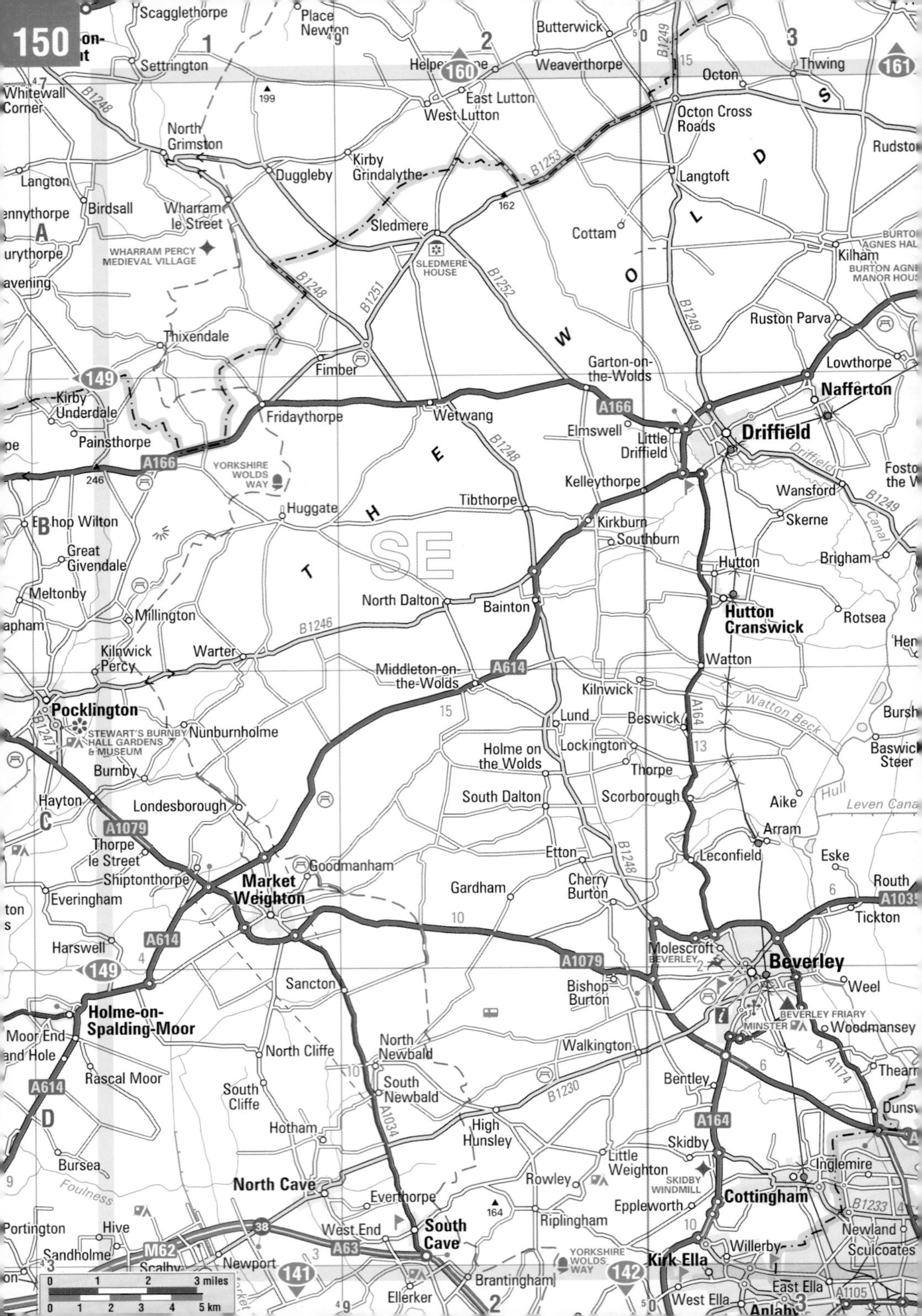

Scagglethorpe
Place Newton
Butterwick
Settrington
Helperthorpe
160
Weaverthorpe
Thwing
161
Octon
Whitewall Corner
B1248
199
East Lutton
West Lutton
Octon Cross Roads
North Grimston
Kirby Grindalythe
B1253
Langtoft
Rudston
Langton
Duggleby
Birdsall
Wharram le Street
Sledmere
162
Cottam
WHARRAM PERCY MEDIEVAL VILLAGE
SLEDMERE HOUSE
Kilham
BURTON AGNES HALL
BURTON AGNES MANOR HOUSE
B1251
B1252
B1249
Ruston Parva
Thixendale
Fimber
Garton-on-the-Wolds
Lowthorpe
149
Kirby Underdale
Fridaythorpe
Wetwang
A166
Nafferton
Elmswell
Little Driffield
Driffield
Painsthorpe
A166
246
YORKSHIRE WOLDS WAY
Kelleythorpe
Wansford
Tibthorpe
Huggate
Kirkburn
Skerne
Bishop Wilton
Southburn
Great Givendale
SE
Hutton
Brigham
Meltonby
North Dalton
Bainton
Hutton Cranswick
Rotsea
Millington
B1246
Kilnwick Percy
Warter
Watton
Middleton-on-the-Wolds
A614
Kilnwick
Pocklington
Lund
Beswick
A164
Watton Beck
STEWART'S BURNBY HALL GARDENS & MUSEUM
Nunburnholme
Holme on the Wolds
Lockington
Thorpe
B1247
Burnby
South Dalton
Scorborough
Aike
Hull
Leven Canal
Hayton
Londesborough
Arram
A1079
Thorpe le Street
Etton
Eske
Leconfield
Shiptonthorpe
Market Weighton
Goodmanham
Cherry Burton
B1248
Routh
Everingham
Gardham
Tickton
A1035
Harswell
A614
Molescroft
BEVERLEY
A1079
Beverley
Weel
Sancton
Bishop Burton
BEVERLEY FRIARY
MINSTER
Woodmansey
Holme-on-Spalding-Moor
Moor End
North Newbald
Walkington
North Cliffe
A1174
Thearne
Rascal Moor
South Newbald
South Cliffe
Bentley
B1230
A1034
A614
High Hunsley
A164
Dunswell
Hotham
Skidby
Bursea
Little Weighton
Inglemire
SKIDBY WINDMILL
Rowley
North Cave
Foulness
Everthorpe
164
Eppleworth
Cottingham
B1233
Riplingham
Portington
Hive
38
West End
South Cave
Newland
M62
A63
Willerby
Sculcoates
Sandholme
Scalby
Newport
YORKSHIRE WOLDS WAY
Kirk Ella
141
142
Brantingham
East Ella
A1105
Ellerker
West Ella
Anlaby
0 1 2 3 miles
0 1 2 3 4 5 km

Grindale
A165
Flamborough
B1255
FLAMBOROUGH HEAD
161
B1259
SEWERBY HALL AND GARDENS
Boynton
PRIORY
Sewerby
BONDVILLE MODEL VILLAGE
BAYLE MUSEUM
Bridlington
Bessingby
West Hill
OLD PENNY MEMORIES
Carnaby
Hilderthorpe
A614
P&R
BRIDLINGTON BIRDS OF PREY & ANIMAL PARK
BRIDLINGTON BAY
Fraisthorpe
Gransmoor
Barmston
Lissett
Ulrome
A165
SKIPSEA CASTLE
Skipsea
B1249
Beeford
Skipsea Brough
B1242
Dunnington
Bewholme
Atwick
North Cliff
Hornsea
Brandesburton
Hornsea Mere
HORNSEA MUSEUM
Seaton
B1244
HORNSEA FREEPORT
Hornsea Bridge
Rolston
Catwick
Sigglesthorne
Goxhill
Mappleton
Little Hatfield
B1243
Rise
Great Hatfield
Great Cowden
Withernwick
New Ellerby
Skirlaugh
Aldbrough
Marton
West Newton
East Newton
Old Ellerby
BURTON CONSTABLE HALL
Flinton
Swine
Coniston
Garton
Grimston
Thirtleby
Sproatley
Humbleton
Fitling
Ganstead
Hilston
Sutton on Hull
B1238
Lelley
Bilton
Owstwick
Tunstall
Sutton Ings
B1240
B1239
Elstronwick
North End
Summergangs
Preston
Burton Pidsea
Roos
B1242
WILBERFORCE HOUSE
West End
142
143
Waxholme
Marfleet
A1033
Saltend
Hedon
B1362
Owthorne
TA
A
B
C
D
4
5
6

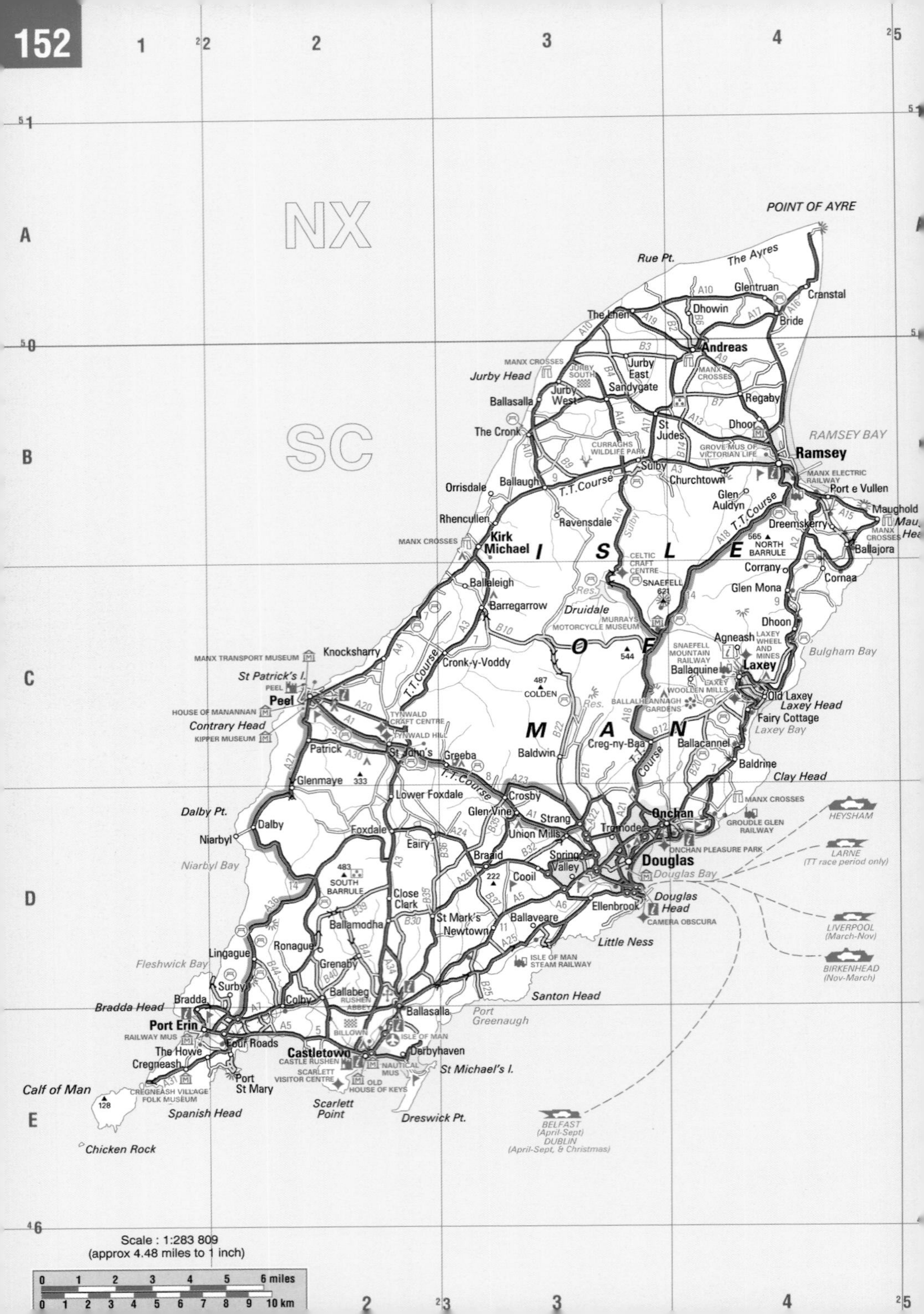

NX
SC
POINT OF AYRE
Rue Pt.
The Ayres
Glentruan
Cranstal
Dhowin
The Lhen
Bride
Andreas
Jurby Head
Jurby East
Sandygate
Jurby West
Ballasalla
Regaby
The Cronk
St Judes
Dhoor
RAMSEY BAY
CURRAGHS WILDLIFE PARK
GROVE MUS OF VICTORIAN LIFE
Ramsey
Sulby
Churchtown
MANX ELECTRIC RAILWAY
Orrisdale
Ballaugh
T.T. Course
Glen Auldyn
Port e Vullen
Maughold
Rhencullen
Ravensdale
Dreemskerry
Kirk Michael
MANX CROSSES
ISLE OF MAN
NORTH BARRULE
Ballajora
CELTIC CRAFT CENTRE
SNAEFELL
Corrany
Ballaleigh
Cornaa
Glen Mona
Barregarrow
Druidale
MURRAYS MOTORCYCLE MUSEUM
Dhoon
Agneash
LAXEY WHEEL AND MINES
Bulgham Bay
MANX TRANSPORT MUSEUM
Knocksharry
SNAEFELL MOUNTAIN RAILWAY
St Patrick's I.
Cronk-y-Voddy
Ballaquine
Laxey
PEEL
COLDEN
LAXEY WOOLLEN MILLS
Peel
Old Laxey
HOUSE OF MANANNAN
TYNWALD CRAFT CENTRE
BALLALHEANNAGH GARDENS
Laxey Head
Fairy Cottage
Contrary Head
TYNWALD HILL
Laxey Bay
KIPPER MUSEUM
Creg-ny-Baa
Ballacannel
Patrick
St John's
Greeba
Baldwin
Baldrine
Glenmaye
Clay Head
Lower Foxdale
Crosby
MANX CROSSES
HEYSHAM
Dalby Pt.
Glen Vine
Strang
Onchan
GROUDLE GLEN RAILWAY
Dalby
Tromode
Niarbyl
Foxdale
Union Mills
ONCHAN PLEASURE PARK
LARNE (TT race period only)
Eairy
Braaid
Spring Valley
Douglas
Niarbyl Bay
Douglas Bay
SOUTH BARRULE
Cooil
Close Clark
Douglas Head
Ellenbrook
St Mark's
Ballaveare
CAMERA OBSCURA
Ballamodha
Newtown
LIVERPOOL (March-Nov)
Little Ness
Lingague
Ronague
Fleshwick Bay
Grenaby
ISLE OF MAN STEAM RAILWAY
BIRKENHEAD (Nov-March)
Surby
Ballabeg
RUSHEN ABBEY
Santon Head
Bradda
Colby
Bradda Head
Ballasalla
Port Greenaugh
Port Erin
RAILWAY MUS
Four Roads
BILLOWN
ISLE OF MAN
The Howe
Castletown
Derbyhaven
CASTLE RUSHEN
NAUTICAL MUS
St Michael's I.
Cregneash
Port St Mary
SCARLETT VISITOR CENTRE
OLD HOUSE OF KEYS
Calf of Man
CREGNEASH VILLAGE FOLK MUSEUM
Spanish Head
Scarlett Point
Dreswick Pt.
BELFAST (April-Sept)
DUBLIN (April-Sept, & Christmas)
Chicken Rock
Scale : 1:283 809
(approx 4.48 miles to 1 inch)
0 1 2 3 4 5 6 miles
0 1 2 3 4 5 6 7 8 9 10 km

FURNESS FELLS
Seascale
Santon Bridge
Eskdale Green
Beckfoot
Boot
Eskdale
Knott Pass
Wrynose Pass
Cockley Beck
Holmrook
Drigg
Irt
Mite
Esk
Harter Fell
Seathwaite Tarn
Coniston Coppermines
Coniston Holly How
The Old Man of Coniston
Birker Fell
Devoke Water
Saltcoats
Ravenglass and Eskdale Railway & Mus
Bath House
Muncaster Castle & World Owl Centre
Ravenglass
Woodend
Hall Dunnerdale
Seathwaite
Bowmanstead
Ulpha Fell
Duddon
Broad Oak
Newbiggin
Lane End
Whitfell
Ulpha
Caw
Hoses
Torver
A595
A593
A5084
Coniston Water
Corney Fell
Corney
Stub Place
Broughton Mills
Hycemoor
Selker Bay
Bootle
Duddon Bridge
Lower Hawthwaite
Water Yeat
Blawith
High Nibthwaite
Broughton in Furness
Black Combe
Lowick Bridge
Hallthwaites
Duddon Mosses
Foxfield
Grizebeck
Lowick Green
A5092
Gawthwaite
Whitbeck
The Green
The Hill
B5281
Penny Bridge
Kirkby-in-Furness
Beck Side
Broughton Beck
Silecroft
Whicham
A5093
Soutergate
Arrad Foot
Millom
Millom Heritage Museum
Kirksanton
Mansriggs
Laurel & Hardy Mus
Haverigg
Duddon Sands
Ulverston
Askam in Furness
Ireleth
Pennington
Swarthmoor
Lindal in Furness
SD
Sandscale Haws
South Lakes Safari Zoo
Great Urswick
Dalton-in-Furness
A590
Dalton Castle
Little Urswick
North Walney
Stainton with Adgarley
Scales
Barrow (Walney Island)
Hawcoat
Bow Bridge
Baycliff
Ormsgill
Newton
Gleaston Watermill
Furness Abbey
Newbarns
Aldingham
Barrow-in-Furness
Dendron
Gleaston
North Scale
Custom Ho
Newbiggin
Leece
The Dock Museum
Vickerstown
Barrow Island
A5087
Roosebeck
Biggar
Rampside
Roa Island
Foulney Island
South End
Piel Island
Isle of Walney
South Channel
South End Point
0 1 2 3 miles
0 1 2 3 4 5 km

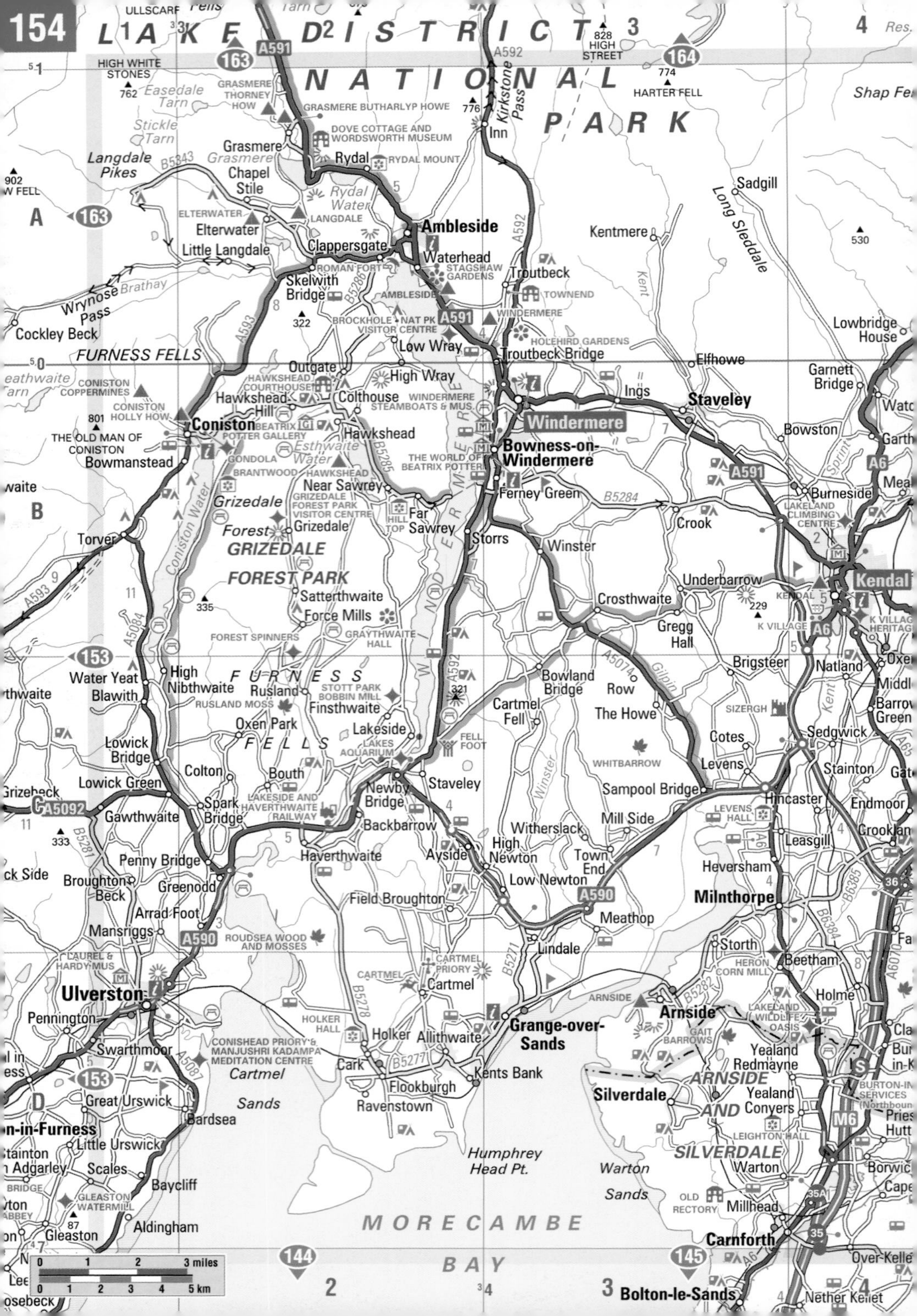
LAKE DISTRICT NATIONAL PARK
163
164
A591
A592
HIGH WHITE STONES
762
Easedale Tarn
GRASMERE THORNEY HOW
GRASMERE BUTHARLYP HOWE
776
Kirkstone Pass
Inn
828 HIGH STREET
774 HARTER FELL
Shap Fell
Stickle Tarn
DOVE COTTAGE AND WORDSWORTH MUSEUM
Grasmere
Langdale Pikes
B5343
Chapel Stile
Rydal
RYDAL MOUNT
Rydal Water
902
A
163
ELTERWATER
Elterwater
LANGDALE
Ambleside
Kentmere
Sadgill
Long Sleddale
530
Little Langdale
Clappersgate
Waterhead
STAGSHAW GARDENS
Troutbeck
TOWNEND
Kent
Wrynose Pass
Brathay
ROMAN FORT
Skelwith Bridge
B5286
AMBLESIDE
322
BROCKHOLE - NAT PK VISITOR CENTRE
A591
WINDERMERE
HOLEHIRD GARDENS
Lowbridge House
Cockley Beck
Low Wray
Troutbeck Bridge
Elfhowe
FURNESS FELLS
Outgate
HAWKSHEAD COURTHOUSE
High Wray
Garnett Bridge
CONISTON COPPERMINES
CONISTON HOLLY HOW
Hawkshead Hill
Colthouse
WINDERMERE STEAMBOATS & MUS.
Ings
Staveley
Windermere
Coniston
801
THE OLD MAN OF CONISTON
BEATRIX POTTER GALLERY
Hawkshead
Esthwaite Water
Bowness-on-Windermere
Bowston
Bowmanstead
GONDOLA
BRANTWOOD
HAWKSHEAD
THE WORLD OF BEATRIX POTTER
A591
A6
Near Sawrey
GRIZEDALE FOREST PARK VISITOR CENTRE
Ferney Green
B5284
Burneside
B
Grizedale
HILL TOP
Far Sawrey
Crook
LAKELAND CLIMBING CENTRE
Forest
Grizedale
Coniston Water
Torver
GRIZEDALE FOREST PARK
Storrs
Winster
WINDERMERE
A593
Satterthwaite
Underbarrow
Kendal
335
Force Mills
Crosthwaite
229
KENDAL
K VILLAGE
Gregg Hall
FOREST SPINNERS
GRAYTHWAITE HALL
A5074
Gilpin
153
Water Yeat
High Nibthwaite
Blawith
FURNESS FELLS
Rusland
RUSLAND MOSS
STOTT PARK BOBBIN MILL
Finsthwaite
321
A592
Bowland Bridge
Row
Brigsteer
Natland
Cartmel Fell
The Howe
SIZERGH
Oxen Park
Lakeside
LAKES AQUARIUM
FELL FOOT
Lowick Bridge
Cotes
Sedgwick
Levens
WHITBARROW
Winster
Colton
Bouth
Staveley
Sampool Bridge
Stainton
Lowick Green
Spark Bridge
LAKESIDE AND HAVERTHWAITE RAILWAY
Newby Bridge
Hincaster
Endmoor
A5092
Gawthwaite
Backbarrow
LEVENS HALL
Witherslack
Mill Side
333
B5281
Haverthwaite
Ayside
High Newton
Town End
Leasgill
Penny Bridge
Heversham
Broughton Beck
Greenodd
Low Newton
A590
Milnthorpe
Field Broughton
Arrad Foot
Meathop
B6385
Mansriggs
A590
ROUDSEA WOOD AND MOSSES
Lindale
B6384
LAUREL & HARDY MUS
B5271
Storth
Beetham
CARTMEL PRIORY
HERON CORN MILL
CARTMEL
Cartmel
B5282
Ulverston
ARNSIDE
Arnside
Holme
Pennington
B5278
HOLKER HALL
Grange-over-Sands
LAKELAND WILDLIFE OASIS
GAIT BARROWS
Holker
Allithwaite
CONISHEAD PRIORY & MANJUSHRI KADAMPA MEDITATION CENTRE
Swarthmoor
A5087
Yealand Redmayne
Cark
B5277
153
Cartmel
Kents Bank
ARNSIDE AND SILVERDALE
Flookburgh
D
Great Urswick
Sands
Silverdale
Yealand Conyers
BURTON-IN-KENDAL SERVICES (Northbound)
Ravenstown
Bardsea
M6
LEIGHTON HALL
Little Urswick
Humphrey Head Pt.
Warton Sands
Warton
Scales
Baycliff
GLEASTON WATERMILL
OLD RECTORY
Millhead
87
Gleaston
Aldingham
MORECAMBE BAY
Carnforth
35
35A
144
145
Over Kellet
0 1 2 3 miles
0 1 2 3 4 5 km
Bolton-le-Sands
Nether Kellet
Sands

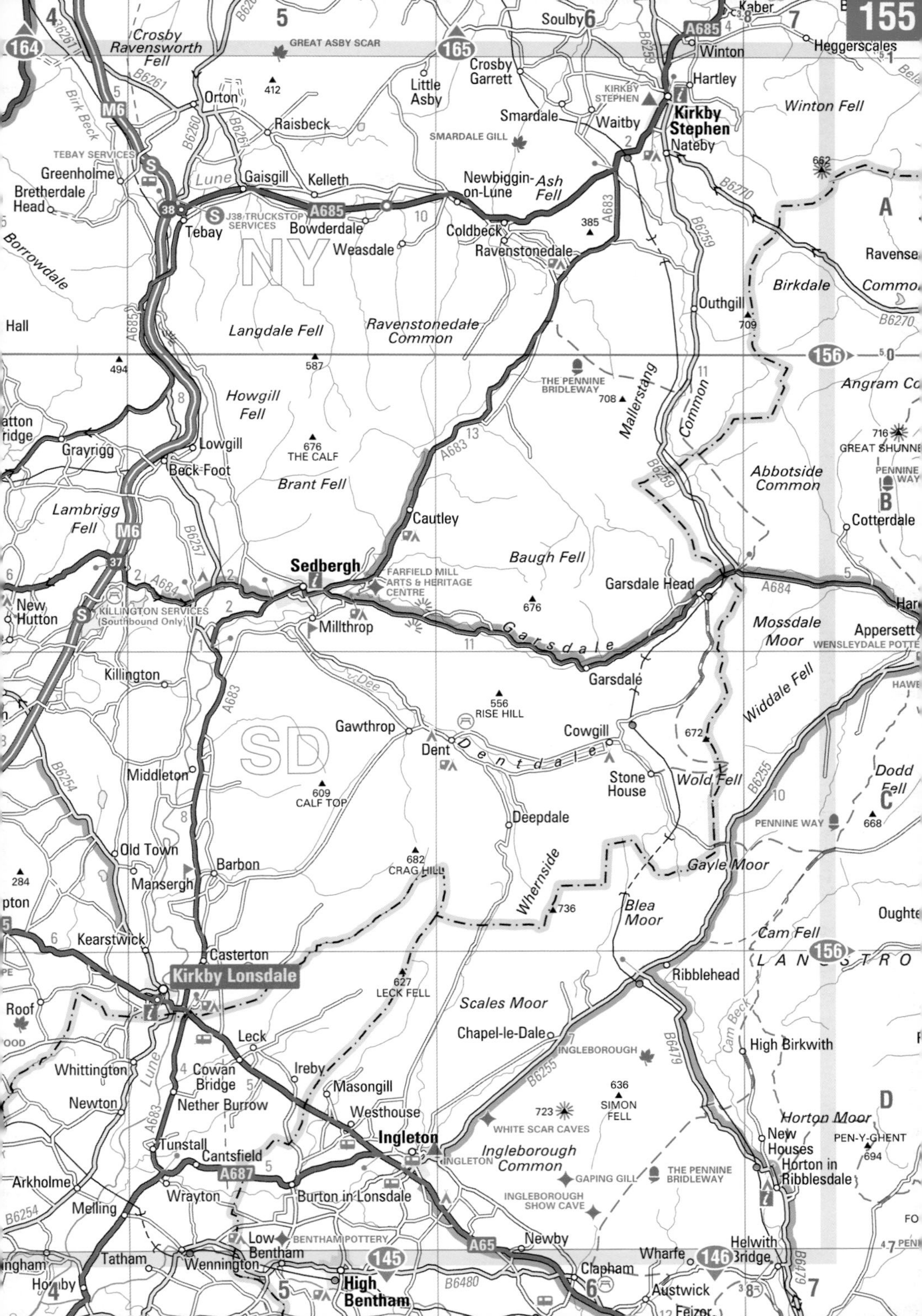

4
5
6
7
164
165
Crosby Ravensworth Fell
GREAT ASBY SCAR
Soulby
Kaber
A685
Winton
Heggerscales
Crosby Garrett
Hartley
Little Asby
Orton
412
Birk Beck
M6
B6261
B6260
B6259
KIRKBY STEPHEN
Kirkby Stephen
Winton Fell
Smardale
Waitby
Raisbeck
SMARDALE GILL
Nateby
TEBAY SERVICES
Greenholme
Bretherdale Head
Lune
Gaisgill
Kelleth
Newbiggin-on-Lune
Ash Fell
662
B6270
A
38
J38 TRUCKSTOP SERVICES
Tebay
Bowderdale
Coldbeck
385
A683
Borrowdale
NY
Weasdale
Ravenstonedale
Ravenseat
Birkdale
Common
Outhgill
709
A685
Hall
Langdale Fell
Ravenstonedale Common
156
Angram Common
494
587
THE PENNINE BRIDLEWAY
708
Mallerstang
Common
Howgill Fell
716
GREAT SHUNNER
Grayrigg
Lowgill
676
THE CALF
Beck Foot
Abbotside Common
PENNINE WAY
Brant Fell
B
Lambrigg Fell
Cautley
Cotterdale
Baugh Fell
B6257
37
A684
Sedbergh
FARFIELD MILL ARTS & HERITAGE CENTRE
Garsdale Head
New Hutton
KILLINGTON SERVICES (Southbound Only)
Millthrop
Garsdale
Mossdale Moor
Appersett
WENSLEYDALE POTTERY
Killington
Dee
Garsdale
556
RISE HILL
Widdale Fell
Gawthrop
Cowgill
672
SD
Dent
Dentdale
Middleton
609
CALF TOP
Stone House
Wold Fell
Dodd Fell
B6254
B6255
C
Deepdale
PENNINE WAY
668
Old Town
682
CRAG HILL
Barbon
Gayle Moor
284
Mansergh
Whernside
736
Blea Moor
Oughtershaw
Kearstwick
Cam Fell
Casterton
Kirkby Lonsdale
Ribblehead
LANGSTROTHDALE
627
LECK FELL
Scales Moor
Roof
Chapel-le-Dale
Cam Beck
Leck
INGLEBOROUGH
B6479
High Birkwith
Whittington
Cowan Bridge
Ireby
636
SIMON FELL
Newton
Masongill
Nether Burrow
Westhouse
723
WHITE SCAR CAVES
D
Horton Moor
A683
Tunstall
Ingleton
INGLETON
Ingleborough Common
New Houses
PEN-Y-GHENT
694
Cantsfield
A687
GAPING GILL
THE PENNINE BRIDLEWAY
Horton in Ribblesdale
Arkholme
Wrayton
Burton in Lonsdale
INGLEBOROUGH SHOW CAVE
Melling
Low Bentham
BENTHAM POTTERY
A65
Newby
Helwith Bridge
Wharfe
Tatham
Wennington
145
146
Clapham
Hornby
High Bentham
B6480
Austwick
Feizor

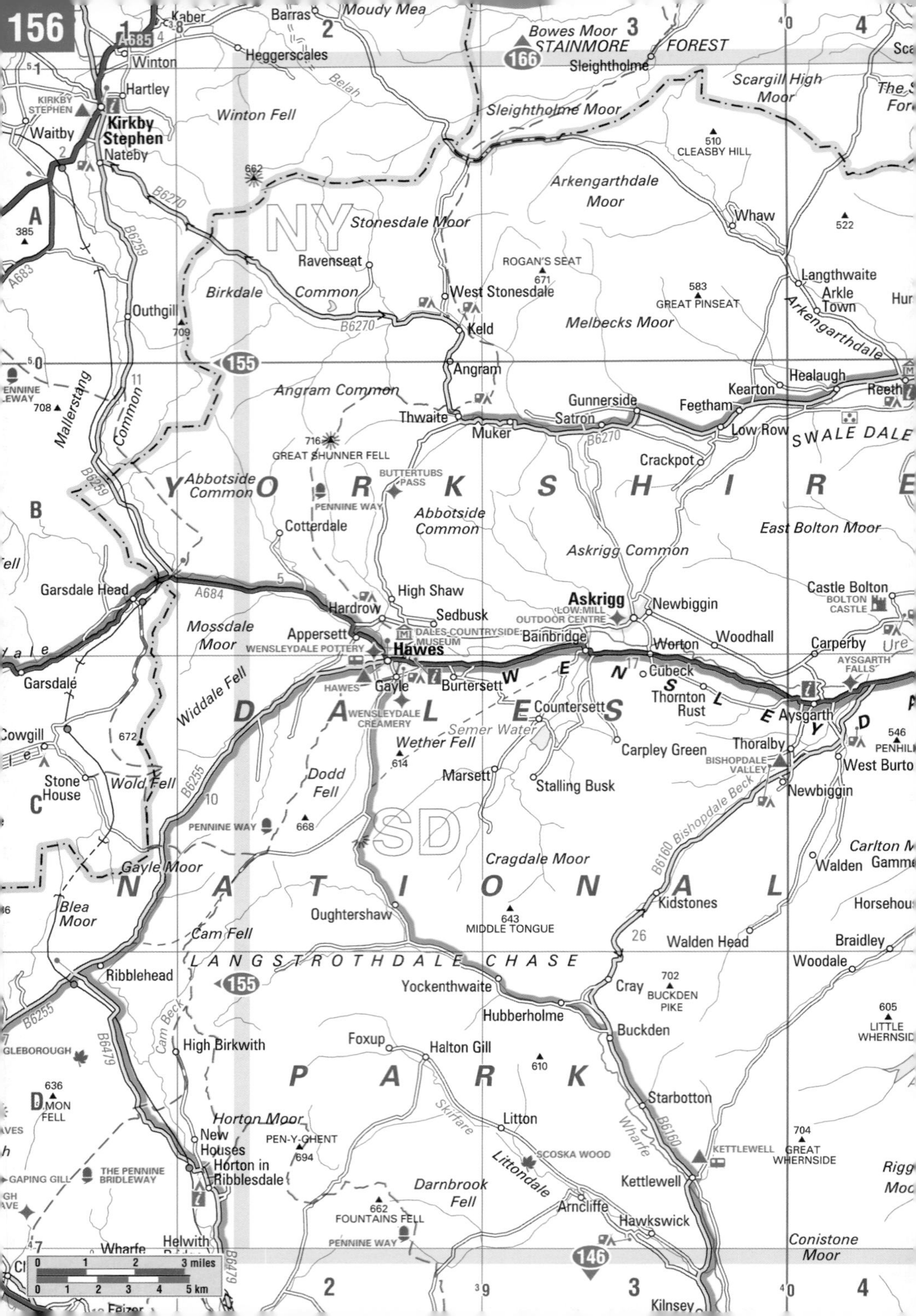

Kaber
Barras
Moudy Mea
Bowes Moor
STAINMORE
FOREST
Sleightholme
Scargill High Moor
Winton
Heggerscales
166
Hartley
KIRKBY STEPHEN
Kirkby Stephen
Waitby
Nateby
Winton Fell
Belah
Sleightholme Moor
510
CLEASBY HILL
662
Arkengarthdale Moor
B6270
B6259
NY
Stonesdale Moor
Whaw
522
A
385
A683
Ravenseat
ROGAN'S SEAT
671
Langthwaite
Arkle Town
583
GREAT PINSEAT
Birkdale
Common
West Stonesdale
Keld
Melbecks Moor
Arkengarthdale
Outhgill
709
B6270
155
Angram
Healaugh
Kearton
Reeth
Mallerstang
Common
708
Angram Common
Gunnerside
Feetham
Thwaite
Satron
Muker
Low Row
SWALE DALE
716
GREAT SHUNNER FELL
B6270
Crackpot
BUTTERTUBS PASS
Abbotside Common
Y O R K S H I R E
PENNINE WAY
B6259
B
Abbotside Common
East Bolton Moor
Cotterdale
Askrigg Common
Garsdale Head
A684
5
High Shaw
Askrigg
Newbiggin
Castle Bolton
BOLTON CASTLE
Hardrow
Sedbusk
LOW MILL OUTDOOR CENTRE
Mossdale Moor
Appersett
DALES COUNTRYSIDE MUSEUM
Bainbridge
Woodhall
Carperby
Worton
Ure
WENSLEYDALE POTTERY
Hawes
17
Cubeck
AYSGARTH FALLS
Garsdale
HAWES
Gayle
Burtersett
W E N S L E Y D A L E
Thornton Rust
Aysgarth
Widdale Fell
Countersett
D A L E S
WENSLEYDALE CREAMERY
Semer Water
Cowgill
672
Wether Fell
614
Carpley Green
Thoralby
546
BISHOPDALE VALLEY
West Burto
Stone House
C
Wold Fell
Dodd Fell
Marsett
Stalling Busk
Newbiggin
B6255
10
PENNINE WAY
668
SD
Bishopdale Beck
B6160
Carlton M
Gayle Moor
Cragdale Moor
Walden
N A T I O N A L
Kidstones
Horsehous
Blea Moor
Oughtershaw
643
MIDDLE TONGUE
Cam Fell
26
Walden Head
Braidley
L A N G S T R O T H D A L E   C H A S E
Woodale
Ribblehead
155
Yockenthwaite
Cray
702
BUCKDEN PIKE
Hubberholme
605
LITTLE WHERNSIDE
B6255
Cam Beck
Buckden
B6479
High Birkwith
Foxup
Halton Gill
610
636
D
P A R K
Starbotton
Skirfare
Horton Moor
Litton
Wharfe
New Houses
PEN-Y-GHENT
694
B6160
704
GREAT WHERNSIDE
KETTLEWELL
THE PENNINE BRIDLEWAY
GAPING GILL
Horton in Ribblesdale
Littondale
SCOSKA WOOD
Kettlewell
Darnbrook Fell
662
FOUNTAINS FELL
Arncliffe
Hawkswick
Wharfe
Helwith Bridge
PENNINE WAY
146
Conistone Moor
0 1 2 3 miles
0 1 2 3 4 5 km
B6479
Kilnsey
1 2 3 4
2 3 4
A B C D

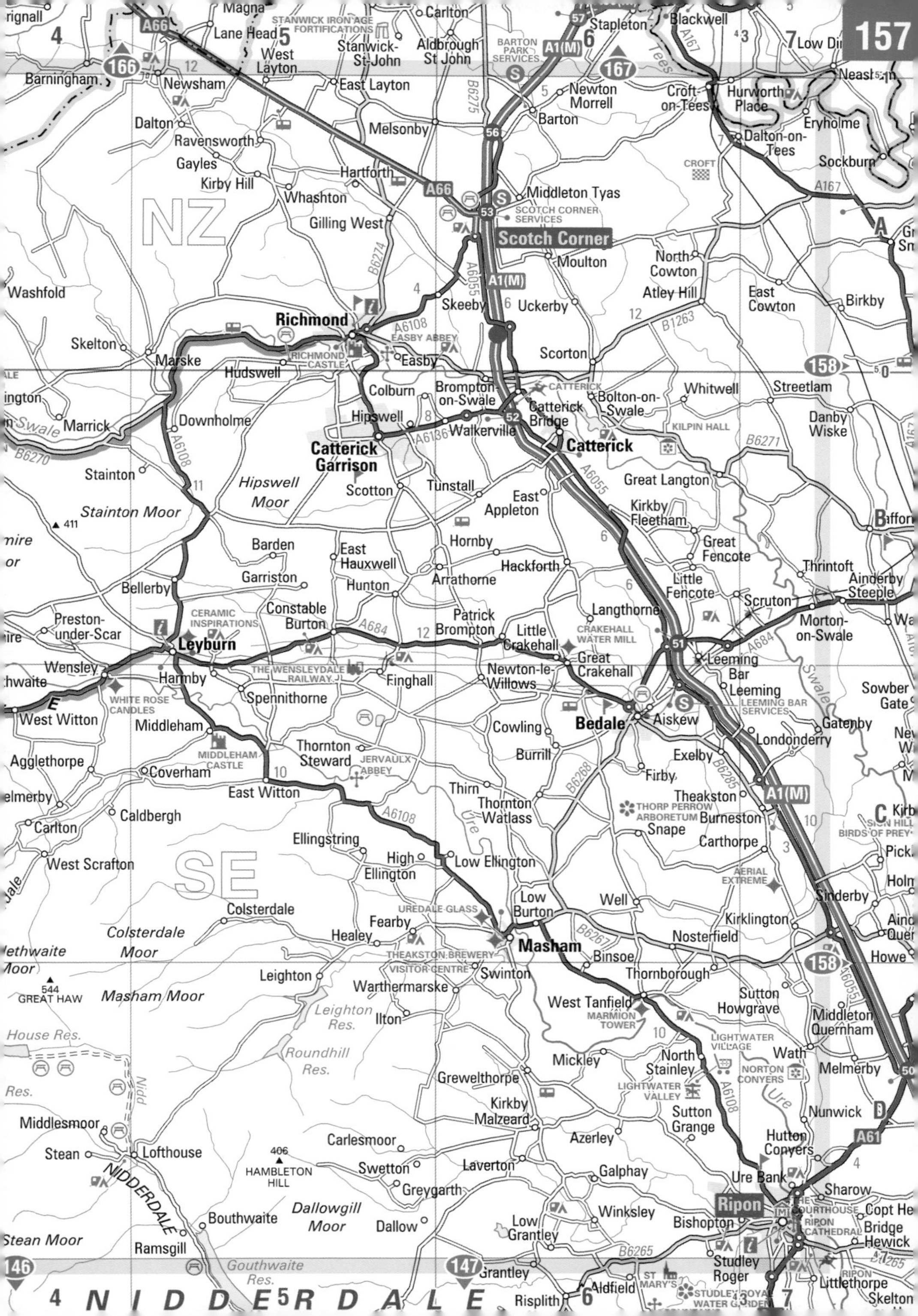
NZ
SE
Scotch Corner
Richmond
Catterick Garrison
Catterick
Leyburn
Bedale
Masham
Ripon
NIDDERDALE
A66
A1(M)
A6108
A684
A6055
A61
Stapleton
Blackwell
Barton
Middleton Tyas
Melsonby
Gilling West
Skeeby
Scorton
Brompton-on-Swale
Catterick Bridge
Marske
Hudswell
Downholme
Hipswell
Colburn
Easby
Scotton
Tunstall
Hornby
Hackforth
East Witton
Middleham
Harmby
Wensley
West Witton
Spennithorne
Finghall
Thornton Steward
Jervaulx Abbey
Well
Snape
Burneston
West Tanfield
North Stainley
Kirkby Malzeard
Grewelthorpe
Lofthouse
Ramsgill
Middlesmoor
Great Haw
Hambleton Hill
Leighton Res.
Roundhill Res.
Gouthwaite Res.
Masham Moor
Colsterdale Moor
Hipswell Moor
Stainton Moor
Dallowgill Moor
Sharow
Bishopton
Studley Roger
Littlethorpe
Aldfield
Risplith
Grantley
Azerley
Laverton
Galphay
Winksley
Sutton Grange
Hutton Conyers
Nunwick
Melmerby
Wath
Middleton Quernham
Sutton Howgrave
Kirklington
Sinderby
Carthorpe
Theakston
Exelby
Londonderry
Leeming
Leeming Bar
Aiskew
Scruton
Ainderby Steeple
Morton-on-Swale
Great Fencote
Little Fencote
Langthorne
Kirkby Fleetham
Great Langton
Bolton-on-Swale
Whitwell
Streetlam
Danby Wiske
East Cowton
North Cowton
Atley Hill
Moulton
Uckerby
Croft-on-Tees
Hurworth Place
Dalton-on-Tees
Eryholme
Sockburn
Newton Morrell
Aldbrough St John
Stanwick-St-John
East Layton
West Layton
Newsham
Barningham
Dalton
Ravensworth
Gayles
Kirby Hill
Whashton
Hartforth
Skelton
Marrick
Washfold
Stainton
Bellerby
Preston-under-Scar
Constable Burton
Patrick Brompton
Little Crakehall
Great Crakehall
Newton-le-Willows
Cowling
Burrill
Thirn
Thornton Watlass
Firby
Barden
Garriston
East Hauxwell
Hunton
Arrathorne
East Appleton
Coverham
Agglethorpe
Caldbergh
Carlton
West Scrafton
Ellingstring
High Ellington
Low Ellington
Fearby
Healey
Colsterdale
Leighton
Warthermarske
Swinton
Ilton
Low Burton
Binsoe
Nosterfield
Thornborough
Mickley
Carlesmoor
Swetton
Greygarth
Dallow
Low Grantley
Bouthwaite
Stean
Ure Bank
Copt Hewick
Bridge Hewick
Skelton
Walkerville
Ceramic Inspirations
The Wensleydale Railway
White Rose Candles
Middleham Castle
Thorp Perrow Arboretum
Crakehall Water Mill
Kilpin Hall
Theakston Brewery Visitor Centre
Uredale Glass
Marmion Tower
Lightwater Village
Lightwater Valley
Norton Conyers
Aerial Extreme
Easby Abbey
Richmond Castle
Stanwick Iron Age Fortifications
Barton Park Services
Scotch Corner Services
Leeming Bar Services
Ripon Cathedral
The Courthouse
St Mary's
Studley Royal Water Garden
166
167
158
146
147

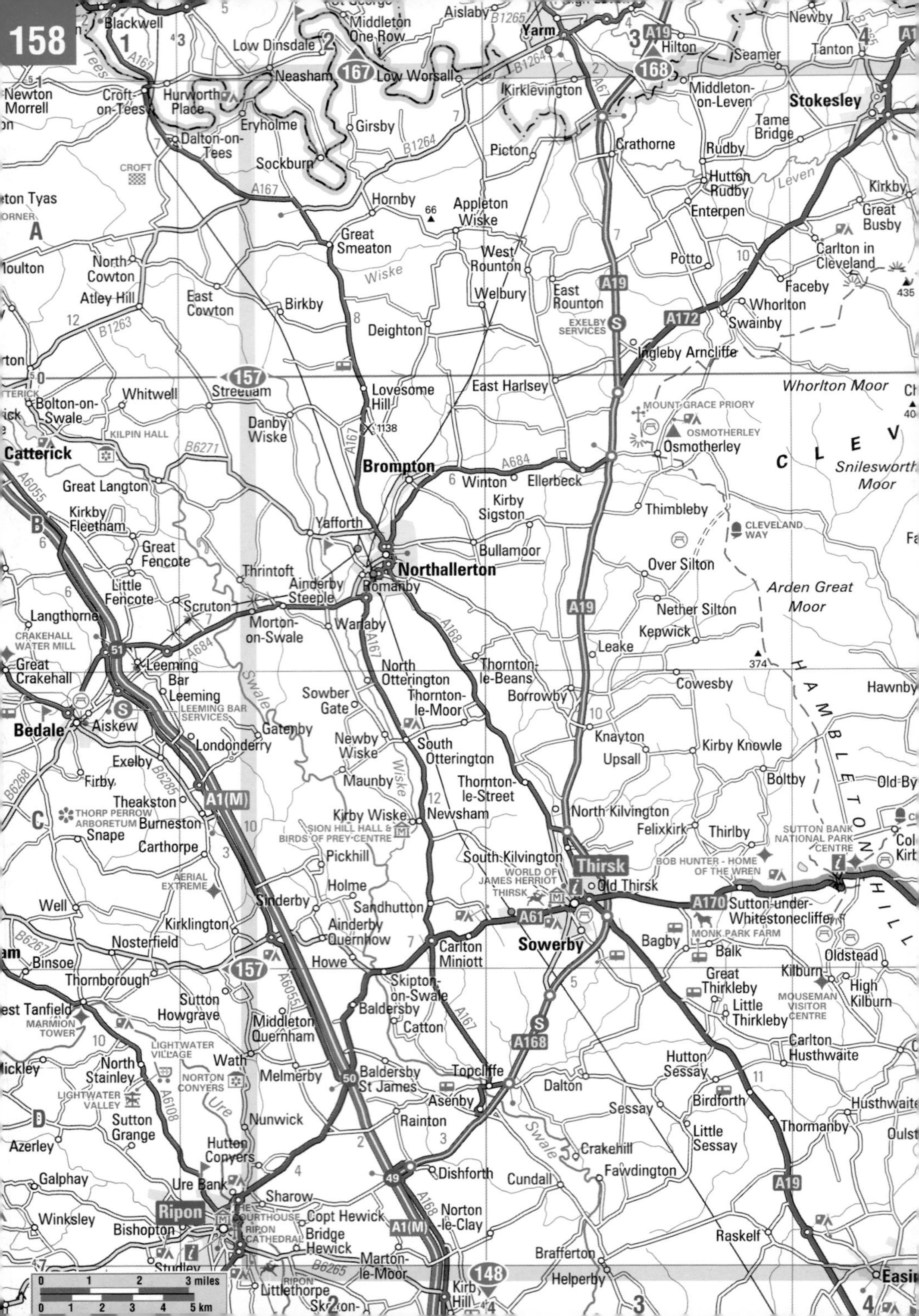

Blackwell
Middleton One Row
Aislaby
Yarm
Newby
Low Dinsdale
Hilton
Seamer
Tanton
Neasham
Low Worsall
Kirklevington
Newton Morrell
Croft-on-Tees
Hurworth Place
Middleton-on-Leven
Stokesley
Eryholme
Girsby
Tame Bridge
Dalton-on-Tees
Picton
Crathorne
Rudby
Sockburn
Hutton Rudby
Hornby
Appleton Wiske
Enterpen
Great Busby
Great Smeaton
West Rounton
Potto
Carlton in Cleveland
North Cowton
Faceby
East Cowton
Welbury
East Rounton
Whorlton
Atley Hill
Birkby
Swainby
Deighton
EXELBY SERVICES
Ingleby Arncliffe
Whitwell
Streetlam
East Harlsey
Whorlton Moor
Bolton-on-Swale
Lovesome Hill
Danby Wiske
KILPIN HALL
MOUNT GRACE PRIORY
OSMOTHERLEY
Osmotherley
Catterick
Brompton
Winton
Ellerbeck
Snilesworth Moor
Great Langton
Kirby Sigston
Thimbleby
Kirkby Fleetham
Yafforth
CLEVELAND WAY
Great Fencote
Bullamoor
Thrintoft
Northallerton
Over Silton
Little Fencote
Ainderby Steeple
Romanby
Arden Great Moor
Scruton
Nether Silton
Langthorne
Morton-on-Swale
Warlaby
Kepwick
CRAKEHALL WATER MILL
Leake
Great Crakehall
Leeming Bar
North Otterington
Thornton-le-Beans
Cowesby
Hawnby
Leeming
Sowber Gate
Thornton-le-Moor
Borrowby
LEEMING BAR SERVICES
Bedale
Aiskew
Gatenby
Newby Wiske
South Otterington
Knayton
Londonderry
Upsall
Kirby Knowle
Exelby
Maunby
Boltby
Firby
Thornton-le-Street
Theakston
Newsham
North Kilvington
THORP PERROW ARBORETUM
Burneston
Kirby Wiske
Felixkirk
Thirlby
Snape
SION HILL HALL & BIRDS OF PREY CENTRE
SUTTON BANK NATIONAL PARK CENTRE
Carthorpe
Pickhill
South Kilvington
Thirsk
BOB HUNTER - HOME OF THE WREN
AERIAL EXTREME
WORLD OF JAMES HERRIOT THIRSK
Old Thirsk
Holme
Well
Sinderby
Sandhutton
Sutton-under-Whitestonecliffe
Kirklington
Ainderby Quernhow
Sowerby
Nosterfield
Carlton Miniott
Bagby
MONK PARK FARM
Binsoe
Howe
Balk
Oldstead
Thornborough
Skipton-on-Swale
Great Thirkleby
Kilburn
Sutton Howgrave
Baldersby
High Kilburn
MOUSEMAN VISITOR CENTRE
Little Thirkleby
West Tanfield
MARMION TOWER
Middleton Quernham
Catton
LIGHTWATER VILLAGE
Carlton Husthwaite
Wath
Hutton Sessay
North Stainley
NORTON CONYERS
Melmerby
Baldersby St James
Topcliffe
Dalton
LIGHTWATER VALLEY
Asenby
Birdforth
Husthwaite
Sutton Grange
Sessay
Nunwick
Rainton
Thormanby
Little Sessay
Azerley
Hutton Conyers
Crakehill
Dishforth
Fawdington
Galphay
Ure Bank
Cundall
Sharow
Ripon
Norton-le-Clay
Winksley
THE COURTHOUSE
Copt Hewick
Raskelf
Bishopton
RIPON CATHEDRAL
Bridge Hewick
Brafferton
Studley
Marton-le-Moor
Helperby
RIPON
Littlethorpe
Kirby Hill
Skelton-
CROFT
CLEVELAND
HAMBLETON HILLS
Tees
Leven
Wiske
Swale
Ure
A167
A19
A67
A172
A684
A6055
A1(M)
A61
A170
A168
A6108
B1264
B1265
B1263
B6271
B6285
B6268
B6267
B6265
157
167
168
148
51
50
49
66
435
1138
374
0
1
2
3 miles
3
4
5 km

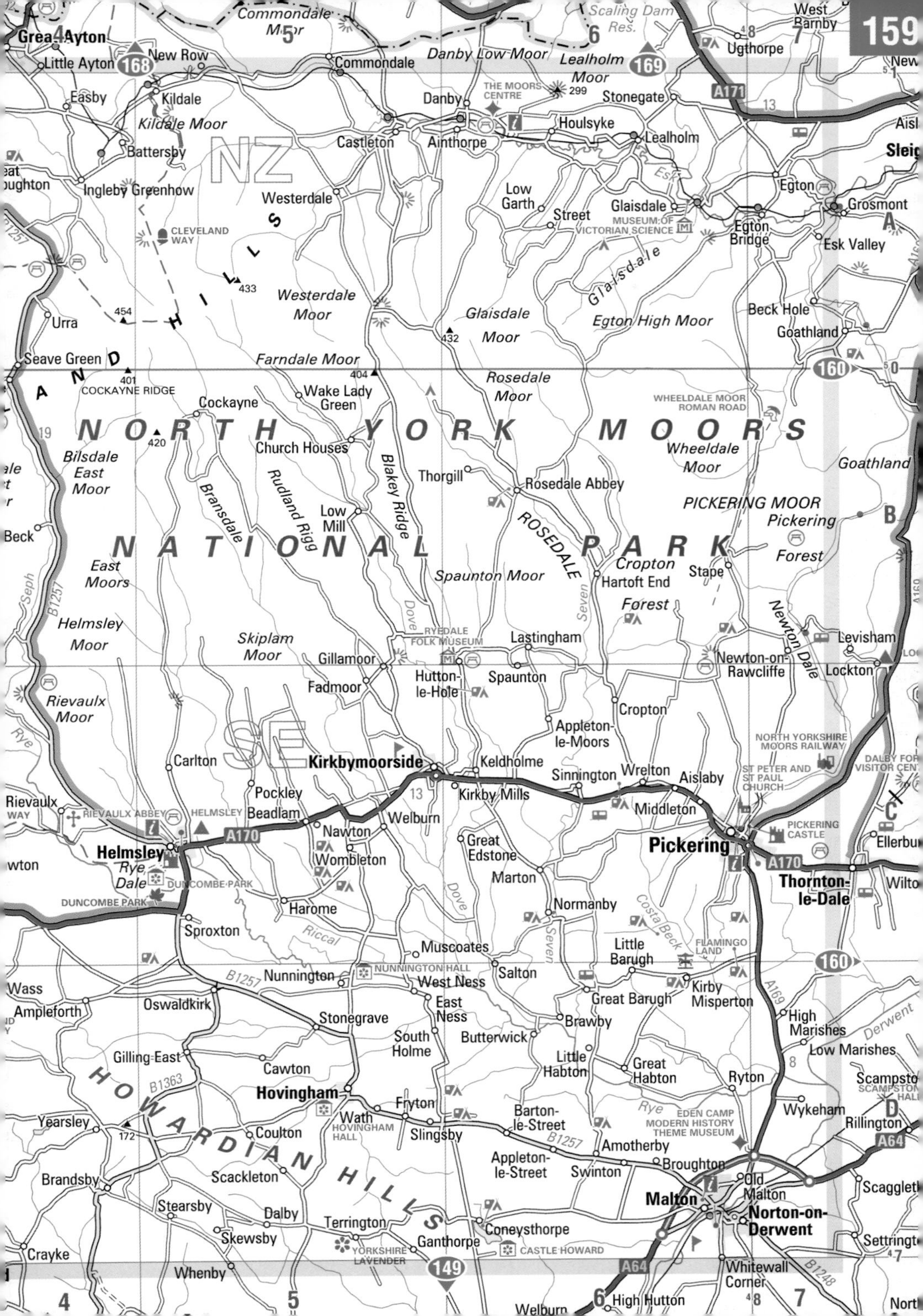
NORTH YORK MOORS NATIONAL PARK
HOWARDIAN HILLS
Great Ayton
Little Ayton
Commondale Moor
Commondale
Danby Low Moor
Lealholm Moor
Scaling Dam Res.
Ugthorpe
West Barnby
Kildale
Easby
Kildale Moor
Battersby
Ingleby Greenhow
Danby
Castleton
Ainthorpe
Houlsyke
Lealholm
Stonegate
THE MOORS CENTRE
Westerdale
Low Garth
Street
Glaisdale
MUSEUM OF VICTORIAN SCIENCE
Egton
Grosmont
Egton Bridge
Esk Valley
CLEVELAND WAY
Westerdale Moor
Glaisdale Moor
Egton High Moor
Beck Hole
Goathland
Urra
Seave Green
Farndale Moor
Rosedale Moor
COCKAYNE RIDGE
Cockayne
Wake Lady Green
WHEELDALE MOOR ROMAN ROAD
Wheeldale Moor
Church Houses
Bilsdale East Moor
Thorgill
Rosedale Abbey
Goathland
Bransdale
Rudland Rigg
Blakey Ridge
Low Mill
ROSEDALE
PICKERING MOOR
Pickering Forest
East Moors
Spaunton Moor
Cropton
Hartoft End
Forest
Stape
Newton Dale
Helmsley Moor
Skiplam Moor
RYEDALE FOLK MUSEUM
Lastingham
Levisham
Gillamoor
Fadmoor
Hutton-le-Hole
Spaunton
Newton-on-Rawcliffe
Lockton
Rievaulx Moor
Cropton
Appleton-le-Moors
NORTH YORKSHIRE MOORS RAILWAY
Carlton
Kirkbymoorside
Keldholme
Sinnington
Wrelton
Aislaby
ST PETER AND ST PAUL CHURCH
Pockley
Kirkby Mills
Middleton
Rievaulx
RIEVAULX ABBEY
HELMSLEY
Beadlam
Welburn
Nawton
PICKERING CASTLE
Ellerburn
Helmsley
Great Edstone
Pickering
Wombleton
Thornton-le-Dale
Rye Dale
DUNCOMBE PARK
Marton
Normanby
Harome
Sproxton
Riccal
Little Barugh
FLAMINGO LAND
Muscoates
Nunnington
NUNNINGTON HALL
West Ness
Salton
Great Barugh
Kirby Misperton
Wass
Oswaldkirk
East Ness
Ampleforth
Stonegrave
Brawby
High Marishes
Butterwick
South Holme
Low Marishes
Gilling East
Cawton
Little Habton
Great Habton
Ryton
Scampston
Hovingham
Fryton
Wykeham
Wath
HOVINGHAM HALL
Barton-le-Street
EDEN CAMP MODERN HISTORY THEME MUSEUM
Rillington
Yearsley
Coulton
Slingsby
Amotherby
Appleton-le-Street
Swinton
Broughton
Brandsby
Scackleton
Old Malton
Malton
Norton-on-Derwent
Stearsby
Dalby
Terrington
Coneysthorpe
Skewsby
Ganthorpe
CASTLE HOWARD
Settrington
Crayke
YORKSHIRE LAVENDER
Whenby
Whitewall Corner
High Hutton
Welburn
Derwent
Rye
Dove
Seven
Costa Beck
Esk
A170
A169
A171
A64
B1257
B1363
B1248
168
169
160
149

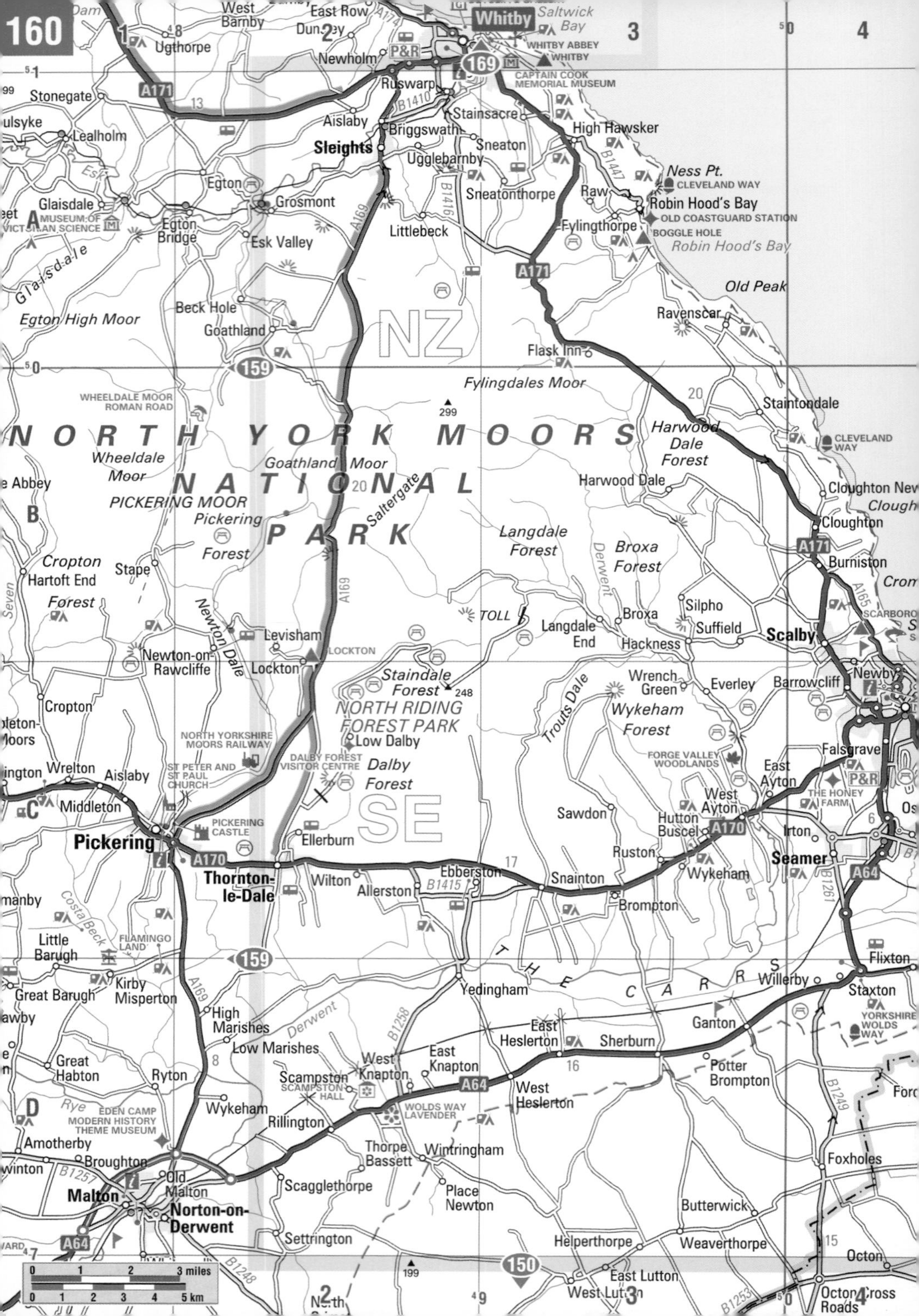
Whitby
Saltwick Bay
WHITBY ABBEY
CAPTAIN COOK MEMORIAL MUSEUM
West Barnby
East Row
Dunsley
Ugthorpe
Newholm
Ruswarp
Stonegate
Aislaby
Briggswath
Stainsacre
High Hawsker
Lealholm
Sleights
Sneaton
Ugglebarnby
Egton
Sneatonthorpe
Ness Pt.
CLEVELAND WAY
Glaisdale
Grosmont
Raw
Robin Hood's Bay
MUSEUM OF VICTORIAN SCIENCE
Egton Bridge
OLD COASTGUARD STATION
Littlebeck
Fylingthorpe
Esk Valley
BOGGLE HOLE
Glaisdale
Egton High Moor
Old Peak
Beck Hole
Ravenscar
Goathland
NZ
Flask Inn
Fylingdales Moor
WHEELDALE MOOR ROMAN ROAD
Staintondale
NORTH YORK MOORS NATIONAL PARK
Harwood Dale Forest
Wheeldale Moor
Goathland Moor
Saltergate
Harwood Dale
Cloughton
Burniston
PICKERING MOOR
Pickering Forest
Langdale Forest
Broxa Forest
Cropton
Hartoft End
Stape
Forest
Newton Dale
Silpho
Broxa
TOLL
Langdale End
Suffield
Hackness
Scalby
Levisham
LOCKTON
Newton-on-Rawcliffe
Lockton
Staindale Forest
Wrench Green
Everley
Barrowcliff
Newby
NORTH RIDING FOREST PARK
Trouts Dale
Wykeham Forest
Cropton
NORTH YORKSHIRE MOORS RAILWAY
Low Dalby
DALBY FOREST VISITOR CENTRE
Dalby Forest
FORGE VALLEY WOODLANDS
Falsgrave
Wrelton
Aislaby
ST PETER AND ST PAUL CHURCH
East Ayton
Middleton
THE HONEY FARM
SE
West Ayton
Sawdon
PICKERING CASTLE
Hutton Buscel
Irton
Pickering
Ellerburn
Ruston
Seamer
Thornton-le-Dale
Wilton
Ebberston
Snainton
Wykeham
Allerston
Brompton
Costa Beck
FLAMINGO LAND
Little Barugh
THE CARRS
Flixton
Kirby Misperton
Great Barugh
Yedingham
Willerby
Staxton
High Marishes
Derwent
East Heslerton
Ganton
YORKSHIRE WOLDS WAY
Low Marishes
Sherburn
Great Habton
West Knapton
East Knapton
Potter Brompton
Ryton
Scampston
SCAMPSTON HALL
West Heslerton
Wykeham
WOLDS WAY LAVENDER
Rye
EDEN CAMP MODERN HISTORY THEME MUSEUM
Rillington
Amotherby
Broughton
Thorpe Bassett
Wintringham
Foxholes
Old Malton
Scagglethorpe
Place Newton
Malton
Norton-on-Derwent
Butterwick
Settrington
Helperthorpe
Weaverthorpe
Octon
East Lutton
West Lutton
Octon Cross Roads
A171
A169
A170
A64
A165
B1410
B1416
B1447
B1415
B1258
B1261
B1249
B1257
B1248
B1253
169
159
150
0 1 2 3 miles
0 1 2 3 4 5 km

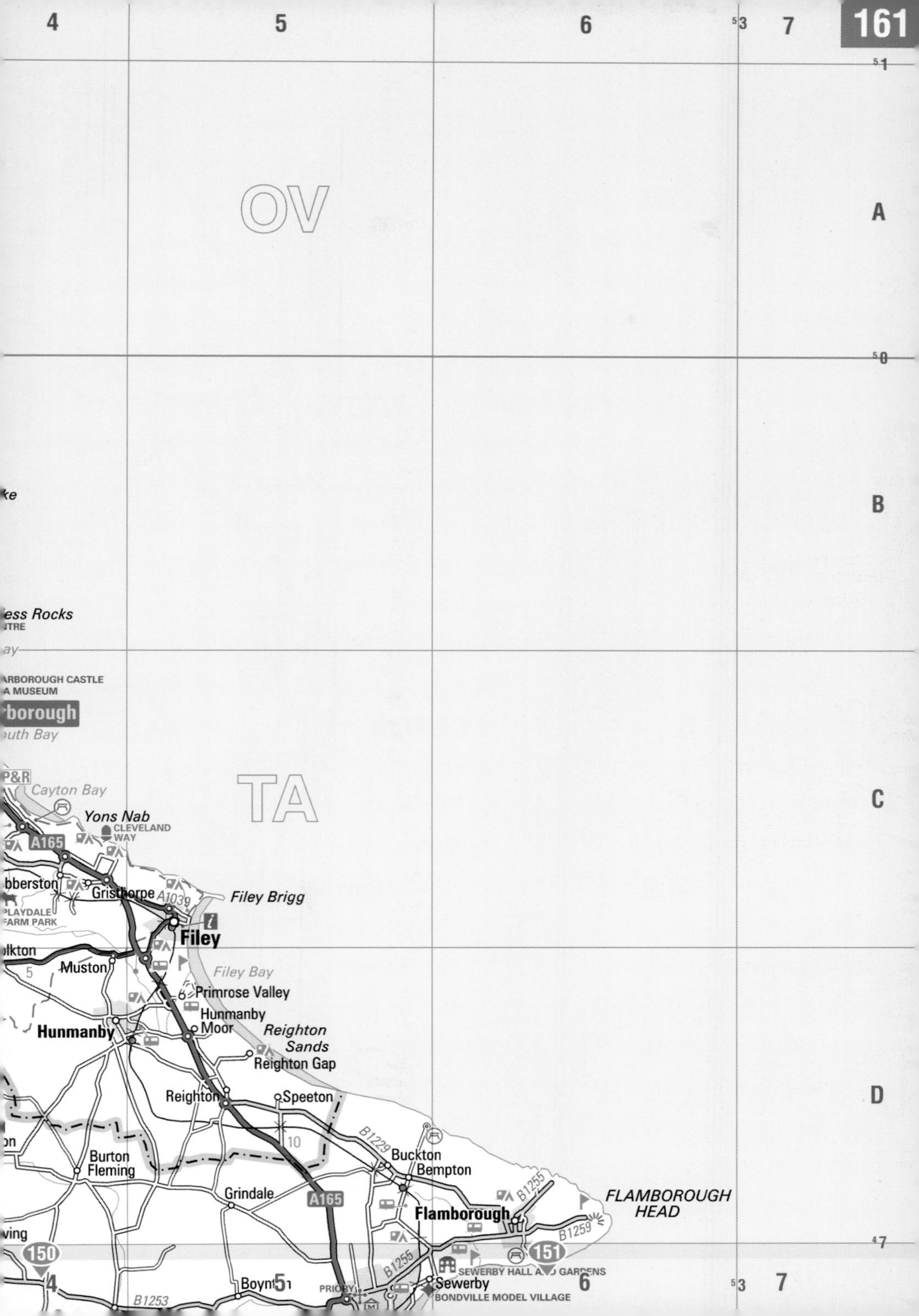

4
5
6
7
A
B
C
D
OV
TA
Rocks
SCARBOROUGH CASTLE
borough
South Bay
P&R
Cayton Bay
Yons Nab
CLEVELAND WAY
A165
Gristhorpe
A1039
Filey Brigg
PLAYDALE FARM PARK
Filey
Muston
Filey Bay
Primrose Valley
Hunmanby
Hunmanby Moor
Reighton Sands
Reighton Gap
Reighton
Speeton
B1229
Buckton
Bempton
Burton Fleming
Grindale
A165
Flamborough
B1255
FLAMBOROUGH HEAD
B1259
150
151
SEWERBY HALL AND GARDENS
Sewerby
BONDVILLE MODEL VILLAGE
PRIORY
B1253

173
174
153
NX
A
B
C
D
Allonby Bay
Allerby
Crosscanonby
Crosby
MARYPORT MARITIME MUSEUM
Maryport
Dearham
Flimby
Broughton Moor
Standingstone
Dovenby
Great Broughton
Siddick
Camerton
Seaton
Great Clifton
Derwent
North Side
Bridgefoot
Greysouthen
Workington
Stainburn
HELENA THOMPSON MUS
Little Clifton
Eaglesfield
Westfield
Mossbay
Deanscales
Marron
Winscales
Harrington
High Harrington
Branthwaite
Dean
Distington
Ullock
Lowca
Pica
Moresby
Keekle
247
Asby
Parton
Bransty
Moresby Parks
Arlecdon
WALK MILL
THE RUM STORY
Rowrah
HIGH LEYS
Kirkland
Whitehaven
Frizington
Ehen
Hensingham
Cleator Moor
Saltom Bay
Mirehouse
Ennerdale Bridge
ST BEES HEAD
Sandwith
Moor Row
Wath Brow
Rottington
Cleator
LONGLANDS LAKE
St Bees
Egremont
Wilton
Coulderton
Thornhill
Middletown
Haile
Calder
Nethertown
Beckermet
322
Braystones
Calder Bridge
High Sellafield
Calder Hall
Well
Gosforth
Seascale
Holmrook
Drigg
A596
A595
A594
A5086
B5300
B5294
B5295
B5345
B5344
0 1 2 3 miles
0 1 2 3 4 5 km

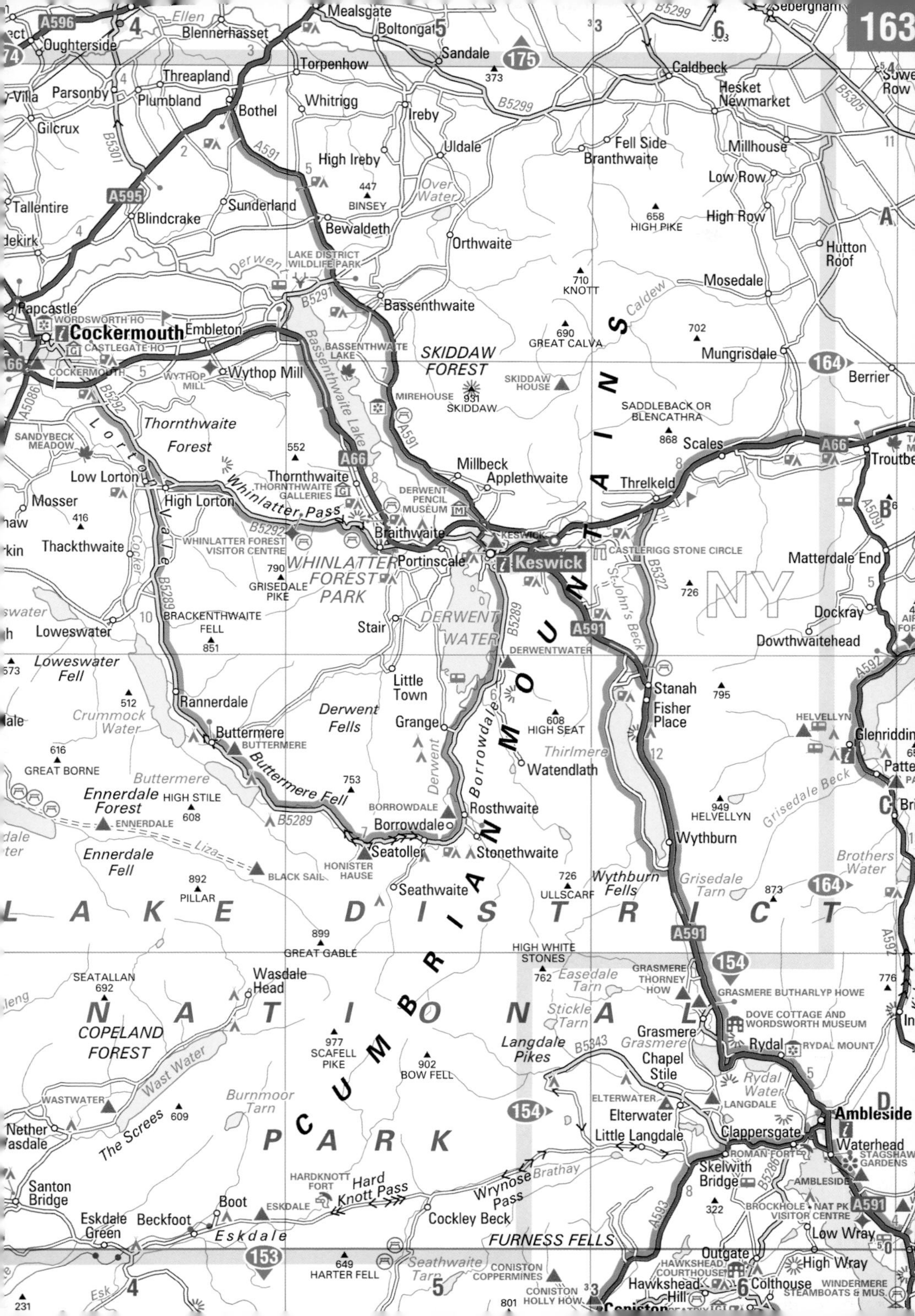

Mealsgate
Boltongate
Sebergham
Oughterside
Ellen
Blennerhasset
Torpenhow
Sandale
175
Caldbeck
Threapland
Parsonby
Plumbland
Bothel
Whitrigg
Ireby
Hesket Newmarket
Sowerby Row
Gilcrux
Fell Side
Branthwaite
Uldale
Millhouse
High Ireby
Low Row
447
BINSEY
Over Water
Tallentire
Sunderland
658
HIGH PIKE
High Row
Blindcrake
Bewaldeth
Orthwaite
Hutton Roof
LAKE DISTRICT WILDLIFE PARK
Derwent
710
KNOTT
Mosedale
Bassenthwaite
Caldew
Papcastle
WORDSWORTH HO
Cockermouth
Embleton
CASTLEGATE HO
690
GREAT CALVA
702
Mungrisdale
BASSENTHWAITE LAKE
SKIDDAW FOREST
164
Berrier
COCKERMOUTH
Wythop Mill
WYTHOP MILL
SKIDDAW HOUSE
MIREHOUSE
931
SKIDDAW
SADDLEBACK OR BLENCATHRA
Bassenthwaite Lake
SANDYBECK MEADOW
Thornthwaite Forest
552
868
Scales
Troutbeck
Lorton
Low Lorton
Thornthwaite
THORNTHWAITE GALLERIES
Millbeck
Applethwaite
Threlkeld
Mosser
High Lorton
Whinlatter Pass
DERWENT PENCIL MUSEUM
416
Thackthwaite
WHINLATTER FOREST VISITOR CENTRE
Braithwaite
KESWICK
CASTLERIGG STONE CIRCLE
Matterdale End
WHINLATTER FOREST PARK
Portinscale
Keswick
790
GRISEDALE PIKE
726
NY
Dockray
Loweswater
BRACKENTHWAITE FELL
Stair
DERWENT WATER
851
Dowthwaitehead
St John's Beck
DERWENTWATER
Loweswater Fell
Little Town
Stanah
795
512
Rannerdale
Fisher Place
Crummock Water
Derwent Fells
Grange
608
HIGH SEAT
HELVELLYN
Glenridding
Buttermere
BUTTERMERE
Thirlmere
616
GREAT BORNE
Watendlath
Patterdale
Buttermere Fell
753
Grisedale Beck
Ennerdale Forest
HIGH STILE
608
ENNERDALE
BORROWDALE
Rosthwaite
949
HELVELLYN
Borrowdale
Wythburn
Liza
Seatoller
Stonethwaite
Ennerdale Fell
BLACK SAIL
HONISTER HAUSE
726
Wythburn Fells
Grisedale Tarn
Brothers Water
892
PILLAR
Seathwaite
ULLSCARF
873
LAKE DISTRICT
899
GREAT GABLE
HIGH WHITE STONES
154
SEATALLAN
692
Wasdale Head
762
Easedale Tarn
GRASMERE THORNEY HOW
776
GRASMERE BUTHARLYP HOWE
NATIONAL
Stickle Tarn
DOVE COTTAGE AND WORDSWORTH MUSEUM
COPELAND FOREST
977
SCAFELL PIKE
Langdale Pikes
Grasmere
Rydal
RYDAL MOUNT
Wast Water
902
BOW FELL
Chapel Stile
Rydal Water
Burnmoor Tarn
WASTWATER
ELTERWATER
LANGDALE
Ambleside
154
Elterwater
Nether Wasdale
The Screes
609
CUMBRIAN MOUNTAINS
PARK
Little Langdale
Clappersgate
Waterhead
ROMAN FORT
STAGSHAW GARDENS
Skelwith Bridge
Brathay
AMBLESIDE
HARDKNOTT FORT
Hard Knott Pass
Wrynose Pass
Santon Bridge
Boot
ESKDALE
322
BROCKHOLE - NAT PK VISITOR CENTRE
Eskdale Green
Beckfoot
Cockley Beck
Low Wray
Eskdale
FURNESS FELLS
153
649
HARTER FELL
Seathwaite Tarn
CONISTON COPPERMINES
Outgate
HAWKSHEAD COURTHOUSE
High Wray
Esk
231
CONISTON HOLLY HOW
801
Hawkshead Hill
Colthouse
WINDERMERE STEAMBOATS & MUS.
A596
A595
A591
B5291
B5299
B5305
B5301
A66
B5292
A5086
B5289
B5322
A592
A5091
A593
B5343
B5286

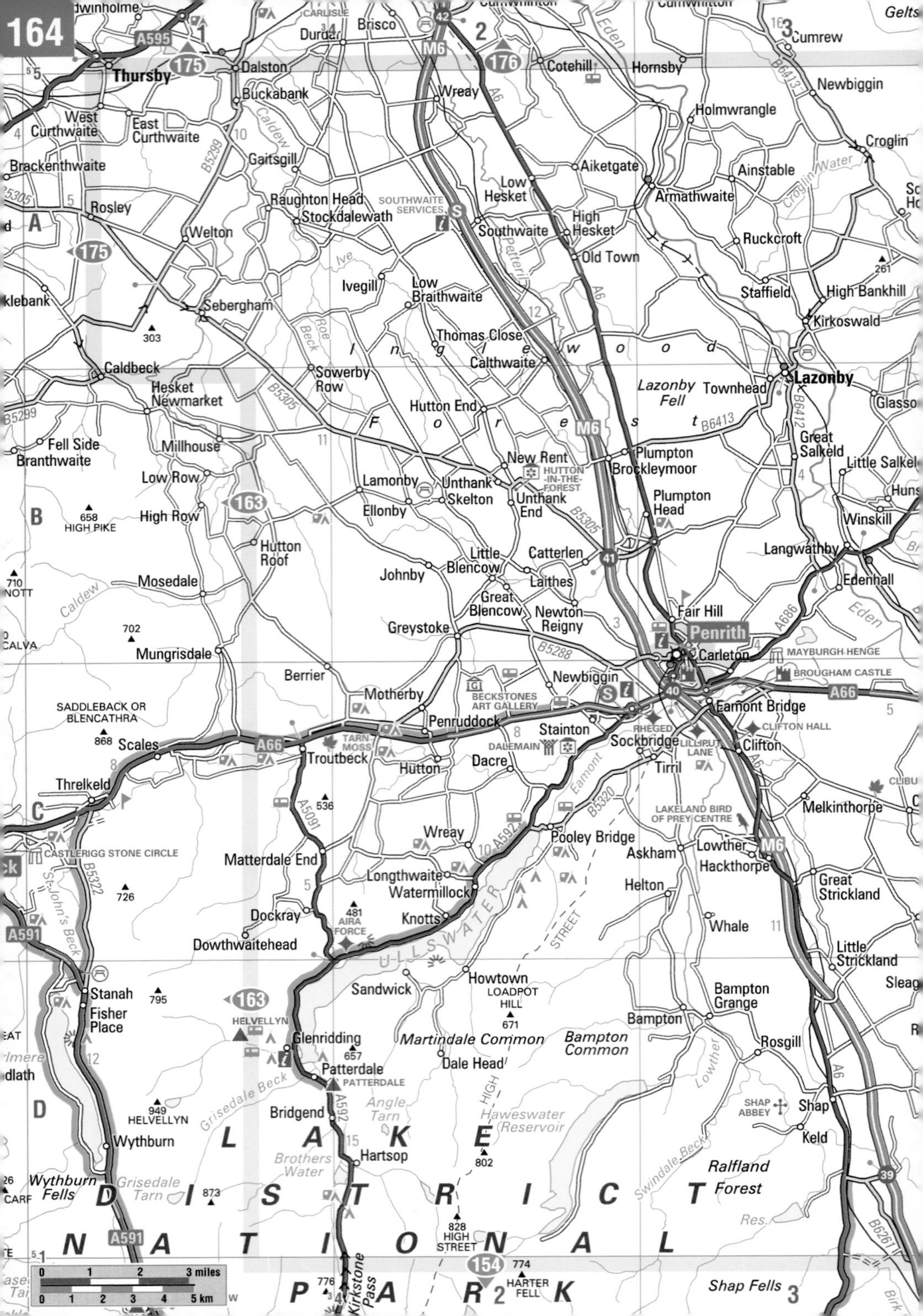
Thursby
Dalston
Buckabank
Wreay
Cotehill
Hornsby
Cumrew
Newbiggin
Holmwrangle
Croglin
West Curthwaite
East Curthwaite
Brackenthwaite
Gaitsgill
Aiketgate
Ainstable
Armathwaite
Rosley
Raughton Head
Stockdalewath
Southwaite Services
Low Hesket
High Hesket
Southwaite
Welton
Old Town
Ruckcroft
Ivegill
Low Braithwaite
Staffield
High Bankhill
Kirkoswald
Sebergham
Thomas Close
Calthwaite
Caldbeck
Hesket Newmarket
Sowerby Row
Hutton End
Lazonby Fell
Townhead
Lazonby
Inglewood Forest
Fell Side
Branthwaite
Millhouse
Low Row
High Row
New Rent
Hutton-in-the-Forest
Plumpton
Brockleymoor
Great Salkeld
Little Salkeld
Lamonby
Unthank
Skelton
Ellonby
Unthank End
Plumpton Head
Winskill
658 HIGH PIKE
Hutton Roof
Little Blencow
Catterlen
Langwathby
Mosedale
Johnby
Laithes
Edenhall
Great Blencow
Newton Reigny
Fair Hill
Greystoke
Penrith
Carleton
Mayburgh Henge
Brougham Castle
Mungrisdale
Berrier
Newbiggin
Motherby
Beckstones Art Gallery
Eamont Bridge
Saddleback or Blencathra
Penruddock
Stainton
Rheged
Sockbridge
Clifton Hall
Clifton
868 Scales
Troutbeck
Tarn Moss
Hutton
Dacre
Dalemain
Tirril
Lilliput Lane
Threlkeld
Melkinthorpe
Lakeland Bird of Prey Centre
Castlerigg Stone Circle
Wreay
Pooley Bridge
Askham
Lowther
Hackthorpe
Matterdale End
Longthwaite
Watermillock
Helton
Great Strickland
Dockray
Aira Force
Knotts
Whale
Dowthwaitehead
Ullswater
Little Strickland
Stanah
Howtown
Loadpot Hill
Sandwick
Bampton Grange
Fisher Place
Helvellyn
Bampton
Glenridding
Martindale Common
Bampton Common
Rosgill
Dale Head
Patterdale
Grisedale Beck
Angle Tarn
Haweswater Reservoir
Shap Abbey
Shap
949 HELVELLYN
Bridgend
Wythburn
Hartsop
Brothers Water
Keld
Lake District National Park
Ralfland Forest
Wythburn Fells
Grisedale Tarn
828 HIGH STREET
774 HARTER FELL
776
Kirkstone Pass
Shap Fells
M6
A6
A66
A591
A592
A5091
B5305
B5288
B5320
B5322
B6413
B6412
A686
B6261
Eden
Caldew
Eamont
Lowther
3 miles
5 km

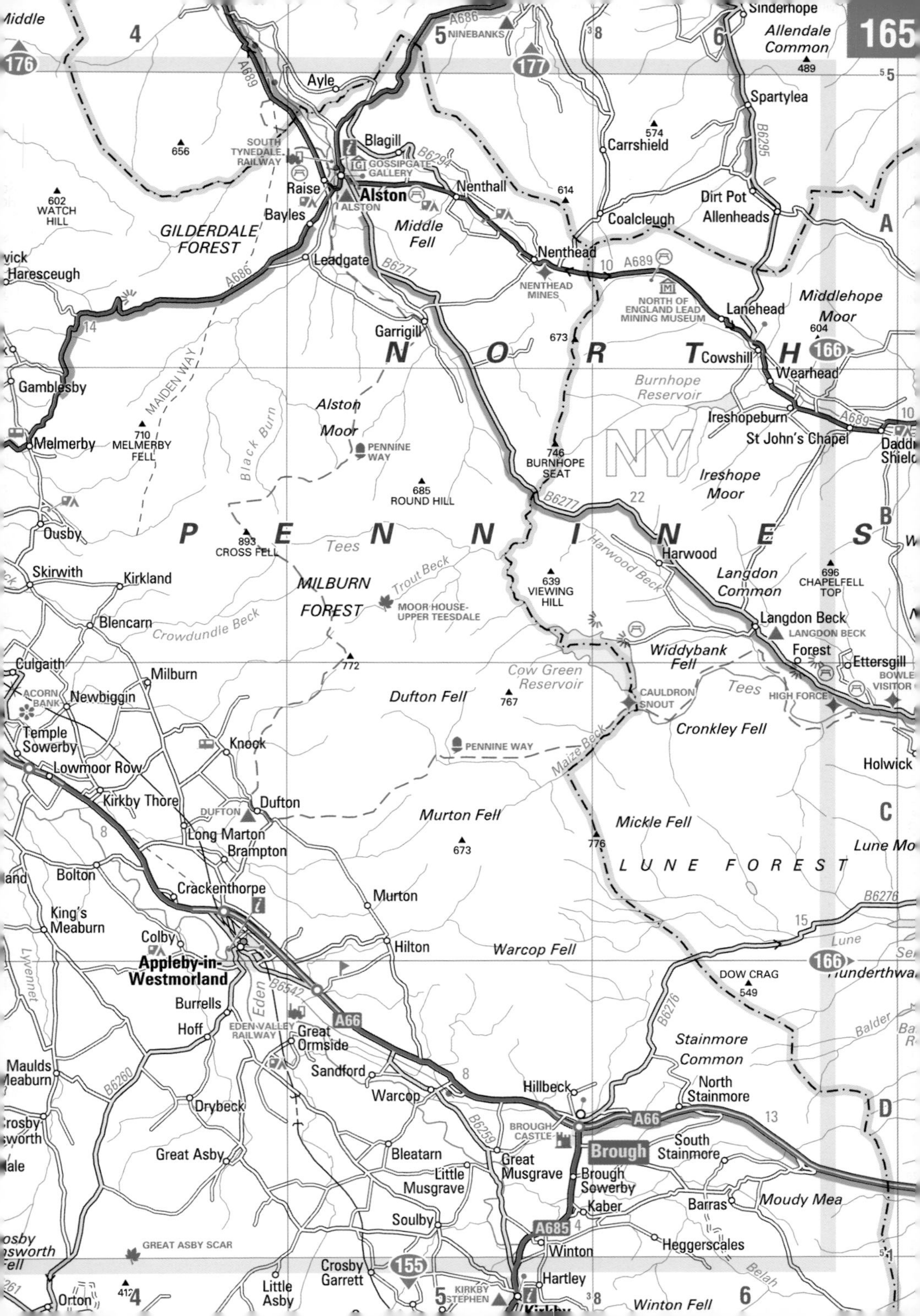

Middle
4
176
A689
Ayle
A686
5
NINEBANKS
177
8
6
Sinderhope
Allendale Common
489
5
Spartylea
656
SOUTH TYNEDALE RAILWAY
Blagill
B6294
GOSSIPGATE GALLERY
574
Carrshield
B6295
602 WATCH HILL
Raise
Alston
ALSTON
Nenthall
614
Dirt Pot
Allenheads
Bayles
Middle Fell
Coalcleugh
A
GILDERDALE FOREST
Nenthead
10
A689
NENTHEAD MINES
NORTH OF ENGLAND LEAD MINING MUSEUM
Leadgate
B6277
A686
Harescеugh
Lanehead
Middlehope Moor
604
14
Garrigill
673
166
N O R T H
Cowshill
Wearhead
MAIDEN WAY
Gamblesby
Burnhope Reservoir
Ireshopeburn
A689
Alston Moor
Black Burn
710 MELMERBY FELL
Melmerby
PENNINE WAY
746 BURNHOPE SEAT
NY
St John's Chapel
Ireshope Moor
685 ROUND HILL
B6277
22
B
P E N N I N E S
Ousby
893 CROSS FELL
Tees
Harwood
Harwood Beck
Skirwith
Kirkland
MILBURN FOREST
Trout Beck
639 VIEWING HILL
Langdon Common
696 CHAPELFELL TOP
MOOR HOUSE-UPPER TEESDALE
Blencarn
Crowdundle Beck
Langdon Beck
LANGDON BECK
Widdybank Fell
Forest
Ettersgill
Culgaith
772
Milburn
Cow Green Reservoir
Tees
HIGH FORCE
ACORN BANK
Newbiggin
Dufton Fell
767
CAULDRON SNOUT
Cronkley Fell
Temple Sowerby
Knock
PENNINE WAY
Maize Beck
Holwick
Lowmoor Row
Kirkby Thore
Dufton
DUFTON
Murton Fell
C
8
Long Marton
Mickle Fell
Brampton
673
776
Lune Moor
LUNE FOREST
Bolton
Crackenthorpe
B6276
Murton
King's Meaburn
15
Colby
Hilton
Lune
Appleby-in-Westmorland
Warcop Fell
166
Lyvennet
Eden
B6542
DOW CRAG 549
Burrells
B6276
Hoff
EDEN VALLEY RAILWAY
A66
Great Ormside
Stainmore Common
Balder
Maulds Meaburn
Sandford
8
B6260
Warcop
Hillbeck
North Stainmore
Drybeck
D
B6259
A66
13
BROUGH CASTLE
Brough
South Stainmore
Bleatarn
Great Asby
Little Musgrave
Great Musgrave
Brough Sowerby
Moudy Mea
Kaber
Barras
Soulby
A685
4
Winton
Heggerscales
GREAT ASBY SCAR
Crosby Garrett
155
Hartley
Belah
412
4
Little Asby
Orton
5
KIRKBY STEPHEN
8
Winton Fell
6

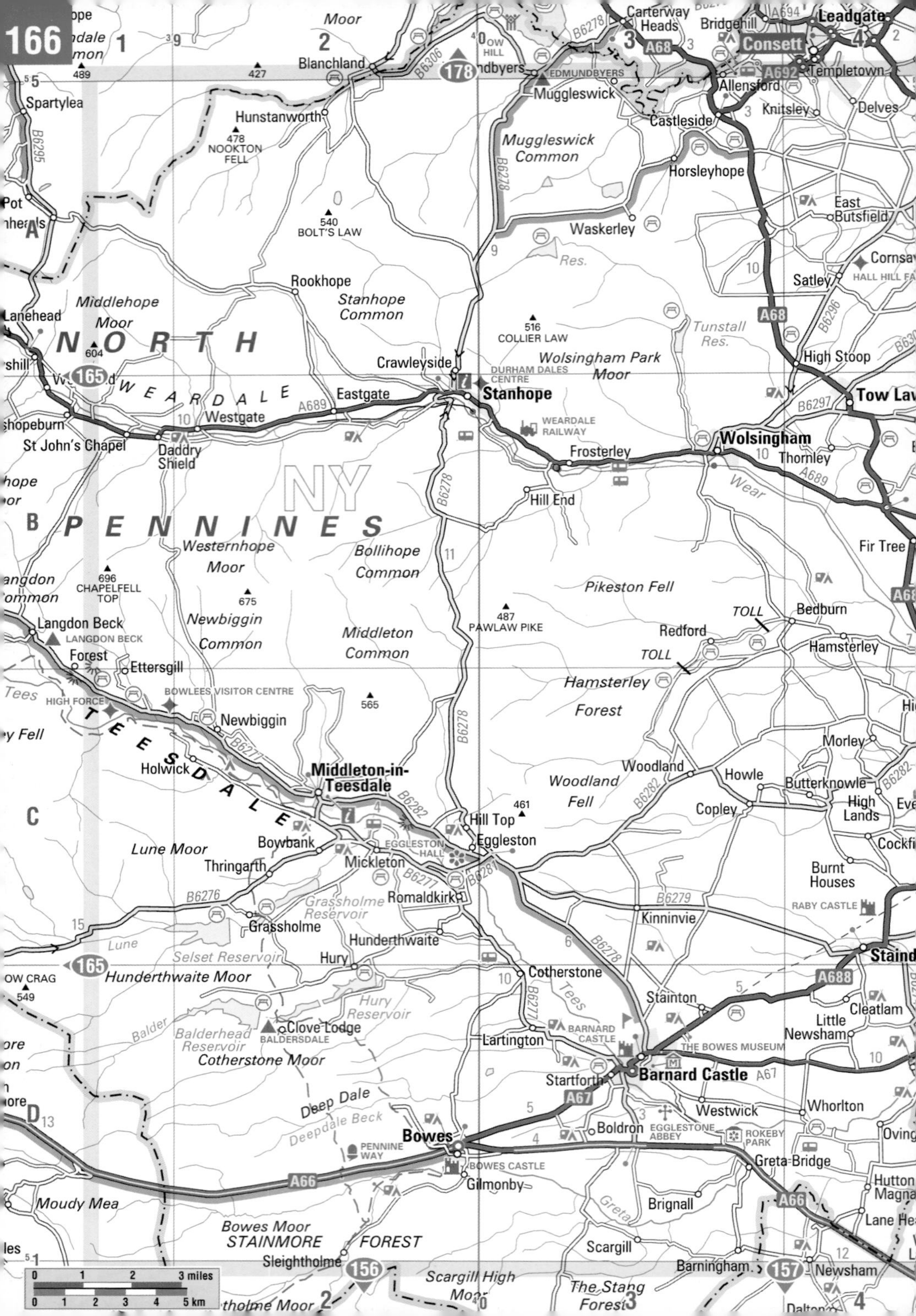

NORTH PENNINES
WEARDALE
TEESDALE
NY
Blanchland
Hunstanworth
Spartylea
Rookhope
Stanhope Common
Middlehope Moor
Lanehead
Crawleyside
Stanhope
Eastgate
Westgate
St John's Chapel
Daddry Shield
Frosterley
Wolsingham
Thornley
Hill End
Westernhope Moor
Bollihope Common
Newbiggin Common
Middleton Common
Pikeston Fell
Pawlaw Pike
Langdon Beck
Forest
Ettersgill
High Force
Bowlees Visitor Centre
Newbiggin
Holwick
Middleton-in-Teesdale
Hamsterley Forest
Woodland Fell
Woodland
Hill Top
Eggleston
Eggleston Hall
Lune Moor
Bowbank
Thringarth
Mickleton
Romaldkirk
Grassholme Reservoir
Grassholme
Hunderthwaite
Selset Reservoir
Hury
Hunderthwaite Moor
Cotherstone
Kinninvie
Balderhead Reservoir
Clove Lodge
Hury Reservoir
Cotherstone Moor
Lartington
Barnard Castle
The Bowes Museum
Startforth
Deep Dale
Deepdale Beck
Bowes
Bowes Castle
Pennine Way
Boldron
Egglestone Abbey
Rokeby Park
Greta Bridge
Gilmonby
Brignall
Moudy Mea
Bowes Moor
Stainmore Forest
Sleightholme
Scargill
Barningham
Newsham
Scargill High Moor
The Stang Forest
Muggleswick
Muggleswick Common
Edmundbyers
Castleside
Horsleyhope
Waskerley
Carterway Heads
Bridgehill
Consett
Leadgate
Templetown
Allensford
Knitsley
Delves
East Butsfield
Cornsay
Satley
Tunstall Res.
Collier Law
Wolsingham Park Moor
High Stoop
Tow Law
Weardale Railway
Durham Dales Centre
Fir Tree
Bedburn
Redford
Hamsterley
Morley
Howle
Butterknowle
High Lands
Copley
Cockfield
Burnt Houses
Raby Castle
Staindrop
Stainton
Cleatlam
Little Newsham
Westwick
Whorlton
Ovington
Hutton Magna
Lane Head
Chapelfell Top
Langdon Common
Nookton Fell
Bolt's Law
Lune
Tees
Wear
Greta
Balder

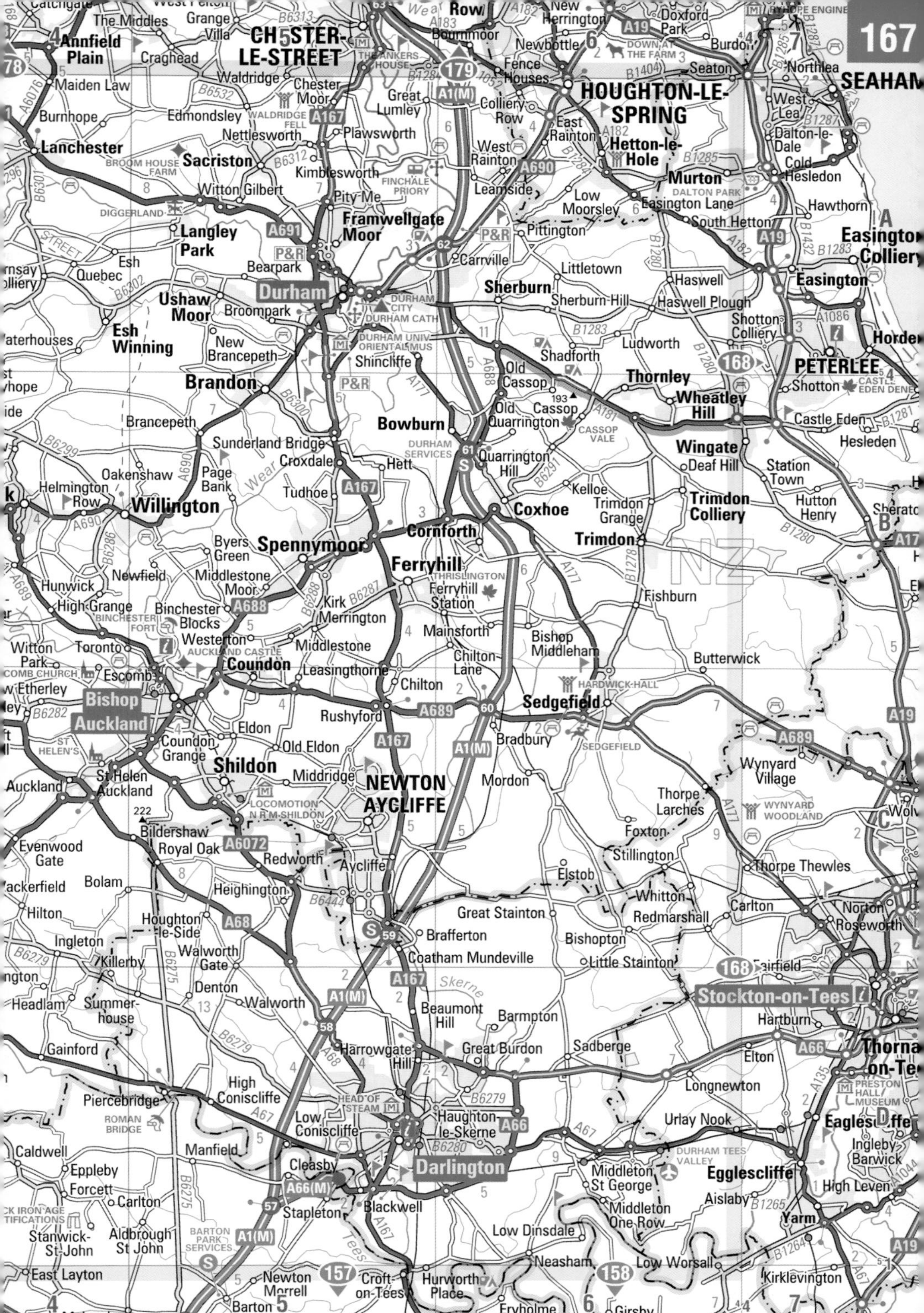
CHESTER-LE-STREET
HOUGHTON-LE-SPRING
SEAHAM
Annfield Plain
Lanchester
Sacriston
Durham
Ushaw Moor
Esh Winning
Brandon
Bowburn
Sherburn
Easington Colliery
Easington
PETERLEE
Wheatley Hill
Thornley
Wingate
Trimdon Colliery
Trimdon
Coxhoe
Cornforth
Ferryhill
Spennymoor
Willington
Coundon
Bishop Auckland
Shildon
NEWTON AYCLIFFE
Sedgefield
Stockton-on-Tees
Darlington
Eaglescliffe
Egglescliffe
Yarm
Murton
Hetton-le-Hole
Langley Park
Framwellgate Moor
A1(M)
A19
A167
A689
A688
A68
A66
A66(M)
A691
A690
A6072
179
168
157
158

168
2
3
4
SEAHAM
179
HOUGHTON-LE-SPRING
Doxford Park
Burdon
Seaton
Northlea
West Lea
Dalton-le-Dale
Cold Hesledon
Hetton-le-Hole
Murton
DALTON PARK
Easington Lane
South Hetton
Hawthorn
Beacon Pt.
Low Moorsley
A
Easington Colliery
Easington
Haswell
Haswell Plough
Shotton Colliery
Horden
Ludworth
PETERLEE
167
Thornley
Wheatley Hill
Shotton
CASTLE EDEN DENE
Blackhall Colliery
Blackhall Rocks
Castle Eden
High Hesleden
Hesleden
CASSOP VALE
Wingate
Deaf Hill
DURHAM COAST
Station Town
Hart Station
Kelloe
Trimdon Grange
Trimdon Colliery
Hutton Henry
Sheraton
Hart
B
Trimdon
A179
High Throston
ST HILDA'S PARISH CHURCH
HARTLEPOOL'S MARITIME EXPERIENCE
Hartlepool Bay
Fishburn
Elwick
West Park
SUMMERHILL
Hartlepool
Dalton Piercy
Rift House
Butterwick
Seaton Carew
HARDWICK HALL
Tees Bay
A689
Greatham
A19
SEDGEFIELD
Graythorp
Wynyard Village
Newton Bewley
Salt Scar
REDCAR
Thorpe Larches
WYNYARD WOODLAND
Wolviston
COWPEN BEWLEY
TEESMOUTH
C
Foxton
Cowpen Bewley
Coatham
Stillington
BILLINGHAM ART GALLERY
Thorpe Thewles
BILLINGHAM
Dormanstown
Marske-by-the-Sea
Haverton Hill
KIRKLEATHAM OLD HALL MUSEUM
Whitton
Redmarshall
Norton
Port Clarence
South Bank
Kirkleatham
Roseworth
BILLINGHAM BECK
TOLL
Grangetown
Yearby
New Marske
Bishopton
North Ormesby
A66
Lazenby
Little Stainton
Fairfield
Wilton
A1053
Upleatham
Stockton-on-Tees
Middlesbrough
Eston
Dunsdale
DORMAN MUSEUM
TOCKETTS WATER MILL
Hartburn
Normanby
Sadberge
Thornaby-on-Tees
Acklam
Park End
Ormesby
242
Elton
FLATTS LANE WOODLAND
GUISBOROUGH PRIORY
Longnewton
PRESTON HALL MUSEUM
ORMESBY HALL
Guisborough
Marton
A171
Charltons
D
Urlay Nook
Eaglescliffe
CAPTAIN COOK BIRTHPLACE
Coulby Newham
A1043
GUISBOROUGH FOREST
Hutton Gate
Nunthorpe
Ingleby Barwick
Stainton
Hemlington
DURHAM TEES VALLEY
Thornton
Hutton Village
Gisborough M
Middleton St George
Egglescliffe
Maltby
Newton under Roseberry
High Leven
Middleton One Row
Aislaby
Newby
Yarm
A172
Hilton
Tanton
Great Ayton
Seamer
New Row
Low Worsall
Little Ayton
Middleton-on-Leven
158
Stokesley
Easby
Kildale
159
0 1 2 3 miles
0 1 2 3 4 5 km

4
5
6
7
A
B
C
D
NZ
MINIATURE RAILWAY
Saltburn-by-the-Sea
166
CHRIS BIRKBECK INTERNATIONAL RALLY SCHOOL
Brotton
Skinningrove
ENGLAND COAST PATH
Boulby
Carlin How
Loftus
A174
Staithes
North Skelton
Kilton Thorpe
Easington
Port Mulgrave
Runswick Bay
Lingdale
Hinderwell
Runswick Bay
Margrove Park
Stanghow
Liverton
Roxby
Newton Mulgrave
Kettleness
Goldsborough
B1366
Ellerby
Moorsholm
Scaling
A171
A174
Lythe
Sandsend
Res.
B1266
Mickleby
East Barnby
Sandsend Wyke
SUTCLIFFE GALLERY
West Barnby
East Row
Whitby
Saltwick Bay
Scaling Dam Res.
Dunsley
Ugthorpe
P&R
WHITBY ABBEY
Commondale
Danby Low Moor
Lealholm Moor
Newholm
WHITBY
CAPTAIN COOK MEMORIAL MUSEUM
159
160
299
Danby
Stonegate
Ruswarp
B1410
A171
Stainsacre

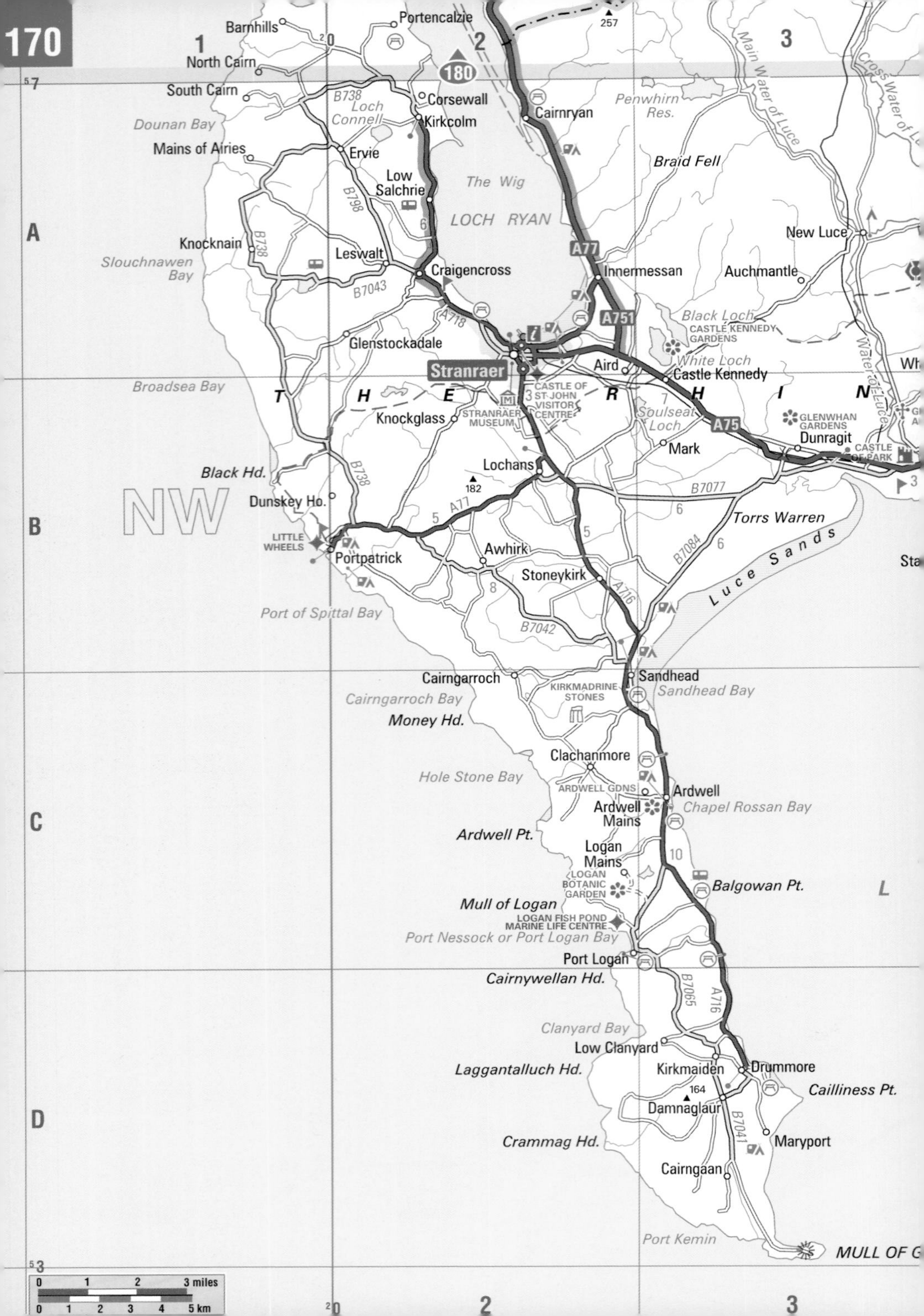

Barnhills
Portencalzie
North Cairn
South Cairn
Corsewall
Loch Connell
Kirkcolm
Dounan Bay
Mains of Airies
Ervie
Low Salchrie
The Wig
LOCH RYAN
Cairnryan
Penwhirn Res.
Braid Fell
Main Water of Luce
Cross Water of Luce
New Luce
Knocknain
Slouchnawen Bay
Leswalt
Craigencross
Innermessan
Auchmantle
Glenstockadale
Black Loch
CASTLE KENNEDY GARDENS
White Loch
Stranraer
Aird
Castle Kennedy
Broadsea Bay
T H E R H I N
CASTLE OF ST JOHN VISITOR CENTRE
STRANRAER MUSEUM
Knockglass
Soulseat Loch
GLENWHAN GARDENS
Dunragit
CASTLE OF PARK
Mark
Lochans
Black Hd.
NW
Dunskey Ho.
Torrs Warren
LITTLE WHEELS
Portpatrick
Awhirk
Stoneykirk
Luce Sands
Port of Spittal Bay
Cairngarroch
Sandhead
KIRKMADRINE STONES
Sandhead Bay
Cairngarroch Bay
Money Hd.
Clachanmore
Hole Stone Bay
ARDWELL GDNS
Ardwell
Ardwell Mains
Chapel Rossan Bay
Ardwell Pt.
Logan Mains
LOGAN BOTANIC GARDEN
Balgowan Pt.
Mull of Logan
LOGAN FISH POND MARINE LIFE CENTRE
Port Nessock or Port Logan Bay
Port Logan
Cairnywellan Hd.
Clanyard Bay
Low Clanyard
Laggantalluch Hd.
Kirkmaiden
Drummore
Cailliness Pt.
Damnaglaur
Crammag Hd.
Maryport
Cairngaan
Port Kemin
MULL OF G
A77
A751
A75
A716
A718
B738
B798
B7043
B7077
B7084
B7042
B7065
B7041
180
257
182
164
0 1 2 3 miles
0 1 2 3 4 5 km

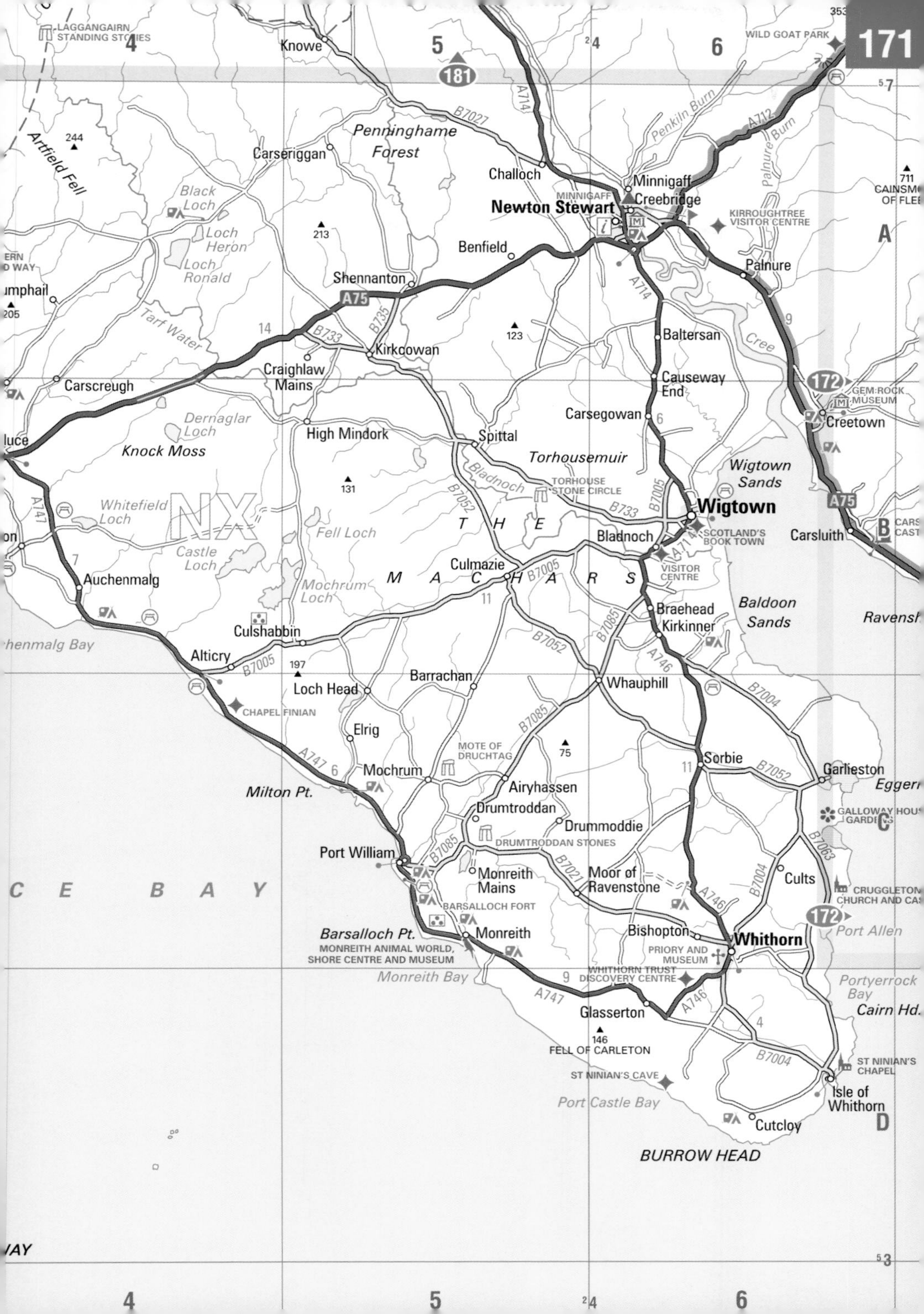
LAGGANGAIRN STANDING STONES
Knowe
181
WILD GOAT PARK
Artfield Fell
Penninghame Forest
Carseriggan
Challoch
Minnigaff
Newton Stewart
Creebridge
KIRROUGHTREE VISITOR CENTRE
Black Loch
Loch Heron
Loch Ronald
Benfield
Shennanton
Palnure
Tarf Water
Kirkcowan
Craighlaw Mains
Baltersan
Cree
Carscreugh
Causeway End
Carsegowan
172
GEM ROCK MUSEUM
Creetown
Dernaglar Loch
Knock Moss
High Mindork
Spittal
Torhousemuir
Wigtown Sands
TORHOUSE STONE CIRCLE
Wigtown
SCOTLAND'S BOOK TOWN
Whitefield Loch
NX
Fell Loch
THE MACHARS
Bladnoch
Carsluith
Castle Loch
Culmazie
VISITOR CENTRE
Auchenmalg
Mochrum Loch
Braehead
Kirkinner
Baldoon Sands
Culshabbin
Alticry
Barrachan
Loch Head
Whauphill
CHAPEL FINIAN
Elrig
MOTE OF DRUCHTAG
Sorbie
Garlieston
Mochrum
Airyhassen
Milton Pt.
Drumtroddan
Drummoddie
GALLOWAY HOUSE GARDENS
DRUMTRODDAN STONES
Port William
Monreith Mains
Moor of Ravenstone
Cults
CRUGGLETON CHURCH AND CASTLE
BARSALLOCH FORT
Barsalloch Pt.
Monreith
Bishopton
Whithorn
Port Allen
MONREITH ANIMAL WORLD, SHORE CENTRE AND MUSEUM
PRIORY AND MUSEUM
WHITHORN TRUST DISCOVERY CENTRE
Monreith Bay
Portyerrock Bay
Glasserton
Cairn Hd.
FELL OF CARLETON
ST NINIAN'S CHAPEL
ST NINIAN'S CAVE
Port Castle Bay
Isle of Whithorn
Cutcloy
BURROW HEAD

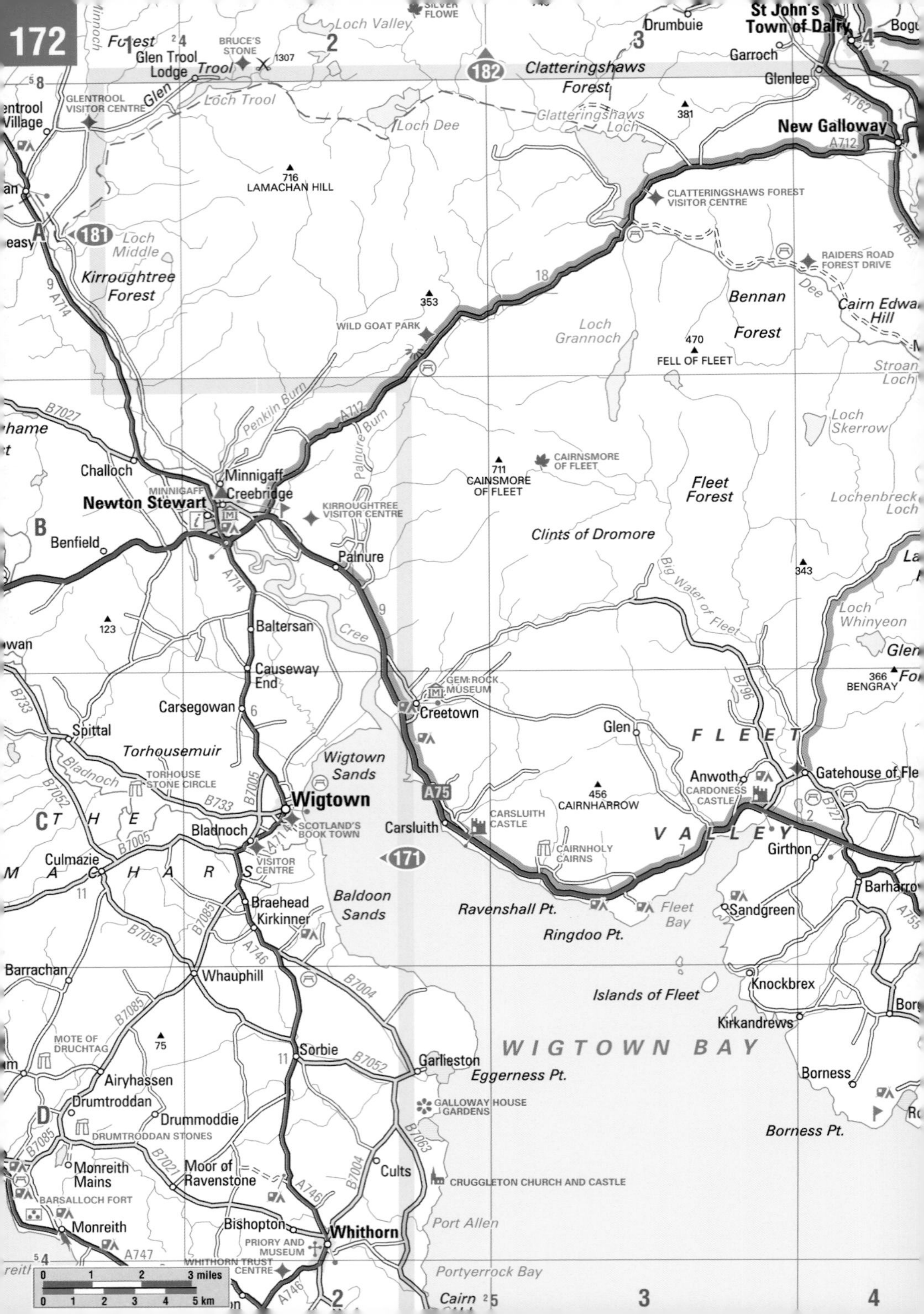
Loch Valley
SILVER FLOWE
Drumbuie
St John's Town of Dalry
Forest
Glen Trool Lodge
BRUCE'S STONE
1307
Trool
182
Clatteringshaws Forest
Garroch
Glenlee
GLENTROOL VISITOR CENTRE
Glen
Loch Trool
Glentrool Village
Loch Dee
Glatteringshaws Loch
381
New Galloway
A712
A762
716
LAMACHAN HILL
CLATTERINGSHAWS FOREST VISITOR CENTRE
181
Loch Middle
RAIDERS ROAD FOREST DRIVE
Kirroughtree Forest
A714
18
Dee
Bennan
Cairn Edward Hill
353
WILD GOAT PARK
Loch Grannoch
470
Forest
FELL OF FLEET
Stroan Loch
B7027
Penkiln Burn
A712
Palnure Burn
Loch Skerrow
Challoch
Minnigaff
711
CAINSMORE OF FLEET
CAIRNSMORE OF FLEET
Fleet Forest
Lochenbreck Loch
MINNIGAFF
Creebridge
Newton Stewart
KIRROUGHTREE VISITOR CENTRE
Benfield
Clints of Dromore
Palnure
343
Big Water of Fleet
A714
Loch Whinyeon
123
Baltersan
Cree
Causeway End
GEM ROCK MUSEUM
366
BENGRAY
B733
Carsegowan
Creetown
Glen
B796
Spittal
F L E E T
Torhousemuir
Wigtown Sands
Anwoth
Gatehouse of Fleet
Bladnoch
TORHOUSE STONE CIRCLE
B7005
456
CAIRNHARROW
CARDONESS CASTLE
B7052
A75
B733
Wigtown
CARSLUITH CASTLE
B727
C T H E
SCOTLAND'S BOOK TOWN
Bladnoch
Carsluith
V A L L E Y
B7005
A714
CAIRNHOLY CAIRNS
Girthon
Culmazie
VISITOR CENTRE
171
M A C H A R S
Barharrow
11
Baldoon Sands
Braehead
Ravenshall Pt.
Fleet Bay
Sandgreen
B7085
Kirkinner
B7052
A746
Ringdoo Pt.
A755
Barrachan
Whauphill
B7004
Islands of Fleet
Knockbrex
B7085
Kirkandrews
MOTE OF DRUCHTAG
75
Sorbie
WIGTOWN BAY
11
B7052
Garlieston
Eggerness Pt.
Airyhassen
Borness
Drumtroddan
GALLOWAY HOUSE GARDENS
Drummoddie
DRUMTRODDAN STONES
B7063
Borness Pt.
B7085
B7021
Monreith Mains
Moor of Ravenstone
B7004
Cults
CRUGGLETON CHURCH AND CASTLE
A746
BARSALLOCH FORT
Monreith
Bishopton
Whithorn
Port Allen
PRIORY AND MUSEUM
A747
WHITHORN TRUST CENTRE
Portyerrock Bay
A746
0 1 2 3 miles
0 1 2 3 4 5 km
Cairn
A B C D
1 2 3 4

Blackcraig
Knocklearn
Gibbshill
Corsock
Craig
Merkland
Drumrash
Parton
Crossmichael
Craig
Laurieston
Loch Glentoo
Loch Bargatton
Bridge of Dee
Ringford
Valleyfield
Twynholm
Tongland
GALLOWAY HYDRO VISITOR CENTRE
BROUGHTON HOUSE AND GARDEN
Kirkcudbright
STEWARTRY MUSEUM
St Mary's Island
Mutehill
Townhead
Balmae
Little Ross
Kirkcudbright Bay
Whinnieliggate
Kirkcarswell
Dundrennan
DUNDRENNAN ABBEY
Netherlaw
Abbey Hd.
Port Mary
Orroland
Rascarrel
Rascarrel Bay
Balcary Pt.
Auchencairn
Auchencairn Bay
Hestan I.
EAST STEWARTRY COAST
Castlehill Pt.
Rough I.
ROUGH ISLAND
MOTE OF MARK
Rockcliffe
Kippford or Scaur
ORCHARDTON TOWER
Palnackie
Airieland
Gelston
BENGAIRN
Rhonehouse or Kelton Hill
THREAVE GARDENS
KELTON MAINS OPEN FARM
THREAVE CASTLE
Castle Douglas
Carlingwark Loch
Townhead of Greenlaw
Clarebrand
Old Bridge of Urr
Kirkpatrick Durham
Auchenreoch Loch
Springholm
Brooklands
Crocketford or Ninemile Bar
Milton Loch
Milton
Haugh of Urr
MOTE OF URR
OLD BUITTLE TOWER
Dalbeattie
Barhill
Dalbeattie Forest
Barnbarroch
Colvend
Sandyhills
Portling
Mersehead Sands
MERSEHEAD RSPB NATURE RESERVE
Mainsriddle
Caulkerbush
Drumstinchall
Prestonn
Kirkgunzeon
DRUMCOLTRAN TOWER
Beeswing
Loch Arthur
Lochaber Loch
Mabie Forest
Mabie
LONG FELL
NX
Lochrutton Loch
Lochfoot
Brae
Cargenbridge
Maxwellto
Shawhead
Glen
Glenkiln
Glenkiln Res.
Drumpark
Irongray
Newbridge
Terregles Banks
Lincluder
Newtonairds
Holywood
Urr Water
Loch Ken
SOLWAY FIRTH
A712
A713
A75
A711
A762
A745
A710
B794
B795
B736
B721
B727
B793
183
174
162

Newtonairds
Drumpark
Holywood
Kirkton
Tinwald
Locharbriggs
Heathhall
Lochmaben Castle
Castle Loch
Heck
Hightae
Glenkiln Res.
Irongray
Newbridge
Lincluden College
The Grove
Dumfries and Galloway Aviation Mus
Torthorwald
Birkshaw Forest
Lincluden
Old Bridge House Mus
Terregles Banks
Dumfries
Greystone
Rammerscales House
Kettleholm
Middleshaw
Shawhead
Maxwelltown
Collin
Greenlea
Cargenbridge
Burns House
Robert Burns Centre
Dumfries Museum & Camera Obscura
Racks
Cleughbrae
Dalton
Brae
Lochfoot
Lochrutton Loch
Kingholm Quay
Islesteps
Mouswald
Carrutherstown
Milton Loch
Lochar Moss
Lochar Water
Mabie Forest
Mabie
Kelton
Milton
Kirkconnell Flow
Loch Arthur
Lochaber Loch
Beeswing
Glencaple
Bankend
Clarencefield
Ruthwell Cross
Kirkconnell
River Nith
Ruthwell
Duncan Savings Bank Museum
Cummertrees
Kirkgunzeon
New Abbey
Sweetheart Abbey
New Abbey Pow
New Abbey Corn Mill
Shearington
Blackshaw
Caerlaverock Castle
Eastpark
Bowhouse
Wildfowl and Wetland Centre
Caerlaverock
Nith Estuary
Overton
383 Long Fell
Loch Kindar
Blackshaw Bank
Drumburn
569 Criffell
Carsethorn
Kirkbean
Arbigland Gardens
Drumstinchall
Prestonmill
Caulkerbush
Forest
Barnbarroch
Mainsriddle
Mersehead RSPB Nature Reserve
John Paul Jones Cottage Museum
Sandyhills
Colvend
Southerness
Southerness Pt.
Rockcliffe
Portling
Rough I.
Mersehead Sands
Castlehill Pt.
NX
Skinburness
Silloth
Greenrow
Causewayhead
Blitterlees
Solway Firth
Beckfoot
Highlaws
Pelutho
Newtown
Holme St Cuthbert
Mawbray
Dubmill Pt.
Edderside
New Cowper
Allonby
Aspatria
Allonby Bay
Hayton
Prospect
Oughterside
Allerby
Crosscanonby
Crosby Villa
Parsonby
Crosby
A75
A76
A701
A709
A711
A710
B725
B724
B793
B7020
B5300
B5301
184
173
162
0 1 2 3 miles
0 1 2 3 4 5 km

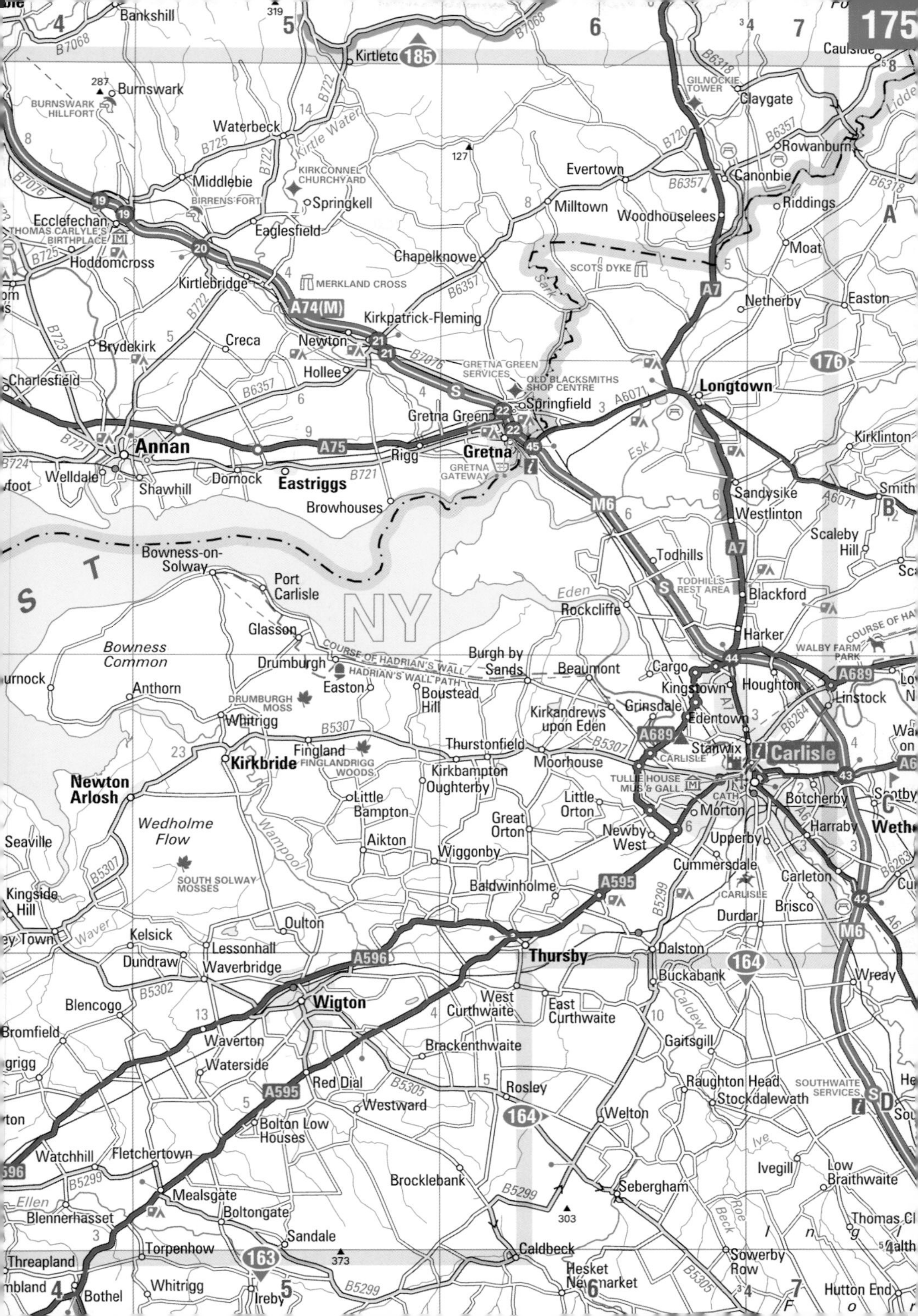
175
Bankshill
Kirtleton
185
Burnswark
BURNSWARK HILLFORT
Waterbeck
Kirtle Water
Middlebie
KIRKCONNEL CHURCHYARD
Springkell
BIRRENS FORT
Ecclefechan
THOMAS CARLYLE'S BIRTHPLACE
Eaglesfield
Hoddomcross
Kirtlebridge
MERKLAND CROSS
A74(M)
Kirkpatrick-Fleming
Brydekirk
Creca
Newton
Hollee
Charlesfield
Annan
Welldale
Shawhill
Dornock
Eastriggs
Rigg
Gretna
GRETNA GATEWAY
Gretna Green
Springfield
GRETNA GREEN SERVICES
OLD BLACKSMITHS SHOP CENTRE
Browhouses
Chapelknowe
Milltown
Evertown
Woodhouselees
SCOTS DYKE
Sark
GILNOCKIE TOWER
Claygate
Rowanburn
Canonbie
Riddings
Moat
Netherby
Easton
Longtown
176
Kirklinton
Sandysike
Westlinton
Scaleby Hill
Todhills
TODHILLS REST AREA
Blackford
Harker
Esk
Eden
Bowness-on-Solway
Port Carlisle
NY
Glasson
Rockcliffe
Bowness Common
Drumburgh
COURSE OF HADRIAN'S WALL
HADRIAN'S WALL PATH
Burgh by Sands
Beaumont
Cargo
Kingstown
Houghton
WALBY FARM PARK
Linstock
Anthorn
Easton
Boustead Hill
DRUMBURGH MOSS
Whitrigg
Kirkandrews upon Eden
Grinsdale
Edentown
Stanwix
Carlisle
Fingland
FINGLANDRIGG WOODS
Kirkbride
Thurstonfield
Kirkbampton
Moorhouse
TULLIE HOUSE MUS & GALL.
Newton Arlosh
Oughterby
Little Bampton
Little Orton
Morton
Botcherby
Wedholme Flow
Great Orton
Newby West
Harraby
Upperby
Aikton
Wiggonby
Wampool
Cummersdale
Carleton
SOUTH SOLWAY MOSSES
Baldwinholme
Seaville
Kingside Hill
Oulton
Durdar
Brisco
Kelsick
Lessonhall
Dundraw
Waverbridge
Waver
Thursby
Dalston
Buckabank
164
Wreay
Blencogo
Wigton
West Curthwaite
East Curthwaite
Caldew
Bromfield
Waverton
Gaitsgill
Brackenthwaite
Waterside
Red Dial
Rosley
Raughton Head
Stockdalewath
SOUTHWAITE SERVICES
Westward
Bolton Low Houses
Welton
Watchhill
Fletchertown
Brocklebank
Ivegill
Low Braithwaite
Mealsgate
Sebergham
Ellen
Blennerhasset
Boltongate
Roe Beck
Thomas Close
Sandale
Torpenhow
Caldbeck
Threapland
163
Sowerby Row
Whitrigg
Hesket Newmarket
Bothel
Ireby
Hutton End
M6
A7
A75
A595
A596
A689
A6071
B7068
B722
B725
B7076
B6357
B721
B5307
B5302
B5299
B5305
B6318
B6264
B6263

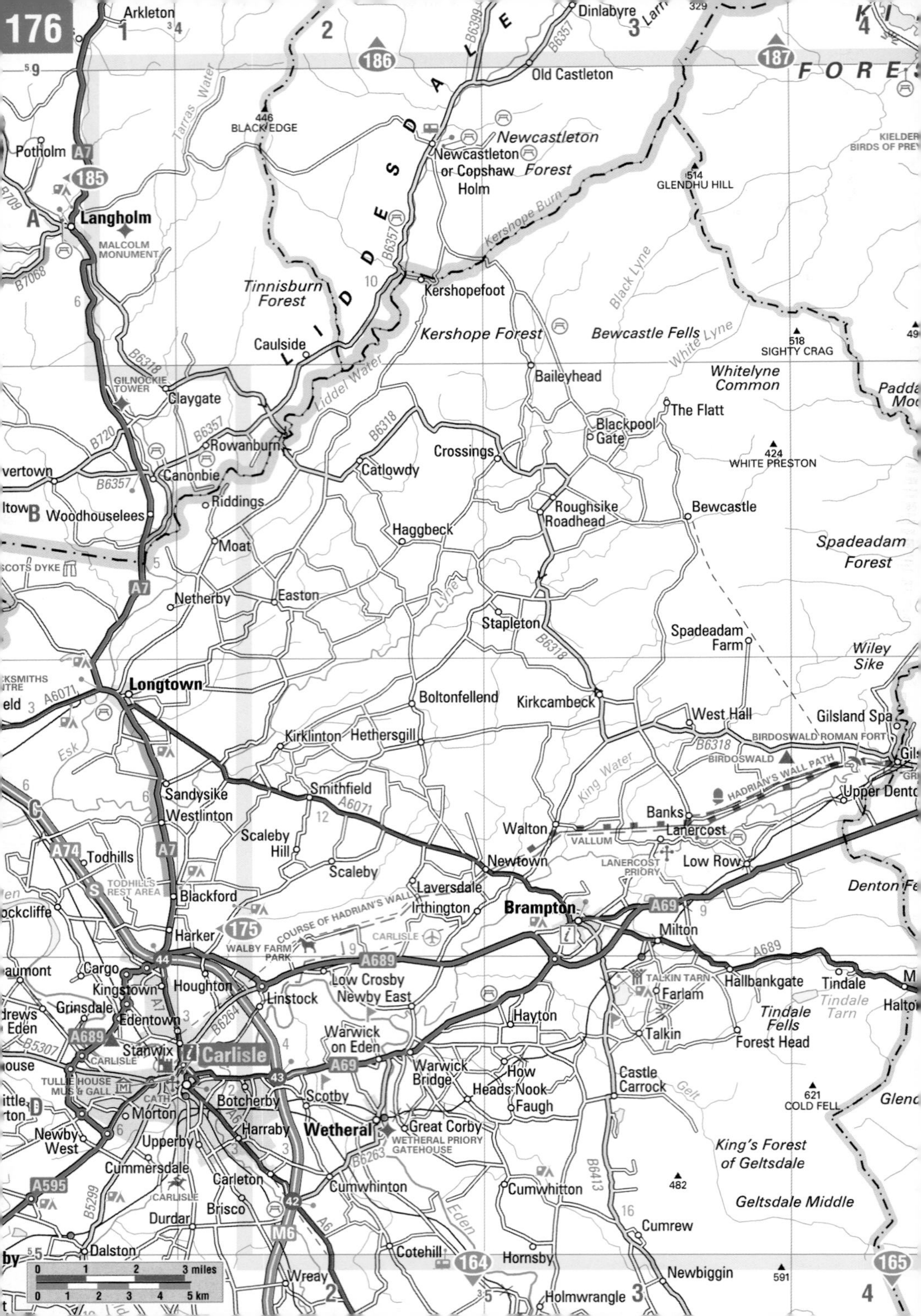

Arkleton
Dinlabyre
Old Castleton
LIDDESDALE
FOREST
BLACK EDGE
Newcastleton
Newcastleton or Copshaw Holm
Newcastleton Forest
KIELDER BIRDS OF PREY
GLENDHU HILL
Potholm
Langholm
MALCOLM MONUMENT
Tinnisburn Forest
Kershopefoot
Kershope Forest
Bewcastle Fells
SIGHTY CRAG
Caulside
Baileyhead
Whitelyne Common
GILNOCKIE TOWER
Claygate
The Flatt
Blackpool Gate
Rowanburn
Crossings
WHITE PRESTON
Canonbie
Catlowdy
Riddings
Roughsike
Roadhead
Bewcastle
Woodhouselees
Haggbeck
Spadeadam Forest
Moat
SCOTS DYKE
Netherby
Easton
Stapleton
Spadeadam Farm
Wiley Sike
Longtown
Boltonfellend
Kirkcambeck
West Hall
Gilsland Spa
Kirklinton
Hethersgill
BIRDOSWALD ROMAN FORT
BIRDOSWALD
HADRIAN'S WALL PATH
Smithfield
Sandysike
Westlinton
Upper Denton
Banks
Scaleby Hill
Walton
Lanercost
VALLUM
Todhills
Newtown
Low Row
Scaleby
LANERCOST PRIORY
TODHILLS REST AREA
Laversdale
Denton Fell
Blackford
Irthington
Brampton
COURSE OF HADRIAN'S WALL
Harker
Milton
WALBY FARM PARK
CARLISLE
Cargo
Low Crosby
TALKIN TARN
Hallbankgate
Tindale
Kingstown
Houghton
Newby East
Farlam
Tindale Tarn
Linstock
Grinsdale
Tindale Fells
Edentown
Hayton
Talkin
Forest Head
Stanwix
Warwick on Eden
Carlisle
TULLIE HOUSE MUS & GALL
CATH
Warwick Bridge
How
Castle Carrock
Heads Nook
Botcherby
COLD FELL
Scotby
Faugh
Morton
Great Corby
Wetheral
WETHERAL PRIORY GATEHOUSE
Newby West
Harraby
Upperby
King's Forest of Geltsdale
Cummersdale
Carleton
Cumwhinton
Cumwhitton
Geltsdale Middle
Durdar
Brisco
Cumrew
Dalston
Cotehill
Hornsby
Newbiggin
Wreay
Holmwrangle
Kershope Burn
Liddel Water
Black Lyne
White Lyne
Lyne
King Water
Esk
Eden
Gelt
Tarras Water
A7
A74
A6071
A689
A69
A595
A6
M6
B6357
B6318
B6399
B720
B7068
B6264
B6263
B6413
B5299
B5307
185
186
187
175
164
165
0 1 2 3 miles
0 1 2 3 4 5 km

NORTHUMBERLAND NATIONAL PARK
Kielder Water
Falstone
Tower Knowe Visitor Centre
Black Middens Bastle House
Shipley Shiels
Gatehouse
Greenhaugh
Lanehead
The Eals
Charlton
Bower
Hesleyside
Bellingham
Redesmouth
Troughend Common
Hareshaw Head
West Woodburn
East Woodburn
Ridsdale
Sweethope Loughs
Kielder Mires
Wark Forest
Blacka Burn
Warks Burn
Birtley
Wark
Whygate
Stonehaugh
Pennine Way
Park End
Colt Crag Reservoir
Great Swinburne
Gunnerton
Barrasford
Chollerton
Simonburn
Black Fell
Haughton Common
Haughton Castle
Humshaugh
Chollerford
Course of Hadrian's Wall
Hadrian's Wall Path
Broomlee Lough
Greenlee Lough
Grindon
Walwick
Low Brunton
Brunton Turret
Chesters Roman Fort
Wall
Hill Head
Whiteside
Housesteads Roman Fort Visitor Centre
Vallum
Roman Army Museum
Fourstones
Newbrough
Warden
Acomb
Greenhead
Once Brewed
Chesterholm Museum (Vindolanda)
Bardon Mill
Chesterwood
Henshaw
Haltwhistle
Melkridge
Redburn
Haydon Bridge
Low Gate
Moothall
Abbey
Hexham
Border History Mus
Plenmeller
South Tyne
Plenmellar Common
Langley
Rowfoot
Lambley
Stonehouse
Whitfield
Dye House
Dalton
Catton
Whitley Chapel
Bearsbridge
West Allen
Eals
Allendale Town
Slaley Forest
Whitfield Moor
Hexhamshire Common
Broadwell House
Slaggyford
Ninebanks
Sinderhope
Allendale Common
Ninebanks
Blanchland Moor
Ayle
Spartylea
Blanchland
Hunstanworth
Maiden Way
Devil's Water
East Allen
NY
A68
A69
A686
A689
A6079
A696
B6320
B6318
B6319
B6305
B6304
B6295
B6303
B6306
187
188
178
165
166

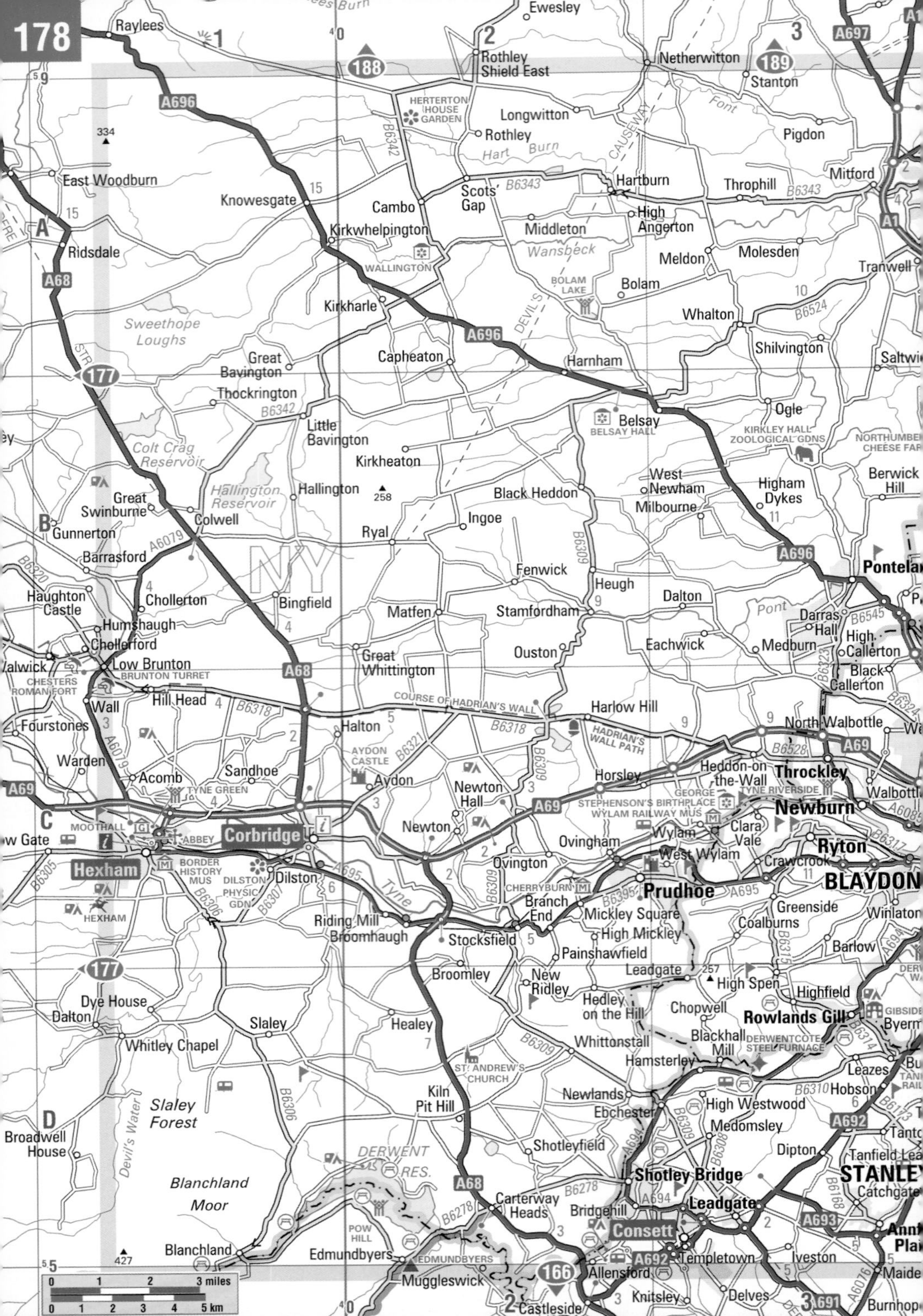
Raylees
Ewesley
Rothley Shield East
Netherwitton
Stanton
188
189
A696
A697
Herterton House Garden
Longwitton
Rothley
Pigdon
Hart Burn
East Woodburn
Knowesgate
Cambo
Scots' Gap
Hartburn
Throphill
Mitford
B6343
B6342
High Angerton
Middleton
Ridsdale
Kirkwhelpington
Wansbeck
Meldon
Molesden
Tranwell
Wallington
Bolam Lake
Bolam
A68
Kirkharle
Whalton
B6524
Sweethope Loughs
Capheaton
Shilvington
Great Bavington
Harnham
177
Thockrington
Little Bavington
Belsay
Ogle
Belsay Hall
Kirkley Hall Zoological Gdns
Colt Crag Reservoir
Kirkheaton
Hallington Reservoir
Hallington
Black Heddon
West Newham
Higham Dykes
Berwick Hill
Great Swinburne
Milbourne
Gunnerton
Colwell
Ryal
Ingoe
Barrasford
A6079
NY
Fenwick
Ponteland
Haughton Castle
Chollerton
Bingfield
Heugh
Dalton
Humshaugh
Matfen
Stamfordham
Darras Hall
Chollerford
Great Whittington
Ouston
Eachwick
Medburn
High Callerton
Walwick
Low Brunton
Brunton Turret
Black Callerton
Chesters Roman Fort
Wall
Hill Head
B6318
Course of Hadrian's Wall
Harlow Hill
North Walbottle
Fourstones
Halton
Hadrian's Wall Path
B6528
A69
Warden
Aydon Castle
B6321
B6309
Horsley
Heddon-on-the-Wall
Throckley
Acomb
Sandhoe
Aydon
Newton Hall
Tyne Green
George Stephenson's Birthplace
Wylam Railway Mus
Tyne Riverside
Walbottle
Newburn
Moothall
Corbridge
Newton
Wylam
Clara Vale
Abbey
Ovingham
Ryton
Hexham
Border History Mus
West Wylam
Crawcrook
Dilston
A695
Tyne
Ovington
Prudhoe
BLAYDON
Dilston Physic Gdn
Cherryburn
B6395
Greenside
B6305
B6306
B6307
Branch End
Mickley Square
Winlaton
Riding Mill
Coalburns
Broomhaugh
Stocksfield
High Mickley
Barlow
Painshawfield
B6315
Leadgate
High Spen
Broomley
New Ridley
Highfield
Dye House
Hedley on the Hill
Chopwell
Rowlands Gill
Gibside
Dalton
Slaley
Healey
Blackhall Mill
Derwentcote Steel Furnace
Whitley Chapel
Whittonstall
Hamsterley
Leazes
St Andrew's Church
Newlands
B6310
Hobson
Kiln Pit Hill
Slaley Forest
Ebchester
High Westwood
D
Broadwell House
Devil's Water
Medomsley
A692
Shotleyfield
Dipton
Tanfield Lea
Derwent Res.
A694
B6308
Shotley Bridge
STANLEY
Blanchland Moor
Carterway Heads
B6278
Bridgehill
Leadgate
Catchgate
Pow Hill
Consett
A693
Blanchland
Edmundbyers
Templetown
Iveston
427
Muggleswick
166
Allensford
Knitsley
Delves
Castleside
Burnhope
A6076
A691
0 1 2 3 miles
0 1 2 3 4 5 km

4
5
6
A
B
C
D
NZ
Ulgham
Linton
Ellington
Lynemouth
189
COLLIERY MUSEUM
Beacon Pt.
QUEEN ELIZABETH II
Woodhorn
Ashington
Pegswood
Newbiggin-by-the-Sea
Bothal
WANSBECK
Hirst
North Seaton
Stakeford
A196
Guide Post
Scotland Gate
Choppington
Hepscott
West Sleekburn
Cambois
Bedlington
Bedlington Station
East Sleekburn
Cowpen
BLYTH
Nedderton
BEDLINGTON
Bebside
East Hartford
Newsham
New Delaval
PLESSEY WOODS
Shankhouse
Nelson Village
ENGLAND COAST PATH
New Hartley
Seaton
Seaton Sluice
SEATON DELAVAL HALL
Cramlington
Southfield
East Cramlington
Seaton Delaval
Hartley
ST MARY'S LIGHTHOUSE
St Mary's or Bait I.
Seaton Burn
Seghill
Holywell
Dinnington
Dudley
Annitsford
Brunswick Village
Wide Open
Burradon
Backworth
Earsdon
WHITLEY BAY
Hazlerigg
NEWCASTLE
Killingworth
Camperdown
Monkseaton
Shiremoor
Marden
Cullercoats
AMSTERDAM
BLUE REEF AQUARIUM
TYNEMOUTH CASTLE & PRIORY
Longbenton
STEPHENSON RAILWAY MUSEUM
Tynemouth
THE RISING SUN
North Shields
Gosforth
Kenton
Jesmond
Willington
ROYAL QUAYS
ARBEIA ROMAN FORT AND MUSEUM
South Shields
WALLSEND
SOUTH SHIELDS MUSEUM
Heaton
TOLL
Tyne Tunnel
THE LEAS AND MARSDEN ROCK
Marsden Bay
NEWCASTLE UPON TYNE
Byker
Jarrow
SEGEDUNUM FORT
JARROW HALL
ST PAUL'S MONASTERY
Westoe
Harton
Marsden
Walker
CASTLE KEEP
Hebburn
NEWCASTLE DISCOVERY
Gateshead
INTERNATIONAL STADIUM
SOUTER LIGHTHOUSE
METROLAND
Dunston
Bensham
Tyne
Hedworth
Whiteleas
Cleadon
Whitburn Colliery
Boldon Colliery
Pelaw
Whitburn
SHIPLEY ART GAL
Felling
Boldon
FULWELL WINDMILL
Carr Hill
Low Fell
Downhill
Fulwell
Roker
Street Gate
Chowdene
Hylton Castle
Southwick
Wrekenton
BOWES RLY
Monkwearmouth
NATIONAL GLASS CENTRE
Lamesley
Springwell
Usworth
Castletown
ST PETER'S CHURCH
ANGEL OF THE NORTH
Blackfell
OLD HALL
South Hylton
Pallion
SUNDERLAND MINSTER
Kibblesworth
Birtley
WASHINGTON
High Barnes
Sunderland
WASHINGTON SERVICES
Pennywell
Hendon
BEAMISH
Ouston
Lambton
THE WILDFOWL & WETLANDS TRUST
PENSHAW MON
Urpeth
Beamish
Perkinsville
Barley Mow
Fatfield
New Silksworth
Rickleton
Penshaw
East Herrington
Ryhope
Pelton
Shiney Row
Tunstall
West Pelton
Wear
New Herrington
Doxford Park
RYHOPE ENGINES MUS
Grange Villa
CHESTER-LE-STREET
Bournmoor
Newbottle
DOWN AT THE FARM
Burdon
THE ANKERS HOUSE
Fence Houses
Seaton
Northlea
Waldridge
Chester Moor
Great Lumley
167
HOUGHTON-LE-SPRING
SEAHAM
Colliery Row
East
West Lea
Edmondsley
A189
A1068
A197
A193
A1061
A192
A1172
A19
A190
A1056
A191
A186
A1058
A187
A185
A1300
A194
A184
A1018
A183
A194(M)
A1290
A195
A1231
A167
A692
A1
A693
A182
A690
A19
A1(M)
A1052
B1337
B1331
B1329
B1505
B1325
B1426
B1288
B1296
B6313
B1284
B1404
B1286
B1285
B1287
B6532

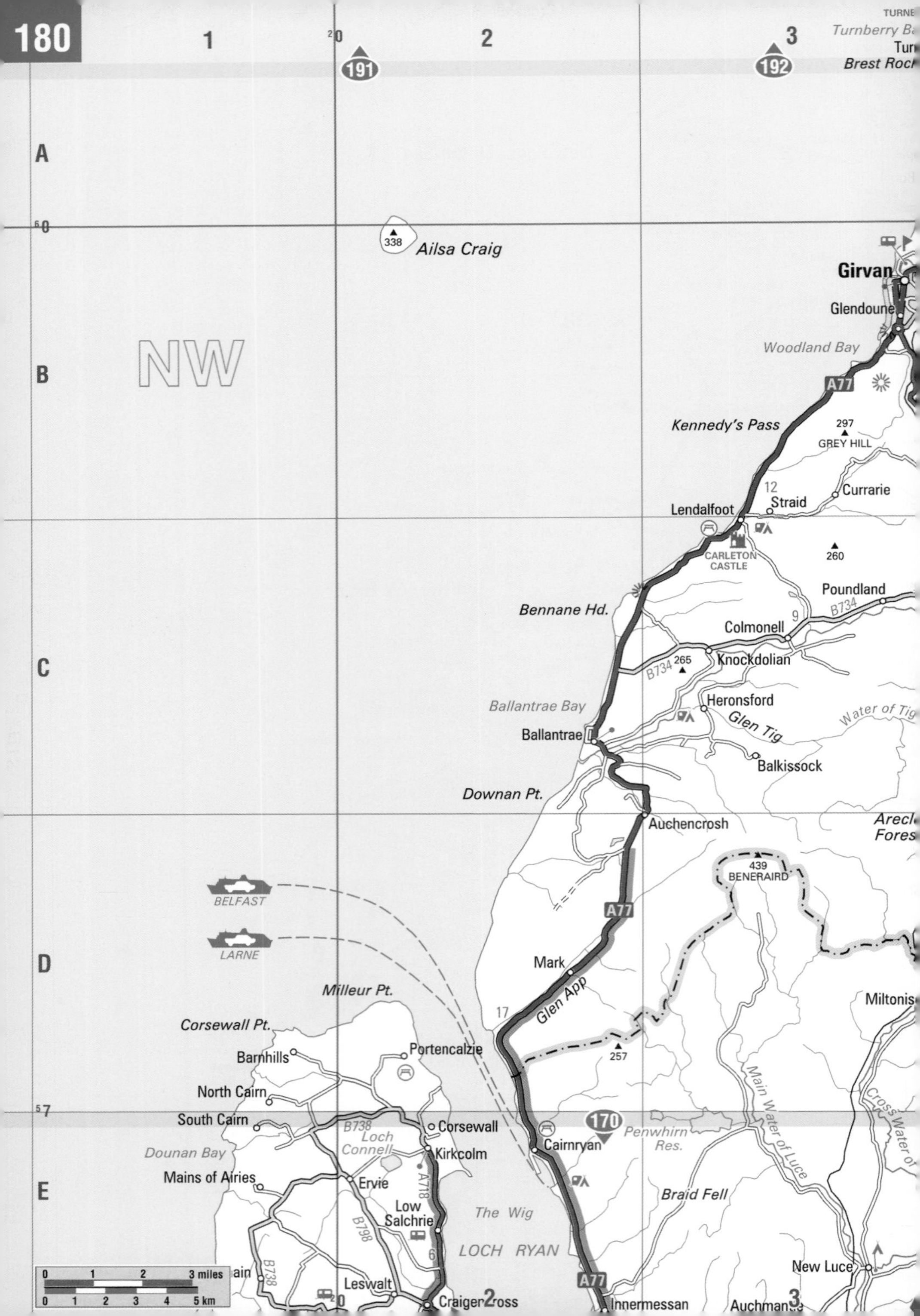

1
2
3
A
B
C
D
E
191
192
NW
Turnberry Bay
Brest Rock
Ailsa Craig
338
Girvan
Glendoune
Woodland Bay
A77
Kennedy's Pass
297
GREY HILL
Currarie
Straid
Lendalfoot
CARLETON CASTLE
260
Poundland
B734
Bennane Hd.
Colmonell
Knockdolian
265
Ballantrae Bay
Heronsford
Glen Tig
Water of Tig
Ballantrae
Balkissock
Downan Pt.
Auchencrosh
Arecleoch Forest
439
BENERAIRD
BELFAST
LARNE
Mark
Glen App
Milleur Pt.
Miltonise
Corsewall Pt.
257
Barnhills
Portencalzie
North Cairn
South Cairn
B738
Loch Connell
Corsewall
170
Penwhirn Res.
Cairnryan
Main Water of Luce
Cross Water of Luce
Dounan Bay
Kirkcolm
Mains of Airies
Ervie
A718
Braid Fell
Low Salchrie
B798
The Wig
LOCH RYAN
New Luce
Leswalt
Craigencross
Innermessan
Auchmantle
0 1 2 3 miles
0 1 2 3 4 5 km

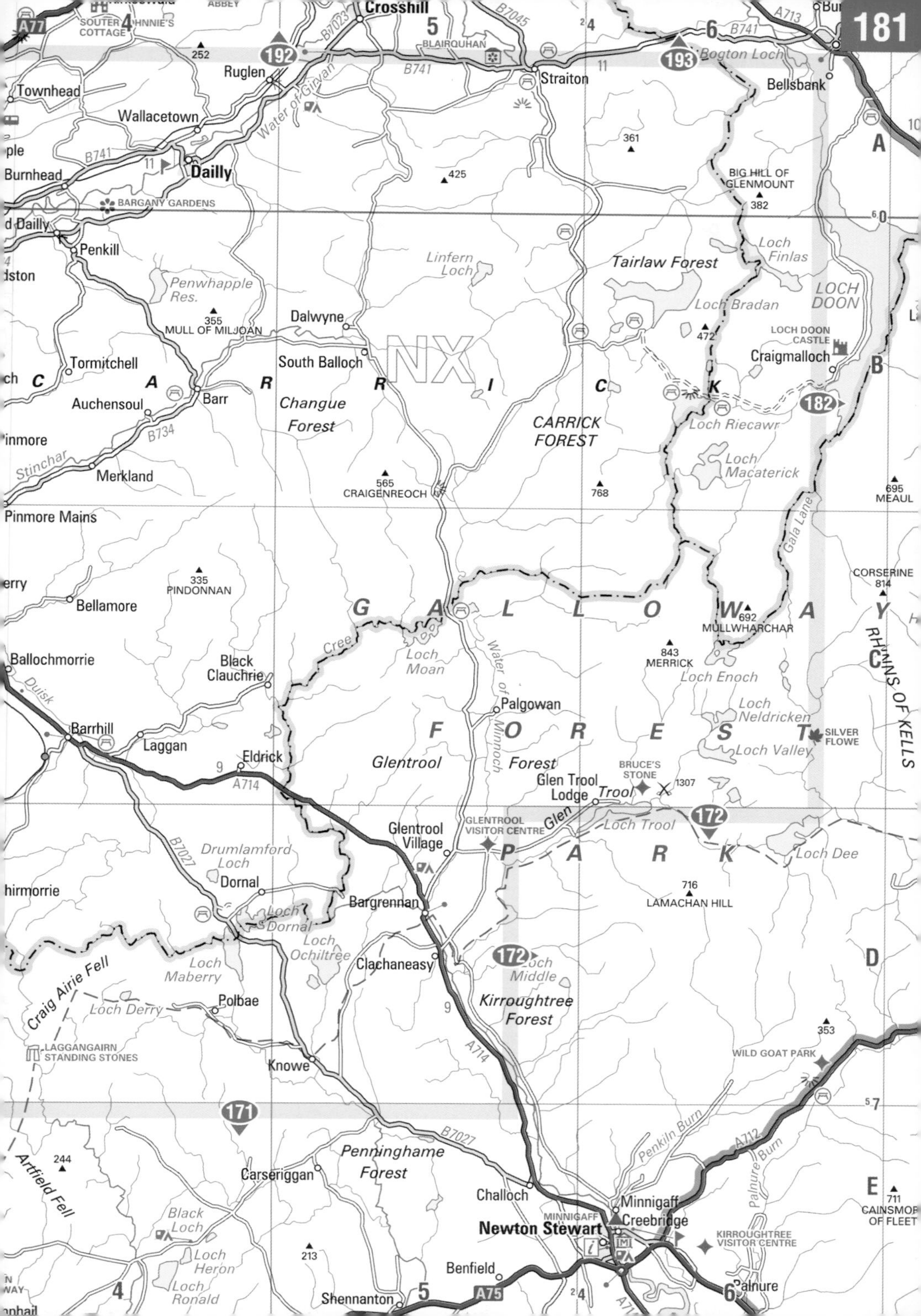
Crosshill
5
4
SOUTER JOHNNIE'S COTTAGE
BLAIRQUHAN
192
193
Ruglen
Straiton
Bogton Loch
Bellsbank
Townhead
Wallacetown
Water of Girvan
Dailly
Burnhead
BARGANY GARDENS
Penkill
BIG HILL OF GLENMOUNT
382
Loch Finlas
Tairlaw Forest
Linfern Loch
Penwhapple Res.
355
MULL OF MILJOAN
Dalwyne
South Balloch
NX
Loch Bradan
LOCH DOON
LOCH DOON CASTLE
Craigmalloch
Tormitchell
C A R R I C K
Barr
Auchensoul
Changue Forest
CARRICK FOREST
Loch Riecawr
182
Merkland
Stinchar
Loch Macaterick
565
CRAIGENREOCH
768
695
MEAUL
Pinmore Mains
Gala Lane
335
PINDONNAN
CORSERINE
814
Bellamore
G A L L O W A Y
MULLWHARCHAR
692
843
MERRICK
Ballochmorrie
Black Clauchrie
Cree
Loch Moan
Water of Minnoch
Loch Enoch
Loch Neldricken
RHINNS OF KELLS
Palgowan
Barrhill
Laggan
F O R E S T
SILVER FLOWE
Loch Valley
Eldrick
Glentrool
Forest
A714
BRUCE'S STONE
1307
Glen Trool Lodge
Trool
172
Loch Trool
Glen
GLENTROOL VISITOR CENTRE
Glentrool Village
B7027
Drumlamford Loch
P A R K
Loch Dee
Dornal
716
LAMACHAN HILL
Bargrennan
Loch Dornal
Loch Ochiltree
Clachaneasy
Loch Middle
Loch Maberry
Craig Airie Fell
Polbae
Loch Derry
Kirroughtree Forest
LAGGANGAIRN STANDING STONES
353
WILD GOAT PARK
Knowe
171
Penkiln Burn
A712
Palnure Burn
244
Artfield Fell
Penninghame Forest
Carseriggan
Challoch
Minnigaff
711
CAINSMORE OF FLEET
MINNIGAFF
Creebridge
Newton Stewart
Black Loch
KIRROUGHTREE VISITOR CENTRE
Loch Heron
213
Benfield
Loch Ronald
Shennanton
A75
Palnure
A
B
C
D
E
6
A713
B741
B7045
B7023
B734
A77
252
361
425
472
11
9

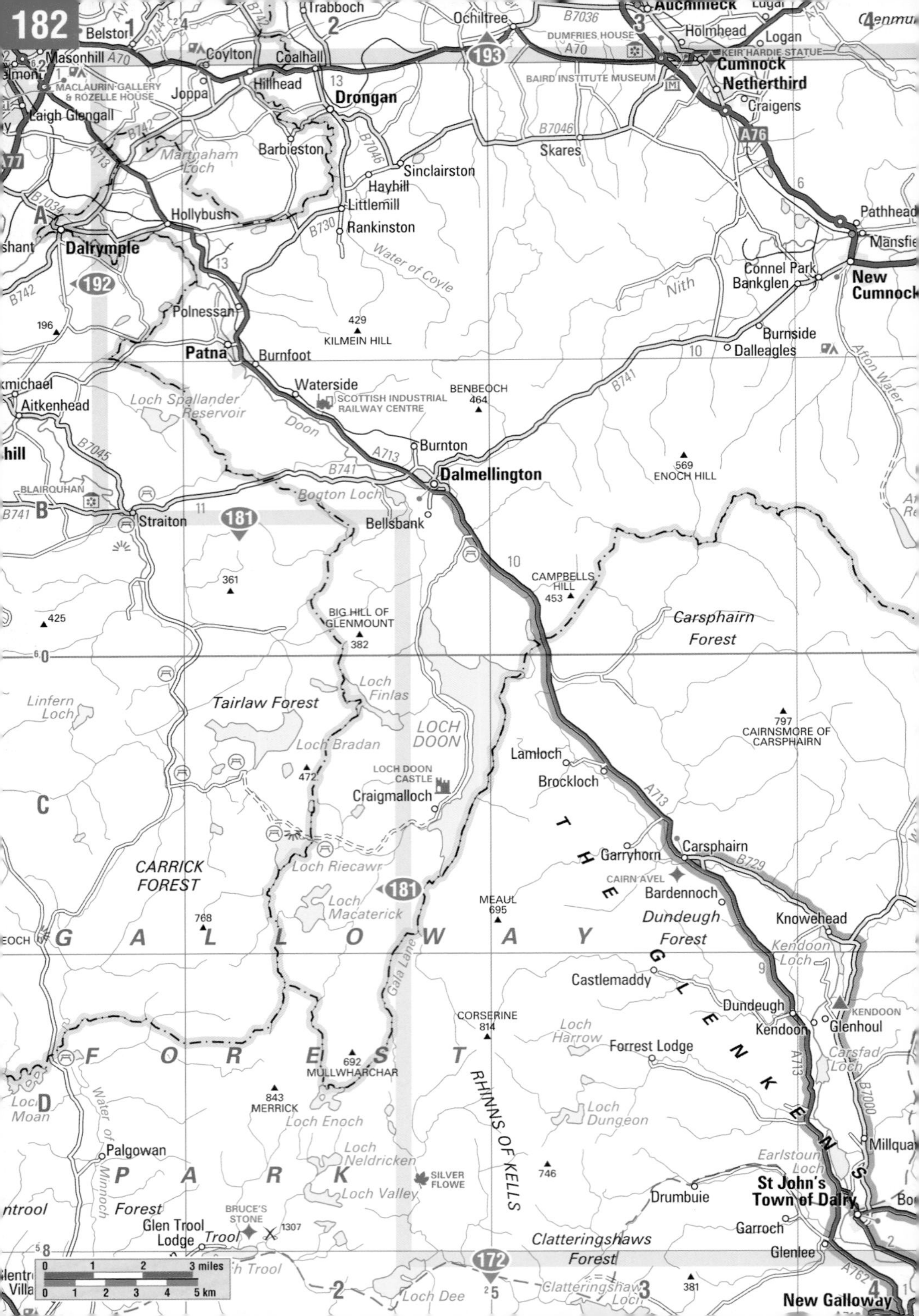

Belston
Trabboch
Ochiltree
Auchinleck
Holmhead
Logan
Masonhill
Coylton
Coalhall
DUMFRIES HOUSE
KEIR HARDIE STATUE
Cumnock
MACLAURIN GALLERY & ROZELLE HOUSE
Joppa
Hillhead
Drongan
BAIRD INSTITUTE MUSEUM
Netherthird
Craigens
Laigh Glengall
Martnaham Loch
Barbieston
Skares
Sinclairston
Hayhill
Littlemill
Hollybush
Rankinston
Pathhead
Dalrymple
Water of Coyle
Nith
Connel Park
Bankglen
New Cumnock
Polnessan
Burnside
Dalleagles
KILMEIN HILL
Patna
Burnfoot
Afton Water
Waterside
SCOTTISH INDUSTRIAL RAILWAY CENTRE
BENBEOCH
Aitkenhead
Loch Spallander Reservoir
Doon
Burnton
ENOCH HILL
Dalmellington
BLAIRQUHAN
Bogton Loch
Straiton
Bellsbank
CAMPBELLS HILL
BIG HILL OF GLENMOUNT
Carsphairn Forest
Linfern Loch
Loch Finlas
Tairlaw Forest
LOCH DOON
CAIRNSMORE OF CARSPHAIRN
Loch Bradan
Lamloch
LOCH DOON CASTLE
Brockloch
Craigmalloch
Garryhorn
Carsphairn
CARRICK FOREST
Loch Riecawr
CAIRN AVEL
Bardennoch
Loch Macaterick
MEAUL
Dundeugh Forest
Knowehead
GALLOWAY FOREST PARK
THE GLENKENS
Kendoon Loch
Castlemaddy
Gala Lane
CORSERINE
Dundeugh
KENDOON
Glenhoul
Kendoon
Loch Harrow
Forrest Lodge
MULLWHARCHAR
Carsfad Loch
RHINNS OF KELLS
MERRICK
Loch Moan
Loch Enoch
Loch Dungeon
Water of Minnoch
Palgowan
Millquarter
Loch Neldricken
Earlstoun Loch
SILVER FLOWE
St John's Town of Dalry
Loch Valley
Drumbuie
Forest
BRUCE'S STONE
Glen Trool Lodge
Trool
Garroch
Clatteringshaws Forest
Glenlee
Loch Trool
Loch Dee
Clatteringshaws Loch
New Galloway
0 1 2 3 miles
0 1 2 3 4 5 km

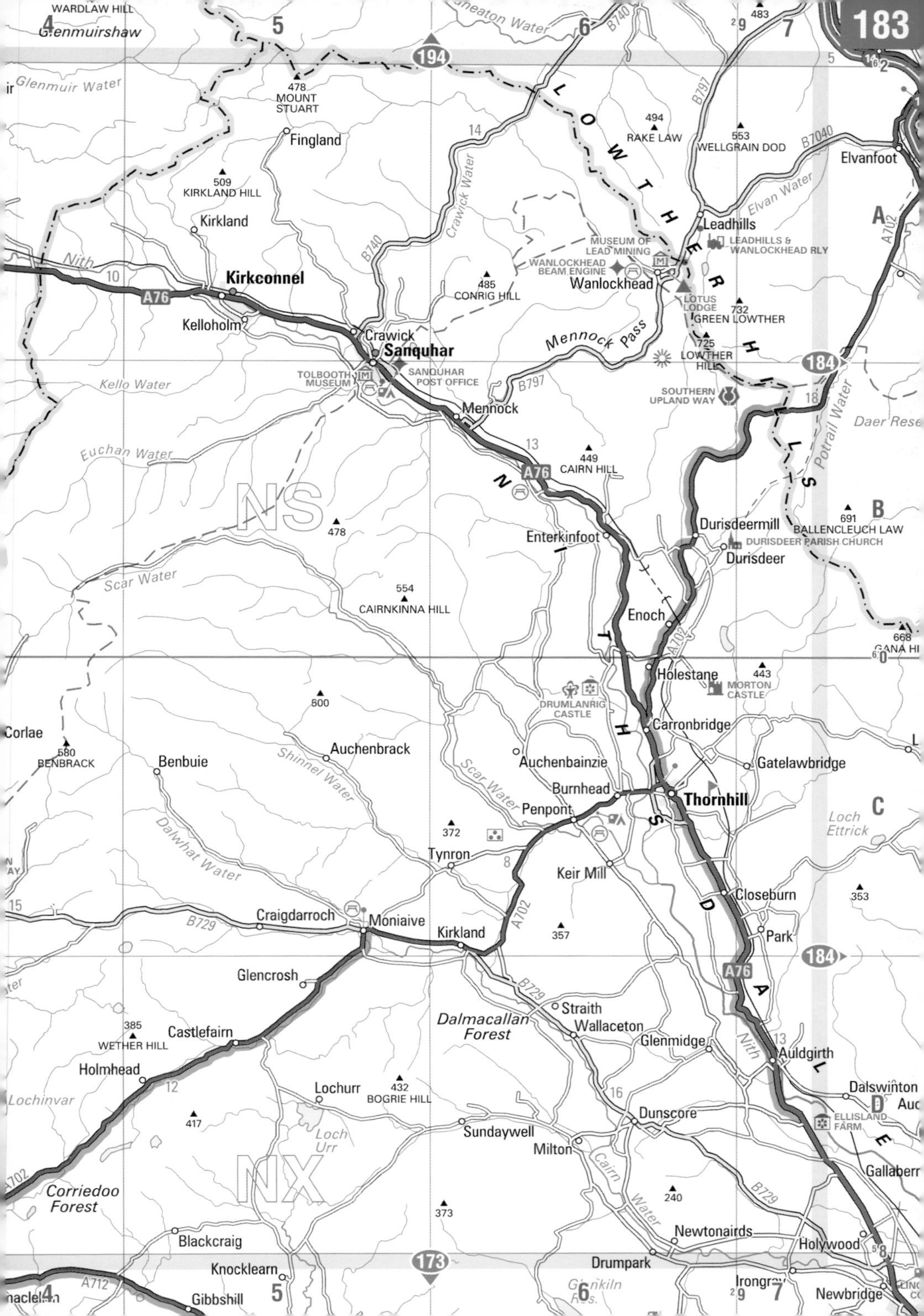

194
184
184
173

Glenbreck
Kirkton
Crawford
195
550
483
B740
B797
LOWTHER HILLS
494
RAKE LAW
553
WELLGRAIN DOD
B7040
Elvanfoot
546
CLYDE LAW
553
CRAIGMAID
A701
Source of River Tweed
Crawick Water
Elvan Water
Leadhills
LEADHILLS & WANLOCKHEAD RLY
MUSEUM OF LEAD MINING
WANLOCKHEAD BEAM ENGINE
Wanlockhead
A702
March
Watermeetings
DEVIL'S BEEF TUB
485
CONRIG HILL
LOTUS LODGE
732
GREEN LOWTHER
Nether Howecleuch
Ericstane
Mennock Pass
725
LOWTHER HILL
183
Sanquhar
SANQUHAR POST OFFICE
B797
Grantshouse
SOUTHERN UPLAND WAY
B719
Mennock
Potrail Water
Daer Reservoir
SOUTHERN UPLAND WAY
A74(M)
13
449
CAIRN HILL
A76
NS
Coatsgate
Durisdeermill
691
BALLENCLEUCH LAW
DURISDEER PARISH CHURCH
Durisdeer
Garpol Water
407
Easter Earshaig
Beattock
Enterkinfoot
Kinnelhead
Enoch
NITHSDALE
668
GANA HILL
Holestane
443
MORTON CASTLE
512
QUEENSBERRY
DRUMLANRIG CASTLE
A701
Carronbridge
Locherben
399
Auchenbainzie
Gatelawbridge
Scar Water
Burnhead
Thornhill
NX
Kinnel Water
Penpont
372
Loch Ettrick
B7020
Tynron
Keir Mill
St Ann's
Closeburn
353
Forest of Ae
Johnstonebridge
Blackacre
Chapelhill
Kirkland
357
Park
A76
183
Courance
B729
Ae Village
Water of Ae
Straith
Nethermill
Dalmacallan Forest
Wallaceton
Glenmidge
Nith
Parkgate
Auldgirth
B7020
Dalswinton
Shieldhill
Auchencairn
A701
Dunscore
ELLISLAND FARM
Sundaywell
Duncow
Applegarth
Milton
Cairn Water
Lochmaben
Gallaberry
Amisfield
240
B729
Kirkton
Tinwald
373
LOCHMABEN CASTLE
Newtonairds
Holywood
Locharbriggs
Heathhall
174
DUMFRIES AND GALLOWAY AVIATION MUS
A709
Irongray
LINCLUDEN COLLEGE
Newbridge
The Grove
Torthorwald
0 1 2 3 miles
0 1 2 3 4 5 km

185
Meggethead
Talla
Linnfoots
Megget Reservoir
St. Mary's Loch
589
THE WISS
Gilmanscleuch
Loch of the Lowes
Crosslee
Newburgh
Tushielaw
Ettrick Water
Fruid Reservoir
LOCHCRAIG HEAD
800
690
Ramsey Knowe
471
Loch Skeen
Birkhill
Wardlaw
Redfordgreen
Hellmoor Loch
GREY MARE'S TAIL WATERFALLS
882
WHITE COOMB
590
Ettrick
Ettrickhill
Ramseycleuch
Buccleuch
808
HART FELL
677
JAMES HOGG MONUMENT
498
Borthwickbrae
Burnfoot
753
SADDLE YOKE
Blackhope Burn
Deanburnhaugh
549
BLACK KNOWE
Glenkerry
390
REDCLEUCH EDGE
Craik Forest
Borthwick Water
Capplegill
Roundstonefoot
Nether Dalgliesh
Craik
Howpasley
RIDDELL MONUMENT
678
CAPEL FELL
692
ETTRICK PEN
488
Moffat Water
688
LOCH FELL
NT
417
PIKE HILL
Teviot
Davington
477
KAGYU SAMYE LING TIBETAN CENTRE
Wamphray Water
484
Laverhay
Eskdalemuir Forest
White Esk
Eskdalemuir
WISP HILL
Jamestown
Black Esk Reservoir
NY
Meggat Water
Ewes Water
Waterhead
Sandyford
Castle O'er Forest
492
Black Esk
Castle O'er
ANNANDALE WATER SERVICES
Dinwoodie Mains
Boreland
Georgefield
Arkleton
Ewes
Bentpath
Dryfe Water
ESKDALE
Esk
Sibbaldbie
331
HART FELL
450
CALKIN RIG
Potholm
Corrie Common
Langholm
MALCOLM MONUMENT
A74(M)
Paddockhole
Water of Milk
Lockerbie
Bankshill
319
Kirtleton
287
Burnswark
BURNSWARK HILLFORT
GILNOCKIE TOWER
Claygate
Tarras
A708
B709
B7009
B711
B723
B709
B7068
B7076
B722
B6318
A7
A709
195
196
186
176
175

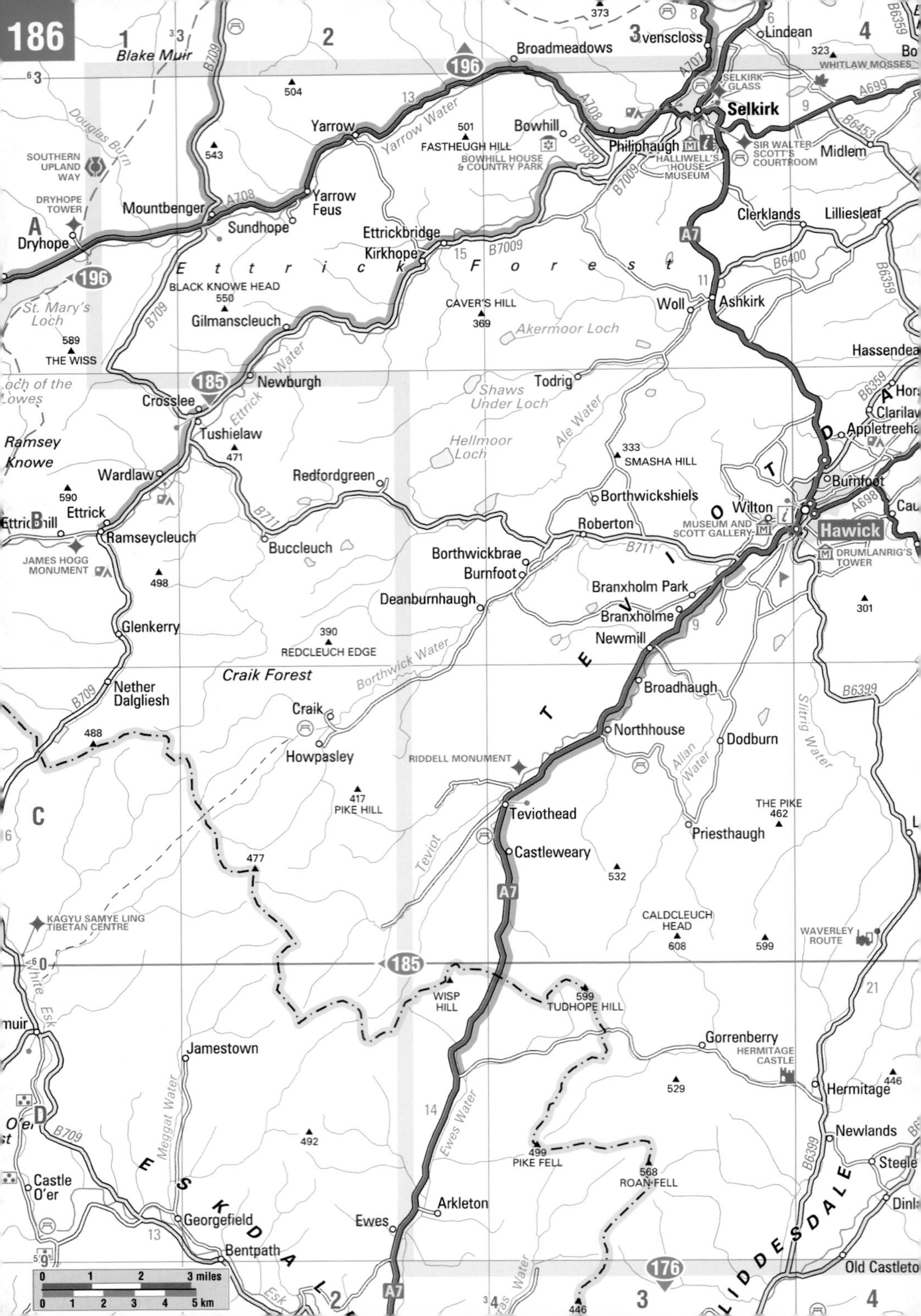

Blake Muir
Broadmeadows
Lindean
Selkirk
Yarrow
Yarrow Water
FASTHEUGH HILL
Bowhill
BOWHILL HOUSE & COUNTRY PARK
Philiphaugh
HALLIWELL'S HOUSE MUSEUM
SELKIRK GLASS
SIR WALTER SCOTT'S COURTROOM
Midlem
WHITLAW MOSSES
SOUTHERN UPLAND WAY
DRYHOPE TOWER
Dryhope
Mountbenger
Yarrow Feus
Sundhope
Ettrickbridge
Kirkhope
Clerklands
Lilliesleaf
Ettrick Forest
BLACK KNOWE HEAD
Gilmanscleuch
CAVER'S HILL
Akermoor Loch
Woll
Ashkirk
St. Mary's Loch
THE WISS
Hassendean
Loch of the Lowes
Newburgh
Crosslee
Todrig
Shaws Under Loch
Ettrick Water
Ale Water
Tushielaw
Hellmoor Loch
SMASHA HILL
Ramsey Knowe
Wardlaw
Redfordgreen
Borthwickshiels
Burnfoot
Appletreehall
Clarilaw
Ettrick
Ettrickhill
Ramseycleuch
Buccleuch
Roberton
Wilton
Hawick
MUSEUM AND SCOTT GALLERY
DRUMLANRIG'S TOWER
JAMES HOGG MONUMENT
Borthwickbrae
Burnfoot
Branxholm Park
Deanburnhaugh
Branxholme
Glenkerry
Newmill
REDCLEUCH EDGE
Craik Forest
Borthwick Water
Nether Dalgliesh
Broadhaugh
Craik
Northhouse
Dodburn
Howpasley
RIDDELL MONUMENT
Allan Water
Slitrig Water
TEVIOT DALE
Teviothead
PIKE HILL
THE PIKE
Priesthaugh
Castleweary
Teviot
KAGYU SAMYE LING TIBETAN CENTRE
CALDCLEUCH HEAD
WAVERLEY ROUTE
WISP HILL
TUDHOPE HILL
White Esk
Jamestown
Gorrenberry
HERMITAGE CASTLE
Hermitage
Meggat Water
Ewes Water
Newlands
PIKE FELL
ROAN FELL
Castle O'er
Arkleton
Steele Road
Georgefield
Ewes
Bentpath
ESKDALE
LIDDESDALE
Old Castleton
0 1 2 3 miles
0 1 2 3 4 5 km

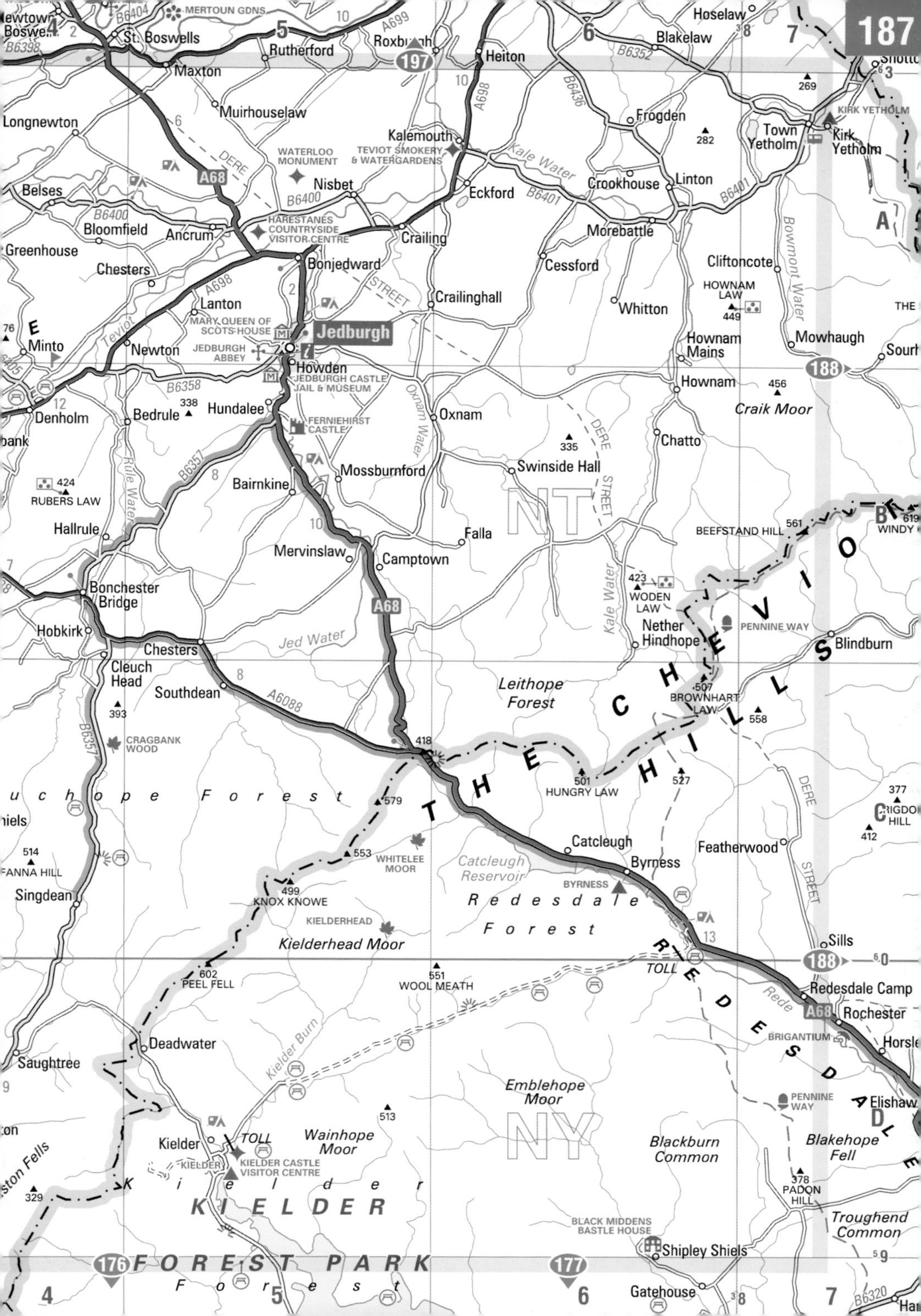

St. Boswells
MERTOUN GDNS
Rutherford
Roxburgh
197
Heiton
Hoselaw
Blakelaw
Maxton
Muirhouselaw
Longnewton
Frogden
Kalemouth
TEVIOT SMOKERY & WATERGARDENS
WATERLOO MONUMENT
Kale Water
Town Yetholm
Kirk Yetholm
KIRK YETHOLM
Linton
Crookhouse
Belses
Nisbet
Eckford
Bloomfield
Ancrum
HARESTANES COUNTRYSIDE VISITOR CENTRE
Crailing
Morebattle
Greenhouse
Chesters
Bonjedward
Cessford
Cliftoncote
Bowmont Water
Lanton
Crailinghall
Whitton
HOWNAM LAW
MARY QUEEN OF SCOTS' HOUSE
Jedburgh
Minto
Newton
JEDBURGH ABBEY
Howden
JEDBURGH CASTLE JAIL & MUSEUM
Hownam Mains
Mowhaugh
Hownam
188
Craik Moor
Denholm
Bedrule
Hundalee
FERNIEHIRST CASTLE
Oxnam
Oxnam Water
Chatto
Swinside Hall
Mossburnford
RUBERS LAW
Bairnkine
Rule Water
NT
DERE STREET
Hallrule
Falla
BEEFSTAND HILL
WINDY
Mervinslaw
Camptown
WODEN LAW
Bonchester Bridge
Hobkirk
Chesters
Jed Water
Kale Water
Nether Hindhope
PENNINE WAY
Blindburn
Cleuch Head
Southdean
Leithope Forest
BROWNHART LAW
THE CHEVIOT HILLS
CRAGBANK WOOD
HUNGRY LAW
Wauchope Forest
FANNA HILL
Catcleugh
Byrness
Featherwood
Catcleugh Reservoir
WHITELEE MOOR
BYRNESS
KNOX KNOWE
Singdean
Redesdale Forest
KIELDERHEAD
Kielderhead Moor
REDESDALE
Sills
TOLL
PEEL FELL
WOOL MEATH
Redesdale Camp
Rochester
Rede
BRIGANTIUM
Deadwater
Saughtree
Kielder Burn
Emblehope Moor
PENNINE WAY
Elishaw
NY
Blakehope Fell
Kielder
TOLL
Wainhope Moor
Blackburn Common
KIELDER CASTLE VISITOR CENTRE
PADON HILL
KIELDER FOREST PARK
BLACK MIDDENS BASTLE HOUSE
Troughend Common
Shipley Shiels
176
177
Gatehouse
Kielder Forest

Kilham
Lanton
Coupland
Newtown
West Horton
Hazelrigg
East Horton
Shotton
Westnewton
198
Kirknewton
Akeld
1402
Weetwood Hall
269
Chatton
Greendikes
KIRK YETHOLM
Town Yetholm
Kirk Yetholm
Hethpool
College Burn
Humbleton
Wooler
WOOLER
166
537
Earle
Haugh Head
CHILLINGHAM CASTLE
Chillingham
WILD CATTLE CHILLINGHAM
Middleton Hall
Newtown
A697
Lilburn Tower
315
Hepburn
PENNINE WAY
COLD LAW 452
North Middleton
East Lilburn
South Middleton
DEVIL'S CAUSEWAY
Bowmont Water
601
THE SCHIL
MOUNTHOOLEY
Langleeford
Ilderton
Roseden
Old Bewick
Mowhaugh
Sourhope
Roddam
Wooperton
Breamish
B6346
New Bewick
726
815
187
AUCHOPE CAIRN
THE CHEVIOT
Harthope Burn
1464
Eglingham
456
Craik Moor
NT
569
DUNMOOR HILL
Brandon
Powburn
Greensidehill
Ingram
Branton
233
Breamish
Shill Moor
Glanton
619
WINDY GYLE
561
NORTHUMBERLAND
335
Glanton Pike
616
CUSHAT LAW
Great Ryle
Prendwick
Usway
Kidland Forest
Whittingham
PENNINE WAY
Barrowburn
Alnham
Aln
Thrunton
Blindburn
NATIONAL PARK
214
Little Ryle
Yetlington
Burn
501
Scrainwood
Callaly
Thrunton Wood
Alwin
Biddlestone
558
Netherton
Lorbottle Hall
Shillmoor
Burradon
Lorbottle
319
Alwinton
Linshiels
High Trewhitt
377
CRIGDON HILL
DERE STREET
Cartington
B6341
412
Coquet
Harbottle
Sharperton
LADY'S WELL
Warton
Snitter
WATTY BELL'S CAIRN
361
Holystone
Flotterton
Rothbury
355
B6341
Caistron
Thropton
CRAGSIDE HOUSE
Hepple
Newtown
Whitton
Sills
14
Great Tosson
187
Redesdale Camp
Rede
NY
A68
Rochester
440
TOSSON HILL
ROTHBURY FOREST
BRIGANTIUM
Horsley
B6342
Forestburn Gate
REDESDALE
274
Otterburn Camp
Harwood
PENNINE WAY
Elishaw
B6341
386
Forest
Blakehope Fell
1388
256
Otterburn
Fallowlees Burn
Fontburn Res.
378
PADON HILL
Elsdon
Ewesley
Raylees
Troughend Common
A68
Old Town
Rothley Shield East
177
178
B6342
HERTERTON HOUSE GARDEN
A696
Longwitton
0 1 2 3 miles
0 1 2 3 4 5 km

NORTHUMBERLAND COAST
Seahouses
Bellshill
Adderstone
Lucker
Elford
North Sunderland
Beadnell
Newham Hall
Warenford
Newham
Swinhoe
Benthall
Fleetham
Beadnell Bay
Newstead
Chathill
Rosebrough
Ellingham
Preston
High Newton-by-the-Sea
Brunton
PRESTON TOWER
Low Newton-by-the-Sea
Brownyside
Christon Bank
North Charlton
Embleton Bay
Embleton
Dunstan Steads
Castle Point
DUNSTANBURGH CASTLE
West Ditchburn
South Charlton
Rock
Craster
Dunstan
Rennington
Littlemill
Howick
NU
Littlehoughton
Shipley
Howick Haven
HULNE PRIORY
Longhoughton
ALNWICK ABBEY
Denwick
Boulmer
Alnwick
Abberwick
Boulmer Haven
Broome Park
Hawkhill
Lesbury
Lemmington Hall
WILLOWTREE
ALN VALLEY RAILWAY
Bilton
Alnmouth
Alnmouth Bay
High Buston
Shilbottle
Low Buston
Birling
Eastfield Hall
Warkworth
Newton-on-the-Moor
Coquet I.
Gloster Hill
Amble
Hazon
Swarland Estate
Guyzance
Hauxley
Brainshaugh
North Togston
Swarland
Acklington
Radcliffe
Togston
Broomhill
Felton
South Broomhill
LONGFRAMLINGTON GARDENS
West Thirston
East Thirston
DRURIDGE BAY
Red Row
ENGLAND COAST PATH
Weldon
Eshott
Druridge Bay
NZ
West Chevington
Helm
Widdrington
Stobswood
Longhorsley
Causey Park Bridge
Widdrington Station
The Scars
Cresswell
Fenrother
Tritlington
Ellington
Ulgham
Lynemouth
Linton
Stanton
Beacon Pt.
Hebron
Longhirst
QUEEN ELIZABETH II
Woodhorn
Ashington
CAUSEWAY
A1
A697
A1068
A189
B6347
B6346
B6341
B1340
B1339
B6345
B6344
B1337
178
179
199

GIGHA
Gigalum Island
Cara Island
SOUND OF GIGHA
Tayinloan
Killean
Beacharr
Muasdale
201
202
322 CNOC NAN CRAOBH
CRUACH MHIC-AN T-SAOIR 364
354 CRUACH NAN GABHAR
BEINN BHREAC
Carradale Water
Grogport
Brackley
Clachaig Water
A83
Glenacardoch Pt.
Amod
Belloch
426 BEINN BHREAC
Carradale
Port Righ
Bridgend
Torrisdale-Square
Carradale Bay
Glenbarr
CLAN MACALISTER CENTRE
Barr Water
454 BEINN AN TUIRC
Cleongart
Saddell Glen
Saddell
SADDELL ABBEY
341 A'CHRUACH
Saddell Bay
Bellochantuy Bay
Bellochantuy
Killocraw
Lussa Loch
397 SGREADAN HILL
Ugadale
Tangy Loch
Skeroblingarry
B842
Black Bay
Westport
Kilchenzie
Glenlussa Water
Peninver
Ardnacross Bay
West Darlochan
Kilmichael
Low Smerby
Machrihanish Bay
CAMPBELTOWN
CAMPBELTOWN HERITAGE CENTRE
Machrihanish
Trodigal
Campbeltown
Campbeltown Loch
Island Davaar
DAVAAR ISLAND CAVE PAINTING
Drumlemble
B843
Stewarton
CAMPBELTOWN BUCKHOUSE
Kilkerran
Kildalloig
ARDROSSAN (May-Sept)
BRODICK (May-Sept, Sat o
Knocknaha
Earadale Pt.
352 BEINN GHUILEAN
Achinhoan Hd.
385 THE SLATE
Woodbank
446 CNOC MOY
BALLYCASTLE
Feochaig
Rubh'a'Mharaiche
Glen Breackerie
277 CNOC ODHAR
Conie Glen
Johnston's Pt.
Keprigan
North Carrine
Strone Glen
Polliwilline Bay
Macharioch
428
Southend
Carskiey
Cove Pt.
Brunerican Bay
MULL OF KINTYRE
Port Mean
Rubha Chlachan
Sheep I.
123
Sanda Island
KINTYRE
KILBRANNAN
0 1 2 3 miles
0 1 2 3 4 5 km

NORTH SANNOX FARM PARK
Sannox
Sannox Bay
MEALL NAN DAMH
Thundergay
573
NORTH
Pirnmill
Loch Tanna
859
Glen Sannox
Corrie
798
CIR MHÔR
721
BEINN BHARRAIN
874
BEINN TARSUINN
825
GOAT FELL
Imachar
ISLE
202
203
ARRAN
ARDROSSAN
BRODICK
BRODICK CASTLE
Glen Iorsa
Glen Rosa
Dougarie
228
OF
Machrie Water
ISLE OF ARRAN HERITAGE MUSEUM
Brodick Bay
Brodick
Strathwhillan
Auchagallon
Glenloig
Machrie Bay
B880
A'CHRUACH
512
Glen Cloy
A841
ARRAN
Clauchlands Pt.
Tormore
MACHRIE MOOR STANDING STONES
Blairbeg
Margnaheglish
Lamlash
Lamlash Bay
KING'S CAVE
503
Balmichael
CAMPBELTOWN (May-Sept Sat only)
Holy Island
Cordon
Torbeg
Shiskine
314
Drumadoon Pt.
Kingscross Pt.
Kingscross
Blackwaterfoot
Kilpatrick
KILPATRICK DUN
Drumadoon Bay
458
TIGHVEIN
Auchencairn
Knockenkelly
Whiting Bay
Sliddery Water
North Kiscadale
South Kiscadale
Largymore
Glenree
Brown Hd.
CARN BAN
Corriecravie
GLENASHDALE FALLS
Kilmory Water
Largybeg
Dippin
Sliddery
Lagg
Levencorroch
Dippin Head
Kilmory
Bennan
TORRYLINN CAIRN
Bennan Hd.
Kildonan
Sound of Pladda
Pladda
NR
NS
192
180
A
B
C
D
E
4
5
6
7

Seamill
Auchentiber
Dalgarven
AYRSHIRE MUSEUM OF COUNTRY LIFE & COSTUME
Kilwinning
Torranyard
Chapelhill
Dykesmains
Horse Isle
Benslie
EGLINTON
Cunninghamhead
CAMPBELTOWN
(May-Sept)
BRODICK
Ardrossan
NORTH AYRSHIRE MUSEUM
Stevenston
Saltcoats
Girdle Toll
Perceton
Irvine
GLASGOW VENNEL MUS
Springside
Knockentiber
SCOTTISH MARITIME MUSEUM
Fullarton
Dreghorn
Irvine Bay
Drybridge
Gatehead
NS
Dundonald
DUNDONALD CASTLE
Barassie
North Bay
Muirhead
Loans
Symington
Bogend
Troon
South Bay
ROYAL TROON
Lady Isle
Monkton
GLASGOW PRESTWICK
Prestwick
Woodfield
St Quivox
Newton on Ayr
Wallacetown
Whitletts
Ayr
Belston
Seafield
Masonhill
ROBERT BURNS BIRTHPLACE MUS
Belmont
Heads of Ayr
HEADS OF AYR FARM PARK
Doonfoot
MACLAURIN GALLERY & ROZELLE HOUSE
Alloway
Laigh Glengall
BURNS NATIONAL HERITAGE PARK
Fisherton
Dunure
287
Culroy
Minishant
Dalrymple
ELECTRIC BRAE
Culzean Bay
196
CULZEAN CASTLE
270
Whitefaulds
Maybole
CULZEAN
COLLEGIATE CHURCH
Maidenhead Bay
Kirkmichael
Aitkenhead
Maidens
TURNBERRY
Kirkoswald
CROSSRAGUEL ABBEY
Crosshill
Turnberry Bay
SOUTER JOHNNIE'S COTTAGE
Turnberry
BLAIRQUHAN
252
Brest Rocks
Ruglen
Townhead
Wallacetown
A737
A78
A738
A759
A77
A79
A719
A713
B714
B780
B778
B7080
B7081
B749
B743
B7024
B7034
B742
B7045
B7023
B741
204
191
182
180
181
0 1 2 3 miles
0 1 2 3 4 5 km

Stewarton
Laighmuir
Flow Moss
CORSE HILL
Carnduff
JOHN HASTIE MUS.
Strathaven
M77
Waterside
Fenwick
Laigh Fenwick
CRINS HILL
Whitelaw
Caldermill
Calder Water
Avon Water
Wallacegill Muir
Moscow
Onthank
Knockinlaw
DEAN CASTLE
Kilmarnock
Stobieside
Gilmourton
Drumclog
Greenholm
DICK INSTITUTE
Crookedholm
Hurlford
Galston
Newmilns
Darvel
A71
Rough Moss
MILL RIG
Glengavel Reservoir
Sornhill
Crossroads
Craigie
A76
WEDDER HILL
MIDDLEFIELD LAW
Cessnock Water
Auchmillan
Millburn
Mossgiel
BACHELOR'S CLUB
BURNS HOUSE MUSEUM
Mauchline
SORN CASTLE
Catrine
Sorn
Ayr
Netherwood
Muirkirk
Smallburn
Kames
Failford
AYR GORGE WOODLANDS
Haugh
Airds Moss
Crosshill
Stair
Lugar Water
Cronberry
Back Rogerton
Auchinleck
Lugar
Trabboch
Ochiltree
DUMFRIES HOUSE
Holmhead
Logan
Glenmuir
WARDLAW HILL
Glenmuirshaw
Coalhall
Hillhead
KEIR HARDIE STATUE
Cumnock
Netherthird
BAIRD INSTITUTE MUSEUM
Craigens
Dalblair
Drongan
Barbieston
Skares
Sinclairston
Hayhill
Littlemill
Rankinston
Water of Coyle
Pathhead
Mansfield
Connel Park
Bankglen
New Cumnock
Nith
KILMEIN HILL
Burnfoot
Burnside
Dalleagles
THE KNIPE
Afton Water
Waterside
SCOTTISH INDUSTRIAL RAILWAY CENTRE
BENBEOCH
Doon
Burnton
Dalmellington
ENOCH HILL
BLACKCRAIG HILL
Bogton Loch
Bellsbank
Afton Reservoir
Kello Water
Euchan Water

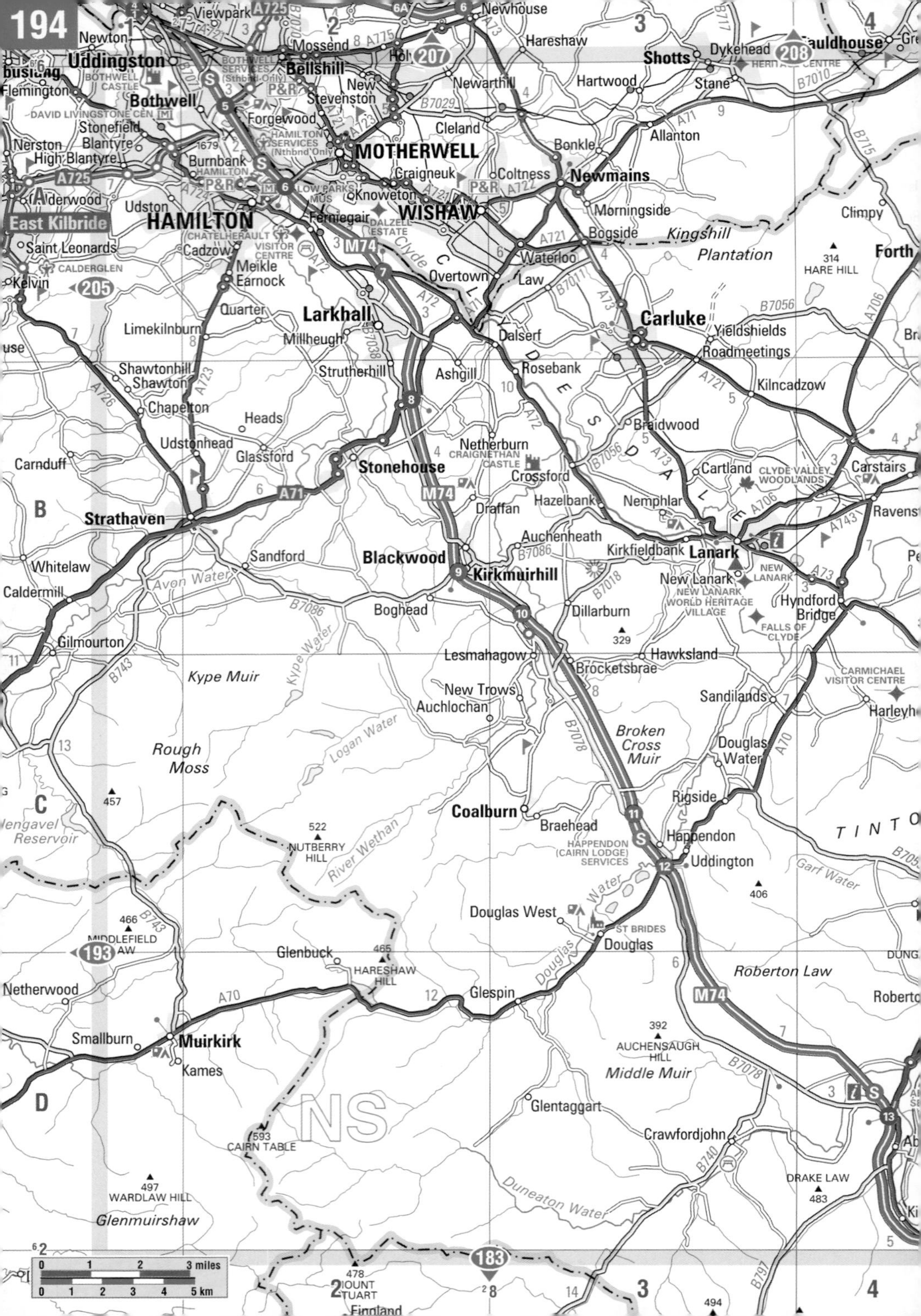
Viewpark
Newton
Uddingston
Bothwell Castle
Flemington
Bothwell
David Livingstone Cen.
Stonefield
Nerston
Blantyre
High Blantyre
Burnbank
Hamilton
A725
Alderwood
Udston
East Kilbride
HAMILTON
Chatelherault
Visitor Centre
Saint Leonards
Cadzow
Calderglen
Meikle
Earnock
Kelvin
205
Quarter
Limekilnburn
Shawtonhill
Shawton
Chapelton
Heads
Udstonhead
Glassford
Carnduff
Strathaven
Whitelaw
Caldermill
Gilmourton
Sandford
Avon Water
Kype Muir
Kype Water
Rough Moss
457
Glengavel Reservoir
466
Middlefield Law
193
Netherwood
Smallburn
Muirkirk
Kames
497
Wardlaw Hill
Glenmuirshaw
Bothwell Services (Sthbnd Only)
Hamilton Services (Nthbnd Only)
Bellshill
Mossend
New Stevenston
Forgewood
MOTHERWELL
Craigneuk
Low Parks Mus
Knowetop
Ferniegair
Dalzell Estate
M74
Clyde
Larkhall
Millheugh
Strutherhill
Stonehouse
Blackwood
Kirkmuirhill
Boghead
Lesmahagow
New Trows
Auchlochan
Logan Water
522
Nutberry Hill
River Wethan
Coalburn
Braehead
Glenbuck
465
Hareshaw Hill
A70
Glespin
NS
593
Cairn Table
478
Mount Stuart
Fingland
183
207
Newhouse
Hareshaw
Holytown
Newarthill
Cleland
Coltness
WISHAW
Overtown
Waterloo
Law
Dalserf
Ashgill
Rosebank
Netherburn
Craignethan Castle
Crossford
Draffan
Auchenheath
Clydesdale
Newmains
Morningside
Bogside
Bonkle
Hartwood
Shotts
Allanton
Dykehead
Stane
Heritage Centre
Fauldhouse
208
Kingshill Plantation
Climpy
314
Hare Hill
Forth
Carluke
Yieldshields
Roadmeetings
Kilncadzow
Braidwood
Cartland
Clyde Valley Woodlands
Carstairs
Hazelbank
Nemphlar
Kirkfieldbank
Lanark
New Lanark
New Lanark World Heritage Village
Hyndford Bridge
Falls of Clyde
Dillarburn
329
Hawksland
Brocketsbrae
Carmichael Visitor Centre
Sandilands
Harleyhead
Broken Cross Muir
Douglas Water
Rigside
Happendon
Happendon (Cairn Lodge) Services
Uddington
Tinto
406
Garf Water
Douglas West
St Brides
Douglas
Roberton Law
Roberton
392
Auchensaugh Hill
Middle Muir
Glentaggart
Crawfordjohn
Duneaton Water
Drake Law
483
494
0 1 2 3 miles
0 1 2 3 4 5 km

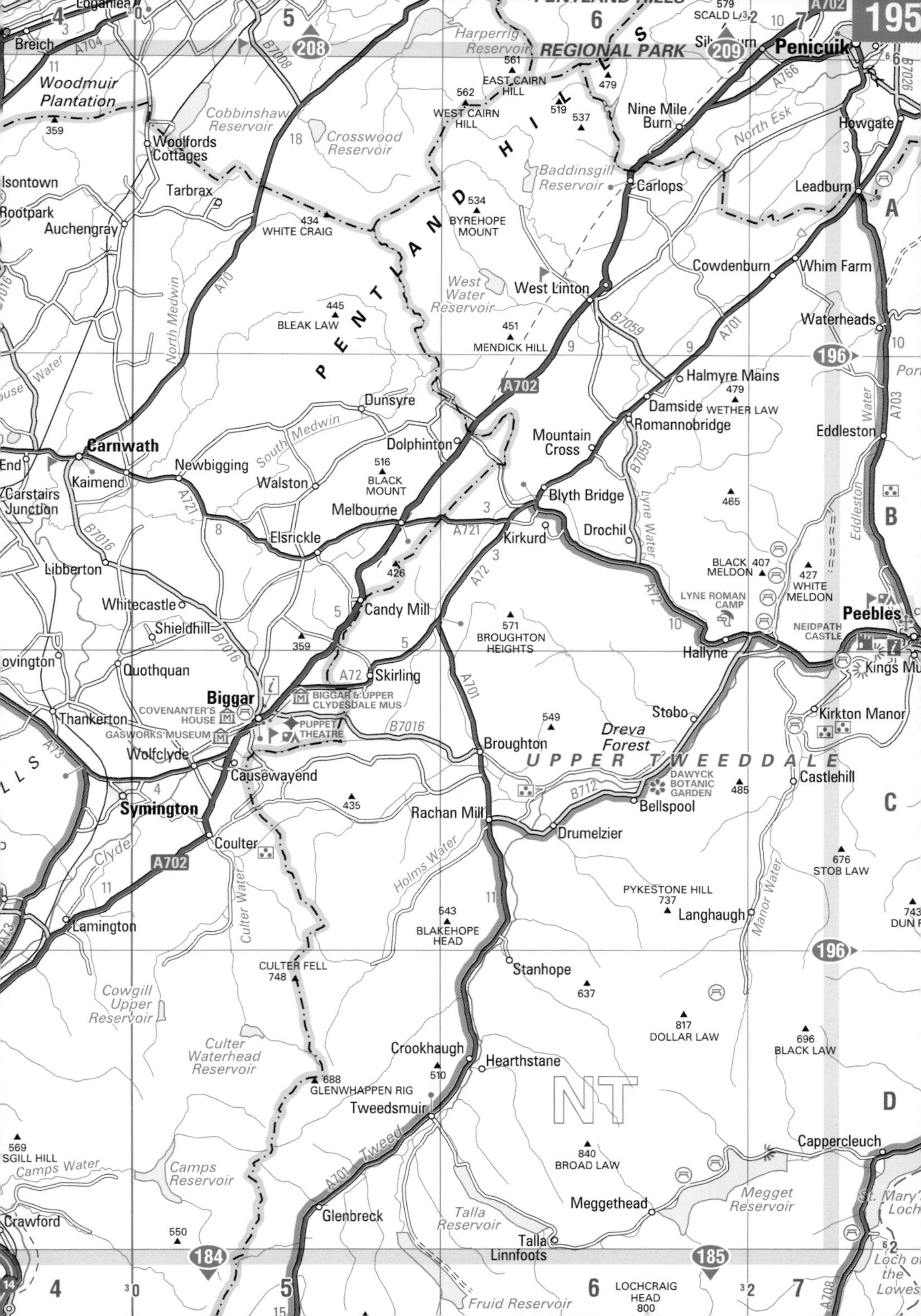
PENTLAND HILLS REGIONAL PARK
Penicuik
Loganlea
Breich
Woodmuir Plantation
Harperrig Reservoir
Cobbinshaw Reservoir
Crosswood Reservoir
Woolfords Cottages
Tarbrax
Rootpark
Auchengray
EAST CAIRN HILL
WEST CAIRN HILL
SCALD LAW
Nine Mile Burn
Howgate
North Esk
Baddinsgill Reservoir
Carlops
Leadburn
WHITE CRAIG
BYREHOPE MOUNT
West Water Reservoir
West Linton
Cowdenburn
Whim Farm
BLEAK LAW
MENDICK HILL
Waterheads
Halmyre Mains
WETHER LAW
Damside
Romannobridge
Dunsyre
Dolphinton
Mountain Cross
Eddleston
Carnwath
Kaimend
Newbigging
Walston
BLACK MOUNT
Blyth Bridge
Carstairs Junction
Melbourne
Elsrickle
Kirkurd
Drochil
Libberton
BLACK MELDON
WHITE MELDON
LYNE ROMAN CAMP
Whitecastle
Candy Mill
Shieldhill
BROUGHTON HEIGHTS
Peebles
NEIDPATH CASTLE
Hallyne
Quothquan
Skirling
Biggar
BIGGAR & UPPER CLYDESDALE MUS
COVENANTER'S HOUSE
Thankerton
PUPPET THEATRE
GASWORKS MUSEUM
Stobo
Kirkton Manor
Broughton
Dreva Forest
Wolfclyde
UPPER TWEEDDALE
Causewayend
DAWYCK BOTANIC GARDEN
Castlehill
Symington
Rachan Mill
Bellspool
Drumelzier
Coulter
Clyde
STOB LAW
Holms Water
PYKESTONE HILL
Langhaugh
Manor Water
Culter Water
Lamington
BLAKEHOPE HEAD
Stanhope
CULTER FELL
Cowgill Upper Reservoir
DOLLAR LAW
BLACK LAW
Culter Waterhead Reservoir
Crookhaugh
Hearthstane
GLENWHAPPEN RIG
Tweedsmuir
NT
SGILL HILL
Cappercleuch
Camps Water
Camps Reservoir
BROAD LAW
Megget Reservoir
St. Mary's Loch
Crawford
Glenbreck
Meggethead
Talla Reservoir
Talla Linnfoots
Loch of the Lowes
LOCHCRAIG HEAD
Fruid Reservoir
Kings Muir
Tweed
A702
A701
A72
A721
A703
A70
A73
A766
A704
A708
B7016
B7059
B712
B7008
B7026
208
209
196
184
185

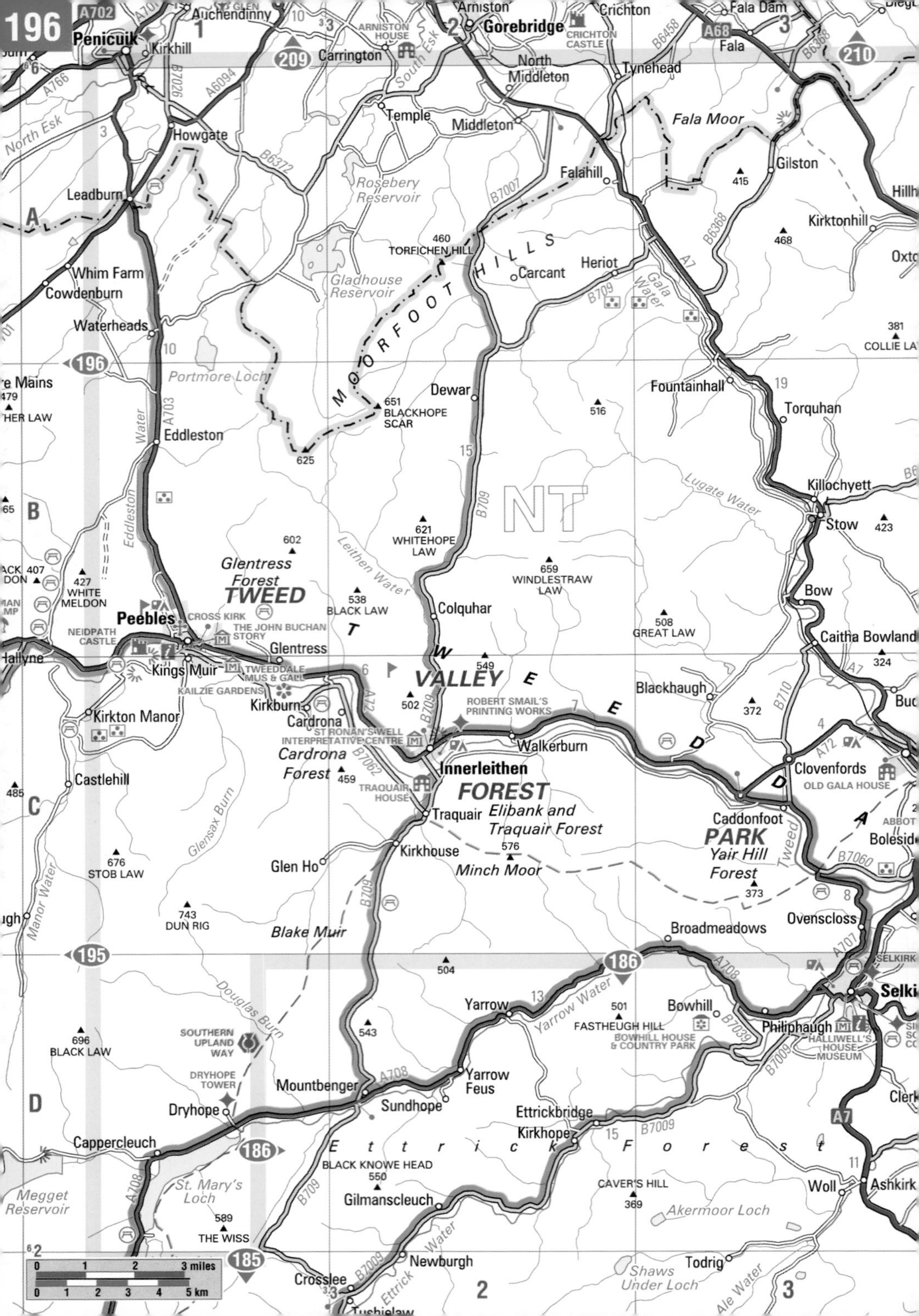
Penicuik
Kirkhill
Auchendinny
Carrington
Arniston House
Arniston
Gorebridge
Crichton
Crichton Castle
Fala Dam
Fala
North Middleton
Tynehead
Temple
Middleton
Howgate
North Esk
Fala Moor
Gilston
Leadburn
Rosebery Reservoir
Falahill
Kirktonhill
Whim Farm
Cowdenburn
460
Torfichen Hill
Moorfoot Hills
Carcant
Heriot
Gladhouse Reservoir
Gala Water
Waterheads
Portmore Loch
381
Collie Law
Dewar
Fountainhall
Torquhan
651
Blackhope Scar
516
Eddleston
625
Eddleston Water
Lugate Water
Killochyett
NT
Stow
423
621
Whitehope Law
602
Glentress Forest
Tweed
659
Windlestraw Law
Leithen Water
427
White Meldon
538
Black Law
Colquhar
Bow
508
Great Law
Peebles
Cross Kirk
Neidpath Castle
The John Buchan Story
Glentress
Caitha Bowland
Tweed Valley
Kings Muir
Tweeddale Mus & Gall
Kailzie Gardens
549
324
Blackhaugh
Kirkburn
Cardrona
502
Robert Smail's Printing Works
372
Kirkton Manor
St Ronan's Well Interpretative Centre
Walkerburn
Cardrona Forest
459
Innerleithen
Clovenfords
Old Gala House
Castlehill
Traquair House
Forest
Traquair
Elibank and Traquair Forest
Caddonfoot
Tweed Forest Park
Yair Hill Forest
Boleside
485
Glensax Burn
676
Stob Law
Kirkhouse
576
Minch Moor
Glen Ho
373
Manor Water
743
Dun Rig
Blake Muir
Broadmeadows
Ovenscloss
504
Selkirk
Yarrow
Yarrow Water
501
Fastheugh Hill
Bowhill
Bowhill House & Country Park
Philiphaugh
Halliwell's House Museum
696
Black Law
Southern Upland Way
Douglas Burn
543
Dryhope Tower
Mountbenger
Yarrow Feus
Sundhope
Dryhope
Ettrickbridge
Kirkhope
Cappercleuch
Ettrick Forest
Black Knowe Head
550
St. Mary's Loch
Caver's Hill
369
Megget Reservoir
Gilmanscleuch
Akermoor Loch
Woll
Ashkirk
589
The Wiss
Ettrick Water
Newburgh
Todrig
Crosslee
Shaws Under Loch
Ale Water
Tushielaw
0 1 2 3 miles
0 1 2 3 4 5 km
209
210
196
195
186
185
A702
A703
A7
A72
A68
A708
B709
B7007
B6372
A6094
B7026
A766
B6368
B7009
B7062
B7060
B710
A707
B6458

527
LAMMER LAW
MEIKLE SAYS LAW
Hopes Reservoir
379
CRANSHAWS HILL
Cranshaws
Whiteadder Water
Abbey St. Bathans
Ellemford
210
211
EDINSHALL BROCH
509
495
HUNT LAW
Dye Water
L A M M E R M U I R
Longformacus
Watch Water Reservoir
Soonhope Burn
448
HOG'S LAW
398
DIRRINGTON GREAT LAW
Preston
B6355
B6365
A6112
JIM CLARK ROOM
Buxley
Duns
Clockmill
Cheeklaw
Addinston
L A U D E R D A L E
A697
Leader Water
389
A68
Wedderlie
Choicelee
Gavinton
A6105
B6456
285
Westruther
Polwarth
Blythe
Thornydykes
Halliburton
Fogo
Boge
Lauder
Whiteburn
Sisterpath
Fogorig
Thirlestane
Houndslow
Blackadder Water
B6460
Swinton
Boon
A6089
Eden Water
Greenlaw
198
Leitholm
Nether Blainslie
Legerwood
Huntlywood
272
GREEN KNOWE TOWER
Gordon
Middlethird
Easter Howlaws
Lambden
Orange Lane
West Morriston
Hume
HUME CASTLE
Eccles
SOUTHERN UPLAND WAY
Fans
Falsidehill
245
223
Langshaw
B6397
B6364
B6461
Birgham
MELLERSTAIN HOUSE
Stichill
A698
Carham
Earlston
Galashiels
Nenthorn
Ednam
Tweed
281
B6356
Smailholm
B6350
Hadden
EILDON AND LEADERFOOT
Redpath
Brotherstone
Kerchesters
Gattonside
ABBEY
B6360
Sprouston
Newstead
SMAILHOLM TOWER
KELSO MUS
FLOORS CASTLE
Kelso
Darnick
A6091
KELSO ABBEY
Windywalls
Holefield
Melrose
PRIORWOOD GDNS
Bemersyde
Clintmains
Maxwellheugh
Lempitlaw
B6404
Manorhill
Trows
ROXBURGH CASTLE
422
THE THREE HILLS ROMAN HERITAGE CTR
Dryburgh
ABBEY
Eildon Hills
MERTOUN GDNS
Hoselaw
B6359
Newtown St. Boswells
A699
Roxburgh
Blakelaw
St. Boswells
B6396
323
Bowden
B6398
Rutherford
Heiton
B6352
WHITLAW MOSSES
Maxton
187
Muirhouselaw
B6436
B6453
Longnewton
Frogden
282
Midlem
Kalemouth
WATERLOO MONUMENT
TEVIOT SMOKERY & WATERGARDENS
Kale Water
DERE STREET
Crookhouse
Linton
Belses
Nisbet
Eckford
B6401
B6400
Lilliesleaf
Bloomfield
Ancrum
HARESTANES COUNTRYSIDE VISITOR CENTRE
Crailing
Morebattle
Greenhouse
Bonjedward
Cessford
Cliftoncote
Chesters
HOWNAM LAW
449
Crailinghall
Lanton
Whitton
276
Teviot
MARY QUEEN OF SCOTS HOUSE
Jedburgh
Hownam Mains
Hassendean
Minto
Newton
JEDBURGH ABBEY
Howden
B6405
Hownam
Horsleyhill
JEDBURGH CASTLE JAIL & MUSEUM
B6358
338
Hundalee
Oxnam
Clarilaw

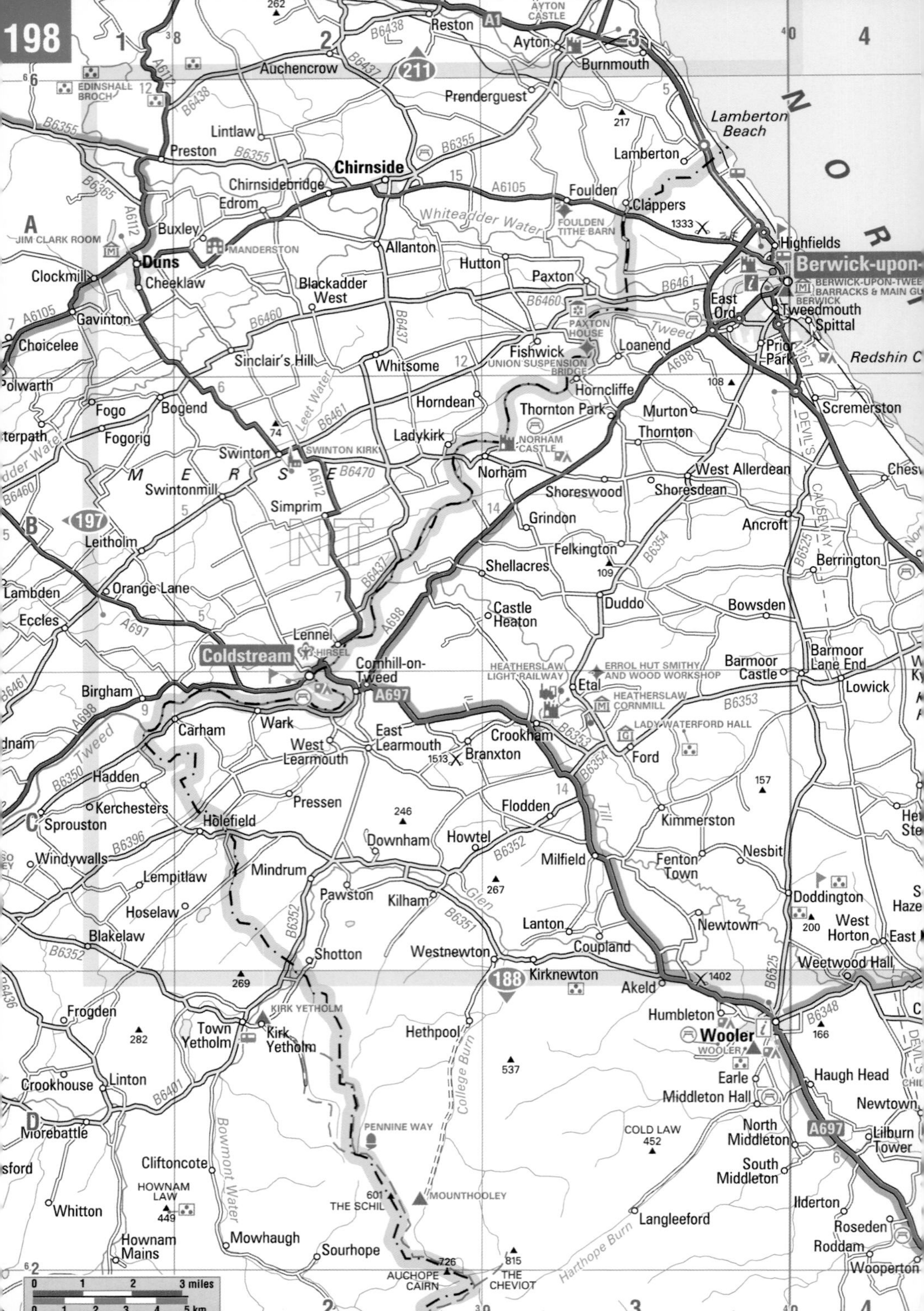

Reston
Ayton
AYTON CASTLE
Burnmouth
Auchencrow
Prenderguest
EDINSHALL BROCH
Lamberton Beach
Lamberton
Lintlaw
Preston
Chirnside
Chirnsidebridge
Edrom
Foulden
Clappers
Whiteadder Water
FOULDEN TITHE BARN
JIM CLARK ROOM
Buxley
MANDERSTON
Allanton
Highfields
Berwick-upon-
Duns
Clockmill
Cheeklaw
Hutton
Paxton
Blackadder West
BERWICK-UPON-TWEED BARRACKS & MAIN GU
BERWICK
East Ord
Tweedmouth
Spittal
Gavinton
Choicelee
PAXTON HOUSE
Tweed
Loanend
Fishwick
Sinclair's Hill
Whitsome
UNION SUSPENSION BRIDGE
Prior Park
Redshin C
Polwarth
Horncliffe
Horndean
Thornton Park
Murton
Scremerston
Fogo
Bogend
Leet Water
Ladykirk
Thornton
Fogorig
NORHAM CASTLE
Swinton
SWINTON KIRK
Norham
West Allerdean
Shoreswood
Shoresdean
M E R S E
Swintonmill
Simprim
Grindon
Ancroft
NT
Leitholm
Felkington
Berrington
Shellacres
Lambden
Orange Lane
Duddo
Bowsden
Castle Heaton
Eccles
Lennel
Coldstream
HIRSEL
HEATHERSLAW LIGHT RAILWAY
ERROL HUT SMITHY AND WOOD WORKSHOP
Barmoor Castle
Barmoor Lane End
Lowick
Cornhill-on-Tweed
Etal
Birgham
HEATHERSLAW CORNMILL
Carham
Wark
LADY WATERFORD HALL
East Learmouth
Crookham
West Learmouth
Branxton
Ford
Hadden
Kerchesters
Sprouston
Holefield
Pressen
Flodden
Till
Kimmerston
Downham
Howtel
Windywalls
Milfield
Nesbit
Fenton Town
Lempitlaw
Mindrum
Pawston
Kilham
Glen
Doddington
Hoselaw
Lanton
Newtown
West Horton
East
Blakelaw
Shotton
Westnewton
Coupland
Weetwood Hall
Kirknewton
Akeld
Frogden
KIRK YETHOLM
Humbleton
Town Yetholm
Kirk Yetholm
Hethpool
Wooler
WOOLER
College Burn
Earle
Haugh Head
Crookhouse
Linton
Middleton Hall
Newtown
Morebattle
PENNINE WAY
COLD LAW
North Middleton
Lilburn Tower
Bowmont Water
Cliftoncote
South Middleton
HOWNAM LAW
THE SCHIL
MOUNTHOOLEY
Whitton
Ilderton
Langleeford
Roseden
Mowhaugh
Harthope Burn
Hownam Mains
Sourhope
Roddam
Wooperton
AUCHOPE CAIRN
THE CHEVIOT
0 1 2 3 miles
0 1 2 3 4 5 km

4
5
6
7
NU
NORTHUMBERLAND
COAST
Goswick
Emmanuel Hd.
Holy Island (Lindisfarne)
LINDISFARNE
LINDISFARNE CASTLE
Beal
Causeway
Holy Island
Holy Island Sands
Castle Pt.
HERITAGE CENTRE
LINDISFARNE PRIORY
Fenham
Guile Pt.
Fenwick
East Kyloe
Buckton
Farne Islands
Staple Sound
Elwick
Ross
Budle Bay
Detchant
BAMBURGH CASTLE
FARNE ISLANDS
Middleton
Budle
Inner Sound
Bamburgh
Belford
Easington
Waren Mill
B1340
B1342
Burton
Spindlestone
Glororum
B6349
Mousen
Bradford
Seahouses
B1341
Elford
North Sunderland
Bellshill
Warenton
Adderstone
ADDERSTONE
Lucker
B6348
Newham Hall
Beadnell
Swinhoe
Warenford
Benthall
Greendikes
Newham
Fleetham
A1
Newstead
Beadnell Bay
Rosebrough
Chathill
Chillingham
WILD CATTLE OF CHILLINGHAM
Ellingham
High Newton-by-the-Sea
Preston
B1340
Brunton
PRESTON TOWER
Low Newton-by-the-Sea
Hepburn
Brownyside
Christon Bank
Embleton Bay
North Charlton
Embleton
B6347
Dunstan Steads
Castle Point
B1339
DUNSTANBURGH CASTLE
Old Bewick
West Ditchburn
South Charlton
B6346
Harehope
Rock
Craster
New Bewick
Eglingham
B6347
B6341
Dunstan
Rennington
189
169
A
B
C
D

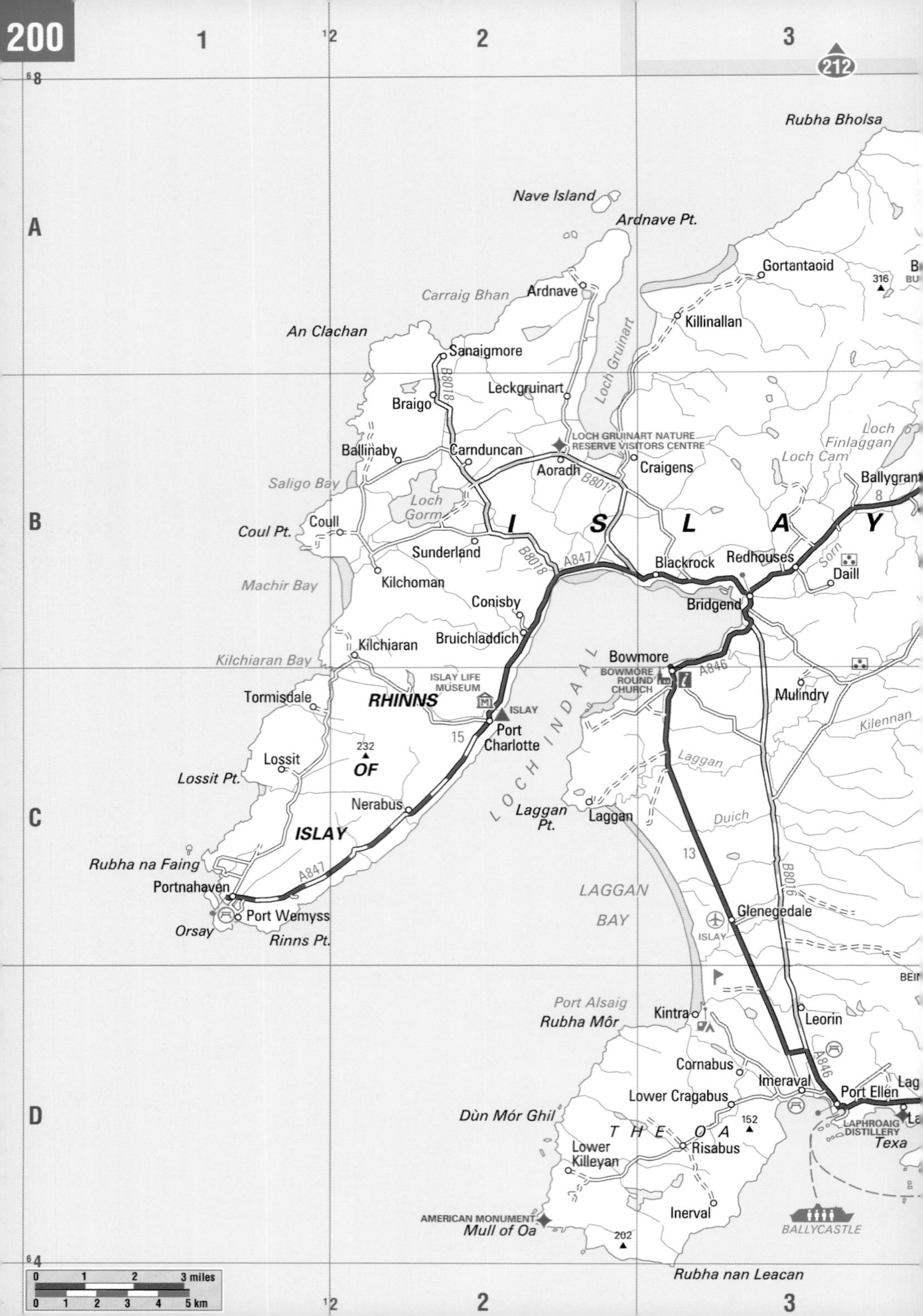

1
2
3
A
B
C
D
212
Rubha Bholsa
Nave Island
Ardnave Pt.
Gortantaoid
316
Carraig Bhan
Ardnave
Killinallan
An Clachan
Sanaigmore
Loch Gruinart
B8018
Leckgruinart
Braigo
LOCH GRUINART NATURE RESERVE VISITORS CENTRE
Loch Finlaggan
Ballinaby
Carnduncan
Loch Cam
Aoradh
Craigens
Saligo Bay
B8017
Ballygrant
Loch Gorm
I S L A Y
Coull
Coul Pt.
Sunderland
B8018
A847
Blackrock
Redhouses
Daill
Machir Bay
Kilchoman
Bridgend
Conisby
Bruichladdich
Kilchiaran
Bowmore
Kilchiaran Bay
BOWMORE ROUND CHURCH
A846
ISLAY LIFE MUSEUM
Mulindry
Tormisdale
RHINNS
ISLAY
Port Charlotte
Kilennan
232
Lossit
OF
LOCH INDAAL
Laggan
Lossit Pt.
Nerabus
Laggan Pt.
Laggan
Duich
ISLAY
Rubha na Faing
13
A847
B8016
Portnahaven
LAGGAN BAY
Glenegedale
Port Wemyss
Orsay
Rinns Pt.
ISLAY
Port Alsaig
Kintra
Leorin
Rubha Môr
A846
Cornabus
Imeraval
Lower Cragabus
Port Ellen
Dùn Mór Ghil
152
THE OA
LAPHROAIG DISTILLERY
Lower Killeyan
Risabus
Texa
Inerval
AMERICAN MONUMENT
Mull of Oa
BALLYCASTLE
202
Rubha nan Leacan
0 1 2 3 miles
0 1 2 3 4 5 km

COLONSAY
4
5
6
Loch Tarbert
Tarbert
212
213
Keillmore
Rubha Lang-aoinidh
Rubha a'Mhail
Loch na Cille
Island
Lagg
439
Loch an Aircill
Loch Lesgamaill
JURA
Eilean Mòr
CHAPEL
ST CORMAC'S CHAPEL
Kilmory Bay
785
755
PAPS OF JURA
Loch a Chnuic Bhric
A846
15
SOUND OF JURA
SOUND OF ISLAY
JURA FOREST
Corran
An Dùnan
Knockrome
Lowlandman's Bay
Leargybreck
Pt. of Knap
Gleann Astaile
Loch na Mile
Caol Ila
DISTILLERY
Port Askaig
Feolin Ferry
561
202
Keills
Keils
Craighouse
Small Isles
ISLE OF JURA DISTILLERY
Miller's Bay
Loch Ballygrant
Gleann Ullibh
342
BRAT BHEINN
NR
B
Kilberry Hd.
SCULPTURED STONES
8
Cabrach
267
BEINN DUBH
Rubha na Tràille
Am Fraoch Eilean
Brosdale I.
McArthur's Hd.
KENNACRAIG
Carraig Mhór
491
BEINN BHEIGEIR
Ardtalla
C
Claggain Bay
Eilean Garbh
West Tarbert Bay
East Tarbert Bay
Tarbert
Kintour
Ardmore Pt.
KILDALTON CHURCH AND CROSSES
Gigha Island
100
Druimyeon More
Eilean Craobhach
Eilean a'Chuirn
KENNACRAIG
Ardminish
Ardminish Bay
SOUND OF GIGHA
Eilean Bhride
ACHAMORE GARDENS
Ardbeg
Eilean Imersay
GAVULIN DISTILLERY
Tayinloan
D
Gigalum Island
Cara Island
Beachar
A83
Muasdale
190
4
5
6

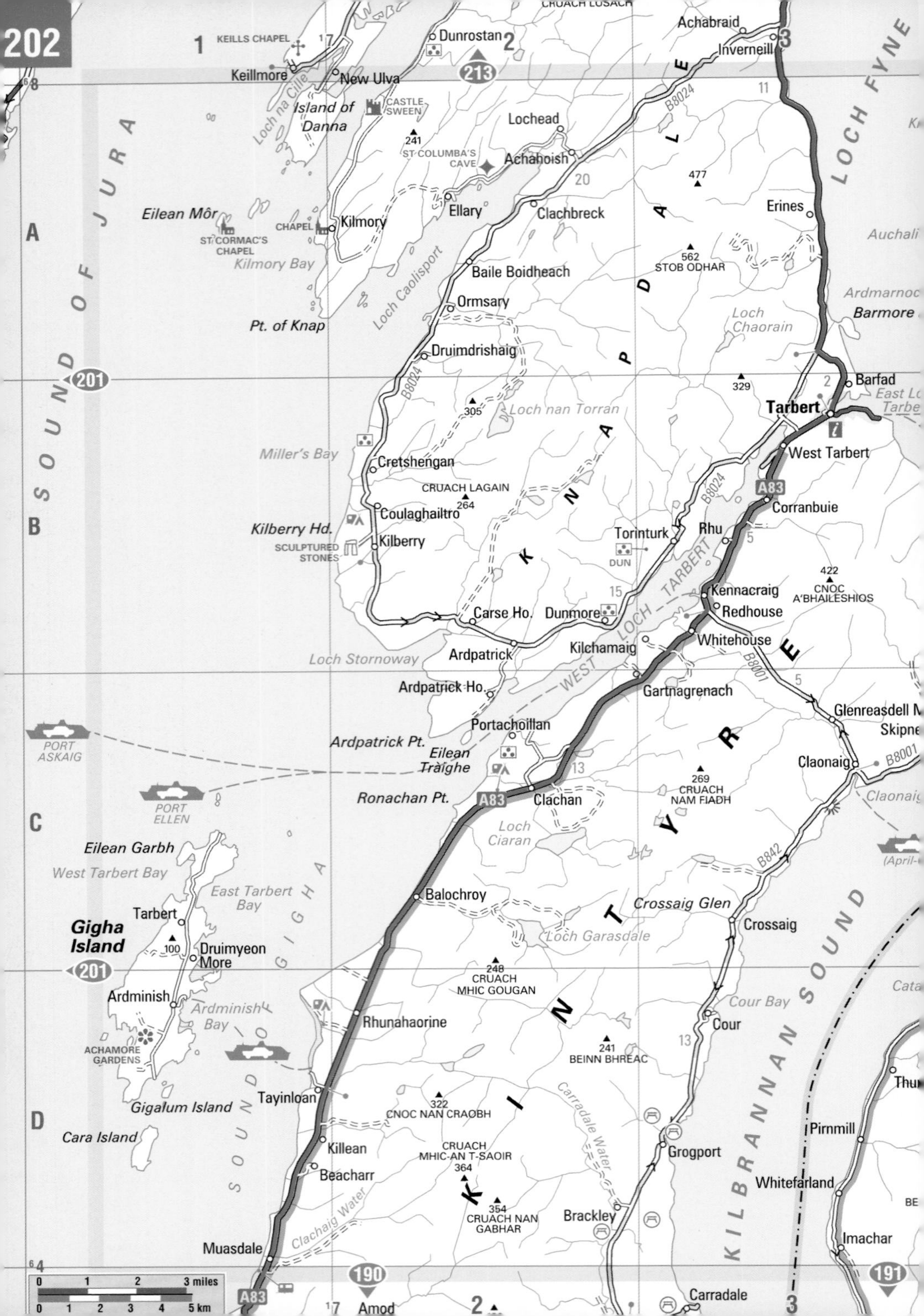
CRUACH LUSACH
KEILLS CHAPEL
Dunrostan
Achabraid
Inverneill
Keillmore
New Ulva
213
Loch na Cille
Island of Danna
CASTLE SWEEN
Lochead
241
ST COLUMBA'S CAVE
Achahoish
LOCH FYNE
SOUND OF JURA
Eilean Mòr
ST CORMAC'S CHAPEL
CHAPEL
Kilmory
Ellary
Clachbreck
477
Erines
Kilmory Bay
Loch Caolisport
562
STOB ODHAR
Baile Boidheach
Auchali
Ardmarnoc
Barmore
Ormsary
Pt. of Knap
Loch Chaorain
Druimdrishaig
B8024
B8024
201
329
Barfad
East Lo Tarbe
Tarbert
KNAPDALE
305
Loch nan Torran
Miller's Bay
West Tarbert
Cretshengan
CRUACH LAGAIN
264
A83
Corranbuie
Coulaghailtro
Kilberry Hd.
Torinturk
Rhu
SCULPTURED STONES
Kilberry
DUN
422
CNOC A'BHAILESHIOS
Kennacraig
Redhouse
WEST LOCH TARBERT
Carse Ho.
Dunmore
Whitehouse
Loch Stornoway
Ardpatrick
Kilchamaig
B8001
Ardpatrick Ho.
Gartnagrenach
Glenreasdell M
Skipne
PORT ASKAIG
Portachoillan
Ardpatrick Pt.
Eilean Traighe
KINTYRE
269
CRUACH NAM FIADH
Claonaig
B8001
PORT ELLEN
Ronachan Pt.
A83
Clachan
Claonaig
Loch Ciaran
Eilean Garbh
West Tarbert Bay
B842
(April–
East Tarbert Bay
Balochroy
Crossaig Glen
Tarbert
Gigha Island
100
Druimyeon More
Crossaig
Loch Garasdale
201
248
CRUACH MHIC GOUGAN
Ardminish
Ardminish Bay
SOUND OF GIGHA
Cour Bay
Cour
Rhunahaorine
ACHAMORE GARDENS
241
BEINN BHREAC
KILBRANNAN SOUND
Carradale Water
Tayinloan
Gigalum Island
322
CNOC NAN CRAOBH
Cara Island
Killean
CRUACH MHIC-AN T-SAOIR
364
Grogport
Pirnmill
Beacharr
Whitefarland
354
CRUACH NAN GABHAR
Brackley
Clachaig Water
Muasdale
Imachar
190
191
A83
Amod
Carradale
Thu
0 1 2 3 miles
0 1 2 3 4 5 km

Auchnaha
Kilfinan
Drum
Melldalloch
Port Driseach
Tighnabruaich
Auchenlochan
Kames
Millhouse
Portavadie
Blair's Ferry
Asgog Loch
Asgog Bay
Kilbride Bay
Ardlamont Ho.
Ardlamont Pt.
NR
NS
Rubha Leathan
Auchenbreck
CRUACH NAN CAORACH
BEINN BHREAC
KYLES OF BUTE
Loch Riddon
Ardentraive
Colintraive
Algaltraig
ISLAND OF BUTE
Glen More
WINDY HILL
St Colmac
Ettrick Bay
Kames B.
Port Bannatyne
Rothesay Bay
ROTHESAY CASTLE
Rothesay
Craigmore
ARDENCRAIG GARDENS
Montford
VICTORIAN FERNERY
Ascog
Straad
Loch Fad
Kerrycroy
Scoulag
MOUNT STUART HOUSE AND GARDEN
Loch Quien
Scalpsie
Inchmarnock
Ardscalpsie Pt.
Scalpsie Bay
Stravanan Bay
Kingarth
Kilchattan Bay
ST BLANE'S CHAPEL
Garroch Hd.
SOUND OF BUTE
SKIPNESS CASTLE
Skipness Pt.
Skipness Bay
(Oct-Mar)
Cock of Arran
Dalinlongart
Clachaig
Glen Kin
Sandbank
Holy Loch
CRUACH NAN CAPULL
Glenstriven
LOCH STRIVEN
BEINN BHREAC
BLACK CRAIG
Inverchaolain
Glen Fyne
CORLARACH HILL
Corlarach Forest
Port Lamont
Ardyne Pt.
Toward
Toward Pt.
Newton Park
Innellan
Bullwood
Dunoon
Kirn
Hunter's Q
Ardnadam
ST JOHN'S CHURCH
HIGHLAND MARY'S STATUE
Cloch Pt.
Lunderston Bay
Wemyss Bay
Skelmorlie
Largs Bay
Largs
Tomont End
Great Cumbrae Island
CHRISTIAN HERITAGE MUSEUM
Downcraig Ferry
Millport
MUSEUM OF THE CUMBRAES
Fairlie Roads
The Tan
FIRTH OF CLYDE
HUNTERSTON POWER STATION VISITOR CENTRE
Little Cumbrae Island
Thirdpart
Portencross
Farland Hd.
West Kilbride
Seamill
Horse Isle
LOCHRANZA CASTLE
Lochranza
Catacol
ISLE OF ARRAN DISTILLERY
Millstone Pt.
Sannox
Sannox Bay
Glen Sannox
Corrie
Loch Tanna
CIR MHÒR
BEINN TARSUINN
GOAT FELL
NORTH ARRAN
NORTH OF ARRAN
SLE
ARRAN
BRODICK
A815
A880
A885
A886
A8003
B8000
B875
A844
B878
B881
A78
B896
B899
A841
214
204
191
192

Helensburgh
Dunoon
Gourock
Greenock
PORT GLASGOW
ALEXANDRIA
Kilmacolm
Bridge of Weir
Wemyss Bay
Skelmorlie
Largs
Great Cumbrae Island
Millport
Fairlie
Lochwinnoch
Kilbirnie
Beith
Dalry
West Kilbride
Kilwinning
Ardrossan
Saltcoats
Stevenston
Irvine
CLYDE-MUIRSHIEL REGIONAL PARK
FIRTH OF CLYDE
CUNNINGHAME
Little Cumbrae Island
Sandbank
Innellan
Kilcreggan
Inverkip
Toward
Rothesay
Kingarth
Kilchattan Bay
Ascog
Montford
Craigmore
Portencross
Seamill
Glengarnock
Longbar
Dalgarven
Torranyard
0 1 2 3 miles
0 1 2 3 4 5 km

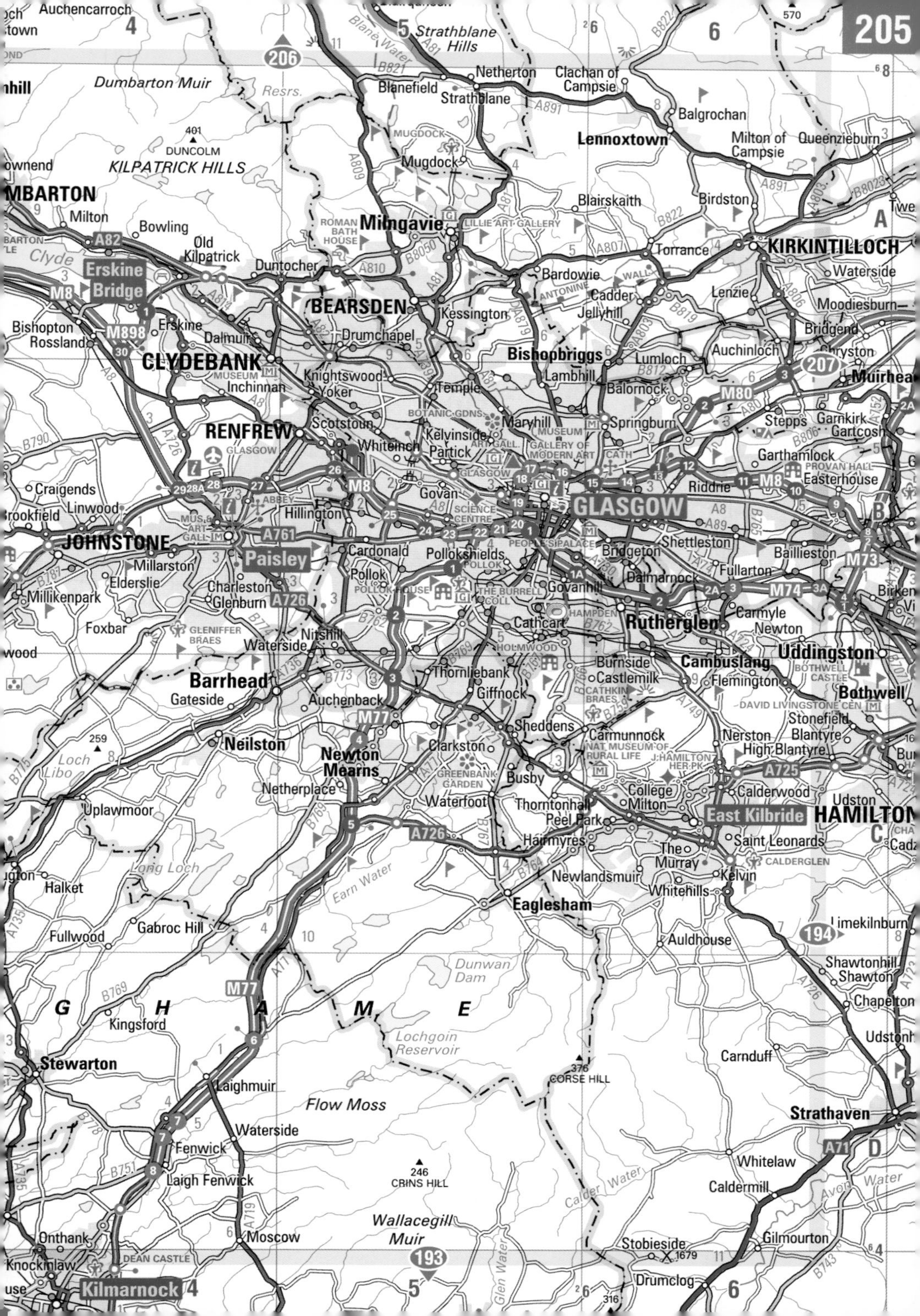

Auchencarroch
Strathblane Hills
Blane Water
Netherton
Clachan of Campsie
Blanefield
Strathblane
Dumbarton Muir
Resrs.
Balgrochan
Lennoxtown
Milton of Campsie
Queenzieburn
DUNCOLM
KILPATRICK HILLS
MUGDOCK
Mugdock
DUMBARTON
Milton
Bowling
Old Kilpatrick
Milngavie
ROMAN BATH HOUSE
LILLIE ART GALLERY
Blairskaith
Birdston
KIRKINTILLOCH
Torrance
Clyde
Erskine Bridge
Duntocher
Bardowie
Waterside
ANTONINE WALL
Cadder
Lenzie
BEARSDEN
Kessington
Jellyhill
Moodiesburn
Bishopton
Rossland
Erskine
Dalmuir
Drumchapel
Bridgend
CLYDEBANK
Bishopbriggs
Lumloch
Auchinloch
Chryston
MUSEUM
Inchinnan
Knightswood
Yoker
Temple
Lambhill
Balornock
Muirhead
BOTANIC GDNS.
Maryhill
Springburn
Stepps
Garnkirk
Gartcosh
RENFREW
Scotstoun
Whiteinch
Kelvinside
Partick
ART GALL.
GALLERY OF MODERN ART
CATH
GLASGOW
Garthamlock
PROVAN HALL
Easterhouse
Craigends
Linwood
ABBEY
Hillington
Govan
SCIENCE CENTRE
Riddrie
Brookfield
JOHNSTONE
MUS.& ART GALL.
PEOPLE'S PALACE
Shettleston
Baillieston
Millarston
Paisley
Cardonald
Pollokshields
POLLOK
Bridgeton
Dalmarnock
Fullarton
Elderslie
Charleston
Pollok
POLLOK HOUSE
THE BURRELL COLL
Govanhill
Millikenpark
Glenburn
HAMPDEN
Rutherglen
Carmyle
Newton
Foxbar
GLENIFFER BRAES
Cathcart
Nitshill
Waterside
HOLMWOOD
Uddingston
BOTHWELL CASTLE
Barrhead
Gateside
Thornliebank
Burnside
Castlemilk
Cambuslang
Flemington
Bothwell
Auchenback
Giffnock
CATHKIN BRAES
DAVID LIVINGSTONE CEN.
Stonefield
Neilston
Sheddens
Carmunnock
Nerston
Blantyre
Loch Libo
Newton Mearns
Clarkston
NAT. MUSEUM OF RURAL LIFE
J. HAMILTON HER. PK
High Blantyre
GREENBANK GARDEN
Busby
Netherplace
College Milton
Calderwood
Uplawmoor
Waterfoot
Thorntonhall
Peel Park
East Kilbride
HAMILTON
Udston
Hairmyres
Saint Leonards
The Murray
CALDERGLEN
Long Loch
Earn Water
Halket
Newlandsmuir
Kelvin
Whitehills
Eaglesham
Fullwood
Gabroc Hill
Auldhouse
Limekilnburn
Dunwan Dam
Shawtonhill
Shawton
G H A M E
Kingsford
Chapelton
Lochgoin Reservoir
Udston
Stewarton
Carnduff
CORSE HILL
Laighmuir
Flow Moss
Strathaven
Waterside
Fenwick
Whitelaw
CRINS HILL
Laigh Fenwick
Calder Water
Caldermill
Avon Water
Wallacegill Muir
Onthank
Moscow
Gilmourton
Stobieside
Knockinlaw
DEAN CASTLE
Glen Water
Drumclog
Kilmarnock

216
217
215
204
205

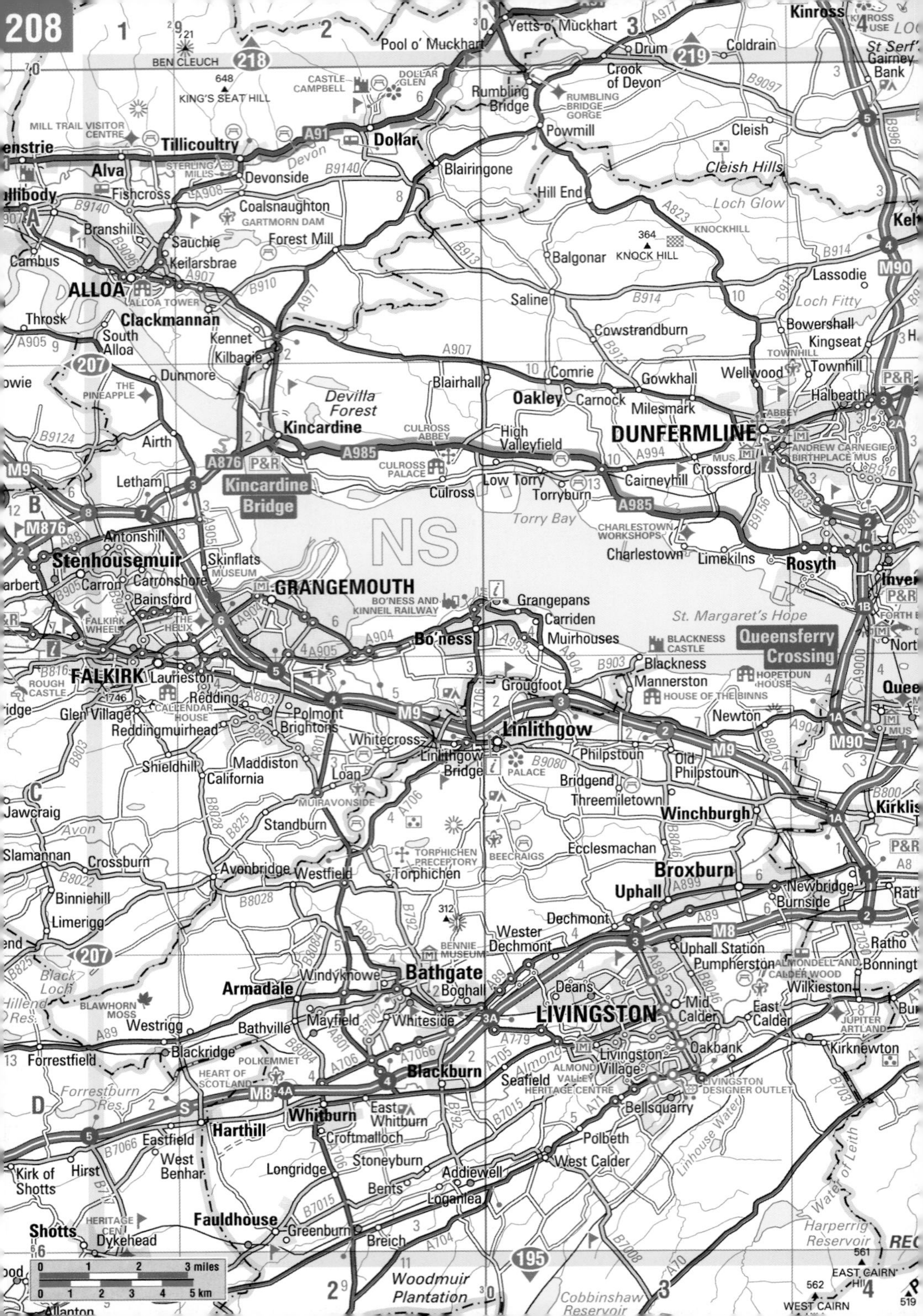
BEN CLEUCH
721
648
KING'S SEAT HILL
218
Pool o' Muckhart
Yetts o' Muckhart
Drum
219
Coldrain
Kinross
KINROSS HOUSE
St Serf's
Gairney Bank
Crook of Devon
Rumbling Bridge
RUMBLING BRIDGE GORGE
CASTLE CAMPBELL
DOLLAR GLEN
MILL TRAIL VISITOR CENTRE
Tillicoultry
Dollar
Powmill
Cleish
Cleish Hills
Alva
STERLING MILLS
Devonside
Blairingone
Hill End
Fishcross
Coalsnaughton
GARTMORN DAM
Loch Glow
KNOCKHILL
Branshill
Sauchie
Forest Mill
364
KNOCK HILL
Balgonar
Cambus
Keilarsbrae
ALLOA
ALLOA TOWER
Lassodie
Loch Fitty
Saline
Throsk
Clackmannan
South Alloa
Kennet
Kilbagie
Cowstrandburn
Bowershall
Kingseat
TOWNHILL
Townhill
207
Dunmore
THE PINEAPPLE
Blairhall
Comrie
Gowkhall
Wellwood
Halbeath
Oakley
Carnock
Milesmark
Devilla Forest
Kincardine
CULROSS ABBEY
High Valleyfield
DUNFERMLINE
ABBEY
ANDREW CARNEGIE BIRTHPLACE MUS
Airth
CULROSS PALACE
MUS.
Crossford
Letham
Kincardine Bridge
Culross
Low Torry
Torryburn
Cairneyhill
Torry Bay
NS
CHARLESTOWN WORKSHOPS
Charlestown
Limekilns
Rosyth
Antonshill
Stenhousemuir
Skinflats
MUSEUM
Carron
Carronshore
GRANGEMOUTH
Grangepans
Bainsford
BO'NESS AND KINNEIL RAILWAY
Carriden
FALKIRK WHEEL
THE HELIX
St. Margaret's Hope
Bo'ness
Muirhouses
BLACKNESS CASTLE
Queensferry Crossing
FALKIRK
Laurieston
Blackness
ROUGH CASTLE
1746
Grougfoot
Mannerston
HOPETOUN HOUSE
Redding
HOUSE OF THE BINNS
Glen Village
CALLENDAR HOUSE
Polmont
Brightons
Reddingmuirhead
Newton
Linlithgow
Whitecross
Philpstoun
Old Philpstoun
Shieldhill
Maddiston
Linlithgow Bridge
California
Loan
PALACE
Bridgend
Threemiletown
MUIRAVONSIDE
Jawcraig
Winchburgh
Kirkliston
Avon
Standburn
Ecclesmachan
Slamannan
Crossburn
TORPHICHEN PRECEPTORY
BEECRAIGS
Avonbridge
Westfield
Torphichen
Broxburn
Binniehill
Uphall
Newbridge
Burnside
Limerigg
312
Dechmont
Wester Dechmont
BENNIE MUSEUM
Uphall Station
Pumpherston
ALMONDELL AND CALDER WOOD
Ratho
Bonnington
Black Loch
Windyknowe
Bathgate
Armadale
Boghall
Deans
Mid Calder
Wilkieston
Hillend Res.
BLAWHORN MOSS
Westrigg
Bathville
Mayfield
Whiteside
LIVINGSTON
East Calder
JUPITER ARTLAND
Forrestfield
Blackridge
POLKEMMET
Livingston Village
Oakbank
Kirknewton
HEART OF SCOTLAND
Blackburn
Seafield
ALMOND VALLEY HERITAGE CENTRE
LIVINGSTON DESIGNER OUTLET
Forrestburn Res.
Whitburn
East Whitburn
Bellsquarry
Harthill
Croftmalloch
Eastfield
West Benhar
Polbeth
Kirk of Shotts
Hirst
Longridge
Stoneyburn
Addiewell
West Calder
Bents
Loganlea
Linhouse Water
Water of Leith
Fauldhouse
HERITAGE CENTRE
Shotts
Dykehead
Greenburn
Breich
Harperrig Reservoir
195
561
EAST CAIRN HILL
562
WEST CAIRN HILL
519
Woodmuir Plantation
Cobbinshaw Reservoir
Allanton
M9
M8
M90
M876
A91
A977
A823
A907
A985
A876
A905
A904
A706
A801
A800
A89
A899
A71
A70
A704
B9140
0 1 2 3 miles
0 1 2 3 4 5 km

Auchmuirbridge
Scotlandwell
Leslie
GLENROTHES
Markinch
BALGONIE CASTLE
Balcurvie
Milton of Balgonie
Scoonie
SILVERBURN ESTATE
LETHAM GLEN
Leven
Largo Bay
Windygates
Innerleven
Methil
Coaltown of Balgonie
Kinglassie
Stenton
Thornton
MUSEUM
Buckhaven
Ballingry
DOGTON STONE
FIFE
Lochore
FIFE COASTAL PATH
East Wemyss
Auchterderran
Cluny
Crosshill
Glencraig
Coaltown of Wemyss
Loch Ore
Cardenden
Gallatown
West Wemyss
Lochgelly
Chapel
Templehall
Dysart
RAVENSCRAIG CASTLE
Lumphinnans
Loch Gelly
KIRKCALDY GALLERIES
Hayfield
Pathhead
Cowdenbeath
Kirkcaldy
Auchtertool
Linktown
FIFE COASTAL PATH
Donibristle
Balmule
NT
Kinghorn
Burntisland
Pettycur
ALEXANDER III MONUMENT
ABERDOUR CASTLE
Aberdour
ST BRIDGET'S CHURCH
Dalgety Bay
Inchkeith
ST COLM'S ABBEY
Inchcolm
FIRTH OF FORTH
Inchmickery
Aberlady Bay
Craigielaw
Cramond I.
Drum Sands
DALMENY HOUSE
Gosford Bay
LAURISTON CASTLE
Black Rocks
Granton
Newhaven
HMY BRITANNIA
Cramond
Leith
Cockenzie and Port Seton
SETON COLLEGIATE CHURCH
Davidson's Mains
ROYAL BOTANIC GARDEN
Drylaw
Barnton
EDINBURGH
Longniddry
Prestonpans
MUSSELBURGH
Fisherrow Sands
INDUSTRIAL HERITAGE MUSEUM
RZSS EDINBURGH ZOO
PALACE OF HOLYROOD HOUSE
Portobello
Joppa
Musselburgh
Murrayfield
Duddingston
251
NAT MUS OF SCOTLAND
Corstorphine
BT MURRAYFIELD
NEWHAILES
INVERESK LODGE GDNS
Wallyford
Tranent
Penston
Macmerry
Gorgie
Morningside
Craigmillar
Newcraighall
Inveresk
CRAIGMILLAR CASTLE
EDINBURGH SERVICES
Elphinstone
New Winton
New Town
Sighthill
Craiglockhart
ROYAL OBSERVATORY
Hermiston
Braid
Danderhall
Whitecraig
Ormiston
Colinton
Liberton
Millerhill
Crossgatehall
Juniper Green
DREGHORN SERVICES
Fairmilehead
Gilmerton
DALKEITH PARK
Cousland
Pencaitland
Currie
Kaimes
Dalkeith
GLENKINCHIE DISTILLERY
SNOWSPORTS CENTRE
HILLEND
Straiton
BUTTERFLY FARM
Eskbank
MALLENY GARDEN
493
BONALY
Loanhead
Newbattle
Peastonbank
Malleny Mills
ALLERMUIR HILL
Harlaw Reservoir
Woodhouselee
Bilston
Polton
Easthouses
Mayfield
Peaston
Bonnyrigg and Lasswade
Pathhead
PENTLAND
499
CASTLELAW FORT
Glencorse Res.
Easter Howgate
Roslin
NAT MINING MUS SCOTLAND
VOGRIE
Newtongrange
Threipmuir Reservoir
Milton Bridge
ROSSLYN CHAPEL
ROSLIN GLEN
Newlandrig
Tyne Water
Humbie
Crichton
HILLS
579
SCALD LAW
Auchendinny
Rosewell
Arniston
Fala Dam
ARNISTON HOUSE
Gorebridge
CRICHTON CASTLE
Silverburn
Penicuik
Kirkhill
PARK
Carrington
Fala
North Middleton
Tynehead
South Esk
Nine Mile Burn
North Esk
Howgate
Temple
Middleton
Fala Moor
PENTLAND HILLS REGIONAL PARK
A
B
C
D
4
5
6
7
210
220
195
196

Largo Bay
Ruddons Pt.
Earlsferry
Elie
Chapel Ness
Sauchar Pt.
Ardross
St Monans
ST MONAN'S WINDMILL
ST MONAN'S CHURCH
221
Isle of May
ISLE OF MAY
FIRTH OF FORTH
209
Fidra
Craigleith
Bass Rock
Eyebroughy
North Berwick
SCOTTISH SEABIRD CENTRE
MUSEUM
TANTALLON CASTLE
Auldhame
DIRLETON CASTLE & GARDENS
MUIRFIELD
Dirleton
Gullane Bay
Gullane
Scoughall
West Fenton
Kingston
Whitekirk
Fenton Barns
St. Baldred's Cradle
Aberlady Bay
Aberlady
Tyne Mouth
MYRETON MOTOR MUSEUM
Craigielaw
Drem
JOHN MUIR
Tyninghame
East Fortune
THE CHESTERS FORT
NATIONAL MUS OF FLIGHT
Belhaven
West Barns
Gosford Bay
GOSFORD HOUSE
Ballencrieff
Preston
Peffer Burn
Athelstaneford
East Linton
Spittal
Cockenzie and Port Seton
HOPETOUN MON
JANE WELSH CARLYLE MUSEUM
PRESTON MILL & PHANTASSIE DOOCOT
Longniddry
Biel Water
HAILES CASTLE
Traprain
Pitcox
Spott
Huntington
Elvingston
SETON COLLEGIATE CHURCH
ST MARY'S COLLEGIATE CH
Tyne
Luggate Burn
Stenton
Haddington
Gladsmuir
Halls
Tranent
Penston
Macmerry
Papple
New Winton
New Town
Samuelston
Garvald
Bolton
Dunbar Common
Ormiston
BRANSLY HILL
Carfrae
Pencaitland
Gifford
Danskine
GLENKINCHIE DISTILLERY
East Saltoun
West Saltoun
Peastonbank
Bothwell Water
Gilchriston
Quarryford
Spartleton Edge
Peaston
Pathhead
Long Newton
Longyester
Birns Water
LAMMERMUIR HILLS
Whiteadder Reservoir
Humbie
Stobshiel
Crichton
Fala Dam
Blegbie
LAMMER LAW
MEIKLE SAYS LAW
Hopes Reservoir
CRANSHAWS HILL
Fala
Fala Moor
196
197
0 1 2 3 miles
0 1 2 3 4 5 km

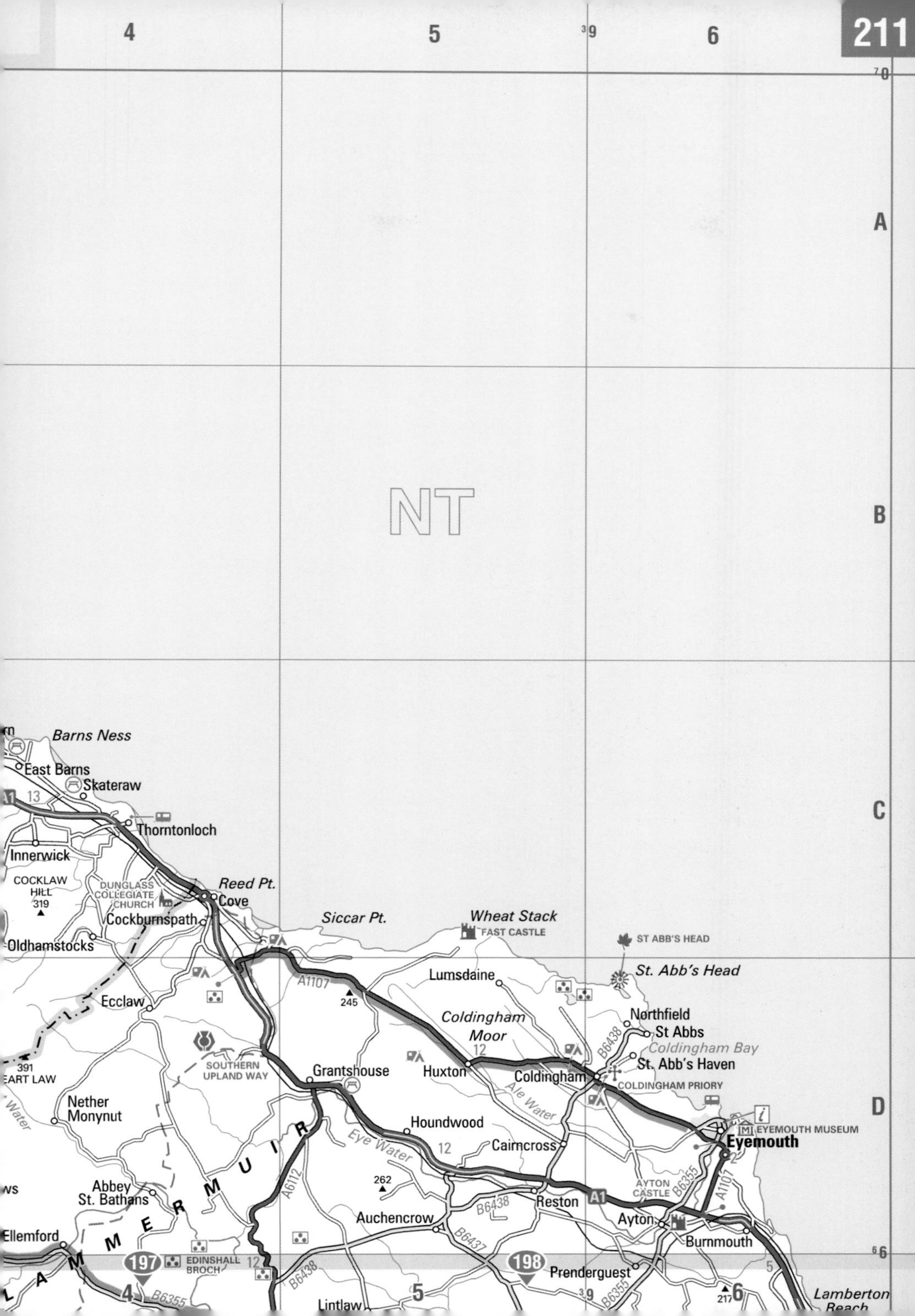
4
5
6
A
B
C
D
NT
Barns Ness
East Barns
Skateraw
Thorntonloch
Innerwick
COCKLAW HILL
319
DUNGLASS COLLEGIATE CHURCH
Reed Pt.
Cove
Cockburnspath
Oldhamstocks
Siccar Pt.
Wheat Stack
FAST CASTLE
ST ABB'S HEAD
St. Abb's Head
Lumsdaine
A1107
245
Ecclaw
Coldingham Moor
Northfield
St Abbs
Coldingham Bay
St. Abb's Haven
391
SOUTHERN UPLAND WAY
Grantshouse
Huxton
Coldingham
Ale Water
COLDINGHAM PRIORY
Nether Monynut
Houndwood
Eye Water
Cairncross
EYEMOUTH MUSEUM
Eyemouth
262
Abbey St. Bathans
A6112
B6438
Reston
A1
AYTON CASTLE
B6355
A1107
Auchencrow
Ayton
Ellemford
Burnmouth
B6437
LAMMERMUIR
197
EDINSHALL BROCH
198
Prenderguest
B6355
217
Lintlaw
Lamberton Beach

Tiraghoil
A849
Bunessan
Lee
376
CRUACHAN MIN
376
Carsaig
Rubha Dubh
224
Loch Assapol
225
Carsaig Bay
ROSS OF MULL
Ardalanish
Uisken
Scoor
Ardchiavaig
CARSAIG ARCHES
Malcolm's Pt.
125
Eilean a'Chalmain
Rubha nam Braithrean
Rubh Ardalanish
A
OBAN
B
NM
Rubh'a'Geadha
Balnahard
Kiloran Bay
KILORAN GARDENS
Kiloran
B8086
B8087
Kilchattan
136
C
COLONSAY
Scalasaig
NR
Loch Staosnaig
Corpach Bay
Garvard
B8085
Rubha Dubh
PRIORY
Dubh Eilean
Oronsay
Shian Bay
453
RAINBERG MOR
Eilean nan Ron
Loch Righ Mòr
D
318
Rubh'an t-Sàilein
PORT ASKAIG
Loch Tarbert
Rubha Lang-aoinidh
200
201
Rubha Bholsa
Rubha a'Mhail
439
0 1 2 3 miles
0 1 2 3 4 5 km

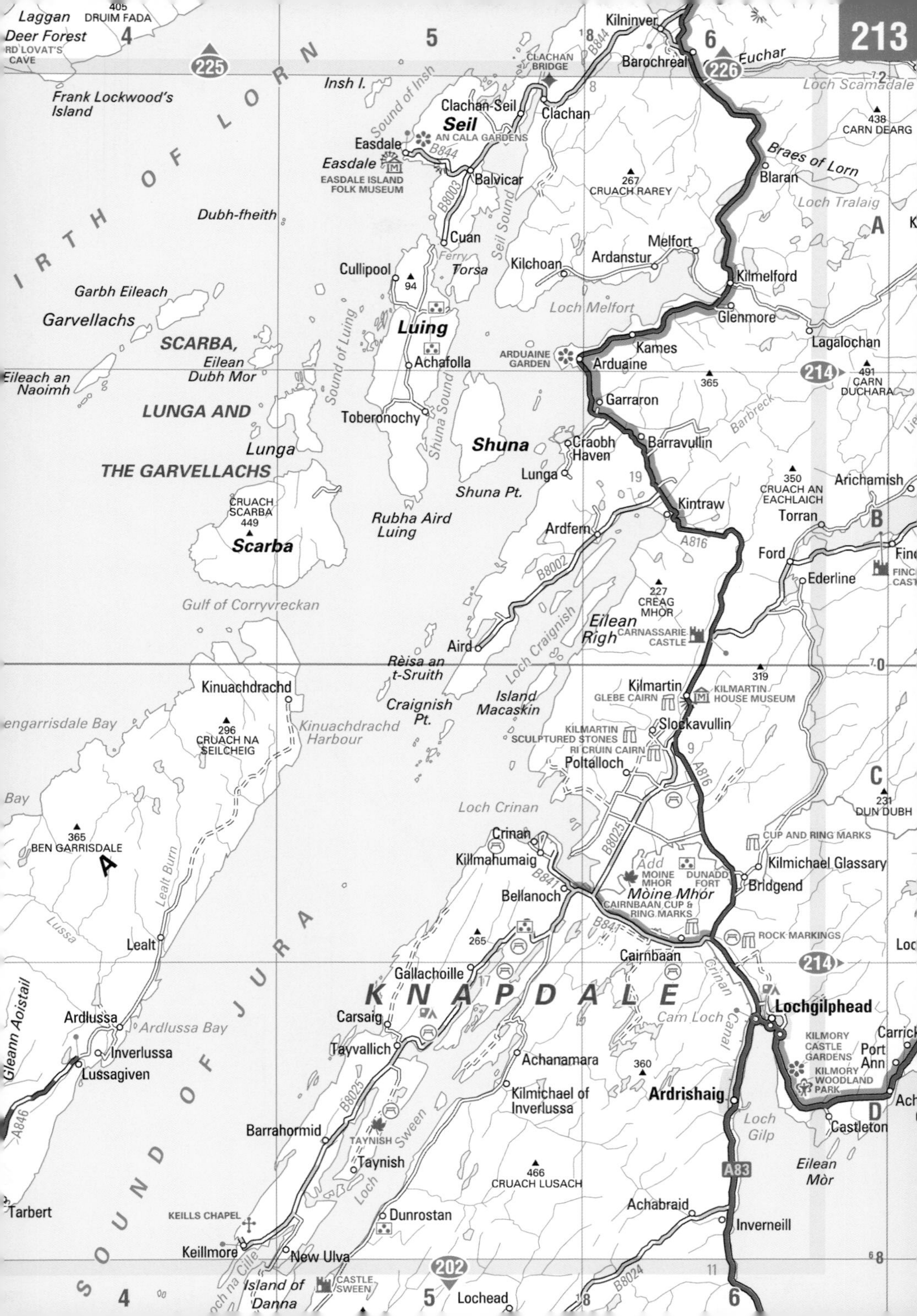

Laggan
Deer Forest
FIRTH OF LORN
Frank Lockwood's Island
Insh I.
Sound of Insh
Clachan-Seil
Seil
Clachan
Clachan Bridge
Kilninver
Barochreal
Euchar
Loch Scamadale
Carn Dearg
Easdale
Eilean Easdale
An Cala Gardens
Easdale Island Folk Museum
Balvicar
Braes of Lorn
Blaran
Cruach Rarey
Loch Tralaig
Dubh-fheith
Cuan
Seil Sound
Melfort
Ardanstur
Kilchoan
Kilmelford
Torsa
Cullipool
Garbh Eileach
Garvellachs
Loch Melfort
Glenmore
Luing
Scarba, Lunga and the Garvellachs
Eilean Dubh Mor
Eileach an Naoimh
Achafolla
Arduaine Garden
Arduaine
Kames
Lagalochan
Carn Duchara
Sound of Luing
Garraron
Toberonochy
Shuna Sound
Barbreck
Lunga
Shuna
Craobh Haven
Barravullin
Lunga
Shuna Pt.
Cruach an Eachlaich
Arichamish
Cruach Scarba
Scarba
Rubha Aird Luing
Kintraw
Torran
Ardfern
Ford
Ederline
A816
B8002
Creag Mhor
Gulf of Corryvreckan
Loch Craignish
Eilean Righ
Carnassarie Castle
Aird
Rèisa an t-Sruith
Kinuachdrachd
Kilmartin
Glebe Cairn
Kilmartin House Museum
Craignish Pt.
Island Macaskin
Lengarrisdale Bay
Kinuachdrachd Harbour
Cruach na Seilcheig
Kilmartin Sculptured Stones
Ri Cruin Cairn
Slockavullin
Poltalloch
Dun Dubh
Loch Crinan
Bay
Ben Garrisdale
Crinan
Cup and Ring Marks
Killmahumaig
Kilmichael Glassary
Add
Moine Mhor
Dunadd Fort
Bridgend
Lealt Burn
B841
Bellanoch
Mòine Mhor
Cairnbaan Cup & Ring Marks
B8025
Lussa
Rock Markings
Lealt
Cairnbaan
Gallachoille
Crinan Canal
Knapdale
Lochgilphead
Carsaig
Cam Loch
Ardlussa
Ardlussa Bay
Gleann Aoistail
Inverlussa
Tayvallich
Kilmory Castle Gardens
Kilmory Woodland Park
Carrick
Port Ann
Lussagiven
Achanamara
Kilmichael of Inverlussa
Ardrishaig
A846
Barrahormid
Loch Sween
Taynish
Loch Gilp
Castleton
Eilean Mòr
A83
Cruach Lusach
Achabraid
Inverneill
Sound of Jura
Tarbert
Keills Chapel
Dunrostan
Keillmore
New Ulva
Loch na Cille
Island of Danna
Castle Sween
Lochead
B8024
225
226
214
202

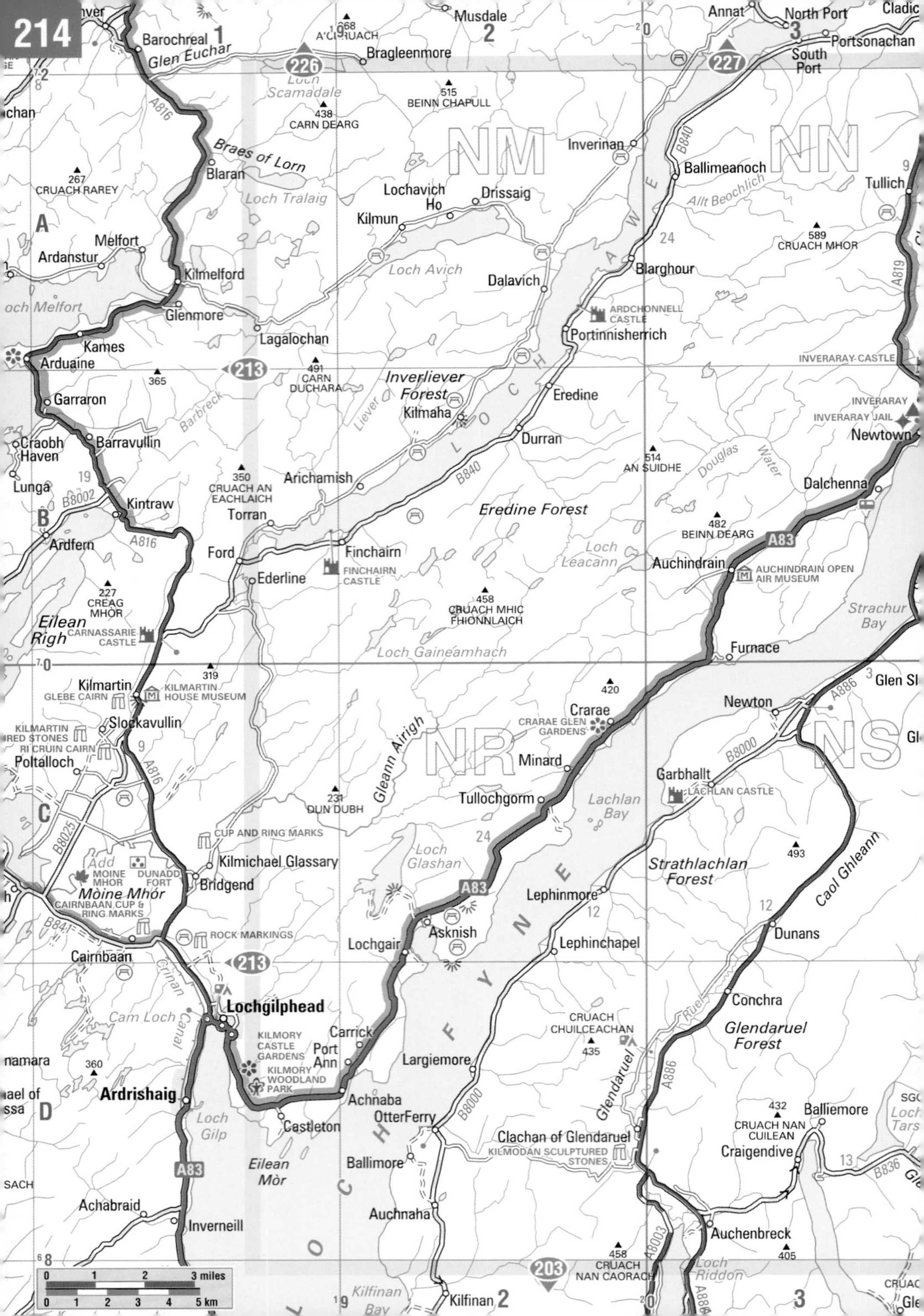

Lochgilphead
Ardrishaig
Kilmartin
Kilmelford
Inveraray
Furnace
Loch Fyne
Loch Awe
Loch Avich
Eredine Forest
Inverliever Forest
Strathlachlan Forest
Glendaruel Forest
Mòine Mhòr
Crinan Canal
Loch Gilp
0 1 2 3 miles
0 1 2 3 4 5 km

LOCH LOMOND AND THE TROSSACHS NATIONAL PARK
ARGYLL FOREST PARK
Lochan Shira
Loch Stron Mor
Glen Shira
Kilblaan Burn
Brannie Burn
550 BEINN GHLAS
948 BEINN BHUIDHE
Glen Fyne
Fyne
Allt na Lairige
Glenfyne Lodge
645 MAOL BREAC
733 TROISGEACH
Inverarnan
Glen Falloch
Falls of Falloch
Ben Glas Burn
940 BEINN A'CHROIN
Ardlui
Clachan
Drishaig
A83
Cairndow
ARDKINGLAS WOODLAND GARDEN
811
Loch Sloy
941 BEN VORLICH
770
Stronachlachar
ROB ROY'S CAVE
916
Inveruglas
Glen Kinglas
Ardno
A815
St Catherine's
901 BEINN AN LOCHAIN
B839
Hell's Glen
Rest and Be Thankful
B828
1011 BEINN IME
849
A82
Inversnaid Hotel
Loch Arklet
216
WEST HIGHLAND WAY
598
Frenich
565 CRUACH NAN CAPULL
Monevechadan
Glen Croe
881
Succoth
Tarbet
Arrochar
Forest
Ardgartan
Ardgartan Forest
847 BEN DONICH
LOCH LOMOND
Craig Rostan
Stuckgowan
Ardmay
974 BEN LOMOND
Drimsynie
Lochgoilhead
703 BEINN LOCHAIN
Corrow
CNOC COINNICH
Ptarmigan Lodge
681
Blairlomond
Loch Goil
Glen Douglas
Rowardennan
ROWARDENNAN LODGE
596 BEINN UIRD
779 BEINN BHEULA
Invernoaden
Ardgoil Forest
A814
DOUNE HILL 734
Inverbeg
INVERBEG GALLERY
519 THE SADDLE
Glenmallan
Rowardennan Forest
Carrick Castle
CARRICK CASTLE
BEINN EICH 702
Edentaggart
618 BEINN BHEAG
Loch Eck
Whistlefield
Forest
LOCH LONG
Portincaple
Whistlefield
713 BEINN CHAORACH
Glen Luss
Inchlonaig
NAT PARK CENTRE
Luss
THISTLE BAGPIPE WORKS
Bernice
659 CREACHAN MOR
Garelochhead
593 BEINN RUISG
Aldochlay
Inchfad
Inchcailloch
206
Glen Finart
BEINN RUADH 664
B883
Faslane Port
Glen Fruin
Inchmurrin
Glenfinart
Ardentinny
Coulport
Rahane
GARE LOCH
A817
Duchlage
Blairglas
BENMORE BOTANIC GARDEN
Ardpeaton
Shandon
Glen Massan
Benmore
Uig
GLENARN GARDEN
THE HILL HOUSE
Arden
Clynder
202
Rhu
A818
Bannachra Muir
BALLOCH CASTLE
Ardbeg
KILMUN ARBORETUM
Invereck
Dalinlongart
A880
Blairmore
LINN BOTANIC GARDENS
Rosneath
THE ROWAN GALLERY
Helensburgh
Cove
Cove Bay
Kilmun
Rosneath Pt.
Craigendoran
NAT PK GATEWAY CENTRE
A811
Holy Loch
Strone
Portkil
Sandbank
Strone Pt.
Kilcreggan
Colgrain
Ardnadam
204
GEILSTON
ALEXANDRIA
Bonhill
Glen Kin
Hunter's Quay
A885
A815
Geilston
ST JOHN'S CHURCH
Gourock
227
216
4
5
6

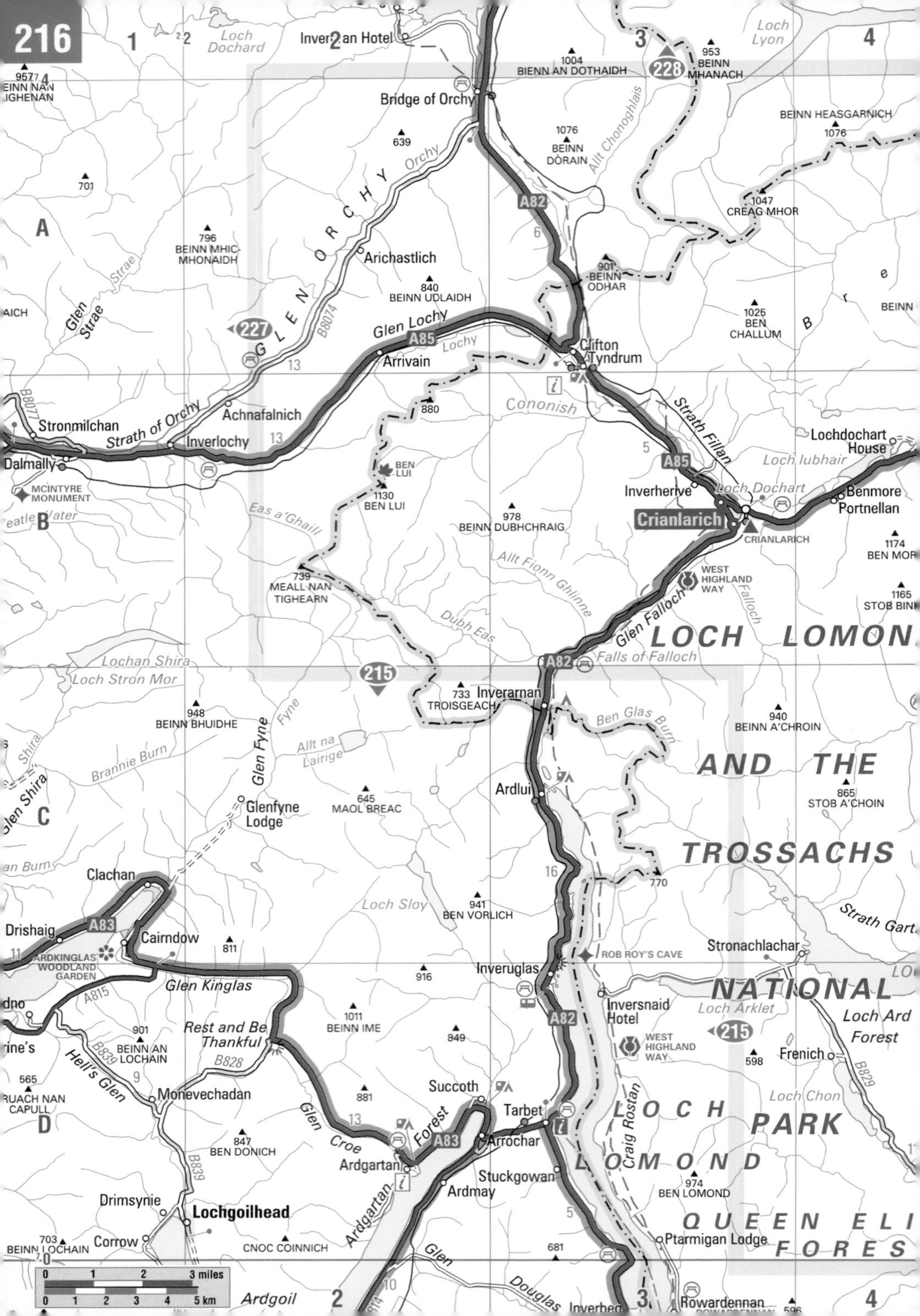
Loch Dochard
Inveroran Hotel
Loch Lyon
BIENN AN DOTHAIDH
BEINN MHANACH
228
Bridge of Orchy
BEINN HEASGARNICH
BEINN DÒRAIN
Allt Chonoghlais
GLEN ORCHY
Orchy
A82
CREAG MHOR
BEINN MHIC-MHONAIDH
Arichastlich
BEINN ODHAR
BEINN UDLAIDH
BEN CHALLUM
Glen Strae
Strae
227
B8074
Glen Lochy
A85
Lochy
Clifton
Tyndrum
Arrivain
Cononish
Strath Fillan
Stronmilchan
Achnafalnich
Strath of Orchy
Inverlochy
Lochdochart House
Dalmally
B8077
BEN LUI
Loch Iubhair
MCINTYRE MONUMENT
Inverherive
Loch Dochart
Benmore
Portnellan
Eas a'Ghaill
BEINN DUBHCHRAIG
Crianlarich
CRIANLARICH
BEN MORE
Allt Fionn Ghlinne
WEST HIGHLAND WAY
MEALL NAN TIGHEARN
Glen Falloch
Falloch
STOB BINNEIN
Dubh Eas
LOCH LOMOND
Falls of Falloch
Lochan Shira
Loch Stron Mor
215
Inverarnan
TROISGEACH
BEINN BHUIDHE
Fyne
Ben Glas Burn
BEINN A'CHROIN
Allt na Lairige
Brannie Burn
Glen Fyne
AND THE
Glen Shira
Shira
Ardlui
STOB A'CHOIN
Glenfyne Lodge
MAOL BREAC
TROSSACHS
Clachan
Loch Sloy
BEN VORLICH
Strath Gartney
Drishaig
A83
Cairndow
Stronachlachar
ARDKINGLAS WOODLAND GARDEN
ROB ROY'S CAVE
Inveruglas
Glen Kinglas
NATIONAL
A815
Inversnaid Hotel
Loch Arklet
Loch Ard Forest
Rest and Be Thankful
BEINN IME
BEINN AN LOCHAIN
WEST HIGHLAND WAY
Hell's Glen
B839
B828
Frenich
B829
RUACH NAN CAPULL
Monevechadan
Succoth
Glen Croe
Tarbet
LOCH LOMOND
Craig Rostan
Loch Chon
PARK
Forest
Arrochar
BEN DONICH
Ardgartan
Stuckgowan
BEN LOMOND
Drimsynie
Ardmay
Lochgoilhead
Ardgartan Forest
QUEEN ELIZABETH FOREST
BEINN LOCHAIN
Corrow
Ptarmigan Lodge
CNOC COINNICH
Glen Douglas
Ardgoil
Inverbeg
Rowardennan
0 1 2 3 miles
0 1 2 3 4 5 km

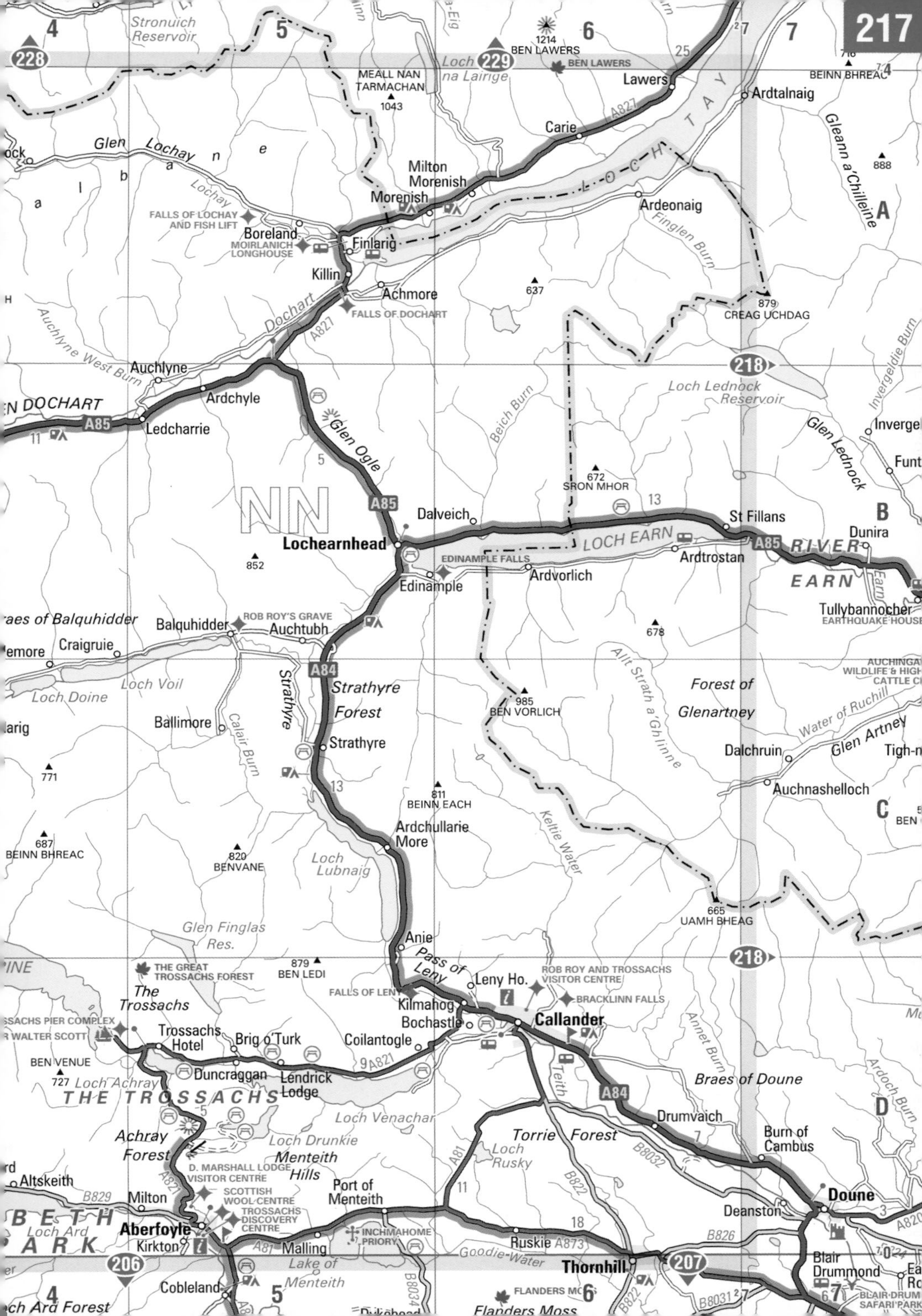
Stronuich Reservoir
228
229
218
206
207
MEALL NAN TARMACHAN
1043
BEN LAWERS
1214
Loch na Lairige
Lawers
Carie
Ardtalnaig
LOCH TAY
Glen Lochay
Milton Morenish
Morenish
Ardeonaig
FALLS OF LOCHAY AND FISH LIFT
Boreland
MOIRLANICH LONGHOUSE
Finlarig
Killin
Achmore
FALLS OF DOCHART
CREAG UCHDAG
Auchlyne
Ardchyle
Ledcharrie
GLEN DOCHART
Loch Lednock Reservoir
Glen Ogle
Glen Lednock
Dalveich
Lochearnhead
SRON MHOR
St Fillans
LOCH EARN
EDINAMPLE FALLS
Edinample
Ardvorlich
Ardtrostan
RIVER EARN
Dunira
Tullybannocher
EARTHQUAKE HOUSE
Braes of Balquhidder
ROB ROY'S GRAVE
Balquhidder
Auchtubh
Craigruie
Loch Voil
Loch Doine
Strathyre Forest
Strathyre
Ballimore
Calair Burn
BEN VORLICH
Allt Strath a'Ghlinne
Forest of Glenartney
Water of Ruchill
Glen Artney
Dalchruin
Auchnashelloch
BEINN EACH
Ardchullarie More
BEINN BHREAC
BENVANE
Loch Lubnaig
Keltie Water
UAMH BHEAG
Glen Finglas Res.
Anie
Pass of Leny
THE GREAT TROSSACHS FOREST
BEN LEDI
ROB ROY AND TROSSACHS VISITOR CENTRE
Leny Ho.
BRACKLINN FALLS
The Trossachs
FALLS OF LENY
Kilmahog
Bochastle
Callander
Trossachs Hotel
Brig o'Turk
Coilantogle
BEN VENUE
Duncraggan
Lendrick Lodge
Loch Achray
THE TROSSACHS
Loch Venachar
Braes of Doune
Drumvaich
Achray Forest
Loch Drunkie
Menteith Hills
Torrie Forest
Loch Rusky
Burn of Cambus
D. MARSHALL LODGE VISITOR CENTRE
SCOTTISH WOOL CENTRE
TROSSACHS DISCOVERY CENTRE
Altskeith
Milton
Port of Menteith
Doune
Deanston
Aberfoyle
Kirkton
Malling
INCHMAHOME PRIORY
Ruskie
Lake of Menteith
Goodie Water
Thornhill
Blair Drummond
Cobleland
FLANDERS MOSS
Flanders Moss
A85
A84
A827
A821
A81
A873
B8032
B822
B829
B826
B8034
NN

Lawers
Ardtalnaig
Carie
Garrow
BEINN BHREAC
Loch Freuchie
Glen Quaich
Cablea
Amulree
Ardeonaig
Gleann a'Chilleine
MEALL NAM FUARAN
Corrymuckloch
Almond
MEALL NAN CAORAICH
Newton
CREAG UCHDAG
BEN CHONZIE
GLEN ALMOND
Sma' Glen
MEALL TARSUINN
Loch Lednock Reservoir
Glen Lednock
Invergeldie
Funtullich
Loch Turret Reservoir
Glen Turret
Shaggie Burn
NN
SRON MHOR
St Fillans
LOCH EARN
Ardtrostan
Dunira
MELVILLE MONUMENT
RIVER EARN
Comrie
Lawers
COMRIE CROFT
Ochtertyre
Quoig
FALLS OF TURRET
Monzie
Monzie Castle
Hosh
Gilmerton
Fowlis Wester
STANDING STONES
GLENTURRET DISTILLERY
Crieff
Tullybannocher
EARTHQUAKE HOUSE
Ross
Dalginross
Lochlane
CRIEFF VISITORS' CENTRE
AUCHINGARRICH WILDLIFE & HIGHLAND CATTLE CENTRE
The Balloch
Forest of Glenartney
Water of Ruchill
Culloch
Torlum Wood
DRUMMOND CASTLE GARDENS
OLD CHURCH & TOWER
Muthill
INNERPEFFRAY LIBRARY
STRATHEARN
Dalchruin
Glen Artney
Tigh-na-Blair
Ochtermuthill
Machany Water
Auchnashelloch
BEN CLACH
Langside
TULLIBARDINE CHAPEL
Auchterarder
Glenlichorn
Knaik
Garrick
Muirton
UAMH BHEAG
BLACKHALL ROMAN CAMPS
Gleneagles Hotel
ARDOCH ROMAN CAMP
GLENEAGLES
Braco
Blackford
BRACLINN FALLS
Bullie Burn
Muckle Burn
Greenloaning
TULLIBARDINE DISTILLERY
Braes of Ogilvie
Glen Eagles
Allan Water
STRATHALLAN
Braes of Doune
Glendevon Resvrs.
Kinbuck
Balhaldie
Drumvaich
Torrie Forest
Burn of Cambus
Ashfield
Sheriff Muir
Doune
CATHEDRAL
Dunblane
Deanston
BLAIRDENON HILL
Pisgah
LEIGHTON LIBRARY
BEN CLEUCH
Blair Drummond
Easter Row
BLAIR DRUMMOND SAFARI PARK
KING'S SEAT HILL
0 1 2 3 miles
0 1 2 3 4 5 km

Coupar Angus
Stanley
Perth
Scone
Methven
Bridge of Earn
Newburgh
Auchtermuchty
Milnathort
Kinross
Falkland
Leslie
Ballingry
Caputh
Murthly
Meikleour
Kinclaven
Cargill
Woodside
Burrelton
Kettins
Markethill
Hallyburton House
Leys
Campmuir
Pitcur
Whitefield
Saucher
Collace
Kirkton of Collace
KING'S SEAT
377
Abernyte
Bandirran
Balbeggie
Ballindean
Kinnaird
Rait
Kilspindie
BRAES OF THE CARSE
Myreside
Kinfauns Forest
Glendoick
Kinfauns
Glencarse
Errol
St Madoes
Chapelhill
Mugdrum I.
Obney Hills
Upper Obney
Balquharn
Waterloo
Bankfoot
Airntully
West Tofts
Muir of Thorn
Ardoch
Gellyburn
Little Glenshee
Tullybelton
Logiealmond Lodge
Chapelhill
Harrietfield
Moneydie
Luncarty
Downhill
Redgorton
Pitcairngreen
Almondbank
Huntingtower
Lochty
Tulloch
Muirton
Keillour
Braegrum
Tibbermore
HUNTINGTOWER CASTLE
Letham
Cherrybank
BROXDEN SERVICES
Craigie
Friarton
BELL'S CHERRYBANK GARDENS
Milltown of Aberdalgie
Aberdalgie
Tarsappie
ELCHO
Elcho
Inchyra
Rhynd
Craigend
Dupplin Castle
Findo Gask
Clathy
Kirkton
Forteviot
Forgandenny
Kintillo
Dron
Aberargie
Abernethy
ROUND TOWER
Glenfoot
Grange of Lindores
Pitmedden Forest
Easter Rhynd
LAING MUSEUM
Ardargie House Hotel
Dunning
Rossie Ochill
Pathstruie
Path of Condie
Glenfarg Res.
Glenfarg
Newton of Balcanquhal
Arngask
Duncrievie
Gateside
Nether Urquhart
Burnside
Strathmiglo
Dunshalt
Common of Dunning
Middle Rigg
485
497
INNERDOUNY HILL
Middleton
Craigow
Upper Tillyrie
Dalqueich
Glendevon
Burnfoot
Castle Hill Reservoir
611
Carnbo
KINROSS SERVICES
BURLEIGH CASTLE
Wester Balgedie
MICHAEL BRUCE'S COTTAGE
Kinnesswood
LOCH LEVEN
LOCHLEVEN CASTLE
KINROSS HOUSE
St Serf's Island
Gairney Bank
Scotlandwell
Auchmuirbridge
Kinglassie
Pool o' Muckhart
Yetts o' Muckhart
Drum
Coldrain
Crook of Devon
Rumbling Bridge
RUMBLING BRIDGE GORGE
DOLLAR GLEN
Cleish
WEST LOMOND
522
LOMOND HILLS
FIFE
REGIONAL PARK
Pitkevy
Glasslie
FALKLAND
PERTH
SCONE PALACE
PERTH MART VISITOR CENTRE
MUSEUM & ART GALLERY
FERGUSSON GALLERY
BRANKLYN GARDEN
Gannochy
POLE HILL
288
MEGGINCH CASTLE GARDENS
Trochry
Ballinlick
Inver
Little Dunkeld
Birnam
Kirkton of Lethendy
Spittalfield
Delvine
404
TAY
Guildtown
Wolfhill
Kinrossie
Newmiln
St Martins
NO
A9
A85
A90
A93
A94
A91
A912
A913
A977
A911
M90
B867
B9099
B8063
B934
B9112
B935
B9141
B8062
B996
B919
B920
B953
B936
B9097
B947
A984
A923
230
231
220
208

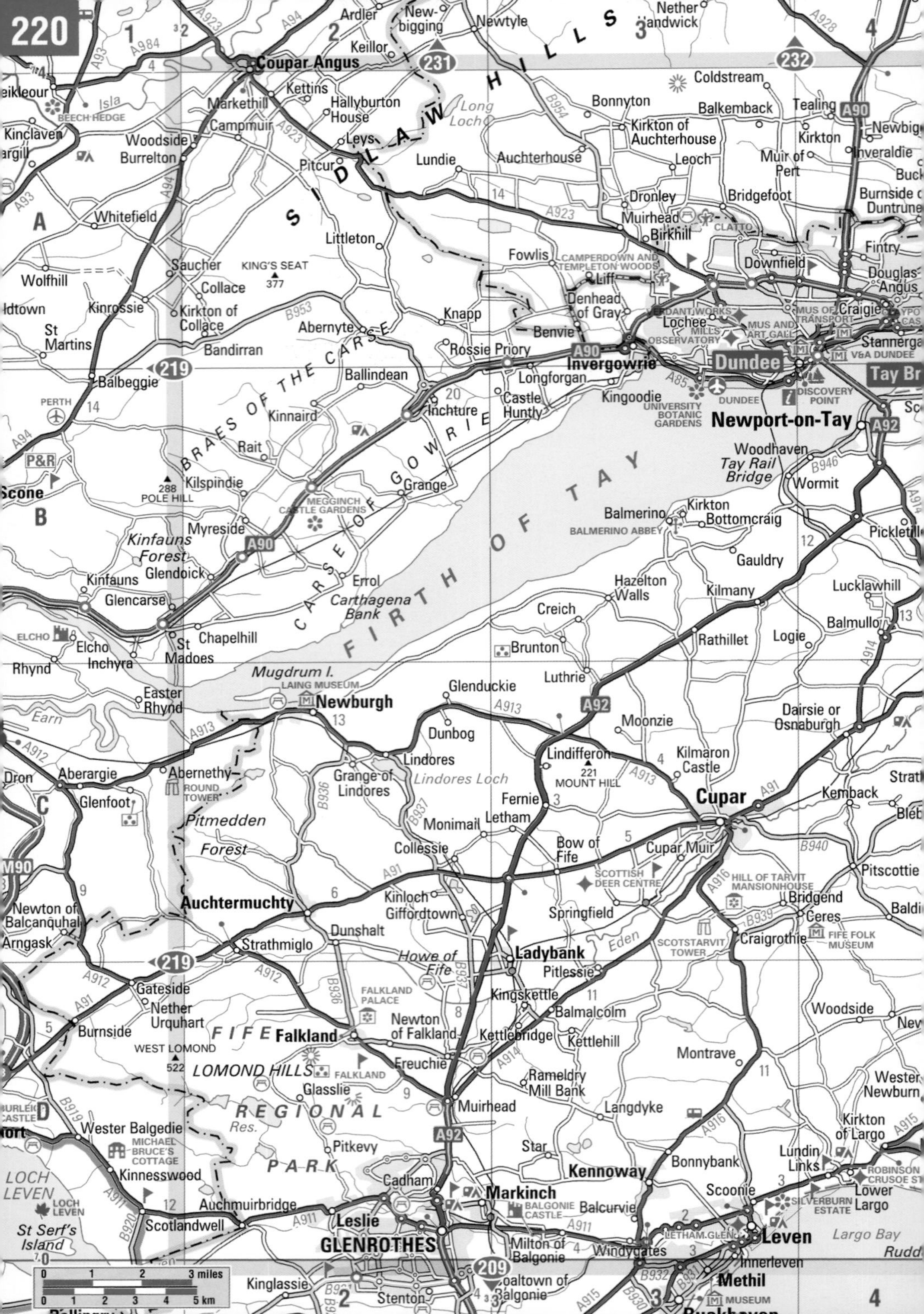

SIDLAW HILLS
Ardler
New-bigging
Newtyle
Nether Handwick
Keillor
231
232
Coupar Angus
Meikleour
Isla
BEECH HEDGE
Kettins
Markethill
Hallyburton House
Long Loch
Coldstream
Bonnyton
Balkemback
Tealing
A90
Kinclaven
Campmuir
Woodside
Burrelton
Leys
Kirkton of Auchterhouse
Kirkton
Newbigging
Muir of Pert
Inveraldie
Pitcur
Lundie
Auchterhouse
Leoch
Dronley
Bridgefoot
Burnside of Duntrune
Whitefield
Muirhead
Birkhill
CLATTO
Littleton
Fowlis
CAMPERDOWN AND TEMPLETON WOODS
Downfield
Fintry
Douglas and Angus
Saucher
KING'S SEAT 377
Wolfhill
Collace
Liff
Kinrossie
Kirkton of Collace
Denhead of Gray
VERDANT WORKS
MUS OF TRANSPORT
Craigie
Lochee
MILLS OBSERVATORY
MUS AND ART GALL
St Martins
Abernyte
Knapp
Benvie
Stannergate
Bandirran
Rossie Priory
A90
Invergowrie
Dundee
V&A DUNDEE
219
Balbeggie
Ballindean
Longforgan
A85
Tay Br
PERTH
BRAES OF THE CARSE
Kinnaird
Inchture
Castle Huntly
Kingoodie
UNIVERSITY BOTANIC GARDENS
DUNDEE
DISCOVERY POINT
Newport-on-Tay
A92
Rait
Woodhaven
Tay Rail Bridge
B946
Wormit
P&R
Scone
Kilspindie
288 POLE HILL
MEGGINCH CASTLE GARDENS
Grange
CARSE OF GOWRIE
FIRTH OF TAY
Balmerino
Kirkton
Bottomcraig
BALMERINO ABBEY
Myreside
Kinfauns Forest
Gauldry
Pickletillem
A90
Glendoick
Errol
Hazelton Walls
Kilmany
Lucklawhill
Kinfauns
Glencarse
Carthagena Bank
Creich
Balmullo
ELCHO
Elcho
Inchyra
Chapelhill
St Madoes
Brunton
Rathillet
Logie
A914
Rhynd
Mugdrum I.
LAING MUSEUM
Newburgh
Glenduckie
Luthrie
A913
A92
Easter Rhynd
Earn
Dunbog
Moonzie
Dairsie or Osnaburgh
A913
Lindores
Lindifferon
221 MOUNT HILL
Kilmaron Castle
A912
Dron
Aberargie
Abernethy
ROUND TOWER
Grange of Lindores
Lindores Loch
Fernie
Cupar
A91
Kemback
Strathkinness
Glenfoot
Pitmedden Forest
Monimail
Letham
Bow of Fife
Cupar Muir
B940
M90
Collessie
SCOTTISH DEER CENTRE
HILL OF TARVIT MANSIONHOUSE
Pitscottie
Auchtermuchty
Kinloch
Giffordtown
Springfield
Bridgend
Ceres
Newton of Balcanquhal
A916
B939
Craigrothie
FIFE FOLK MUSEUM
Arngask
Dunshalt
Strathmiglo
Ladybank
Eden
SCOTSTARVIT TOWER
219
Howe of Fife
Pitlessie
A912
FALKLAND PALACE
Kingskettle
Gateside
Nether Urquhart
Balmalcolm
Woodside
A91
Burnside
FIFE
Falkland
Newton of Falkland
Kettlebridge
Kettlehill
WEST LOMOND 522
LOMOND HILLS
FALKLAND
Freuchie
A914
Montrave
Ramelrdy Mill Bank
Wester Newburn
Glasslie
Muirhead
Langdyke
B919
Wester Balgedie
REGIONAL
Res.
A92
Kirkton of Largo
A915
MICHAEL BRUCE'S COTTAGE
Pitkevy
PARK
Star
Bonnybank
Lundin Links
LOCH LEVEN
Kinnesswood
Kennoway
ROBINSON CRUSOE ST
Cadham
Markinch
Scoonie
LOCH LEVEN
A911
Auchmuirbridge
BALGONIE CASTLE
Balcurvie
SILVERBURN ESTATE
Lower Largo
B920
Scotlandwell
A911
Leslie
A911
LETHAM GLEN
Leven
Largo Bay
St Serf's Island
GLENROTHES
Milton of Balgonie
Windygates
Innerleven
209
Kinglassie
Coaltown of Balgonie
B932
Methil
Stenton
A915
B930
MUSEUM
0 1 2 3 miles
0 1 2 3 4 5 km
A B C D
1 2 3 4

Hayhillock
Carmyllie
Denhead of Arbilot
Hayshead
Cliffburn
The Deil's Heid
ARBROATH ABBEY
Arbroath
CROMBIE
Arbirlot
SIGNAL TOWER MUSEUM
Kirkton of Monikie
Balmirmer
Elliot
Monikie
MONIKIE
Craigton
Monikie Burn
Salmond's Muir
Wellbank
CARLUNGIE SOUTERRAIN
Muirdrum
Drumsturdy
East Haven
Kellas
Newbigging
Panbride
BARRY MILL
SOUTERRAIN ARDESTIE
Barry
Carnoustie
Mains of Ardestie
CARNOUSTIE
Barry Links
Monifieth
Barnhill
BROUGHTY CASTLE MUSEUM
Buddon Ness
Tayport
TENTSMUIR
Tentsmuir Forest
NO
EUCHARS NORMAN CHURCH
Eden Mouth
EN ESTUARY CENTRE
ST ANDREWS BAY
ST ANDREWS
ST ANDREWS AQUARIUM
St Andrews
CATH & ST RULE'S TOWER
Newpark
Buddo Ness
Brownhills
Boarhills
Babbet Ness
Balone
ST ANDREWS BOTANIC GARDEN
Denhead
Prior Muir
Kingsbarns
Cameron Res.
Cameron Burn
Stravithie
Cambo Ness
CAMBO GARDENS
Carr Brigs
Dunino
Tullybothy Craigs
Balcomie
Craighead
Fife Ness
Kingsmuir
CRAIL TOLBOOTH
SCOTLAND'S SECRET BUNKER
Lathones
Lochty
Crail
CRAIL MUSEUM AND HERITAGE CENTRE
Largoward
Pitcorthie
Carnbee
Pitkierie
West Ness
KELLIE CASTLE AND GARDEN
FIFE COASTAL PATH
Kilrenny
Arncroach
Anstruther Easter
Colinsburgh
SCOTTISH FISHERIES MUSEUM
Abercrombie
Pittenweem
Anstruther Wester
Kilconquhar
ST FILLAN'S CAVE
ST MONAN'S WINDMILL
Ardross
St Monans
ST MONAN'S CHURCH
Isle of May
ISLE OF MAY
Elie
Sauchar Pt.
Chapel Ness
A92
A930
A91
A915
A917
B961
B9128
B978
B939
B9131
B940
B941
B9171
B942
232
233
210
A
B
C
D
4
5
6
7

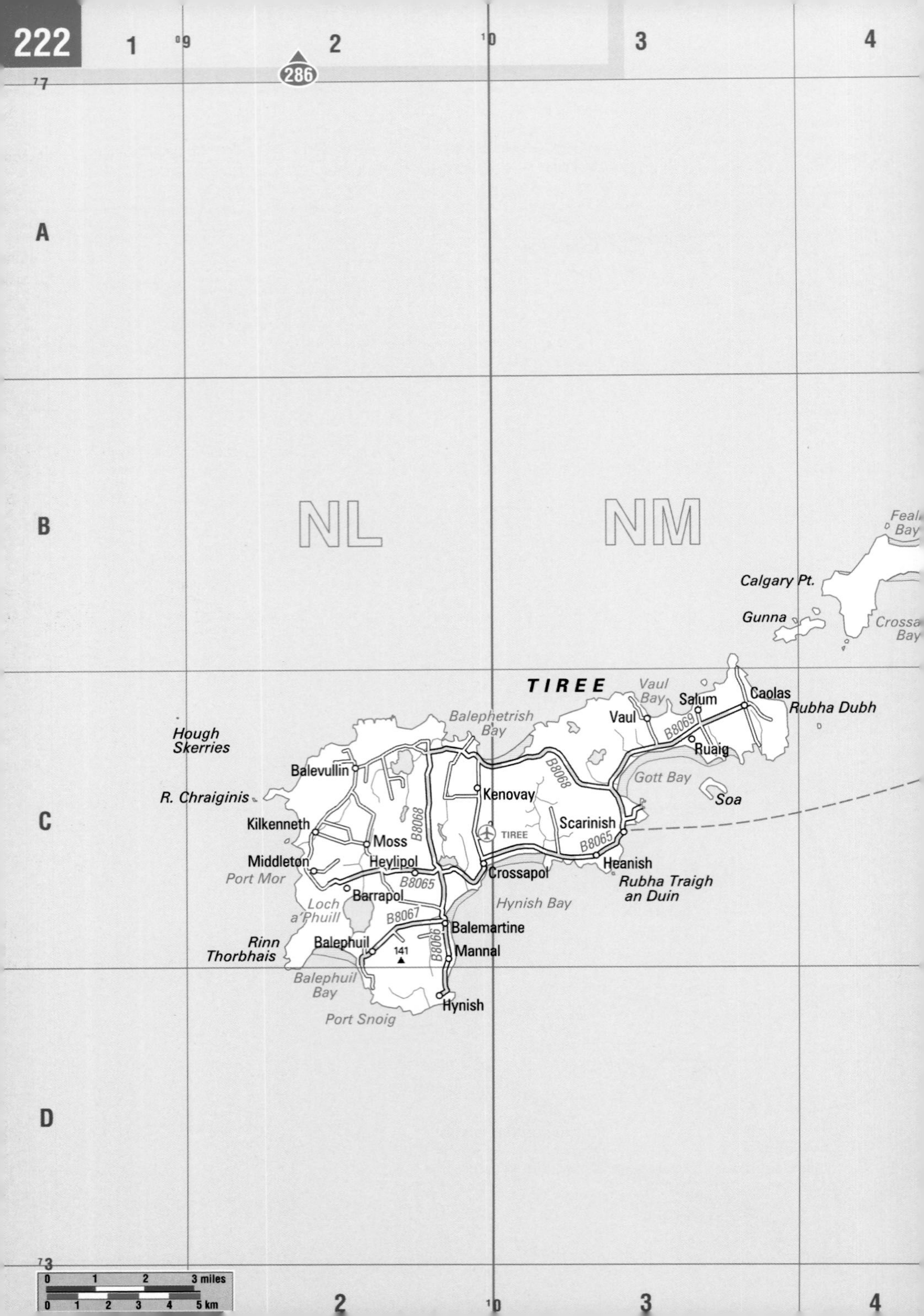
286
NL
NM
Feal Bay
Calgary Pt.
Gunna
Crossa Bay
TIREE
Vaul Bay
Salum
Caolas
Rubha Dubh
Vaul
B8069
Ruaig
Balephetrish Bay
Hough Skerries
Balevullin
B8068
Gott Bay
Kenovay
Soa
R. Chraiginis
Kilkenneth
Scarinish
TIREE
Moss
B8065
Middleton
Heylipol
Heanish
Port Mor
B8065
Crossapol
Rubha Traigh an Duin
Barrapol
Loch a'Phuill
Hynish Bay
B8067
Balemartine
Rinn Thorbhais
Balephuil
141
B8066
Mannal
Balephuil Bay
Hynish
Port Snoig
0 1 2 3 miles
0 1 2 3 4 5 km

4
5
6
7
A
B
C
D
Sanna Point
Sanna Bay
Portuairk
Point of Ardnamurchan
ARDNAMURCHAN LIGHTHOUSE
An Acairseid
Ormsaig
Cairns of Coll
234
Eilean Mor
Rubha Mor
Sorisdale
Bousd
B8072
Cliad Bay
Arnabost
Gallanach
Grishipoll
B8071
Loch Cliad
73
104
COLL
OBAN
Arinagour
Totronald
B8070
Acha
Loch Eatharna
Eilean Ornsay
Breachacha Castle
Friesland
Loch Breachacha
Soa
Ardmore Bay
Quinish Pt.
Glengorm Castle
Mishnish
Quinish
Rubha an Aird
Caliach Pt.
Sunipol
Mornish
Penmore Mill
MULL THEATRE
Calgary
Dervaig
Calgary Bay
THE OLD BYRE HERITAGE CENTRE
Treshnish Pt.
Ensay
342
CARN MOR
Haunn
B8073
Rubh a'Chaoil
224
Burg
Kilninian
Achleck
23
Fanmore
390
Treshnish Isles
Fladda
LOCH TUATH
Ballygown
EAS FORS WATERFALL
Eilean Dioghlum
Lunga
Gometra
Laggan Bay
Bearnus
313
Ulva
Ulva House
Bac Mor
Little Colonsay
Staffa
STAFFA
FINGAL'S CAVE
INCH KENNETH CHAPEL
Inch Kenneth
MACKINNON'S CAVE
Erisgeir
ARDMEANACH
224

COLL
Gallanach
Loch Cliad
Arinagour
Loch Eatharna
Eilean Ornsay
Friesland
TIREE
OBAN
234
Ardmore Bay
Quinish Pt.
Glengorm Castle
MULL MUSEUM
Tobermory
Rubha an Aird
Caliach Pt.
Sunipol
Mornish
Quinish
Mishnish
'S AIRDE-BEINN
292
MULL THEATRE
Penmore Mill
Dervaig
Achnadrish
Calgary
Calgary Bay
THE OLD BYRE HERITAGE CENTRE
Loch Frisa
Treshnish Pt.
Ensay
342
CARN MOR
Haunn
Bellart
Achnacraig
Rubh a'Chaoil
223
Burg
Kilninian
Achleck
Fanmore
390
Treshnish Isles
Fladda
LOCH TUATH
Ballygown
EAS FORS WATERFALL
424
BEINN NA DRISE
Eilean Dioghlum
Lunga
Gometra
Lagganulva
Laggan Bay
Bearnus
313
Oskamull
Ulva
Ulva House
Sound of Ulva
Bac Mor
LOCH NA KEAL
Eorsa
Little Colonsay
ISLE OF
INCH KENNETH CHAPEL
Inch Kenneth
Staffa
STAFFA
FINGAL'S CAVE
Balnahard
MACKINNON'S CAVE
561
Erisgeir
519
BEINN NA SREINE
Glen Seilisdeir
ARDMEANACH
Kilfinichen Bay
THE BURG
Eilean Annraidh
MACLEAN'S CROSS
Rubha nan Cearc
LOCH SCRIDAIN
IONA ABBEY AND CATHEDRAL
100
IONA HERITAGE CENTRE
Loch na Lathaich
Kintra
Iona
Baile Mor
ST COLUMBA EXHIBITION & WELCOME CENTRE
Stac an Aoineidh
Aridhglas
Eorabus
Fionnphort
A849
Sound of Iona
Fidden
Tiraghoil
Bunessan
Lee
376
CRUACHAN MIN
Loch Assapol
Erraid
212
ROSS OF MULL
Ardalanish
Ardchiavaig
Uisken
Scoor
0 1 2 3 miles
0 1 2 3 4 5 km

ISLAND OF MULL
MORVERN
SOUND OF MULL
FIRTH OF LORN
NM
Ardslignish
Glenborrodale
BEN LAGA
Laga
235
Eilean Mor
Oronsay
Carna
Glencripesdale
Camuschoirk
Liddesdale
Auliston Pt.
169
516 MEALL AN DAMHAIN
582 BEINN NAM BEATHRACH
Loch Teacuis
571 BEINN IADAIN
Lochuisge
Loch Uisge
Beach
TOBERMORY
Calve I.
TOBERMORY DISTILLERY
Drimnin
Bonnavoulin
Upper Druimfin
451 BEINN BHUIDHE
Gleann Dubh
Loch Arienas
550 STITHEAN NA RAPLAICH
Acharn
739 BEINN MHEADH
Rhemore
Ardnacross
Killundine
Gleann Geal
Claggan
Larachbeg
KINLOCHALINE CASTLE
ARDTORNISH GARDENS
Achranich
Loch Tearnait
437 BEINN A' CHAISIL
Fiunary
Savary
Loch Aline
Rannoch
226
Loch nan Clach
Aros Mains
Lochaline
GLAIS BHEINN 479
AN SLEAGHACH 513
Eignai
Rubha Mor
ARDTORNISH CASTLE
Salen
Fishnish Bay
Ardtornish Pt.
Pennygown
Killiechronan
Kellan
Gruline
Killbeg
Corrynachenchy
Inninmore Bay
Garbh Shlios
Camas Gorm
412
Garmony
Scallastle Bay
Rubha an Ridire
Bernera I.
Knock
Loch Bà
Forsa
Scallastle
Java
Craignure Bay
OBAN
Craignure
591 BEINN A'GHRAIG
766 DUN DA GHAOITHE
Duart Bay
Duart Pt.
DUART CASTLE
Eilean Musdile
Glen Cannel
761 BEINN TALAIDH
Lochdon
966 BEN MORE
704 CORRA-BHEINN
Glen More
Lussa
Loch Don
Grass Pt.
Strathcoil
Coladoir
Loch Airdeglais
Kerrera
248
Loch Spelve
Ardmore
Bach I.
BEN BUIE 717
698 CREACH BEINN
Loch Fuaron
Croggan
Rubha nan Sailthean
Kinlochspelve
Pennycross
Lochbuie
Barachandroman
Rubha Seanach
503 BEINN NA CROISE
Loch Uisg
Leidle
Loch Buie
405 DRUIM FADA
Carsaig
376
Laggan Deer Forest
Rubha Dubh
Carsaig Bay
LORD LOVAT'S CAVE
CLACHAN BRIDGE
212
213
Insh I.
Sound of Insh
Frank Lockwood's Island
Clachan-Seil
Seil
Clachan
A848
A849
A884
B8035
B849
B8043
B844

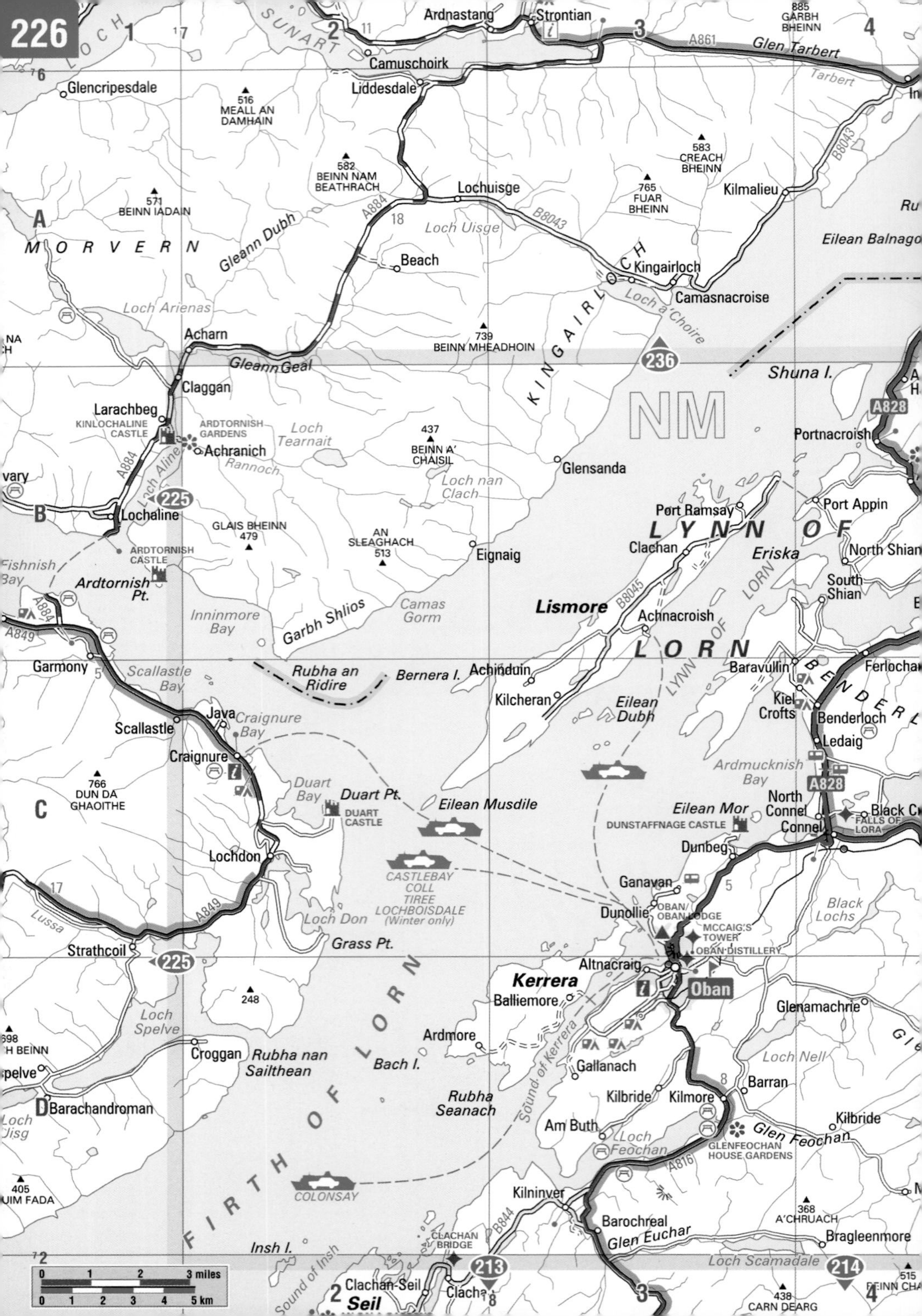
Ardnastang
Strontian
885 GARBH BHEINN
Camuschoirk
Glen Tarbert
A861
Tarbert
Liddesdale
Glencripesdale
516 MEALL AN DAMHAIN
582 BEINN NAM BEATHRACH
583 CREACH BHEINN
765 FUAR BHEINN
571 BEINN IADAIN
Lochuisge
Loch Uisge
B8043
Kilmalieu
A884
M O R V E R N
Gleann Dubh
Beach
Kingairloch
KINGAIRLOCH
Camasnacroise
Loch a' Choire
Eilean Balnagowan
Loch Arienas
Acharn
739 BEINN MHEADHOIN
Gleann Geal
236
Shuna I.
Claggan
NM
Larachbeg
KINLOCHALINE CASTLE
ARDTORNISH GARDENS
Achranich
Loch Tearnait
Rannoch
437 BEINN A' CHAISIL
Glensanda
Portnacroish
A828
Loch Aline
Loch nan Clach
225
Lochaline
GLAIS BHEINN 479
AN SLEAGHACH 513
Port Ramsay
Port Appin
LYNN OF
Clachan
Eignaig
North Shian
Fishnish Bay
ARDTORNISH CASTLE
Ardtornish Pt.
Eriska
South Shian
Lismore
B8045
LYNN OF LORN
Camas Gorm
Garbh Shlios
Inninmore Bay
A849
Achnacroish
LORN
Garmony
Rubha an Ridire
Bernera I.
Achinduin
Baravullin
Ferlochan
Scallastle Bay
BENDERLOCH
Kilcheran
Eilean Dubh
Kiel Crofts
Benderloch
Java
Craignure Bay
Scallastle
Ledaig
Craignure
Ardmucknish Bay
766 DUN DA GHAOITHE
Duart Bay
Duart Pt.
Eilean Musdile
DUART CASTLE
Eilean Mor
North Connel
Black Crofts
DUNSTAFFNAGE CASTLE
Connel
FALLS OF LORA
Lochdon
Dunbeg
CASTLEBAY COLL TIREE LOCHBOISDALE (Winter only)
Ganavan
Lussa
Loch Don
Dunollie
OBAN/OBAN LODGE
MCCAIG'S TOWER
OBAN DISTILLERY
Black Lochs
Strathcoil
Grass Pt.
Altnacraig
Kerrera
Oban
Balliemore
Glenamachrie
248
Loch Spelve
Ardmore
698
Croggan
Rubha nan Sailthean
Bach I.
Loch Nell
Gallanach
Sound of Kerrera
FIRTH OF LORN
Barran
Barachandroman
Rubha Seanach
Kilbride
Kilmore
Kilbride
Loch Uisg
Am Buth
Loch Feochan
Glen Feochan
A816
GLENFEOCHAN HOUSE GARDENS
405
COLONSAY
Kilninver
368 A'CHRUACH
Barochreal
B844
CLACHAN BRIDGE
Glen Euchar
Bragleenmore
Insh I.
Sound of Insh
213
Loch Scamadale
214
515
Clachan-Seil
Seil
438 CARN DEARG
0 1 2 3 miles
0 1 2 3 4 5 km

Onich
North Ballachulish
Kinlochleven
ALUMINIUM STORY VISITOR CENTRE
MAM NA GUALAINN
LOCH LINNHE
Sallachan Pt.
Loch Leven
GLENCOE AND NORTH LORN FOLK MUSEUM
Glencoe
South Ballachulish
Ballachulish
Kentallen
AONACH
Glenduror Forest
GLENCOE VISITOR CENTRE
Glen an Fhiodh
Glen Coe
Altnafeadh
BEINN A' CHRULAIST
Duror
Beinn a'Bheithir
BEN NEVIS AND GLEN COE
Keil
Glen Duror
Salachan Glen
BIDEAN NAM BIAN
Royal Forest
Coupall
Etive
FRAOCHAIDH
SGOR NA H-ULAIDH
Dalness
Glen Etive
Alltchaorunn
Elleric
Glen Creran
BEINN FHIONNLAIDH
STOB DUBH
CLACH LEATHAD
Fasnacloich
Invercreran
An Iola
Inverchanan
Glenceitlein
Glen Ure
BEINN CHURALAIN
GLASDRUM WOOD
Glasdrum
BEINN SGULAIRD
Gualachulain
Allt Coire a'Chaolain
Creagan
Druimavuic
Allt Dochard
STOB GHABHAR
South Creagan
NN
Allt Easach
BEINN TRILLEACHAN
STOB COIR'AN ALBANNAICH
BEN STARAV
CREACH BHEINN
Abhainn Dalach
Loch Dochard
Barcaldine Forest
Allt Hallater
BEINN NAN AIGHENAN
Gleann Salach
B845
LOCH ETIVE
BEINN MHEADHONACH
ARDCHATTAN PRIORY
Glen Kinglass
Glen Liver
BEINN MHIC-MHONAIDH
GLEN ORCHY
Achnacloich
ACHNACLOICH GARDEN
Bonawe
Glen Noe
BONAWE IRON FURNACE
INVERAWE FISHERIES AND SMOKERIES EXHIBITION
Brochroy
A85
BEINN EUNAICH
Glen Strae
Strae
B8074
Taynuilt
BEN CRUACHAN
Allt Mhoille
Ichrachan
Bridge of Awe
Pass of Brander
Cruachan Reservoir
BARGUILLEAN GARDENS
GLEN NANT
Glen Nant
Awe
B8077
KILCHURN CASTLE
Lochawe
Falls of Cruachan
Stronmilchan
Strath of Orchy
Achnafalnich
Inverlochy
Dalmally
CRUACHAN DAM VISITOR CENTRE
MCINTYRE MONUMENT
Loch Nant
Loch Tromlee
ARDANAISEIG GARDENS
Innis Chonain
Ardanaiseig
INISHAIL CHAPEL
Inishail
Teatle Water
Eas a'Ghaill
A819
Kilchrenan
Sior Loch
Annat
North Port
Cladich
Allt Fearna
MEALL NAN TIGHEARN
Portsonachan
South Port
Cladich
Lochan Shira
Loch Stron Mor
B840
237
228
216
214
215

Bridge
Inverroy
Roybridge
Achluachrach
Murlaggan
Roughburn
Killiechonate
A86
239
240
Spean
MONESSIE FALLS
Lochaber
GLEN SPEAN
Leanachan Forest
724
BEINN CHLIANAIG
Fersit
Allt Loraich
1087
BEINN A'CHLACHAIR
The Cour
EXPERIENCE
Allt Làire
Loch Ghuilbinn
1114
AONACH BEAG
1046
CHNO DEARG
1177
STOB CHOIRE CLAURIGH
1106
1115
STOB COIRE EASAIN
Lairig Leacach
Allt na Lairige
LOCH TREIG
Ossian
1234
1094
Uisge Labhair
937
BEINN NA LAP
Creaguaineach Lodge
Corrour Shooting Lodge
Amhainn Rath
LOCH OSSIAN
Loch Ossian
Corrour Forest
237
952
SGOR GAIBHRE
583
630
1130
BINNEIN MOR
MAMORE FOREST
Loch Eilde Beag
Allt na Caim
Rannoch Forest
789
Loch Eilde Mor
906
LEUM UILLEIM
Ciaran Water
Black Water
BLACKWATER RESERVOIR
Leven
BEN NEVIS
Rannoch Station
B846
Altnafeadh
857
BEINN A' CHRULAISTE
Black Corries Lodge
739
STOB NA CRUAICHE
Loch Eigheach
Gaur
Coupall
Kingshouse Hotel
Loch Laidon
Loch Gaineamhach
AND
Royal Forest
Etive
GLENCOE SKI CENTRE
A82
RANNOCH MOOR
547
Alltchaorunn
1188
Loch Bà
GLEN COE
1099
CLACH LEATHAD
Allt Coire a' Chaolain
Bà
Loch na h-Achlaise
Water of Tulla
Loch an Daimh
BLACK MOUNT
Eas Daimh
1090
STOB GHABHAR
WEST HIGHLAND WAY
907
MEALL BUIDHE
960
STUCHD AN LOCHAIN
227
Loch Tulla
Achallader
1081
BEINN A' CHREACHAIN
Black Mount
Forest Lodge
Pubil
Cashlie
Loch Lyon
Loch Dochard
Inveroran Hotel
1004
BIENN AN DOTHAIDH
953
BEINN MHANACH
216
217
Bridge of Orchy
BEINN HEASGARNICH
0 1 2 3 miles
0 1 2 3 4 5 km

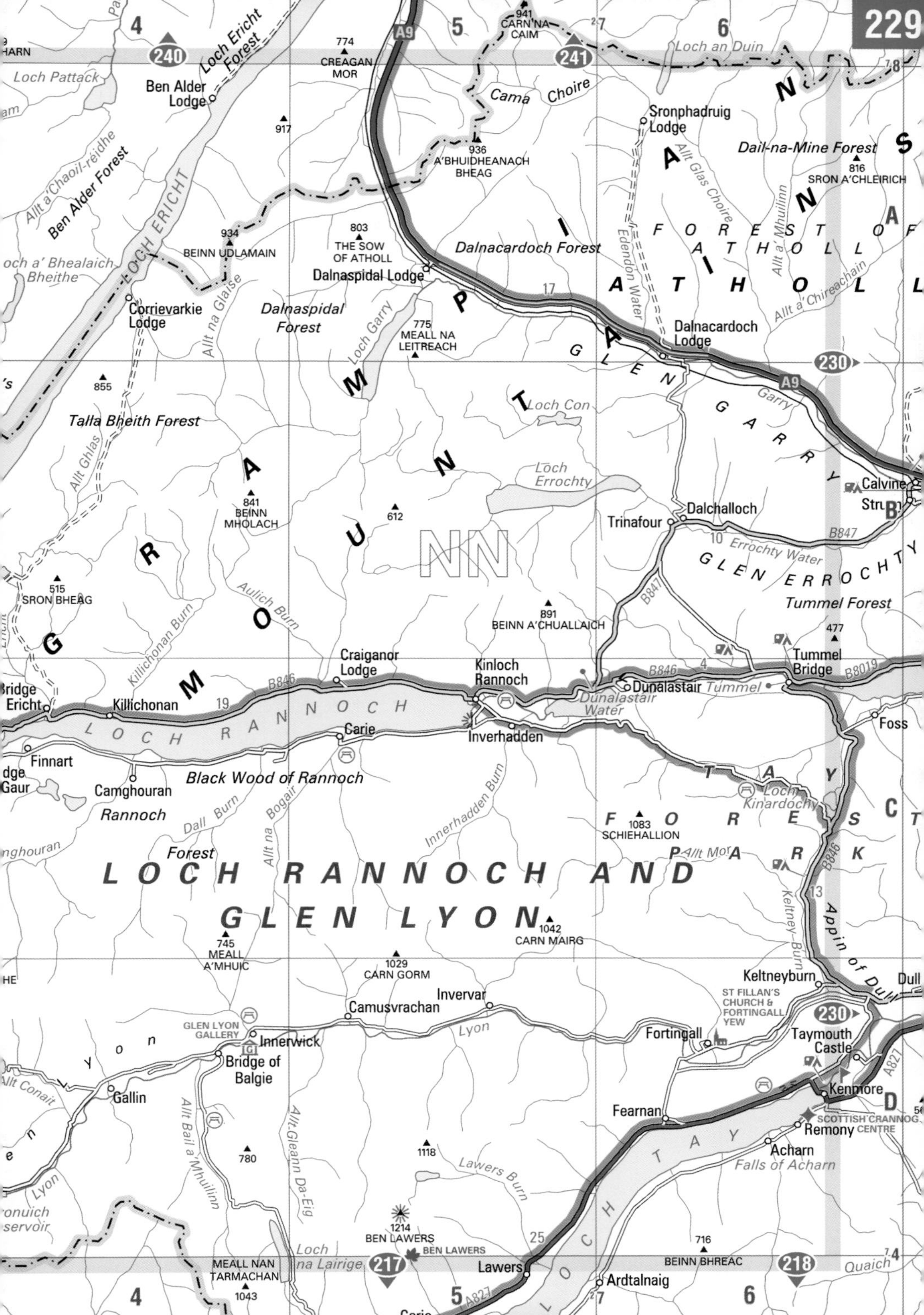
4
5
6
240
241
230
218
217
A9
Loch Ericht Forest
Ben Alder Lodge
Loch Pattack
774
CREAGAN MOR
941
CARN NA CAIM
Loch an Duin
Cama Choire
917
Sronphadruig Lodge
936
A'BHUIDHEANACH BHEAG
Dail-na-Mine Forest
816
SRON A'CHLEIRICH
Allt a' Chaoil-reidhe
Ben Alder Forest
LOCH ERICHT
934
BEINN UDLAMAIN
803
THE SOW OF ATHOLL
Dalnacardoch Forest
Allt Glas Choire
Edendon Water
Allt a' Mhuilinn
FOREST OF ATHOLL
ATHOLL
Allt a' Chireachain
Loch a' Bhealaich Bheithe
Dalnaspidal Lodge
17
Corrievarkie Lodge
Allt na Glaise
Dalnaspidal Forest
Loch Garry
775
MEALL NA LEITREACH
Dalnacardoch Lodge
GLEN GARRY
Garry
855
Talla Bheith Forest
Loch Con
Allt Ghlas
Loch Errochty
Calvine
Struan
841
BEINN MHOLACH
612
NN
Dalchalloch
Trinafour
10
B847
Errochty Water
GLEN ERROCHTY
Tummel Forest
515
SRON BHEAG
Aulich Burn
Killichonan Burn
891
BEINN A'CHUALLAICH
477
GRAMPIAN MOUNTAINS
Craiganor Lodge
Kinloch Rannoch
B846
4
Tummel Bridge
B8019
Bridge of Ericht
Killichonan
19
LOCH RANNOCH
Dunalastair
Tummel
Dunalastair Water
Carie
Inverhadden
Foss
Finnart
Bridge of Gaur
Camghouran
Black Wood of Rannoch
Allt na Bogair
Innerhadden Burn
Loch Kinardochy
Rannoch
Dall Burn
Forest
1083
SCHIEHALLION
Allt Mor
TAY FOREST PARK
Keltney Burn
13
Appin of Dull
LOCH RANNOCH AND GLEN LYON
1042
CARN MAIRG
745
MEALL A'MHUIC
1029
CARN GORM
Keltneyburn
Dull
ST FILLAN'S CHURCH & FORTINGALL YEW
Invervar
Camusvrachan
GLEN LYON GALLERY
Innerwick
Lyon
Fortingall
Taymouth Castle
Bridge of Balgie
Glen Lyon
Alt Conait
Gallin
A827
Kenmore
Fearnan
SCOTTISH CRANNOG CENTRE
Remony
Acharn
Falls of Acharn
Allt Bail a' Mhuilinn
Allt Gleann Da-Eig
780
1118
Lawers Burn
LOCH TAY
1214
BEN LAWERS
25
716
BEINN BHREAC
Loch na Lairige
MEALL NAN TARMACHAN
1043
Lawers
Ardtalnaig
Quaich

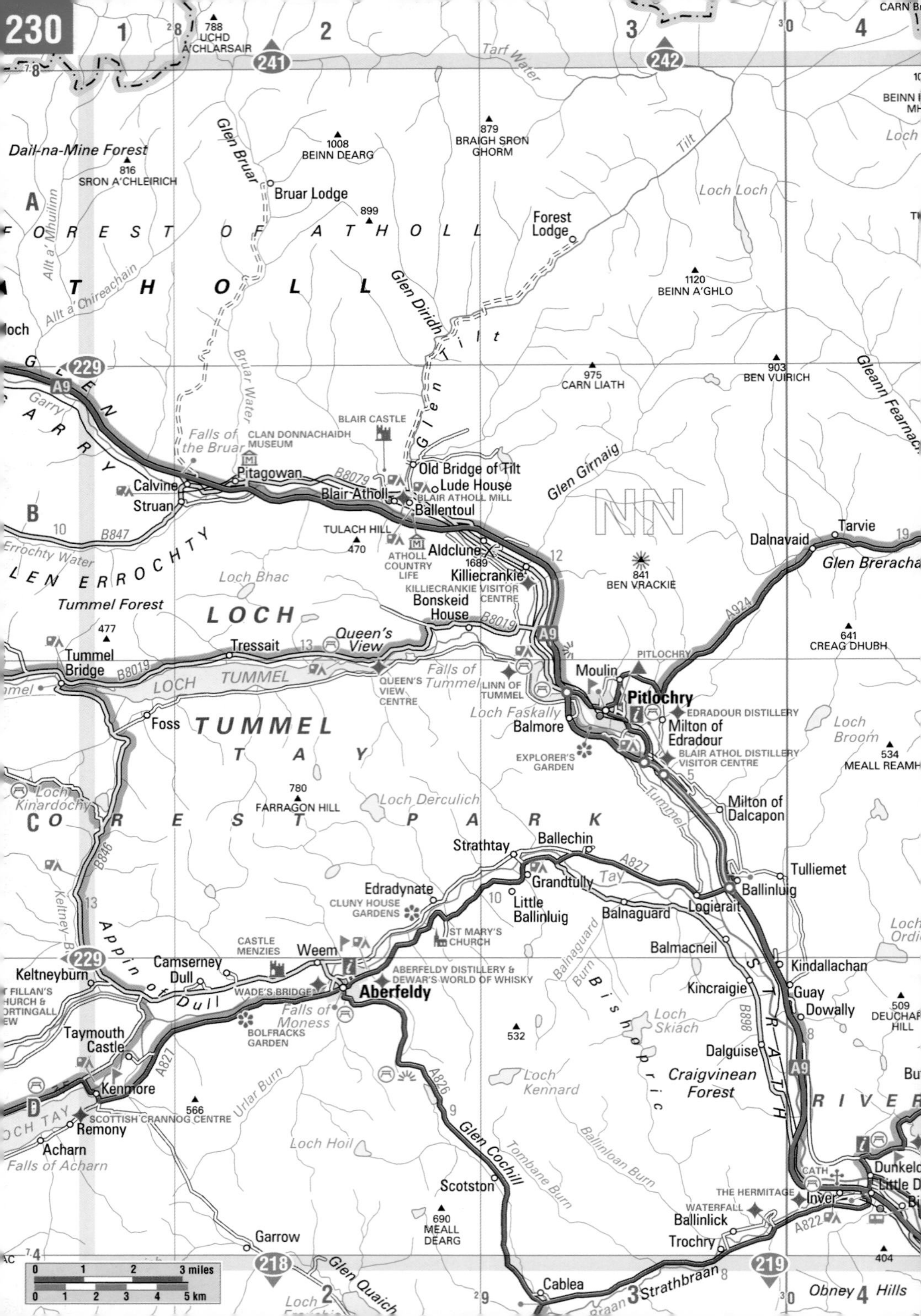

241
242
229
218
219
FOREST OF ATHOLL
ATHOLL
GLEN GARRY
GLEN ERROCHTY
LOCH TUMMEL
TAY FOREST PARK
Dail-na-Mine Forest
SRON A'CHLEIRICH
UCHD A'CHLARSAIR
BEINN DEARG
BRAIGH SRON GHORM
Glen Bruar
Bruar Lodge
Forest Lodge
BEINN A'GHLO
Loch Loch
Tarf Water
Tilt
Glen Tilt
Glen Diridh
CARN LIATH
BEN VUIRICH
Gleann Fearnach
BLAIR CASTLE
CLAN DONNACHAIDH MUSEUM
Falls of the Bruar
Bruar Water
Calvine
Struan
Pitagowan
Blair Atholl
Old Bridge of Tilt
Lude House
BLAIR ATHOLL MILL
Ballentoul
Glen Girnaig
NN
TULACH HILL
ATHOLL COUNTRY LIFE
Aldclune
Killiecrankie
KILLIECRANKIE VISITOR CENTRE
Bonskeid House
BEN VRACKIE
Dalnavaid
Tarvie
Glen Brerachan
A924
CREAG DHUBH
Tummel Forest
Loch Bhac
Tummel Bridge
Tressait
Queen's View
QUEEN'S VIEW CENTRE
Falls of Tummel
LINN OF TUMMEL
Moulin
PITLOCHRY
Pitlochry
EDRADOUR DISTILLERY
Milton of Edradour
BLAIR ATHOL DISTILLERY VISITOR CENTRE
Loch Faskally
Balmore
EXPLORER'S GARDEN
Loch Broom
MEALL REAMH
Foss
Loch Kinardochy
FARRAGON HILL
Loch Derculich
Milton of Dalcapon
Strathtay
Ballechin
Grandtully
Little Ballinluig
Edradynate
CLUNY HOUSE GARDENS
Balnaguard
Logierait
Ballinluig
Tulliemet
ST MARY'S CHURCH
CASTLE MENZIES
Weem
Camserney
Dull
Keltneyburn
Appin of Dull
WADE'S BRIDGE
ABERFELDY DISTILLERY & DEWAR'S WORLD OF WHISKY
Aberfeldy
Falls of Moness
BOLFRACKS GARDEN
Balmacneil
Kindallachan
Kincraigie
Guay
Dowally
DEUCHARY HILL
Bishopric
Loch Skiach
Dalguise
Craigvinean Forest
STRATH
RIVER
Taymouth Castle
Kenmore
SCOTTISH CRANNOG CENTRE
Remony
Acharn
Falls of Acharn
Loch Hoil
Loch Kennard
Urlar Burn
Glen Cochill
Tombane Burn
Ballinloan Burn
Scotston
MEALL DEARG
Garrow
Glen Quaich
Cablea
Strathbraan
Trochry
Ballinlick
WATERFALL
THE HERMITAGE
Inver
Dunkeld
Obney Hills
A9
A827
A826
A821
A822
B8079
B847
B8019
B846
B898
0 1 2 3 miles
0 1 2 3 4 5 km

4
5
6
7
242
243
232
219
220
939 AN SOCACH
1019 CARN AN TUIRC
958 TOLMOUNT
998 BROAD CAIRN
BANNOCH
Clunie Water
Loch Vrotachan
GLENSHEE SKI CENTRE
933 THE CAIRNWELL
Devil's Elbow
1068 GLAS MAOL
Caenlochan Forest
Glen Doll
Glendoll Lodge
Glendoll Forest
Braedownie
832 LAIR OF ALDARARIE
Loch Brandy
CORRIE FEE
905 FINALTY HILL
947 DRIESH
Clova
758
GLEN CLOVA
B955
Wheen
Kilburn
BEN GULABIN 806
Glenlochsie
808 MONAMEANACH
Spittal of Glenshee
801 BEN EARB
Loch Beanie
Auchavan
Glen Prosen
Glenprosen Lodge
Balnaboth
PROSEN
Glenprosen Village
794 MEALL UAINE
702 DUCHRAY HILL
740 BADENDUN HILL
Glen Shee
A93
Dalnaglar Castle
Meikle Forter
Glenisla Forest
611
Folda
B951
Cray
Enochdhu
Ashintully Castle
744 MOUNT BLAIR
Brewlands Bridge
Backwater Res.
Glenhead Farm
Easter Lednathie
Freuchies
CAPTAIN SCOTT DR WILSON
668 CAT LAW
Kirkmichael
Blacklunans
Kirkton of Glenisla
Bellaty
497 CREIGH HILL
Balintore
Pearsie
STRATHARDLE
B950
520 CAIRN GIBBS
Dykends
KNOCK OF BALMYLE 444
Black Water
Forest of Alyth
NO
409 MILE HILL
Isla
B954
Loch of Lintrathen
PEEL FARM TRAIL
Bridgend of Lintrathen
Kirkton of Kingoldrum
LOCH OF KINNORDY NATURE RESERVE
Ballintuim
BALDUFF HILL 425
REEKIE LINN WATERFALL
Ardle
A924
Netherton
Tullymurdoch
Bridge of Craigisla
Auchrannie
Kirkton of Airlie
A926
Blackcraig Forest
Forest of Clunie
Loch Benachally
Bridge of Cally
Bamff
Shanzie
Craigton
Cochrage Muir
Tullyfergus
Ruthven
Ruthven House
EASSIE SCULPTURED STONE
Lornty Burn
Middleton
308
Alyth
New Alyth
Riechip
Westfields of Rattray
Lornty
Balhary
Castleton
A94
Forneth
Achalader
A923
Blairgowrie
Kinloch
Rattray
Leitfie
MEIGLE MUSEUM
Balkeerie
Eassie
Concraigie
Loch of Clunie
Loch of Drumellie
Loch of Lowes
LOCH OF LOWES NATURE RESERVE
Kirkinch
Clunie
Craigie
Muirton of Ardblair
Rosemount
River Ericht
Kinloch
Meigle
Arthurstone
Wester Denoon
Snaigow House
Kirkton of Lethendy
B947
Lunan Burn
Ardler
New-bigging
Newtyle
SIDLAW HILLS
Spittalfield
A984
Delvine
Keillor
Coupar Angus
Caputh
TAY
Tay
Meikleour
BEECH HEDGE
Kinclaver
Isla
Kettins
Markethill
Campmuir
Hallyburton House
Long Loch
Bonnyton
Kirkton
Gellyburn
Muir of Thorn
Murthly
A
B
C
D

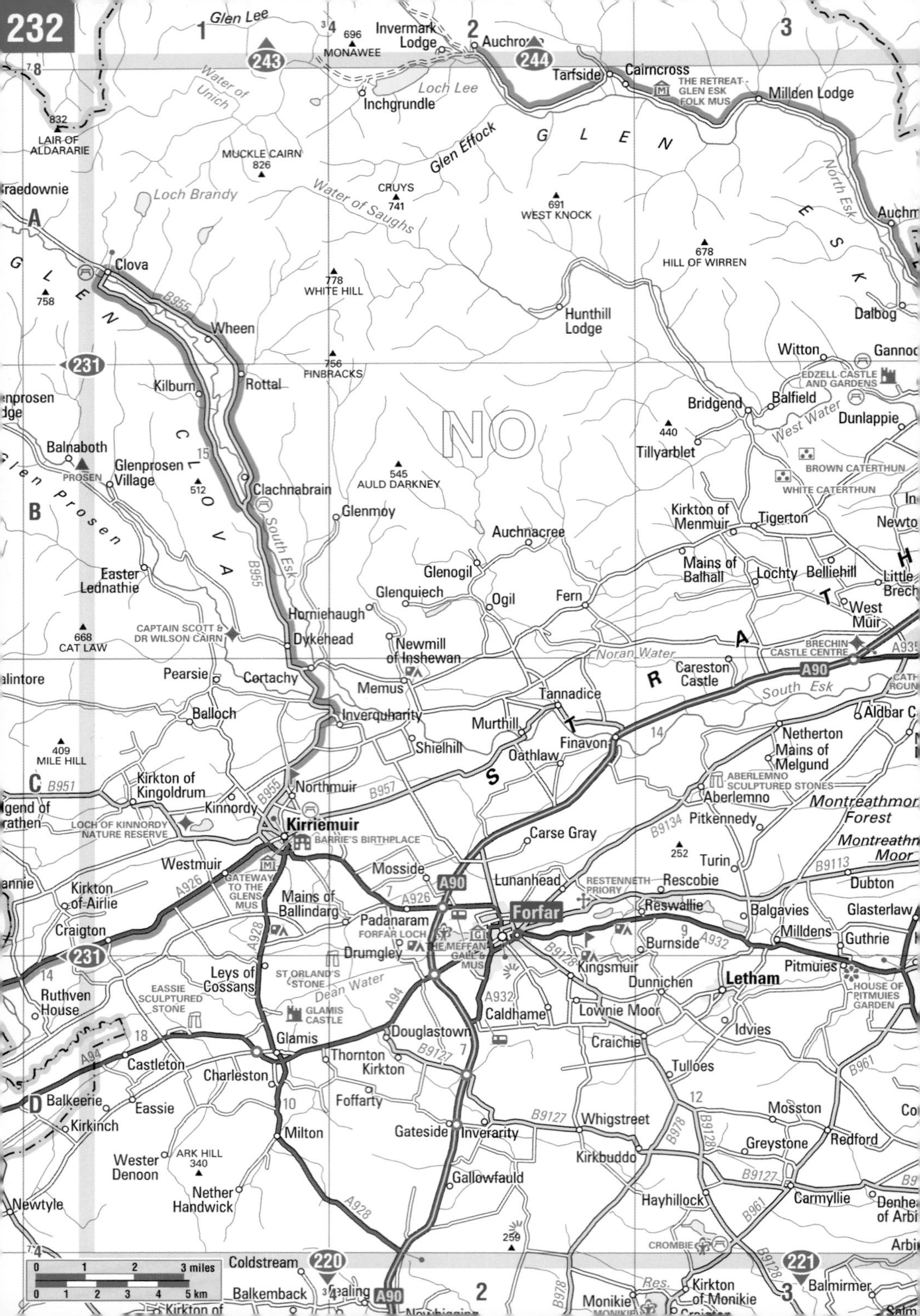
Glen Lee
696
MONAWEE
Invermark Lodge
Auchronie
243
244
Tarfside
Cairncross
THE RETREAT GLEN ESK FOLK MUS
Millden Lodge
Water of Unich
Loch Lee
Inchgrundle
832
LAIR OF ALDARARIE
MUCKLE CAIRN
826
Glen Effock
GLEN ESK
North Esk
Braedownie
Loch Brandy
Water of Saughs
CRUYS
741
691
WEST KNOCK
Auchmull
678
HILL OF WIRREN
Clova
778
WHITE HILL
GLEN CLOVA
758
B955
Wheen
Hunthill Lodge
Dalbog
231
756
FINBRACKS
Witton
Gannochy
EDZELL CASTLE AND GARDENS
Kilburn
Rottal
Balfield
Bridgend
Dunlappie
NO
West Water
440
Tillyarblet
Balnaboth
PROSEN
Glenprosen Village
512
545
AULD DARKNEY
BROWN CATERTHUN
WHITE CATERTHUN
Glen Prosen
Clachnabrain
South Esk
Glenmoy
Kirkton of Menmuir
Tigerton
Newton
Auchnacree
Easter Lednathie
Glenogil
Mains of Balhall
Lochty
Belliehill
Little Brechin
Glenquiech
Ogil
Fern
West Muir
Horniehaugh
CAPTAIN SCOTT & DR WILSON CAIRN
668
CAT LAW
Dykehead
Newmill of Inshewan
STRATHMORE
Noran Water
BRECHIN CASTLE CENTRE
A935
Balintore
Pearsie
Cortachy
Memus
Careston Castle
A90
South Esk
Tannadice
Balloch
Inverquharity
Murthill
Aldbar Castle
Finavon
Netherton
409
MILE HILL
Shielhill
Oathlaw
Mains of Melgund
B951
Kirkton of Kingoldrum
B955
Northmuir
B957
ABERLEMNO SCULPTURED STONES
Aberlemno
Montreathmont Forest
Bridgend of Lintrathen
Kinnordy
LOCH OF KINNORDY NATURE RESERVE
Kirriemuir
BARRIE'S BIRTHPLACE
Carse Gray
B9134
Pitkennedy
Montreathmont Moor
252
Westmuir
GATEWAY TO THE GLENS MUS
Mosside
Turin
B9113
A926
A90
Lunanhead
RESTENNETH PRIORY
Rescobie
Dubton
Kirkton of Airlie
Mains of Ballindarg
A926
Reswallie
Balgavies
Glasterlaw
Forfar
Padanaram
FORFAR LOCH
THE MEFFAN GALL & MUS
Milldens
Guthrie
Craigton
A928
Burnside
A932
231
Drumgley
B9128
Kingsmuir
Pitmuies
ST ORLAND'S STONE
Leys of Cossans
Dean Water
Dunnichen
Letham
HOUSE OF PITMUIES GARDEN
Ruthven House
EASSIE SCULPTURED STONE
A94
GLAMIS CASTLE
A932
Caldhame
Lowrie Moor
Idvies
Glamis
Douglastown
Craichie
A94
Castleton
Thornton
Kirkton
B9127
Charleston
Tulloes
B961
Balkeerie
Eassie
Foffarty
Mosston
Kirkinch
Milton
Gateside
Inverarity
B9127
Whigstreet
B978
B9128
Greystone
Redford
Wester Denoon
ARK HILL
340
Kirkbuddo
B9127
Gallowfauld
Carmyllie
Newtyle
Nether Handwick
A928
Hayhillock
B961
Denhead of Arbirlot
259
CROMBIE
B9128
Arbirlot
Coldstream
220
221
Balkemback
Tealing
A90
B978
Res.
Kirkton of Monikie
Monikie
Balmirmer
Kirkton of
Newbigging
Craigton
3 miles
5 km

Cairn o' Mount
Drumtochty Forest
Drumtochty Castle
Glenfarquhar Lodge
Dellavaird
BURNS FAMILY MEMORIALS
Glenbervie
Drumlithie
Fiddes
Barras
Mill of Uras
Crawton
FOWLSHEUGH NATURE RESERVE
Crawton Bay
Strath Finella
Clatterin Bridge
Glensaugh
Auchenblae
Monboddo House
Mondynes
Pitforthie
Roadside of Catterline
Catterline
Braidon Bay
Todhead Point
Brownmuir
East Cairnbeg
Fordoun
Parkneuk
Arbuthnott
Roadside of Kinneff
Kinneff
Mains of Balnakettle
Thainston
FETTERCAIRN DISTILLERY VISITOR CENTRE
Fettercairn
Howe of the Mearns
GRASSIC GIBBON CENTRE
ARBUTHNOTT CHURCH
ARBUTHNOTT HOUSE GARDENS
Mains of Allardice
Little John's Haven
Scotston
Bent
Inverbervie
Bervie Bay
Mains of Thornton
Meikle Strath
Inch of Arnhall
Laurencekirk
Tulloch
Garvock
Garvock Hill
Redford
Gourdon
Sauchieburn
Luther Water
Luthermuir
Dykelands
Benholm
MILL OF BENHOLM
Johnshaven
North Water Bridge
North Esk
Pert
Marykirk
Ecclesgreig
Craigo
Lochside
St Cyrus
Milton Ness
Logie Pert
Logie
Morphie
ST CYRUS
Keithock
Muirton of Ballochy
Pathhead
Trinity
Hillside
Brechin
HOUSE OF DUN
Kirkhill
Dun
CALEDONIAN RAILWAY
Bridge of Dun
Montrose Basin
Montrose
MUSEUM AND ART GALLERY
Kinnaird Castle
Barnhead
Inchbraoch
Scurdie Ness
MONTROSE BASIN VISITOR CENTRE
WILLIAM LAMB MEMORIAL STUDIO
Ferryden
Farnell
Bonnyton
Maryton
Kirkton of Craig
Carcary
Long Craig
Dunninald
Fishtown of Usan
Rossie Moor
Westerton
Boddin Pt.
Braehead of Lunan
Bolshan
Lunan
LUNAN BAY
Redcastle
Boysack
Inverkeilor
Lunan Water
Lang Craig
Ethie Mains
Cauldcots
Red Head
Ethie Castle
Drunkendub
Letham Grange
Auchmithie
Marywell
Meg's Craig
St Vigeans
ST VIGEANS MUSEUM
Hayshead
The Deil's Heid
Cliffburn
ARBROATH ABBEY
Arbroath
SIGNAL TOWER MUSEUM
Elliot
NO
221

1
2
3
Guirdil Bay
388
246
CANNA
Kilmory Glen
Kinloch Glen
Rubha na Roinne
A'Bhrideanach
Kinloch
Loch Scresort
571
ORVAL
R Ù M
KINLOCH CASTLE
Rubha Port na Caranean
RÙM
Schooner Pt.
Harris
Glen Harris
812
ASKIVAL
781
AINSHVAL
Rubha Sgorr an t-Snidhe
Rubha nam Meirleach
THE SMALL ISLES
SOUND OF RÙM
Bay of Laig
Rubha an Fhasaidh
Eigg
393
AN SGURR
SOUND OF EIGG
Eilean nan Each
137
Port Mor
Muck
A
B
C
D
Sanna Point
Sanna
Sanna Bay
Achnaha
Portuairk
Point of Ardnamurchan
ARDNAMURCHAN LIGHTHOUSE
Achosnich
B8007
Ormsaigmore
Ormsaigbeg
An Acairseid
Kilchoan Bay
223
Cairns of Coll
Eilean Mor
Rubha Mor
Sorisdale
Bousd
COLL
B8072
Gallanach
224
Ardmore Bay
0 1 2 3 miles
0 1 2 3 4 5 km

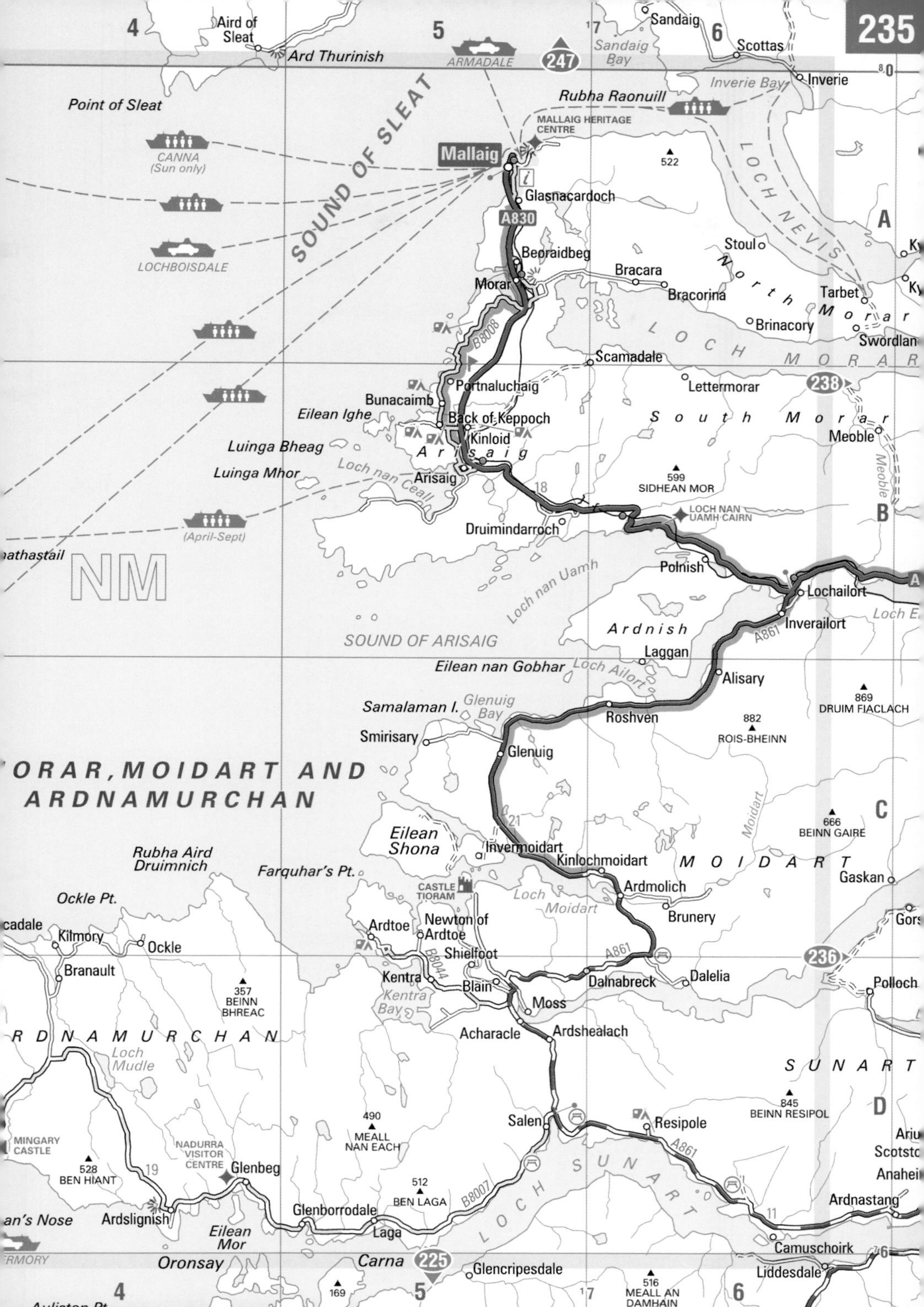

Aird of Sleat
Ard Thurinish
ARMADALE
247
Sandaig
Sandaig Bay
Scottas
Inverie
Inverie Bay
Point of Sleat
Rubha Raonuill
MALLAIG HERITAGE CENTRE
Mallaig
CANNA (Sun only)
SOUND OF SLEAT
522
LOCH NEVIS
Glasnacardoch
A830
LOCHBOISDALE
Beoraidbeg
Stoul
Morar
Bracara
Bracorina
North Morar
Tarbet
Brinacory
Swordlan
LOCH MORAR
B8008
Scamadale
Lettermorar
238
Portnaluchaig
Bunacaimb
Eilean Ighe
Back of Keppoch
South Morar
Kinloid
Meoble
Luinga Bheag
Arisaig
Luinga Mhor
Loch nan Ceall
Arisaig
599
SIDHEAN MOR
Meoble
LOCH NAN UAMH CAIRN
(April-Sept)
Druimindarroch
Polnish
NM
Loch nan Uamh
Lochailort
Loch E
Inverailort
Ardnish
A861
SOUND OF ARISAIG
Laggan
Eilean nan Gobhar
Loch Ailort
Alisary
869
DRUIM FIACLACH
Samalaman I.
Glenuig Bay
Roshven
882
ROIS-BHEINN
Smirisary
Glenuig
MORAR, MOIDART AND ARDNAMURCHAN
Moidart
666
BEINN GAIRE
Eilean Shona
Invermoidart
Rubha Aird Druimnich
Kinlochmoidart
MOIDART
Gaskan
Farquhar's Pt.
CASTLE TIORAM
Ardmolich
Ockle Pt.
Loch Moidart
Brunery
cadale
Kilmory
Ockle
Ardtoe
Newton of Ardtoe
Gors
A861
236
Shielfoot
B8044
Branault
Kentra
Blain
Dalnabreck
Dalelia
Polloch
357
BEINN BHREAC
Kentra Bay
Moss
ARDNAMURCHAN
Acharacle
Ardshealach
Loch Mudle
SUNART
845
BEINN RESIPOL
490
MEALL NAN EACH
Salen
Resipole
MINGARY CASTLE
NADURRA VISITOR CENTRE
528
BEN HIANT
Glenbeg
LOCH SUNART
A861
Ariu
Scotsto
Anahei
512
BEN LAGA
B8007
Ardnastang
an's Nose
Ardslignish
Eilean Mor
Glenborrodale
Laga
Camuschoirk
RMORY
Oronsay
Carna
225
Glencripesdale
Liddesdale
169
516
MEALL AN DAMHAIN
Auliston Pt

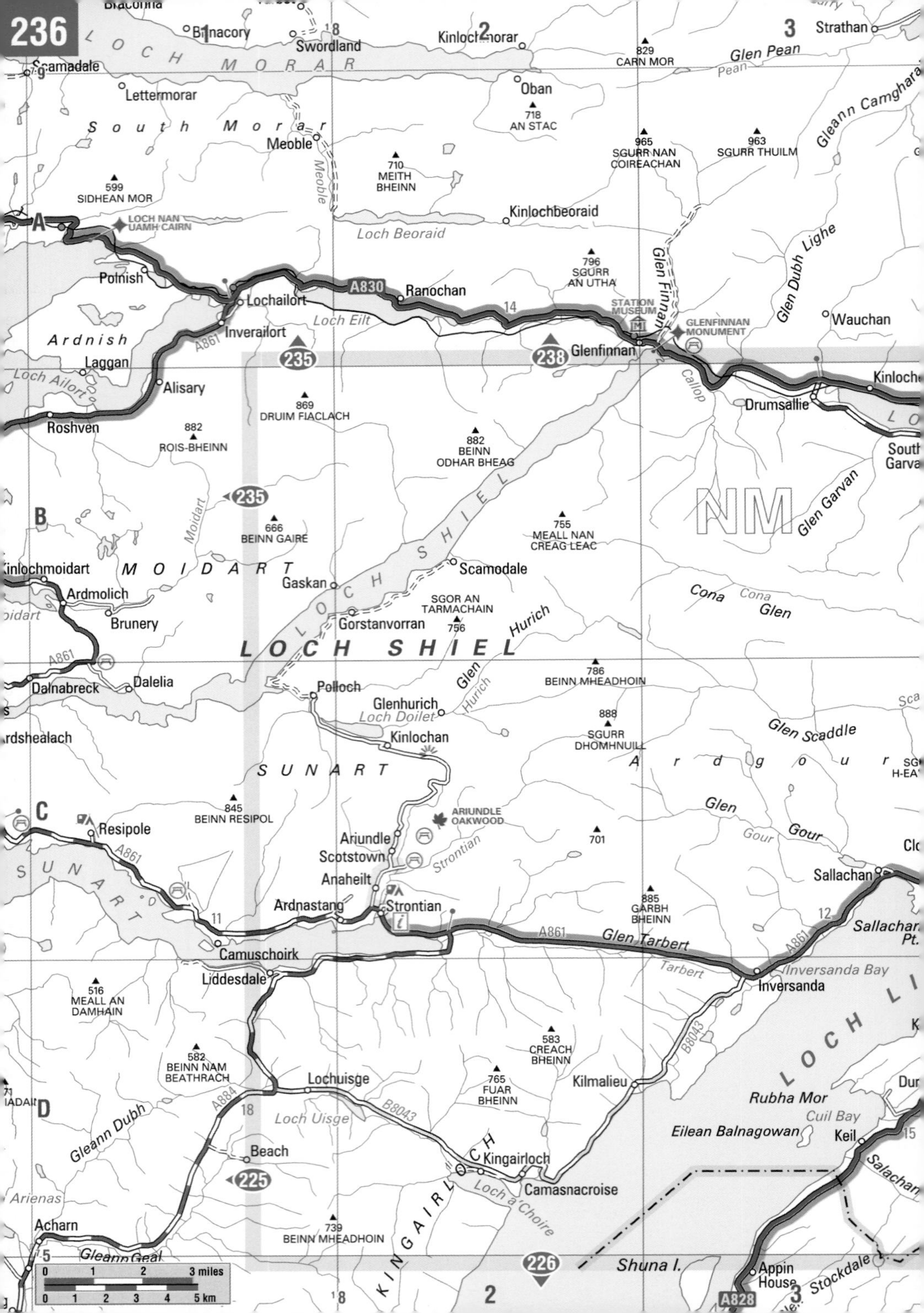
Bracorina
Brinacory
Swordland
Kinlochmorar
Strathan
LOCH MORAR
829
CARN MOR
Glen Pean
Pean
Scamadale
Lettermorar
Oban
718
AN STAC
Gleann Camgharaidh
South Morar
Meoble
965
SGURR NAN
COIREACHAN
963
SGURR THUILM
710
MEITH
BHEINN
599
SIDHEAN MOR
Meoble
Kinlochbeoraid
A
LOCH NAN
UAMH CAIRN
Loch Beoraid
Glen Dubh Lighe
796
SGURR
AN UTHA
Polnish
A830
Ranochan
Lochailort
Loch Eilt
14
STATION
MUSEUM
Glen Finnan
GLENFINNAN
MONUMENT
Wauchan
Ardnish
Inverailort
A861
235
238
Glenfinnan
Laggan
Loch Ailort
Alisary
Callop
Kinloch
Drumsallie
869
DRUIM FIACLACH
Roshven
882
ROIS-BHEINN
882
BEINN
ODHAR BHEAG
South
Garva
235
NM
Glen Garvan
B
Moidart
666
BEINN GAIRE
755
MEALL NAN
CREAG LEAC
LOCH SHIEL
Kinlochmoidart
MOIDART
Scamodale
Gaskan
Ardmolich
SGOR AN
TARMACHAIN
756
Cona
Cona
Glen
Brunery
Gorstanvorran
Glen Hurich
LOCH SHIEL
A861
786
BEINN MHEADHOIN
Dalnabreck
Dalelia
Polloch
Glenhurich
Loch Doilet
Hurich
888
SGURR
DHOMHNUILL
Ardshealach
Kinlochan
Glen Scaddle
SUNART
Ardgour
C
Resipole
845
BEINN RESIPOL
ARIUNDLE
OAKWOOD
Glen
Gour
Gour
Ariundle
701
Scotstown
Strontian
A861
SUNART
Anaheilt
Sallachan
885
GARBH
BHEINN
Ardnastang
Strontian
11
12
Sallachan
Pt.
A861
Glen Tarbert
A861
Camuschoirk
Tarbert
Inversanda Bay
Liddesdale
Inversanda
516
MEALL AN
DAMHAIN
LOCH LINNHE
583
CREACH
BHEINN
582
BEINN NAM
BEATHRACH
B8043
765
FUAR
BHEINN
Lochuisge
Kilmalieu
A884
18
Rubha Mor
D
Loch Uisge
B8043
Cuil Bay
Gleann Dubh
Eilean Balnagowan
Keil
15
Beach
LOCH
Kingairloch
Salachan
225
Camasnacroise
Arienas
Loch a' Choire
KINGAIRLOCH
739
BEINN MHEADHOIN
Acharn
5
Gleann Geal
226
Shuna I.
Appin
House
Stockdale
0
1
2
3 miles
0
1
2
3
4
5 km
18
2
A828
3

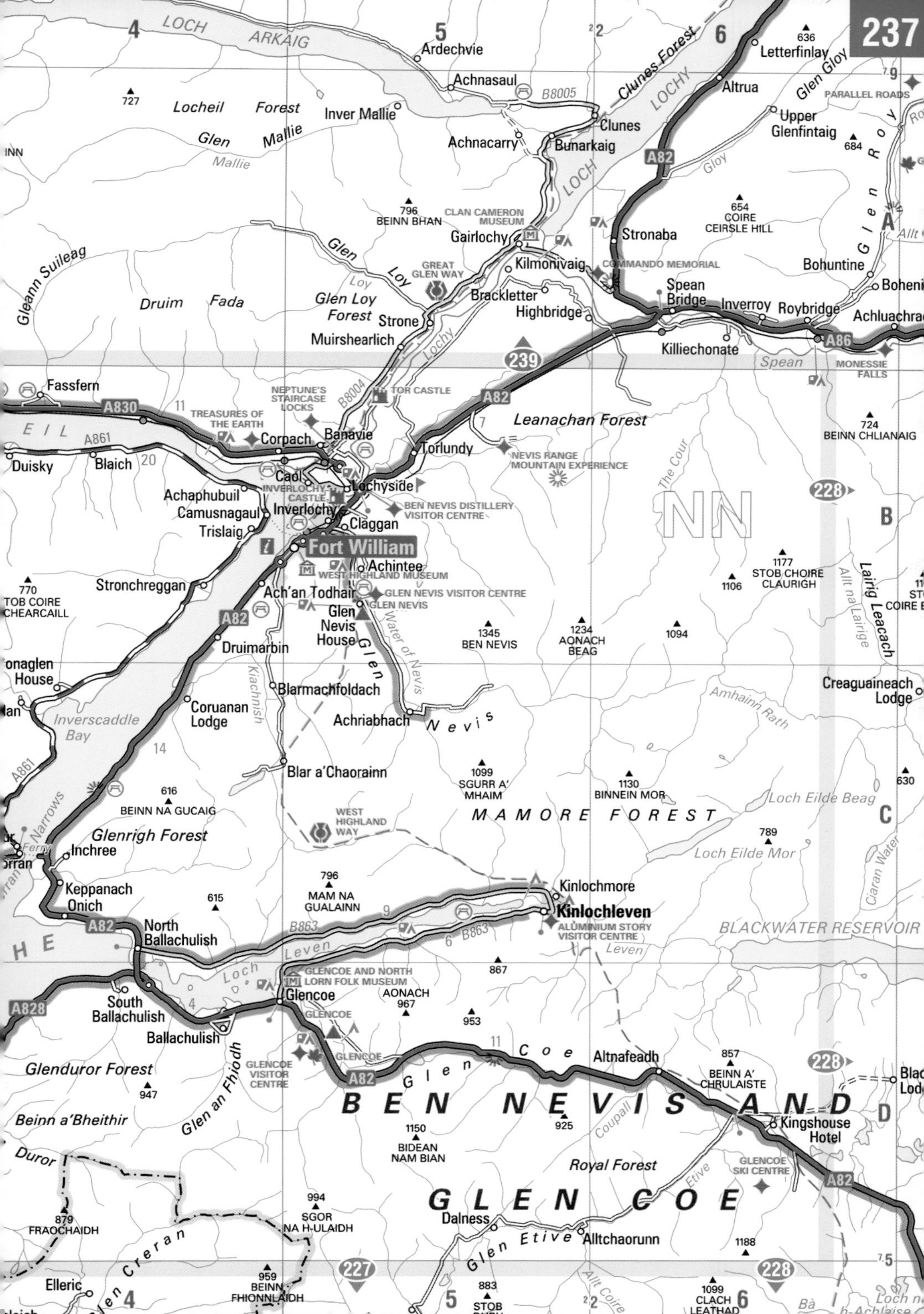

LOCH ARKAIG
Ardechvie
Achnasaul
B8005
Clunes Forest
LOCH LOCHY
Letterfinlay
636
Glen Gloy
Altrua
PARALLEL ROADS
727
Locheil Forest
Inver Mallie
Glen Mallie
Mallie
Clunes
Upper Glenfintaig
684
Achnacarry
Bunarkaig
A82
Gloy
Glen Roy
796
BEINN BHAN
CLAN CAMERON MUSEUM
654
COIRE CEIRSLE HILL
Gairlochy
Stronaba
Glen Loy
Loy
GREAT GLEN WAY
Kilmonivaig
COMMANDO MEMORIAL
Bohuntine
Gleann Suileag
Druim Fada
Glen Loy Forest
Brackletter
Spean Bridge
Inverroy
Roybridge
Achluachra
Strone
Highbridge
Muirshearlich
Lochy
Killiechonate
A86
Spean
MONESSIE FALLS
239
Fassfern
NEPTUNE'S STAIRCASE LOCKS
TOR CASTLE
B8004
A830
TREASURES OF THE EARTH
Leanachan Forest
724
BEINN CHLIANAIG
EIL
A861
Corpach
Banavie
Torlundy
Duisky
Blaich
NEVIS RANGE MOUNTAIN EXPERIENCE
The Cour
Caol
Lochyside
228
Achaphubuil
INVERLOCHY CASTLE
Camusnagaul
Inverlochy
BEN NEVIS DISTILLERY VISITOR CENTRE
NN
Trislaig
Claggan
Fort William
Achintee
WEST HIGHLAND MUSEUM
1177
STOB CHOIRE CLAURIGH
1106
770
STOB COIRE CHEARCAILL
Stronchreggan
Ach'an Todhair
GLEN NEVIS VISITOR CENTRE
GLEN NEVIS
Glen Nevis House
Allt na Lairige
Lairig Leacach
Water of Nevis
1345
BEN NEVIS
1234
AONACH BEAG
1094
Druimarbin
Conaglen House
Kiachnish
Blarmachfoldach
Creaguaineach Lodge
Coruanan Lodge
Inverscaddle Bay
Achriabhach
Nevis
Amhainn Rath
14
Blar a'Chaorainn
1099
SGURR A' MHAIM
1130
BINNEIN MOR
630
616
BEINN NA GUCAIG
Loch Eilde Beag
Narrows
MAMORE FOREST
WEST HIGHLAND WAY
Glenrigh Forest
789
Ferry
Inchree
Loch Eilde Mor
796
MAM NA GUALAINN
Keppanach
Onich
615
Kinlochmore
Kinlochleven
B863
ALUMINIUM STORY VISITOR CENTRE
North Ballachulish
BLACKWATER RESERVOIR
Loch Leven
Leven
867
A828
GLENCOE AND NORTH LORN FOLK MUSEUM
Glencoe
AONACH 967
953
South Ballachulish
Ballachulish
GLENCOE
GLENCOE VISITOR CENTRE
Glen Coe
Altnafeadh
857
BEINN A' CHRULAISTE
Glenduror Forest
947
Glen an Fhiodh
BEN NEVIS AND GLEN COE
Beinn a'Bheithir
925
Coupall
Kingshouse Hotel
1150
BIDEAN NAM BIAN
Royal Forest
Duror
Etive
GLENCOE SKI CENTRE
879
FRAOCHAIDH
994
SGOR NA H-ULAIDH
Dalness
Glen Creran
Glen Etive
Alltchaorunn
1188
959
BEINN FHIONNLAIDH
227
883
STOB DUBH
Allt Coire
1099
CLACH LEATHAD
Elleric
4
5
6
A
B
C
D

KYLERHEA
OTTER HAVEN
Ferry
Kylerhea
Bernera
Galltair
Glenelg
BERNERA BARRACKS
Glenelg Bay
610
BEN ASLAK
Eilanreach
GLENELG BROCHS
Abhainn a' Ghlinne Bhig
Balvraid
Upper Sandaig
Sandaig Is.
742
BEINN A'CHAPAILL
974
BEINN SGRITHEALL
BEINN NAN CAORACH
774
603
BEINN A'CHUIRN
249
Glen More
Loch Duich
Ruarach
Morvich
Carn-gorm
Ault a'chruinn
Ratagan
RATAGAN
Inverschiel
Shiel Bridge
779
KINTAIL
Kintail Forest
BEINN FADA OR BEN ATTOW
1032
1067
FIVE SISTERS
1027
1719
Glenshiel Forest
GLEN SHIEL
Shiel
31
1010
THE SADDLE
918
SGURR AN LOCHAIN
1004
Arnisdale
LOCH HOURN
247
Glen Arnisdale
Corran
Kinlochhourn Forest
Cluanie
713
DRUIM FADA
879
BUIDHE BHEINN
906
SGURR THIONAIL
Glen Quoich
Kinloch Hourn
Inverguseran
785
BEINN NA CAILLICH
Barrisdale Bay
1027
SGURR A'MHAORAICH
NG
NH
GLEOUR
KNOYDART
894
Glen Barrisdale
1020
LADHAR BHEINN
Gleann na Guiserein
Abhainn Chosaidh
LOCH QUOICH
Gleann an Dubh-Lochain
LUINNE BHEINN
939
Scottas
Inverie
Inverie Bay
MALLAIG
946
MEALL BUIDHE
919
GAIRICH
Glen
1003
SGURR MOR
BEINN BHUIDHE
855
LOCH NEVIS
Carnach
1040
SGURR NA CICHE
Camusrory
NN
NM
880
SGURR MHURLAGAIN
858
Stoul
Kylesknoydart
Kylesmorar
859
Glen Dessarry
Dessarry
Murlaggan
Tarbet
North Morar
Brinacory
Swordland
Kinlochmorar
Strathan
829
CARN MOR
Glen Pean
Pean
LOCH MORAR
235
Oban
718
AN STAC
Gleann Camgharaidh
South Morar
Meoble
965
SGURR NAN COIREACHAN
963
SGURR THUILM
987
GAOR BHEINN
710
MEITH BHEINN
Kinlochbeoraid
Loch Beoraid
796
SGURR AN UTHA
Glen Finnan
Glen Dubh Lighe
Gleann Suileag
A830
Ranochan
Lochailort
Inverailort
A861
Loch Eilt
14
STATION MUSEUM
GLENFINNAN MONUMENT
Glenfinnan
Wauchan
Callop
236
Kinlocheil
Fassfern
Drumsallie
Alisary
0 1 2 3 miles
0 1 2 3 4 5 km

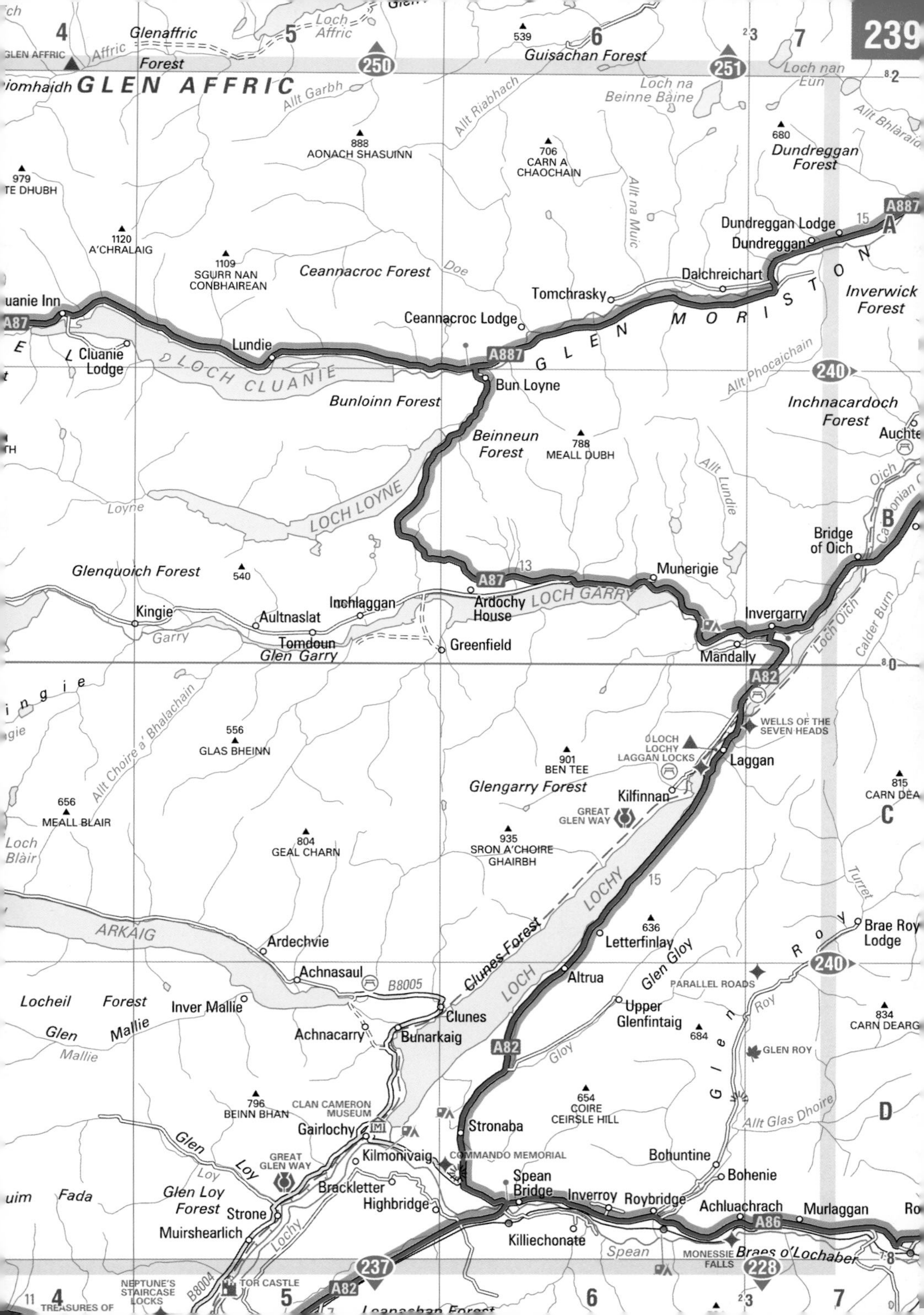

Glenaffric
Loch Affric
Forest
GLEN AFFRIC
250
Guisachan Forest
251
Loch nan Eun
Loch na Beinne Bàine
Allt Garbh
Allt Riabhach
888
AONACH SHASUINN
706
CARN A CHAOCHAIN
680
Dundreggan Forest
979
1120
A'CHRALAIG
1109
SGURR NAN CONBHAIREAN
Ceannacroc Forest
Doe
Allt na Muic
A887
Dundreggan Lodge
Dundreggan
Dalchreichart
Tomchrasky
Inverwick Forest
Cluanie Inn
A87
Cluanie Lodge
Lundie
LOCH CLUANIE
Ceannacroc Lodge
A887
GLEN MORISTON
Bun Loyne
Allt Phocaichain
240
Bunloinn Forest
Inchnacardoch Forest
Beinneun Forest
788
MEALL DUBH
Allt Lundie
Oich
LOCH LOYNE
Loyne
Bridge of Oich
Glenquoich Forest
540
13
A87
Munerigie
Kingie
Aultnaslat
Inchlaggan
Ardochy House
LOCH GARRY
Invergarry
Garry
Tomdoun
Glen Garry
Greenfield
Mandally
Loch Oich
Calder Burn
A82
WELLS OF THE SEVEN HEADS
556
GLAS BHEINN
Allt Choire a' Bhalachain
LOCH LOCHY
LAGGAN LOCKS
901
BEN TEE
Laggan
Glengarry Forest
Kilfinnan
815
GREAT GLEN WAY
656
MEALL BLAIR
Loch Blàir
804
GEAL CHARN
935
SRON A'CHOIRE GHAIRBH
LOCHY
15
Turret
ARKAIG
636
Ardechvie
Clunes Forest
Letterfinlay
Brae Roy Lodge
Glen Gloy
Glen Roy
240
Achnasaul
B8005
Altrua
PARALLEL ROADS
LOCH
Locheil Forest
Inver Mallie
Clunes
Upper Glenfintaig
834
CARN DEARG
Glen Mallie
Mallie
Achnacarry
Bunarkaig
684
A82
Gloy
GLEN ROY
Roy
796
BEINN BHAN
CLAN CAMERON MUSEUM
654
COIRE CEIRSLE HILL
Allt Glas Dhoire
Glen Loy
Gairlochy
Stronaba
GREAT GLEN WAY
Kilmonivaig
COMMANDO MEMORIAL
Bohuntine
Loy
Spean Bridge
Bohenie
Glen Loy Forest
Fada
Brackletter
Inverroy
Roybridge
Achluachrach
Murlaggan
Strone
Highbridge
A86
Muirshearlich
Killiechonate
Lochy
Spean
MONESSIE FALLS
Braes o' Lochaber
237
228
NEPTUNE'S STAIRCASE LOCKS
TOR CASTLE
B8004
A82
4
5
6
7
A
B
C
D

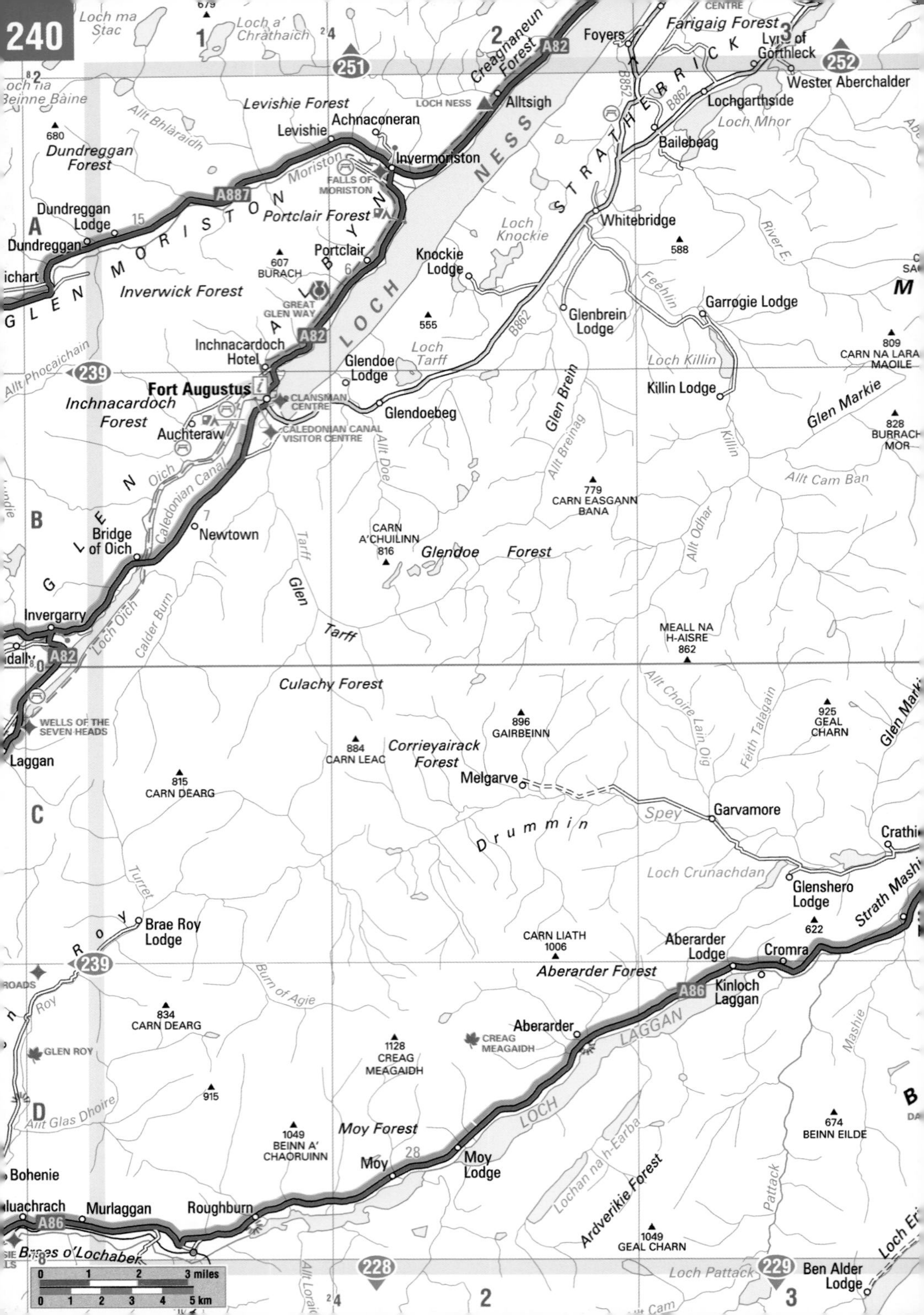

Loch ma Stac
Loch a' Chràthaich
Creagnaneun Forest
A82
Foyers
Farigaig Forest
Lyne of Gorthleck
252
251
Wester Aberchalder
Loch na Beinne Bàine
Levishie Forest
LOCH NESS
Alltsigh
Lochgarthside
Loch Mhor
Allt Bhlàraidh
Levishie
Achnaconeran
680
Dundreggan Forest
Invermoriston
Bailebeag
STRATHERRICK
B852
B862
Moriston
FALLS OF MORISTON
GLEN MORISTON
A887
Dundreggan Lodge
Portclair Forest
Whitebridge
Loch Knockie
Dundreggan
Portclair
588
607 BURACH
Knockie Lodge
River E.
Inverwick Forest
GREAT GLEN WAY
LOCH NESS
GLEN
Feehlin
Garrogie Lodge
555
Glenbrein Lodge
809 CARN NA LARAIG MAOILE
A82
Inchnacardoch Hotel
Glendoe Lodge
Loch Tarff
Loch Killin
239
Allt Phocaichain
Fort Augustus
CLANSMAN CENTRE
Killin Lodge
Inchnacardoch Forest
Glendoebeg
Glen Brein
Glen Markie
Auchteraw
CALEDONIAN CANAL VISITOR CENTRE
828 BURRACH MOR
Allt Doe
Allt Breinag
Killin
Oich
Caledonian Canal
Allt Cam Ban
779 CARN EASGANN BANA
Newtown
Bridge of Oich
CARN A'CHUILINN 816
Glendoe Forest
Allt Odhar
Tarff
Glen Tarff
Invergarry
Calder Burn
Loch Oich
MEALL NA H-AISRE 862
A82
Culachy Forest
Allt Choire Lain Oig
Feith Talagain
WELLS OF THE SEVEN HEADS
896 GAIRBEINN
925 GEAL CHARN
Laggan
884 CARN LEAC
Corrieyairack Forest
815 CARN DEARG
Melgarve
Spey
Garvamore
Drummin
Crathie
Loch Crunachdan
Glenshero Lodge
Turret
Strath Mashie
Brae Roy Lodge
Glen Roy
622
CARN LIATH 1006
Aberarder Lodge
Cromra
239
Aberarder Forest
Burn of Agie
A86
Kinloch Laggan
Roy
834 CARN DEARG
Aberarder
LAGGAN
CREAG MEAGAIDH
1128 CREAG MEAGAIDH
GLEN ROY
Mashie
915
LOCH
Allt Glas Dhoire
674 BEINN EILDE
1049 BEINN A' CHAORUINN
Moy Forest
Lochan na h-Earba
Ardverikie Forest
Moy
Moy Lodge
Bohenie
Pattack
Murlaggan
Roughburn
A86
1049 GEAL CHARN
Braes o' Lochaber
Loch Pattack
228
229
Ben Alder Lodge
Allt Loraic
0 1 2 3 miles
0 1 2 3 4 5 km

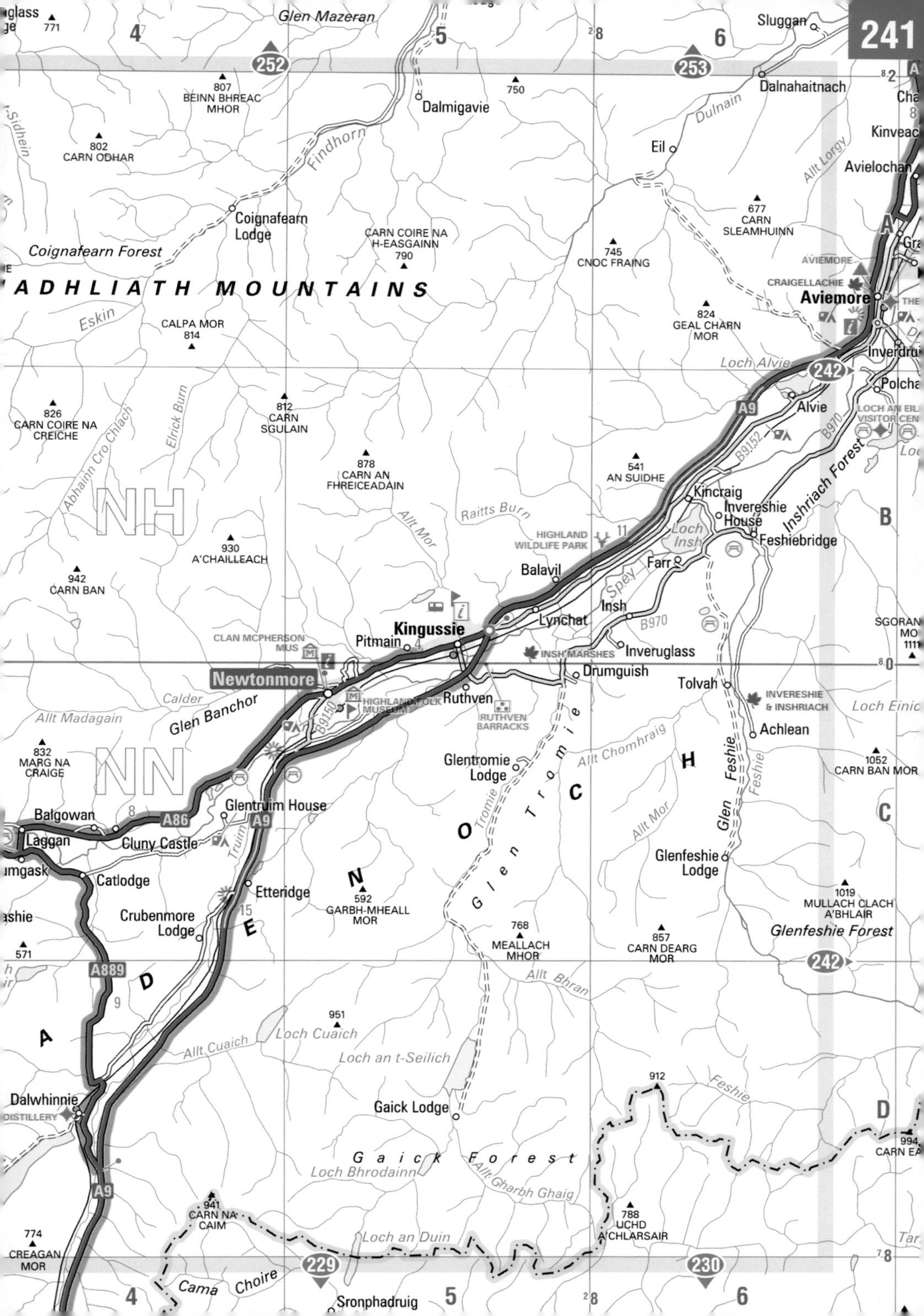
Glen Mazeran
252
253
Sluggan
Dalnahaitnach
807
BEINN BHREAC
MHOR
750
Dalmigavie
802
CARN ODHAR
Findhorn
Dulnain
Eil
Allt Lorgy
Kinveac
Avielochan
Coignafearn
Lodge
Coignafearn Forest
CARN COIRE NA
H-EASGAINN
790
745
CNOC FRAING
677
CARN
SLEAMHUINN
ADHLIATH MOUNTAINS
AVIEMORE
CRAIGELLACHIE
Aviemore
Eskin
CALPA MOR
814
824
GEAL CHARN
MOR
Inverdrui
Loch Alvie
242
Polcha
826
CARN COIRE NA
CREICHE
Elrick Burn
812
CARN
SGULAIN
A9
Alvie
LOCH AN EIL
VISITOR CEN
B9152
B970
Abhainn Cro Chlach
878
CARN AN
FHREICEADAIN
541
AN SUIDHE
Inshriach Forest
NH
Allt Mor
Raitts Burn
Kincraig
Invereshie
House
B
HIGHLAND
WILDLIFE PARK
11
Loch
Insh
Feshiebridge
930
A'CHAILLEACH
942
CARN BAN
Balavil
Farr
Spey
Insh
Lynchat
Kingussie
B970
SGORAN
MOR
1111
CLAN MCPHERSON
MUS
Pitmain
4
INSH MARSHES
Inveruglass
Newtonmore
Drumguish
Tolvah
Calder
HIGHLAND FOLK
MUSEUM
Ruthven
INVERESHIE
& INSHRIACH
Loch Einic
Allt Madagain
Glen Banchor
B9150
RUTHVEN
BARRACKS
Achlean
Glen Tromie
Allt Chomhraig
832
MARG NA
CRAIGE
NN
Glentromie
Lodge
H
Glen Feshie
Feshie
1052
CARN BAN MOR
C
Tromie
Glentruim House
Balgowan
8
A86
A9
O
Laggan
Cluny Castle
Truim
Allt Mor
Glenfeshie
Lodge
mgask
Catlodge
N
Etteridge
592
GARBH-MHEALL
MOR
1019
MULLACH CLACH
A'BHLAIR
15
ashie
Crubenmore
Lodge
E
768
MEALLACH
MHOR
857
CARN DEARG
MOR
Glenfeshie Forest
571
A889
D
242
Allt Bhran
9
A
951
Loch Cuaich
Allt Cuaich
Loch an t-Seilich
912
Feshie
Dalwhinnie
DISTILLERY
Gaick Lodge
D
994
CARN EA
Gaick Forest
Loch Bhrodainn
Allt Gharbh Ghaig
A9
941
CARN NA
CAIM
788
UCHD
A'CHLARSAIR
774
CREAGAN
MOR
Loch an Duin
229
230
4
Cama Choire
Sronphadruig
5
6

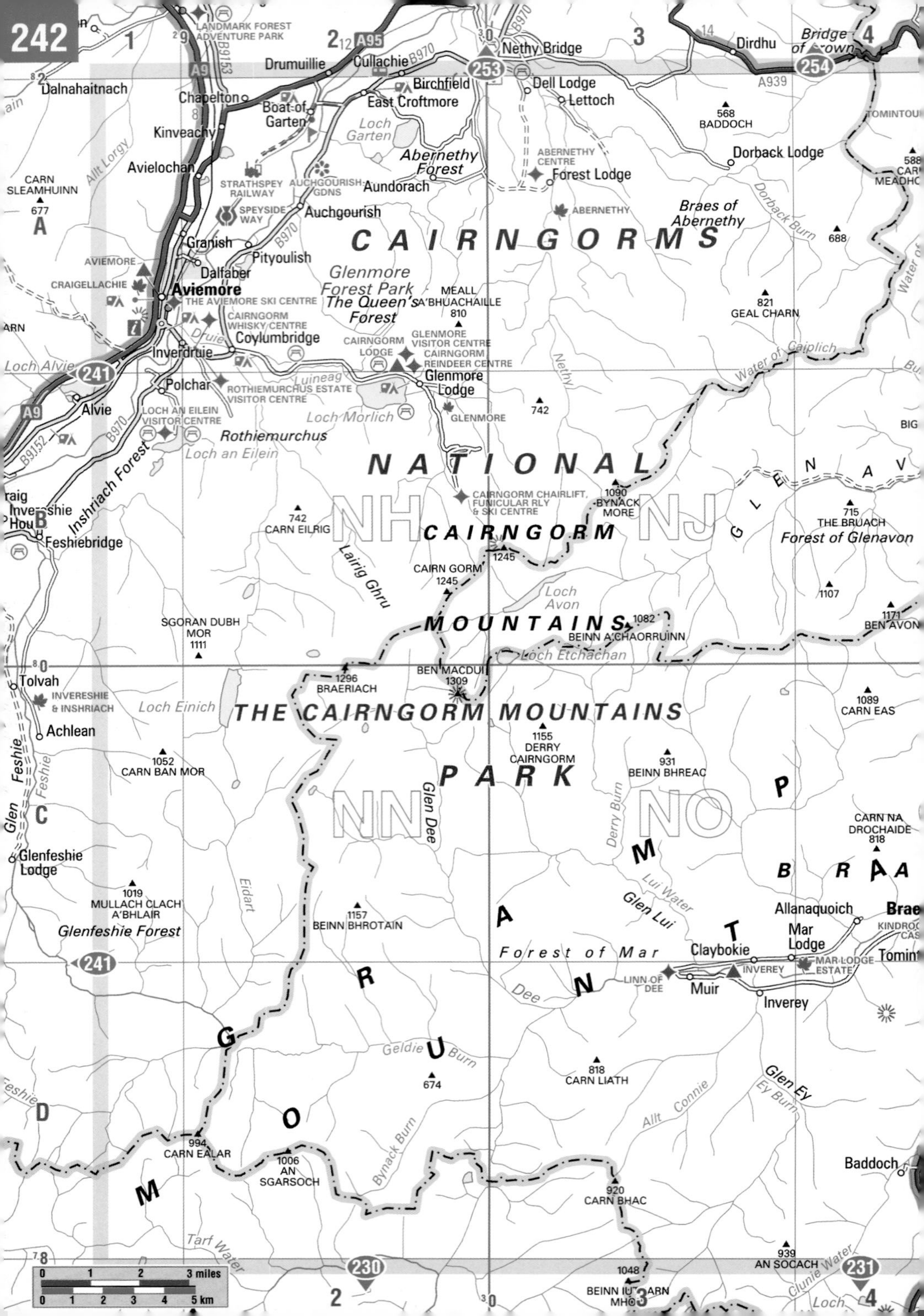
LANDMARK FOREST ADVENTURE PARK
Nethy Bridge
Dirdhu
Bridge of Brown
Drumuillie
Cullachie
Dalnahaitnach
Chapelton
Birchfield
Dell Lodge
Boat of Garten
East Croftmore
Lettoch
Kinveachy
Loch Garten
568 BADDOCH
Avielochan
Abernethy Forest
ABERNETHY CENTRE
Forest Lodge
Dorback Lodge
CARN SLEAMHUINN 677
STRATHSPEY RAILWAY
AUCHGOURISH GDNS
Aundorach
SPEYSIDE WAY
Auchgourish
ABERNETHY
Braes of Abernethy
Dorback Burn
688
Granish
Pityoulish
CAIRNGORMS
AVIEMORE
Dalfaber
CRAIGELLACHIE
Aviemore
THE AVIEMORE SKI CENTRE
Glenmore Forest Park
The Queen's Forest
MEALL A'BHUACHAILLE 810
821 GEAL CHARN
CAIRNGORM WHISKY CENTRE
Coylumbridge
Inverdruie
CAIRNGORM LODGE
GLENMORE VISITOR CENTRE
CAIRNGORM REINDEER CENTRE
Water of Caiplich
Loch Alvie
Polchar
ROTHIEMURCHUS ESTATE VISITOR CENTRE
Luineag
Glenmore Lodge
Nethy
Alvie
LOCH AN EILEIN VISITOR CENTRE
Loch Morlich
GLENMORE
742
Rothiemurchus
Loch an Eilein
NATIONAL
GLEN AVON
Inshriach Forest
CAIRNGORM CHAIRLIFT, FUNICULAR RLY & SKI CENTRE
1090 BYNACK MORE
Invereshie
Feshiebridge
742 CARN EILRIG
NH
CAIRNGORM
NJ
715 THE BRUACH
Forest of Glenavon
1245
Lairig Ghru
CAIRN GORM 1245
Loch Avon
1107
SGORAN DUBH MOR 1111
MOUNTAINS
1082 BEINN A'CHAORRUINN
1171 BEN AVON
Loch Etchachan
Tolvah
1296 BRAERIACH
BEN MACDUI 1309
INVERESHIE & INSHRIACH
Loch Einich
THE CAIRNGORM MOUNTAINS
1089 CARN EAS
Achlean
1155 DERRY CAIRNGORM
1052 CARN BAN MOR
931 BEINN BHREAC
PARK
Glen Feshie
NN
Glen Dee
Derry Burn
NO
CARN NA DROCHAIDE 818
Glenfeshie Lodge
Eidart
Lui Water
Glen Lui
1019 MULLACH CLACH A'BHLAIR
1157 BEINN BHROTAIN
Allanaquoich
Glenfeshie Forest
Mar Lodge
Forest of Mar
Claybokie
MAR LODGE ESTATE
INVEREY
LINN OF DEE
Muir
Inverey
Dee
Geldie Burn
674
818 CARN LIATH
Glen Ey
Ey Burn
Allt Connie
Bynack Burn
994 CARN EALAR
1006 AN SGARSOCH
Baddoch
920 CARN BHAC
Tarf Water
939 AN SOCACH
Clunie Water
1048 BEINN IUTHARN MHOR
0 1 2 3 miles
0 1 2 3 4 5 km

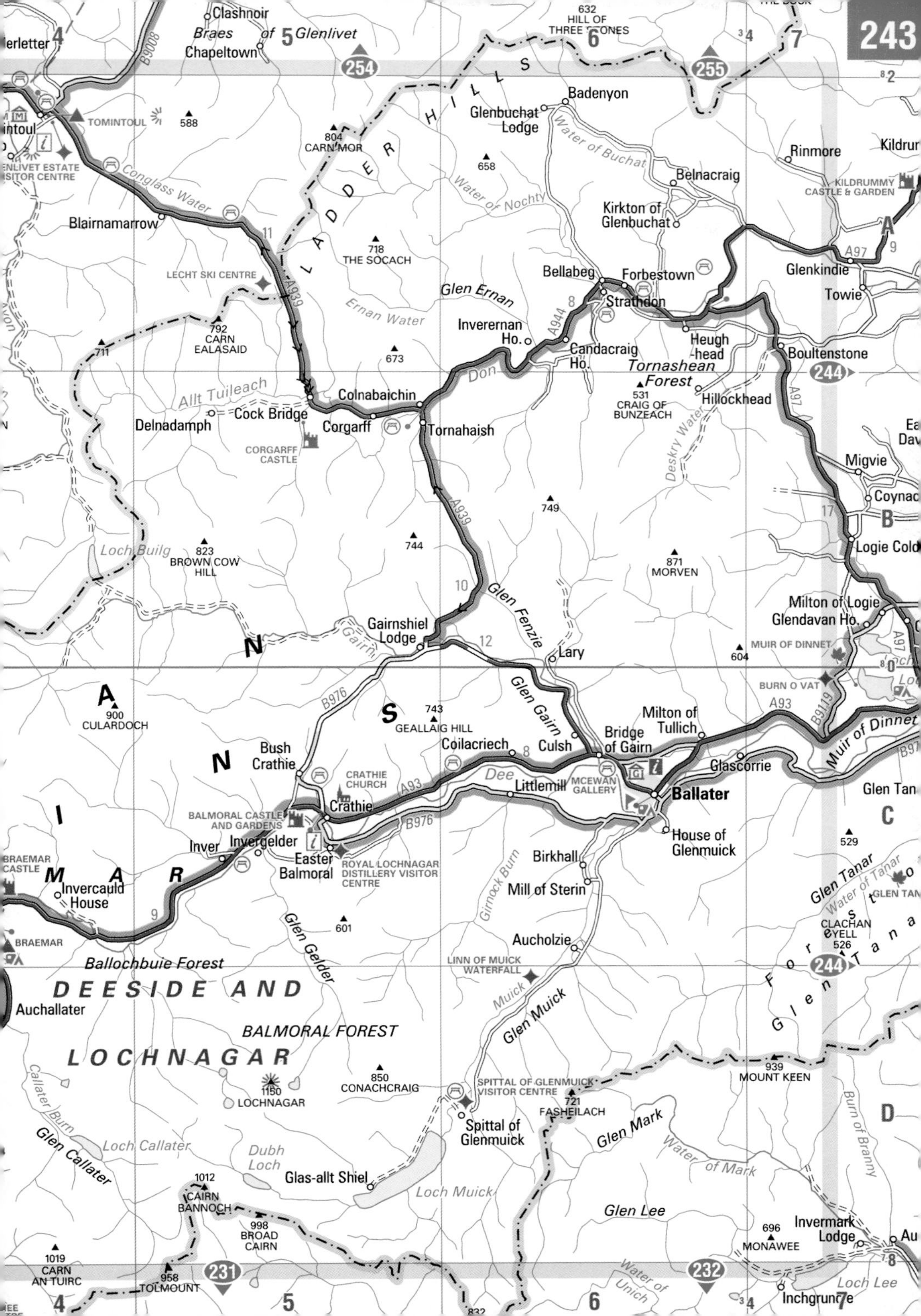

Clashnoir
Braes of Glenlivet
Chapeltown
Tomintoul
Blairnamarrow
Conglass Water
LECHT SKI CENTRE
LADDER HILLS
Badenyon
Glenbuchat Lodge
Water of Buchat
Belnacraig
Kirkton of Glenbuchat
Rinmore
Kildrummy Castle & Garden
Glenkindie
Towie
Bellabeg
Forbestown
Strathdon
Inverernan Ho.
Candacraig Ho.
Heugh-head
Boultenstone
Tornashean Forest
Hillockhead
CRAIG OF BUNZEACH
Colnabaichin
Cock Bridge
Delnadamph
Corgarff
CORGARFF CASTLE
Tornahaish
Allt Tuileach
Glen Ernan
Ernan Water
THE SOCACH
CARN EALASAID
CARN MOR
Migvie
Coynach
Logie Coldstone
Loch Builg
BROWN COW HILL
MORVEN
Glen Fenzie
Milton of Logie
Glendavan Ho.
Gairnshiel Lodge
Lary
MUIR OF DINNET
BURN O VAT
CULARDOCH
GEALLAIG HILL
Glen Gairn
Milton of Tullich
Bridge of Gairn
Culsh
Coilacriech
Bush Crathie
CRATHIE CHURCH
Littlemill
MCEWAN GALLERY
Ballater
Glascorrie
Muir of Dinnet
Glen Tanar
BALMORAL CASTLE AND GARDENS
Crathie
House of Glenmuick
Inver
Invergelder
Easter Balmoral
ROYAL LOCHNAGAR DISTILLERY VISITOR CENTRE
Birkhall
Mill of Sterin
BRAEMAR CASTLE
Invercauld House
BRAEMAR
Glen Gelder
Girnock Burn
Aucholzie
CLACHAN YELL
LINN OF MUICK WATERFALL
Ballochbuie Forest
DEESIDE AND LOCHNAGAR
Auchallater
BALMORAL FOREST
Glen Muick
Forest of Glen Tanar
CONACHCRAIG
LOCHNAGAR
SPITTAL OF GLENMUICK VISITOR CENTRE
Spittal of Glenmuick
FASHEILACH
MOUNT KEEN
Glen Callater
Loch Callater
Dubh Loch
Glas-allt Shiel
Loch Muick
Glen Mark
Water of Mark
Burn of Branny
CAIRN BANNOCH
BROAD CAIRN
Glen Lee
MONAWEE
Invermark Lodge
CARN AN TUIRC
TOLMOUNT
Water of Unich
Inchgrundle
Loch Lee
CAIRNGORMS
254
255
244
231
232

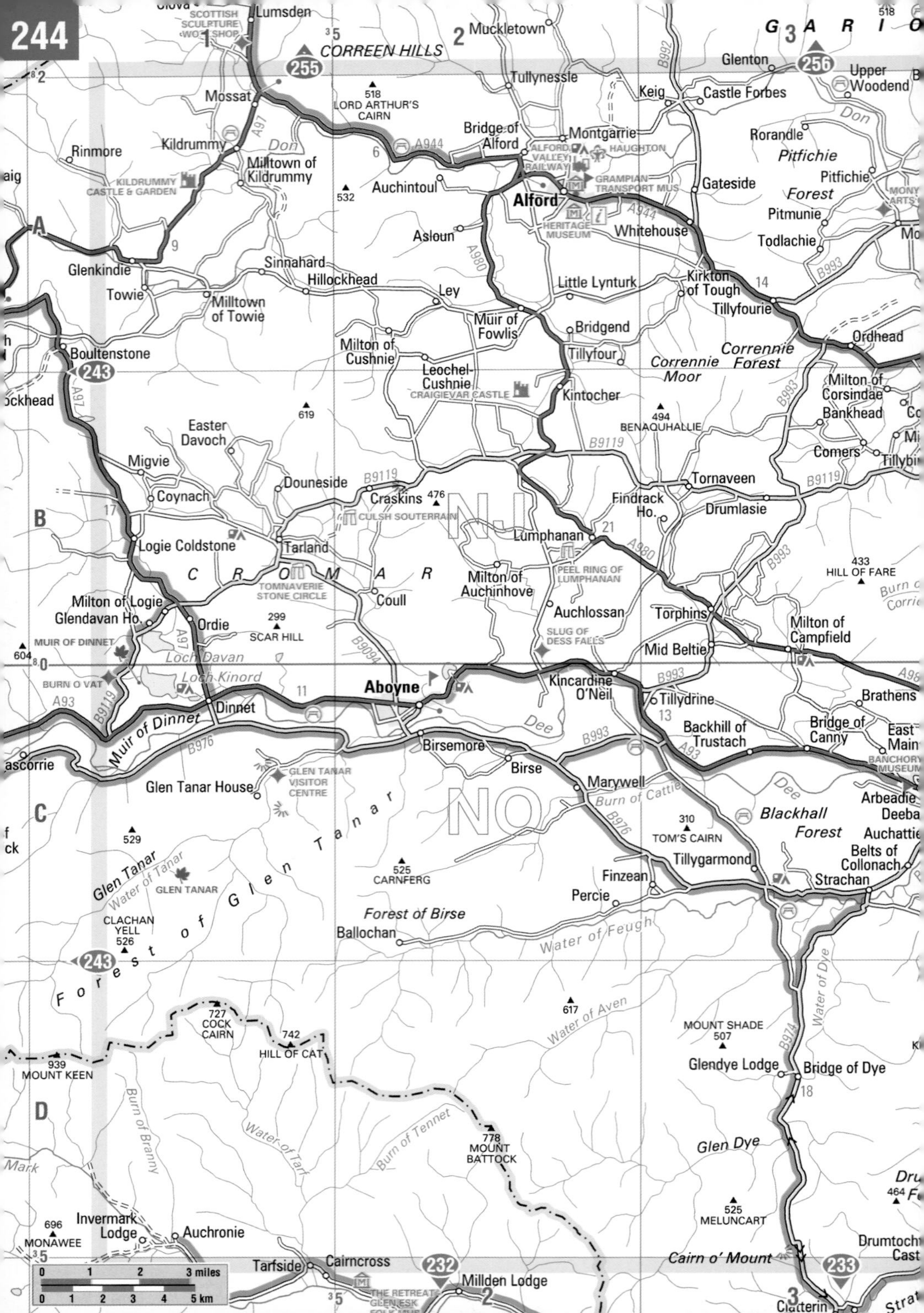
Lumsden
SCOTTISH SCULPTURE WORKSHOP
CORREEN HILLS
255
Muckletown
GARIOCH
256
Glenton
Upper Woodend
Tullynessle
Keig
Castle Forbes
Mossat
518
LORD ARTHUR'S CAIRN
Bridge of Alford
Montgarrie
Rorandle
Rinmore
Kildrummy
A97
Don
A944
ALFORD VALLEY RAILWAY
HAUGHTON
Pitfichie
Milltown of Kildrummy
KILDRUMMY CASTLE & GARDEN
532
Auchintoul
GRAMPIAN TRANSPORT MUS
Gateside
Pitfichie Forest
Alford
HERITAGE MUSEUM
Pitmunie
Asloun
Whitehouse
Todlachie
A980
Glenkindie
Sinnahard
Hillockhead
Little Lynturk
Kirkton of Tough
B993
Towie
Milltown of Towie
Ley
Tillyfourie
Muir of Fowlis
Bridgend
Ordhead
Boultenstone
Milton of Cushnie
Tillyfour
Corrennie Forest
Corrennie Moor
243
Leochel-Cushnie
CRAIGIEVAR CASTLE
Kintocher
Milton of Corsindae
Bankhead
619
494
BENAQUHALLIE
Easter Davoch
B9119
Comers
Migvie
Douneside
Tornaveen
Coynach
Craskins
476
Findrack Ho.
Drumlasie
CULSH SOUTERRAIN
NJ
Logie Coldstone
Lumphanan
Tarland
433
HILL OF FARE
CROMAR
PEEL RING OF LUMPHANAN
Milton of Auchinhove
TOMNAVERIE STONE CIRCLE
Coull
Milton of Logie
Glendavan Ho.
Ordie
299
SCAR HILL
Auchlossan
Torphins
Milton of Campfield
MUIR OF DINNET
SLUG OF DESS FALLS
Mid Beltie
604
Loch Davan
B9094
Loch Kinord
Aboyne
Kincardine O'Neil
BURN O VAT
Tillydrine
Brathens
A93
Dinnet
Muir of Dinnet
Dee
Backhill of Trustach
Bridge of Canny
B976
Birsemore
B993
BANCHORY MUSEUM
Birse
Marywell
GLEN TANAR VISITOR CENTRE
Glen Tanar House
Burn of Cattie
Arbeadie
NO
Blackhall Forest
310
TOM'S CAIRN
529
Forest of Glen Tanar
Auchattie
Belts of Collonach
Glen Tanar
Water of Tanar
525
CARNFERG
Tillygarmond
Finzean
Strachan
GLEN TANAR
Percie
Forest of Birse
CLACHAN YELL
526
Ballochan
Water of Feugh
617
Water of Aven
727
COCK CAIRN
742
HILL OF CAT
MOUNT SHADE
507
939
MOUNT KEEN
Glendye Lodge
Bridge of Dye
B974
Water of Dye
Burn of Branny
Water of Tarf
Burn of Tennet
778
MOUNT BATTOCK
Glen Dye
Mark
696
MONAWEE
Invermark Lodge
Auchronie
525
MELUNCART
464
Drumtochty Castle
Cairn o' Mount
Tarfside
Cairncross
232
Millden Lodge
233
Clatterin
THE RETREAT GLEN ESK FOLK MUS
0 1 2 3 miles
0 1 2 3 4 5 km

Inverurie
Kintore
Kemnay
Newmachar
Dyce
Westhill
Aberdeen
Bridge of Don
Cults
Peterculter
Cove Bay
Portlethen
Newtonhill
Stonehaven
Balmedie
Blackdog
Girdle Ness
Nigg Bay
Greg Ness
Hare Ness
Findon Ness
Cammachmore Bay
Garron Pt.
Castle Haven
Thornyhive Bay
Crawton Bay
Durris Forest
Fetteresso Forest
Loch of Skene
KIRKWALL LERWICK
DUNNOTTAR CASTLE
TOLBOOTH MUSEUM
DRUM CASTLE
CRATHES CASTLE AND GARDENS
CASTLE FRASER
ABERDEEN SCIENCE CENTRE
MARISCHAL MUSEUM
KING'S COLLEGE VISITOR CENTRE
ST MACHAR'S CATHEDRAL
BRIG O' BALGOWNIE
CRUICKSHANK BOTANIC GARDEN
DAVID WELCH WINTER GARDENS
DOONIES FARM
GORDON HIGHLANDERS MUSEUM
RAEDYKES ROMAN CAMP
BURNS FAMILY MEMORIALS
ROYAL DEESIDE RLY
A90
A96
A92
A956
A93
256
257
233

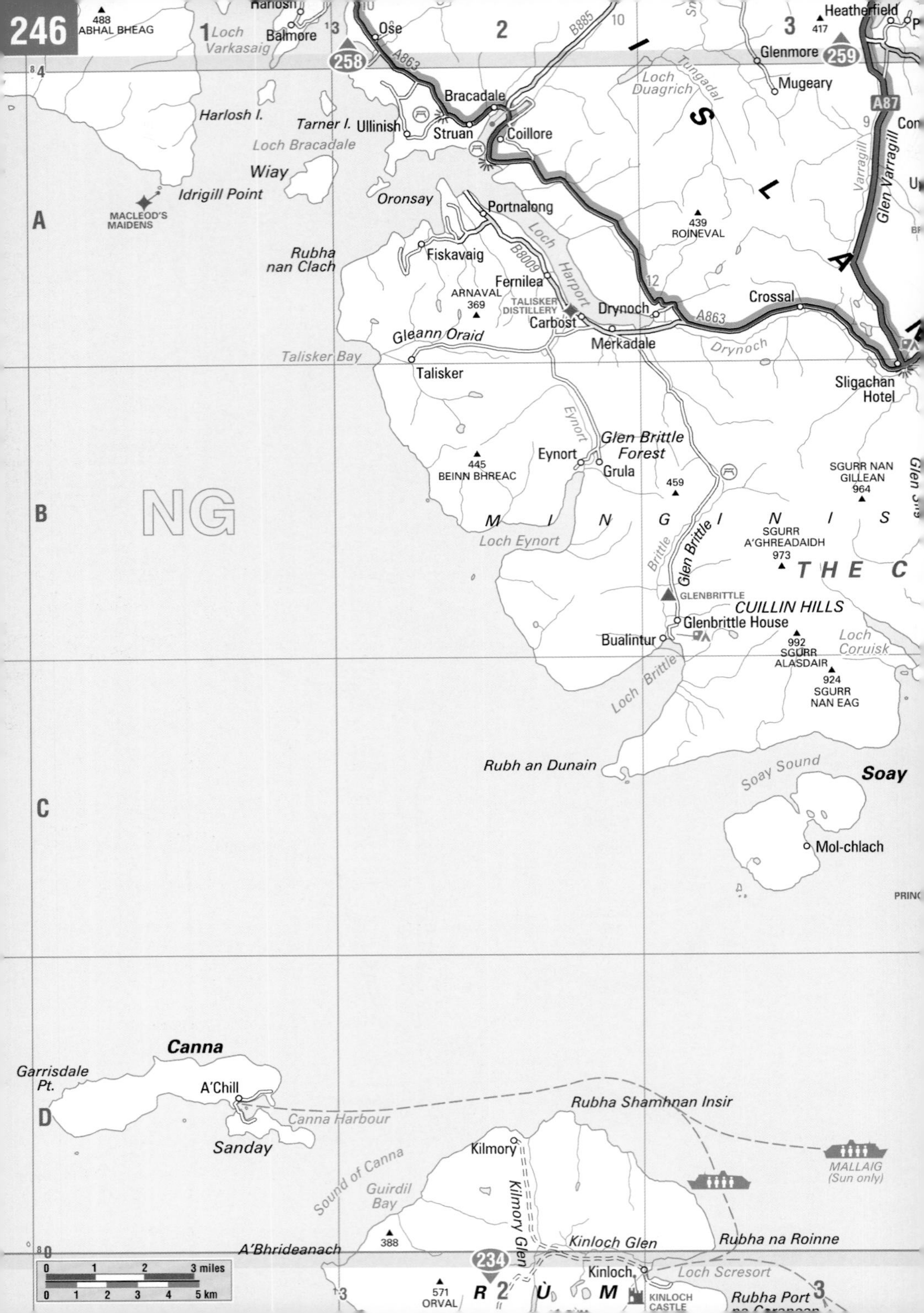

488
ABHAL BHEAG
Loch Varkasaig
Balmore
Ose
258
A863
B885
Heatherfield
417
Glenmore
259
Loch Duagrich
Tungadal
Mugeary
A87
Harlosh I.
Tarner I.
Ullinish
Bracadale
Struan
Coillore
Loch Bracadale
Wiay
Idrigill Point
MACLEOD'S MAIDENS
Oronsay
Portnalong
Varragill
Glen Varragill
439
ROINEVAL
Rubha nan Clach
Fiskavaig
B8009
Loch Harport
Fernilea
ARNAVAL 369
TALISKER DISTILLERY
Carbost
Drynoch
A863
Crossal
Gleann Oraid
Merkadale
Drynoch
Talisker Bay
Talisker
Sligachan Hotel
Eynort
Glen Brittle Forest
Eynort
Grula
445
BEINN BHREAC
459
SGURR NAN GILLEAN 964
NG
M I N G I N I S
Loch Eynort
Brittle
Glen Brittle
SGURR A'GHREADAIDH 973
THE C
GLENBRITTLE
CUILLIN HILLS
Glenbrittle House
Bualintur
992 SGURR ALASDAIR
Loch Coruisk
924 SGURR NAN EAG
Loch Brittle
Rubh an Dunain
Soay Sound
Soay
Mol-chlach
Canna
Garrisdale Pt.
A'Chill
Rubha Shamhnan Insir
Canna Harbour
Sanday
Kilmory
MALLAIG (Sun only)
Sound of Canna
Guirdil Bay
Kilmory Glen
388
A'Bhrideanach
Kinloch Glen
Rubha na Roinne
234
Kinloch
Loch Scresort
571 ORVAL
R U M
KINLOCH CASTLE
Rubha Port
0 1 2 3 miles
0 1 2 3 4 5 km

ISLAND
OF
RAASAY
INNER SOUND
Camusteel
Camusterrach
Ard-dhubh
Culduie
710
MEALL GORM
Balmeanach
Balachuirn
259
413
BEN
NAVAIG
Holoman
Bay
443
DUN CAAN
amastianavaig
Tianavaig
Bay
Oskaig
Rubha na'Leac
Eilean na Bà
Toscaig
Toscaig
Kishorn I.
Lower Ollach
RAASAY
Raasay Ho.
Clachan
RAASAY
OUTDOOR
CENTRE
North Fearns
The
Braes
Narrows of
Raasay
Inverarish
East
Suisnish
Eyre Point
Eyre
Caol Mór
Crowlin
Islands
Caolas Mór
Uags
A
An Dubh-aird
Eilean Mór
Peinchorran
Loch Sligachan
Sconser
LAMAIG
775
Moll
Scalpay
249
Longay
Port Cam
Duirinish
Drumbuie
Erbusaig
Black Is.
Badicaul
Loch Ainort
Luib
Dunan
Scalpay Ho.
Guillamon I.
Pabay
Kyle of Lochalsh
A87
CASTLE MOIL
Balma
LOCHALSH
WOODLAND
Caolas Scalpay
16
570
GLAS
BHEINN MHOR
RED HILLS
A87
Corry
Broadford
Bay
Waterloo
Kyleakin
BRIGHTWATER
VISITOR CENTRE
B
BROADFORD
732
Broadford
Lower Breakish
Upper Breakish
Skulamus
SGURR
NA COINNICH
739
LIN HILLS
BLA BHEINN
928
15
Harrapool
INTERNATIONAL
OTTER SURVIVAL
FUND
Suardal
A851
Allt Mór
Glen Arroch
KYLERHEA
OTTER HAVEN
Kyle Rhea
Ferry
Loch na
Crèitheach
Torrin
B8083
249
Kylerhea
Kilbride
Strathaird
Loch Slapin
Strath
SKYE
610
BEN ASLAK
Glenel
Glenelg
Bay
Kirkibost
Kilmarie
BEN
MEABOST
346
301
Heast
Kinloch
Drumfearn
Loch na Dal
Rubha
Suisnish
Loch Eishort
B8083
Sandaig Is.
C
Upper
Sandaig
Elgol
Glasnakille
Ord
16
Duisdalemore
Ornsay
DUNSCAITH
CASTLE
Isleornsay
Camuscross
S CAVE
Tokavaig
Rubha na h-
Easgainne
Tarskavaig
A851
SLEAT
238
Tarskavaig Pt.
Achnacloich
Teangue
KNOCK CASTLE
Rubha Ard
Slisneach
Knock
Bay
Ferindonald
Inverguseran
Kilmore
Kilbeg
SOUND OF SLEAT
785
BEINN NA CAILLICH
Armadale
Castle
Airor
D
Glen Meadhonach
ARMADALE GARDENS
CLAN DONALD CENTRE
Armadale
Bay
Rubha Charn
nan Cearc
Gleann na Guiserein
280
Calligarry
Ardvasar
Sandaig
KNOYDART
Aird of
Sleat
MALLAIG
Sandaig
Bay
Scottas
Ard Thurinish
235
Inverie Bay
Inverie
4
Point of
Sleat
5
Rubha Raonuill
6
MALLAIG

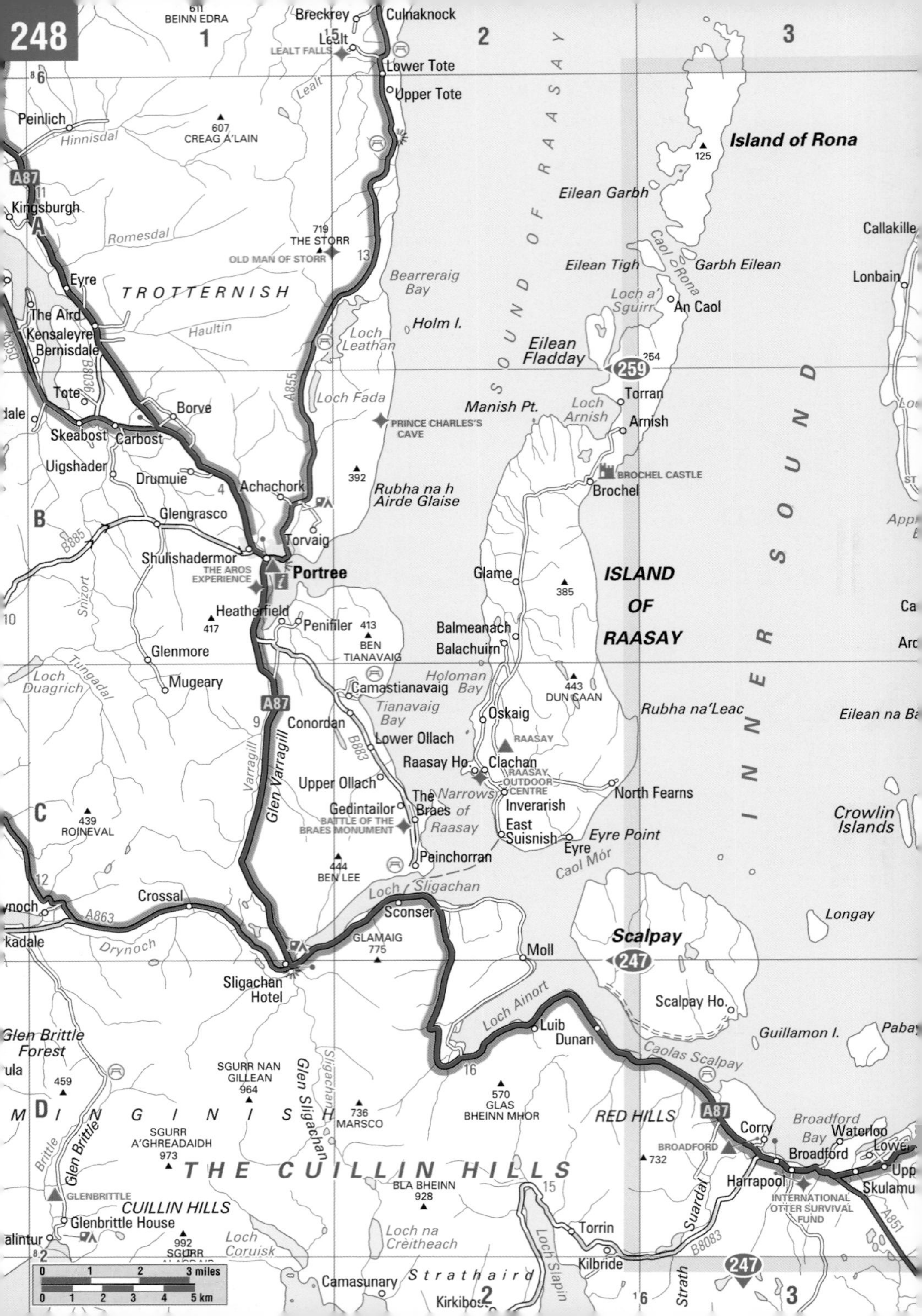

Culnaknock
Breckrey
Lealt
LEALT FALLS
Lower Tote
Upper Tote
BEINN EDRA
607
CREAG A'LAIN
Peinlich
Hinnisdal
Island of Rona
125
Eilean Garbh
Kingsburgh
A87
719
THE STORR
OLD MAN OF STORR
Romesdal
Callakille
Eilean Tigh
Garbh Eilean
Caol Rona
Lonbain
Eyre
TROTTERNISH
Bearreraig Bay
Loch a' Sguirr
An Caol
The Aird
Kensaleyre
Bernisdale
Haultin
Holm I.
Loch Leathan
SOUND OF RAASAY
Eilean Fladday
254
259
Tote
B8036
A855
Loch Fada
Torran
Borve
Manish Pt.
Loch Arnish
Arnish
Skeabost
Carbost
PRINCE CHARLES'S CAVE
Uigshader
Drumuie
392
BROCHEL CASTLE
Brochel
Achachork
Rubha na h Airde Glaise
Glengrasco
B885
Torvaig
Shulishadermor
THE AROS EXPERIENCE
Portree
Glame
385
ISLAND OF RAASAY
INNER SOUND
Snizort
Heatherfield
417
Penifiler
413
BEN TIANAVAIG
Balmeanach
Balachuirn
Glenmore
Loch Duagrich
Tungadal
Mugeary
Holoman Bay
Camastianavaig
443
DUN CAAN
Tianavaig Bay
A87
Conordan
Oskaig
Rubha na'Leac
Eilean na Ba
Lower Ollach
B883
RAASAY
Raasay Ho.
Clachan
RAASAY OUTDOOR CENTRE
Varragill
Glen Varragill
Upper Ollach
The Braes
Narrows of Raasay
North Fearns
Gedintailor
Inverarish
439
ROINEVAL
BATTLE OF THE BRAES MONUMENT
East Suisnish
Eyre
Eyre Point
Crowlin Islands
Peinchorran
444
BEN LEE
Caol Mór
Loch Sligachan
Crossal
A863
Sconser
Drynoch
GLAMAIG
775
Moll
Scalpay
247
Longay
Sligachan Hotel
Loch Ainort
Scalpay Ho.
Glen Brittle Forest
Luib
Dunan
Guillamon I.
Pabay
Caolas Scalpay
459
SGURR NAN GILLEAN
964
Glen Sligachan
736
MARSCO
570
GLAS BHEINN MHOR
RED HILLS
A87
MINGINISH
Glen Brittle
SGURR A'GHREADAIDH
973
THE CUILLIN HILLS
Corry
Broadford Bay
Waterloo
BROADFORD
Broadford
732
Harrapool
INTERNATIONAL OTTER SURVIVAL FUND
Skulamus
A851
BLA BHEINN
928
GLENBRITTLE
CUILLIN HILLS
Glenbrittle House
Suardal
B8083
Torrin
992
Loch Coruisk
Loch na Crèitheach
Loch Slapin
Kilbride
247
Camasunary
Strathaird
Strath
Kirkibost
0 1 2 3 miles
0 1 2 3 4 5 km

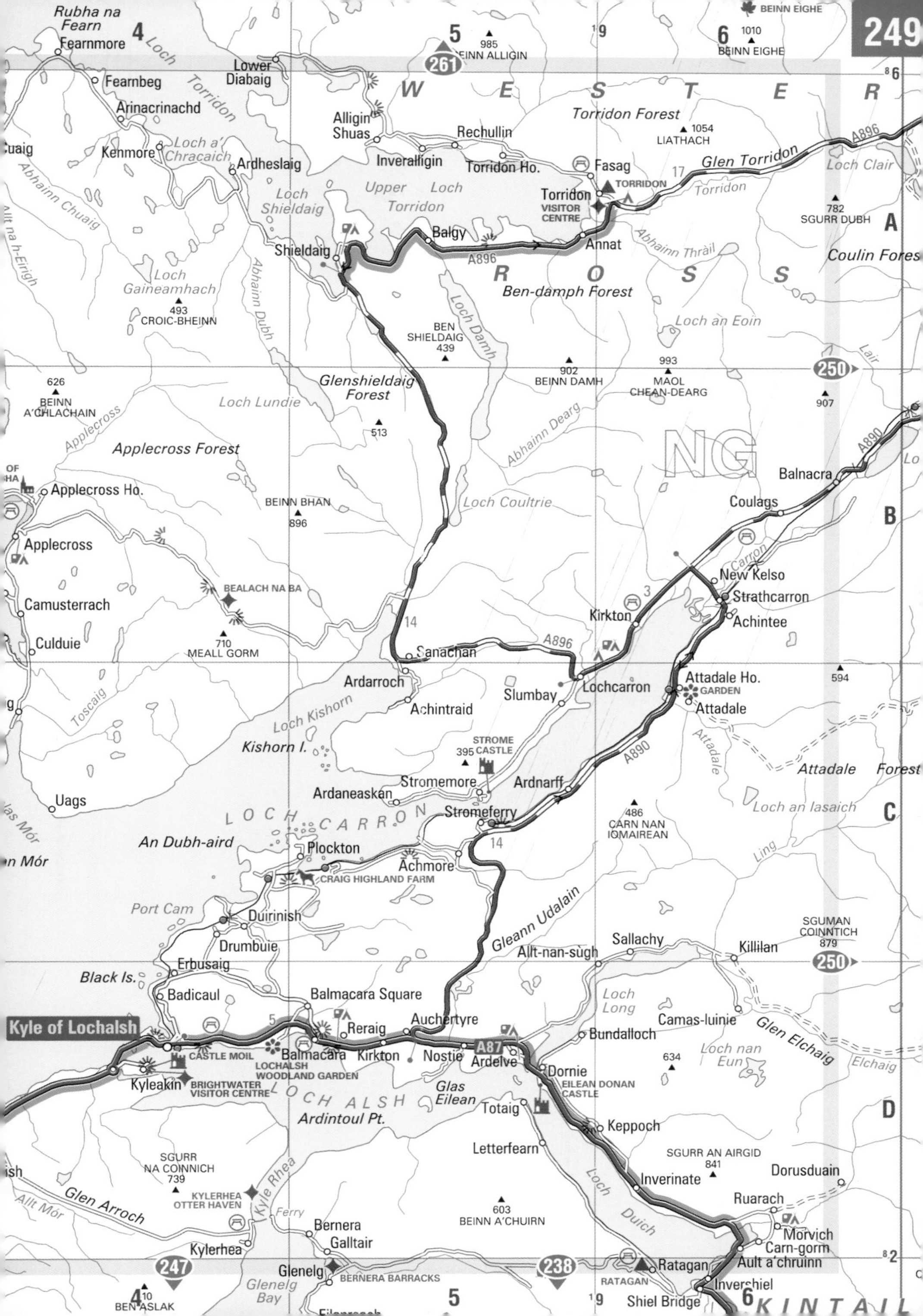

Rubha na Fearn
Fearnmore
Loch Torridon
Lower Diabaig
Fearnbeg
Arinacrinachd
Kenmore
Loch a' Chracaich
Ardheslaig
Alligin Shuas
Inveralligin
Rechullin
Torridon Ho.
Torridon Forest
LIATHACH
Fasag
Glen Torridon
A896
Loch Clair
Torridon
VISITOR CENTRE
TORRIDON
SGURR DUBH
Upper Loch Torridon
Loch Shieldaig
Shieldaig
Balgy
Annat
Abhainn Thràil
Coulin Forest
A896
Ben-damph Forest
WESTER ROSS
Loch Gaineamhach
CROIC-BHEINN
Abhainn Dubh
Abhainn Chuaig
Cuaig
Loch an Eoin
BEN SHIELDAIG
Loch Damh
BEINN DAMH
MAOL CHEAN-DEARG
Lair
Glenshieldaig Forest
BEINN A'CHLACHAIN
Loch Lundie
Applecross
Applecross Forest
Abhainn Dearg
Applecross Ho.
Balnacra
A890
Coulags
BEINN BHAN
Loch Coultrie
Applecross
Carron
New Kelso
BEALACH NA BA
Strathcarron
Camusterrach
Kirkton
Achintee
Culduie
MEALL GORM
Sanachan
A896
Ardarroch
Toscaig
Slumbay
Lochcarron
Attadale Ho.
GARDEN
Attadale
Achintraid
Loch Kishorn
Kishorn I.
STROME CASTLE
A890
Attadale Forest
Stromemore
Ardaneaskan
Ardnarff
Uags
Loch an Iasaich
LOCH CARRON
Stromeferry
CARN NAN IOMAIREAN
An Dubh-aird
Plockton
Achmore
CRAIG HIGHLAND FARM
Ling
Port Cam
Duirinish
Gleann Udalain
SGUMAN COINNTICH
Drumbuie
Sallachy
Killilan
Allt-nan-sugh
Erbusaig
Black Is.
Badicaul
Balmacara Square
Loch Long
Kyle of Lochalsh
Reraig
Auchertyre
Camas-luinie
Bundalloch
Glen Elchaig
CASTLE MOIL
Balmacara
Kirkton
Nostie
A87
Ardelve
Dornie
Loch nan Eun
Elchaig
LOCHALSH WOODLAND GARDEN
Kyleakin
BRIGHTWATER VISITOR CENTRE
EILEAN DONAN CASTLE
LOCH ALSH
Glas Eilean
Totaig
Ardintoul Pt.
Keppoch
Letterfearn
SGURR NA COINNICH
SGURR AN AIRGID
Dorusdluain
Inverinate
Loch Duich
Glen Arroch
KYLERHEA OTTER HAVEN
Kyle Rhea
Ferry
BEINN A'CHUIRN
Ruarach
Bernera
Morvich
Galltair
Carn-gorm
Kylerhea
Glenelg
Ratagan
Ault a'chruinn
BERNERA BARRACKS
RATAGAN
Glenelg Bay
Invershiel
BEN ASLAK
Shiel Bridge
KINTAIL
A
B
C
D

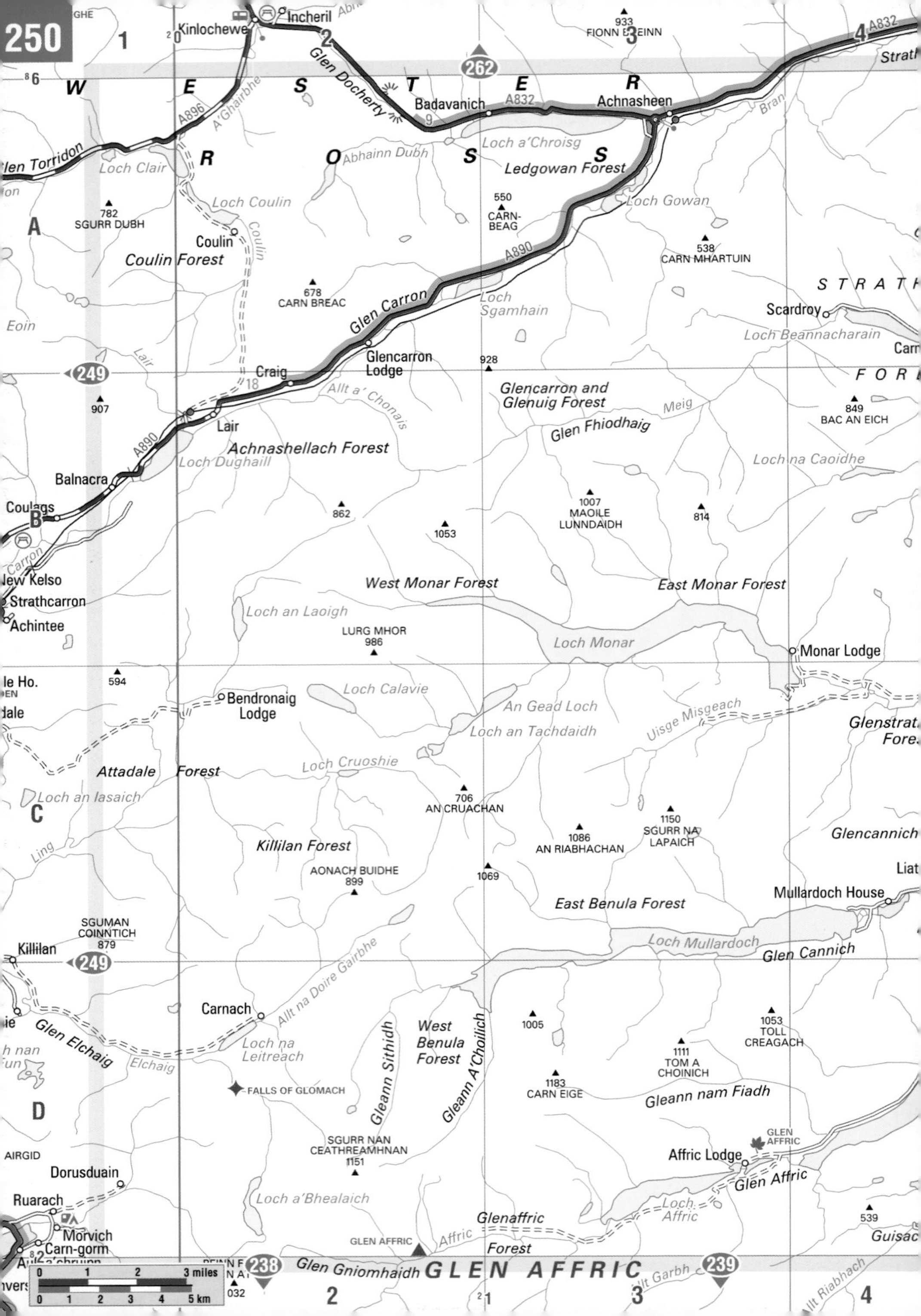

Kinlochewe
Incheril
Glen Docherty
FIONN BEINN 933
262
WESTER ROSS
A832
Badavanich
Achnasheen
Glen Torridon
A896
Loch Clair
Loch Coulin
Loch a'Chroisg
Abhainn Dubh
Ledgowan Forest
Loch Gowan
782 SGURR DUBH
Coulin
Coulin Forest
550 CARN-BEAG
538 CARN MHARTUIN
A890
678 CARN BREAC
Glen Carron
Loch Sgamhain
Scardroy
Loch Beannacharain
STRATH
249
Craig
Glencarron Lodge
928
Glencarron and Glenuig Forest
Meig
Glen Fhiodhaig
849 BAC AN EICH
907
Lair
Allt a' Chonais
Achnashellach Forest
Loch Dughaill
Loch na Caoidhe
Balnacra
Coulags
862
1053
1007 MAOILE LUNNDAIDH
814
Carron
New Kelso
Strathcarron
Achintee
West Monar Forest
East Monar Forest
Loch an Laoigh
LURG MHOR 986
Loch Monar
Monar Lodge
594
Bendronaig Lodge
Loch Calavie
An Gead Loch
Loch an Tachdaidh
Uisge Misgeach
Attadale Forest
Loch Cruoshie
Loch an Iasaich
706 AN CRUACHAN
1150 SGURR NA LAPAICH
1086 AN RIABHACHAN
Glencannich
Killilan Forest
AONACH BUIDHE 899
1069
Mullardoch House
East Benula Forest
SGUMAN COINNTICH 879
Killilan
Loch Mullardoch
Glen Cannich
Carnach
Allt na Doire Gairbhe
1005
1053 TOLL CREAGACH
Glen Elchaig
Elchaig
Loch na Leitreach
West Benula Forest
Gleann Sithidh
Gleann A'Choilich
1111 TOM A CHOINICH
1183 CARN EIGE
Gleann nam Fiadh
FALLS OF GLOMACH
AIRGID
SGURR NAN CEATHREAMHNAN 1151
GLEN AFFRIC
Affric Lodge
Glen Affric
Dorusduain
Ruarach
Loch a'Bhealaich
Loch Affric
Morvich
Carn-gorm
Glenaffric Forest
Affric
539
238
239
GLEN AFFRIC
Glen Gniomhaidh
Allt Garbh
Allt Riabhach
0 1 2 3 miles
0 1 2 3 4 5 km
032

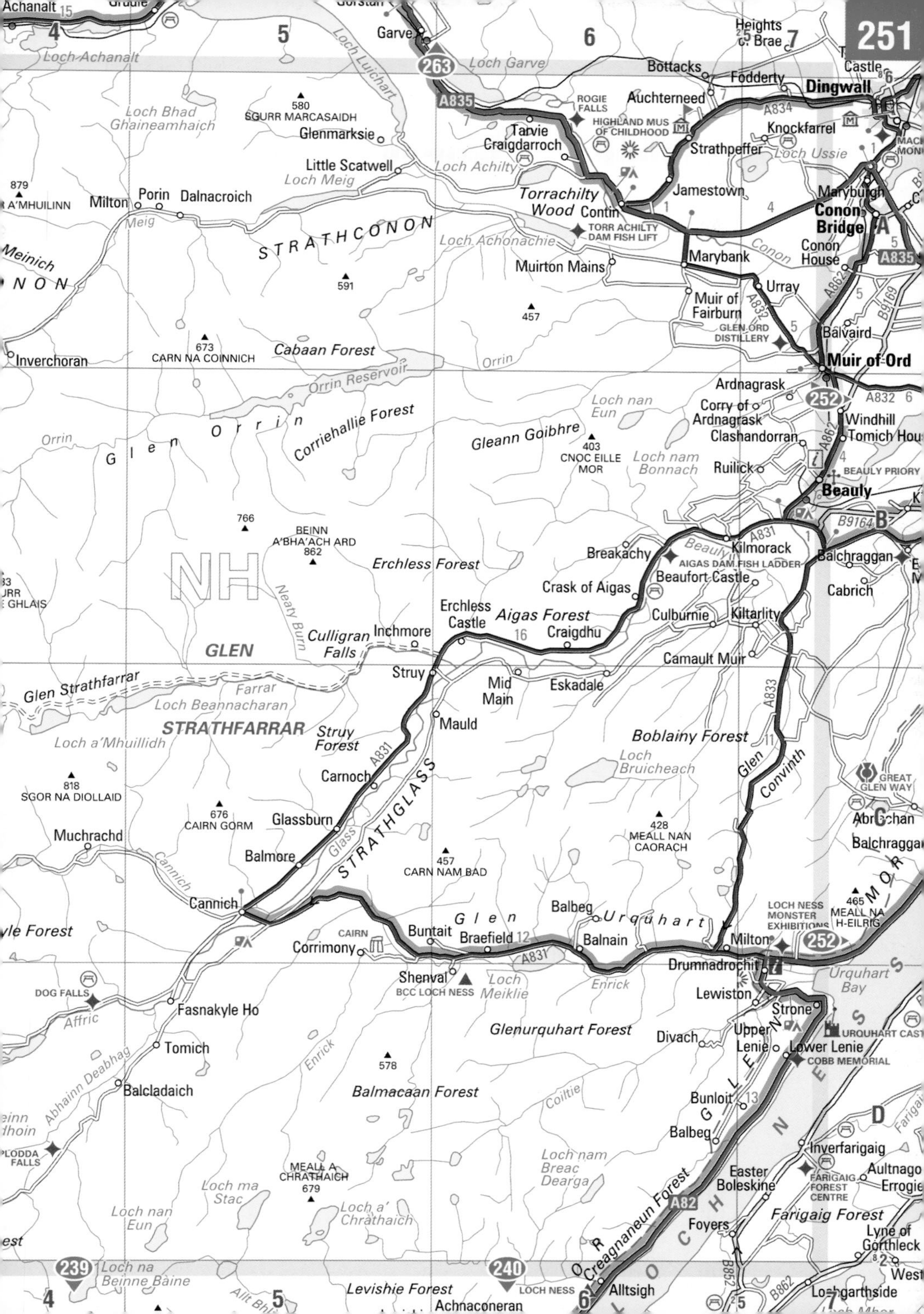

Achanalt
Garve
263
Loch Garve
Heights
Brae
Bottacks
Fodderty
Castle
Dingwall
Loch Achanalt
Loch Luichart
A835
ROGIE FALLS
Auchterneed
A834
Loch Bhad Ghaineamhaich
580
SGURR MARCASAIDH
Glenmarksie
Tarvie
Craigdarroch
HIGHLAND MUS OF CHILDHOOD
Strathpeffer
Knockfarrel
Loch Ussie
Little Scatwell
Loch Meig
Loch Achilty
Torrachilty Wood
Contin
Jamestown
Maryburgh
Conon Bridge
879
A'MHUILINN
Milton
Porin
Dalnacroich
Meig
STRATHCONON
TORR ACHILTY DAM FISH LIFT
Loch Achonachie
Conon
Conon House
Marybank
A835
Meinich
NON
Muirton Mains
591
Urray
Muir of Fairburn
A832
A862
B9169
457
GLEN ORD DISTILLERY
Balvaird
673
CARN NA COINNICH
Cabaan Forest
Inverchoran
Orrin
Muir of Ord
Orrin Reservoir
Ardnagrask
252
A832
Loch nan Eun
Corry of Ardnagrask
Windhill
Corriehallie Forest
Glen Orrin
Gleann Goibhre
403
CNOC EILLE MOR
Loch nam Bonnach
Clashandorran
Tomich House
Orrin
Ruilick
BEAULY PRIORY
Beauly
766
BEINN A'BHA'ACH ARD
862
NH
B9164
Beauly
Kilmorack
A831
Breakachy
AIGAS DAM FISH LADDER
Erchless Forest
Balchraggan
Beaufort Castle
Crask of Aigas
Cabrich
GHLAIS
Neaty Burn
Erchless Castle
Aigas Forest
Culburnie
Kiltarlity
Culligran Falls
Inchmore
16
Craigdhu
GLEN
Camault Muir
Struy
Mid Main
Eskadale
Glen Strathfarrar
Farrar
Loch Beannacharan
STRATHFARRAR
Mauld
A833
Loch a'Mhuillidh
Struy Forest
Boblainy Forest
Loch Bruicheach
Carnoch
A831
818
SGOR NA DIOLLAID
STRATHGLASS
Glen Convinth
GREAT GLEN WAY
676
CAIRN GORM
Glassburn
428
MEALL NAN CAORACH
Abriachan
Muchrachd
Balchraggan
Glass
457
CARN NAM BAD
Balmore
Cannich
Cannich
MOR
465
MEALL NA H-EILRIG
LOCH NESS MONSTER EXHIBITIONS
Balbeg
Glen Urquhart
Forest
CAIRN
Buntait
Braefield
12
Balnain
Milton
252
Corrimony
A831
Drumnadrochit
Shenval
BCC LOCH NESS
Loch Meiklie
Enrick
Urquhart Bay
DOG FALLS
Fasnakyle Ho
Lewiston
Strone
Affric
Glenurquhart Forest
Divach
Upper Lenie
URQUHART CASTLE
Lower Lenie
COBB MEMORIAL
Tomich
Enrick
578
Abhainn Deabhag
Balcladaich
Balmacaan Forest
Coiltie
Bunloit
13
GLEN
Balbeg
D
PLODDA FALLS
Inverfarigaig
Loch nam Breac Dearga
MEALL A CHRATHAICH
679
Easter Boleskine
Aultnagoire
FARIGAIG FOREST CENTRE
Errogie
Loch ma Stac
Creagnaneun Forest
A82
Loch nan Eun
Loch a' Chràthaich
Foyers
Farigaig Forest
Lyne of Gorthleck
239
Loch na Beinne Baine
240
LOCH NESS
Alltsigh
Levishie Forest
Achnaconeran
B862
West
Lochgarthside
LOCH NESS
4
5
6
7

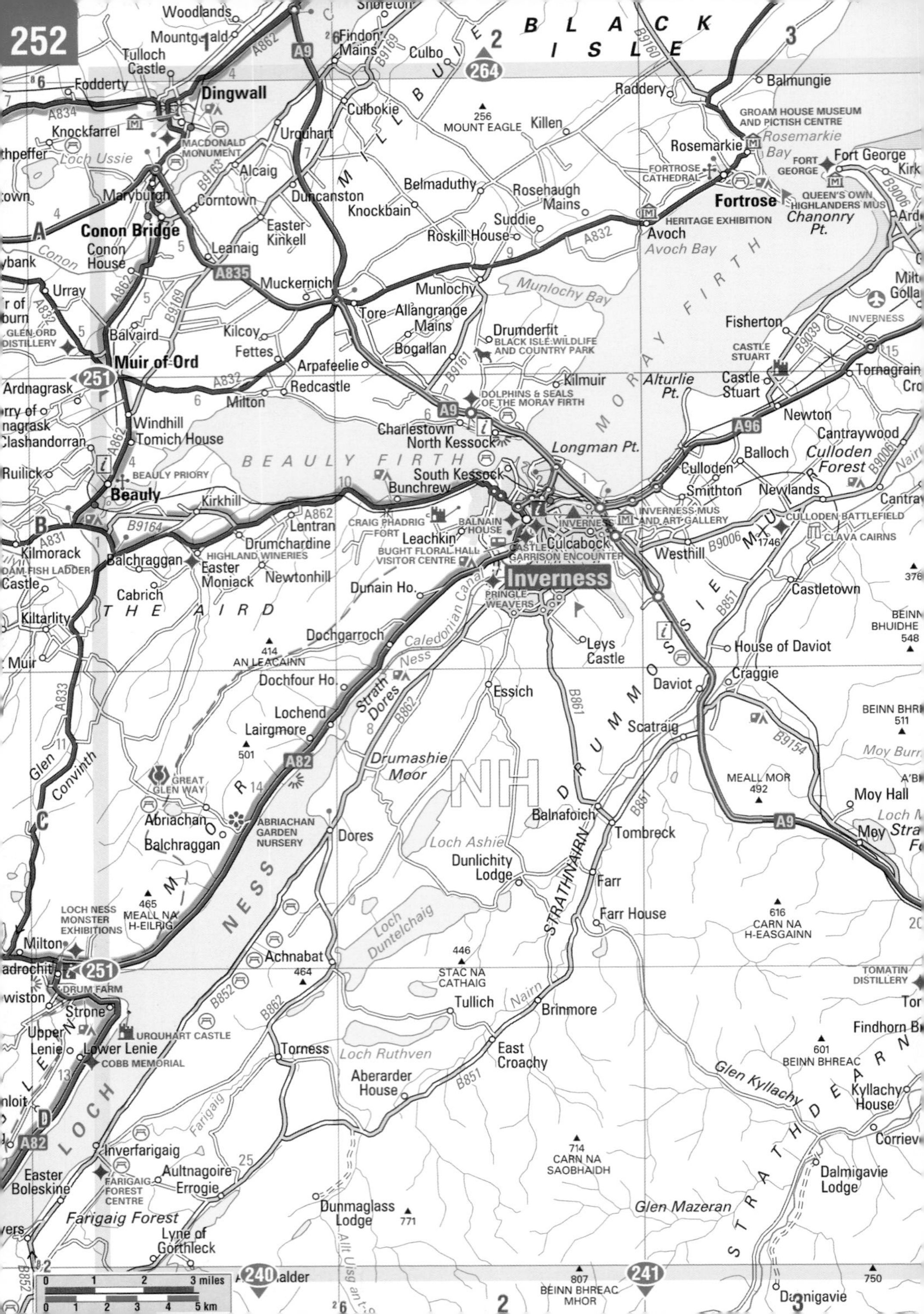

264
251
240
241

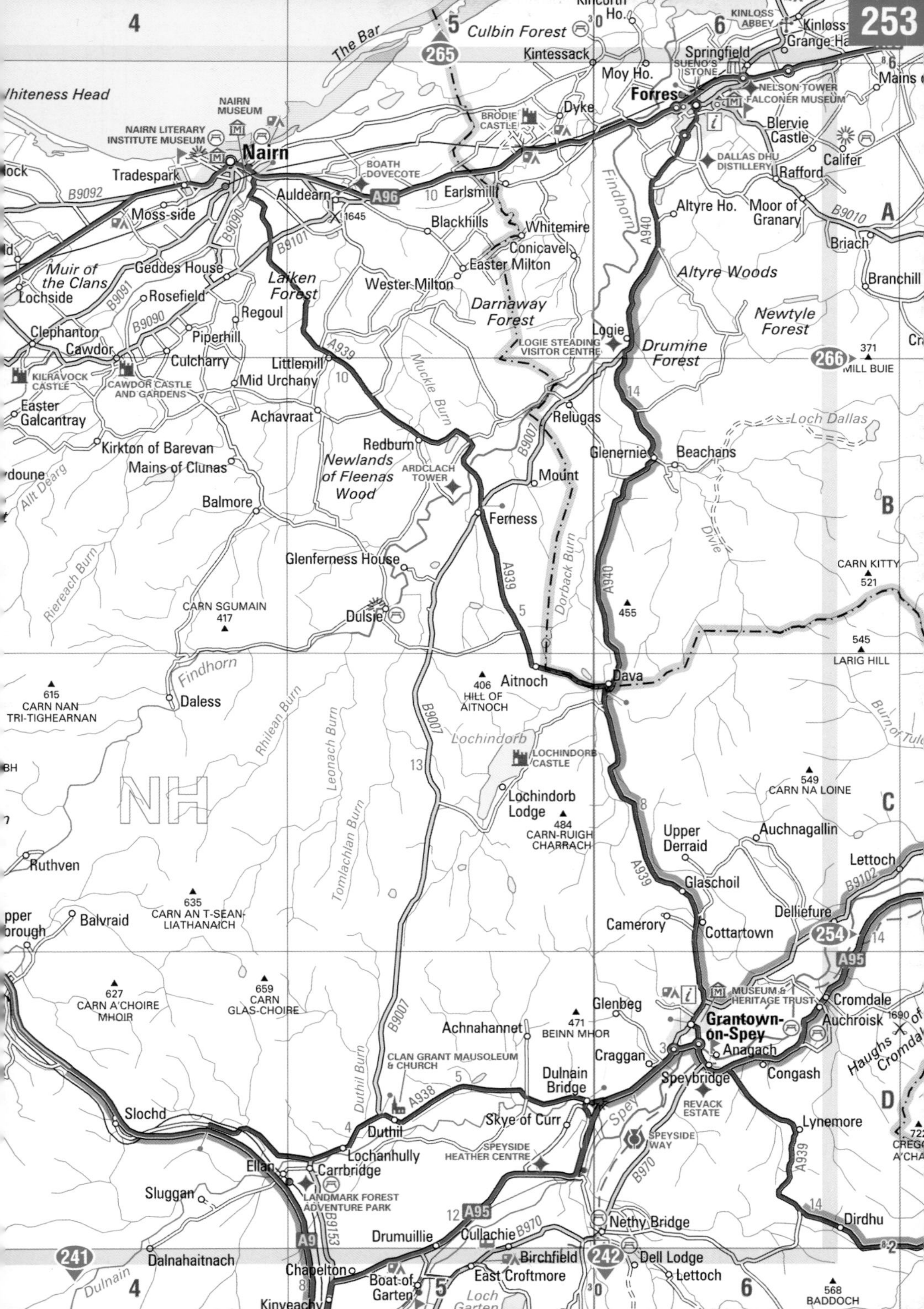
Culbin Forest
The Bar
Kintessack
Moy Ho.
Springfield
Kinloss
Forres
Whiteness Head
NAIRN MUSEUM
NAIRN LITERARY INSTITUTE MUSEUM
Nairn
BRODIE CASTLE
Dyke
NELSON TOWER
FALCONER MUSEUM
Blervie Castle
Califer
DALLAS DHU DISTILLERY
Rafford
Tradespark
BOATH DOVECOTE
Auldearn
Earlsmill
Moss-side
Blackhills
Whitemire
Altyre Ho.
Moor of Granary
Briach
Conicavel
Easter Milton
Wester Milton
Muir of the Clans
Geddes House
Laiken Forest
Lochside
Rosefield
Regoul
Altyre Woods
Branchill
Darnaway Forest
Newtyle Forest
Clephanton
Cawdor
Piperhill
Logie
LOGIE STEADING VISITOR CENTRE
Drumine Forest
MILL BUIE
KILRAVOCK CASTLE
CAWDOR CASTLE AND GARDENS
Culcharry
Littlemill
Mid Urchany
Muckle Burn
Easter Galcantray
Achavraat
Relugas
Loch Dallas
Kirkton of Barevan
Redburn
Mains of Clunas
Newlands of Fleenas Wood
ARDCLACH TOWER
Mount
Glenernie
Beachans
Balmore
Ferness
Allt Dearg
Riereach Burn
Glenferness House
Dorback Burn
Divie
CARN KITTY
CARN SGUMAIN
Dulsie
Aitnoch
HILL OF AITNOCH
Dava
LARIG HILL
Findhorn
CARN NAN TRI-TIGHEARNAN
Daless
Rhilean Burn
Leonach Burn
Lochindorb
LOCHINDORB CASTLE
Lochindorb Lodge
CARN-RUIGH CHARRACH
CARN NA LOINE
NH
Upper Derraid
Auchnagallin
Ruthven
Tomlachlan Burn
Glaschoil
Lettoch
CARN AN T-SEAN-LIATHANAICH
Balvraid
Camerory
Cottartown
Delliefure
CARN A'CHOIRE MHOIR
CARN GLAS-CHOIRE
Glenbeg
MUSEUM & HERITAGE TRUST
Cromdale
Achnahannet
BEINN MHOR
Grantown-on-Spey
Auchroisk
Haughs of Cromdale
Anagach
CLAN GRANT MAUSOLEUM & CHURCH
Craggan
Congash
Dulnain Bridge
Speybridge
REVACK ESTATE
Duthil Burn
Slochd
Skye of Curr
Lynemore
Duthil
SPEYSIDE WAY
Spey
Lochanhully
SPEYSIDE HEATHER CENTRE
Ellan
Carrbridge
Sluggan
LANDMARK FOREST ADVENTURE PARK
Nethy Bridge
Dirdhu
Drumuillie
Cullachie
Dalnahaitnach
Birchfield
Dell Lodge
Chapelton
Boat of Garten
East Croftmore
Lettoch
Dulnain
Loch Garten
Kinveachy
BADDOCH
A96
A939
A940
A938
A95
A9
B9090
B9091
B9092
B9101
B9007
B9010
B9102
B970
B9153
265
266
254
241
242

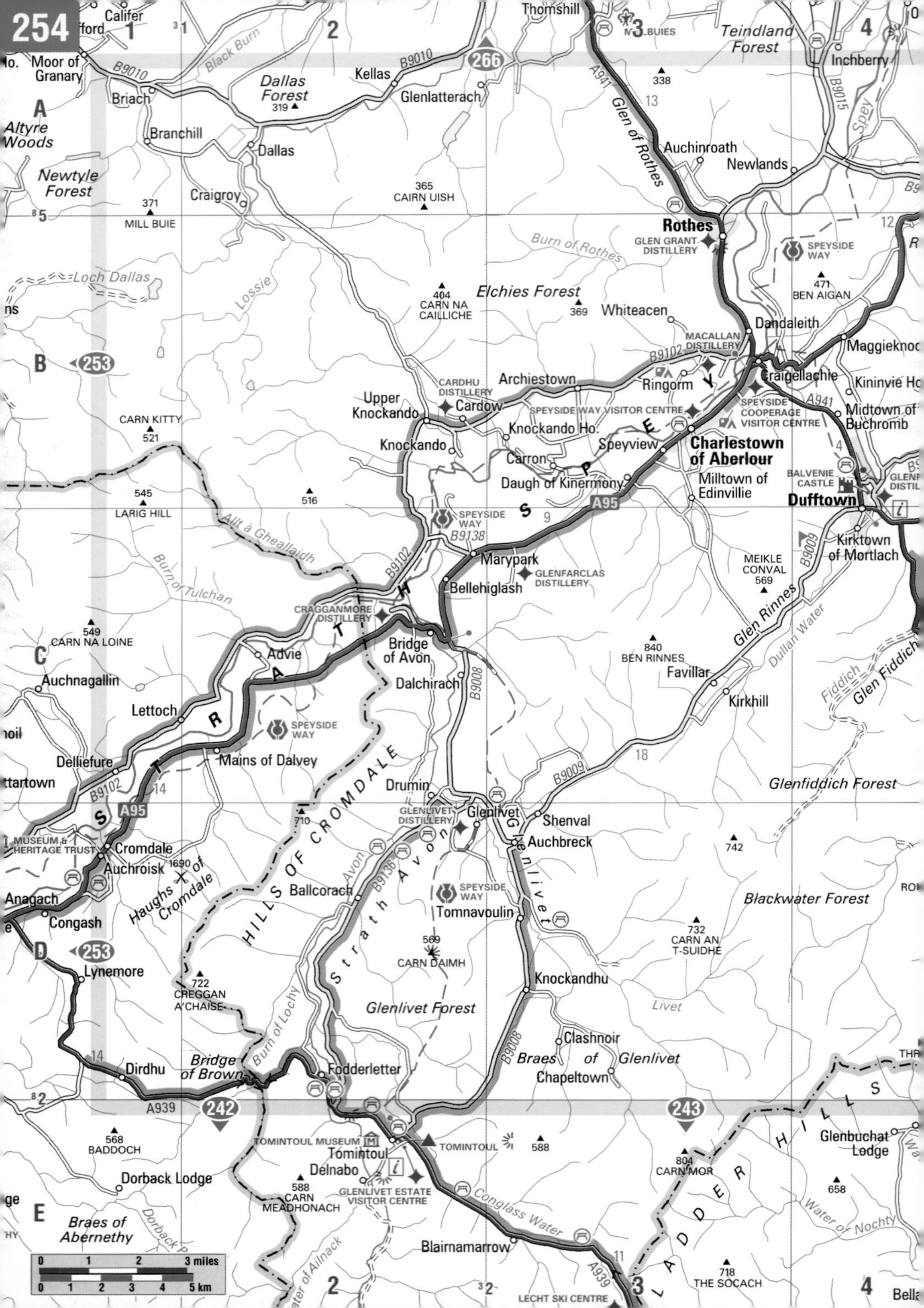
Moor of Granary
Briach
Branchill
Dallas
Dallas Forest
Kellas
Glenlatterach
Altyre Woods
Newtyle Forest
Craigroy
MILL BUIE
Loch Dallas
Lossie
CARN NA CAILLICHE
Elchies Forest
Whiteacen
Glen of Rothes
Auchinroath
Newlands
Rothes
GLEN GRANT DISTILLERY
SPEYSIDE WAY
BEN AIGAN
Dandaleith
MACALLAN DISTILLERY
Maggieknockater
Craigellachie
Kininvie House
Midtown of Buchromb
Teindland Forest
Inchberry
CARN KITTY
LARIG HILL
CARDHU DISTILLERY
Archiestown
Ringorm
Upper Knockando
Cardow
SPEYSIDE WAY VISITOR CENTRE
SPEYSIDE COOPERAGE VISITOR CENTRE
Knockando Ho.
Knockando
Carron
Speyview
Charlestown of Aberlour
Daugh of Kinermony
Milltown of Edinvillie
BALVENIE CASTLE
Dufftown
Kirktown of Mortlach
MEIKLE CONVAL
Marypark
GLENFARCLAS DISTILLERY
Bellehiglash
CRAGGANMORE DISTILLERY
Allt à Ghealláidh
Burn of Tulchan
CARN NA LOINE
Advie
Bridge of Avon
Dalchirach
BEN RINNES
Favillar
Glen Rinnes
Dullan Water
Kirkhill
Glen Fiddich
Auchnagallin
Lettoch
Delliefure
Mains of Dalvey
STRATH SPEY
HILLS OF CROMDALE
Drumin
Glenfiddich Forest
GLENLIVET DISTILLERY
Glenlivet
Shenval
Auchbreck
MUSEUM & HERITAGE TRUST
Cromdale
Auchroisk
Haughs of Cromdale
Ballcorach
Strath Avon
Tomnavoulin
Blackwater Forest
Anagach
Congash
CARN DAIMH
CARN AN T-SUIDHE
Lynemore
CREGGAN A'CHAISE
Knockandhu
Glenlivet Forest
Livet
Clashnoir
Braes of Glenlivet
Chapeltown
Burn of Lochy
Bridge of Brown
Dirdhu
Fodderletter
TOMINTOUL MUSEUM
Tomintoul
TOMINTOUL
BADDOCH
Dorback Lodge
Delnabo
GLENLIVET ESTATE VISITOR CENTRE
CARN MEADHONACH
CARN MOR
Glenbuchat Lodge
LADDER HILLS
Braes of Abernethy
Conglass Water
Water of Nochty
Blairnamarrow
THE SOCACH
LECHT SKI CENTRE
0 1 2 3 miles
0 1 2 3 4 5 km

MILLSTONE HILL
Mains of Edingight
Gordontown
Weachyburn
Deerhill
Grange Crossroads
267
Edingight Ho.
KNOCK HILL
430
Blacklaw
Finnygaud
Broadrashes
Forgie
B9016
Crannoch
Sillyearn
Knowes of Elrick
Aultmore
A96
B9018
Bracobrae
Knock
Glen Barry
Cranna
Newmill
Davoch of Grange
Drumnagorrach
Aberchirder
311
Farmtown
Old Crombie
Mulben
Keith
STRATHISLA DISTILLERY
I S L A
A95
B9022
Knauchland
Marnoch
Clunie
B9014
B9117
265
366
Deveron
Forest
KEITH AND DUFFTOWN RLY
Balloch Wood
Isla
Milltown of Rothiemay
Mains of Mayen
Hillbrae
Inverkeithny
339
S T R A T H
Edintore
Glen of Coachford
Ruthven
Yonder Bognie
Towiemore
Bogniebrae
344
FOURMAN HILL
Little Pitlurg
Coachford
Cairnie
256
Castle
B9115
Drummuir
313
THE BIN
GLENDRONACH DISTILLERY
Drumblair
A96
The Bin Forest
Corse of Kinnoir
A97
B9001
Daugh of Cairnborrow
417
NORDIC SKI CENTRE
HUNTLY CASTLE
Lessendrum
Milltown of Auchindoun
Cairnborrow
A920
Huntly
Drumblade
Corse
Aucharnie
Torry
BRANDER MUSEUM
A920
Deveron
Brideswell
Haugh of Glass
Slioch
Denend
Ythanwells
AUCHINDOUN CASTLE
S T R A T H B O G I E
Thomastown
487
THE SCALP
Bailiesward
Bridgend
Hillhead
Tillathrowie
Succoth
Kirkstile
Shanquhar
Bainshole
A96
381
Ballochford
525
Blackburn
Glens of Foudland
Tomnaven
NJ
Coynachie
Culdrain
467
HILL OF FOUDLAND
Colpy
Clashindarroch Forest
Kirkney
Clashindarroch Forest
Bridgend
Clashindarroch
Gartly
Largie
Inverharroch
Cults
434
KNOCKANDY HILL
Wrangham
Kirkney Water
LEITH HALL
B992
Milton of Lesmore
Milton of Noth
Kennethmont
The Shevock
Aulton
B9002
Oldtown
Insch
Auchmair
505
Ardlair
A941
Ardoyne
Belhinnie
Cabrach
Cottown
Rhynie
B9002
Aldunie
Wheedlemont
Clatt
Duncanstone
Craig Castle
A97
Leslie
Kirkton
B9002
256
Auchleven
ST MARY'S CHURCH
Knockespock Ho.
721
THE BUCK
Coldwells Croft
Whitehaugh Forest
Clova
Lumsden
SCOTTISH SCULPTURE WORKSHOP
CORREEN HILLS
Muckletown
B992
Glenton
243
Tullynessle
244
518
Mossat
LORD ARTHUR'S CAIRN
Keig
Castle Forbes
Bridge of Alford
Montgarrie
Rorandle
Kildrummy
A97
Don
A944
ALFORD VALLEY RAILWAY
HAUGHTON
Rinmore
Milltown of Kildrummy
Belnacraig
GRAMPIAN TRANSPORT MUS
KILDRUMMY CASTLE & GARDEN
532
Auchintoul
Gateside
Kirkton of Glenbuchat
Alford
A980
A944
HERITAGE MUSEUM
Whitehouse
Asloun
Forbestown
Glenkindie
Sinnahard
Hillockhead
Kirkton
4
5
6
7
A
B
C
D
E

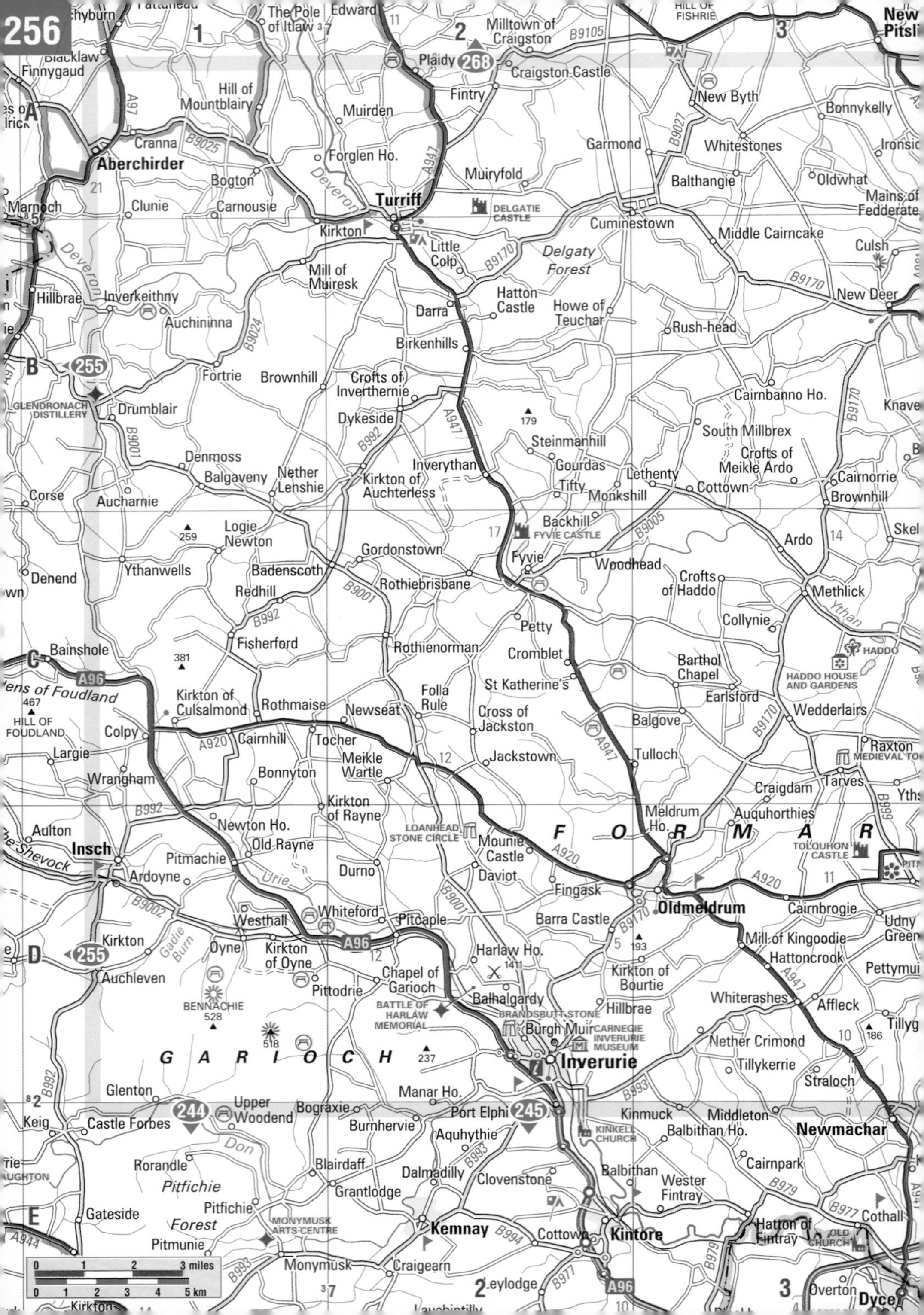
The Pole of Itlaw
Edward
Milltown of Craigston
HILL OF FISHRIE
New Pitsligo
Blacklaw
Finnygaud
Plaidy
268
Craigston Castle
B9105
Hill of Mountblairy
Muirden
Fintry
New Byth
Bonnykelly
Cranna
B9025
Aberchirder
Forglen Ho.
A947
Garmond
B9027
Whitestones
Balthangie
Oldwhat
Muiryfold
Bogton
Clunie
Carnousie
Deveron
Turriff
DELGATIE CASTLE
Marnoch
Cuminestown
Middle Cairncake
Mains of Fedderate
Kirkton
Little Colp
B9170
Delgaty Forest
Culsh
Mill of Muiresk
New Deer
Hillbrae
Inverkeithny
Auchininna
B9024
Darra
Hatton Castle
Howe of Teuchar
Rush-head
Birkenhills
255
Fortrie
Brownhill
Crofts of Inverthernie
Cairnbanno Ho.
GLENDRONACH DISTILLERY
Drumblair
Dykeside
A947
179
South Millbrex
B992
B9001
Steinmanhill
Gourdas
Crofts of Meikle Ardo
Denmoss
Inverythan
Lethenty
Cairnorrie
Balgaveny
Nether Lenshie
Kirkton of Auchterless
Tifty
Monkshill
Cottown
Brownhill
Corse
Aucharnie
Backhill
FYVIE CASTLE
B9005
Ardo
259
Logie Newton
Gordonstown
Fyvie
Denend
Ythanwells
Badenscoth
Woodhead
Crofts of Haddo
Methlick
Rothiebrisbane
Redhill
B9001
Ythan
B992
Petty
Collynie
Fisherford
Rothienorman
Cromblet
HADDO
381
Bainshole
Barthol Chapel
HADDO HOUSE AND GARDENS
A96
St Katherine's
Kirkton of Culsalmond
Folla Rule
Earlsford
467
HILL OF FOUDLAND
Rothmaise
Newseat
Cross of Jackston
Balgove
Wedderlairs
B9170
Colpy
Cairnhill
Tocher
A920
Largie
Meikle Wartle
Jackstown
Tulloch
Raxton
MEDIEVAL
Bonnyton
Wrangham
Craigdam
Tarves
B992
Kirkton of Rayne
Meldrum Ho.
Auquhorthies
B999
Aulton
Newton Ho.
LOANHEAD STONE CIRCLE
F O R M A R T I N E
Insch
Old Rayne
Mounie Castle
TOLQUHON CASTLE
Pitmachie
A920
Ardoyne
Durno
Daviot
Urie
Fingask
A920
B9002
Oldmeldrum
Cairnbrogie
Whiteford
B9001
Barra Castle
Westhall
Pitcaple
B9170
Udny Green
Kirkton
A96
193
Mill of Kingoodie
Oyne
Kirkton of Oyne
Harlaw Ho.
Hattoncrook
255
Gadie Burn
1411
Kirkton of Bourtie
Pettymuick
Auchleven
Chapel of Garioch
A947
Pittodrie
Whiterashes
Affleck
BENNACHIE
BATTLE OF HARLAW MEMORIAL
Balhalgardy
Hillbrae
528
BRANDSBUTT STONE
Tillygreig
Burgh Muir
CARNEGIE INVERURIE MUSEUM
186
518
Nether Crimond
G A R I O C H
237
Inverurie
Tillykerrie
Straloch
Glenton
Manar Ho.
B993
B992
Upper Woodend
Bograxie
244
Port Elphinstone
245
Kinmuck
Middleton
Keig
Castle Forbes
Burnhervie
Aquhythie
KINKELL CHURCH
Balbithan Ho.
Newmachar
Don
B993
Rorandle
Blairdaff
Cairnpark
Pitfichie
Dalmadilly
Clovenstone
Balbithan
Wester Fintray
B979
Grantlodge
Gateside
Pitfichie Forest
MONYMUSK ARTS CENTRE
B977
Cothall
Kemnay
B994
Cottown
Kintore
Hatton of Fintray
OLD CHURCH
A944
Pitmunie
B979
Monymusk
Craigearn
B993
B977
Leylodge
A96
Overton
Dyce
0 1 2 3 miles
0 1 2 3 4 5 km
A B C D E
1 2 3

Knowhead
Strichen
MORMOND HILL
Nether Park
Crimond
Rattray
Blackhill
269
A90
New Leeds
Longhill
Balearn
St Fergus Moss
Adziel
North Ugie Water
Leys
Little Skillymarno
Denhead
Backfolds
Kirktown
St Fergus
Scotstown Hd.
Fetterangus
Hythie
Rora Moss
North Kirkton
Forest of Deer
Toux
Rora
Lunderton
Kirkton Hd.
DEER ABBEY
Dunshillock
Woodside
Maud
B U C H A N
Mintlaw
Newseat
Inverugie
INVERUGIE CASTLE
UGIE SALMON FISH HOUSE
Buchanhaven
ADEN
Backhill of Clackriach
Old Deer
Longside
Torterston
Flushing
ABERDEENSHIRE FARMING MUSEUM
South Ugie
Peterhead
Stuartfield
Inverquhomery
A950
ARBUTHNOT MUSEUM & ART GALLERY
Drymuir
Bulwark
Mains of Crichie
Millbreck
Hillhead of Cocklaw
Keith Inch
Nether Kinmundy
Peterhead Bay
Nethermuir
Crichie
Invernettie
Sandford Bay
Kinnadie
Clola
Little Dens
Skelmuir
Blackhill
Millbank
Boddam
Mains of Annochie
Buchan Ness
Kinknockie
Stirling
Backhill of Fortree
Smallburn
Sandfordhill
Moss of Cruden
Coldwells
Backhill
Stoneygate
Teuchan
Longhaven
Milton Coldwells
A90
North Haven
Auchiries
BULLERS OF BUCHAN
Hatton
Muirtack
Twa Havens
Drumwhindle
Eastertown of Auchleuchries
Cruden Bay
Arthrath
SLAINS CASTLE
Toll of Birness
Port Erroll
Chapel Hill
Bogbrae
NJ
NK
Bay of Cruden
A952
A948
A975
Hilton
Mains of Birness
Nether Leask
Inverebrie
Whinnyfold
Broomfield
A90
West Arrachie
P&R
Artrochie
Auchmacoy
Ellon
A920
I N E
Kirkton of Logie Buchan
VISITOR CENTRE
Kirktown of Slains
Collieston
Waterside
St Catherine's Dub
Meikle Tarty
Tipperty
B9000
FORVIE
Sands of Forvie
Hackley Hd. or Forvie Ness
Tarty Burn
B9000
Newburgh
Cultercullen
Foveran
Foveran Burn
Minnes
Newburgh Bar
A975
Drums
Tillycorthie
Rashiereive
B999
Ardo Ho.
Delfrigs
Middlemuir
245
Craigie
Causeyend
Whitecairns
Belhelvie
B977
BALMEDIE
Balmedie
A90
Potterton
Blackdog
Corby Loch
Mundurno
B9093
A981
A950
B9029
B9106
B9030
A982
4
5
6
A
B
C
D
E

Fladda-chùain
Rubha
TARBERT
LOCHMADDY
287
Hungladder
Borneskętaig
Kilmuir
FLORA MACDONALD'S MEMORIAL
Waternish Point
Totscore
Kilbride Point
Ascrib Islands
Idrigill
Uig Bay
Ru Chorachan
BEN GEARY 284
Geary
Ard Beag
TRUMPAN CHURCH
Trumpan
Knockbreck
Gillen
LOCH SNIZORT
Ardmore Pt.
Lower Halistra
Upper Halistra
Hallin
WATERNISH
ISLE OF SKYE
Lyndale Pt.
Greshornish Pt.
Mingay
Isay
Dunvegan Head
Stein
Lusta
LOCH DUNVEGAN
Loch Bay
B886
Loch Greshornish
Lyndale Ho.
Galtrigill
Claigan
Greshornish
Treaslane
Borreraig
Uig
327 BEINN BHREAC
Bay River
Flashader
Suladale
Husabost
Edinbane
An Ceannaich
Loch Pooltiel
Feriniquarrie
DUNVEGAN CASTLE
Blackhill
Lower Milovaig
Totaig
Glasphein
Oisgill Bay
Upper Milovaig
Lephin
B884
COLBOST FOLK MUSEUM
Colbost
A850
Glen Bernisdale
Holmisdale
GIANT ANGUS MACASKILL MUSEUM
LIGHTHOUSE
Neist Point
Glen Dale
Hamara
Skinidin
Dunvegan
Kilmuir
CRUACHAN BEINN A'CHEARCAILL 266
Lonmore
Moonen Bay
HEALABHAL MHOR 468
Roskhill
Ramasaig
Roag
Vatten
Loch Connan
Hoe Rape
Macleod's Tables
Orbost
Harlosh
Ose
488 HEALABHAL BHEAG
Loch Varkasaig
Balmore
Loch Caroy
B885
Hoe Point
A863
246
Bracadale
Geodha Mor
Harlosh I.
0 1 2 3 miles
0 1 2 3 4 5 km

4
5
6
260
261
249
248
A
B
C
D
Eilean Trodday
Rubha na h-Aiseig
Balmacqueen
Kilmaluag
MUSEUM OF ISLAND LIFE
Eilean Flodigarry
Flodigarry
MEALL NA SUIRAMACH 543
Digg
Staffin Bay
Staffin I.
THE QUIRAING
Glashvin
Brogaig
Stenscholl
Staffin
TROTTERNISH
Kilt Rock
KILT ROCK & MEALT FALLS
466 BIOD BUIDHE
Elishader
Maligar
Loch Mealt
NG
Valtos
A855
Marishader
Conon
Garros
Rubha nam Brathairean
Balnaknock
611 BEINN EDRA
Breckrey
Culnaknock
Lealt
LEALT FALLS
Lower Tote
Upper Tote
Lealt
Hinnisdal
607 CREAG A'LAIN
SOUND OF RAASAY
Island of Rona
125
Eilean Garbh
Romesdal
719 THE STORR
OLD MAN OF STORR
Callakille
Eyre
Caol Rona
Eilean Tigh
Garbh Eilean
TROTTERNISH
Bearreraig Bay
Lonbain
Loch a' Sguirr
An Caol
Haultin
Holm I.
Loch Leathan
Eilean Fladday
B8036
Tote
Loch Fada
Torran
Manish Pt.
Loch Arnish
Arnish
Borve
Skeabost
Carbost
PRINCE CHARLES'S CAVE
INNER SOUND
Loch nan Eun
Uigshader
Drumuie
392
BROCHEL CASTLE
CHAPEL ST MAELRUBHA
Achachork
Brochel
Rubha na h Airde Glaise
Glengrasco
Torvaig
Applecross Bay
Shulishadermor
THE AROS EXPERIENCE
Portree
Glame
385
ISLAND OF RAASAY
Snizort
Heatherfield
417
Penifiler
413 BEN TIANAVAIG
Camusteel
Balmeanach
Balachuirn
Glenmore
Ard-dhubh
Tungadal
Mugeary
B883
Camastianavaig
Holoman Bay
443 DUN CAAN
A87
Tianavaig
Toscaig

1
2
3
Garbh Eilean
Eilean Mhuire
Eilean an Tighe
Na h-Eileanan Mòra (Shiant Islands)
A
288
288
B
NG
259
Eilean Trodday
Rubha Hunish
Rubha na h-Aiseig
C
DUNTULM CASTLE
Duntulm
Balmacqueen
Kilmaluag
MUSEUM OF ISLAND LIFE
Eilean Flodigarry
Flodigarry
MEALL NA SUIRAMACH
543
259
Digg
Staffin Bay
Staffin I.
Glashvin
THE QUIRAING
Brogaig
Stenscholl
Staffin
TROTTERNISH
Kilt Rock
KILT ROCK & MEALT FALLS
466
BIOD BUIDHE
D
Elishader
Maligar
Loch Mealt
A855
Valtos
Uig
UIG
Conon
Marishader
Garros
Rubha nam Brathairean
Balnaknock
611
BEINN EDRA
Breckrey
Culnaknock
Island of Rona
Lealt
LEALT FALLS
Lower Tote
Upper Tote
Earlish
Linicro
Kilvaxter
Kilmuir
0 1 2 3 miles
0 1 2 3 4 5 km

Greenstone Point
Rubha Beag
Cailleach Hd.
Opinan
Rubha Mor
Mellon Udrigle
Stattic Pt.
Gruinard I.
Badluarach
Mungasdale
Achgarve
Gruinard Bay
Gruinard House
Laide
Mellon Charles
Sand
First Coast
Second Coast
Inchina
Ormiscaig
Little Gruinard
Tighnafiline
Aultbea
Drumchork
Isle of Ewe
Eilean Furadh Mór
Sròn a' Gheodha Dhuibh
Camas Mór
Rubha Reidh
Loch an Draing
Cove
296 AN CUAIDH
Loch Sguod
Loch a' Bhaid-luachraich
Melvaig
Inverasdale
Midtown
LOCH EWE
Aultgrishan
Seana Chamas
Loch Fada
Little Gruinard
Brae
B8057
Rubha 'Ard na Bà
Naast
Tournaig
A832
Peterburn
Aird Dubh
INVEREWE GARDEN
Loch Bad a' Chreamh
680 BEINN A'CHAISGEIN BEAG
B8021
Londubh
Port Erradale
North Erradale
Poolewe
Loch Kernsary
Fisherfield Forest
Rubha Bàn
Big Sand
Ewe
FIONN LOCH
Longa Island
Caolas Beag
CARN DEARG
Strath
Loch Tolláidh
Smithstown
GAIRLOCH HERITAGE MUSEUM
Gairloch
MEALL AN DOIREAN 420
Dubh Loch
LOCH GAIRLOCH
791 BEINN AIRIGH CHARR
Charlestown
A832
Port Henderson
Aird
B8056
Badachro
Kerrysdale
BEINN LAIR 860
Letterewe Forest
Opinan
Shieldaig
LOCH MAREE
Eilean Subhainn
LOCH MAREE ISLANDS
Kerry
Loch Bad an Sgalaig
Letterewe
Loch Clàir
South Erradale
VICTORIA FALLS
Talladale
Loch Garbhaig
Abhainn a' Gharbh Choire
Redpoint
Erradale
Abhainn Braigh-horrisdale
Dubh Loch
A832
Loch Gaineamhach
WESTER ROSS
Flowerdale Forest
Glen Grudie
Loch na h-Oidhche
875 BAOSBHEINN
Shieldaig Forest
Craig
878
624 BEINN BHREAC
Loch a'Bhealaich
Kinlochewe Forest
BEINN EIGHE
Rubha na Fearn
Loch Torridon
WESTER
985 BEINN ALLIGIN
1010 BEINN EIGHE
Fearnmore
Lower Diabaig
Fearnbeg
Arinacrinachd
Alligin
Torridon Forest
1054
302
4
5
6
A
B
C
D
270
262
249

262
Carn nan Sgeir
Strathcanaird
Strath Kanaird
Strath nan Lon
270
271
Camas Mór
Isle Martin
Loch Kanaird
A835
415
Allt-Beinn Dor
Cailleach Hd.
STORNOWAY
Ardmair
Rhue
Rhidorroc
Annat Bay
Stattic Pt.
Scoraig
Carnach
Rireavach
LITTLE LOCH BROOM
Morefield
Ullapool
Loch Achall
Rhidorroch Ho.
548
ULLAPOOL MUSEUM
ULLAPOOL
Ullapool
Glen Achall
Rhidorroch
A
Badluarach
635
BEINN GHOBHLACH
LOCH BROOM
Eas
Mungasdale
Durnamuck
Allt na h-Airbhe
558
BEINN EILIDEACH
Gruinard House
A832
Badcaul
Badrallach
LECKMELM SHRUBBERY AND ARBORETUM
Inchina
Leckmelm
Blarnalearoch
642
261
Camusnagaul
Strath Beag
MEALL DUBH
302
Ardessie
Rhiroy
Gruinard
767
SAIL MHOR
Ardcharnich
Ardindrean
29
Dundonnell Hotel
Eilean Darach
Dundonnell
Letters
12
Inverlael Fore
Dundonnell House
Strathnasheallag Forest
B
AN TEALLACH
1062
Inverlael
LAEL FOREST GARDEN
Lael Forest
Inverbroom
Lael
Loch na Sealga
Strath More
Broom
680
BEINN A'CHAISGEIN BEAG
Dundonnell Forest
Fisherfield Forest
Auchindrean
889
908
BEINN DEARG MHOR
Strath na Sealga
Fain
Braemore
Dundonnell
CORRIESHALLOCH GORGE
Abhainn Cuileig
MEALL LEACA
LOCH
Dubh Loch
914
BEINN A' CHLAIDHEIMH
Abhainn Droma
Braemore Forest
C
807
Loch a'Bhraoin
BEINN LAIR
860
Letterewe Forest
1019
MULLACH COIRE MHIC FHEARCHAIR
934
1110
SGURR MOR
Letterewe
Lochan Fada
748
GROBAN
999
A'CHAILLEACH
Loch Garbhaig
949
MEALL GORM
980
SLIOCH
Abhainn a'Chadh'Bhuidhe
Fannich Forest
WESTER ROSS
BEINN NAN RAMH
711
Fannich Lodge
Glen Grudie
692
Kinlochewe Forest
LOCH FANNICH
D
Heights of Kinlochewe
Leckie
Strath Chrombuill
Taagan
878
Lochrosque Forest
Abhainn Bruachaig
Kinlochewe Forest
Anancaun
WESTER ROSS
BEINN EIGHE
Incheril
Kinlochewe
933
FIONN BHEINN
1010
BEINN EIGHE
Glen Docherty
A832
Strath
Gharbhe
250
Badavanich
Achnasheen
Bran
0 1 2 3 miles
0 1 2 3 4 5 km
2
4
1
3

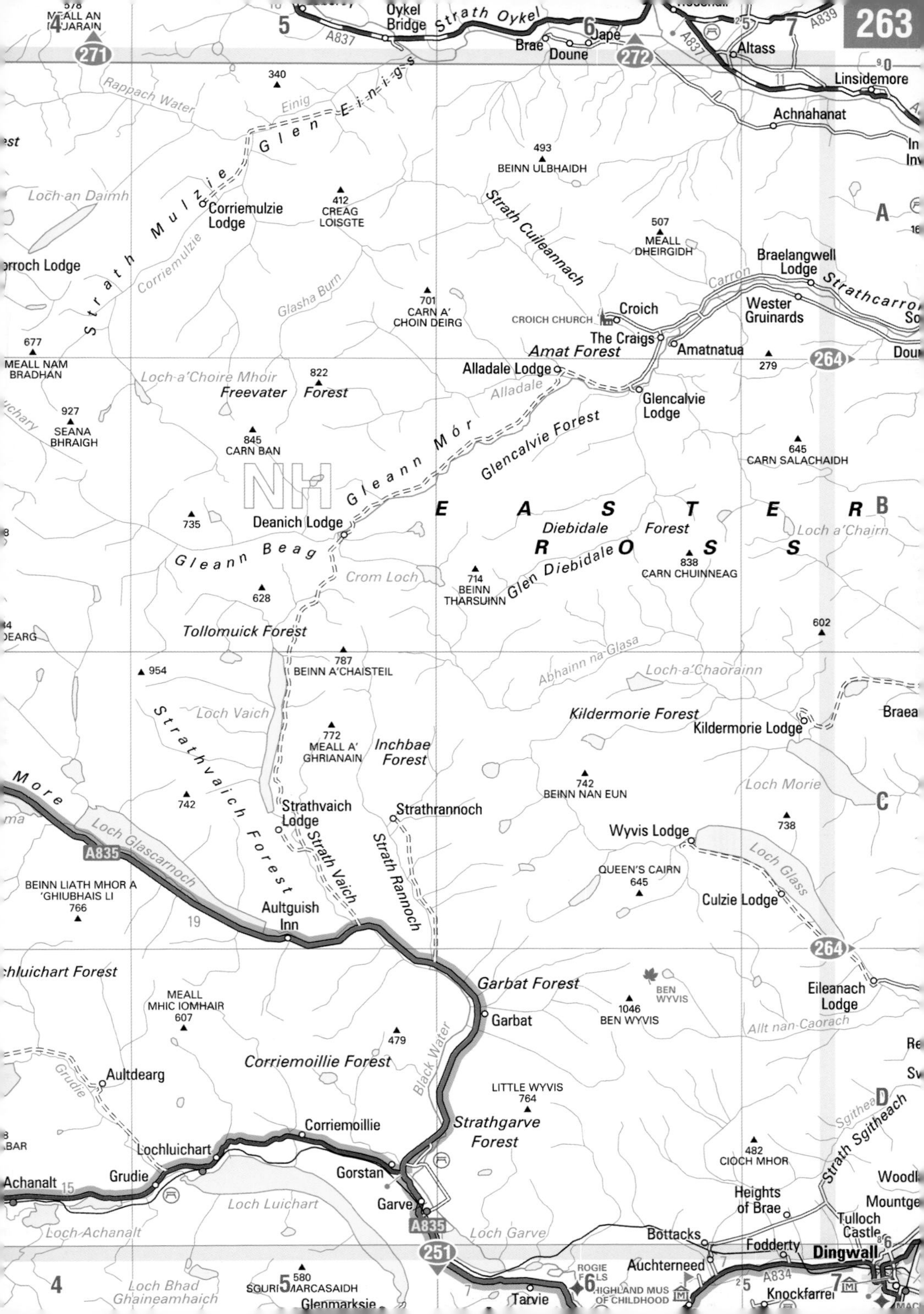
MEALL AN
Oykel Bridge
Strath Oykel
A837
Brae
Doune
Jape
272
271
Altass
A839
Linsidemore
Rappach Water
340
Einig
Glen Einig
Achnahanat
493
BEINN ULBHAIDH
Strath Mulzie
Loch an Daimh
Corriemulzie Lodge
412
CREAG LOISGTE
Strath Cuileannach
507
MEALL DHEIRGIDH
Corriemulzie
Braelangwell Lodge
Carron
Strathcarron
Glasha Burn
701
CARN A' CHOIN DEIRG
CROICH CHURCH
Croich
Wester Gruinards
The Craigs
Amatnatua
Amat Forest
677
MEALL NAM BRADHAN
279
264
Loch a'Choire Mhoir
822
Alladale Lodge
Freevater Forest
Alladale
Glencalvie Lodge
927
SEANA BHRAIGH
845
CARN BAN
Gleann Mór
Glencalvie Forest
645
CARN SALACHAIDH
NH
735
Deanich Lodge
EASTER ROSS
Diebidale Forest
B
Loch a'Chairn
Gleann Beag
Crom Loch
714
BEINN THARSUINN
Glen Diebidale
838
CARN CHUINNEAG
628
Tollomuick Forest
602
787
BEINN A'CHAISTEIL
954
Abhainn na Glasa
Loch a'Chaorainn
Loch Vaich
Kildermorie Forest
Kildermorie Lodge
772
MEALL A' GHRIANAIN
Inchbae Forest
Strathvaich Forest
Loch Morie
742
BEINN NAN EUN
C
742
Strathvaich Lodge
Strathrannoch
Loch Glascarnoch
A835
Strath Vaich
Strath Rannoch
Wyvis Lodge
738
Loch Glass
QUEEN'S CAIRN
645
BEINN LIATH MHOR A 'GHIUBHAIS LI
766
Culzie Lodge
Aultguish Inn
19
264
Garbat Forest
BEN WYVIS
Eileanach Lodge
MEALL MHIC IOMHAIR
607
Garbat
1046
BEN WYVIS
Allt nan-Caorach
479
Black Water
Corriemoillie Forest
Aultdearg
Grudie
LITTLE WYVIS
764
D
Strathgarve Forest
Strath Sgitheach
Corriemoillie
482
CIOCH MHOR
Lochluichart
Grudie
Gorstan
Achanalt
15
Loch Luichart
Garve
Heights of Brae
Loch Achanalt
A835
Loch Garve
Bottacks
Tulloch Castle
251
Fodderty
Dingwall
ROGIE FALLS
Auchterneed
A834
580
SGURR MARCASAIDH
Loch Bhad Ghaineamhaich
HIGHLAND MUS OF CHILDHOOD
Knockfarrel
Tarvie
Glenmarksie
4
5
6
7
A

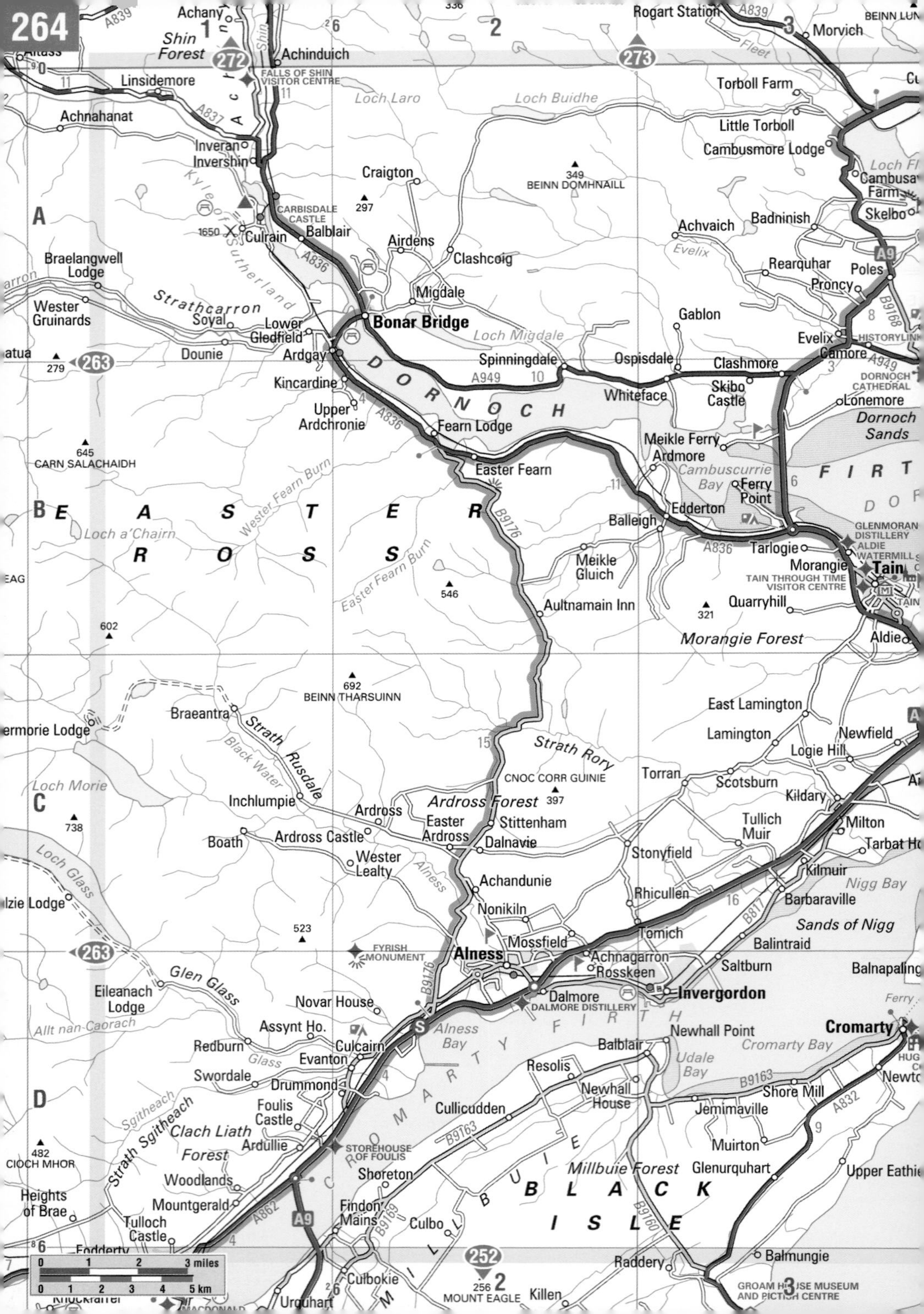

Achany
Shin Forest
272
Achinduich
FALLS OF SHIN VISITOR CENTRE
Rogart Station
273
Morvich
A839
Fleet
Torboll Farm
Little Torboll
Cambusmore Lodge
Loch Laro
Loch Buidhe
Linsidemore
A837
Achnahanat
Inveran
Invershin
Craigton
297
349
BEINN DOMHNAILL
Kyle of Sutherland
CARBISDALE CASTLE
1650
Culrain
Balblair
Airdens
Clashcoig
Achvaich
Badninish
Skelbo
Evelix
Rearquhar
Poles
Proncy
A9
Braelangwell Lodge
Wester Gruinards
Strathcarron
Soyal
Lower Gledfield
Dounie
Ardgay
279
263
Migdale
Bonar Bridge
Loch Migdale
Gablon
Evelix
HISTORYLINKS
Camore
B9168
Spinningdale
Ospisdale
Clashmore
A949
DORNOCH CATHEDRAL
Lonemore
Dornoch Sands
Kincardine
Upper Ardchronie
A836
DORNOCH
Whiteface
Skibo Castle
Fearn Lodge
Meikle Ferry
Ardmore
Cambuscurrie Bay
Ferry Point
FIRT
645
CARN SALACHAIDH
Easter Fearn
Wester Fearn Burn
EASTER ROSS
Loch a'Chairn
B9176
Edderton
Balleigh
GLENMORANGIE DISTILLERY
ALDIE WATERMILL
Tarlogie
Morangie
Tain
TAIN THROUGH TIME VISITOR CENTRE
Meikle Gluich
Easter Fearn Burn
546
Aultnamain Inn
321
Quarryhill
Morangie Forest
Aldie
602
692
BEINN THARSUINN
East Lamington
Lamington
Newfield
Logie Hill
Braeantra
Strath Rusdale
Black Water
Strath Rory
CNOC CORR GUINIE
397
Torran
Scotsburn
Kildary
Loch Morie
Inchlumpie
Ardross
Ardross Forest
Easter Ardross
Stittenham
Tullich Muir
Milton
Tarbat Ho
738
Boath
Ardross Castle
Dalnavie
Stonyfield
Kilmuir
Loch Glass
Wester Lealty
Alness
Achandunie
Rhicullen
Nigg Bay
Barbaraville
Nonikiln
Sands of Nigg
B817
523
Mossfield
Tomich
Balintraid
FYRISH MONUMENT
Alness
Achnagarron
Rosskeen
Saltburn
Balnapaling
Glen Glass
Eileanach Lodge
Dalmore
DALMORE DISTILLERY
Invergordon
Novar House
Ferry
Allt nan Caorach
Assynt Ho.
Alness Bay
CROMARTY FIRTH
Cromarty
Redburn
Glass
Culcairn
Evanton
Balblair
Newhall Point
Cromarty Bay
Udale Bay
Swordale
Resolis
B9163
Drummond
Newhall House
Shore Mill
Newton
Foulis Castle
Cullicudden
Jemimaville
A832
Sgitheach
Strath Sgitheach
Clach Liath Forest
Ardullie
STOREHOUSE OF FOULIS
Muirton
482
CIOCH MHOR
Shoreton
Millbuie Forest
Glenurquhart
Upper Eathie
Woodlands
BLACK ISLE
Heights of Brae
Mountgerald
A862
A9
Findon Mains
B9169
Culbo
MILLBUIE
B9160
Tulloch Castle
Fodderty
252
Raddery
Balmungie
Culbokie
256
MOUNT EAGLE
Killen
Urquhart
GROAM HOUSE MUSEUM AND PICTISH CENTRE
0 1 2 3 miles
0 1 2 3 4 5 km

A9
DUNROBIN CASTLE MUSEUM & GARDENS
Golspie
274
NH
NJ
A
B
C
D
Littleferry
Fourpenny
Embo
Embo Street
WITCHES STONE
OLD POST OFFICE VISITOR CENTRE
Whiteness Sands
Tarbat Ness
TARBAT NESS LIGHTHOUSE
Wilkhaven
TARBAT DISCOVERY CENTRE
Bindal
Portmahomack
Rockfield
Inver
Arboll
Balnagall
Tarrel
Lochslin
Loch Eye
Geanies House
B9165
Rhynie
Fearn Station
Hill of Fearn
Fearn
FEARN ABBEY
B9166
Hilton of Cadboll
Loans of Tullich
Balintore
SHANDWICK STONE
Shandwick
B9175
Ankerville
Chapelhill
Pitcalnie
Port an Righ
Nigg
203
King's Cave
Castlecraig
Sutors of Cromarty
MORAY FIRTH
266
Burghead
BURGHEAD BAY
Findhorn
Lower Hempriggs
B9011
Findhorn Bay
Miltonhill
Kincorth Ho.
KINLOSS ABBEY
Kinloss
The Bar
Culbin Forest
Grange Hall
A96
Kintessack
Springfield
SUENO'S STONE
253
Moy Ho.
NELSON TOWER
FALCONER MUSEUM
Mains
Whiteness Head
Forres
Dyke
BRODIE
4
5
6

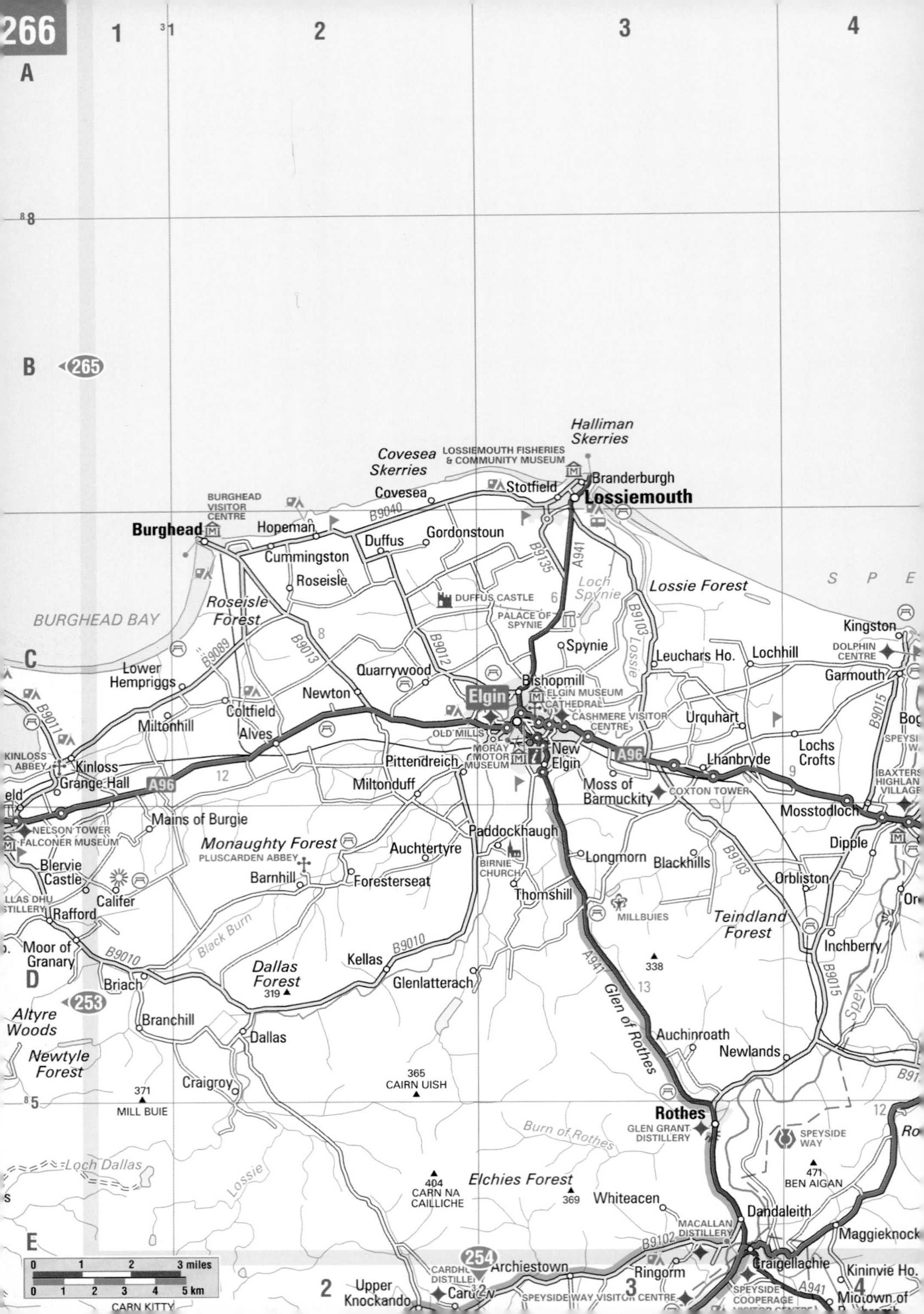

Halliman Skerries
Covesea Skerries
LOSSIEMOUTH FISHERIES & COMMUNITY MUSEUM
Branderburgh
Lossiemouth
Stotfield
Covesea
BURGHEAD VISITOR CENTRE
Burghead
Hopeman
Duffus
Gordonstoun
Cummingston
Roseisle
DUFFUS CASTLE
Loch Spynie
Lossie Forest
PALACE OF SPYNIE
Roseisle Forest
BURGHEAD BAY
Kingston
Spynie
Leuchars Ho.
Lochhill
DOLPHIN CENTRE
Garmouth
Lower Hempriggs
Quarrywood
Newton
Bishopmill
Elgin
ELGIN MUSEUM
CATHEDRAL
CASHMERE VISITOR CENTRE
Coltfield
Miltonhill
Alves
OLD MILLS
Urquhart
Lochs Crofts
KINLOSS ABBEY
Kinloss
Grange Hall
MORAY MOTOR MUSEUM
New Elgin
Pittendreich
Lhanbryde
Miltonduff
Moss of Barmuckity
COXTON TOWER
Mosstodloch
Mains of Burgie
NELSON TOWER
FALCONER MUSEUM
Paddockhaugh
Monaughty Forest
PLUSCARDEN ABBEY
Auchtertyre
Longmorn
Blackhills
Dipple
Blervie Castle
Barnhill
Foresterseat
BIRNIE CHURCH
Orbliston
Thomshill
Califer
Rafford
MILLBUIES
Teindland Forest
Black Burn
Moor of Granary
Inchberry
Kellas
Dallas Forest
Briach
Glenlatterach
Glen of Rothes
338
Altyre Woods
Branchill
Dallas
Auchinroath
Newlands
Newtyle Forest
Craigroy
365 CAIRN UISH
371 MILL BUIE
Rothes
GLEN GRANT DISTILLERY
Burn of Rothes
SPEYSIDE WAY
471 BEN AIGAN
Loch Dallas
Lossie
404 CARN NA CAILLICHE
Elchies Forest
369
Whiteacen
Dandaleith
MACALLAN DISTILLERY
Maggieknock
Archiestown
Ringorm
Craigellachie
Kininvie Ho.
Upper Knockando
SPEYSIDE WAY VISITOR CENTRE
SPEYSIDE COOPERAGE
CARN KITTY
A96
A941
B9040
B9135
B9103
B9013
B9012
B9089
B9011
B9010
B9015
B9102
0 1 2 3 miles
0 1 2 3 4 5 km

265
253
254

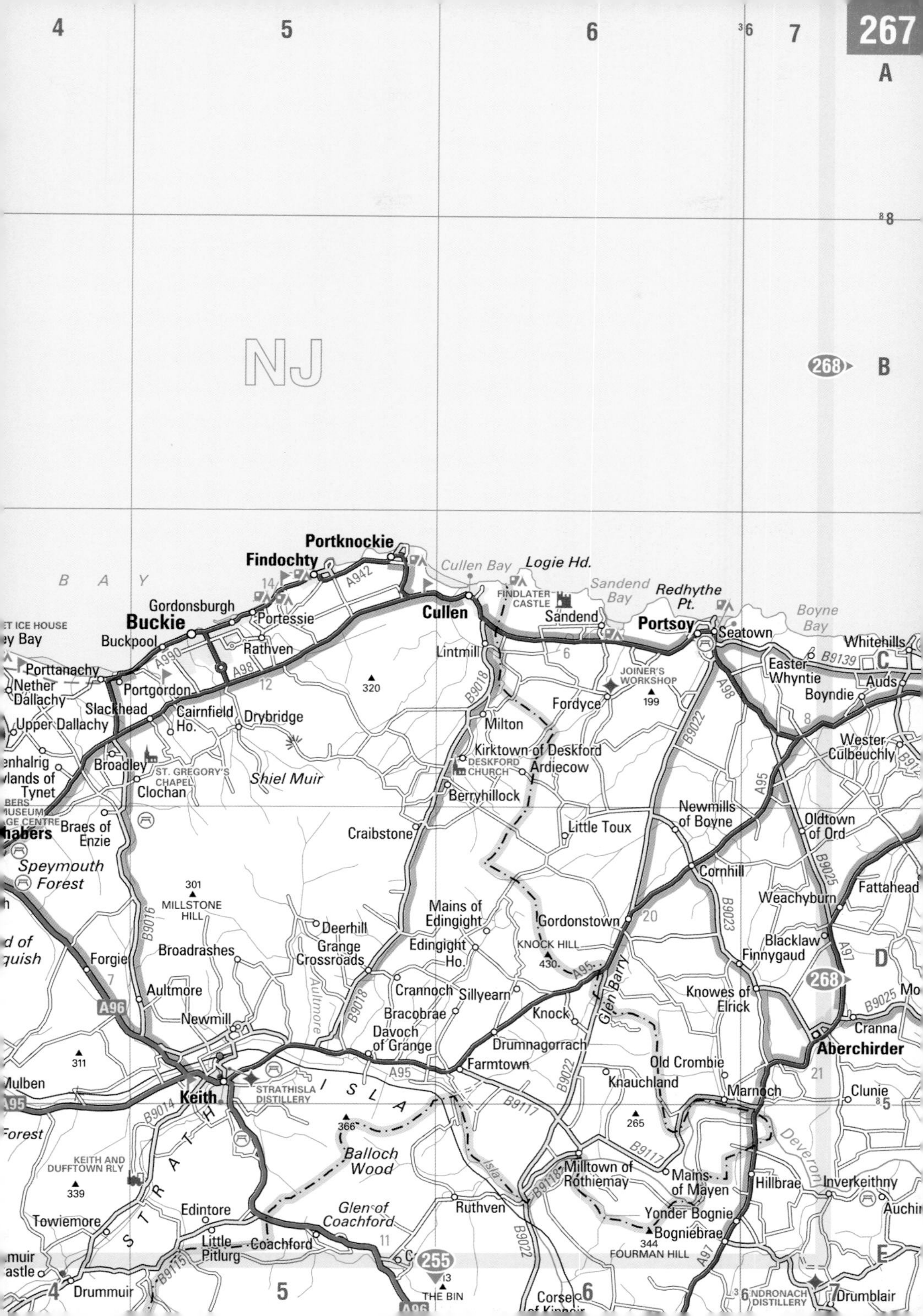
NJ
Portknockie
Findochty
Cullen Bay
Logie Hd.
Sandend Bay
Redhythe Pt.
Boyne Bay
Gordonsburgh
Buckie
Portessie
Cullen
Findlater Castle
Sandend
Portsoy
Seatown
Buckpool
Rathven
Lintmill
Whitehills
Portgordon
Slackhead
Cairnfield Ho.
Drybridge
Milton
Fordyce
Joiner's Workshop
Easter Whyntie
Auds
Boyndie
Upper Dallachy
Nether Dallachy
Porttanachy
Broadley
St. Gregory's Chapel
Clochan
Shiel Muir
Kirktown of Deskford
Deskford Church
Ardiecow
Berryhillock
Wester Culbeuchly
Braes of Enzie
Speymouth Forest
Craibstone
Little Toux
Newmills of Boyne
Oldtown of Ord
Cornhill
Fattahead
Weachyburn
Millstone Hill
Mains of Edingight
Gordonstown
Deerhill
Grange Crossroads
Edingight Ho.
Knock Hill
Blacklaw
Finnygaud
Broadrashes
Forgie
Aultmore
Crannoch
Sillyearn
Knowes of Elrick
Glen Barry
Newmill
Bracobrae
Knock
Davoch of Grange
Drumnagorrach
Cranna
Aberchirder
Farmtown
Old Crombie
Knauchland
Marnoch
Clunie
Mulben
Keith
Strathisla Distillery
Strath Isla
Balloch Wood
Deveron
Keith and Dufftown Rly
Milltown of Rothiemay
Mains of Mayen
Hillbrae
Inverkeithny
Edintore
Glen of Coachford
Ruthven
Yonder Bognie
Towiemore
Bogniebrae
Fourman Hill
Little Pitlurg
Coachford
Drummuir
The Bin
Corse of Kinnoir
Drumblair
Glendronach Distillery
A96
A95
A98
A990
A942
A97
B9016
B9018
B9022
B9023
B9025
B9139
B9117
B9118
B9014
B9115
B9022
255
268
320
199
301
430
311
265
339
344
366
4
5
6
7
A
B
C
D
E

1
2
3
A
B
C
D
E
267
256
Troup Hd.
Pennan Hd.
Boyne Bay
Knock Hd.
Boyndie Bay
Head of Garness
Gamrie Bay
Seatown
Whitehills
Macduff
MACDUFF MARINE AQUARIUM
Crovie
Gardenstown
Pennan
Easter Whyntie
Inverboyndie
Auds
Boyndie
Banff
BANFF MUSEUM
DUFF HOUSE
Easter Silverford
West Greenskares
Dubford
Towie
Longmanhill
Doune Park
Wester Culbeuchly
Cushnie
231 WINDYHEADS HILL
Montcoffer Ho.
Minnonie
Nether Glasslaw
Oldtown of Ord
Kirktown of Alvah
Keilhill
Netherbrae
Mid Cloch Forbie
Craigmaud
Gorrachie
227 HILL OF FISHRIE
Fattahead
Greenlaw
King Edward
The Pole of Itlaw
Weachyburn
Milltown of Craigston
Blacklaw
Plaidy
Craigston Castle
Finnygaud
Hill of Mountblairy
Fintry
New Byth
Bonnykelly
Muirden
Cranna
Aberchirder
Forglen Ho.
Garmond
Whitestones
Bogton
Muiryfold
Balthangie
Oldwhat
Clunie
Carnousie
Turriff
DELGATIE CASTLE
Marnoch
Kirkton
Cuminestown
Middle Cairncake
Culsh
Deveron
Little Colp
Delgaty Forest
Mill of Muiresk
Hillbrae
Inverkeithny
Hatton Castle
Howe of Teuchar
New Deer
Darra
Auchininna
Rush-head
Birkenhills
Fortrie
Brownhill
Crofts of Inverthernie
Cairnbanno Ho.
Dykeside
179
A98
A95
A97
A947
B9139
B9121
B9031
B9025
B9023
B9027
B9105
B9170
B9024
0 1 2 3 miles
0 1 2 3 4 5 km

NJ
NK
Fraserburgh
FRASERBURGH HERITAGE CENTRE
SANDHAVEN MEAL MILL
Pittulie
Broadsea
Kinnaird Head
KINNAIRD CASTLE LIGHTHOUSE & SCOTLAND'S LIGHTHOUSE MUSEUM
sehearty
PITSLIGO CASTLE
Sandhaven
Peathill
Fraserburgh Bay
Cairnbulg Pt.
Inverallochy
Percyhorner
Pitblae
Coburty
MAGGIE'S HOOSIE
Upper Boyndlie
Mid Ardlaw
Cairnbulg Castle
St Combs
Inzie Head
Gowanhill
Tyrie
Memsie
Whitewell
MEMSIE BURIAL CAIRN
Strathellie
Rathen
Cairness
Loch of Strathbeg
Hillhead of Auchentumb
Newburgh
Crimonmogate
Lonmay
Rattray Head
Old Rattray
Crimond
230
MORMOND HILL
Knowhead
Nether Park
Blackhill
Strichen
New Leeds
Longhill
Balearn
Adziel
St Fergus Moss
North Ugie Water
Leys
Little Skillymarno
Backfolds
Kirktown
St Fergus
Scotstown Hd.
Denhead
Fetterangus
Hythie
Rora Moss
North Kirkton
Forest of Deer
Toux
Rora
Lunderton
Kirkton Hd.
DEER ABBEY
Dunshillock
Woodside
Ugie
BUCHAN
Maud
Mintlaw
ADEN
Newseat
Inverugie
INVERUGIE CASTLE
UGIE SALMON FISH HOUSE
Buchanhaven
Water
Backhill of Clackriach
Old Deer
Longside
Torterston
Flushing
Peterhead
ABERDEENSHIRE FARMING MUSEUM
South Ugie
Stuartfield
Inverquhomery
ARBUTHNOT MUSEUM & ART GALLERY
Drymuir
Bulwark
Keith Inch
Mains of Crichie
Millbreck
Hillhead of Cocklaw
Crichie
Nethermuir
Neth
Kinmundy
257
Peterhead Bay
Invernettie
Sandford
Kinnadie
Clola
Little Dens
A90
A98
A981
A952
A950
A982
B9031
B9032
B9033
B9107
B9093
B9029
B9106
B9030

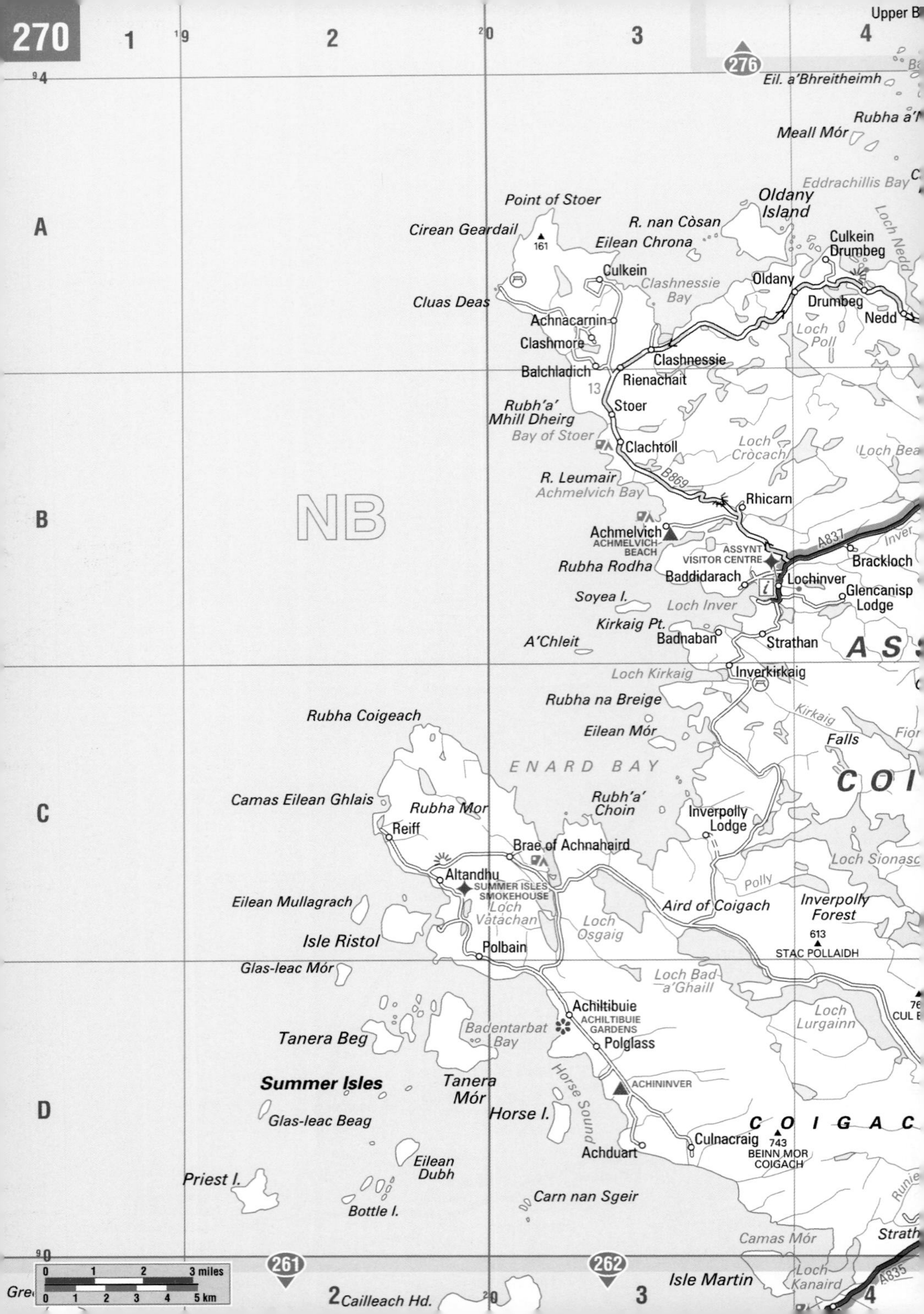
1
2
3
4
A
B
C
D
NB
276
261
262
Upper B
Eil. a'Bhreitheimh
Rubha a'
Meall Mór
Eddrachillis Bay
Point of Stoer
Oldany Island
R. nan Còsan
Cirean Geardail
161
Eilean Chrona
Culkein Drumbeg
Loch Nedd
Culkein
Clashnessie Bay
Oldany
Drumbeg
Nedd
Cluas Deas
Achnacarnin
Loch Poll
Clashmore
Clashnessie
Balchladich
Rienachait
13
Rubh'a' Mhill Dheirg
Stoer
Bay of Stoer
Clachtoll
Loch Cròcach
Loch Bea
R. Leumair
B869
Achmelvich Bay
Rhicarn
Achmelvich
ACHMELVICH BEACH
ASSYNT VISITOR CENTRE
A837
Inver
Brackloch
Rubha Rodha
Baddidarach
Lochinver
Glencanisp Lodge
Soyea I.
Loch Inver
Kirkaig Pt.
Badnaban
Strathan
A'Chleit
A S S
Loch Kirkaig
Inverkirkaig
Rubha na Breige
Rubha Coigeach
Kirkaig
Falls
Eilean Mór
ENARD BAY
C O I
Camas Eilean Ghlais
Rubha Mor
Rubh'a' Choin
Inverpolly Lodge
Reiff
Brae of Achnahaird
Loch Sionasc
Altandhu
SUMMER ISLES SMOKEHOUSE
Polly
Eilean Mullagrach
Loch Vatachan
Loch Osgaig
Aird of Coigach
Inverpolly Forest
Isle Ristol
613
STAC POLLAIDH
Polbain
Glas-leac Mór
Loch Bad a'Ghaill
Achiltibuie
ACHILTIBUIE GARDENS
Loch Lurgainn
CUL B
Tanera Beg
Badentarbat Bay
Polglass
Horse Sound
Summer Isles
Tanera Mór
ACHININVER
Horse I.
C O I G A C
Glas-leac Beag
Culnacraig
743
BEINN MOR COIGACH
Achduart
Eilean Dubh
Priest I.
Carn nan Sgeir
Bottle I.
Camas Mór
Strath
Isle Martin
Loch Kanaird
A835
Caillleach Hd.
0 1 2 3 miles
0 1 2 3 4 5 km

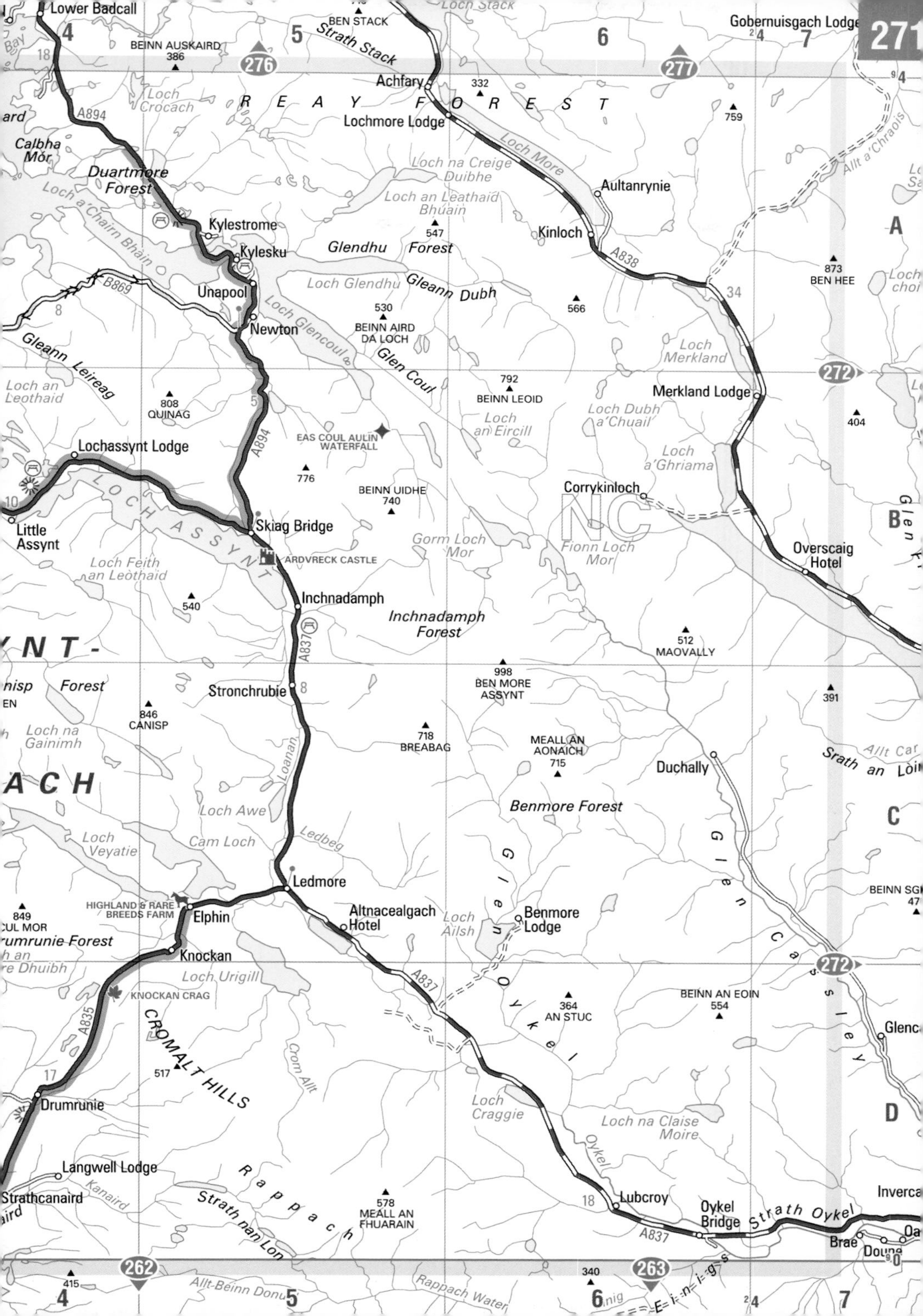
Lower Badcall
BEN STACK
Strath Stack
BEINN AUSKAIRD
386
Gobernuisgach Lodge
Achfary
332
R E A Y F O R E S T
Lochmore Lodge
Loch More
759
Loch Crocach
A894
Calbha Mór
Duartmore Forest
Loch a'Chàirn Bhàin
Loch na Creige Duibhe
Loch an Leathaid Bhuain
547
Aultanrynie
Kylestrome
Kylesku
Glendhu Forest
Kinloch
A838
873
BEN HEE
Unapool
B869
Loch Glendhu
Gleann Dubh
566
Newton
Loch Glencoul
530
BEINN AIRD DA LOCH
Glen Coul
Gleann Leireag
Loch an Leothaid
808
QUINAG
792
BEINN LEOID
Loch Merkland
Merkland Lodge
Loch Dubh a'Chuail
Loch an Eircill
404
Lochassynt Lodge
EAS COUL AULIN WATERFALL
776
Loch a'Ghriama
BEINN UIDHE
740
Corrykinloch
LOCH ASSYNT
Little Assynt
Skiag Bridge
NC
Overscaig Hotel
ARDVRECK CASTLE
Gorm Loch Mor
Fionn Loch Mor
Loch Feith an Leòthaid
540
Inchnadamph
Inchnadamph Forest
A837
512
MAOVALLY
Stronchrubie
998
BEN MORE ASSYNT
391
Forest
846
CANISP
Loch na Gainimh
718
BREABAG
MEALL AN AONAICH
715
Duchally
Strath an Loin
Loanan
Loch Awe
Benmore Forest
Loch Veyatie
Cam Loch
Ledbeg
Glen Cassley
Ledmore
849
CUL MOR
HIGHLAND & RARE BREEDS FARM
Elphin
Altnacealgach Hotel
Loch Ailsh
Benmore Lodge
Drumrunie Forest
Knockan
Loch Urigill
KNOCKAN CRAG
Glen Oykel
364
AN STUC
BEINN AN EOIN
554
A835
CROMALT HILLS
Crom Allt
517
Drumrunie
Loch Craggie
Loch na Claise Moire
Oykel
Langwell Lodge
Rappach
Strathcanaird
Kanaird
Strath nan Lon
578
MEALL AN FHUARAIN
Lubcroy
Oykel Bridge
Strath Oykel
Brae
Doune
Invercassley
415
Allt-Beinn Donu
Rappach Water
340
4
5
6
7
A
B
C
D

Gobernuisgach Lodge
277
271
263
Loch More
Aultanrynie
Kinloch
A838
Loch Merkland
Merkland Lodge
BEINN LEOID
BEN HEE
Loch Fiag
Corrykinloch
Overscaig Hotel
Fiag Plantation
Glen Fiag
Fiag Bridge
MAOVALLY
BEN MORE ASSYNT
MEALL AN AONAICH
Duchally
Srath an Lòin
Benmore Forest
LOCH SHIN
Shinness
Achnairn
BEINN SGEIREACH
Benmore Lodge
Glen Cassley
Glencassley Castle
BEINN AN EOIN
AN STUC
Loch Craggie
Loch na Claise Moire
Lubcroy
Oykel Bridge
Strath Oykel
A837
Brae
Doune
Oape
Invercassley
Rosehall
Altass
Oykel Forest
Glenrossal
CNOC A'CHOIRE
A839
Achany
Shin Forest
Linsidemore
Achnahanat
Lairg
Claonel
Gruids
Sallachy
Colaboll
Dalchork
Rhian
Strath Tirry
Crask Inn
Strath Vagastie
A836
Altnaharra
Mudale
B873
Loch Meadie
Meadie Burn
Loch Coire na Saidhe Dùibhe
Loch a'Ghorm-choire
CNOC AN ALASKIE
MEALL NAN CON
Loch Gaineamhach
Kilbreck Burn
Allt a'Chraois
Loch Dubh a'Chuail
Loch an Eircill
Loch a'Ghriama
Fionn Loch Mor
Allt Car
Allt a'Bhunn
Loch na Fuaralaich
Grudie Burn
B864
Loch Ailsh
Glen Oykel

Naver Forest
Pole Hill
Garvault Hotel
Achentoul Forest
Ben Griam Beg
Ben Griam More
Loch Rimsdale
Loch nan Clàr
Badanloch Forest
Loch an Ruathair
Lochside
Loch Badanloch
Loch Arichlinie
Achentoul
Loch Truderscaig
Loch an Alltan Fhearna
Badanloch Lodge
Strath Beg
Kinbrace
Helmsdale
Loch Choire Lodge
Loch Choire
Abhainn na Frithe
Borrobol Forest
Ben Armine
Gorm-loch Beag
Meall a'Bhata
Altanduin
Borrobol Lodge
Gorm-loch Mór
Creag Mhór
Creag nam Fiadh
Ben Armine Forest
Skinsdale
Strath Skinsdale
Tuarie Burn
Glas-loch Mor
Ben Armine Lodge
Craggie
Craggie Burn
Strath na Seilge
Meallan Liath Mor
Dalnessie
Black Water
Glen Sletdale
Brora
Balnacoil
Col-Bheinn
Achnaluachrach
West Langwell
Strath Brora
Gordonbush
Allt na Luibe
Dalreavoch
Loch Brora
Loch Craggie
Rhilochan
Ben Horn
Achrimsdale
East Clyne
East Langwell
Farlary
West Clyne
Loch Horn
Clynelish
Clynelish Distillery
Muie
Strath Fleet
Brora
Ardachu
Rogart
Cagar Feosaig
Golspie Burn
Doll
Pittentrail
Backies
Hector Macdonald Monument
Rogart Station
Beinn Lunndaidh
Morvich
Dunrobin Castle Museum & Gardens
Golspie
Torboll Farm
Culmaily
Loch Buidhe
Kirkton

Loch Druim a'Chliabhain
FORSINARD FLOWS
279
580 BEN GRIAM BEG
Rumsdale Water
Dalnav
Garvault Hotel
509 BEN GRIAM MORE
Allt Airigh-dhamh
Achentoul Forest
A897
Loch an Ruathair
Badanloch Forest
Lochside
373
438
Glutt Lodge
Glutt Water
Loch nan Clàr
Loch Arichlinie
Knockfin Heights
Loch Badanloch
Badanloch Lodge
Achentoul
Strath Beg
Kinbrace
B871
Helmsdale
328
318 CNOC LOCH MHADADH
273
Kinbrace Burn
438 CNOC COIRE NA PEARNA
705 MORVEN
Borrobol Forest
Abhainn na Frithe
517 CNOC AN EIREANNAICH
Suisgill Burn
Wag
Langwell
Altanduin
Borrobol Lodge
A897
NC
365
STRATH OF KILDONAN
17
Kildonan Burn
387 CREAG NAM FIADH
555 CREAG SCALABSDALE
Kildonan Lodge
BAILE AN ÒR GOLDRUSH SITE
BEINN DUBHAIN 414
Skinsdale
Strath Skinsdale
Tuarie Burn
Craggie
Craggie Burn
Helmsdale
Torrish
Kilphedir
A897
ELDRABLE HILL 417
HELMSDALE
Marrel
West Helmsdale
345
628 BEINN DHORAIN
592
Gartymore
Black Water
Glen Loth
Glen Sletdale
Portgower
Lothmore
Balnacoil
11
538 COL-BHEINN
Lothbeg
273
Gordonbush
Lothbeg Pt.
A9
Loch Brora
Dalreavoch
Rhilochan
BEN HORN 521
Achrimsdale
East Clyne
Farlary
Loch Horn
West Clyne
Dalchalm
Clynelish
CLYNELISH DISTILLERY
377 CAGAR FEOSAIG
Brora
Rogart
Golspie Burn
Doll
466 BEINN LUNNDAIDH
Backies
9
A839
Morvich
DUNROBIN CASTLE MUSEUM & GARDENS
Golspie
265
Farm
0 1 2 3 miles
0 1 2 3 4 5 km

Loch Sand
Loch Thulachan
Loch Rangag
248
STEMSTER HILL
Camster
Ulbster
CAIRN OF GET
Whaligoe
280
281
A9
Crofts of Benachielt
Roster
HILL O' MANY STANES
Bruan
Loch Breac
Rumster Forest
Upper Lybster
Mid Clyth
Braehungie
287
Loch Dubh
269 CNOCAN CONACHREAG
Reisgill Burn
West Clyth
Forse Ho.
Swiney
Lybster
Houstry
WAG OF FORSE
A99
Burn of Houstry
Smerral
Latheron
Forse
CLAN GUNN HERITAGE CENTRE
Dunbeath Water
Latheronwheel Ho.
Latheronwheel
Braemore
LAIDHAY CROFT MUSEUM
Balnabruich
283
DUNBEATH HERITAGE CENTRE
Dunbeath
Dunbeath Bay
Knockally
DUNBEATH CASTLE
Ramscraigs
626 CARABEN
Borgue
ND
Newport
Ceann Leathad nam Bò
19
Langwell Ho.
Berriedale
BADBEA CLEARANCE VILLAGE
422
A9
Ousdale
Ord Point
A
B
C
D
4
5
6
7
33
94
90
17

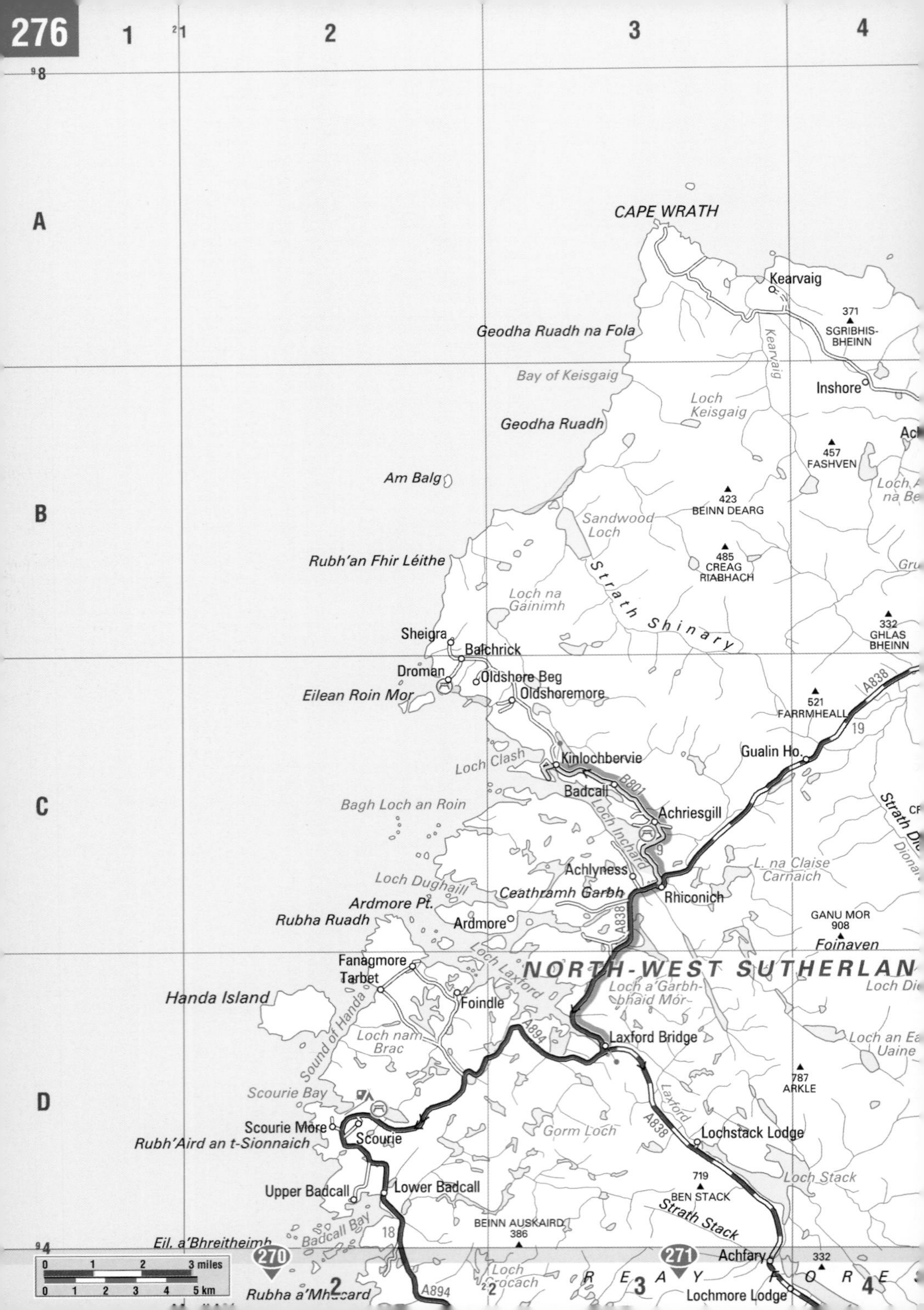

CAPE WRATH
Kearvaig
371
SGRIBHIS-BHEINN
Geodha Ruadh na Fola
Bay of Keisgaig
Kearvaig
Inshore
Loch Keisgaig
Geodha Ruadh
457
FASHVEN
Am Balg
423
BEINN DEARG
Sandwood Loch
485
CREAG RIABHACH
Rubh'an Fhir Léithe
Loch na Gainimh
Strath Shinary
332
GHLAS BHEINN
Sheigra
Balchrick
Droman
Oldshore Beg
Eilean Roin Mor
Oldshoremore
521
FARRMHEALL
A838
19
Kinlochbervie
Loch Clash
Gualin Ho.
Badcall
B801
Bagh Loch an Roin
Achriesgill
Loch Inchard
Strath Dionard
L. na Claise Carnaich
Achlyness
Loch Dughaill
Ceathramh Garbh
Rhiconich
Ardmore Pt.
Rubha Ruadh
Ardmore
A838
GANU MOR
908
Foinaven
Fanagmore
Tarbet
NORTH-WEST SUTHERLAN
Loch Laxford
Loch a'Garbh-bhaid Mór
Handa Island
Foindle
Sound of Handa
A894
Laxford Bridge
Loch nam Brac
Loch an Ea Uaine
787
ARKLE
Scourie Bay
Laxford
A838
Scourie More
Gorm Loch
Lochstack Lodge
Scourie
Rubh'Aird an t-Sionnaich
719
BEN STACK
Loch Stack
Upper Badcall
Lower Badcall
Strath Stack
Badcall Bay
18
BEINN AUSKAIRD
386
Eil. a'Bhreitheimh
270
271
Achfary
332
Loch Crocach
REAY FORE
Rubha a'Mhecard
A894
Lochmore Lodge
0 1 2 3 miles
0 1 2 3 4 5 km

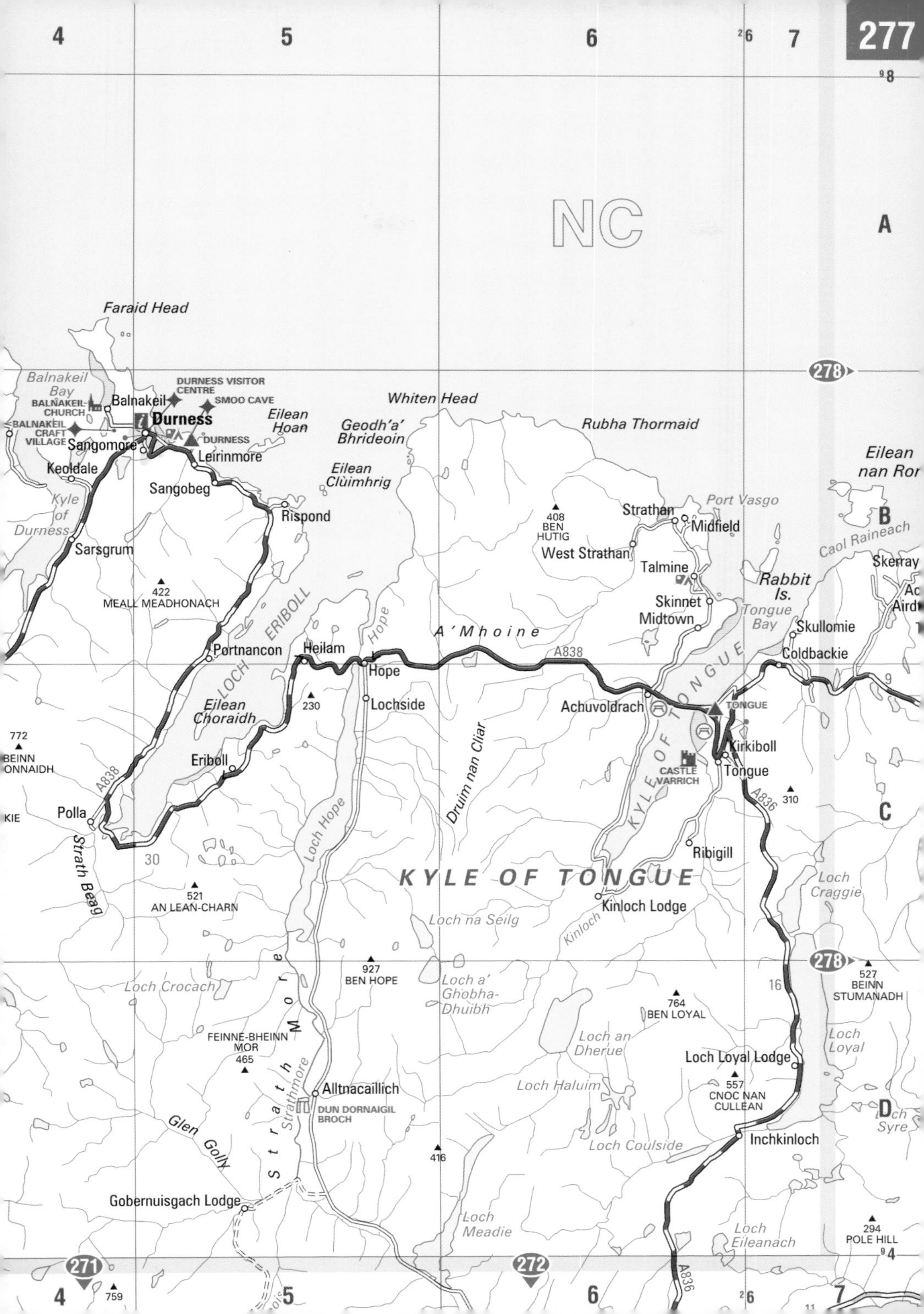

278 278 271 272

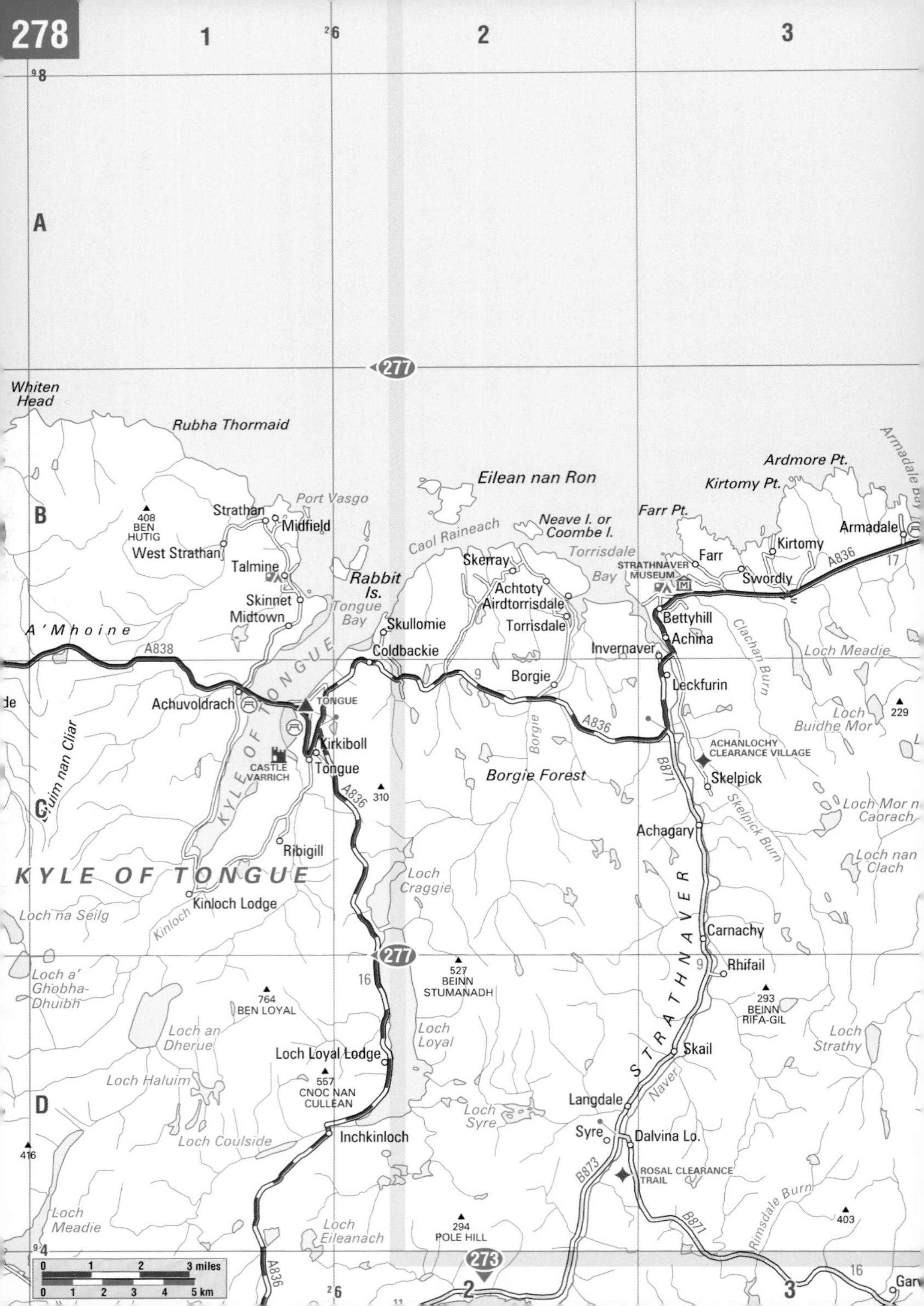
1
2
3
A
B
C
D
277
Whiten Head
Rubha Thormaid
Eilean nan Ron
Ardmore Pt.
Kirtomy Pt.
Armadale Bay
Port Vasgo
Farr Pt.
Strathan
Midfield
408 BEN HUTIG
West Strathan
Caol Raineach
Neave I. or Coombe I.
Armadale
Kirtomy
Talmine
Skerray
Torrisdale Bay
Farr
STRATHNAVER MUSEUM
Swordly
A836
Rabbit Is.
Achtoty
Airdtorrisdale
Skinnet
Midtown
Tongue Bay
Torrisdale
Bettyhill
Skullomie
Achina
A'Mhoine
A838
KYLE OF TONGUE
Coldbackie
Invernaver
Clachan Burn
Loch Meadie
Borgie
Leckfurin
Achuvoldrach
TONGUE
A836
229
Loch Buidhe Mor
Kirkiboll
CASTLE VARRICH
Tongue
ACHANLOCHY CLEARANCE VILLAGE
Skelpick
Borgie Forest
B871
310
Loch Mor na Caorach
Achagary
Skelpick Burn
Ribigill
Loch nan Clach
Loch Craggie
Kinloch Lodge
Loch na Seilg
Kinloch
STRATHNAVER
Carnachy
Rhifail
Loch a' Ghobha-Dhuibh
764 BEN LOYAL
527 BEINN STUMANADH
293 BEINN RIFA-GIL
Loch an Dherue
Loch Loyal
Loch Strathy
Loch Loyal Lodge
Skail
Loch Haluim
557 CNOC NAN CULLEAN
Naver
Langdale
Loch Syre
Syre
Dalvina Lo.
Loch Coulside
Inchkinloch
416
B873
ROSAL CLEARANCE TRAIL
Rimsdale Burn
Loch Meadie
Loch Eileanach
294 POLE HILL
403
273
0 1 2 3 miles
0 1 2 3 4 5 km
Garv

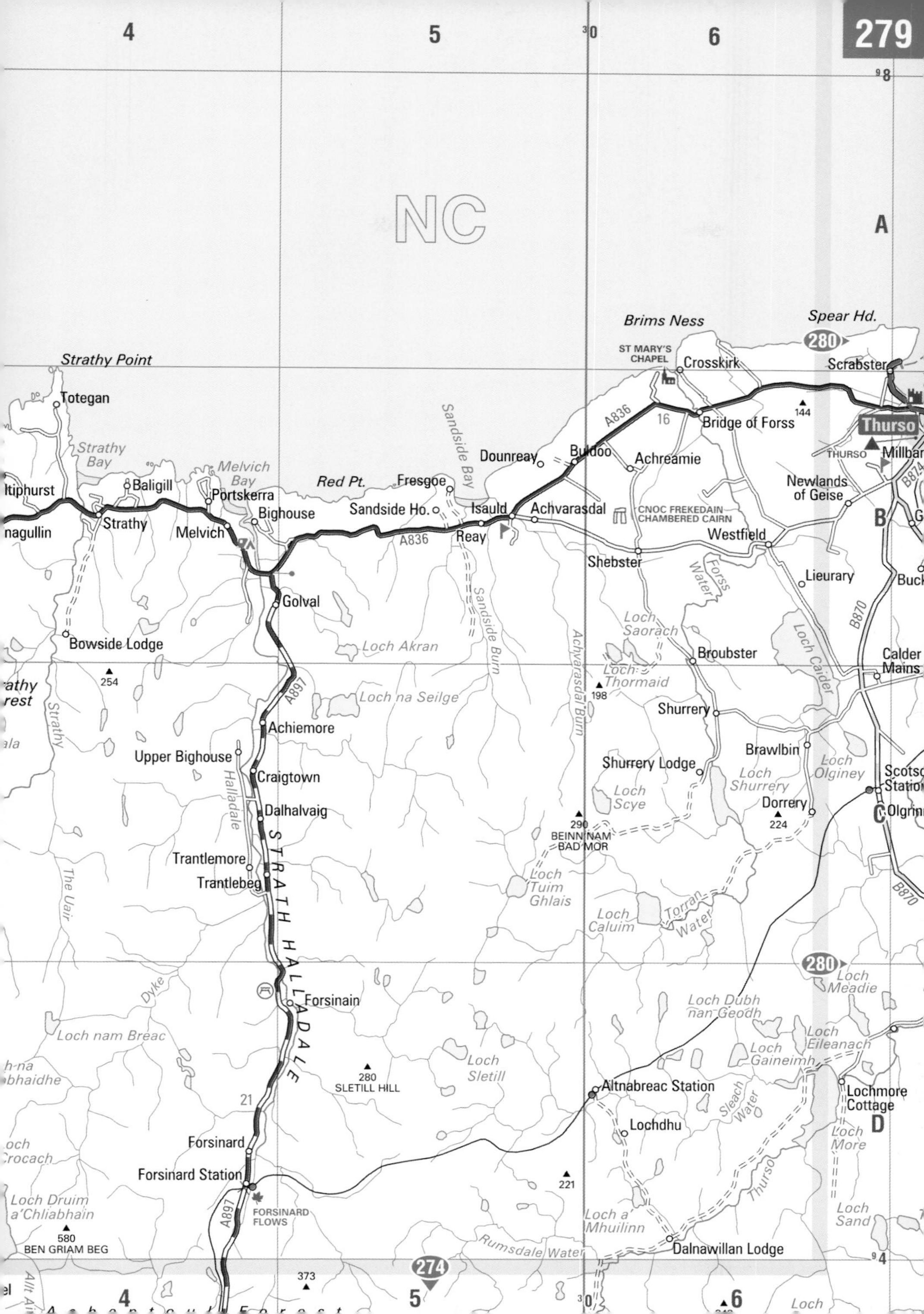

NC
Strathy Point
Totegan
Strathy Bay
Melvich Bay
Baligill
Portskerra
Strathy
Melvich
Bighouse
Red Pt.
Fresgoe
Sandside Bay
Sandside Ho.
Isauld
Reay
A836
Dounreay
Buldoo
Achreamie
Achvarasdal
CNOC FREKEDAIN CHAMBERED CAIRN
Brims Ness
ST MARY'S CHAPEL
Crosskirk
Bridge of Forss
16
Spear Hd.
280
Scrabster
144
Thurso
THURSO
Millbar
Newlands of Geise
B874
Westfield
Shebster
Forss Water
Lieurary
B870
Golval
Bowside Lodge
254
Loch Akran
Loch Saorach
Broubster
Loch Calder
Calder Mains
Loch Thormaid
198
Sandside Burn
Achvarasdal Burn
Loch na Seilge
A897
Achiemore
Shurrery
Brawlbin
Loch Olginey
Upper Bighouse
Craigtown
Shurrery Lodge
Loch Shurrery
Loch Scye
Dorrery
224
Dalhalvaig
Halladale
290
BEINN NAM BAD MOR
Trantlemore
Trantlebeg
STRATH HALLADALE
Loch Tuim Ghlais
Loch Caluim
Torran Water
B870
Strathy
The Uair
Dyke
Forsinain
Loch nam Breac
Loch Dubh nan Geodh
Loch Meadie
Loch Eileanach
Loch Gaineimh
Loch Sletill
280
SLETILL HILL
Altnabreac Station
Sleach Water
Lochmore Cottage
Lochdhu
21
Forsinard
Forsinard Station
221
Loch More
Loch Druim a'Chliabhain
FORSINARD FLOWS
580
BEN GRIAM BEG
Loch a' Mhuilinn
Thurso
Loch Sand
Rumsdale Water
Dalnawillan Lodge
274
373
A
B
C
D
4
5
6
30
98
94

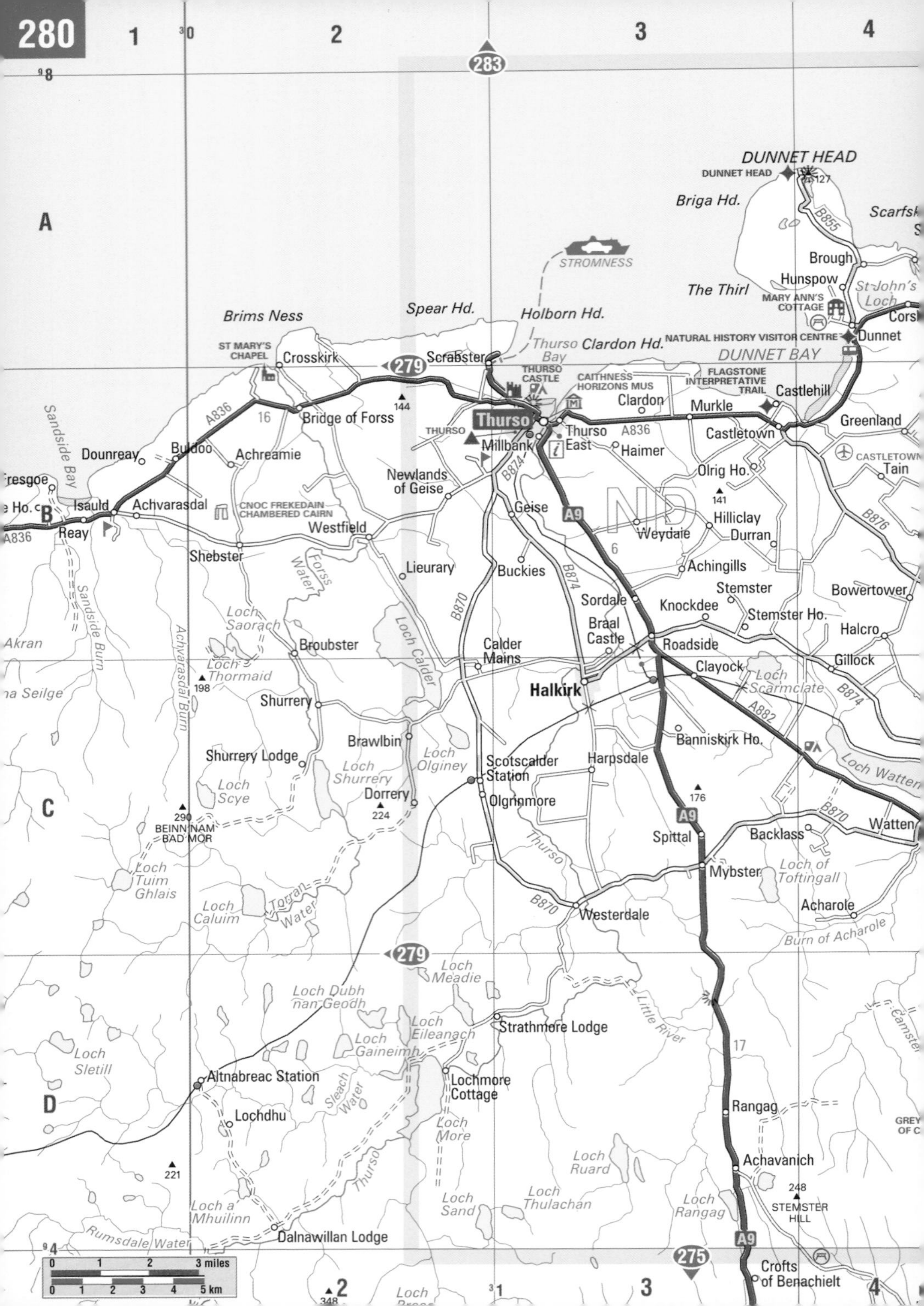

1
2
3
4
A
B
C
D
283
279
275
DUNNET HEAD
Briga Hd.
Scarfsk
Brough
Hunspow
The Thirl
St John's Loch
MARY ANN'S COTTAGE
Corsb
Dunnet
NATURAL HISTORY VISITOR CENTRE
DUNNET BAY
STROMNESS
Brims Ness
Spear Hd.
Holborn Hd.
Thurso Bay
Clardon Hd.
ST MARY'S CHAPEL
Crosskirk
Scrabster
THURSO CASTLE
CAITHNESS HORIZONS MUS
FLAGSTONE INTERPRETATIVE TRAIL
Clardon
Murkle
Castlehill
Greenland
Castletown
CASTLETOWN
Tain
A836
Bridge of Forss
144
Thurso
THURSO
Millbank
Thurso East
Haimer
Olrig Ho.
Sandside Bay
Dounreay
Buldoo
Achreamie
Newlands of Geise
Fresgoe
Isauld
Achvarasdal
CNOC FREKEDAIN CHAMBERED CAIRN
Reay
Westfield
B874
Geise
141
Hilliclay
Weydale
Durran
B876
Shebster
Forss Water
Lieurary
Buckies
Achingills
Stemster
Bowertower
Sordale
Knockdee
Stemster Ho.
Loch Saorach
Loch Calder
B870
Braal Castle
Roadside
Halcro
Akran
Sandside Burn
Achvarasdal Burn
Broubster
Calder Mains
Clayock
Gillock
Loch Thormaid
198
Halkirk
Loch Scarmclate
Seilge
Shurrery
A882
Brawlbin
Banniskirk Ho.
Shurrery Lodge
Loch Olginey
Loch Shurrery
Scotscalder Station
Harpsdale
Loch Watten
Loch Scye
Dorrery
224
Olgrinmore
176
290
BEINN NAM BAD MOR
A9
Spittal
Backlass
Watten
Loch Tuim Ghlais
Mybster
Loch of Toftingall
Loch Caluim
Torran Water
Westerdale
Acharole
Burn of Acharole
Loch Meadie
Loch Dubh nan Geodh
Little River
Camster
Loch Sletill
Loch Eileanach
Strathmore Lodge
Loch Gaineimh
17
Altnabreac Station
Sleach Water
Lochmore Cottage
Lochdhu
Loch More
Rangag
GREY OF C
Loch Ruard
Achavanich
221
248
STEMSTER HILL
Loch a Mhuilinn
Loch Sand
Loch Thulachan
Loch Rangag
Rumsdale Water
Dalnawillan Lodge
Crofts of Benachielt
0 1 2 3 miles
0 1 2 3 4 5 km
348
Loch

Langaton Point
Nethertown
Red Head
Island of Stroma
Mell Head
Uppertown
ST. MARGARET'S HOPE
BURWICK (May-Sept)
Muckle Skerry
Pentland Skerries
Men of Mey
St John's Pt.
Boars of Duncansby
Gills Bay
East Mey
CASTLE OF MEY
Huna
DUNCANSBY HEAD
Kirkstyle
Gills
Mey
A836
Canisbay
John o' Groats
Stacks of Duncansby
Barrock
Inkstack
Brabster
Lochend
Gill Burn
Tofts
Skirza
Skirza Head
Freswick
Freswick Bay
Slickly
Ness Head
Reaster
BUCHOLLY CASTLE
ND
Alterwall
CAITHNESS BROCH CENTRE
Auckengill
Lyth
LYTH ARTS CENTRE
Sortat
Nybster
Barrock Ho.
Brough Head
Howe
Keiss
KEISS CASTLE
Mireland
Burn of Lyth
Kirk
Loch of Wester
B870
Myrelandhorn
SINCLAIR'S BAY
Killimster
B876
CASTLE SINCLAIR
CASTLE GIRNIGOE
Noss Head
Reiss
Winless
A99
Sealky Head
Ackergill
B874
WICK
Staxigoe
Bilbster
WICK HERITAGE MUS
Papigoe
Strath
A882
Wick
Broadhaven
Stirkoke Ho.
Milton
Wick Bay
Achairn Burn
Old Wick
South Hd.
Newton
CASTLE OF OLD WICK
Whiterow
Gote O'Tram
Tannach
Hempriggs House
Loch Hempriggs
Helman Hd.
HILL OF OLICLETT
Thrumster
Gansclet
Sarclet
Loch of Yarrows
Sarclet Hd.
Ulbster
CAIRN OF GET
Whaligoe
HILL O' MANY STANES
Bruan
Mid
283
275
A
B
C
D

Scale : 1:425 700
(approx 6.72 miles to 1 inch)
0 2 4 6 miles
0 2 4 6 8 10 km
HY
ORKNEY ISLANDS
North Ronaldsay
NORTH RONALDSAY
Hollandstoun
BROCH OF BURRIAN
NORTH RONALDSAY FIRTH
Papa Westray
Holm of Papa
PAPA WESTRAY
KNAP OF HOWAR
WESTRAY
Aikerness
Backaskaill
Holland
Gayfield
NOUP HEAD
PIEROWALL CHURCH
Rackwick
Pierowall
Broughton
Braehead
NOLTLAND CASTLE
104
WESTRAY
B9067
B9066
FITTY HILL
169
Midbea
Skelwick
Langskaill
WESTSIDE CHURCH
Rapness
Sulland
THE NORTH SOUND
KIRKWALL
WESTRAY FIRTH
Faray
Calf of Eday
Carrick Ho.
CARRICK HOUSE
76
Calfsound
Braeswick
Guith
B9063
Millbounds
Loth
EDAY
Backaland
101
Veness
Scar
Burness
B9068
Lettan
START PT.
Sellibister
Newark
SANDAY
B9069
Lady
Broughtown
SANDAY
Overbister
B9070
Kettletoft
Laminess
65
Stove
QUOYNESS CHAMBERED CAIRN
SANDAY SOUND
Odie
STRONSAY
Papa Stronsay
Whitehall Village
B9062
Wardhill
STRONSAY
Everbay
B9061
Grobister
B9060
Kirbister
Rothiesholm
Dishes
Holland
Linga Holm
Muckle Green Holm
Auskerry
STRONSAY FIRTH
Edmonstone
Shapinsay
B9058
64
BALFOUR CASTLE
Balfour
B9059
Newlot
ABERDEEN LERWICK
Wasbister
ROUSAY
MIDHOWE BROCH
Eynhallow
EYNHALLOW CHURCH
Sourin
B9064
Westness
227
KNOWE OF YARSO CAIRN
Frotoft
Brinian
CUBBIE'S ROO'S CASTLE AND ST MARY'S CHAPEL
Skaill
ST MAGNUS CHURCH
Egilsay
Wyre
102
Gairsay
BROUGH HEAD
BROUGH OF BIRSAY
A966
Abune-the-Hill
Costa
Burgar
EARL'S PALACE
The Barony
MARWICK HEAD NATURE RESERVE
Kirbuster
11
159
Stenso
BROCH OF GURNESS
Redland
Marwick
Stara
A967
Twatt
B9057
A986
Tingwall
Isbister
Beaquoy
Click Mill
CLICK MILL
A966
B9056
Scarwell
Quoyloo
Hackland
Northdyke
Skeabrae
Dounby
Mirbister
221
Skaill
Kierfiold Ho
B9057
12
CORRIGALL FARM MUSEUM
Gorseness
SKAILL HOUSE
Brough
Settiscarth
6
Isbister
Aith
Hestwall
Tenston
Breck of Cruan
Netherbrough
Bimbister
Yesnaby
13
A967
A986
Arion
Voy
B9055
Finstown
158
RING OF BRODGAR
STANDING STONES
TORMISTON MILL
Grimbister
A965
WIRELESS MUSEUM
ORKNEY MUSEUM
Work
Craigiefield
Quholm
Bridge of Waith
A965
MAES HOWE
Heddle
Kirkwall
MAINLAND
30
38
106
A B C D E F
1 2 3 4 5 6 7 8

ND
SCAPA FLOW
PENTLAND FIRTH
HOY AND WEST MAINLAND
HOY
SOUTH WALLS
SOUTH RONALDSAY
Burray
Flotta
Fara
Cava
Rysa Little
Swona
Switha
Copinsay
Island of Stroma
DUNNET HEAD
DUNCANSBY HEAD
RORA HEAD
DUNNET BAY
SINCLAIR'S BAY
Kirbister
Hobbister
Waulkmill
Lodge
Greenigoe
Tradespark
Whitecleat
Toab
Foubister
Deerness
North Halley
Skaill
Grindigar
Gritley
Upper Sanday
Braehead
Cornquoy
North Dawn
St Mary's
Northtown
Southtown
Grimness
Hunda
Hillside
Burray Village
St. Margaret's Hope
Quindry
Papley
Aikers
Lythes
Linklater
Cleat
Liddel
Herston
Widewall
Sandwick
Suckquoy
Dundas Ho.
Burwick
Cairnton
Smoogro
Swanbister
Gyre
Crya
Clestrain
Petertown
Houton
Breckan
Graemsay
Linksness
Quoyness
Murra
Hoy
Rackwick
Lyness
Rinnigill
Bow
Crockness
Little Ayre
Wyng
Hackness
Longhope
Melsetter
Hurliness
Brims
Pan
Uppertown
ST NICHOLAS CHURCH
DWARFIE STANE
WARD HILL
KNAP OF TROWIEGLEN
NORTH HOY NATURE RESERVE
OLD MAN OF HOY
SCAPA FLOW VISITOR CENTRE
MARTELLO TOWERS
FOSSIL AND VINTAGE CENTRE
ITALIAN CHAPEL
TOMB OF THE EAGLES AND BRONZE AGE HOUSE
STROMNESS MUSEUM
SCRABSTER
STROMNESS
(May-Sept)
Nethertown
Uppertown
John o' Groats
Huna
Canisbay
Kirkstyle
Gills
East Mey
Mey
CASTLE OF MEY
Scarfskerry
Rattar
Ham
Brough
Corsback
Barrock
Dunnet
Inkstack
Lochend
Hunspow
MARY-ANN'S COTTAGE
Greenland
CASTLETOWN
Castlehill
Castletown
Murkle
Clardon
East Haimer
Thurso
Scrabster
Millbank
THURSO CASTLE
CAITHNESS HORIZONS MUS
FLAGSTONE INTERPRETATIVE TRAIL
NATURAL HISTORY VISITOR CENTRE
ST MARY'S CHAPEL
Crosskirk
Bridge of Forss
Achreamie
Buldoo
Dounreay
Achvarasdal
CNOC FREKEDAIN CHAMBERED CAIRN
Shebster
Westfield
Newlands of Geise
Lieurary
Geise
Buckies
Sordale
Braal Castle
Olrig Ho.
Tain
Hilliclay
Weydale
Achingills
Durran
Knockdee
Stemster Ho.
Bowertower
Halcro
Gillock
Hastigrow
Roadside
Calder Mains
Halkirk
Clayock
Banniskirk Ho.
Harpsdale
Scotscalder Station
Olgrinmore
Broubster
Shurrery
Shurrery Lodge
Brawlbin
Dorrery
BEINN NAM BAD MOR
Forss Water
Torran Water
Thurso
Spittal
Backlass
Mybster
Acharole
Westerdale
Watten
Strath
Bilbster
Badlipster
Stirkoke Ho.
Milton
Newton
Wick
Old Wick
CASTLE OF OLD WICK
Broadhaven
Papigoe
Staxigoe
WICK HERITAGE CENTRE
Ackergill
CASTLE SINCLAIR
CASTLE GIRNIGOE
Winless
Reiss
Killimster
Mains of Watten
North Watten
Kirk
Myrelandhorn
Mireland
Keiss
KEISS CASTLE
Nybster
Auckengill
CAITHNESS BROCH CENTRE
BUCHOLLY CASTLE
Freswick
Tofts
Skirza
Brabster
Slickly
Reaster
Alterwall
LYTH ARTS CENTRE
Bowermadden
Lyth
Sortat
Barrock Ho.
Howe
A964
A961
A960
A99
A9
A836
A882
B9044
B9041
B9042
B9043
B9045
B9047
B9050
B9051
B9052
B855
B874
B876
B870
280
281
G
H
J
K
L
M
1
2
3
4
5
6
7
8
283

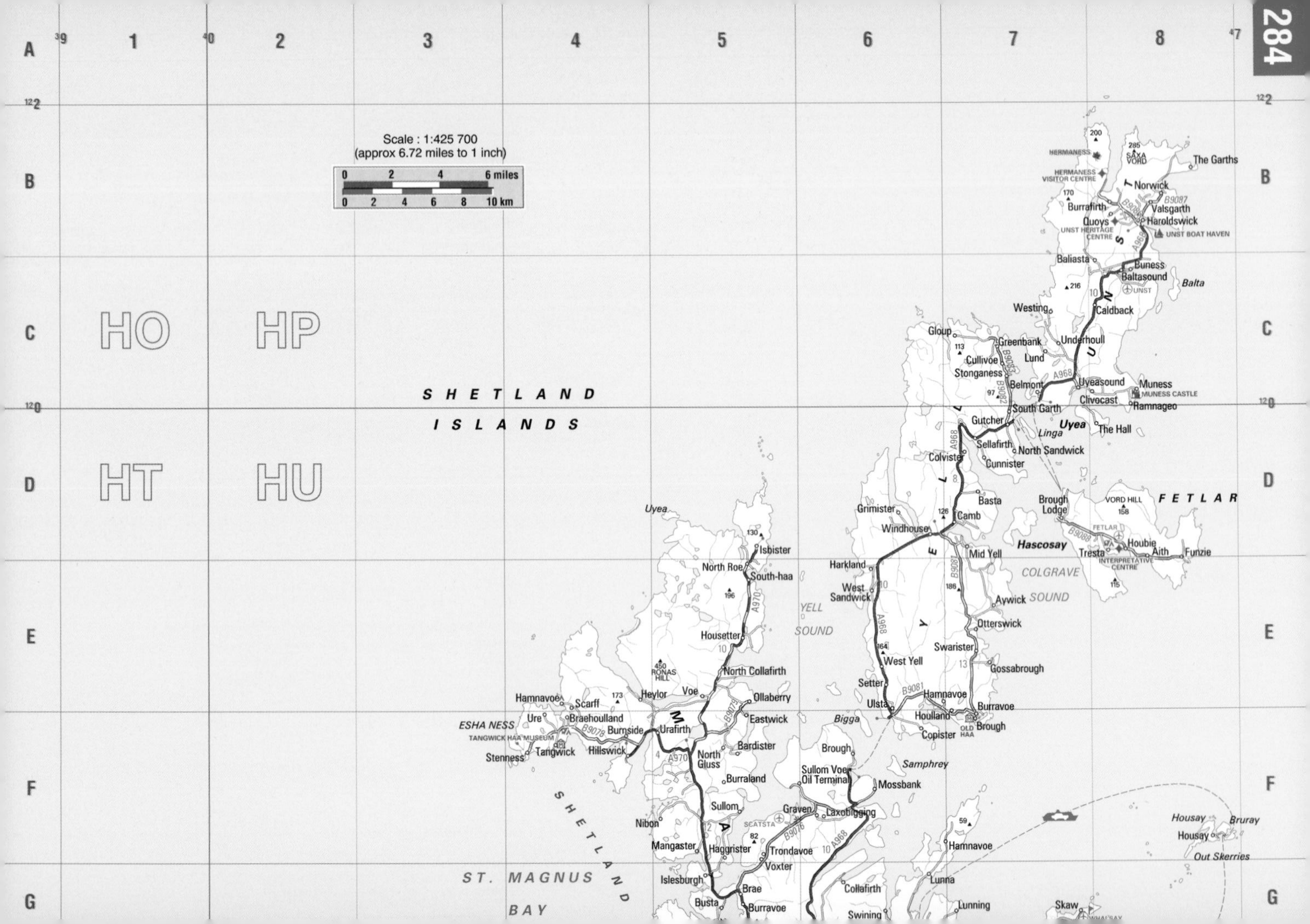
Scale : 1:425 700
(approx 6.72 miles to 1 inch)
0 2 4 6 miles
0 2 4 6 8 10 km
HO
HP
HT
HU
SHETLAND ISLANDS
UNST
YELL
FETLAR
MAINLAND
Hermaness
Hermaness Visitor Centre
Saxa Vord
The Garths
Norwick
Burrafirth
Valsgarth
Haroldswick
Quoys
Unst Heritage Centre
Unst Boat Haven
Baliasta
Buness
Baltasound
Balta
Unst
Westing
Caldback
Gloup
Greenbank
Underhoull
Cullivoe
Lund
Stonganess
Belmont
Uyeasound
Muness
Muness Castle
Clivocast
Ramnageo
South Garth
Gutcher
Uyea
The Hall
Linga
Sellafirth
North Sandwick
Colvister
Cunnister
Basta
Grimister
Camb
Brough Lodge
Vord Hill
Windhouse
Hascosay
Tresta
Houbie
Aith
Funzie
Fetlar Interpretative Centre
Mid Yell
Colgrave Sound
Harkland
West Sandwick
Aywick
Otterswick
Swarister
West Yell
Gossabrough
Setter
Hamnavoe
Burravoe
Ulsta
Houlland
Brough
Old Haa
Copister
Bigga
Yell Sound
Uyea
Isbister
North Roe
South-haa
Housetter
Ronas Hill
North Collafirth
Heylor
Voe
Ollaberry
Hamnavoe
Scarff
Ure
Braehoulland
Eastwick
Esha Ness
Tangwick Haa Museum
Burnside
Urafirth
Bardister
Stenness
Tangwick
Hillswick
North Gluss
Brough
Samphrey
Sullom Voe Oil Terminal
Burraland
Mossbank
Sullom
Graven
Laxobigging
Nibon
Scatsta
Mangaster
Haggrister
Trondavoe
Hamnavoe
Housay
Bruray
Housay
Out Skerries
Voxter
Islesburgh
Brae
Collafirth
Lunna
Busta
Burravoe
Swining
Lunning
Skaw
St. Magnus Bay
Shetland
A968
A970
B9081
B9082
B9083
B9084
B9086
B9087
B9088
B9076
B9078
B9079

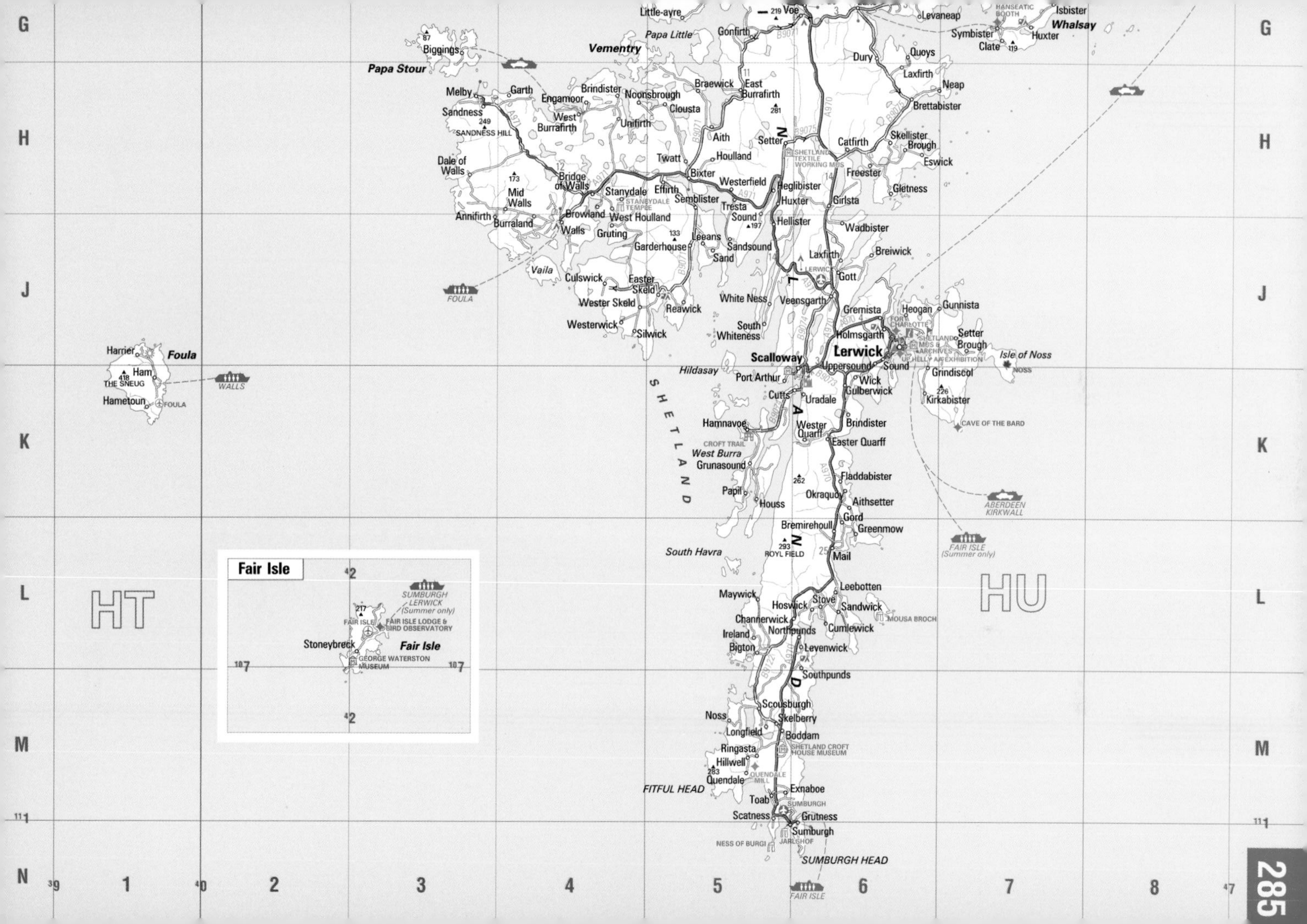

G
H
J
K
L
M
N
1
2
3
4
5
6
7
8
HT
HU
SHETLAND
Fair Isle
Stoneybreck
FAIR ISLE LODGE & BIRD OBSERVATORY
GEORGE WATERSTON MUSEUM
SUMBURGH LERWICK (Summer only)
Foula
Harrier
Ham
Hametoun
418 THE SNEUG
WALLS
FOULA
Papa Stour
Biggings
Vementry
Papa Little
Little-ayre
Voe
Gonfirth
Melby
Sandness
SANDNESS HILL
Garth
Engamoor
Brindister
Noonsbrough
Clousta
West Burrafirth
Unifirth
Braewick
East Burrafirth
Aith
Setter
Houlland
Twatt
Bixter
Westerfield
Dale of Walls
Mid Walls
Bridge of Walls
Stanydale
STANYDALE TEMPLE
Effirth
Semblister
Tresta
Sound
Annifirth
Burraland
Browland
West Houlland
Walls
Gruting
Garderhouse
Leeans
Sandsound
Sand
Vaila
Culswick
Easter Skeld
Wester Skeld
Reawick
Westerwick
Silwick
White Ness
South Whiteness
Veensgarth
Heglibister
Huxter
Hellister
Laxfirth
Gott
Scalloway
Hildasay
Port Arthur
Cutts
Uradale
Hamnavoe
CROFT TRAIL
West Burra
Grunasound
Papil
Houss
South Havra
Bremirehoull
ROYL FIELD
Levaneap
Symbister
Clate
Huxter
Isbister
Whalsay
HANSEATIC BOOTH
Dury
Quoys
Laxfirth
Neap
Brettabister
Catfirth
Skellister
Brough
Eswick
SHETLAND TEXTILE WORKING MUS
Freester
Gletness
Girlsta
Wadbister
Breiwick
Gremista
Heogan
Gunnista
Holmsgarth
FORT CHARLOTTE
SHETLAND MUS & ARCHIVES
UP HELLY AA EXHIBITION
Lerwick
Setter
Brough
Isle of Noss
NOSS
Uppersound
Sound
Wick
Gulberwick
Grindiscol
Kirkabister
CAVE OF THE BARD
Wester Quarff
Brindister
Easter Quarff
Fladdabister
Okraquoy
Aithsetter
Gord
Greenmow
Mail
ABERDEEN KIRKWALL
FAIR ISLE (Summer only)
Maywick
Leebotten
Hoswick
Stove
Sandwick
MOUSA BROCH
Channerwick
Ireland
Northpunds
Cumlewick
Bigton
Levenwick
Southpunds
Scousburgh
Skelberry
Noss
Longfield
Boddam
SHETLAND CROFT HOUSE MUSEUM
Ringasta
Hillwell
Quendale
QUENDALE MILL
FITFUL HEAD
Exnaboe
Toab
SUMBURGH
Scatness
Grutness
Sumburgh
JARLSHOF
NESS OF BURGI
SUMBURGH HEAD
FAIR ISLE

Na h-eileanan Monach
(Heisker or Monach Islands)
287
Baile Sear
(Baleshare)
Clachan na Luib
Loch Euphoirt
Saighdinis
Teanna Mhachair
Samhla
Corunna
Bail Uachdraich
Cairinis
Baile Glas
Iochdrach
Griomasaigh
(Grimsay)
Scotbheinn
Bagh Mor
Ronay
Uachdar
Baile a Mhanaich
Baile nan Cailleach
Gramsdal
Flodaigh
BEINN NA FAOGHLA
(BENBECULA)
Griminis
Torlum
Lionacleit
Creag Ghoraidh
Iochdar
Aird a Mhachair
Clachan
Fuidhaigh
(Wiay)
NF
Sanndabhaig
Loch a Charnain
Geirinis
OUR LADY OF THE ISLES STATUE
Stadhlaigearraidh
Loch Sgioport
Dreumasdal
Tobha Mor
LOCH DRUIDIBEG NATURE RESERVE
HECLA
Sniseabhal
Staoinebrig
Ormiclate Castle
BEINN MHOR
SOUTH UIST MACHAIR
Bornais
Taobh a Thuath Loch Aineort
UIBHIST A DEAS
(SOUTH UIST)
Cill Donnain
KILDONAN MUSEUM
Unasary
Minngearraidh
Gearraidh Bhailteas
FLORA MACDONALD'S BIRTHPLACE
OUTER HEBRIDES
Aisgernis
STULAVAL
Dalabrog
Taobh a Tuath Loch Baghasdail
Crois Dughaill
Loch Baghasdail
(Lochboisdale)
Cille Pheadair
Baghasdal
Ceann a Deas Loch Baghasdail
Gearraidh na Monadh
Trosaraidh
Cille Bhrighde
Smercleit
South Glendale
MALLAIG
OBAN
(Winter only)
Pol a Charra
Taobh a Chaolais
Ludag
Bun a'Mhuillin
Am Baile
Haunn
Coilleag
Eiriosgaigh
(Eriskay)
Fuideigh
(Fuday)
Eolaigearraidh
CILLE BHARRA
EILEAN BHARRAIGH
(BARRA)
BARRA
Cliaid
BEN CLIAD
Aird Mhor
Cuidhir
Allathasdal
Aird Mhidhinis
Bagh Shiarabhagh
Bruairnis
Baile na Creige
CRAIGSTON MUSEUM
Buaile nam Bodach
Borgh
Tangasdal
HEAVAL
Earsairidh
BARRA HERITAGE CENTRE
Breibhig
Bagh a Chaisteil
(Castlebay)
KIESSIMUL (KISIMUL) CASTLE
Bhatarsaigh
(Vatersay)
Uidh
Bhatarsaigh
OBAN
Sanndraigh
(Sandray)
Pabaidh
(Pabbay)
NL
Scale : 1:425 700
(approx 6.72 miles to 1 inch)
6 miles
10 km
Miùgh Laigh
(Mingulay)
Bearnaraigh
(Berneray)

Scale : 1:425 700
(approx 6.72 miles to 1 inch)
0 2 4 6 miles
0 2 4 6 8 10 km
St. Kilda
NA
NF
Boreray
ST KILDA
Soay
CONACHAIR
St Kilda or Hirta (Hiort)
MULLACH BI
ST KILDA
OUTER HEBRIDES
NB
NF
NG
SOUTH LEWIS,
HARRIS AND
NORTH UIST
LOCH A SIAR
CEANN A TUATH NA HEARADH
NA HEARADH (HARRIS)
UIBHIST A TUATH (NORTH UIST)
CAOLAS NA HEARADH
AN CAOLAS MHONACH
AN CAOLAS
Aird Uig
Cliobh
Bhaltos
Timsgearraidh
Miabhig
Uigen
Riof
Cradhlastadh
Carnais
Cairisiadar
Eadar Dha Fhadhail
Mangurstadh
SUAINAVAL
Geisiadar
Islibhig
Breanais
MEALISVAL
Einacleite
Giosla
BEINN MHEADHONACH
Mealasta Island
Scarp
Huisinis
TIRGA MOR
ULLAVAL
STULAVAL
Gobhaig
Abhainn Suidhe
UISGNAVAL MORE
CLISHAM
Cliasmol
Miabhag
Bun Abhainn Eadarra
OLD WHALING STATION
Aird Asaig
Tarasaigh (Taransay)
BEN LUSKENTYRE
Paible
Losgaintir
Tairbeart (Tarbert)
LUSKENTYRE BEACH
Seilebost
Borve Lodge
SCARISTA STANDING STONE
Buirgh
CHAIPAVAL
Sgarasta Mhor
Aird Mhighe
Liceasto
Geocrab
BLEAVAL
Beacrabhaic
Caolas Stocinis
Taobh Tuath
SEALLAM
Fleoideabhagh
Manais
Aird Mhighe
Cuidhtinis
Fionnsbhagh
Boirseam
Ensay
An t-Ob (Leverburgh)
ROINEABHAL
Lingreabhagh
Killegray
Cairminis
Srannda
ST CLEMENT'S CHURCH
Roghadal
Pabaidh (Pabbay)
Eilean Bhearnaraigh (Berneray)
Ruisigearraidh
Boreray
Borgh
Baile
IRON AGE HOUSE
Tobson
BERNERA
Breacleit
Tacleit
Crulabh
Vallay
Oronsay
Port nan Long
Baile Mhic Phail
Scolpaig
SCOLPAIG TOWER
Solas
Greinetobht
Trumaisgearraidh
Hermetray
Baile Mhartainn
Malacleit
Taigh a Ghearraidh
Hosta
Lochportain
Hogha Gearraidh
Baile Raghaill
MARRIVAL
Loch nam Madadh (Lochmaddy)
TAIGH CHEARSABHAGH MUSEUM
UIG
Ceann a Bhaigh
Claddach-knockline
Paibeil
Baile Mor
CLACH MHOR A CHE STANDING STONES
Cladach Chireboist
BARPA LANGASS CAIRN
Na h-eileanan Monach (Heisker or Monach Islands)
Kirkibost Island
SOUTH LEE
Clachan na Luib
Loch Euphoirt
Saighdinis
Teanna Mhachair
Samhla
Corunna
Baile Sear (Baleshare)
TRINITY TEMPLE
Bail Uachdraich
Cairinis
EAVAL
Bail Iochdrach
Baile Glas
Griomasaigh (Grimsay)
BENBECULA
Uachdar
Scotbheinn

Scale : 1:425 700
(approx 6.72 miles to 1 inch)
0 2 4 6 miles
0 2 4 6 8 10 km
NB
NG
RUBHA ROBHANAIS
CHURCH OF ST MOULAG
Eòropaidh
Coig Peighinnean
HARBOUR VIEW GALLERY
Port Nis
Lional
Suainebost
Aird Dhail
Tabost
Dail bho Dheas
Cros
Sgiogarstaigh
Dail bho Thuath
Gabhsann bho Thuath
Gabhsann bho Dheas
Mealabost Bhuirgh
Cuiashader
Coig Peighinnean Bhuirgh
Bail Àrd Bhuirgh
Siadar
Siadar Iarach
TRUSHAL STONE
Siadar Uarach
Baile an Truiseil
BLACK HOUSE MUSEUM
Barabhas Iarach
Barabhas Uarach
Brù
Barabhas
Labost
Arnol
Bragar
Siabost bho Thuath
MUIRNEAG
Bail' Ur Tholastaidh
Tolastadh bho Thuath
SHAWBOST NORSE MILL
SHAWBOST MUSEUM
Siabost bho Dheas
Pairc Shiaboist
GEARRANNAN BLACKHOUSE VILLAGE
Dail Beag
Dail Mor
Na Gearrannan
Borghastan
Gleann Tholàstaidh
BEINN BRAGAR
DUN CARLOWAY BROCH
Carlabhagh
Griais
Ciribhig
Dun Charlabhaigh
Bac
Col
IRON AGE HOUSE
AN CAOLAS
Tobson
Crothair
Col Uarach
Breibhig
NORSE MILL
Great Bernera
Tolastadh a Chaolais
BEINN MHOLACH
BROAD BAY OR LOCH A TUATH
Port Nan Giùran
Aird Uig
Cliobh
Bhaltos
Breacleit
Aird Thunga
Tunga
Cnoc Amhlaigh
Port Mholair
Timsgearraidh
Miabhig
Riof
Circebost
Breascleit
Grianan
Newmarket
An Gleann Ur
Sulaisiadar
Aird
Cradhlastadh
Uigen
Tacleit
Barraglom
Tobhtarol
CALANAIS VISITOR CENTRE
LEWS CASTLE MUS NAN EILEAN
LEWIS LOOM CENTRE
Lacasdal
STORNOWAY
Garrabost
EYE PENINSULA
Seisiadar
Calanais
CALANAIS STANDING STONES
CALANAIS SMALL STONE CIRCLES
Stornoway
Mealabost
Aiginis
Càrnais
Cairisiadar
Crulabhig
Sanndabhaig
ST COLUMBA'S
Pabail Uarach
Eadar Dha Fhadhail
AN LANNTAIR GALLERY
Mangurstadh
Linsiadar
Gearraidh na h-Aibhne
Tolm
An Cnoc
Pabail Iarach
Geisiadar
SUAINAVAL
Suardail
Acha Mor
ACHMORE STONE CIRCLE
BONNIE PRINCE CHARLIE'S MONUMENT
287
Loch a' Ghainmhich
Eisgean
Islibhig
MEALISVAL
Einacleite
Liurbost
Griomsidar
ULLAPOOL
Breanais
Giosla
Ben Casgro
Ranais
Soval Lodge
Crosbost
BEINN MHEADHONACH
EILEAN LEODHAIS ISLE OF LEWIS
Lacasaidh
Ceos
Cromor
Baile Ailein
Gearraidh Bhaird
Sildinis
Cearsiadair
Tabost
Cabharstadh
LOCH LANGABHAT
Ceann Tarabhaigh
Marbhig
Airidh a Bhruaich
Ceann Shiphoirt
Calbost
Taobh a' Ghlinne
Grabhair
PARK OR PAIRC
STULAVAL
Orasaigh
Huisinis
SOUTH LEWIS,
Aline Lodge
Leumrabhagh
TIRGA MOR
ULLAVAL
Eisgean
Aird a' Mhulaidh
Seaforth I.
Gobhaig
UISGNAVAL MORE
BEINN MHOR
Eilean Iubhard
Abhainn Suidhe
CLISHAM
HARRIS AND CEANN A TUATH NA HEARADH
CRIONAIG
Cliasmol
Maraig
LOCH A SIAR
Miabhag
Bun Abhainn Eadarra
OLD WHALING STATION
NORTH UIST
Aird Asaig
CAOLAS NAN EILEAN
Tarasaigh (Taransay)
Reinigeadal
BEN LUSKENTYRE
Urgha
Losgaintir
Tairbeart (Tarbert)
Paible
LUSKENTYRE BEACH
Carragraich
Caolas Scalpaigh
Carnach
Na h-Eileanan Mòra (Shiant Islands)
Seilebost
Miabhag
Scalpay
Eilean Scalpaigh (Scalpay)
Borve Lodge
NA HEARADH (HARRIS)
Drinisiadar
Kennacley
SCARISTA STANDING STONE
Buirgh
Aird Mhighe
Greosabhagh
Plocrapol
Sgarasta Mhor
Liceasto
Leac a Li
Scadabhagh
UIG
BLEAVAL
Geocrab
Cliuthar
Beacrabhaic
Caolas Stocinis
Fleoideabhagh
Manais
Aird Mhighe
Ghidhtinis
Fionnsbhagh

Index to road maps

How to use the index

Example

Thistleton Rutland **116** D2

- grid square
- page number
- county or unitary authority (only shown for duplicate names)

Abbreviations used in the index

Aberdeen **Aberdeen City**
Aberds **Aberdeenshire**
Ald **Alderney**
Anglesey **Isle of Anglesey**
Angus **Angus**
Argyll **Argyll and Bute**
Bath **Bath and North East Somerset**
Bedford **Bedford**
Bl Gwent **Blaenau Gwent**
Blackburn **Blackburn with Darwen**
Blackpool **Blackpool**
Bmouth **Bournemouth**
Borders **Scottish Borders**
Brack **Bracknell**
Bridgend **Bridgend**
Brighton **City of Brighton and Hove**
Bristol **City and County of Bristol**
Bucks **Buckinghamshire**
C Beds **Central Bedfordshire**
Caerph **Caerphilly**
Cambs **Cambridgeshire**
Cardiff **Cardiff**
Carms **Carmarthenshire**
Ceredig **Ceredigion**
Ches E **Cheshire East**
Ches W **Cheshire West and Chester**
Clack **Clackmannanshire**
Conwy **Conwy**
Corn **Cornwall**
Cumb **Cumbria**
Darl **Darlington**
Denb **Denbighshire**
Derby **City of Derby**
Derbys **Derbyshire**
Devon **Devon**
Dorset **Dorset**
Dumfries **Dumfries and Galloway**
Dundee **Dundee City**
Durham **Durham**
E Ayrs **East Ayrshire**
E Dunb **East Dunbartonshire**
E Loth **East Lothian**
E Renf **East Renfrewshire**
E Sus **East Sussex**
E Yorks **East Riding of Yorkshire**
Edin **City of Edinburgh**
Essex **Essex**
Falk **Falkirk**
Fife **Fife**
Flint **Flintshire**
Glasgow **City of Glasgow**
Glos **Gloucestershire**
Gtr Man **Greater Manchester**
Guern **Guernsey**
Gwyn **Gwynedd**
Halton **Halton**
Hants **Hampshire**
Hereford **Herefordshire**
Herts **Hertfordshire**
Highld **Highland**
Hrtlpl **Hartlepool**
Hull **Hull**
IoM **Isle of Man**
IoW **Isle of Wight**
Invclyd **Inverclyde**
Jersey **Jersey**
Kent **Kent**
Lancs **Lancashire**
Leicester **City of Leicester**
Leics **Leicestershire**
Lincs **Lincolnshire**
London **Greater London**
Luton **Luton**
M Keynes **Milton Keynes**
M Tydf **Merthyr Tydfil**
Mbro **Middlesbrough**
Medway **Medway**
Mers **Merseyside**
Midloth **Midlothian**
Mon **Monmouthshire**
Moray **Moray**
N Ayrs **North Ayrshire**
N Lincs **North Lincolnshire**
N Lanark **North Lanarkshire**
N Som **North Somerset**
N Yorks **North Yorkshire**
NE Lincs **North East Lincolnshire**
Neath **Neath Port Talbot**
Newport **City and County of Newport**
Norf **Norfolk**
Northants **Northamptonshire**
Northumb **Northumberland**
Nottingham **City of Nottingham**
Notts **Nottinghamshire**
Orkney **Orkney**
Oxon **Oxfordshire**
Pboro **Peterborough**
Pembs **Pembrokeshire**
Perth **Perth and Kinross**
Plym **Plymouth**
Poole **Poole**
Powys **Powys**
Ptsmth **Portsmouth**
Reading **Reading**
Redcar **Redcar and Cleveland**
Renfs **Renfrewshire**
Rhondda **Rhondda Cynon Taff**
Rutland **Rutland**
S Ayrs **South Ayrshire**
S Glos **South Gloucestershire**
S Lanark **South Lanarkshire**
S Yorks **South Yorkshire**
Scilly **Scilly**
Shetland **Shetland**
Shrops **Shropshire**
Slough **Slough**
Som **Somerset**
Soton **Southampton**
Staffs **Staffordshire**
Southend **Southend-on-Sea**
Stirling **Stirling**
Stockton **Stockton-on-Tees**
Stoke **Stoke-on-Trent**
Suff **Suffolk**
Sur **Surrey**
Swansea **Swansea**
Swindon **Swindon**
T&W **Tyne and Wear**
Telford **Telford and Wrekin**
Thurrock **Thurrock**
Torbay **Torbay**
Torf **Torfaen**
V Glam **The Vale of Glamorgan**
W Berks **West Berkshire**
W Dunb **West Dunbartonshire**
W Isles **Western Isles**
W Loth **West Lothian**
W Mid **West Midlands**
W Sus **West Sussex**
W Yorks **West Yorkshire**
Warks **Warwickshire**
Warr **Warrington**
Wilts **Wiltshire**
Windsor **Windsor and Maidenhead**
Wokingham **Wokingham**
Worcs **Worcestershire**
Wrex **Wrexham**
York **City of York**

A

B

C

D

E

F

H

I

J

K

L

M

N

O

P

S

T

U

Y

Z